The Fifties in America

The Fifties in America

Volume II
Pancho Gonzáles—Ringling
Brothers and Barnum and
Bailey Circus

Editor
John C. Super
West Virginia University

Managing Editor
R. Kent Rasmussen

SALEM PRESS, INC.
Pasadena, California
Hackensack, New Jersey

Editorial Director: Christina J. Moose

Managing Editor: R. Kent Rasmussen   *Photograph Editor:* Philip Bader

Copy Editor: Sarah M. Hilbert   *Production Editor:* Joyce I. Buchea

Assistant Editors: Andrea E. Miller   *Acquisitions Editor:* Mark Rehn

Elizabeth Ferry Slocum   *Graphics and Design:* James Hutson

Indexer: R. Kent Rasmussen   *Layout:* Eddie Murillo

Title page photo: *Richard M. Nixon campaigning for California's junior seat in the U.S. Senate in 1950.* (AP/Wide World Photos)

Library of Congress Cataloging-in-Publication Data

The fifties in America / edited by John C. Super.
    p. cm.
    Includes bibliographical references and index.
    ISBN 1-58765-202-1 (set : alk. paper) — ISBN 1-58765-203-X (v. 1 : alk. paper) — ISBN 1-58765-204-8 (v. 2 : alk. paper) — ISBN 1-58765-205-6 (v. 3 : alk. paper)
    1. United States—Civilization—1945—Encyclopedias. 2. United States—History—1945-1953—Encyclopedias. 3. United States—History—1953-1961—Encyclopedias. 4. Nineteen fifties—Encyclopedias. I. Super, John C., 1944-
    E169.12.F498 2005
    973.92'03—dc22

2004024559

First Printing

Table of Contents

■ Complete List of Contents

Volume I

Volume II

Volume III

The Fifties in America

■ Gonzáles, Pancho

Identification Mexican American tennis player
Born May 9, 1928; Los Angeles, California
Died July 3, 1995; Las Vegas, Nevada

Pancho Gonzáles overcame racial prejudice to rise to the pinnacle of world professional tennis from 1953 to 1961.

Richard Alonzo Gonzáles was the oldest of seven children, born to parents who emigrated from Mexico during the early twentieth century. Affectionately nicknamed "Pancho" by a fellow competitor, he was largely self-taught and became the top tennis player in Southern California in 1943, only four years after taking up the game. However, his truancy from school inhibited his acceptance by the tennis establishment, and he eventually joined the Navy.

Gonzáles turned professional after defending his U.S. Championship title in 1949. Possessing a blistering serve and competitive temperament, he nevertheless delivered a disappointing performance during his early career on the pro circuit, and he was dropped from competition. In 1952, he returned to elite play and earned a reputation as one of the game's truly dominant players of all time. Gonzáles won eight world professional championships (1953-1959 and 1961) and stayed competitive with the top players until he was in his mid-forties.

As professional tennis consisted of world tours and fierce competition among a select few, Gonzáles was unable to participate in the grand-slam events again until the advent of "open" tennis in 1968. He is recognized as one of the top-ten players worldwide across three decades. One of the few athletes to be inducted into his sport's hall of fame while still actively playing, Gonzáles was a perennial fan favorite, both for his skill and for his fiery nature.

Impact Gonzáles ranked in the U.S. top ten for twenty-four consecutive years (1948-1972). His determination as a boy to overcome obstacles was channeled into a competitiveness that earned him the admiration of all who witnessed his tremendous talent.

Further Reading
Christopher, Andre. *Top-Ten Tennis Players.* Berkeley Heights, N.J.: Enslow, 1998. A book for young adults that profiles famous tennis players, including Gonzáles.
Gonzáles, Doreen. *Richard "Pancho" Gonzáles: Tennis Champion.* Berkeley Heights, N.J.: Enslow, 1998. Details his playing career.
Gonzáles, Pancho. *Man with a Racket.* New York: A. S. Barnes, 1959. Autobiography.

P. Graham Hatcher

See also Connolly, Maureen; Gibson, Althea; Kramer, Jack; Sports; Tennis.

■ Goren, Charles

Identification Champion contract bridge player and authority
Born March 4, 1901; Philadelphia, Pennsylvania
Died April 3, 1991; Encino, California

By the 1950's, Charles Goren was the leading expert on contract bridge and was popular for his world championship win in 1950.

Charles Goren received his law degree from McGill University in 1923 and practiced law in his native Philadelphia until 1936, when he wrote his first bridge book, *Winning Bridge Made Easy.* One secret of Goren's success was a new "point" system in which the top cards were given numerical values. Another was his own success at the bridge table. He won the world contract bridge championship in 1950 and more than two thousand other bridge trophies, including eight victories in the prestigious McKenney competition.

The rummylike game of canasta became popular during the early 1950's, and Goren wrote guides to that game as well, but that game proved to be a passing fancy; Goren and the nation returned to contract bridge. To promote the game, he played with such celebrity amateurs as author W. Somerset Maugham (who wrote an introduction to one of Goren's books) and President Dwight D. Eisenhower. Goren was also the master of ceremonies and commentator on the television show *Championship Bridge with Charles Goren* from 1959 to 1962.

During the 1960's, however, Goren's bidding system was supplanted by one created by Edgar Kaplan and Alfred Sheinwold, which used Goren's point count system but had stricter requirements for bidding a suit. Goren was officially given the title of "Mr. Bridge" by the American Contract Bridge League in 1969.

Impact Goren developed a system that enabled average players to bid confidently, thus popularizing the game of bridge, and he served as its genial promoter during the 1950's.

Further Reading

Goren, Charles, and Jack Olsen. *Bridge Is My Game: Lessons of a Lifetime.* New York: Doubleday, 1965. Goren's autobiography, which also includes secrets of his success with bridge.

Olsen, Jack. *The Mad World of Bridge.* New York: Holt, 1960. Details the game's popularity as well as Goren's contributions to it.

Arthur D. Hlavaty

See also Eisenhower, Dwight D.; Fads; Scrabble.

■ Graham, Billy

Identification American Protestant evangelist
Born November 7, 1918; near Charlotte, North Carolina

As an evangelist, Billy Graham came to prominence during the early 1950's with his touring campaigns and his founding of the Billy Graham Evangelistic Association in 1950, thus beginning his tenure as a major figure in American religious life throughout the next several decades.

William "Billy" Franklin Graham, Jr., grew up on the family dairy farm. He experienced a religious conversion at an evangelistic meeting in 1934, attended Bob Jones College, graduated from the Florida Bible Institute, and was ordained as a Baptist minister. Later he earned a degree in anthropology from Wheaton College in Illinois, where he met his wife, Ruth Bell, daughter of Protestant missionaries to China. He was a pastor, an evangelist for Youth for Christ, and president of Northwestern Baptist Bible College in Minneapolis, Minnesota. His message was fundamentalist, moralistic, and patriotic. An eight-week evangelistic campaign in his "canvas cathedral" in Los Angeles in 1949 made him a national figure when newspaper mogul William Randolph Hearst ordered his reporters to "puff Graham" and give him favorable coverage and promotion.

National and International Prominence In 1950, Graham established the Billy Graham Evangelistic Association and the Hour of Decision radio program. A March, 1950, campaign in South Carolina received support from then-governor and future senator Strom Thurmond and prominent fundamentalists Bob Jones, Sr., and Bob Jones, Jr., who hosted two meetings. Graham enjoyed friendly relations with fundamentalists until a major breach occurred over Graham's tactics and his desire for a more inclusive focus, which included working with theological liberals in preparation for his New York City campaign of 1957.

Evangelist Billy Graham preaching before forty thousand people at New York City's Polo Grounds in 1957. (AP/Wide World Photos)

Graham cultivated friendships with prominent political figures beginning in 1950, although a meeting with President Harry S. Truman did not go well because later Graham divulged contents of their conversation to reporters. Graham's close ties to presidents nevertheless made him an unofficial spiritual adviser to the nation. Graham met General Dwight D. Eisenhower in Europe in 1951 and remained close during Eisenhower's presidency as Eisenhower publicly supported Graham's ministry and invited him to the White House. Lifelong relationships with Richard M. Nixon and Lyndon B. Johnson continued throughout their vice presidencies and presidencies.

Graham's message of the early 1950's was strongly anticommunist. He visited American troops in Korea in 1952 to demonstrate support for United States policy and publicly praised Senator Joseph McCarthy's efforts to expose communists and communist sympathizers. In 1954, Graham led his first major evangelistic campaign outside the United States with a twelve-week series of meetings in London. This campaign attracted huge crowds, made him an international figure, and helped him move beyond the label of "fundamentalist." He began to refer to himself as a "constructionist" or "evangelical."

Graham worked to persuade southern white pastors and politicians to end segregation. In his campaigns in southern states, he had an open seating policy that allowed black followers to sit where they wanted. In 1956, he established *Christianity Today*, which remained a leading evangelical Christian magazine in subsequent decades. A huge watershed was his 1957 New York City Crusade, which finalized his break with the fundamentalists after he accepted support from the Protestant Council of New York instead of leading fundamentalists. More than two million people attended his meetings at Madison Square Garden. He had Dr. Martin Luther King, Jr., lead in prayer, and he integrated his staff. In 1959, Graham held massive rallies in Australia and New Zealand, and at the height of the Cold War, he made his first visit to the Soviet Union.

Impact By the end of the 1950's, Graham had become a major figure in American religious and public life and garnered an international reputation. He had created an evangelical organization and radio program, published books, and founded a magazine

without a hint of financial scandal or accusation of impropriety.

Further Reading
Graham, Billy. *Just as I Am*. San Francisco: Harper, 1997. Graham's autobiography.
Martin, William. *A Prophet with Honor: The Billy Graham Story*. New York: William Morrow, 1991. One of the most extensive scholarly studies of Graham and his impact on American religion.

Mark C. Herman
See also Civil Rights movement; Cold War; Eisenhower, Dwight D.; King, Martin Luther, Jr.; Korean War; Nixon, Richard M.; Peale, Norman Vincent; Religion in the United States; Sheen, Fulton J.; Truman, Harry S.

■ Grand Canyon airliner collision

The Event Collision of two commercial aircraft over the Grand Canyon
Date June 30, 1956
Place Grand Canyon, northern Arizona

The 128 people who died in the Grand Canyon collision made it the worst airline accident since the advent of commercial flight to that date. The tragedy spurred official agencies to reform air safety standards.

At 9:01 A.M. on June 30, 1956, Trans World Airlines (TWA) Flight 2 left Los Angeles carrying seventy people on a flight to Kansas City. Three minutes later United Airlines (UA) Flight 718 left Los Angeles on its way to Chicago, carrying fifty-eight passengers and crew. Both pilots were flying under instrument flight rules (IFR), requiring them to fly prearranged routes, check in with air traffic control, and receive permission to fly at specific altitudes. According to their flight plans, the two aircraft should have been at different altitudes when their paths crossed.

Shortly after takeoff, TWA pilot Jack Gandy and UA pilot Robert Shirley changed to visual flight rules (VFR). Under VFR, pilots could fly at higher altitudes in uncontrolled (unsupervised) airspace but were expected to visually identify and avoid nearby planes. TWA pilot Gandy had received permission from flight control to fly one thousand feet above the highest clouds. Flight controllers on the ground did not realize this could place TWA Flight 2 at the same altitude as UA Flight 718.

At 10:31 A.M., flight controllers received a garbled radio message, later identified as the last transmission from the United Airlines flight; there were no further radio communications from either plane. A private pilot spotted wreckage from both planes in a remote area of the Grand Canyon along the Colorado River. Air Force and Army helicopters reached the crash sites on July 1 but found no survivors.

The Investigation The United States Civil Aeronautics Board (CAB), the Air Line Pilots Association, and the Air Transport Association conducted a ten-month investigation of the accident. CAB reconstructed the accident from the condition of debris at the crash sites, taking into account weather conditions, cloud cover, the physical layout of each plane's cockpit, and human limitations. CAB concluded that neither pilot had seen the other plane until it was too late to avoid a midair collision.

One flight controller had warned Gandy that Shirley's plane was nearby, but Shirley had not been similarly warned about the proximity of the TWA flight. CAB noted that flight controllers were not required to keep pilots informed about nearby air traffic; the Civil Aeronautics Administration did not have the necessary funding or staffing to provide more extensive air traffic control.

Impact The Grand Canyon collision increased public awareness of air safety standards. Soon after the incident, the Air Line Pilots Association and Air Transport Association agreed pilots should avoid flying by visual flight rules. Several more commercial flights nearly collided following the Grand Canyon crash. Congress allocated funds to improve air traffic control with more personnel and better radar equipment. The independent Federal Aviation Administration was created in 1958 as part of a movement to improve air safety, replacing the government-run Civil Aeronautics Administration.

Further Reading

Knight, Clayton, and K. S. Knight. "Collision Hazards." In *Plane Crash: The Mysteries of Major Air Disasters and How They Were Solved.* New York: Greenberg, 1958. Provides a detailed description of the crash.

Mallan, Lloyd. *Great Air Disasters.* Greenwich, Conn.: Fawcett, 1962. Discusses several air disasters, including the Grand Canyon crash, with a thorough

account of the subsequent Civil Aeronautics Administration investigation.

Maureen J. Puffer-Rothenberg

See also Aircraft design and development; *Andrea Doria* sinking; Boeing 707; Federal Aviation Administration.

■ Great Books movement

Identification Movement surrounding a set of books whose influence peaked during the 1950's, especially in the reform of adult education in North America

The Great Books movement reintroduced a number of Western classics to the American literary canon, influenced higher education curriculum, and sparked a popular interest in what were widely regarded as literary "masterpieces."

The Great Books movement that became popular in North America during the 1950's began as a modest educational reform at Columbia University in 1921. English professor John Erskine introduced an innovative general honors course after concluding that the university's undergraduate curriculum was too specialized and too focused on practical, vocational goals to provide an adequate general education. He sought to remedy this defect by devising a course based on a broad and rigorous set of readings that consisted of "classic" works drawn from what he called the Western tradition—books that embodied ideas and values characteristic of Western civilization as found in Europe and the Americas.

Erskine's curriculum consisted of selected classics of literature and philosophy that ranged from the ancient Greek poet Homer to works from the nineteenth century. Each week his students discussed a book under review in a required two-hour seminar. Erskine believed that the skills of careful reading, informed discussion, and logical thinking derived from the study of the Great Books would prove invaluable, regardless of the specialized studies or the particular vocation a student might later pursue.

Among the students in Erskine's first Great Books class was a brash, intense young man named Mortimer Adler. Adler was inspired to make a career of teaching the Great Books and preaching their educational value. By 1930, Adler was on the University of Chicago faculty, where he quickly convinced the new university president Robert Hutchins to adopt the Great Books approach to general education. For several years Adler co-taught, on the Erskine model, a popular Great Books course with Hutchins himself. Because the movement generated a great deal of debate and dissent among the University of Chicago faculty, Adler and Hutchins turned their attention toward adult nondegree education in the Great Books. Adler left the university in 1946, and Hutchins resigned as president in 1950. They continued their collaboration on Great Books projects for years to come, however.

The heyday of the Great Books movement came in the 1950's. The era witnessed a dramatic expansion of adult Great Books education across the United States and into Canada. Hundreds of Great Books discussion groups formed and met regularly in homes, schools, and community centers. The cornerstone of this venture under Adler and Hutchins was the publication in early 1952 of a massive collection of classic readings titled *Great Books of the Western World*. Contained in its fifty-one volumes were some seventy-four authors and more than three hundred writings. To give more coherence to such a diverse collection, Adler edited a two-volume index, the *Syntopican*, in which he cross-referenced 102 "master ideas" that were contained in the authors' writings. The *Syntopican* demonstrated clearly the interconnection of the major ideas in what Hutchins called the Great Conversation.

Impact Skillful promotion, including the help of the newly created Great Books Foundation, helped to ensure the remarkable financial success of the *Great Books of the Western World* set for years to come. Thousands of readers now had access to texts often inaccessible in preceding years. However, mounting criticism of the Great Books series and curriculum took its toll. The popularity of the movement waned. Nonetheless, adult Great Books classes remained active into the twenty-first century, when nearly forty colleges in the United States and Canada continued to teach the Great Books in some form. The Great Books Foundation also introduced programs at the primary and secondary school levels. In sum, despite an occasionally checkered history, the Great Books movement in general education, which reached the summit of its influence in the 1950's, continues to have a significant impact.

Great Books of the Western World: Selected Titles in 1952

Chaucer, Geoffrey, *Troilus and Criseyde* (1382)
Dante, *The Divine Comedy* (1320)
Darwin, Charles, *On the Origin of Species by Means of Natural Selection* (1859)
Euripides, *Medea* (431)
Galilei, Galileo, *Dialogue Concerning the Two Chief World Systems, Ptolemaic and Copernican* (1632)
Gibbon, Edward, *The History of the Decline and Fall of the Roman Empire* (1779)
Hamilton, Alexander, James Madison, and John Jay, *The Federalist* (1788)
Homer, *Iliad* (c. 725 B.C.E.) and *Odyssey* (c. 725 B.C.E.)
Machiavelli, Niccolò, *The Prince* (1532)
Marx, Karl, and Friedrich Engels, *The Communist Manifesto* (1848)
Melville, Herman, *Moby Dick: Or, The Whale* (1851)
Mill, John Stuart, *On Liberty* (1859)
Plutarch, *Parallel Lives*, also known as *The Lives of the Noble Grecians and Romans* (c. 105-115)
Rabelais, Francois, *Pantagruel* (1532) and *Gargantua* (1534)
Shakespeare, William, *Hamlet, Prince of Denmark* (1600-1601)
Smith, Adam, *An Inquiry into the Nature and Causes of the Wealth of Nations* (1776)
Swift, Jonathan, *Gulliver's Travels* (1726)
Tacitus, Cornelius, *Annals* (c. 116)
Tolstoy, Leo, *War and Peace* (1865-1869)

Further Reading

Allen, James S. *The Renaissance of Commerce and Culture*. Chicago: University of Chicago Press, 1983. Contains a concise, objective account of the evolution of the Great Books movement from Erskine to Adler.

Campbell, W. John. *The Book of Great Books*. New York: Barnes and Noble Books, 2003. Examines one hundred of the world's most enduring novels, plays, and epic poems and discusses why they have remained influential over the years.

Hutchins, Robert, and Mortimer Adler, eds. *Great Books of the Western World*. 2d. ed. 61 volumes. Chicago: Encyclopedia Britannica, 1990. A later version of the series.

Donald Sullivan

See also Book publishing; Education in the United States; Literature in the United States.

■ Greco, José

Identification Flamenco dancer and choreographer
Born December 23, 1918; Montorio nei Frentani, Italy
Died December 31, 2000; Lancaster, Pennsylvania

The best-known Spanish dancer in the world, José Greco rose to greater prominence during the 1950's after the creation of his own dance company, a successful run on Broadway, and appearances in films.

Born of Spanish-Italian parents, Costanzo "Gus" Greco moved to New York at the age of ten. During his teenage years, he began developing his talent by practicing for hours in the basement after his parents were asleep. After adopting the name José, he danced with various partners in the United States and Europe and continued to perfect his vibrant choreography. In 1951, he formed the José Greco Spanish Dance Company, successfully integrating the intensely passionate "gypsy style" with the elegance and strength of classical ballet. After the company's first year at New York City's Shubert Theatre, he was named New Broadway Personality of the Year. Greco so delighted audiences with his flamboyant style that during his performances they often shouted "Ole!"—an accolade previously reserved for courageous bullfighters.

Impact The popularity of flamenco increased as television brought the flash, excitement, and magnetism of dancers into family living rooms everywhere. By 1958, after dancing in several films, including *Sombrero* (1953) and *Around the World in Eighty Days* (1956), Greco was a frequent and highly paid guest on television, often appearing on variety shows and even teaching flamenco to the puppets on the 1950's children's program *Kukla, Fran and Ollie.*

Greco retired from dance during the 1960's, was knighted by the Spanish government in 1962, and served as adjunct professor at a college in Pennsylvania until his death at age eighty-two.

Further Reading

Derezinski, Amelia. *Star Turns: Dancing on Broadway.* New York: Rosen, 2004. A general book that explores the historical traditions of New York theater.

Greco, José, with Harvey Ardman. *The Gypsy in My Soul: The Autobiography of José Greco.* Garden City, N.Y.: Doubleday, 1977. A vivid personal account of Greco's rise to stardom, featuring the tempestuous women who danced with him and loved him.

Gale M. Thompson

See also Ailey, Alvin, Jr.; *Around the World in Eighty Days*; Film in the United States; *Kukla, Fran and Ollie*; Television in the United States; Theater in the United States.

■ Gross national product of Canada

Definition Canada's national total of consumption outlays, private investment inside the country, and expenditures of governments for both goods and services, minus imported goods and services

The growth of Canada's economy during the 1950's marked its inclusion among the developed countries of the world, especially as the Canadian standard of living began to approximate that in the United States.

During the 1950's, Canada's gross national product (GNP) grew substantially. Between 1950 and 1959, the GNP grew by two-thirds. Measured in 1971 dollars, Canada's gross national product grew in 1950 from C$33.7 billion to C$51.7 billion in 1959. The real gross domestic product (GDP), that is, the GNP adjusted for price inflation, grew during the decade at a rate never before attained—6.55 percent per year. The real GDP per capita also grew at a rate higher than ever before—3.77 percent per year.

The Canadian dollar, initially pegged to the U.S. dollar, fluctuated at around par for most of the decade until the Bank of Canada loosened monetary policy as the economy slowed down during the late 1950's. The Canadian dollar then declined to around $0.92 (U.S.).

During the early 1950's, growth was propelled partly by inflation and partly by the stimulus of the Korean War. Unemployment ran at about 4.7 percent per year. However, by the late 1950's, growth diminished and unemployment began to rise. This was due in part to a restriction in some of the export markets that earlier had fueled Canadian growth, notably the growth of competition for Canada's grain exports and its exports of minerals.

Impact The growth of Canada's gross national product was fueled in large measure by new investment, both public and private. The government undertook the development of the country's infrastructure, notably with the building of the Trans-Canada Highway and the construction, in cooperation with the United States, of the St. Lawrence Seaway, which opened up the provinces of Quebec and Ontario to world commerce. In particular, the seaway facilitated shipments of grain, oil, and ore from the center of the country to the outside world.

Subsequent Events The investments of the 1950's enabled Canada's economy to recover during the 1960's from the modest downturn of the late 1950's. The country's production of minerals continued to expand sharply—Canada was the world's largest producer of nickel—and the development of new mines fueled further expansion. Public expenditure continued to rise at the provincial and municipal levels.

Further Reading

Bothwell, Robert, Ian Drummond, and John English. *Canada Since 1945: Power, Politics, and Provincialism.* Rev. ed. Toronto: University of Toronto Press, 1989. Although the book covers politics primarily, it has several chapters on the development of the economy.

Lamontagne, Maurice. *Business Cycles in Canada: The Postwar Experience and Policy Directions.* Toronto: James Lorimer, 1984. Provides the historical figures for GNP.

Marr, William L., and Donald G. Paterson. *Canada: An Economic History.* Toronto: Macmillan, 1980. Provides data on growth rates in comparison to earlier periods as well as the 1960's.

Rea, K. J. *The Prosperous Years: The Economic History of Ontario, 1939-1975.* Toronto: University of Toronto Press, 1985. Although focused primarily on Ontario, Canada's most populous and most in-

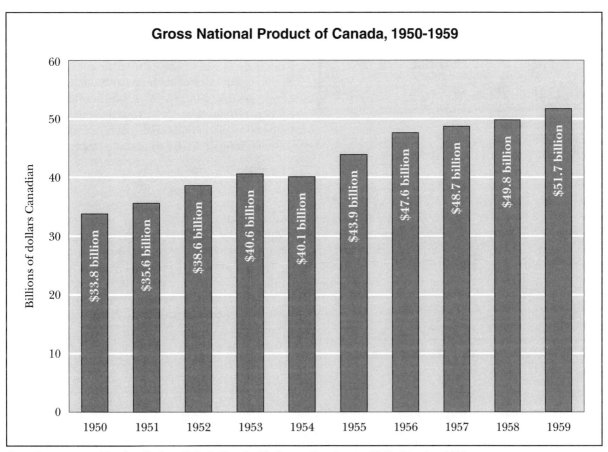

Gross National Product of Canada, 1950-1959

Source: Lamontagne, Maurice. *Business Cycles in Canada: The Postwar Experience and Policy Directions,* 1984.

Casting room in a Canadian nickel plant during the early 1950's. (Hulton Archive | by Getty Images)

dustrialized province, it gives a good picture of overall development.

Nancy M. Gordon

See also Agriculture in Canada; Business and the economy in Canada; Canada and U.S. investments; Gross national product of the United States; Income and wages in Canada; Inflation in Canada; Unemployment in Canada; Unionism in Canada; Unionism in the United States.

■ Gross national product of the United States

Definition United States' national total of consumption outlays, private investment inside the country, and expenditures of governments for both goods and services, minus imported goods and services

Gross national product data track the significant growth of national output during the 1950's, contributing to higher living standards, despite some inflation and mild recessions.

Gross national product (GNP) has two dimensions—price and quantity. When price changes are filtered out, one can obtain estimates of real GNP, which show what happened to the quantity of output over time. GNP data are useful in tracking the short-run movements of the business cycle and the long-run growth trend of output. In 1954 and 1958, real GNP actually declined, marking episodes of economic recession. However, both recessionary episodes were mild and brief. Between 1950 and 1959, real output grew at an average annual rate of 3.3 percent. Roughly half of this growth was absorbed by rising population, and half was available to support improvement in living standards for households.

An increase in the U.S. population enabled the labor force to rise by an annual average of 1.2 percent. Thus the larger share of output growth came from higher labor productivity. An important contribution was the major increase in education resulting from the G.I. Bill of Rights. The amount of business capital goods per worker increased, and the technology of production improved. Workers shifted from lower-productivity work (primarily agriculture) into higher-productivity activities. Government added valuable infrastructure, such as highways.

Aggregate Demand GNP is a measure of total expenditures to buy currently produced goods and services, also termed "aggregate demand." One can analyze aggregate demand by looking at the sectors involved. The components are consumption spending by households; investment spending, which includes purchases of currently produced capital goods (housing and other structures, producers' equipment, and additions to business inventories); government purchases of goods and services; and net exports.

Variations in these components of aggregate demand are the chief cause of business fluctuations. The rapid growth of federal defense spending associated with the Korean War of the early 1950's spurred large growth in output and employment, to be followed by a slump in 1954 when spending was reduced. This recession raised unemployment by 2.5 percent of the labor force. The sizable drop in business investment spending (particularly for inventories) brought on another recession in 1958, accompanied by a similar increase in unemployment. Consumption spending increased every year, reflecting the stabilizing influence of government transfer payment programs such as unemployment compensation. Such income supplements allowed household incomes to increase even in years of economic recession.

These variations in aggregate demand were also the immediate cause of inflation, primarily resulting from the Korean War. With relatively low unemployment, business firms were easily able to demand higher prices when buyers increased spending—at least until price controls were imposed. Consumer prices increased by about 10 percent from 1950 to 1952 and rose another 10 percent over the remainder of the decade as price controls were removed.

Economic data indicate the kinds of goods and services that the economy produced. Through most of the 1950's, consumer goods and services accounted for 63-65 percent of national output. Capital goods of all kinds, which contributed importantly to increasing labor productivity, accounted (after abnormally high levels in 1950-1951) for 14-17 percent. Government purchases (which include pay of government employees) shot up from 13 percent in 1950 to 22 percent in 1952-1953 and then leveled off to a slightly lower figure.

Income Shares GNP represents the total of gross income shares generated by the economy. Most of these go to households in the form of labor income, rent, interest, and profits. Some income is retained within the business sector. Business disposable income is estimated as capital consumption allowances plus undistributed corporate profits. House-

Gross National Product of the United States, 1950-1959
(in current prices)

Source: U.S. Department of Commerce, Bureau of the Census.

hold income includes government transfer payments and interest.

All the money spent to buy current output becomes income for one of the sectors of the economy; there is always enough income to buy all the output at current prices. However, not all the income goes to the private sector, since government takes a significant share. About four-fifths of GNP during the 1950's went into the disposable (after-tax) incomes of households and business.

Because the economy's production capacity grows from year to year, it is important that aggregate demand also increase. This can occur only if some sectors spend more than their income. Typically this is the role of business, borrowing in order to finance spending for the capital goods that support higher output and more jobs.

Impact After the major economic disorders of the 1930's and 1940's, gross national product during the 1950's manifested the signs of a healthy economy, with vigorous growth and only mild fluctuations. This good performance was aided by relatively skillful exercise of monetary and fiscal policies by the federal government, pursuant to the Employment Act of 1946.

Further Reading

Hickman, Bert G. *Growth and Stability of the Postwar Economy.* Washington, D.C.: Brookings Institution, 1960. This scholarly study devotes a separate chapter to each major component of aggregate demand.

Stein, Herbert. *The Fiscal Revolution in America.* Chicago: University of Chicago Press, 1969. Chapters 10 through 14 give a lively view of the macroeconomics of the 1950's, narrated by a longtime policy insider.

Vatter, Harold G. *The U.S. Economy in the 1950's: An Economic History.* New York: W. W. Norton, 1963. Data and categories of GNP are at the heart of this readable overview.

Paul B. Trescott

See also *Affluent Society, The*; Agriculture in the United States; Business and the economy in the United States; G.I. Bill; Income and wages in the United States; Inflation in the United States; International trade of the United States; Korean War; Recession of 1957-1958; Unemployment in the United States.

■ Guatemala invasion

The Event U.S.-assisted rebel invasion of Guatemala that overthrew a reformist president

Date June, 1954

U.S. confidence in the effectiveness of covert operations as a tool in the Cold War grew as a result of a low-cost victory in Guatemala, but the affair left a residue of anti-American feeling in Latin America.

The 1950 election of Jacobo Arbenz as Guatemalan president set his nation on a collision course with the United States. Arbenz was a determined nationalist who also was married to a communist. Moreover, his associations with the pro-Soviet Guatemalan Workers' Party (PGT) deepened worries in the presidential administrations of both Harry S. Truman and Dwight D. Eisenhower. In 1952 and 1953, Arbenz implemented a sweeping land reform program called Decree 900. It aimed to redistribute to poor peasants all large plantations, a plan that alarmed officials of Boston-based United Fruit Company (UFCO), the largest landholder in Guatemala. UFCO launched an ambitious public relations campaign that labeled Arbenz a communist. Privately, UFCO lobbyists urged the U.S. government to take action, finding sympathetic ears especially with Secretary of State John Foster Dulles and his brother, Central Intelligence Agency (CIA) director Allen Dulles. They and other high officials in the Eisenhower administration had substantial ties to UFCO prior to becoming elected officials.

Official planning for the operation that Eisenhower ultimately would authorize as Operation PBSuccess began in August, 1953. Its purpose was the overthrow of the Arbenz government, and it had several elements. An early goal was to foster alarm and panic in the Guatemalan public and thus to undermine support for Arbenz within the Guatemalan armed forces. Coordinated from Opa-locka, Florida, a CIA-sponsored campaign of psychological warfare dubbed Radio Liberation was launched on a set of news radio stations. Though most of the Radio Liberation transmitters were in neighboring countries, two were inside Guatemala, and one was inside the U.S. embassy. Behind the scenes, subtle approaches were made to senior military officers, urging cooperation with the U.S. goal of stopping Arbenz. To diplomatically isolate Arbenz from neighboring states' support, a March, 1954, Organization of American States conference at Caracas, Venezuela, produced near unanimous support for a U.S.-authored denunciation of communist influence in Guatemala. This influence seemed heightened by the May 15 delivery to Guatemala of more than fifteen thousand cases of military weapons—more than four million pounds—bought from communist Czechoslovakia and delivered by the cargo ship *Alfem,* a freighter of Swedish registry.

The Invasion With the stage set, U.S.-organized rebels, chiefly former military personnel in exile, played a key part in the plan to overthrow Arbenz. Former colonel Carlos Castillo Armas was chosen by the CIA as the rebels' leader. His troops were armed by the United States, trained in Nicaragua with the assistance of its president, Anastasio Somoza, and then moved to the Honduran-Guatemalan border area, where they awaited the go-ahead from Washington, D.C. A CIA air force of numerous planes provided support. On June 15, 1954, Eisenhower gave the green light to the invasion, and two days later, the lightly armed exiles crossed the border. However, they advanced only a few miles into Guatemala before stalling: Castillo Armas's Liberation Army did little militarily to dislodge the Guatemalan army.

To magnify perceptions of a mounting crisis, CIA aircraft then bombed Guatemalan fuel tanks and an important military base near the capital. Radio Liberation broadcasts over the next ten days greatly exaggerated the size of the invading force and its military capabilities, in one instance suggesting that perhaps five thousand invaders were armed, when, in fact, they numbered less than two hundred.

PBSuccess was designed not to conquer Guatemala but to stimu-

late the Guatemalan armed forces to demand a change of government. This event occurred on June 27, when army chief of staff Colonel Carlos Enrique Diaz informed Arbenz that it was time to leave; Arbenz announced his resignation over the radio and requested asylum in the Mexican embassy. Subsequently, Castillo Armas was flown into Guatemala City by the United States and was named president of the country shortly thereafter.

Impact The absence of extensive costs or casualties in the Guatemalan operation encouraged U.S. offi-

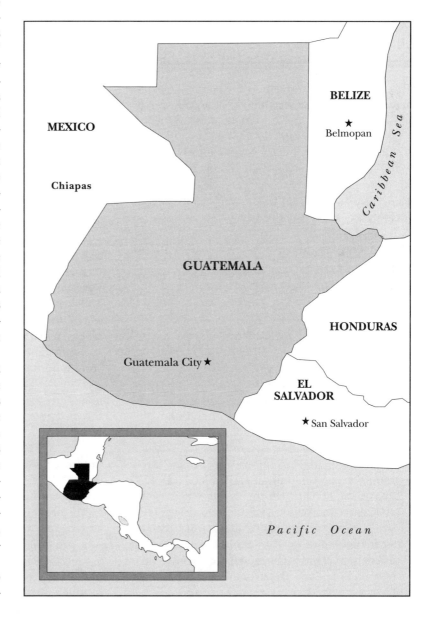

cials to believe that covert operations were an effective way to end anti-American regimes in developing nations. The removal of Arbenz, which was sympathetically reported in the United States' media as a victory for the "forces of freedom" in the Cold War, also built public support for the overall anticommunist policy of that era. While it would be decades before the United States openly would acknowledge its direction of the removal of Arbenz, within Latin America it was broadly perceived as an American operation at the time, casting an ominous shadow over other countries who went against the grain of America's interests.

Subsequent Events An eyewitness to the overthrow of Arbenz, Argentine exile Ernesto "Che" Guevara drew strong lessons from these events. When Guevara and Fidel Castro came to power as rulers of Cuba in 1959, they quickly disbanded the prerevolutionary armed forces, replacing them with a politically reliable and loyal force. Thus, when the very same CIA personnel attempted to replicate Operation PBSuccess in a new operation against Cuba in 1960-1961—an operation that used Guatemala as its training base—a small invading force of Cuban exiles could not stimulate a military coup against Castro. In this very real sense, the United States relied too much on lessons derived from Guatemala: They led the CIA directly to disaster at the Bay of Pigs in April, 1961.

Further Reading

Cullather, Nick. *Secret History: The CIA's Classified Account of Its Operations in Guatemala, 1952-1954.* Stanford, Calif.: Stanford University Press, 1999. Written during the early 1990's as an official CIA in-house history, this volume later was declassified for public use. Despite some deletions for security purposes, these official documents richly convey key features of the U.S. operation.

Schlesinger, Stephen, and Stephen Kinzer. *Bitter Fruit: The Story of the American Coup in Guatemala.* Cambridge, Mass.: Harvard University Press, 1999. Originally published by Doubleday in 1982, this classic book places the fall of Arbenz within an Eisenhower White House agenda driven by desire to protect U.S. economic interests. Includes an updated afterword by Schlesinger and a new assessment of the consequences of the invasion by former U.S. State Department official Richard Nuccio.

Streeter, Stephen M. *Managing the Counterrevolution: The United States and Guatemala, 1954-1961.* Athens: Ohio University Center for International Studies, 2000. A well-documented account that carefully compares the author's thesis about American desire for hegemony with those of earlier works that emphasized economic or Cold War motives behind American actions. Provides extensive analysis of later impact of the 1954 events.

Gordon L. Bowen

See also Castro, Fidel; Central Intelligence Agency; Cuban Revolution; Dulles, John Foster; Eisenhower Doctrine; Latin America; Lodge, Henry Cabot; Mexico; Nixon's Latin America tour; Organization of American States; Truman Doctrine; United Fruit Company.

■ Guggenheim Museum

Identification Modern-art museum
Date Opened in 1959
Place New York City

Designed by Frank Lloyd Wright to showcase modern art, this museum is considered to be one of the great examples of twentieth century architecture.

In 1939, Solomon R. Guggenheim's art collection was opened to the public as the Museum of Non-Objective Painting, located on New York City's East Fifty-fourth Street. Although the museum was originally committed to nonrepresentational modernist works, the 1950's marked a time of transition. The scope of the collection was expanded to include sculpture and more representational examples of contemporary art.

Famed architect Frank Lloyd Wright was selected to design a new building for the collection. In 1950, the purchase of the building site, Fifth Avenue between Eighty-eighth and Eighty-ninth Streets, was completed. Ground was broken in 1956. Wright's unique glass-domed structure of poured concrete departed from rigid rectilinear building styles. Its hollow core was surrounded by a six-story spiral ramp that moved upward and outward to create a continuous, curving space. Although many feared its sloping walls and floors would be unsuitable for artistic display, the new structure, called the Solomon R. Guggenheim Museum in memory of its founder, opened on October 21, 1959.

Interior of Frank Lloyd Wright's Guggenheim Museum in New York City in 1959. (AP/Wide World Photos)

Impact During the 1950's, the Guggenheim evolved from a museum of nonrepresentational art to one in which the entire scope of modernism was represented. Its structure came to be regarded as one of the twentieth century's great buildings and one of the most original in museum architecture. Designed to house an art collection, it became a work of art in itself.

Further Reading

Solomon R. Guggenheim Foundation. *Art of This Century: The Guggenheim Museum and Its Collection.* New York: Guggenheim Museum Publications, 1997. Illustrated essays on the collections provide an overview of twentieth century art.

Spector, Nancy, ed. *Guggenheim Museum Collection A to Z.* New York: Solomon R. Guggenheim Foundation, 2001. Guidebook to the museum and its collections.

Cassandra Lee Tellier

See also Abstract expressionism; Architecture; Art movements; de Kooning, Willem; Getty, J. Paul; Johns, Jasper; Kline, Franz; Motherwell, Robert; Pollock, Jackson; Rauschenberg, Robert.

■ *Gunsmoke*

Identification Long-running television Western series
Producer Norman Macdonnell (1916-1979)
Date Aired from 1955 to 1975

The first major "adult Western" series on television, Gunsmoke portrayed the American West realistically as violent and uncivilized.

Originally popular on radio, *Gunsmoke* successfully made the transition to television, eventually becoming television's longest-running Western series. The show was set in the rough frontier town of Dodge City, Kansas, during the 1880's and depicted the

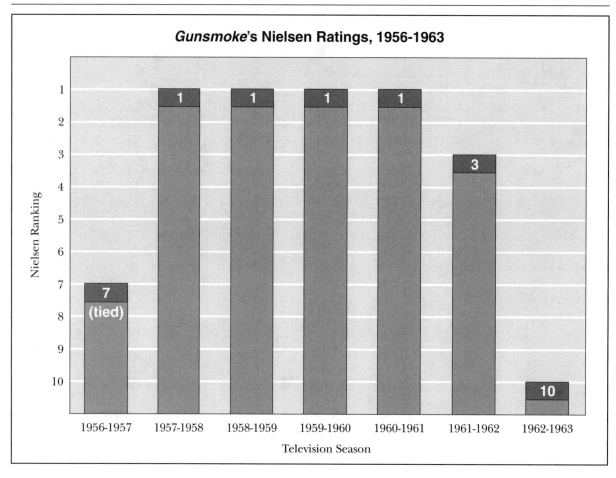

Gunsmoke's Nielsen Ratings, 1956-1963

daily lives of Marshal Matt Dillon (played by James Arness), his deputy Chester Goode (Dennis Weaver), cantankerous Doc Adams (Milburn Stone), and Kitty Russell (Amanda Blake), the proprietor of the Longbranch saloon. Setting the tone with its famous opening gunfight scene, *Gunsmoke* was aimed at adult viewers, unlike *The Lone Ranger* and other contemporary television Westerns, which were typically intended for children. Lawbreakers could be brutally cut down by Marshal Dillion. Episodes included amputations, spousal abuse, and senseless shootings. In *Gunsmoke*'s raw version of the Old West, Dillon did not ride a white horse and rarely turned down a drink in the saloon.

Impact *Gunsmoke*'s stark, unglamorous depiction of the American West was a shock to 1950's audiences, who were accustomed to romanticized Westerns with sanitized heroes. Nonetheless, the show affirmed social values of the decade. The terse, rugged Marshal

Dillon maintained law and order. He championed the virtues of fair play and honesty, and while not a typical 1950's family unit, the core cast was an extended family who showed mutual affection and respect for one another.

Further Reading

Aaker, Everett. *Television Western Players of the Fifties: A Biographical Encyclopedia of All Regular Cast Members in Western Series, 1949-1959.* Jefferson, N.C.: McFarland, 1997. Collection of brief biographies of television actors, including those on *Gunsmoke.*

Barabas, SuzAnne, and Gabor Barabas. *Gunsmoke: A Complete History and Analysis of the Legendary Broadcast Series.* Jefferson, N.C.: McFarland, 1990. The definitive sourcebook, featuring interviews with cast members, abundant photographs, and detailed episode-by-episode guides to the radio and television programs.

Stark, Steven D. "*Gunsmoke* and Television's Lost Wave of Westerns." In *Glued to the Set: The Sixty Television Shows and Events That Made Us What We Are Today.* New York: Free Press, 1997. An engrossing analysis of *Gunsmoke* in the contexts of contemporary social values and the television Western.

Yoggy, Gary A., ed. *Back in the Saddle: Essays on Western Film and Television Actors.* Jefferson, N.C.: McFarland, 1998. Essays on a variety of Western film and television subjects, including a discussion of *Gunsmoke.*

Richard W. Grefrath

See also *Cisco Kid, The*; *Lone Ranger, The*; Radio; *Sergeant Preston of the Yukon*; *Sky King*; Television in the United States; Television Westerns.

Gunsmoke costars Dennis Weaver (left), who played Chester, and James Arness, who played the indomitable Marshal Matt Dillon, in 1956. (AP/Wide World Photos)

■ Gunther, John

Identification American journalist and author
Born August 30, 1901; Chicago, Illinois
Died May 29, 1970; New York, New York

John Gunther's fame, earned in earlier decades as the author of "Inside" books about foreign lands, continued during the 1950's with the publication of his books on Africa and the Soviet Union.

At the beginning of the 1950's, John Gunther was already one of the most famous writers in the United States, primarily because of his series of "Inside" books, in which he presented detailed reports on whole continents or countries. *Inside Europe* (1936) was an instant success and was followed by *Inside Asia* (1939), *Inside Latin America* (1941), and *Inside the U.S.A.* (1947). Gunther also won acclaim for his sensitive memoir about his teenage son's unsuccessful battle against cancer, *Death Be Not Proud* (1949).

In the opening years of the 1950's, however, Gunther issued three less successful books: *Roosevelt in Retrospect* (1950), a study of the late president that some saw as too laudatory and lacking in analysis; *The Riddle of MacArthur: Japan, Korea, and the Far East* (1951), about the controversial American general, which some saw as inaccurate; and *Eisenhower: The Man and the Symbol* (1952), seen by some as mere campaign literature.

However, during the mid-1950's, Gunther returned to what he did best, producing two new Inside books. First came *Inside Africa* (1955), about a continent in the news because of the bloody Mau Mau uprisings in Kenya, the anticolonial movement in Morocco, and the apartheid system in South Africa, which Gunther strongly criticized. Next came *Inside Russia Today* (1958), a balanced and even somewhat positive account of America's Cold War adversary, which had recently moved from the harsh rule of Joseph Stalin to what Gunther saw as an altogether different sort of rule under Nikita Khrushchev. The book came out shortly after the Soviet Union surprised the world with the launch of the *Sputnik* space satellite, an achievement Gunther noted as part of his generally positive evaluation of Soviet science and education.

Both books were huge successes, selling hundreds of thousands of copies, and both were Book-of-the-Month Club selections and were widely praised by reviewers for their readability and their informativeness. When the book on the Soviet Union appeared, *Time* magazine put Gunther on its cover and ran a long feature article on him in which it said that he was more famous than most of the people he interviewed. The following year, he was asked to host a short-lived television series, *John Gunther's High Road.* His name even became a word for a time: to "guntherize" meant to do the sort of sweeping study Gunther produced in his Inside books.

After the 1950's, Gunther's fame receded. His book-length presentations of life in far-off lands began to be superseded by the greater immediacy of television. He completed only one more full-length Inside book, *Inside South America* (1967), though he was working on an "Inside Australia" book when he died.

Impact During the 1950's, continuing the role he had played in the previous two decades, John Gunther was America's eyes and ears in foreign lands. Americans relied on his books to learn about exotic places and important political developments abroad.

Even when criticisms were made of his analyses—some found him too positive or ambivalent about the Soviet Union, for instance—the information he accumulated was usually seen as invaluable. When Vice President Richard M. Nixon visited the Soviet Union in 1959, he took along *Inside Russia Today* as background material for himself and his staff.

Further Reading

Cuthbertson, Ken. *Inside: The Biography of John Gunther.* Chicago: Bonus Books, 1992. The only full-length biography.

Gunther, John. *A Fragment of Autobiography: The Fun of Writing the Inside Books.* New York: Harper & Row, 1962. Gunther's own account of writing his most famous books.

"The Insider." *Time* (April 14, 1958): 44-52. Feature on Gunther at the time that *Inside Russia Today* was published.

Sheldon Goldfarb

See also Cold War; Eisenhower, Dwight D.; Nixon, Richard M.; *Sputnik I.*

H

■ Hairstyles

During the 1950's, hairstyles mirrored the popular idealist American culture while retaining some sense of conservatism for mainstream society.

While North America experienced affluence accompanied by excesses and change in almost every area of life during the 1950's, hairstyles remained subdued for most of the population with the exception of the youth. The G.I. crew cut, also known as the Ivy League cut, was the wholesome and respectable style for men. This parted and brushed, one-inch haircut characterized the 1950's distinguished looking, upwardly mobile man. Hairstyles for most women were fashionably short at the entrance to the 1950's and remained so until near the end of the decade, when a longer style became popular. Even longer-haired styles remained conservative, with hair close to the head and neck or pulled back and held in a chignon. With the rise in the use of acrylic and modacrylic fibers, which easily simulated natural hair, wigs and hairpieces became increasingly popular. Women completed the look with small, close-fitting hats with or without netting trim, but as patronage of beauty salons increased and the longer style emerged, hats decreased in popularity.

The Elvis Look People more than events influenced hairstyles during the 1950's. While politicians had some influence in the hair trends of the decade, theater, film, and television—the new entertainment medium to invade American homes—brought wide public attention to the styles of actors and celebrities. Elvis Presley, a young singer from Memphis, Tennessee, credited with changing a generation of young people, played a huge role in influencing hairstyles of the latter half of the decade. Presley became as well known for his head of dark hair that flopped, fluttered, and fell onto his face as for his frantic hip-swiveling movements. The gyrations that produced the unruly hair made young women wild and young men imitate the Elvis style. The constant adjustment of his hair brought shrills of delight from girls and imitation from teen boys. When the U.S. Army cut his famous sideburns and ducktail, the coal-black clippings set off a bidding frenzy.

At the same time, girls and young women showed their devotion to Elvis by getting haircuts that resembled his pre-G.I. style. Presley began a trend for the youth generation, making it acceptable to spend time grooming and performing tasks such as dyeing, wave setting, and greasing one's hair into a conforming style. While many young men faithfully practiced these techniques so as to acquire the perfect sideburns and ducktail style, the older establishment sometimes viewed this hairstyle as a rebellious act that would ultimately bring about the erosion of morals, work ethics, and all other positive character traits. One young man was sentenced to ten days in jail or "a man's haircut" after being arrested in Tacoma, Washington, for sporting an Elvis style. The military strictly forbade this extreme civilian haircut in favor of the short crew cut of the conservative class. While other men such as the young male star James Dean, who made famous the greaser look, and President Dwight D. Eisenhower, who made acceptable the distinguished bald look, may have influenced hairstyles, it was Elvis Presley who had the strongest and most lasting influence on male hairstyles during the era.

Women's Styles Film and stage stars such as Audrey Hepburn, Mary Martin, Grace Kelly, Faye Emerson, Joan Crawford, and Maria Callas set trends in hairstyles for young women, while First Lady Mamie Eisenhower captured the attention of the older, established generations of women. Audrey Hepburn introduced a short hairdo that became a national craze during the early 1950's, but it was not until Faye Emerson donned the style on television that the name poodle cut was coined and used to describe the short, curled style that resembled a manlike look. The poodle cut was widely received by young and old alike but not by the hairstylist, who dubbed this style as unforgiving because every sag on the face and neck was exposed. Even Mamie Eisenhower adopted a version of the poodle cut that featured bangs framing her forehead. Many stars followed the style to a degree. Elizabeth Taylor cut her luxurious locks to a shorter style, but by the mid- to late decade, she and others were growing long hair styled close to the head in a nonbouffant style.

Throughout the 1950's, chapters in books and articles in magazines were devoted to the best hairstyles to wear with various shapes of faces. The oval-shaped face was deemed the ideal for women, and hairstyles were used to create the illusion of this shape if one was not born with this desired beauty trait.

Trends Chemistry met with fashion to produce innovative hairstyles during the 1950's. Permanent waves for men, curls for women, and straightened hair for African Americans were achieved by the application of chemicals. Toni, a manufacturer of chemical "permanents" (or "perms") for use in the home, became a household word. In addition to shaping hair, chemicals were used to create solutions to add color to hair using rinses, tints, and dyes. Bleaching agents to remove color were also used. Home kits of these solutions and agents, and well as kits for home permanents, were marketed to the consumer.

Many appliances were created or redesigned for hairstyle purposes. The hot curling iron was a favorite among consumers. A portable version of the flexible, plastic-hooded hair dryer met success because it allowed the busy homemaker to continue other tasks while the heating unit either hung from her shoulder or was attached to her waistline.

During the 1950's, wigs and hairpieces were created for men and women. French designer Hubert de Givenchy assisted in the popularization of such items made of synthetic fibers and real human hair when he had models don elaborately styled ones in a 1958 fashion show. Sears Roebuck department stories sent thirty thousand catalogs featuring toupees in unmarked packages to men.

Millinery fashion for women changed drastically during the 1950's. The prevailing styles included the pillbox, bcrct, cloche, and whimsy because they best enhanced the short hairstyles of the time. However, the popularity of the hair salon among middle-class women curtailed the hat market; the American woman rebelled at having to place a hat on a recently created salon hairdo.

Impact Hairstyles of the 1950's both reinforced the conservative culture of the times and, in the case of the Elvis style, simultaneously reflected and promoted the new, rebellious youth culture. The use of hair products and accessories increased rapidly, and hair salons became a great success during the decade despite the relatively slow pace of hairstyle changes.

Further Reading

Cumming, Valerie, et al., eds. *Fashions of a Decade: The 1950's.* New York: Facts on File, 1991. Part of a series for young adults, chronicles the rise of several fashions during the decade.

Marling, Karl Ann. *As Seen on TV: The Visual Culture of Everyday Life in the 1950's.* Cambridge, Mass.: Harvard University Press, 1994. An overview of the influence of television on 1950's culture.

Olian, Joanne. *Everyday Fashions of the Fifties: As Pictured in Sears Catalogs.* New York: Dover, 2002. More than one hundred illustrated entries with captions detail the prevailing styles of middle-class America.

Rooks, Noliwe. *Hair Raising.* New Bunswick, N.J.: Rutgers University Press, 1996. Provides an overview of beauty, culture, and African American women from the nineteenth century through the 1990's.

Sue Bailey

See also Barbie dolls; Conformity, culture of; Fads; Fashions and clothing; Film in the United States; Kelly, Grace; *Life*; *Look*; Presley, Elvis; Women and the roots of the feminist movement.

■ Haley, Bill

Identification American rock-and-roll musician
Born July 6, 1925; Highland Park, Michigan
Died February 9, 1981; Harlingen, Texas

One of the true pioneers of rock-and-roll music, Bill Haley played a major role in popularizing the new musical form during the mid-1950's.

Although his fame was comparatively short-lived, Bill Haley was one of the giants of rock and roll when the new musical form was taking shape. A native of Detroit, Michigan, Haley grew up in a country-and-western musical environment and learned to play the guitar at an early age. He organized his first band while he was a teenager and began touring after he finished high school. By the late 1940's, he was working as a radio disc jockey and recording country songs that went nowhere.

During the early 1950's, Haley began covering rhythm-and-blues hits and was starting to blend rhythm-and-blues with the rhythms that were soon to become characteristic of rock and roll. In 1952, he finally shed the cowboy image his bands had projected and renamed his band Bill Haley and His Comets—a takeoff on the name of the British astronomer Edmond Halley, after whom Halley's comet was named. With the band's new sound and new name, Haley was beginning to get attention, and he signed a recording contract with Decca. The band finally scored its first big success in 1954, with "Rock Around the Clock," whose pulsating beat was to make it an irresistible dance tune. Although the song was released as the B-side of a single, it was used on the sound track of the 1955 film *Blackboard Jungle*, and it soon became the anthem of the current generation of teenagers. The same song was also used in more than a dozen other films and eventually sold twenty-five million records, making it the best-selling rock single of all time.

Meanwhile, Haley capitalized on the success of "Rock Around the Clock" by starring in a film of the same title in 1956. *Rock Around the Clock*, in which Haley's band performed nine songs, lifted Haley to superstar status and helped make most of his records hits. Haley also appeared in a sequel, *Don't Knock the Rock*, in 1957. That same year, he became the first rock-and-roll star to tour abroad—something that Elvis Presley never did. He took his band to England, where he was mobbed by excited fans.

Impact After Haley released his last Top 40 hit, "Skinny Minnie," in 1958, his popularity in the United States waned. His impact on the birth of rock and roll was great, but the music moved on without him because he could not fit the image of a youthful, rebellious rocker.

Bill Haley (second from right) performing with his band in London in 1957. Haley was the first American rock performer to tour in Europe—something that Elvis Presley never did. (Hulton Archive | by Getty Images)

Further Reading

Altschuler, Glenn C. *All Shook Up*. New York: Oxford University Press, 2003. Details the rise of rock-and-roll music during the 1950's, with vivid biographies of countless musicians, including Haley.

Friedlander, Paul. *Rock and Roll: A Social History*. Boulder, Colo.: Westview Press, 1996. A history of the first thirty years of the rock-and-roll era as they related to changes in society.

Haley, John W., and John Von Hoelle. *Sound and Glory: The Incredible Story of Bill Haley, the Father of Rock 'n' Roll and the Music That Shook the World*. Wilmington, Del.: Dyne-American, 1991.

Helander, Brock. *The Rockin' Fifties: The People Who Made the Music*. New York: Schirmer Books, 1998. An overview of the roots of rock and roll and the subgenres that made up the musical landscape during the 1950's.

Knapp, Ron. *American Legends of Rock*. Springfield, N.J.: Enslow Publishers, 1996. This book provides biographies of nearly one dozen American rock stars, including Ritchie Valens, Buddy Holly, Bob Dylan, and Jimi Hendrix.

R. Kent Rasmussen

See also *Blackboard Jungle*; Dance, popular; Diddley, Bo; Lewis, Jerry Lee; Music; Radio; Rock and roll; *Rock Around the Clock*; Sullivan, Ed.

■ Harlem Globetrotters

Identification Professional basketball team
Date Formed in 1927

The Harlem Globetrotters were responsible for accelerating the racial integration of the National Basketball Association (NBA) and entertaining crowds worldwide with their unique style of comedic play.

The Harlem Globetrotters, originally from Chicago, debuted in 1927 under the ownership of Abe Saperstein and joined other Negro League basketball teams in an era of social and sport segregation. Originally a strictly competitive team, the Globetrotters won the World Professional Basketball Championship in 1940. They so dominated their opponents that they gradually inserted comedic routines and amazing feats of skill into their games to maintain fan interest.

The integration of professional basketball in 1950 began with the signing to the NBA of two Globetrotters, Nathaniel "Sweetwater" Clifton and Marques Haynes. As segregated competition lessened, the Globetrotters maintained a high degree of competitiveness, regularly attracting the best basketball talent available and rarely losing against a host of opposition. Their popularity escalated with their entertaining style of play, ball-handling wizardry, and shot-making expertise, as they played before crowds worldwide. Their 1951 performance in Berlin's Olympic Stadium attracted more than seventy-five thousand fans, an attendance record that stood for decades. *The Harlem Globetrotters*, a 1951 film that told the story of player Billy Brown, further piqued interest in the team.

The Globetrotter's trademark theme, "Sweet Georgia Brown," was adopted in 1952 as their Silver Anniversary tour involved more than one hundred games throughout the world. Another film—this one in 1954 and titled *Go, Man, Go!*—chronicled the team's success and bolstered its popularity. By 1956, with the team's popularity soaring, four separate teams were created to serve as touring ambassadors

of goodwill worldwide. One of basketball's dominant players, Wilt Chamberlain, joined the team for one season in 1958 before joining the NBA, and the team enjoyed their first undefeated season in 1959.

Impact The Harlem Globetrotters were at the forefront of social change while perfecting an unequalled blend of sport and entertainment. Throughout history, no sport team has performed before more people in more places (more than twenty thousand games in more than one hundred countries) than the Globetrotters.

Further Reading

Thomas, Ron. *They Cleared the Lane: The NBA's Black Pioneers.* Lincoln: University of Nebraska Press, 2002. Tells the story of the gradual integration of the sport and uses interviews with players, coaches, and fans to explore what the early days of integrated basketball were like for African American players.

Wilker, Josh. *The Harlem Globetrotters.* Broomall, Pa.: Chelsea House, 1996. Overview of the team and its personalities.

P. Graham Hatcher

See also Basketball; Chamberlain, Wilt; Sports.

Globetrotter star Goose Tatum in 1950. (Hulton Archive | by Getty Images)

■ Hawaii statehood

The Event Admission of Hawaii as the fiftieth state
in the Union
Date August 21, 1959

Hawaii's entrance into the United States made it the second of the nation's noncontiguous states (along with Alaska) and the only state with a predominantly nonwhite citizenry.

Even before the overthrow of the Hawaiian monarchy in 1893 and the islands' annexation as a U.S. territory in 1898, Hawaiian statehood was debated on the U.S. mainland and among the *haole* (white) businessmen whose ancestors had come to the islands as Christian missionaries. Since territorial acquisition often implied eventual statehood, for most Americans the question was not if, but when.

The first Hawaiian statehood bill was presented to the U.S. Congress in 1919 by Prince Jonah Kuhio Kalanianaole, Hawaii's first delegate. Similar bills were also introduced in 1920, 1931, and 1935, but they found little congressional support; however, by the mid-1930's, statehood for Hawaii had become a national issue. Opponents claimed geographical distance as an impediment, along with the absence of a strong middle class, the excessive economic and political power of five corporate families, and the large proportion of islanders of Japanese ancestry as barriers to admission. After the Japanese attack on Pearl Harbor in Honolulu on December 7, 1941, and the subsequent entry of the United States into World War II, discussions of statehood were temporarily silenced.

The Postwar Years After World War II, the platforms of both national parties routinely supported "eventual statehood." The economy of Hawaii was robust, bolstered by extensive military spending, a newly diversified industrial base, and a rapidly expanding tourist industry. The loyalty of residents of Asian ancestry to the United States had been clearly demonstrated in World War II and the Korean War. Air travel became available to a growing American middle class, with Hawaii a favored destination. Hollywood films, radio and television programs, popular music, and sports advertising created appealing images of Hawaii as an exotic paradise.

Hawaii Democrats led the campaign for immediate statehood. Southern Democrats, who associated Hawaiian statehood with Civil Rights legislation promising full citizenship for people of color, led congressional opposition. Cold War fears of communist infiltration of labor unions, combined with memories of the sugar workers' strike of 1946, the waterfront strike in 1949, and an associated concern regarding the growing power of the International Longshoremen's and Warehousemen's Union (ILWU) became rallying points for opponents to statehood, both in the islands and on the mainland. Nevertheless, statehood bills for Hawaii passed in the U.S. House of Representatives in 1947 and 1950, only to die in the Senate.

By 1950, migration patterns to Hawaii had changed drastically from early twentieth century trends, when immigrants were primarily Asian nationals. Mid-century newcomers were mostly European Americans. By 1950, almost 90 percent of Hawaii's residents were U.S. citizens; many were of Asian descent, born in the islands. A local *haole* and former police detective, John A. Burns, led working-class Americans of Japanese ancestry and native Hawaiians into an alliance that resulted in the Democratic Revolution of 1954. In 1956, Burns was elected as Hawaii's delegate to Congress. Risking his political career in the islands, Burns agreed to let Alaska go first for statehood consideration, although Alaska's qualifications for statehood were generally thought inferior to those of Hawaii. Alaska was admitted to the Union in January, 1959.

Admission to Statehood In the first session of the Eighty-sixth Congress, the Senate led the way for Hawaii's statehood. Burns persuaded a powerful Texas senator, Lyndon B. Johnson, to support statehood, although even Johnson's influence could not sway staunch segregationists: Fourteen of the fifteen "nay" votes in the Senate came from southern Democrats. In March, 1959, the U.S. Congress approved the statehood bill, and it was signed into law. Ninety percent of voters in a special election in Hawaii supported statehood. Opposition came mostly from *haole*-dominated districts. (Decades later, Hawaiian sovereignty activists would challenge the legitimacy of this plebiscite because voting residents of Hawaii were not offered a means to support free association or independence. Support for statehood, or rejection of statehood—and implied support of continued territorial status—were the only ballot choices.)

A Hawaiian child reading the news of Hawaii's admission to the Union. (George Bacon)

In July, 1959, Hawaii elected its first congressional delegates; two were Asian American. Hiram Fong became the first U.S. senator of Asian ancestry; Daniel Inouye was the first Japanese American elected to the House. After sixty-one years as a territory, Hawaii became the fiftieth state when President Dwight D. Eisenhower signed an executive order on August 21, 1959.

In the first election after statehood, Democrats split their support between Burns and a younger, more liberal and educated opponent, Thomas Gill. Consequently, the appointed territorial governor, Republican William F. Quinn, became the first elected governor of Hawaii. However, affection for the centrist Burns remained; he was elected in 1962, reelected for two more terms, and oversaw a reconfiguration of racial relations that became a model for the United States. Another Republican governor would not be elected in Hawaii until the twenty-first century.

Impact Publicity surrounding statehood and the introduction of jet airline service to Hawaii led to a huge expansion of tourism, which in turn resulted in tremendous growth in the construction and service industries. Because of Hawaii's location and popula-

tion, it became a vital link for U.S. contacts with Pacific Rim nations and cultures. Statehood created many educational and economic opportunities for citizens of Hawaii, but native Hawaiians have benefited least from statehood.

As the first state with a white minority and a large population of citizens of Asian, Polynesian, and mixed-race ancestry, Hawaii during the 1950's foreshadowed the multiracial and multicultural landscape that would characterize much of the United States at the beginning of the twenty-first century.

Further Reading

Bell, Roger. *Last Among Equals: Hawaiian Statehood and American Politics.* Honolulu: University of Hawaii Press, 1984. Chronicles the struggle for statehood.

Coffman, Tom. *The Island Edge of America: A Political History of Hawaii.* Honolulu: University of Hawaii Press, 2003. Details critical events within Hawaii in the twentieth century, including those surrounding the statehood issue.

Carolyn Anderson

See also Alaska statehood; Asian Americans; Continentalism; Eisenhower, Dwight D.; Immigration and Nationality Act of 1952; Immigration to the United States; Puerto Rico as a commonwealth; Racial discrimination; Surfing and beach culture.

■ Health care systems in Canada

In Canada, the provision of government-sponsored health care was a seminal event in the social landscape of the 1950's.

As the 1950's began, health care delivery in Canada closely resembled that in the United States: a patchwork of services provided by a variety of public, private, and religious groups and organizations. Health care expenditures in Canada totaled $502 million in 1950. By the close of the 1950's, it had assumed the form it would take in subsequent decades: nearly universal in access, free in patient cost, and uniform in coverage and quality across different provinces. Health care expenditures in Canada totaled $1.29 billion in 1959.

The Postwar Experience Canada emerged from World War II as a changed nation. Although nominally still a subject of Great Britain, it soon dwarfed its old ruler in economic growth and vitality. Businesses were flush from years of wartime profits, and workers had enjoyed several years of low unemployment and high demand for overtime on the part of their employers. Even mothers were happy, since they had been receiving their family allowances (an additional amount paid directly to them each month for each child they had) since 1944. Although located on the continent of North America, Canada's government and culture had long resembled that of the European continent to which it was still attached, however loosely.

Military spending was greatly reduced after the war, yet federal power was rising in Canada's capital, Ottawa. During federal and provincial conferences held during 1945-1946, the provinces were urged to cede their social policy functions (including health care insurance) to the federal government. Economic diversity among the provinces resulted in great variations in social services as well as other public services. While many provinces in the western half of Canada were quite prosperous and progressive, the Maritime Provinces (Newfoundland, New Brunswick, and Nova Scotia) were relatively poor.

Quebec became urbanized, and under the provincial government of Maurice Duplessis (1944-1959), it seemed committed to a policy of no change. Alone among the provinces, women were still denied the vote. Although the province was predominantly Roman Catholic, the Catholic Church had difficulty providing educational and welfare services for the newly urbanized residents of the province, despite substantial subsidies from the provincial government. At the other extreme, Ontario objected to an increase in federal power and effectively blocked a nationwide hospital insurance program. As the richest of the provinces, it balked at subsidizing the social needs of the less affluent provinces. Quebec balked as well, but for different reasons: Although it would benefit from the effective subsidization of its social service needs by wealthier provinces, it was not about to cede any of its historical independence.

New Federal Support Although the national government did not win all that it wanted in the Federal-Provincial Conferences of 1945-1946, it began making federal grants to the provinces for the improvement of hospitals in 1948. By 1951, using funds freed from reduced military needs, the national government began universal old age pensions of $40 per month to all citizens over seventy years of age (sixty-five if they were needy). By 1956, an Unemployment Assistance Act was passed, and in 1957, the Hospital Insurance and Diagnostic Services Act was passed, providing financial assistance to provinces that established publicly administered hospital insurance programs with universal coverage. Saskatchewan had already been providing its own universal hospital insurance program since 1947, but for the rest of the provinces, this act enabled them to offer universal hospital insurance to their citizens for the first time.

Although the goal of these programs was to alleviate human medical needs, the program founders also intended that they would help to even out fluctuations in the business cycle. According to the Keynesian economic theory of the time, government spending on social services acted as a source of stability in the economy. Increased taxes would prevent runaway economic growth (and its accompanying inflation), while the provision of social services would prevent economic recessions from deepening into economic depressions.

Change in Government Many Canadian provinces accepted the financial assistance offered by the national government and set up their own universal hospital insurance programs. Before all provinces could be persuaded to do so, however, Prime Minister Louis St. Laurent's Liberal Party was voted out of power in the 1957 elections, and John G. Diefenbaker's Tory (Progressive Conservative) Party was voted in. The pace of provincial adoption of universal hospital insurance programs slowed, and it was not until 1961 that all provinces had health insurance plans in place with cost-sharing agreements with the federal government.

Impact Canada came out of World War II in a position similar to that of the United States with little war damage, an enhanced reputation on the world stage, and a financially healthy economy. The Canadian federal government used this fortunate state of affairs to alleviate many differences between its various geographic areas through the provision of uniform social services. In this respect, they were following the European model of governments taking an active role in caring for their citizens. During this period, the United States chose a different course, seeking to expand its role as a world power. In both nations, the 1950's was a decade in which emerging national powers mapped out the courses they would take in subsequent decades.

Further Reading

Armstrong, Pat, et al. *Universal Health Care: What the United States Can Learn from the Canadian Experience.* New York: The New Press, 1999. A study that traces the emergence of Canada's health care system from 1947 onward.

Bothwell, Robert. *A Traveler's History of Canada.* London: Windrush Press, 2001. Contains a good description of the economic and social conditions found in Canada as well as insights into the nation's political climate.

Li, Peter S. *The Making of Post-war Canada.* Toronto: Oxford University Press, 1996. Addresses major social changes in Canada since World War II, including immigration, female labor, and reduced fertility.

McIntosh, Tom, et al., eds. *Governance and Health Care in Canada.* Toronto: University of Toronto, 2003. Not only covers issues pertinent to health care in the twenty-first century but also traces the historical evolution of the system.

Betsy A. Murphy

See also Asian flu epidemic; Business and the economy in Canada; Canadian regionalism; Demographics of Canada; Diefenbaker, John G.; Health care systems in the United States; Hoof-and-mouth epidemic; Medicine; Polio; St. Laurent, Louis.

■ Health care systems in the United States

The postwar years witnessed government and private-sector expansion of separate facets of the health care system: Hospital construction and medical research were supported at the federal level, while the financing of health insurance remained largely in private hands.

By 1950, the discovery of such miracle drugs as penicillin and antibiotics had already made profound inroads into the treatment of many infectious diseases.

As the decade progressed, modern medicine faced the challenges posed by the disease that killed and crippled more children than any other: polio, which reached its peak in 1952. The disease would be contained thanks to medical researchers such as Jonas Salk, whose polio vaccine went into national field trials in 1954. Medical research did much to wipe out the ravages of the disease by the end of the decade.

Focus on Chronic Degenerative Diseases Successes in combatting smallpox and other communicable diseases meant a shift of focus in medical research, from infectious diseases to the biological processes underlying chronic degenerative diseases, such as heart disease and cancer. By the early 1950's, many Americans were afflicted with cardiovascular disease. The enormous interest following President Dwight D. Eisenhower's heart attack in 1955 led to an unparalleled flood of medical research, with particular advances in the development and application of surgery as treatment for heart disorders. The American Heart Association, based on data from the U.S. National Health Survey in 1957, estimated the number of individuals with some form of cardiovascular disease at more than ten million.

Kenneth K. Keown, an early innovator of cardiac anesthesiology, perfected the use of hypothermia and lidocaine to counteract the negative effects during cardiac surgery. Pacemakers implanted within the body were introduced during the late 1950's and outperformed the more cumbersome and awkward external models. Similarly, the successful use of drug treatments to reduce hypertension made significant strides in reducing stroke and stroke-related deaths.

Considerable attention was also given to the escalating rate of cancer deaths, particularly cancer of the lung. Deaths per year from lung cancer had risen from four thousand in 1935 to eleven thousand in 1945. By 1960, the number of annual lung cancer deaths had risen to 36,000. The period witnessed a number of significant medical breakthroughs regarding cancer treatment. In 1954, James Holland led the first randomized clinical cancer trial. James Watson and Francis Crick discovered the structure of DNA in 1953, while during the same period, the Food and Drug Administration (FDA) approved methotrexate, an antimetabolite derived from folic acid, and 6-mercaptopurine as anticancer drugs. In 1955, Roy Hertz and Min Chiu Li successfully achieved a total cure of a solid tumor. During the same period, several epidemiologists, including Ernst Wynder, Evarts Graham, and Sir Richard Doll, confirmed a link between cigarette smoking and lung cancer.

The Expanding Role of Government The end of World War II marked the beginning of the great expansion of the federal government's support of medical research. In 1944, Congress passed the Public Health Service Act and authorized the National Institutes of Health (NIH) to conduct and support medical research. By 1950, NIH had seven institutes under its umbrella, including the National Cancer Institute, the National Heart Institute, and the National Institute of Arthritis and Metabolic Diseases. Between 1955 and 1960, the NIH budget expanded from $81 million to more than $400 million.

During the 1950's, Congress became increasingly alarmed about the hazards of the modern environment. The Air Pollution Control Act of 1955, followed by more legislation in 1956, authorized grants for the construction of waste treatment facilities. The creation of the Division of Radiological Health in 1958 was an important outcome of the government's proactive role regarding health hazards created by industrial development.

The collection of health statistics was another important role set forth by the federal government. The transfer of the National Office of Vital Statistics from the Census Bureau to the Public Health Service marked the beginning of a new era in the collection, analysis, and dissemination of health data. In 1956, Congress authorized the National Health Survey, which set the stage for the development of the National Center for Health Statistics, which began in 1960. The government was now well positioned to track the health and disease patterns of the American people.

Preventive Medicine Government funding was also directed toward programs of health prevention. The American College of Preventive Medicine was established in 1954, along with medical residency programs in preventive medicine. However, health officials disagreed about the implementation of prevention programs. Public health advocates argued that these efforts should be centered in public health departments run by local and state agencies, while physicians argued that screening should be performed within the private sector, preferably within the doctor's office.

Health prevention programs emphasized interventions such as vaccinations and screenings rather than modifying health behavior. In fact, the concept of lifestyle risk factors was relatively unknown to most people. However, in 1957, the National Health Education Committee in conjunction with Harvard doctors issued a statement presenting the public with the first mention of factors predisposing the individual to heart disease. The report, prepared by eight physicians, cited excess weight, elevated blood cholesterol, elevated blood pressure, and excessive smoking as "risk factors" for cardiovascular disease. James Watt, director of the National Institutes of Health, promoted the fact that a number of public health officials linked lifestyle behaviors, such as drinking, smoking, and nutrition, with chronic diseases. The attention to behavioral risk factors, however, did not bring about an immediate change in people's lifestyles because the medical experts often could not agree on the causes of chronic disease. A major reinterpretation of the importance of lifestyle behaviors in the development of disease would not come until the publication of epidemiological evidence linking chronic disease to health behaviors, which was first reported in the Framingham Study during the 1960's.

Hospital Construction The Great Depression and World War II left the United States with a severe shortage of hospital beds as millions of returning veterans needed medical attention. The Hospital Survey and Construction Act, passed by Congress in 1946, provided grants to states to support the construction and modernization of hospital facilities. Better known as the Hill-Burton Act, the federally sponsored program was amended in 1954 to provide grants for the construction of nursing homes and rehabilitation centers.

Hospital expansion meant changes in how patients were treated. During the 1950's, intensive care units first appeared. Initially called critical recovery units, intensive care units began appearing in 1953 and 1954 at facilities such as the North Carolina Memorial Hospital in Chapel Hill, the Manchester (Connecticut) Memorial Hospital, and Chestnut Hill, Philadelphia. By the late 1960's, 90 percent of U.S. hospitals with five hundred or more beds had opened intensive care units. Moreover, the increasing number of critical care nurses soon organized a national group, American Association of Critical

Care Nurses, which developed a core curriculum to educate nurses entering the field and a national examination to ensure competency in critical care.

Hospital expansion also meant a change in health services for new mothers. Prior to the expansion of hospitals, postpartum stays were often twenty-four hours or less. However with increased hospital space, maternity stays were extended to six days. The number of hospital births during the 1950's was assisted by two programs that made a wide range of inpatient care in hospitals more affordable: the Federal Emergency Maternity and Infant Care Act, which financed care for servicemen's wives, and the Blue Cross/Blue Shield program, which included maternity benefits for millions of industrial workers and their wives. By the end of the decade, 96 percent of all births were hospital births and only one in ten contacts with physicians occurred outside the hospital setting in patients' homes.

Doctor Shortages Although hospital facilities and beds were more plentiful, physicians were not. By 1957, hospitals were looking for more than twelve thousand interns annually, but American medical schools were graduating fewer than seven thousand students. Congress was close to approving a five-year program of grants and scholarships for medical schools to increase the nation's supply of physicians. The American Medical Association (AMA) originally supported the bill, but, concerned about setting a precedent, it reversed its position, and the bill died in Congress. The shortage of doctors meant hospitals looked outside the United States to fill their openings. The number of foreign medical students establishing medical practices in the United States increased from 10 percent to 26 percent during this era.

The Korean War exacerbated this shortage. The Selective Service Act was amended in 1950 to include a special registration for medical, dental, and other health specialists. By 1953, an estimated 10,423 physicians and 4,224 dentists were recruited to military service. The infusion of federal money into research programs, which created new jobs at medical schools, also contributed to the doctor shortage. Full-time medical positions doubled nationally, increasing from approximately four thousand in 1951 to more than eleven thousand by 1959. The supply of qualified applicants simply could not keep up with the number of clinical and research openings.

Hospitals also struggled with a nursing shortage, since the shortage of interns and residents increased the workload for nurses. In 1950, the American Hospital Association reported more than 22,000 nursing vacancies. Low pay and long working hours contributed to the problem. Hospitals responded to the shortage with various innovations including offering on-site child care services and an expansion of the duties of licensed practical nurses.

The doctor shortage was particularly severe among general practitioners. The higher income enjoyed by specialists and researchers created a significant shift in training, and consequently, the number of individuals training to be general practioners dropped from 60 to 16 percent between the first and fourth years of medical study. Students training for various medical specialities jumped from 35 to 74 percent, and students interested in research careers increased from 5 to 10 percent. The most significant increases were seen in the highly paid areas of surgical specialists.

As specialization intensified during the 1950's, patients experienced a less personal relationship with the specialist. Malpractice claims increased dramatically, and a 1957 report warned physicians of the hazards of practicing without liability insurance. The report advised all physicians to pay the increasing cost of professional liability insurance.

Private Health Insurance The failure to provide medical care benefits under the Social Security Act of 1935 and the defeat of federal grant-in-aid medical care programs through the states under the Wagner Bill of 1939 shifted medical insurance to private industry. Health care was increasingly seen by unions as a valued part of benefits packages for their employees, and as a result, commercial insurance companies grew substantially. The Liberty Mutual Insurance Company was one of the first to introduce major medical insurance to supplement basic medical care expenses. The number of Americans covered by Blue Cross and other insurance plans increased significantly. In 1940, only 9 percent of the civilian population had any hospital benefits through private medical insurance and only 4 percent had surgical benefits. However, by 1950, 51 percent had hospital insurance and 35 percent had surgical insurance. By 1960, the proportion of persons in the United States covered by private insurance plans increased to 70 percent. The types of insurance offered to employees and their families also expanded. In 1957, vision care benefits were introduced, followed in 1959 by payments for dental care.

The prepaid group practice, the precursor to later decades' popular health maintenance organizations (HMOs), emerged during the period. These plans provided a wide range of comprehensive health care services to subscribers for a predetermined rate. The most successful of these were the Kaiser Health Insurance Plan of California and the Health Insurance Plan of Greater New York.

National Health Insurance Even though many middle-class Americans had some type of voluntary medical insurance coverage, there were millions who had no coverage and were unable to afford medical care. Historically, state governments played the most important governmental role in regulating health care, but after World War I, the federal government would become more involved in health matters. One of the most important examples of federal government involvement was the Social Security Act of 1935. The policy furnished federal grants to states to provide retirement and death benefits and to develop local public health programs. As a result of strong resistance from the AMA, the Social Security Act made no provision for health insurance.

Harry S. Truman was the first president to offer an official administrative proposal for national health insurance to Congress. Although Truman was unsuccessful in gaining support for his national health plan in 1948, attention was increasingly focused on providing health care, at least for the neediest Americans. The report by the Commission on the Health Needs of the Nation, released in 1952, highlighted the critical medical care needs of the elderly and other disadvantaged groups. The Social Security Administration then proposed a government health insurance program limited to beneficiaries of the current social security system, namely the elderly and survivor and disability pensioners.

Interest in a national health plan for all United States citizens did not disappear during the decade. Legislative proposals went before Congress every year regarding some aspect of national health insurance. Most notably, the Forand Bill, introduced in 1957, proposed covering the elderly for expenses up to 60 days in the hospital and 120 days of nursing home care and surgical benefits. Although the bill did not pass, the legislation exemplified the in-

tense political arguments surrounding government-supported health care. The medical profession, typically a politically and socially conservative group, opposed legislation that would give government more responsibility for health. Fearing federally imposed limits on their practices, the AMA waged a successful campaign to fight national health insurance. Although there was still considerable concern about the need for health insurance, especially for the needy, the stringent opposition of organized medicine delayed discussion of health reform until the 1960's.

Impact The health care system of the 1950's reflected the dynamic changes in science, medicine, and politics that would significantly affect the delivery of health care for the short term and position the health care system for two significant social reforms during the 1960's: Medicare, which would provide health care for the elderly, and Medicaid, which would provide health care for the poor.

Moreover, the 1950's brought great prestige to the medical profession for extending and improving the quality of life, while the era also represented a period of significant growth of the health care industry. Between 1950 and 1970, the medical workforce increased from 1.2 million to 3.9 million people. National health care expenditures grew from $12.7 billion to $71.6 billion, and medical care became one of the nation's largest industries. Furthermore, the success of medical research gave new legitimacy to the field of medicine. The National Institutes of Health took the leading role in research, which previously had been supported primarily by foundations and drug companies.

The battle over national health insurance was significant in that it helped to clarify the role of the AMA in shaping the nation's health policy. The association served as a powerful professional lobby that opposed virtually every specific health care reform, including reform in the private sector, contending that it would prevent physicians from receiving adequate compensation and would lead to a lowering of medical standards. Implicit in the AMA's position was the underlying principle that the federal government should support the advancement of medical knowledge but should not be involved in directly coordinating and subsidizing medical care.

The growth of private health insurance had a significant impact on public policy toward health care.

The Republican victory in the presidential election of 1952 somewhat eased the pressure for a national health insurance plan. Measures such as the Flanders-Ives and the Hill-Aiken bills advocated federal support to encourage the development and growth of private health insurance. In turn, the private insurance system provided enough political clout to thwart attempts at a national health insurance plan.

Further Reading

Hollingsworth, J. Rogers. *A Political Economy of Medicine: Great Britain and the United States.* Baltimore: Johns Hopkins University Press, 1986. A comprehensive analysis of the rise of modern medicine in the United States and Great Britain, with particular emphasis on the different attitudes toward national health insurance.

Marcus, Alan I. *Health Care Policy in Contemporary America.* University Park: Pennsylvania State University Press, 1997. Chronicles the radical changes in America's health care delivery, beginning the discussion with the 1950's.

Park, Buhm Soon. "The Development of the Intramural Research Program at the National Institutes of Health After World War II." *Perspectives in Biology and Medicine* 46 (2003): 383-402. A brief account of the rise of medical research sponsored by the federal government.

Rosen, George. *A History of Public Health.* Rev. ed. Baltimore: Johns Hopkins University Press, 1993. One section includes a detailed exploration of the politics of public health during the 1950's.

Starr, Paul. *The Social Transformation of American Medicine.* New York: Basic Books, 1982. The book divides the rise of medicine into two movements: the development of medicine as a profession and the transformation of medicine into an industry.

Mary McElroy

See also Asian flu epidemic; Cancer; Eisenhower's heart attack; Health care systems in Canada; Hearing aids; LaLanne, Jack; Medicine; Polio; Smith, Margaret Chase; Truman, Harry S.

■ Health, Education, and Welfare, Department of

Identification Department of the U.S. federal government

Date Created on April 11, 1953

Creation of the Department of Health, Education, and Welfare (HEW) consolidated many of the federal domestic programs created during the Roosevelt and Truman administrations under one cabinet-level department.

In 1953, under the recommendation of the Hoover Commission on government reorganization, President Dwight D. Eisenhower transferred parts of the Federal Security Agency to the newly created cabinet-level Department of Health, Education, and Welfare (HEW). Included within the new department were the Social Security Administration, the Public Health Service, the Office of Education, and the Food and Drug Administration. In addition, the secretary of HEW was charged to oversee federal aid to the American Printing House for the Blind, Gallaudet College (later University) for the Deaf, and Howard University.

Four years later, when the Soviet Union launched the first Earth-orbiting satellite, *Sputnik I*, in October, 1957, Americans were shocked to realize how advanced Soviet science and technology had become. In response, both the public and the U.S. Congress demanded that the nation place greater emphasis on science education in the United States. One of the first results of this demand was passage of the National Defense Education Act (NDEA) in 1958. This act expanded the role of HEW, which implemented most of the provisions of the new law. The NDEA funded graduate study in the sciences, mathematics, and foreign languages. The act also funded aspects of technical education, educational media centers, library expansion, and the training of librarians. Federal support aided reforms in elementary and secondary education. As the 1950's came to a close, administration of these new and enlarged programs were among HEW's major missions.

Three different people served as secretaries of HEW during the 1950's. The first, Oveta Culp Hobby, had been head of the Women's Army Auxiliary Corps (WAAC) during World War II. Eisenhower chose her because of her proven administrative skills. In 1955, Hobby resigned and was succeeded by Marion B. Folsom, an undersecretary of the Treasury Department with whom Hobby had worked closely to integrate aspects of the Social Security system into the federal tax system. Folsom had the initial responsibility for implementing the provisions of the NDEA and overseeing new federal funding for medical and science research. Arthur S. Flemming succeeded Folsom in 1958 and remained secretary of HEW through the rest of Eisenhower's administration.

Impact The creation of the new department brought most federally funded social welfare programs within a unified structure and facilitated implementation of the National Defense Education Act. However, the new department fell under heavy criticism from conservatives who opposed federal government involvement in education and social services. In 1979, the Department of Education Act created a separate cabinet-level Education Department, and HEW's remaining agencies were reorganized under the new Department of Health and Human Services.

Further Reading

Divine, Robert A. *The Sputnik Challenge: Eisenhower's Response to the Soviet Satellite.* New York: Oxford University Press, 1993. Details the technological crises spurred by *Sputnik*'s launch and the response of United States scientists.

Miles, Rufus E. *The Department of Health, Education, and Welfare.* New York: Praeger, 1974. Full-scale study of the organization and functions of HEW.

Rosen, George. *A History of Public Health.* Rev. ed. Baltimore: Johns Hopkins University Press, 1993. Survey of the history of public health in the United States that includes a section that covers the politics of public health during the 1950's.

Gayle R. Avant

See also Asian flu epidemic; Conservatism in U.S. politics; Education in the United States; Eisenhower, Dwight D.; Health care in the United States; Hoover Commission; Medicine; National Defense Education Act.

■ Hearing aids

Definition Appliances worn on ears to counteract the effects of hearing loss

During the 1950's, hearing aids, along with sign languages, advocacy organizations, and political mobilization, played an important role in transforming the bleak situation of the deaf community.

Life is enhanced by the presence of sound, which may consist of distant waves striking a shingle beach, birds singing overhead, or intimate conversations. Individuals' inability to access this acoustic reper-

toire may range from slight impairment to profound deafness, and the degree of hearing loss may vary depending on the sound's frequency or other factors. The complexity of hearing loss is evidenced by the fact that there is no accepted North American legal definition of deafness, as exists for blindness.

There are some known risk factors, namely that men are more prone to deafness than women, and both sexes are more vulnerable to hearing loss as they age. Current estimates of the North American deaf population are unreliable (because of differences in definition, collection strategies, and other methodological problems), and data from earlier time periods are even less trustworthy.

History Deaf people in the nineteenth century had limited technology that they could employ to amplify sounds, such as hearing trumpets, and these were available only to a small proportion of those who could benefit from their use. By the late nineteenth and early twentieth centuries, tabletop, hearing-assistance devices relying on a carbon transmitter had been patented in the United States and Europe. However, these devices were bulky and inadequate for people with severe hearing loss.

During the late 1930's, vacuum-tube hearing aids provided some assistance to the deaf. However, it was not until the 1950's that hearing aid technology was revolutionized, prompted by the 1947 development of the transistor at Bell Telephone Laboratories. This technological advance was gradually applied to the manufacture of hearing aids, and behind-the-ear, miniaturized transistor models were available for purchase five years later. By 1955, the Dahlberg company had produced an in-the-ear hearing aid, consisting of several components, including a microphone (which absorbed sounds and converted them to electrical impulses), an amplifier (which increased the electrical signal), a receiver (which translated the electrical patterns into sound waves), an ear mold (which focused the sounds into the ear), and a battery (which provided power). This small appliance was a significant advance from the bulky models available several decades earlier.

Impact Prior to the 1950's and the greater availability, power, and miniaturization of hearing aids, members of the deaf community were often treated as though they were mentally subnormal and denied access to educational and employment opportunities. Hearing aids that were less noticeable and more powerful than their bulky predecessors allowed hard-of-hearing individuals to blend into the general population and to improve their educational and job-related attainments. This served to insulate some deaf citizens from the negative effects of a society prejudiced against them. At the same time, greater political agitation and public awareness by groups such as the Canadian Deaf Education Fund (established during the 1950's) helped to improve community attitudes and access to education. These events set the stage for the political activist movement of Deaf Culture (based on sign language use), which matured during the late twentieth century.

Further Reading

Berger, Kenneth W. "History and Development of Hearing Aids." In *Amplification for the Hearing-Impaired*, edited by Michael C. Pollack. 2d ed. New York: Grune & Stratton, 1980. A detailed presentation of the history of hearing aids commencing in the nineteenth century.

Biderman, Beverly. *Wired for Sound: A Journey into Hearing*. Toronto: Trifolium Books, 1998. A fascinating personal account about coping with deafness in Canada and the advent of technological aids since the 1950's.

Dillon, Harvey. *Hearing Aids*. Sydney: Boomerang Press, 2001. An introductory textbook that explains acoustic processes and the functions of hearing aids.

Susan J. Wurtzburg

See also Communications in Canada; Communications in the United States; Health care systems in Canada; Health care systems in the United States.

■ Hemingway, Ernest

Identification American author
Born July 21, 1899; Oak Park, Illinois
Died July 2, 1961; Ketchum, Idaho

One of America's best-known and most popular writers of the decade, Ernest Hemingway was widely recognized not only as a novelist but also as a celebrity, big-game hunter, and Nobel Prize winner.

Ernest Hemingway grew up in suburban Illinois and rural Michigan, where his parents also maintained a summer home. He was wounded while serving as an ambulance driver in Italy in World War I and served as a war correspondent during the Spanish Civil War (1936-1939) and World War II (1939-1945). An established novelist and short-story writer since the 1920's, the well-traveled Hemingway lived and wrote in France, Spain, Africa, and Cuba, as well as the United States.

Hemingway's reputation took an interesting detour in 1950, dropping to its lowest point following the publication of his fifth novel, *Across the River and into the Trees*, which endured harsh reviews. However, two years later, his literary stature increased dramatically with *The Old Man and the Sea* (1952), first published in its entirety in *Life* magazine. The issue, with the author's photograph on the cover, sold out five million copies. In 1953, Hemingway received the Pulitzer Prize for the novel, which traces an old fisherman's struggle to land a great marlin off the coast of Cuba and was inspired by the stoicism of baseball legend Joe DiMaggio.

In January, 1954, reports surfaced from East Africa that Hemingway and his fourth wife, Mary Welsh Hemingway, had been killed in a plane crash while on safari. In fact, they had survived two plane crashes and, although injured, enjoyed the grim irony of reading their own obituaries in the newspapers. Hemingway's account of the accident, "The Christmas Gift," appeared in *Look* magazine. That same year he was awarded the Nobel Prize in Literature; however, because he was still recuperating, he did not attend the public ceremony in Stockholm, Sweden, although he was privately pleased.

Even as his health began to decline, Hemingway continued to work on a massive, uncompleted trilogy. Articles by or about him were published in periodicals as diverse as *The Atlantic, Playboy,* and *McCall's*; his stories were dramatized on television. Seven films based on his fiction were released during the decade, and more would follow. Spencer Tracy starred in the 1958 film version of *The Old Man and the Sea*, the only motion picture with which Hemingway ever allowed himself to become personally involved. In 1959, he traveled again to the bullfights in Spain, ostensibly to update an earlier nonfiction book, *Death in the Afternoon* (1932), but the result was a new volume, released after his death as *The Dangerous Summer* (1985).

Impact Hemingway was perhaps the first American author since Mark Twain to become a genuine celebrity. His love of sports, his war experiences, and

Author Ernest Hemingway with a leopard he shot in Africa in 1953. (AP/Wide World Photos)

multiple marriages marked him as a "man's man," and his reputation as a hard drinker flourished. Critics analyzed his books, which became a significant addition to college literature courses. His terse, understated style influenced young writers immensely; often imitated, it has never been surpassed.

Beginning in 1960, Hemingway's noticeably failing health precipitated two visits to the Mayo Clinic in Rochester, Minnesota. Nevertheless, his suicide in 1961 came as a shock to those who did not know him well.

Further Reading

Laurence, Frank M. *Hemingway and the Movies.* Jackson: University Press of Mississippi, 1981. Examines the history and reception of fifteen motion pictures based on Hemingway's books.

Raeburn, John. *Fame Became of Him: Hemingway as Public Writer.* Bloomington: Indiana University Press, 1984. Focuses on the popular image of Hemingway as celebrity and culture hero.

Reynolds, Michael. *Hemingway: The Final Years.* New York: W. W. Norton, 1999. The fifth and final vol-

ume of this biography details Hemingway's personal life and sources of his work from 1940 until his death.

Joanne McCarthy

See also DiMaggio, Joe; Literature in the United States; Nobel Prizes; Pound, Ezra.

■ Herblock

Identification American editorial cartoonist
Born October 13, 1909; Chicago, Illinois
Died October 7, 2001; Washington, D.C.

During the 1950's, the willingness of Pulitzer Prize-winner Herblock to draw cartoons criticizing U.S. senator Joseph McCarthy and the House Committee on Un-American Activities (HUAC) emboldened others of all political leanings to be similarly outspoken.

One of the few editorial cartoonists who stood up to the 1950's red scare, Herbert Block is credited with coining the term "McCarthyism." Block, who had used the pen name Herblock since he was a teenage cartoonist, was inspired by family members. His father drew for *Judge* and other magazines, and he and Herbert's older brother had been Chicago newspapermen.

After a stint as a police reporter with Chicago's City News Bureau, Block began cartooning with the *Chicago Daily News* when he was nineteen. Four years later, he became the only editorial cartoonist with the Newspapers Enterprise Association (NEA) feature service, where his illustrations commented on poverty, fascism, and other current events. During the early 1940's, the NEA president sought to temper Block's enthusiastic jabs at tyranny, but the cartoonist was spared any censoring. He won the Pulitzer Prize for work done in 1941 and was drafted into the military in 1943. After World War II, Block was hired by *The Washington Post*, where he worked the rest of his career.

Critiquing the Era During the 1950's, Herblock anticipated social issues that lasted for decades, commenting on nuclear proliferation, the Civil Rights movement, and government corruption. He also attacked dictators of all stripes, from Nazis to communists, and criticized what he saw as demagoguery. He targeted such figures as Father Charles Coughlin, a liberal who advocated social justice, the corrupt politician Huey Long, Vice President Richard M.

Nixon, and Joseph R. McCarthy, who became notorious for his witch-hunts of alleged communists. Block upset his Washington employer when he criticized Dwight D. Eisenhower in the 1952 presidential campaign but was noticeably ahead of the press corps concerning McCarthy.

A civil libertarian, Block believed that there was something wrong about a handful of congressmen electing themselves to decide who and what was un-American. In fact, Herblock's caricatures of McCarthy and Nixon, featuring rough, shady faces, reportedly annoyed both men to such an extent that McCarthy started shaving twice a day, and Nixon sought to erase the Herblock image.

Impact "No editorial cartoonist in American history, not even nineteenth century political cartoonist Thomas Nast, has made a more lasting impression on the nation than Herbert Block," wrote Library of Congress curator Harry L. Katz. With humor, wit, and insight, Herblock tackled controversial topics throughout his career, but the Pulitzer Prize he won in 1954—the second of three he earned—was for his running graphic commentaries on the HUAC and McCarthyism. Besides recognition by his peers in the press, Herblock earned widespread popularity: More than three hundred newspapers were using his cartoons by the 1990's. His commitment and consistency encouraged others to take on McCarthy, as well as southern racists, Nixon, and many more targets.

Further Reading

Block, Herbert. *Herblock: A Cartoonist's Life.* New York: Times Books/Random House, 1998. Herblock's memoirs.

_____. *The Herblock Book.* Boston: Beacon Press, 1952. A representative sampling of Herblock's works from the 1950's.

Bill Knight

See also Army-McCarthy hearings; Civil Rights movement; Cold War; McCarthy, Joseph; Newspapers in the United States; Nixon, Richard M.

─────────────────────────────

■ *Hernández v. Texas*

Identification U.S. Supreme Court ruling that barred exclusion of Hispanics from trial juries

Date Decided on May 3, 1954

In Hernández v. Texas, *the Supreme Court struck down state policies that discriminated against Mexican Ameri-*cans in jury selection, a ruling that helped pave the way for later decisions forbidding ethnic discrimination.*

In 1950, Pete Hernández was charged with murder in Jackson County, Texas. He was tried, convicted, and sentenced to life imprisonment. Hernández argued at trial that persons of Mexican descent were systematically excluded from the jury, thus denying him the equal protection of the laws guaranteed by the Fourteenth Amendment.

It had long been established that exclusion of jurors of a defendant's race or color was unconstitutional. Texas argued that Hispanics are "whites" in the interpretation of Texas statutes; consequently, there had been no racial exclusion of jurors in this case. Despite Hernández's showing that no juror with a Spanish surname had served on a Jackson County jury during the prior twenty-five years, he lost in the Texas Court of Criminal Appeals. On Hernández's petition, the U.S. Supreme Court agreed to hear the case.

In an opinion written by Chief Justice Earl Warren, the Court unanimously reversed Hernández's conviction. There was clear evidence that Hispanics were treated as a separate class in Texas and that they had been systematically excluded from service on both grand and petit juries. This ruling stated that Hernández's Fourteenth Amendment right to the equal protection of the laws had been violated.

Impact This decision was an important victory for Hispanic civil rights as it established that anti-Hispanic discrimination is unconstitutional despite the earlier Caucasian-African American bent of state law and federal cases. *Hernández v. Texas* was an important precedent until 1971, when Hispanics were accepted as a discrete minority group in *Cisneros v. Corpus Christi ISD.*

Further Reading

Lewis, Thomas T., and Richard Wilson, eds. *Encyclopedia of the U.S. Supreme Court.* Pasadena, Calif.: Salem Press, 2000. Covers major cases of the Supreme Court and discusses their significance.

Rosales, Francisco A. *Chicano! The History of the Mexican American Civil Rights Movement.* 2d rev. ed. Houston, Tex.: Arte Público Press, 1997. Historical review of the Hispanic civil rights movement; discusses important cases and statutes.

Robert Jacobs

See also Civil Rights Act of 1957; Civil Rights movement; Latinos; Racial discrimination; Warren, Earl.

■ Hersey, John

Identification American journalist and author
Born June 17 1914; Tianjin, China
Died March 24, 1993; Key West, Florida

John Hersey viewed his writing as a moral mission and used his imaginative literature to present historical events to the American public.

Born in China to American missionary parents, John Hersey first came to the United States when he was ten. He eventually graduated from Yale University, lettering in football and writing for the *Yale Daily News.* Afterward, he did graduate study in literature at Cambridge University's Clare College in England. After working on the staff of *Time* magazine in 1937, he became an editor and correspondent for *Life* magazine and a writer for *The New Yorker* and other magazines, covering international news bureaus. Drawing on his experience as a war correspondent during World War II, Hersey published a series of books, including *Men on Bataan* (1942), *Into the Valley: A Skirmish of the Marines* (1943), and *A Bell for Adano* (1944), for which he received the Pulitzer Prize. The U.S. bombing of Hiroshima, Japan, at the end of World War II resulted in *Hiroshima* (1946), which first appeared as a series in *The New Yorker* and was published as a book some months later.

Literary Works of the 1950's In 1950, Hersey published the novel considered by many to be his best work. As one of the first novels written about the Holocaust, *The Wall* (1950) recounts experiences of Jews living in the Warsaw ghetto during the years of German occupation as they learn to depend on one another while struggling with the prospect of possible annihilation. *The Wall* was also dramatized and filmed for television. Following an obscure novel, *The Marmot Drive* (1953), he published *A Single Pebble* (1956), a short, lucid novel set in China about cultural relativism and the need for people to understand one another. In 1959, he published *The War Lover.* In 1953, at the age of thirty-nine, Hersey became the youngest writer ever elected to the American Academy of Arts and Letters, and in 1955, he was named a delegate to the White House Conference on Education. His passion for education led to his membership in various educational councils, boards, and committees and contributed to his last book of the decade, *The Child Buyer* (1960), which presented

a case for individuality, freedom of thought, and faith in the youth of America.

Impact Perhaps better than other novelists of the 1950's, Hersey successfully realized what he believed should be the aims of writers of contemporary history novels: to make readers better able to cope with modern life and to elucidate how human beings coped with their own individual situations, many of which were historical events. Hersey dared to deal with social themes at a time when doing so was suspect.

Subsequent Events Hersey wrote nine more novels between 1960 and 1991, ending with *Antonietta* two years before his death. He also published several nonfiction works during this period. While remembered chiefly as a novelist, he also published *Key West Tales,* a volume of short stories, in 1994.

Further Reading
Sanders, David. *John Hersey.* New York: Twayne, 1967. Provides a chronology of Hersey's life and a critical analysis of his major novels up to 1960.
_____. *John Hersey Revisited.* New York: Twayne, 1991. Sanders updates his previous volume on Hersey's literary accomplishments.
Victoria Price
See also Bomb shelters; Education in the United States; Literature in the United States; War films.

■ Hitchcock films

Definition Films directed by producer-director Alfred Hitchcock (1899-1980)

Alfred Hitchcock's films of the 1950's gave a panoramic view not only of famous or typical American locales but also of key American social, political, and psychic dilemmas.

Born in England, Alfred Hitchcock came to the United States in 1939, working initially for David O. Selznick in an arrangement that offered him not only tremendous resources and opportunities but also many pressures and restrictions. Although such films as *Shadow of a Doubt* (1943) and *Notorious* (1946) contained fascinating reflections on his new American home, Hitchcock did not hit his stride as an American filmmaker until the 1950's. The deepening and broadening of his perspective on contemporary America went hand in hand with his successful struggle to consolidate a relatively stable position within the studio system, establishing a reliable team of collaborators, an efficient production routine, and a substantial amount of independence, power, and creative control as a producer-director.

Social Critic Even a brief survey of his films of this decade gives a good overview of his recurrent focus on crucial American issues. *Strangers on a Train* (1951) is in part a psychological portrait of a pathological character, Bruno, whose plan is to exchange murders with Guy, a successful tennis player he meets by chance. However, Guy is as disturbed and disturbing as Bruno, an ambitious social climber who shares Guy's violent desires. Bruno's well-to-do but dysfunctional family and domineering mother, and Guy's manipulative wife, who keeps him from his new true love, set this film solidly in the realm of 1950's domestic melodrama. However, by using Washington, D.C., as a recurrent backdrop, Hitchcock associated the personal and familial with political corruption, dysfunction, and vulnerability.

I Confess (1953) is set in Montreal, but its portrayal of a priest tortured by the demands of legal authorities and the community to reveal information that he feels compelled by higher principles not to disclose is an oblique but stunning dramatization of McCarthy-era hearings that pressured people to go against their conscience by "naming names" of suspected subversives.

Rear Window (1954) is one of Hitchcock's most important studies of American urban and domestic life. The apartment complex where the film is set becomes a kind of movie theater that displays a cross-section of lonely and frustrated lives, including that of L. B. Jeffries (played by James Stewart), a wheelchair-bound photographer who does most of the watching in the film. Hitchcock portrays voyeurism as a complex psychological and cultural phenomenon, representing both harmless ocular delight and morbid curiosity, a mode of engaging in, but also distancing oneself from, the lives of others. Behind the film lies widespread contemporary concern that America was turning into a nation of watchers rather than doers, that is, not a true community but a mere audience staring at one another.

Americans at Home and Abroad Hitchcock's next three films caught quintessential American characters in odd and picturesque locations. *To Catch a Thief* (1955), set in the French Riviera, features a

Director Alfred Hitchcock. (Arkent Archive)

beautiful but prematurely confident young American woman, played by Grace Kelly, crying out for a kiss and a comeuppance, unaware that she is out of her league in the continental world of love and intrigue. *The Trouble with Harry* (1956) transfers Hitchcock's British sense of humor—dry, droll, and grim—to an autumnal Vermont locale, where the mysterious appearance of a dead body somehow allows a group of down-home characters to display both their irrepressible eccentricity and their life-affirming affection for one another. In *The Man Who Knew Too Much* (1956), Hitchcock modifies his breakthrough thriller of 1934 by placing an American family at its center. They are innocents abroad—first in a sunny French Morocco and then suddenly forced to search for their missing son in a gray London—and their vulnerability and victimization epitomize what many felt was the defining American experience of the 1950's, caught up in Cold War mysteries and machinations not of their making. However, they are also not so innocent, and they carry with them their own set of problems, including provinciality, patriarchal arrogance, and unresolved tension, felt by both the husband and wife, about a woman's claims to self-determination and full partnership in a marriage.

American Culture and Psyche Hitchcock's last four films of the decade collectively lay out a remarkably comprehensive analysis of some of the fundamental cracks in American character and culture. *The Wrong Man* (1956) powerfully dramatizes the double-doom of middle-class families: bound to an ordinary life of interminable work and worry that can never keep impending emotional, physical, and financial ruin more than an arm's length away, and also subject to impersonal and institutional assault, ironically even from institutions (an insurance company, the police department, the law) established for protection. *Vertigo*'s (1958) haunting evocation of human passion and desire in league with death and annihilation gives it transcultural relevance, but Hitchcock carefully framed the film as an American operatic romance, embedding the drama in a culture characterized by abusive power, materialism, and possessiveness as well as by dreams of freedom and love.

North by Northwest (1959) examines the American character and predicament while traversing the American landscape. Using the format of an action-adventure spy story allowed Hitchcock to satirize a society that had lost its way in a Cold War struggle that seemed more chaotic and amoral than clear-cut and principled. The film was also a critique of the dominant culture of advertising and commerce, an enemy from within perhaps as duplicitous, fantastic, and dangerous as any external Cold War foe.

Impact Hitchcock's films of this period became models for some of the most popular emerging genres: later "caper" films such as *Topkapi* (1964) and *Charade* (1963) are clearly indebted to the amiable rogues, romance, international setting, and verbal and pictorial wit of *To Catch a Thief*; while *North by Northwest* is credited as a decisive influence on the James Bond films. Hitchcock often argued that he was not particularly concerned with content, and his films of the 1950's are indeed, broadly speaking, what his films from other decades were: compelling narratives, provocative existential fables of the human predicament, and adventurous exercises of and experiments in cinematic form. His films of the 1950's also form a coherent group and, especially when taken together, offer a complex and far-reaching dramatization and analysis of the American scene that was his recurrent subject and constant reference point during his long stay in the United States.

Further Reading

Freedman, Jonathan, and Richard Millington, eds. *Hitchcock America.* New York: Oxford University Press, 1999. Important anthology of essays focusing on Hitchcock's portrait of the United States in his films of the 1940's and 1950's.

McGilligan, Patrick. *Alfred Hitchcock: A Life in Darkness and Light.* New York: Regan Books, 2003. Extensively documented biography of Hitchcock's life and career, with much information on his working environment and method.

Truffaut, François. *Hitchcock.* New York: Simon & Schuster, 1984. Fascinating and essential book-length interview, covering Hitchcock's entire career.

Wood, Robin. *Hitchcock's Films Revisited.* New York: Columbia University Press, 2002. Revised edition of one of the classic critical books on Hitchcock; particularly good on social, sexual, and political dimensions of the films.

Sidney Gottlieb

See also Academy Awards; Advertising; American Dream; Cold War; Day, Doris; Film in the United States; House Committee on Un-American Activities; Kelly, Grace; McCarthy, Joseph; Wide-screen movies.

■ Hockey

Definition Winter team sport played on ice

A sport played by professionals and amateurs and one that, during the 1950's, was more popular in Canada and the northern United States than elsewhere throughout the continent, hockey changed little during the decade, particularly at the professional level.

Most North Americans during the 1950's would have associated hockey with the main professional league, the National Hockey League (NHL). Founded in 1917, the National Hockey League remained small for decades, consisting of only six teams during the 1950's: the Detroit Red Wings, the New York Rangers, the Chicago Blackhawks, the Toronto Maple Leafs, and the Montreal Canadiens. Because of the nature of the game, it was easy for single teams and a handful of players to dominate it. Thus, the decade showcased two teams and two players from those teams in particular: the Detroit Red Wings with Gordie Howe and the Montreal Canadiens with Maurice "the Rocket" Richard. From the 1950-1951 season to the 1954-1955 season, Detroit finished first each season and did so again during the 1956-1957 season. For the remainder of the decade, the top team was Montreal.

Finishing first did not guarantee a team would win the league's championship trophy, the Stanley Cup. However, between 1950 and 1960, with the exception of 1951, when the Toronto Maple Leafs took home the title, Detroit and Montreal won the titles each year; Montreal, under the direction of Coach Hector "Toe" Blake, won five straight Stanley Cups in the latter half of the decade.

Howe helped earn Detroit its consistent success, and he won the league-scoring title four straight times at the beginning of the decade. Statistically, Richard did not win a single scoring title during the 1950's; however not only was he the dominant player on his team, but also he was the hero to millions of French Canadians across Canada. Richard was so revered among the general populace in the Canadian province of Quebec that in March of 1955, after the NHL commissioner suspended him for the remainder of the season and playoffs for injuring another player, a riot erupted in the arena in Montreal that soon spread across the city. It ended only after Richard took to the radio to plead for calm.

Some aspects of the NHL did change during the 1950's. In Canada, the Canadian Broadcasting Corporation began broadcasting games nationally on television in 1952 in what it called "Hockey Night," which quickly became a tradition across Canada. Other significant changes involved equipment. Near the end of the 1950's, players began experimenting with curved sticks. In 1959, Jacques Plante, a goaltender for the Montreal Canadiens, became the first goalie to wear a protective face mask after a puck in a previous game injured him.

Other Professional Leagues The National Hockey League was not the only existing professional league during the 1950's: The American Hockey League (AHL) was also an important entity in the sport. The league, based in the northeastern United States, began play in 1936, and by the 1950's, it was a feeder league for the dominant National Hockey League. NHL teams controlled AHL teams and used them to develop players. The AHL's annual championship was called the Calder Cup, and only two teams during the 1950's,

Gordie Howe, the leading goal scorer in the NHL during the 1950's, in 1955. (AP/Wide World Photos)

the Hershey Bears and the Pittsburgh Hornets, were repeat winners. Another existing professional league at the time that also served as a source of players for the NHL was the International Hockey League, which featured teams from the central United States and Canada. The Cincinnati Mohawks, an International Hockey League team, won five straight championships during the middle of the decade.

Because only six teams existed in the NHL during the 1950's, it was difficult for players in lower leagues to find a place with top professional teams. It was equally true, however, that in an era before players were drafted by NHL teams, having a solid farm system with high-quality players ready to replace the injured or retired, as the Montreal Canadiens did during the 1950's, was a key factor in producing dominant franchises.

Amateur Hockey Professionals were not the only athletes who played hockey during the 1950's: The game also flourished at the amateur level, and among its major events during the 1950's was the Winter Olympics. Teams from Canada and the United States dominated Olympic hockey in this decade. In 1952, Canada won the gold medal and the United States won the silver; in 1956, the United States won silver and Canada won bronze; and, with Squaw Valley in California as host city in 1960, the U.S. won gold and Canada won silver.

The epicenter for amateur hockey in the United States was at the college level, especially among institutions based in northern states. The National Collegiate Athletic Association (NCAA) began its Division 1 championship in 1948, and from then until the end of the 1950's, the University of Michigan Wolverines won six championships and was the runner-up once. By the end of the 1950's, Canadian players were highly sought after by American university recruiters.

For most players from Canada, however, the path to stardom was not through college hockey but through amateur junior hockey. NHL teams used the top junior league the same way it did the AHL—as a place from which to acquire players or to which it could farm out players if they were not ready to turn professional. The top junior level in Canada, divided into a number of leagues along regional lines, had a large and loyal fan base nonetheless.

Impact Compared with other major North American sports, hockey remained at all levels a regional sport during the 1950's and claimed several professional leagues, including the NHL, and a flourishing amateur game in both Canada and the United States.

Further Reading
Diamond, Dan, and Eric Zweig. *Hockey's Glory Days: The 1950's and '60's.* Toronto: Andrews McMeel, 2003. A popular history of the years before the NHL expanded.
Fischler, Stan. *Golden Ice: The Greatest Teams in Hockey History.* New York: Wynwood Press, 1990. Journalistic study of some of the greatest teams in NHL history, including the Montreal Canadiens of the 1950's.
McKinley, Michael. *Putting a Roof on Winter: Hockey's Rise from Sport to Spectacle.* New York: Greystone Books, 2000. A general history of the rise of hockey as a professional sport with a special focus on the 1940's, 1950's, and 1960's.

Steve Hewitt

See also Canadian Broadcasting Corporation; Continentalism; Olympic Games of 1952; Olympic Games of 1956; O'Ree, Willie; Sports; Television in Canada.

■ Hoffa, Jimmy

Identification President of the International Brotherhood of Teamsters from 1958 to 1971
Born February 14, 1913; Brazil, Indiana
Died July 30, 1975; place unknown

Jimmy Hoffa's tenure as Teamsters president brought scandal to the labor movement through illegal activities and association with crime families. He vanished in 1975, thought to be the victim of foul play.

The son of a coal miner, James Riddle Hoffa was born in Indiana. His family moved to Detroit when Jimmy was seven. A high school dropout, he found work unloading produce at a Kroger's grocery warehouse. Success in organizing a tiny union there led to his affiliation with the American Federation of Labor (AFL) and, in 1935, membership in the International Brotherhood of Teamsters (IBT). Although strong-arm tactics and crime family connections tarnished his public image, within the IBT membership he became lionized as a persecuted champion of workers' rights. When Dave Beck became president of the Teamsters in 1952, Hoffa successfully ran as vice president.

Teamster official Jimmy Hoffa (right) conferring with attorney George S. Fitzgerald (center) and Robert F. Kennedy (left), counsel for the Senate Rackets Investigating Committee, during a break in a Senate hearing, in September, 1957. (AP/Wide World Photos)

A special subcommittee, headed by Arkansas senator John McClellan, brought Beck to trial. Convictions on tax evasion and larceny earned Beck a sentence of five years in federal prison. In late 1957, the Teamsters elected Hoffa president with 73 percent of the vote, and he took office in January the following year. The now-joined AFL-CIO voted to expel the union. As the McClellan Committee investigations continued through 1958, a national television audience watched allegations against Hoffa of shakedowns, mob contacts, illegal loans, and embezzlement. In spite of strong evidence of his guilt, none of the charges resulted in a conviction.

Impact Hoffa's successful bargaining with management resulted in fierce loyalty from his Teamsters. However, his unapologetic brashness and underworld associations, brought to the American public through live television hearings, garnered notoriety for him and tainted the labor movement in general.

Subsequent Events When John F. Kennedy assumed office as U.S. president in 1961, Hoffa's days of skating through criminal charges were numbered. In 1964, the government convicted the Teamster leader of attempting to buy jury votes, conspiracy, and mail and wire fraud. President Richard M. Nixon pardoned him in 1971, but Hoffa mysteriously disappeared four years later en route to a luncheon engagement in suburban Detroit.

Further Reading

Russell, Thaddeus. *Out of the Jungle: Jimmy Hoffa and the Remaking of the American Working Class.* New York: Alfred A. Knopf, 2001. Chronicles Hoffa's involvement with labor and argues that he was motivated by the material well-being of his union members.

Sheridan, Walter. *The Rise and Fall of Jimmy Hoffa.* New York: Saturday Review Press, 1972. Details the life of Hoffa.

Jim Heaney

See also Landrum-Griffin Act of 1959; McClellan Committee; Meany, George; Teamsters Union; Unionism in the United States.

■ Hogan, Ben

Identification American professional golfer
Born August 13, 1912; Dublin, Texas
Died July 25, 1997; Fort Worth, Texas

The winner of sixty-three golf tournaments, including all four major championships, Ben Hogan was perhaps the most outstanding male golfer of the 1950's.

Ben Hogan joined the professional golf tour in 1931 but had to overcome a problem with his swing. He led golfers in earnings for several years during the 1940's and earned the Vardon Trophy for lowest stroke average in 1940, 1941, and 1948. Hogan captured his first major tournament in 1946 at the Professional Golfers Association (PGA) Championship and won a career-high eleven events in 1948, taking both the U.S. Open and the PGA Championship. He was involved in a near-fatal automobile accident in February, 1949, while returning home to Fort Worth, Texas. The movie *Follow the Sun* (1951) details his accident and remarkable comeback.

Hogan triumphed in the 1950 U.S. Open, prevailing in a three-way playoff by four strokes. In 1951, he attained his first Masters title by two strokes and the U.S. Open crown by two strokes. Hogan thereafter concentrated on major golf tournaments. His best season came in 1953, when he took five of six tournaments and three majors, nearly equaling Bobby Jones's grand slam of 1930. He triumphed in the Masters by five strokes, the U.S. Open by six strokes, and his first British Open by four strokes, breaking the Carnoustie, Scotland, course record. He played regularly in major tournaments until 1960 and set a record at the 1967 Masters by shooting the back nine in thirty strokes.

Hogan participated on four Ryder Cup teams and won the PGA Player of the Year Award in 1948, 1950, 1951, and 1953. He wrote *Power of Golf* (1948) and *Five Lessons* (1957) and was elected to the PGA Hall of Fame and World Golf Hall of Fame.

Impact Hogan won nine majors, including four U.S. Opens, two Masters, two PGAs, and one British Open. He is one of only five golfers to take all four grand-slam titles and ranks third with sixty-three ca-reer victories, trailing only Sam Snead and Jack Nicklaus.

Further Reading

Rubinstein, Lorne, and David Leadbetter. *The Fundamentals of Hogan.* New York: Doubleday, 2000. Detailed analysis of Hogan's golf techniques.
Sampson, Curt *Hogan.* Rev. ed. Nashville, Tenn.: Rutledge Hill Press, 2001. A solid biography of Hogan.
Vasquez, Jody. *Afternoons with Mr. Hogan: A Boy, a Golf Legend, and the Lessons of a Lifetime.* New York: Gotham Books, 2004. Anecdotal material about Hogan's playing career collected by a man who shagged balls for him during the 1950's.
David L. Porter

See also Golf; Snead, Sam; Sports.

■ Holiday Inn

Identification American hotel chain
Date First motel opened on August 1, 1952

Holiday Inn launched a revolution in the travel industry by introducing uniform, affordable, and predictable lodgings for American travelers.

Kemmons Wilson conceived the idea for the Holiday Inn in 1952 while on a family vacation. Upset at the dirty, run-down motels available on his trip, he recognized the need for reliable, high-quality lodging, especially since the rapidly developing interstate highway system was putting more people than ever before on the road. Within the year, he had commissioned a design from Eddie Bluestein, who borrowed the name Holiday Inn from a popular Bing Crosby film of the same title. The new hotels were to include amenities such as air conditioning, telephones, restaurants, swimming pools, and free ice. The most important aspect of his vision was standardization, enabling the traveler to know what to expect from lodgings, whether in Topeka or Tallahassee.

The first Holiday Inn opened in Memphis, Tennessee, and proved so successful that by 1972, there were 1,405 in the United States and around the world. Furthermore, chains such as Howard Johnson and Ramada Inn began to copy the pattern of standard amenities at reasonable prices. The distinctive green Holiday Inn sign became a familiar landmark for tourists and business travelers.

Impact Holiday Inn changed the face of automobile travel in the United States by standardizing lodging and making high-quality accommodations available to all middle-class American business and tourist travelers at a reasonable price. An unfortunate side-effect of the Holiday Inn was the gradual disappearance of the smaller, independent roadside inns and motor lodges, which could not compete with the large chain motels.

Further Reading

Jakle, John A. *The Motel in America.* Baltimore: Johns Hopkins University Press, 1996. Informative and comprehensive look at the history of the motel.

Margolies, John. *Home Away from Home: Motels in America.* Boston: Little, Brown, 1995. Full of advertisements, memorabilia, and photos.

Mary Virginia Davis

See also Automobiles and auto manufacturing; Interstate highway system; Motels.

■ Holly, Buddy

Identification Singer-songwriter who recorded under his own name and with the Crickets

Born September 7, 1936; Lubbock, Texas

Died February 3, 1959; Clear Lake, Iowa

Buddy Holly's "Tex-Mex" sound—Western, with just a hint of a Latin beat—had a major influence on later music, and after his untimely death in 1959, Holly became legendary in roll-and-roll history.

Charles Hardin Holley (the "e" was dropped by mistake in his first record contract) was influenced musically by Bob Wills's "Western Swing." With three friends, Holly started the Crickets, whose first single, "That'll Be the Day," was released in 1957 and was an immediate hit. It was followed by "Oh, Boy!" Holly then released "Peggy Sue" under his own name, with "Every Day" on the flip side.

In March, 1958, the Crickets successfully toured Great Britain, one of the first American rock groups to do so. In the summer of that year, Holly met Maria Elena Santiago, a receptionist, and they married two weeks later. In 1959, Holly went on a tour of the Midwest with J. P. Richardson (who performed as the Big Bopper) and singer Ritchie Valens. On February 3, their small chartered plane crashed, killing all three performers. Coral Records, his label, rushed to release Holly's last record, "It Doesn't Matter Anymore."

Buddy Holly shortly before his death in an airplane accident. (AP/Wide World Photos)

Impact Holly was in the public eye for less than two years, but his music influenced many other performers, and his life inspired songs and a movie. He performed with a nervous intensity, even when the lyrics (like those of "Peggy Sue") would seem to require calm or sorrow; the adolescent sexual fervor of "Oh, Boy!" is all but overpowering. Like Elvis Presley and Roy Orbison, he was far from the standards of male attractiveness for the time, but he helped redefine them.

Holly's Tex-Mex sound influenced other musicians, from the Drifters to the Beatles and Freddy Fender. The 1978 movie *The Buddy Holly Story* included a certain amount of Hollywood imagination. Holly's plane crash is the central image of Don McLean's musical history song, "American Pie."

Further Reading

Goldrosen, John. *Remembering Buddy: The Definitive Biography of Buddy Holly.* Rev. ed. New York: DaCapo Press, 2001. Many illustrations, photos, news clippings, and charts accompany this good biography.

Lehmer, Larry. *The Day the Music Died: The Last Tour of Buddy Holly, the Big Bopper, and Ritchie Valens.* New York: Schirmer Books, 1997. This detailed view of Holly's final tour includes biographical material on the performers.

Arthur D. Hlavaty

See also Dance, popular; Diddley, Bo; Domino, Fats; Lewis, Jerry Lee; Music; Rock and roll; Sullivan, Ed; Top 40 radio; Valens, Ritchie.

■ Home appliances

During the 1950's, widespread socioeconomic changes—including a dual rise of affluence and a consumer culture and a demand for new homes for expanding postwar families—created a huge market for home appliances.

North America of the 1950's was poised for the development and consumption of home appliances. New family units were rapidly being established, and the supply of dwellings—especially single-unit homes—was barely keeping up with the demand. Changes in basic house plans, which typically eliminated the front porch and dining room, gave kitchens increased status. In turn, kitchens became places for entertaining and showcasing major and small home appliances, symbols of affluence. During the 1950's, one income often supported a family, and along with easily obtained credit or part-time income, families could afford the new labor-saving and comfort devices that were flooding the market. Moreover, the electrification of North America, even in the most rural of areas, and the availability of gas generated a consumer demand for home appliances and resulted in the growth of the appliance industry.

Major Appliances The development and marketing of major home appliances targeted certain laborious tasks performed in the home. The preparation and preservation of food and the care of clothing were areas in which appliance innovations became prevalent during the 1950's. Oven ranges were offered in a variety of styles, from single-standing to built-in units, and from slide-in units to range tops with a separate mounted oven. Features included tilt-tops, removable oven coverings, and rounded oven corners for easy cleaning. Mounted control panels with removable knobs also provided for ease in the cleaning and operation of the appliance. A

standard feature on the newly designed ranges of the 1950's included oven fans, which directed and dissipated heat and reduced exterior surface temperatures. Extra features available at a much higher cost included self-cleaning options and a timer device on the control panel.

Microwave ovens were introduced during the 1950's but were not used for food preparation during that decade. Automatic dishwashers, introduced during the 1950's and proclaimed by *Better Homes and Gardens* as being "advantage appliances" for their use in cleanup after food preparation and meals, were not considered necessities but luxuries. An unusual appliance with the combined function of cleaning clothes and washing dishes was introduced during the 1950's but failed in the marketplace.

During the decade, designers focused on appliances' shapes and feature placements; the refrigerator typically had the greatest number of styles. Refrigerators were designed with freezing compartments placed above, under, or beside the cold-storage compartments and had single doors, which opened the whole unit, or two doors, which opened the freezer and the cold storage section. In one model, the freezer rolled out for convenience of food storage and selection. Baskets, pull-out drawers, and special containers for food storage were among the other popular features of refrigerators. A high-end refrigerator with an automatic icemaker was available during the 1950's. Stand-alone freezers also were available and came in two basic models—the chest style and the vertical style, which mirrored the style of refrigerators.

Major appliances for the care of clothing included washing machines in three different styles—wringer, spinner, and automatic. Surprisingly, the acceptance of the automatic washer did not displace entirely the other two styles until after the 1950's. Special features on washers included the choice of different washing action (agitation and pulsation) and different settings for fabric types, soil levels, and water levels. Dryers were accepted only as "bad weather helpers" until the later advent of durable press fabrics, which required the automatic dryer for best maintenance and performance.

Small Appliances The market was flooded with small home appliances during the 1950's. Their function ranged from labor-saving devices to specific-

Electrical Appliances in Wired U.S. Homes in 1950 and 1959

Item	Number in homes by 1950 (millions)	Percent of wired homes in 1950	Number in homes by 1959 (millions)	Percent of wired homes in 1959
Televisions	10.6	26.4	45.5	89.9
Refrigerators	33.8	86.4	49.6	98.0
Freezers	2.8	7.2	11.2	22.1
Vacuum cleaners	22.0	56.5	36.7	72.5
Washers	28.1	71.9	47.1	93.1
Driers*	0.6	1.4	9.0	17.8
Air conditioners	0.2	0.6	6.5	12.8

Note: *Includes gas driers.
Source: Harold G. Vatter, *The U.S. Economy in the 1950's*, 1963.

task equipment. With the rise of wall-to-wall carpeting in several rooms of homes, the vacuum cleaner, designed to clean all types of floors, was widely embraced. Their accompanying, special-purpose attachments for such tasks as cleaning corners, dusting, and brushing increased consumers' desires for this product. Small electrical appliances tended to be targeted for kitchen use: blenders, mixers, fry pans, deep fryers, broilers, knives, knife sharpeners, hot trays, ice crushers, coffee makers, can openers, corn poppers, griddles, waffle bakers, toaster ovens, rotisseries, hot plates, and baby-bottle warmers. A number of items were brought to the market to assist with the care of clothing and personal grooming.

The iron—whether used dry or with steam or spray, or a combination of both—was a welcomed product. Other care products included steam wrinkle removers, shoe polishers, stream press valets, and electric clothes brushes. Electrical grooming appliances included vanity mirrors with magnification and lights, salon and bonnet-style hair dryers, hair curlers, hair cutters, heated lather dispensers, shavers, tooth brushes, oral water jets, manicure sets, and electric hair brushes.

Consumers of the 1950's had discretionary incomes and desired appliances for comfort and entertainment. The two most popular luxury appliances included air conditioners and television sets. Other appliances in this category included electric

dehumidifiers, water softeners, electric blankets, massagers, hot pads, warmers, and record players.

Impact The 1950's was an ideal era for the testing of home appliances among consumers. The success of the appliance industry helped create manufacturing empires, including John Oster, Maytag, General Electric, Eureka, and Proctor. The rise of home-appliance use produced a host of spin-off products, including stainless steel cookware, plastic ware, food preparation gadgets, and ceramic, all-purpose dishes. As appliances and related products filled the home, they provided an additional avenue for consumers to display their affluence and express their style sense. The products were designed to mirror cultural interests and to color-coordinate homes. The design lines of the appliances often mirrored the styles of automobiles, satellites, and the jet age. The colors moved from red and chartreuse during the early 1950's to the pastel yellows, pinks, and turquoises by the end of the decade.

Further Reading

Cohen, Elizabeth. *A Consumer's Republic: The Politics of Mass Consumption in Postwar America.* New York: Knopf, 2003. Examines the way in which affluence and consumerism were linked to issues of citizenship (the encouragement to buy for "the good of the nation") in postwar America.

Jackson, Leslie. *Contemporary Architecture and Interiors of the 1950's.* Reprint. London: Phaidon Press,

1998. In its discussion of the Contemporary style in architecture, also explores the styles of the era's kitchens and its appliances.

Matranga, Victor Casaba, and Jerry Renninger, eds. *America at Home: A Celebration of Twentieth-Century Housewares.* Rosemount, Ill.: National Housewares Manufacturers, 1997. An overview of changes in housewares from 1900 to 1997.

Parr, Joy. *Domestic Goods: The Material, the Moral, and the Economic in the Postwar Years.* Toronto: University of Toronto Press, 1999. Examines the differences in the ways American and Canadian housewives used consumer goods and takes a broader look at the production, promotion, and consumption of furniture and appliances in Canada.

Wingate, Isabel, et al. *Know Your Merchandise: For Retailers and Consumers.* New York: McGraw-Hill, 1984. A textbook format is used to present home appliance and furnishings information needed by consumers and retailers.

Sue Bailey

See also Affluence and the new consumerism; Betty Crocker cookbooks; Home furnishings; Housing in the United States; Inventions; *Look*; Tupperware; TV dinners; Women and the roots of the feminist movement.

■ Home furnishings

During the 1950's, home owners turned away from traditional wood veneers, delicate finishes, and fussy upholstery and instead sought the practicality and shine of laminates, plastics, and metal surfaces. Mid-century modern was a dynamic, if short-lived, design aesthetic that enhanced the ergonomics of common objects and introduced a range of inexpensive and durable materials that continue to be widely used.

The housing boom of the 1950's produced an unprecedented large market for middle-class household goods. These included furniture, large and small appliances, flooring, textiles, and ceramics, all of which expressed the optimism of postwar America. As densely developed new housing tracts were filled with growing families, the shape of American homes was altered to accommodate not only large numbers of young children but also their possessions and expectations. Average square footage shrank, but its uses were maximized; floor plans opened up, kitchens expanded, and bathrooms multiplied.

Americans wanted to be in the vanguard of a forward-thinking and better-living modern world, and the stuffed and ruffled trappings of the past fell into popular disfavor. The modern interior was something altogether new.

Embracing the Exotic and the Practical World War II produced a number of effects on the tastes and inclinations of the postwar generation. Military assignment overseas and ensuing improvements in transportation decreased American provincialism, and many homes were salted with exotic memorabilia of the Pacific Islands, India, and Mexico, while suburban yards sported pink flamingos and Tiki torches. European trends in design, such as the nearly spartan Danish modern, were also viewed with interest as alternatives to fussy, expensive, and hard-to-maintain furnishings.

Postwar families generally were upwardly mobile, but wartime rationing and the long economic Depression that preceded the war had impressed upon members of those generations a deep sense of practicality and frugality. Although they could afford a level of well-deserved conspicuous consumption, they rejected ornamentation that smacked of opulence. A stylish home demonstrated simplicity and practicality and was clean, comfortable, and people-friendly. It was also full of natural light and was allowed a bold palette of interior colors.

New Materials and Technologies By the 1950's, middle-class demand for home furnishings was overwhelming. People wanted things that were fresh, modern, and affordable, and they wanted lots of them. Such demand was met by putting to commercial use many of the materials and technologies developed during the war. Charles Eames famously transformed the laminated leg splints he had designed with Finnish American architect Eero Saarinen for battlefield injuries into chairs for civilian repose.

Plywood was first produced during the mid-nineteenth century, but it was steamed, bent, and glued by hand. It was valued during World War II as a lightweight aircraft material, and mass-manufacturing techniques were quickly developed for it. After the war, this moldable laminate became a designer's ideal material for shaping artistic yet functional furniture. Made of multiple thin layers of wood stacked and glued together with the grain of each layer running at a right angle to the layer below it, plywood offered great strength without joints, and it could be pressed into curving or undulating shapes. It was attractive, inexpensive, and abundant. Another laminate that came into its own during the 1950's was Formica, essentially a paper product but impregnated with resin. Perfectly smooth and extremely durable, formica became a premier material for counters and tabletops in American kitchens.

Stainless steel became a popular material for chair and table legs. Durable and colorful new plastics were molded into seats intended to conform to the human posterior rather than cushion it, though these innovative seats were accepted more widely in institutional settings, such as schools. Where upholstery was unquestionably wanted, such as a sofa or easy chair, vinyl or Naugahyde, an imitation leather, made a comfortable, easy-to-clean surface over foam.

Design Revolutionaries Many designers had been working in the modern style before the war, but scarcity of materials and uncertainty about the future did not allow a popular embrace of the style until G.I.'s returned and factories turned from production of wartime necessities to household goods. In 1948, Milo Bougham introduced his California Modern line of furniture, designed for the open-plan homes popular in Los Angeles. The style, which divided room space without the full impediment of a wall, caught on nationwide.

The Cranbrook Academy of Art graduated the most influential modern designers, including Harry Bertoia, Florence Knoll, Saarinen, and Charles and Ray Eames. Saarinen and Charles Eames developed a new production method for molded plywood that was honed during the war for the making of airplane parts and medical supplies, such as sculptural leg splints designed to conform to the patient's leg. The Eameses approached chair design in the same way they designed the leg splints—as dictated by the shape of the human form. The Eameses used brightly colored fiberglass produced by Zenith Plastics for the DAR chair, which was mass-produced by the thousands. The molded shell of the seat and back were mounted on steel legs. The design is still in production (and much imitated) and is ubiquitous in school classrooms and cafeterias. The Eameses were also among the first to produce furniture designed to be assembled at home by the purchaser.

The Eames studio employed a number of talented but more or less uncredited designers. Bertoia left the Eameses in 1946, and by the early 1950's, he was designing fairly autonomously for Knoll International. His steel mesh chairs, including the Diamond and Long-necked Bird designs, were loved for their elegant forms and near transparency and became seminal pieces of modern design. They were, however, uncomfortable; they were made useful with special removable seat covers.

Many of the best-known furniture lines of the 1950's were distributed by Herman Miller. Miller's chairs and sofas were largely complemented with textiles by Alexander Girard, who used bold and often disturbing slashes of color in his designs. Influenced by folk art and handicrafts from Mexico and India, Girard's textiles met head-on the bright, primary color schemes of much modern furniture, while softening its potentially antiseptic effect with whimsy or folksy patterns.

Modernism was not appreciated universally. Untempered, it could be offputting. Edward Wormely produced more conservative furniture designs, which combined the sculptural lines of his more radical competitors with spare but traditional Japanese elements. Isamu Noguchi, an American sculptor of Japanese descent, also found great demand for Japanese accents with his commercially produced white paper lanterns, called Akari, and other household accessories.

The Home of Tomorrow Women of the 1950's embraced the machine. Improvements in refrigerators, clothes washers and dryers, dishwashers, and vacuum cleaners relieved considerable drudgery. Large appliances took up a lot of room in the kitchen and were expected to contribute their proportional share of style, with aerodynamic rounded corners and a mix-and-match color scheme of pink, yellow, aqua, or turquoise. Blenders, toasters, mixers, and even clocks all became designed accessories for the "kitchen of the future." Formica, fiberglass, and melamine made easy-to-clean surfaces for countertops and tables. Smooth waterproof vinyl covered not only the kitchen floor but also the seats. Chrome or stainless steel added shine to chair and table legs, small appliances, trim, handles, and drawer pulls.

Ceramic Fiestaware reached its peak during the 1950's; its Art Deco shapes blended well with simple, often two-toned tableware of the period. Popular taste moved away from expensive china and toward more durable melamine. Formal patterns gave way to abstracted or stylized images, one of the most popular being the Homemaker line, designed for Woolworth by Enid Seeney. The two-tone Homemaker pattern featured cutouts of typical 1950's furnishings, notably a boomerang coffee table, pasted at odd angles over a background of horizontal scratch marks.

In 1950, manufacturers seeking a way to produce a wider, unseamed bedspread discovered that the same technology could produce an inexpensive wall-to-wall carpet. The cotton-tufted carpeting, however, could not rival its older woven-wool competitor in durability until DuPont introduced bulked continuous filament (BCF) nylon in 1957. Area rugs were rolled up, hardwood floors disappeared under an indoor sea of artificial fibers, and the carpet industry boomed. Space-age vacuum cleaners, such as one by Hoover that floated on a cushion of its own exhaust and the Kenmore Commander, shaped conspicuously like an atomic bomb, helped make cleaning the luxurious flooring possible.

An "atomic" aesthetic was possibly the most interesting expression of science in mid-century design. Geometrical shapes, especially spheres, were popular motifs and were often arranged to suggest the orbits of planets or electrons. Coat hooks and clocks held out the promise of a nuclear age.

Impact Modern design soon passed from American homes along with the optimistic view that better living could be achieved through chemicals. Mass production had been developed to bring comfort and quality in the form of affordable goods to the greatest number of people. Its environmental impact, in the form of water and air pollution and landfills that received non-biodegradable garbage, began to become apparent only during the 1960's and 1970's. The bright future of atomic power was soon clouded, and a losing war in Vietnam fractured national pride. The bold color schemes, stylized patterns, and asymmetric lines grew wearisome and annoyingly quaint. Vinyl upholstery, always squeaky and sweaty, tore and did not seem to merit repair.

Subsequent Events While the hallmarks of modern interior design fell out of fashion, many of its tenets continued to drive the middle-class market for home furnishings. Mass production continued to be the rule in subsequent decades, and ergonomics be-

came a top design consideration, particularly in the making of chairs, beds, and small appliances. Home assembly became standard for much of the furniture industry. Scandinavian design, once a core influence on American modern, found thriving markets through major retailers such as Ikea, Herman Miller, and Knoll International.

At the beginning of the twenty-first century, thrift stores began to see renewed interest in discarded items from the 1950's. After a period in which turquoise refrigerators and amoeba-shaped coffee tables were reviled almost universally as the low point of interior design, collectors and decorators began to express a loving appreciation of the soft lines, uninhibited splashes of color and imaginative patterns, and the quirky play between space and balance. Mid-century "retro" brought back to the home market many of the same or similar designs produced fifty years before, this time using refined production methods and overseas labor, as well as a range of new plastics and other inexpensive materials unavailable before.

Further Reading

Albrecht, Donald. *The Work of Charles and Ray Eames.* New York: Abrams, 1997. This exquisite examination of the career of the Eameses was produced by the Library of Congress to accompany an exhibition of their work. It is superbly illustrated and its profile of both designers is appreciative and painstaking.

Bosker, Gideon, Michele Mancini, and John Gramstad. *Fabulous Fabrics of the 1950's.* San Francisco: Chronicle Books, 1992. A thorough and enthusiastic survey of period textiles, this book shows the quirky patterns that characterized 1950's fabrics.

Fiell, Charlotte, and Peter Fiell. *Modern Furniture Classics: Postwar to Postmodern.* New York: Thames and Hudson, 2001. This beautiful reference puts 1950's furniture design in the context of modernism.

Greenberg, Cara, and Tim Street-Porter. *Mid-Century Modern: Furniture of the 1950's.* Rev. ed. New York: Harmony Books, 1995. An overview of the movement that includes material from the Herman Miller archives.

Pina, Leslie. *Fifties Furniture.* Atglen, Pa.: Schiffer, 2000. Indispensable guide to designers and their work. Includes 450 captioned images, plus biographies of seventy designers and a bibliography.

Weaving, Andrew. *Living Modern: Bringing Modernism Home.* San Francisco: Chronicle Books, 2002. Offers visual tours of seminal homes by modernism's architectural masters. Not limited to the 1950's but shows the reader how a high-end modern home might be furnished.

Janet Alice Long

See also Affluence and the new consumerism; American Dream; Architecture; Art movements; Betty Crocker cookbooks; Home appliances; Housing in Canada; Housing in the United States; Inventions; Science and technology; Tupperware; TV dinners.

■ Homosexuality and gay rights

Though gay rights groups were beginning to form during the 1950's, gay and lesbian rights of that decade were limited by stereotyping and public misunderstanding. Groups during the decade gave gays and lesbians a social and political outlet, even though the repression that characterized this era continued until the late 1960's.

During the early twentieth century, gays and lesbians moved from complete isolation to a burgeoning sense of community. World War II brought many people to the cities to work, where they found a new sense of freedom. Lesbians working in factories found themselves, for the first time, in a large community made almost entirely of women, making it easier for them meet one another. Gay men, some of whom were expelled from the army, also gathered in large cities. However, even as they gathered, they struggled to keep secret their sexual orientations and preserve their privacy.

The Homophile Movement McCarthy era repression included prejudice against groups other than alleged communists. Gays and lesbians, already popularly perceived as "perverted," made easy targets for public paranoia. Therefore, early gay and lesbian rights groups were limited in both their ability and desire to promote gay rights. Such groups typically advocated a conservative approach toward gay rights, supporting a move toward public understanding of homosexuality but not necessarily large-scale change. Collectively known as the "homophile movement," members pursued moderate political goals during the 1950's. Later militant gay activists would argue that these groups' conservative attitudes slowed social change, but the homophile movement was nonetheless significant in helping to raise political awareness in gay and lesbian communities before the 1969 Stonewall Inn riots.

The same repressive atmosphere that forced gay and lesbian rights groups to keep their activities clandestine also proved to be the impetus in their initial creation. Surrounded by the paranoia of the "second red scare," homosexuals lived in fear of the House Committee on Un-American Activities (HUAC), which investigated reports of homosexuality. Being called in front of this body invited job loss and public opprobrium. Thousands of gays were fired from government jobs because of HUAC probes. Thus, when homophiles supported gay and lesbian rights, they had to do so very carefully.

Support from Experts The homophile movement searched for medical support to bring about public acceptance of their sexual orientation. They found such support from doctors ranging from Alfred Kinsey to Evelyn Hooker.

During the late 1940's and early 1950's, Dr. Kinsey released two reports, *Sexual Behavior in the Human Male* (1948) and *Sexual Behavior in the Human Female* (1953), which argued that homosexuality, far from being perverted, was perfectly normal human behavior. The Kinsey Reports further stated that a significant percentage of the population was exclusively homosexual. These reports were one of the key factors spurring the homophile movement.

Psychologist Evelyn Hooker became involved with the issue of homosexuality during the early 1950's. Enabled by a grant from the National Institute of Mental Health, Hooker performed a study that demonstrated that homosexual and heterosexual men did not perform significantly differently on standard personality tests. More important, her work demonstrated that it was impossible to distinguish a gay man based on such tests. Also key to the gay rights movement in this era was *The Homosexual in America*, (1951) published by a man named Edward Sagarin under the pseudonym Donald Webster Cory. The book recorded the unjust prejudice experienced by gays and lesbians and promoted public tolerance. As science and scholars began to demonstrate that homosexuality was not abnormal, homosexuals hoped the rest of the population would slowly follow suit.

Henry Hay and the Mattachine Society The two best-known gay and lesbian rights groups were the Mattachine Society and the Daughters of Bilitis. Named for a fifteenth century all-male secret society, the Mattachine Society was founded by Harry Hay and focused on issues faced by gay men. Hay left the group only two years after its creation. Born in Great Britain in 1912, Hay knew that he was attracted to other boys at the age of eleven. After his family moved to the United States, he joined the acting community, first in Los Angeles and later in San Francisco.

The sight of the National Guard shooting two striking dock workers prompted Hay to join the American Communist Party in 1934. The American Communist Party had a strong antigay bias, and Hay ultimately asked to leave, though his request was refused. When, in 1937, a psychiatrist advised him to start dating girls to achieve personal satisfaction, he dutifully married Anita Platky. The marriage was troubled and ultimately doomed, and Hay was busy founding the Mattachine Society even before his divorce was finalized in 1951.

When Hay began organizing the society in 1950, he chose a communist model, with a secretive cell-like structure. He was well aware of the dangers gays faced in McCarthy-era America, and he wanted to offer them a political and social outlet. Gay men during the 1950's faced a unique set of challenges. Drawn to gay bars and beaches, they were easy targets for police entrapment. California (and most other states) forbade homosexual gatherings, and an arrest meant having one's name and address printed in the newspaper. Thus, when the Mattachine Society met, members brought female friends and relatives for cover, and new members were met in public before being driven around several blocks on the way to meetings.

When gays went to bars, they did so carefully, though there was still plenty of cross-dressing and dancing. The militant attitude fostered by these bars arguably prompted the move toward a gay liberation movement, which rose to prominence during the 1970's. However, the idea of gay men meeting in a nonsexual setting was novel. The Mattachine Society gave its members the chance to focus their ideas and take political action.

In 1952, a Mattachine member was involved in an entrapment case in which an undercover officer manipulated him into soliciting sex and then arrested him for homosexuality. With the support of the Mattachines, the man was eventually cleared of all

charges, drawing thousands of new members to the group. However, communist paranoia drew an increasingly conservative group of men to leadership roles in the group, and Hay and some of the other radical founders were forced out of the organization. After Hay's departure, the society was left in a struggle between conservatives and militant radicals. The increased pull between conservatives, who wanted to preserve secrecy above all else, and militants, who wanted to force heterosexual society to deal with gay concerns, would ultimately lead the group to disband at the national level in 1961, though local chapters remained in effect nationwide.

After he was ousted from the society in 1953, Hay was investigated by HUAC in 1955, though he was never convicted of anything. Until his death in 2002 from cancer, Hay believed gays would always stand out as different from heterosexual society, and he did not believe there was any point to their trying to assimilate into mainstream society. Thus, he always intended the Mattachines to help gays and lesbians achieve political goals. He is remembered as one of the founders of the gay rights movement, even though his most-remembered work took place nearly twenty years before the Stonewall Inn riots would catapult the move for gay and lesbian rights into the mainstream spotlight.

The Daughters of Bilitis The Mattachine Society was initially designed to serve the needs of gay men and lesbians alike. However, the differing socialization patterns between the two groups and the Mattachine's increasing patriarchal structure alienated many lesbians and left them without a political outlet. Although gay men tended to congregate in gay bars, lesbians often avoided them because they perpetuated the "butch-femme dichotomy" that many found stereotypical. Moreover, because of their less public lifestyles, lesbians were far less likely to be targeted by the police. They often objected to Mattachine political aims and sought a more social outlet.

In 1955, lesbian couple Del Martin and Phyllis Lyon founded the Daughters of Bilitis (DOB) to address the concerns of the lesbian community. Their primary objective when they founded the DOB was to socialize with other lesbians. They helped to move the group beyond the social sphere, and even after they parted ways with the organization, they both remained heavily involved in lesbian politics.

The DOB rapidly developed political goals. In 1955, the group had only eight members, a number that dwindled to four when the working-class members of the group split away from their white-collar counterparts. The reason for the departure of several members represented a problem that the DOB would struggle with for years: The working-class members felt that secrecy was so important that only lesbians should be involved in the group, while others wanted to involve all women.

In 1956, the DOB began its own publication, *The Ladder.* Thanks to this publication, membership grew, and the group became a nonprofit organization. Nationwide chapters were independent of the parent group and free to pursue their own political agendas. Periodically, DOB partnered with Mattachine members to oppose antihomosexual policies and laws. However, they always did so with an emphasis on member secrecy and with passive policies. The absence of radical political goals eventually led to the departure of founders Martin and Lyon, and *The Ladder* ultimately became a publication devoted to feminist concerns.

Impact Fear of discovery haunted gay men and lesbians alike, and membership in both the Mattachines and the DOB always remained low. Moreover, both groups tended to retain their conservative roots and never really moved beyond the secretive fear that dominated the era of their founding. Though they would be rapidly overshadowed by radical activism during the 1960's, gay rights groups and activists during the 1950's broke ground for their radical activist modern counterparts. They struggled against McCarthy-era repression to achieve a small degree of understanding for gays and lesbians.

Further Reading

Aldrich, Robert, and Garry Wotherspoon. *Who's Who in Contemporary Gay and Lesbian History: From World War II to the Present Day.* New York: Routledge, 2001. Presents a huge biographical dictionary of the people involved in the last sixty years of the gay and lesbian struggle for equal rights.

Cain, Patricia A. *Rainbow Rights: The Role of Lawyers and Courts in the Lesbian and Gay Civil Rights Movement.* Boulder, Colo.: Westview Press, 2000. Examines the judicial system as an arena of recourse for those fighting for gay civil rights.

D'Emilio, John. *Sexual Politics, Sexual Communities: The Making of a Homosexual Minority in the United States, 1940-1970.* Chicago: University of Chicago Press, 1983. A landmark work that examines homosexual communities in the United States in the thirty years before the Stonewall Inn riots.

Doberman, Martin. *Stonewall.* New York: Dutton, 1993. Examines the Stonewall Inn riots but includes some important material on the pre-Stonewall period.

Marcus, Eric. *Making Gay History: The Half Century Fight for Lesbian and Gay Equal Rights.* New York: Perennial, 2002. Starts with the gay rights struggles of the 1940's and tells the story of many people, weaving in a wide variety of perspectives.

Miller, Diane Helene. *Freedom to Differ: The Shaping of the Gay and Lesbian Struggle for Civil Rights.* New York: New York University Press, 1998. Details the efforts undertaken in the courts and elsewhere for gay and lesbian rights.

Scott A. Merriman

See also Beat generation; Clift, Montgomery; *Confidential*; Conformity, culture of; Ginsberg, Allen; Jorgensen, Christine; Kerouac, Jack; Kinsey Report; San Francisco Renaissance; *Second Sex, The*; Sex and sex education; *Streetcar Named Desire, A*; Williams, Tennessee.

■ The Honeymooners

Identification Television series about working-class neighbors

Date Began in 1951 as a segment on the DuMont network's *Cavalcade of Stars*; aired from 1952 to 1955 as part of the variety program *The Jackie Gleason Show*; aired as a thirty-minute program on CBS 1955-1956; sporadic revivals of the series occurred until 1971

Although an often hilarious situation comedy, this program ran contrary to the optimism and bland good cheer that were typical of 1950's entertainment by depicting ordinary people struggling to make ends meet and continually frustrated in their attempts to get ahead financially.

The Honeymooners initially began as a sketch on *Cavalcade of Stars* in 1951 and eventually grew into a series centered on four characters—bus driver Ralph Kramden (played by Jackie Gleason); his wife, Alice (Audrey Meadows); and their neighbors, Ed (Art Carney) and Trixie Norton (Joyce Randolph).

The plots revolved around Kramden and Norton's absurd get-rich-quick-schemes, which inevita-

The cast of The Honeymooners *in 1955, from left to right: Jackie Gleason, Art Carney, Audrey Meadows, and Joyce Randolph. The majority of scenes in the series were shot in this spartan room.* (Hulton Archive | by Getty Images)

bly failed. The shows were an inventive blend of verbal wit, goofy malapropisms, and brilliant physical comedy. The show was performed before a live audience and the minimalist setting never changed—a barely furnished room held a dresser, battered table, and an antiquated refrigerator. The dilapidated apartment and Kramden's futile schemes presented a dystopian view of the United States on its rise to financial security. Although presumably newlyweds, Ralph and Alice come across as weary mid-lifers, struggling and childless, and seem to serve as the antithesis to another scheming but thoroughly happy couple depicted on *I Love Lucy*. Such a formula is hardly the stuff of buoyant comedy, yet the series was initially the second-highest-rated show on television.

Impact Although it lasted only two years in its thirty-minute format, *The Honeymooners* created a formula

that endured in television situation comedies of subsequent decades. Gleason reprised the Kramden sketches in a series of variety shows for another fifteen years. In 1985, Gleason released never-before-seen episodes that went into regular syndication.

Further Reading

Cresenti, Peter, and Bob Columbe. *The Official Honeymooners Treasury*. New York: Perigee, 1985. Truly a fan's resource for information about the show and actors and includes excised script material.

McCrohan, Donna. *The Honeymooners' Companion*. New York: Workman, 1978. An entertaining compendium of photos and trivia.

David W. Madden

See also Berle, Milton; Caesar, Sid; DuMont network; *Explorer I*; *I Love Lucy*; Television in the United States.

■ Hoof-and-mouth epidemic

The Event Outbreak of foot-and-mouth disease among animals on several farms in Saskatchewan
Date Outbreak confirmed on February 24, 1952

The 1952 hoof-and-mouth epidemic was the last of its kind to occur in Canada. The rapid response by the Canadian government limited its impact and provided an example for future containment of disease outbreak.

In February, 1952, on farms east of Regina, Saskatchewan, an outbreak of hoof-and-mouth disease was confirmed among animals. The outbreak was so unexpected that it was three days before the disease could be confirmed. The exact source was never determined but was suspected to have been the result of European imports. The next day, an embargo was placed on the entire 130-million-dollar livestock trade industry with the United States.

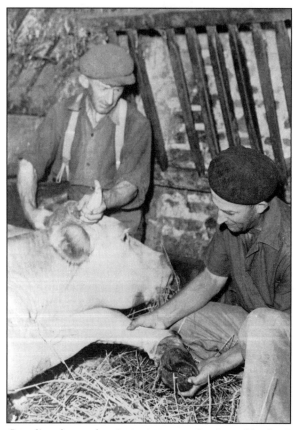

Canadian farmworkers inspecting a cow for signs of hoof-and-mouth disease in 1952. (Hulton Archive | by Getty Images)

Estimates of the number of infected livestock ranged from 800 to 1,300 head. The Canadian government decided the only way to halt the epidemic was to slaughter all potentially infected animals. Among the total of 42 premises, approximately 1,350 cattle, 300 pigs, and 100 sheep were slaughtered. Of the 580 rural municipalities in the province, active infection was limited to only 5 as a result of the rapid response. The last case was diagnosed in May, and by August, the outbreak was declared to be over.

Impact While farmers were reimbursed for their losses, the price of livestock nevertheless plummeted as markets throughout the province were closed. Export of livestock to the United States was also halted.

Further Reading

Animal Foot and Mouth Disease in the UK and Other Affected Countries: Not a Public Health Threat to Travelers. Ottawa: Health Canada, 2001.

Rowlands, David J. *Foot and Mouth Disease.* New York: Elsevier Science, 2003. Presents the story of the disease from the perspective of world experts on the virus.

Richard Adler

See also Canada and Great Britain; Canadian regionalism; Health care systems in Canada; Mexico.

■ Hoover, J. Edgar

Identification Director of the Federal Bureau of Investigation (FBI) from 1924-1972
Born January 1, 1895; Washington, D.C.
Died May 2, 1972; Washington, D.C.

J. Edgar Hoover transformed the FBI into a professional police force and built its image in the public mind, but also created major institutional problems, which would ultimately damage its credibility.

In 1924, when J. Edgar Hoover was appointed director of the Bureau of Investigation (it was renamed Federal Bureau of Investigation in 1935), he was a young and relatively untried administrator. He quickly established himself as a professional with a stern code of ethics and reorganized the bureau with a new breed of trained agents to replace political appointees. He established strict standards for every aspect of agents' appearance and behavior and dismissed anyone who could not or would not meet those standards. During the 1930's, he built the FBI's reputation for capturing notorious gangsters and Prohibition delinquents and used carefully controlled films and newsletters about FBI agents' crime-fighting activities to present to the general public. He cemented this reputation during World War II with the fight against spies and saboteurs. By 1950, the Cold War was in full swing, and Hoover turned his formidable agency to the new threat of communist subversion.

Hoover had regarded communism as a major threat since the first Red Scare in 1919-1920 and believed that the government's loyalty programs were not going far enough. He regarded the Communist Party of the U.S.A. to be directly controlled by the Soviet Union and thus an immediate threat to American security. He therefore ordered the FBI to undertake investigations above and beyond anything Congress had authorized. Throughout the early 1950's, Hoover ordered the FBI to cooperate fully with the investigations of Senator Joseph R. McCarthy, even using surveillance methods of questionable constitutionality to monitor the activities of suspected communists. Among the best known of the people convicted of communist subversion as a result of FBI investigative work were Julius and Ethel Rosenberg, who were subsequently executed for having passed American nuclear secrets to the Soviet Union.

Cracks in the Facade Even as Hoover was doing everything within his power to protect the image of the FBI, his managerial style was creating major institutional weaknesses. His inflexibility in the face of a changing society led the FBI to cling to methods that had been effective in past decades but no longer reflected the realities of the present. He also mistook dissent for subversion. By 1959, the FBI was poised for its unedifying role in the social upheavals of the following decade, attempting to squash the drive for social reform, particularly in the area of race relations, through such extralegal means as the tapping of activists' telephones and the insertion of informers into organizations that called for change.

Impact With his dynamic personality, Hoover placed his indelible stamp upon the FBI for both good and ill. While he built it into a professional federal police force of impeccable reputation, his tendency to micromanage and to act high-handedly created major institutional weaknesses that would ultimately

J. Edgar Hoover in 1957. (Library of Congress)

lead FBI agents to overstep their authority and perform illegal acts in the pursuit of law enforcement.

Further Reading

Dennenberg, Barry. *The True Story of J. Edgar Hoover and the FBI.* New York: Scholastic, 1993. A lively and readable biography and institutional history, balancing Hoover's successes with the very real problems that his managerial style created.

Gentry, Curt. *J. Edgar Hoover: The Man and the Secrets.* New York: W. W. Norton, 2001. A best-selling biography of Hoover that details the ways in which he helped create McCarthyism, influenced the Supreme Court, and compromised the efforts of the Civil Rights movement, among other topics.

Theoharis, Athan. *J. Edgar Hoover, Sex, and Crime: An Historical Antidote.* Chicago: Ivan R. Dee, 1995. Responds to the lurid accusations that Hoover was a closeted homosexual hypocritically persecuting alleged homosexuals and demonstrates that there were pervasive problems in the way the FBI under Hoover handled organized crime and dissent.

Leigh Husband Kimmel

See also Army-McCarthy hearings; Communist Party of the U.S.A.; Espionage and Sabotage Act of 1954; Federal Bureau of Investigation; House Committee on Un-American Activities; McCarthy, Joseph; Nixon, Richard M.; Organized crime; Rosenberg, Julius and Ethel; Truman, Harry S.

■ Hoover Commission

Identification U.S. government commission developed to study the role of government policymaking and to reorganize the executive departments of the federal government
Date Operated from 1953 to 1955

The proposals of the first and second Hoover Commissions resulted in extensive reorganization of the executive branch of the federal government.

In 1947, President Harry S. Truman appointed Herbert Hoover to a commission to reorganize the executive departments. He was appointed chairman of a similar commission, the second Hoover Commission, by President Dwight D. Eisenhower in 1953. Many changes resulted from both commissions' recommendations.

After the Great Depression and World War II, many members of Congress believed that the U.S. government had grown bloated. Both Republicans and Democrats advocated a streamlining of government. Thus, through passage of the Lodge-Brown Act of 1947, President Truman organized the Commission on Organization of the Executive Branch of the Government, which commonly became known as the Hoover Commission after former president Herbert C. Hoover was named as the commission chairman. Hoover's early career as a cost accountant and mining engineer provided him with the business background needed to enhance the efficiency and effectiveness of government operations.

Following the submission of the commission's report in 1949, there was spectacular public and congressional acclaim. By the end of 1950, the alliance between Truman and Hoover had produced one of Truman's most successful reform programs. When Truman left office in 1953, he proudly told reporters that he had done more for administrative reform than all previous presidents combined.

The Second Hoover Commission By the time of Dwight D. Eisenhower's election to the presidency in 1952, massive rearmament as a result of the Cold War and the conflict in Korea had led to government expansion. Though seventy-nine years old, Hoover was again entrusted with the chairmanship of a twelve-member commission to reorganize the executive branch of the federal government. Whereas the first Hoover Commission dealt with how the federal government was organized, the second Hoover Commission addressed whether the government should act in certain realms of policy making. Hoover set up twenty task forces, with hundreds of volunteer workers, to conduct the actual work of the commission. To simplify problems faced with the first commission, Hoover obtained from Congress the authority to subpoena witnesses.

Impact While the reports of the first Hoover Commission had been widely applauded and its proposals led to the creation of the Joint Chiefs of Staff, the Council of Economic Advisors, the Atomic Energy Commission, and the Department of Health, Education, and Welfare, such was not the case with the reports of the second commission. Fewer than 30 percent of the second commission's recommendations were enacted. The one phase of the reports that did win approval was the recommendation to reduce government "red tape." Many federal agencies examined their standard procedures and attempted to simplify them. The second Hoover Commission was moderately successful, and a number of states throughout the nation established their own "Little Hoover Commissions" to study efficiency and effectiveness in state government.

Further Reading

Lyons, Eugene. *Herbert Hoover: A Biography.* Garden City, N.Y.: Doubleday, 1964. Many consider this the best biography ever written on Hoover. Chapter 32 summarizes the activities of the two Hoover Commissions, with particular emphasis on the long hours contributed by Hoover himself.

Moe, Ronald C. *The Hoover Commissions Revisited.* Boulder, Colo.: Westview Press, 1982. This volume provides an in-depth analysis of the two Hoover commissions.

Walch, Timothy, and Dwight M. Miller, eds. *Herbert Hoover and Harry S. Truman: A Documentary History.* Billings, Mont.: High Plains, 1993. Explores the professional relationship between the two presidents.

Dale L. Flesher

See also Congress, U.S.; Eisenhower, Dwight D.; Health, Education, and Welfare, Department of; Truman, Harry S.

■ Hope, Bob

Identification American comedian and actor
Born May 29, 1903; Leslie Town Eltham, England
Died July 27, 2003; Toluca Lake, California

Bob Hope's personal appearances before combat forces in Korea enhanced his already legendary reputation.

Born in England, Bob Hope, the son of William Henry and Avis Townes Hope, came to the United States with his family in 1906, settling in Cleveland, Ohio. The father could not provide for the family, so the oldest boys were sent to work. Bob Hope sold newspapers and professionally boxed. Becoming an accomplished singer and dancer, he succeeded in vaudeville and starred in Broadway musicals including *Roberta* (1933) and the *Ziegfeld Follies of 1936*, before making his first major film, *The Big Broadcast of 1938*. By the 1950's, Hope was a star on radio; his National Broadcasting Company (NBC) contract ran from 1937 through 1955.

Impact Hope's commitment to entertaining American troops made him a legend. He began in World War II with numerous United Service Organization (USO) shows close to battlefields, sometimes under hazardous conditions. He continued his appearances during the Korean War and later, during the Vietnam War in the 1970's and Operation Desert Storm in 1991. His many films during the 1950's were generally weaker than the five "Road" films he made during the 1940's with Bing Crosby and Dorothy Lamour. However, his films still drew large audiences, as did his personal appearances and 1950 television debut. Although his popularity dipped in the 1960's, to his fans, Hope was more than a fine comedian; he was an embodiment of American patriotism. In 1996, the U.S. Congress named him an honorary military veteran, the only American to receive that honor.

Bob Hope surrounded by some of the U.S. troops in Korea whom he came to entertain at the start of the Korean War, in October, 1950. (AP/Wide World Photos)

Further Reading

Faith, William Robert. *Bob Hope: A Life in Comedy.* Cambridge, Mass.: Da Capo Press, 2003. An updated version of a readable 1982 work.

Grudens, Richard. *The Spirit of Bob Hope: One Hundred Years, One Million Laughs.* New York: Celebrities Profiles, 2002. Includes lists of his film, Broadway, and USO show appearances.

Betty Richardson

See also Film in the United States; Korean War; Radio; Television in the United States.

■ House Committee on Un-American Activities

Identification Investigative committee of the U.S. House of Representatives generally known as HUAC

Date Formed in 1938

HUAC investigated suspected threats of communist subversion or propaganda that threatened the Constitution. In the process, the committee blighted reputations and careers of numerous citizens, while uncovering little credible data to back its allegations, and occasioned dramatic confrontations.

The House Committee on Un-American Activities, or HUAC (for the colloquial House Un-American Activities Committee), was formed in 1938. Its first chairman, Texas Democrat Martin Dies, used the committee chiefly to look for subversion in labor unions and in Franklin D. Roosevelt's administration. The committee gained some mainstream attention after 1947, when it began investigating alleged communist subversion in the Hollywood film industry.

The committee stepped up its efforts as the 1950's began. As a pernicious by-product of Cold War paranoia, the committee had a chilling effect on any sort of opinion or activity not in conformity with that of the majority. Those who had some sympathy or involvement with leftists during the Depression of the 1930's or with the Soviet Union during World War II were considered suspect and were often called to testify before the committee. Many people broke ties with friends and associates by informing on them. HUAC witnesses were not deemed "friendly" until after they revealed the names of suspected subversives. Those persons who were named were likely to be blacklisted in their professions or even charged with perjury if they tried concealing their past affiliations when signing loyalty oaths—affidavits required of government employees. Persons signing such oaths declared that they were not, nor ever had been, members of the Communist Party.

In 1950, the most famous member of HUAC, Richard M. Nixon, who had been instrumental in the controversial discrediting of alleged spy Alger Hiss, won election to the U.S. Senate. J. Parnell Thomas, a former HUAC chairman who led the 1947 investigation of the film industry, spent part of the year in prison for conspiracy to defraud the government. Lester Cole and Ring Lardner, Jr., two of the "unfriendly" witnesses before the committee who had been sentenced to prison for contempt of Congress for refusing to answer questions, were in the same prison at the same time. During that same year, Senator Patrick McCarran's Internal Security Act, which had some HUAC input and which the Supreme Court would eventually declare to be unconstitutional, was passed, and Senator Joseph McCarthy became a national figure with his allegations concerning communists in the State Department.

The Hoover Connection The HUAC chairmen of the 1950's, John S. Wood, Harold Velde, and Francis Walter, were all close to Federal Bureau of Investigation (FBI) director J. Edgar Hoover, and Velde himself was a former FBI agent. The connection was kept carefully concealed, and the committee was careful never to compete with Hoover's own publicity efforts. However, it had unlimited access to supposedly secret FBI files, which in turn contained information of varying degrees of reliability gathered by police throughout the country. Thus, police authorities already knew nearly all the names named to the committee, and those whom it was expedient to prosecute were already being prosecuted.

HUAC thus served as an adjunct to Hoover and others dominant during the 1950's in enforcing a culture of conformity. This culture was widely criticized by intellectuals, but it was nevertheless effective. Criticism tended to be indirect, as in the case of Ray Bradbury's 1953 science-fiction novel about a book-burning future, *Fahrenheit 451,* or in Arthur Miller's play about the 1692 Salem witch trials, *The Crucible,* first produced in 1953. Criticism of the committee in films and television was relatively subdued through most of the decade. Meanwhile, literally thousands of Americans were being fired, without due process, from government and defense industry jobs and were being blacklisted from teaching jobs and the entertainment industry. Even critics of HUAC except those obviously about to be convicted were careful not to involve the untouchable Hoover in their criticisms.

The Committee "Ritual" The ritual, and several analysts have used that term, of a committee hearing typically unfolded in this fashion: A witness would be called, sometimes after rumors of the impending session had been leaked to the press. "Friendly" witnesses would testify about their own past actions, respectfully apologize for them, then give the commit-

Poet Langston Hughes testifying before HUAC in March, 1953. Hughes admitted to having been sympathetic to Soviet communism but denied ever joining the Communist Party and refused to name other communist sympathizers. (AP/Wide World Photos)

tee the names of associates involved in leftist activities. Occasionally, witnesses would give their first testimony before executive sessions of the committee from which the press and public were barred, and their later public testimony would mention only those persons whose names were likely to be considered newsworthy.

Friendly testimony occasionally got the names of the witnesses off blacklists, but not always. Unfriendly witnesses were not allowed to refuse to testify on the grounds that the committee was interfering with their freedom of speech guaranteed by the Bill of Rights. They were also not allowed to object that the committee's questions had no bearing on congressional legislation under consideration and were thus improper. Unfriendly witnesses could only cite the Fifth Amendment to the U.S. Constitution, which guaranteed protection against self-incrimination. Witnesses who took that stand were branded "Fifth Amendment communists." Those who resisted testifying on other grounds could be cited for contempt of Congress and could be imprisoned. However, that danger diminished as the decade progressed.

Famous Confrontations and Feuds Several potential witnesses, including actor Larry Parks and playwrights Arthur Miller and Lillian Hellman, offered to testify to their own activities if excused from naming the names of their associates. This offer was not accepted. Hellman wrote to the committee that she did "not like subversion or disloyalty in any form" and that if she saw such activity, she would consider it her duty to report it. However, she added that she considered hurting innocent people in order to save herself would be "inhumane and indecent and intolerable." Although Hellman's associations with the Communist Party were more extensive than she then claimed, she was not cited for contempt. She had a sharp tongue, and committee chairman John S. Wood said of her, "After all, she's a woman." The committee's failure to cite Miller for contempt seems to have stemmed from the desire of some committee members to have their pictures taken with Miller's glamorous wife, actress Marilyn Monroe.

Many of the witnesses who named names found it an agonizing decision. Actor Sterling Hayden said that the testimony he gave to save his own career tortured him ever afterward. Others who had been subject to the enforced conformity and humiliating self-criticism sessions of the Communist Party felt it their duty to expose a danger to the nation. Among these were writer Budd Schulberg and director Elia Kazan, who later collaborated on one of the best films of the 1950's, *On the Waterfront* (1954)—one of whose themes, not coincidentally, is about informing on one's associates. Kazan had been a close associate of Miller, who broke permanently with him over the issue, despite the efforts of Monroe, Kazan's former lover as well as Miller's wife, to reconcile them. The eventual feelings of both Kazan and Miller involved more sadness than anger.

Waning Influence The power of the committee diminished as the 1950's went on. Singer Paul Robeson called members of the committee "Un-Americans" and said that they should be ashamed of themselves. Robeson himself had been blacklisted in the United States, and his passport had been withdrawn in 1950, but in 1958, the U.S. Supreme Court ruled that practice unconstitutional.

Folksinger Pete Seeger was cited for contempt in 1956 after telling HUAC that although he had sung both in hobo jungles and for the wealthy Rockefeller family, he would not perform for the committee. He was sentenced to a year in prison for contempt but managed to avoid serving time until the courts reversed the verdict. In 1956, 1957, and 1958, Academy Awards went to scripts written by blacklisted writers working under other names. In 1959, the Motion Picture Academy of Arts and Sciences repealed its ban on giving awards to those who had refused to cooperate with HUAC. Blacklisted Dalton Trumbo was immediately hired to write the screenplay for *Spartacus* (1960), based on a novel by the blacklisted Howard Fast.

The peak of the Cold War and the peak of HUAC's influence had passed, although those who criticized it were often fired and blacklisted through the efforts of groups such as the John Birch Society well into the next decade.

Impact Although the committee did not get as much publicity during the 1950's as it had in earlier years or as much as the strident chair of the Senate's 1953 Permanent Investigating Committee, Senator Joseph McCarthy, HUAC contributed to a climate of fear among artists and academics. This slowly declined as the decade went on, but many people remained afraid to take stands for peace, civil rights, or freedom of expression, a situation that changed slowly as the 1950's wore on.

Further Reading

Buckley, William F., Jr., ed., *The Committee and Its Critics: A Calm Review of the House Committee on Un-American Activities.* New York: G. P. Putnam's Sons, 1962. Collected essays on the committee.

Goodman, Walter. *The Committee: The Extraordinary Career of the House Committee on Un-American Activities.* New York: Farrar, Straus and Giroux, 1968. Good summary of the committee's history.

O'Reilly, Kenneth. *Hoover and the Un-Americans.* Philadelphia: Temple University Press, 1988. The best account of the special relationship that kept the committee going.

Simmons, Jerold. *Operation Abolition: The Campaign to Abolish the House Un-American Activities Committee, 1938-1975.* New York: Garland, 1986. Study of the growing opposition to the committee's investigations.

J. Quinn Brisben

See also Cold War; Communist Party of the U.S.A.; Congress, U.S.; Faulk, John Henry; Federal Bureau of Investigation; Hoover, J. Edgar; Internal Security Act of 1950; Loyalty oaths; McCarthy, Joseph; Nixon, Richard M.; Red Monday; Rosenberg, Julius and Ethel; Truman Doctrine; *Yates v. United States.*

■ Housing in Canada

The postwar era proved to Canadian officials that the country lacked a sufficient number of homes for low-income families, and the government sought means to increase the construction of affordable, subsidized housing.

Historically, Canadians, like U.S. citizens, have been housed relatively well, with more than 63 percent of the population owning their own homes. Public housing represents a mere 7 percent of the housing in Canada. During the twentieth century, in addition to providing Canadians with a full spectrum of housing from affordable to extravagant, home-ownership programs and public housing projects stimulated economic growth and relieved unemployment during economic downturns. However, gaps in the availability of low- and moderate-income housing remained.

Housing policy in Canada traditionally focused on facilitating the functioning of the private housing and rental markets by developing an effective mortgage finance system; public housing has taken a secondary role in filling the gaps in the market system. During the 1950's, Canada was a relative newcomer to public housing, as compared to Great Britain, the United States, and other Western nations. Until the 1964 and 1973 amendments to the National Housing Act, the government played only a modest role in the creation of new housing, mostly through mortgage guarantees.

In 1919, Canada passed its first housing program, a twenty-five-million-dollar program intended as much to combat post-Word War I unemployment as to meet housing needs. The 1935 Dominion Housing Act and the 1938 National Housing Act were intended to stimulate the private housing construction industry during the Great Depression by providing government guarantees for bank mortgages for new home construction. This emphasis in private home ownership left a shortage of housing for Canada's mobile youth and labor population, off-reservation indigenous Canadians, retired couples and singles, and immigrants. By the end of World War II, all parts of Canada were experiencing an affordable housing crisis and a backlog in residential construction, which public policy analysts believed could not be accommodated by the private housing market operating alone.

The Canadian Mortgage and Housing Corporation (CMHC) was created in 1949 to stimulate construction of new houses, to facilitate the repair and modernization of older houses, and to promote community planning. The CMHC facilitated the construction of 250,000 units by 1986. CMHC housing is primarily funded by the national government, with provincial governments contributing 10 to 20 percent of the capital. Loans were secured by fifty-year, fixed-rate mortgages.

Public Housing By the late 1940's, homelessness and families housed in emergency accommodations

were such a problem that the Toronto City Council told those who sought new housing to stay away from the city. In 1948, Toronto constructed its first major public housing project, Regency Park, a program also providing slum clearance. Government-funded public housing was constructed throughout Canada beginning during the early 1950's; twelve thousand units were constructed by 1964. Most public housing was built and managed by public housing authorities and was funded jointly by national and provincial governments, with occasional participation by municipalities. Much of this housing was located in areas of urban renewal and was seen as a cure for urban blight.

The CMHC funded private construction of affordable rental housing by underwriting fifty-year bank mortgages. Residents in these housing projects paid rent based on their income levels. The difference between the rent collected and the full operating costs (including the mortgage payment) was covered by a government subsidy, which was cost-shared by the federal government and the provincial or municipal government. The mortgage interest rate was based on the government's long-term borrowing rate plus administrative costs.

As in the United States, large-scale projects focused on low-income households, which led to the labeling of these projects as "ghettos." Low-income households paid between 25 and 30 percent of their income to live in public housing. When the household income rose sufficiently to allow the household to enter the private rental or home ownership market, the household was required to move out, making the unit available for new families in need. This meant that housing projects held concentrations of low-income households.

Also as in the United States, tax provisions in Canada were important in encouraging home ownership and the production of rental housing. Canada has not used tax-exempt bonds and low-income tax credits, as has the United States, and does not permit mortgage interest deductions on homes, but Canada also does not impose capital gains taxes on the sale of principal residences.

Impact Government programs that encouraged home ownership and private residences left Canada with a recurring shortage in available and affordable housing for low-income households. Mortgage programs and public housing projects during the 1950's were inadequate to meet the needs. In spite of efforts since the 1950's, as of 2004, 30 percent of Canadian households remained in inadequate housing based on standards of affordability, physical condition of the accommodation, and its suitability to the household. Of those living in inadequate housing, 60 percent had the income necessary to afford better housing, should homes become available. Improved, modernized, and affordable public housing is needed by 12 percent of Canada's population, most of which are renter households of seniors, singles, and one-parent families.

Subsequent Events Amendments to the National Housing Act in 1972 sought to improve the social mix in public housing by limiting the expulsion feature as income rose. This led to criticism that middle- and high-income households benefited from government housing. Income mixing was therefore discontinued as an objective in housing act amendments during the 1980's. The 1972 amendments also initiated a new type of public housing, owned and operated by nongovernmental, nonprofit, and cooperative associations, that eventually accounted for more than two-thirds of public housing in Canada, with the government-owned-and-operated housing accounting for less than one-third of public housing. Other affordable housing included First Nations on-reservation and urban housing, and rent-restricted, government-managed but privately constructed and owned rental housing.

Further Reading

Dennis, Michael. *Low Income Housing: Programs in Search of a Policy.* Ottawa: Canadian Mortgage and Housing Corporation, 1972. Discussion of problems unresolved from the 1950's and 1960's.

Fallick, Arthur L., and H. Peter Oberlander. *Housing a Nation: The Evolution of Canadian Housing Policy.* Ottawa: Canadian Mortgage and Housing Corporation, 1992. History of housing problems and solutions.

A National Affordable Housing Strategy. Ottawa: Federation of Canadian Municipalities, 2000. A review of the past housing efforts with proposals for the future.

Gordon Neal Diem

See also Home furnishings; Housing in the United States; Television in Canada; Television in the United States; Urbanization in Canada.

■ Housing in the United States

The 1950's was a decade of home construction, family formation, and rapid suburbanization, all of which followed the Depression, world wars, and decades of economic stagnation, weak housing resales and construction markets, and family fragmentation. Americans during the 1950's were well housed—more than 60 percent owned their own homes. Public housing represented less than 2 percent of housing during the 1950's.

Through the first half of the twentieth century, the percentage of families in owner-occupied housing hovered around the 45 percent range. Throughout the 1950's, however, the percentage increased each year to well over 60 percent by the end of the decade, nearing 70 percent in the following decades.

Annual starts for new single-family homes doubled in the postwar years of the latter 1940's, doubled again during the early 1950's, and remained consistently strong for the remainder of the decade. New two-family and multifamily rental housing doubled from prewar years and remained consistently strong. New public housing was insignificant prior to the war, but it boomed between 1949 and 1952, then subsided for the remainder of the decade.

Larger American Homes Prior to the 1950's, the composition of the country's housing stock tended to reflect the social classes in the United States. Homes of the wealthy were spacious, rambling, conspicuous mansions, constructed with rooms reserved for specific uses—dining, billiards, reading, or guest bedrooms, for example. These mansions sat on large urban lots, some consuming an entire city block, or on rural estates of one or more acres.

Homes of the middle-class were large, comfortable villas, constructed with five or more large rooms, each serving multiple functions. Typical homes included the four-room-over-four urban or suburban family home and the three-room-over-three-over-two urban town house. Homes were constructed on narrow urban or suburban lots, usually with a shed in back or, later, a detached garage, or as row homes, each abutting the house next door.

Homes of the working class and the poor were small, cramped, and limited to one to four rooms. Typical homes included the one-room sod house or log cabin; the two-room "dog trot" home with an enclosed breezeway between the rooms; the two-or-three-room ranch house; the one-over-one colonial home, often with a lean-to kitchen in the back; the two-room efficiency apartment of the industrial village; the three-room "shotgun house" or tenement apartment with three rooms aligned in order; and the relatively comfortable two-over-two farmhouse or village bungalow with center or side stairs and a kitchen in the rear. Many working-class and poor families lived in 300 to 800 square feet of living space.

During the 1950's, the housing of the working class and the poor underwent a substantial upgrade. The four-room Cape Cod or ranch home on a small lot became standard for new home construction for the working class. The Cape Cod could often be modified by the home owner into a two-story, two-over-four home to comfortably accommodate a family of four to six people. The average new single-family home of the 1950's was 983 square feet, spacious by previous standards but small in comparison to the average 1,500 square feet of the 1970's and the average 2,329 square feet by the turn of the twenty-first century.

The typical new home included a twelve-by-sixteen-foot living room, a twelve-by-twelve-foot bedroom for the married couple, an eight-by-ten-foot bedroom or nursery for the children, a small but efficient ten-by-ten-foot kitchen, a dining area, one small bathroom, and an unfinished attic with room for two eight-by-ten-foot bedrooms, stairs, and a second bath, especially if roof dormers were added. Some homes had basements with additional room for expansion to construct laundry rooms, recreation rooms, and dens. The typical home was constructed so that workers with a weekly income of $55 to $65 could afford to pay 25 percent of their income on their monthly mortgage. Do-it-yourself books and men's magazines such as *Popular Mechanics* helped men undertake home improvement projects themselves at minimum cost. Women's magazines such as *Better Homes and Gardens* and *Good Housekeeping* helped women maintain the home, undertake home beautification projects, and stretch the family budget. Hubbard Cobb's *Your Dream Home: How to Build It for Less than $3500* appeared in 1950, offering instructions on everything from selecting the site to landscaping for war-weary newlyweds "tired of waiting for high costs to go down."

Emphasis on House and Family During the period from the 1890's through the 1920's, young people,

often in their early teens and younger, left home and flocked to the industrial cities. During the 1930's, families fragmented as both adults and teens migrated in search of employment in public works projects and government labor camps. During the 1940's, families were torn apart by service in the military or in the war industries. The 1950's became the first decade of the twentieth century to experience a period of true family solidarity.

Family became a primary value of Americans. The media, church, popular culture, and schools taught that adults could achieve the greatest satisfaction and fulfillment as members of a family, that child rearing was a primary value and the avenue for a sense of personal achievement, and that marital love and sexual fidelity were the primary ways to achieve personal happiness and satisfaction.

The family ideal was broadcast weekly on television in programs such as *The Adventures of Ozzie and Harriet* and *Leave It to Beaver.* The popular *I Love Lucy* and *The Honeymooners* depicted childless, renting couples with yearnings for houses and children to make their lives complete. Wives and children were integrated into story lines in shows such as *Roy Rogers* and *Sky King.* Even award-winning motion pictures such as *Shane* and *High Noon* featured subtle themes emphasizing the value of family. Popular movie themes included the rich seeking happiness in simple family life and Western homesteaders defending their homes against various enemies.

Each growing American family wanted a house of its own. Most children had their own spaces—backyards and bedroom sanctuaries. Properties were delineated with fences and hedges. Each family tended and landscaped their own space, and each man improved his property with myriad home improvement projects, as did the woman inside, with the purchase of new appliances, gadgets, and furnishings.

Suburbanization and the Decline of Urban Housing
Americans followed the trolley tracks out of the city during the late nineteenth century in the first wave of suburbanization. They followed the automobile and the paved roads out of the city during the early twentieth century in the second wave of this process. The third wave of suburbanization came during the 1950's with the creation of suburban housing developments and tract housing projects such as Levittown. Hundreds of nearly identical homes were constructed on large expanses of land, populated

Typical American housing tract constructed during the mid-1950's. (Hulton Archive I by Getty Images)

with nearly identical families, and provided with convenient, nearby community shopping centers, schools, parks, green spaces, and recreation facilities for the children.

Tract housing sprang up at the edge of each city and town. In the 1950 census, the suburban population exceeded that of both the urban and rural areas. Suburban housing often surrounded the outer fringes of an urban core, adding an outer circle to the concentric circle pattern of development seen in many cities. In other instances, suburban tracts centered on transportation hubs or claimed the most attractive and vista-blessed real estate, creating a sector pattern of development. Newly developed urban land-use plans and zoning regulations reinforced these patterns of development and ensured that the beauty, uniformity, and tranquillity of these new suburban havens would not be disturbed.

Suburbanization was largely a white, middle- and working-class phenomenon. As these groups de-

parted the city, they left behind urban housing to be occupied by the new underclass. During the late nineteenth century and through the early twentieth century, this underclass was largely immigrant labor from Europe, followed by rural African Americans from the American South. During the 1950's, this underclass was largely African American or Spanish-speaking residents.

The increase in the number of available urban homes and rental units led to a decrease in the value of those units as supply outstripped demand. Even with low purchase prices, new owners often lacked the income to maintain the homes. Rent values declined, providing the landlords with less income for maintenance. Poorer families had incomes too low to pay rent even on older units, leading to a low level of maintenance and repair for continued habitation. The depreciation provisions in tax policy also encouraged landlords to take rapid depreciation on the properties, then sell the property without repairs to another landlord, who would subsequently depreciate the property and resell it; the process was called "milking" the property.

The 1937 Housing Act authorized loans and subsidies to local government for construction of public housing but required the demolition of dilapidated dwelling units in a number equal to the new units constructed. This meant that the number of units available to the poor did not increase. The shortage of homes following World War II led to the passage of the 1949 Housing Act, which removed this provision. Congress authorized construction of 810,000 public low-rent units over six years; however, the construction was not completed until the 1970's.

Urban Renewal and Federal Housing The Housing Act of 1949 was, according to its congressional sponsors, primarily a housing act, with urban improvement a secondary interest. However, the act did provide grants to local governments to cover two-thirds of the loss involved in acquiring and clearing blighted properties. More than one thousand cities participated in the program. The professional planning community, fueled by economist Miles Colean's 1953 book, *Renewing Our Cities*, from which the term "urban renewal" originated, believed that removal of blight, rather than replacing housing, should be a priority. However, rather than replacing the demolished homes and properties with new rental units and retail shops for the poor, most of the replacement buildings were built as high-rise apartments for high-income families and trendy retail shops, many privately funded. A revision to the Housing Act in 1954 required city planning for slum clearance and community development and permitted 10 percent of federal funds to be used for nonresidential projects; this was subsequently increased to 30 percent. A 1959 revision authorized funding of long-range community renewal programs. By the 1960's, public resistance to further demolition in the urban core led to a shift to conservation, rehabilitation, and adaptive re-uses of the older buildings rather than demolition and new construction.

The U.S. government only reluctantly developed public-owned housing for the poor. The first public housing act was the 1937 Wagner-Steagall Act, which produced few dwelling units. In 1949, Congress passed a more comprehensive bill combining urban renewal and public housing with the goal of ensuring a decent home and a suitable living environment for every American family. Government construction of housing for defense workers and military families during World War II set a precedent for federal involvement in housing construction.

By the end of the 1950's, public-owned rental housing was available to less than 6 percent of low-income families, and most of that housing went to the elderly. During the 1960's, emphasis shifted to providing income-based subsidies to residents in privately owned rental units. By the 1970's, President Richard Nixon's administration declared both the federal housing construction and urban renewal programs to be failures.

Federal Programs for Home Ownership The most successful federal programs of the 1940's and 1950's were designed to provide home ownership and not merely housing. These programs propelled veterans and the working class into the middle class, reducing the potential for political radicalism and militancy seen occasionally during the Great Depression and in Europe. By providing this opportunity for home ownership, the government reduced the class consciousness of the working class, undermined unions, largely extinguished interest in socialist and communist politics, and expanded the middle-class backbone of the United States. The programs gave millions more people a material stake in their own country.

These federal programs also smoothed the transition from military production to civilian production and prevented chaos in the economy. The productive capacity built during the war years was put to the task of new home construction and to producing all the appliances and furnishings to fill the home. Since most of the houses were structurally similar, it was the furnishings that made each house personal and distinctive. Vance Packard's book *The Status Seekers*, published in 1959, examined the patterns of home furnishings and decoration that reflected the various social-class and ethnic origins of the home owners.

The Home Owners Loan Corporation, created in 1933, was designed to protect home ownership by extending the terms of mortgages and preventing foreclosures. The program worked well to protect home ownership for the upper and middle classes. Its appraisal methods and policies had long-term impacts on housing for the poor, urban renewal, housing segregation, and the denial of home ownership opportunities for the poor and minorities through the 1950's. Neighborhoods were assigned color-coded grades based not only on the dominant occupations, income levels, and ethnicity of the inhabitants but also the market demand, value, and type of construction of the housing stock. This led to the "redlining" of poor and nonwhite neighborhoods and denial of loan extensions and guarantees for housing in those neighborhoods.

G.I. Bill and FHA Housing The Servicemen's Readjustment Act, or G. I. Bill, took effect in 1944, providing demobilized veterans with education and housing benefits. Veterans, most of whom had no money for a down payment on a home, were offered private ownership of newly constructed single-family dwellings, financed by banks whose risk was underwritten by the federal government. The government had some fear that returning veterans could be a source of disruption in society, especially if they believed their sacrifice in the war was not adequately rewarded and if they called on their military-life behavior while adjusting to civilian life. Many in the government felt that returning veterans needed to be settled down with a home and family and that women needed to leave their wartime employment and resettle in the domestic arena.

Most of the houses constructed under G.I. Bill financing were four-room Cape Cod cottages, with one bathroom and space for expansion in the attic or the basement. The homes were designed to economize on plumbing, wiring, and heating and were affordable to the burgeoning middle class. They were simple, functional, nearly identical and interchangeable, and suitable for do-it-yourself maintenance and improvement. The only real differences among the new homes were in the facades.

The Federal Housing Act of 1934, with post–World War II revisions, provided a home-owning opportunity for the working class through Federal Housing Administration (FHA) mortgage insurance underwriting on low down-payment loans made by FHA-approved private lenders on FHA-approved properties, including single-family and multifamily homes, new and existing homes, and manufactured homes. The primary objective of the FHA was to stimulate the housing market and housing industry. A secondary objective was to increase the housing stock.

During the 1940's and 1950's, the FHA, along with the G.I. Bill, helped finance homes for veterans. It not only helped finance homes for the working class and the poor but also financed privately owned apartments for elderly, handicapped, and poor Americans.

Impact Two federal programs, the G. I. Bill and the FHA, enabled the working class to become members of the home-owning middle class in society. As new members of the middle class, they were then expected to uphold the traditions, values, and institutions supported by this class. Government home ownership programs shifted America's politics to the right, encouraged an emphasis on marriage and family as a lifestyle ideal, and led to profound changes in the social-class structure.

Further Reading

Abbott, Carl. *Urban America in the Modern Age, 1920 to the Present.* Arlington Heights, Ill.: Harlan Davidson, 1987. Explores the evolution of the American city, including the changing composition of the urban population.

Clarke, Graham. *The American City: Literary Sources and Documents.* New York: Routledge, 1997. Essays on selected large American cities, commenting especially on African Americans' experience within them.

Gillette, Howard, and Zane Miller, eds. *American Urbanism: A Histographical Review.* Westport, Conn.: Greenwood, 1987. A series of articles summarizing the history of a wide variety of themes related to housing.

Mason, Joseph B. *History of Housing in the U. S., 1930-1980.* Houston, Tex.: Gulf, 1982. History of housing, housing policy, and domestic architecture from 1930 to 1980.

Mitchell, J. Paul. *Federal Housing Policy and Program: Past and Present.* New Brunswick, N.J.: Rutgers University Press, 1985. Examination of the philosophy of postwar housing policies.

VanVliet, William. *The Encyclopedia of Housing.* Thousand Oaks, Calif.: Sage, 1998. An award-winning encyclopedia of definitions and descriptions related to housing.

Weiss, Marc. *The Rise of Community Builders: The American Real Estate Industry and Urban Land Planning.* New York: Columbia University Press, 1987. Gives a good history of tract housing and the landmark changes that occurred during the 1940's and 1950's.

Wright, Gwendolyn. *Building the Dream: A Social History of Housing in America.* Cambridge, Mass.: MIT Press, 1983. An important work on the rich diversity of American architecture and housing from the colonial era through 1980.

Gordon Neal Diem

See also Affluence and the new consumerism; Architecture; Demographics of the United States; G.I. Bill; Home appliances; Home furnishings; Income and wages in the United States; Levittown; Racial discrimination; Urbanization in the United States.

■ *Howdy Doody Show*

Identification Long-running children's television program
Producer Roger Muir
Date Aired from 1947 to 1960

A groundbreaking program produced live for most of its thirteen years, it was a unique blend of human-puppet interaction, cartoons, and a screaming audience of children referred to as the Peanut Gallery.

Bob Smith had been active in radio for several years when he helped create a program titled *The Triple B Ranch Show,* which featured a voice (Smith's) of a none-too-bright farmhand named Elmer, who became memorable for constantly uttering the phrase "howdy doody."

Elmer's name was changed to Howdy Doody, and a puppet was created to give the voice a body. The decision was made by Smith and the fledgling NBC television network to broadcast the program, now to be titled *Puppet Playhouse.* The show successfully premiered December 27, 1947, and was immediately popular. *Puppet Playhouse* became the *Howdy Doody Show* in 1949, and each episode featured fast-paced timing and a barrage of live commercials. The program endured and survived a variety of crises through the years but could not survive changing times. In 1957, its ratings slipped because of competition from a new ABC program, the *Mickey Mouse Club.* NBC executives were concerned about rising production costs of the *Howdy Doody Show* and complaints about its alleged racial stereotyping of characters. The show was canceled and aired for the last time on September 30, 1960. In that last show, the famously mute clown, Clarabell, uttered the only words he ever said, "Goodbye, kids."

Howdy Doody and Princess Summerfall Winterspring during the early 1950's. Howdy Doody was always a marionette on his television show, but the princess puppet was replaced by live actors. (Hulton Archive | by Getty Images)

Impact The *Howdy Doody Show* was a broadcast pioneer. It was the first show to produce more than two thousand episodes, to be regularly broadcast in color, and to achieve split-screen, cross-country broadcasts on a regular basis—a technology later used during the Kennedy-Nixon presidential debates. The *Howdy Doody Show* also reflected America's fascination with technology, using wizardry such as the Electromindomizer, which read minds, and the Honkadoodle, which translated Mother Goose's honks into English. The educational content of the show helped promote both the program and the sale of television sets, while mass marketing also got a boost from the program: The show's producers allowed the endorsement of certain products by incorporating product messaging into songs and skits. The marketing of Howdy Doody comic books, wind-up toys, and clothing also became a legacy of the show.

Further Reading

Davis, Stephen. *Say Kids! What Time Is It? Notes from the Peanut Gallery.* Boston: Little, Brown, 1987. An insider's view; Davis's father directed the show from 1952 to 1956.

Wilk, Max. *The Golden Age of Television: Notes from the Survivors.* Washington, D.C.: Diane, 1999. Wilk, one of television's first writers, details television's first decade, from 1947 through the 1950's.

Thomas W. Buchanan

See also *Captain Kangaroo; Kukla, Fran and Ollie; Mickey Mouse Club;* Silly Putty; Television for children; Television Westerns.

■ Hudson, Rock

Identification American film actor
Born November 17, 1925; Winnetka, Illinois
Died October 2, 1985; Beverly Hills, California

An engagingly handsome and beloved screen star, Rock Hudson epitomized the masculine Hollywood leading man during the 1950's and 1960's.

Rock Hudson was born Leroy Harold Scherer, Jr. His parents divorced when he was eight years old, and he later changed his name to Roy Fitzgerald when his mother remarried. He worked as a mail carrier and served in World War II as a Navy airplane mechanic. After an aggressive agent recognized his star potential and encouraged him to pursue acting, Fitzgerald assumed the name Rock Hudson and launched his film career.

Though it took no less than thirty-eight takes to complete successfully one line of dialogue in his first picture, *Fighter Squadron* (1948), Hudson's alluring presence and rugged good looks quickly propelled him to stardom. During the early 1950's, Hudson began to win more major roles, and following the release of *Magnificent Obsession* in 1954, he became one of Hollywood's leading men. He earned an Oscar nomination in 1956 after starring with James Dean and Elizabeth Taylor in *Giant.* In 1957, he acted in the film adaptation of Ernest Hemingway's *A Farewell to Arms* and was named Star of the Year by *Look* magazine the following year.

Impact In an acting career that later extended to television and spanned some thirty years, Hudson was twice voted Hollywood's top box-office draw. His death at age fifty-nine from complications of AIDS astounded many of his fans, who were unaware of his homosexuality, and focused worldwide attention on finding a cure for the disease.

Further Reading

Hudson, Rock, with Sara Davidson. *Rock Hudson: His Story.* New York: Avon, 1987. Hudson's posthumous autobiography.

Oppenheimer, Jerry. *Idol, Rock Hudson: The True Story of an American Film Hero.* New York: John Curley, 1987. A good biography of Hudson.

Jan Giel

See also Academy Awards; *Confidential;* Dean, James; Film in the United States; *Giant;* Taylor, Elizabeth.

■ Hula hoops

Identification Lightweight toys in the shape of a hoop, constructed of plastic tubing connected with wooden plugs and staples
Manufacturer Wham-O
Date First marketed in 1958

The hula hoop was one of the best-selling American toys of the 1950's, and its widespread popularity sparked one of the decade's most memorable fads.

Inspired by exercising devices used in gym classes in Australia, Richard Knerr and Arthur Melin designed the first hula hoops in 1957. They gave the large polyurethane circle the name "hula hoop" because the spinning and twisting required to keep the plastic loops in motion around the body reminded them of the moves of the traditional Hawaiian dance, the hula. Although hoops had been used as toys for centuries, the brightly colored hula hoops caught the public's imagination and sense of fun during the late 1950's. At the height of the craze, in the summer of 1958, 25 million hoops were sold in little more than three months, and 75 million more would be sold before the fad waned the following year. Eventually the hula hoop craze spread to Europe, Asia, and the Middle East.

Impact More than simply adding a new item to the roster of classic toys that is characteristic of an American childhood, the hula hoop virtually became the prototype of the many must-have toys that would follow in its wake throughout the twentieth century. It not only became a traditional toy but it also began the tradition of American toy crazes. In 1958, Knerr and Melin went on to invent the Frisbee.

At the peak of the hula hoop craze in 1958, scores of young hula-hoopers competed for prizes on Art Linkletter's House Party *television show.* (AP/Wide World Photos)

Further Reading

Asakawa, Gil, and Leland Rucker. *The Toy Book.* New York: Knopf, 1992. Useful information on hula hoops specifically within the larger discussion of American toys.

Schwarcz, Joe. *Radar, Hula Hoops, and Playful Pigs.* New York: Henry Holt, 2001. Interesting look at hula hoops and other common objects from a scientific standpoint.

Thomas Du Bose

See also Baby boomers; Fads; Inventions; Silly Putty.

■ Human growth hormone

The Event Isolation of the human growth hormone from the anterior pituitary gland by Choh Hao Li and Harold Papkoff

Date Isolated in 1956

During the 1950's, the isolation of the human growth hormone and the elucidation of its chemical structure held promise for the treatment of pituitary dwarfism.

As early as the 1920's, scientists knew about the existence of growth hormones. Choh Hao Li and other researchers had isolated the bovine growth hormone during the mid-1940's using a method that produced pure and potent samples. By 1960, growth hormones from six species—beef, sheep, whale, pig, monkey, and human—had been isolated, and their roles in metabolism and growth were elucidated. Li and Harold Papkoff tested the efficacy of human growth hormones in rats and mice in which the pituitary had been excised. By measuring the increase in the width of the tibia, they determined the relative effect of varying doses.

Impact As research had revealed that human beings did not respond to the growth hormone of any other species, the isolation of the human growth hormone raised the possibility of human therapy. In 1958, Maurice Raben of Tufts Medical School administered human growth hormone extracted from cadavers to a young male dwarf, who subsequently grew two inches in ten months. News of this success gave hope to the parents of children of abnormally short stature. In 1963, the National Hormone and Pituitary Program was established, ultimately treating some eight thousand patients, until it became apparent in 1985 that the hormone, when derived from a cadaver, could transmit Creutzfeldt-Jakob disease. In late 1985, recombinant human growth hormone became available.

Further Reading

Frasier, S. D. "The Not-So-Good Old Days: Working with Pituitary Growth Hormone in North America, 1956 to 1985." *The Journal of Pediatrics* 131, no. 1, part II (1997): S1-S4. Account of cases of Creutzfeldt-Jakob disease in patients treated with human growth hormone obtained from cadavers.

Henry, Stephen, Colin G. Scanes, and William H. Daughaday. *Growth Hormone*. Boca Raton, Fla.: CRC Press, 1995. Fairly technical account of growth hormone.

Kristen L. Zacharias

See also Inventions; Medicine; Science and technology.

■ Hungarian revolt

The Event National uprising for freedom from Soviet influence that was crushed violently

Date October-November, 1956

Military violence used by the Soviet Union in its invasion of Hungary demonstrated its aggressive nature during the Cold War, prompting nearly 100,000 refugees from communist Hungary to find safety in the United States and Canada.

Hungary was first occupied by the Soviets as World War II concluded in 1945, and local communists of the Hungarian Socialist Workers' Party (HSWP) gained dictatorial control by 1948. Direct Soviet rule was avoided. After May, 1953, tensions grew between a new, moderate socialist leader of the government, Imre Nagy, and more pro-Soviet elements of the HSWP. Nagy initiated policies called the New Course, which favored limited capitalism for farmers, open trade with Western Europe, better wages for factory workers, and release of political prisoners. Nagy announced plans for free multiparty elections, the right to create unions independent of communist control, freedom of the press, and other measures that challenged the established one-party communist dictatorship.

In foreign relations, Nagy challenged Soviet dominance by demanding the return of Hungarian citizens whom the Red Army had abducted ten years earlier and by announcing a plan to withdraw Hungary from the Warsaw Pact, an alliance of Soviet-controlled countries. He also requested the United Nations to act to protect Hungarian sovereignty.

Hard-line Stalinists in the HSWP fired Premier Nagy in January, 1955, but nationalist resistance to communism continued to grow at universities and among intellectuals of the Petőfi Circle and others. These elements received encouragement from the United States through broadcasts from Radio Free Europe.

On October 23, 1956, mass university student protests in Budapest in support of similar nationalist protests in Poland were fired on by security forces, igniting a riot. Joseph Stalin's statue was pulled down, and crowds began to confront the hated secret police. Support quickly broadened to include workers and other urban residents, all demanding basic changes in the system of communism. Jailed Roman Catholic Cardinal József Mindszenty escaped and gave open support to the protests. To try to calm the growing revolution, HSWP leaders agreed to reappoint Nagy as premier, and on day six of the riots, Soviet Red Army troops began to withdraw.

Khrushchev Responds to Hungary's Revolution Soviet armored forces never actually left Hungary but had only pulled back from visible urban centers. On November 3-4, 1956, at Soviet leader Nikita Khrushchev's direction, the Red Army surged forward to confront the unrest. Elements of the Hungarian army, notably led by General Pal Maleter, had joined the people's rebellion earlier, and arms were given to crowds of freedom fighters. Despite valiant resistance, the small arms of the disorganized bands of Hungarians proved no match for the five thousand Soviet tanks. Within weeks, the Hungarian revolt was crushed: Roughly 32,000 people were killed, and approximately 15,000 were wounded. Internment camps were created, and of the 35,000 people detained, 25,000 ultimately were jailed.

Impact Soviet violence in Hungary created a strongly negative impression in the West. News weeklies such as *Life* and *Look* magazines showered readers with photographs of the repression and destruction; *Reader's Digest* and other mass circulation magazines ran frequent first-person accounts of the Soviets' violence in Hungary. Roughly 200,000 Hungarians fled across the border into Austria; 80,000 of these refugees immigrated to the United States, and several thousand more went to Canada.

No amount of talk from Soviet leaders about their desire for "peaceful coexistence" could overcome the direct testimony that the refugees relayed to their new North American neighbors about the dictatorial essence of Soviet Communism. Some American conservatives and Hungarian American advocates, however, were embittered by failure of the United States to lend military assistance to the rebels in their time of greatest need. These views found strongest voice in the pages of the *National Review* magazine. Defenders of American nonintervention in Hungary pointed to the fact that this crisis unfolded simultaneously with the crisis in Egypt's Suez Canal, requiring careful effort to prevent a general escalation in East-West confrontation in order to avoid general war.

Subsequent Events Suppression of the Hungarian revolt demonstrated that the Soviet Union, not allied local communist parties, actually ruled east of the Iron Curtain. These violent events ended hope for reform in Communist-dominated Central Europe for a generation. Nagy and Maleter were arrested in late November by Soviet troops despite having been given a promise of safe conduct out of the country by the new Hungarian administration of János Kádár. Tried in secret in Romania by the Soviets on charges of treason along with other revolutionaries, the two officials were executed on June 16, 1958, and were buried in an unmarked grave inside the prison on Kozma Street. Later, Maleter and Nagy were reburied in a second unmarked grave at Lot 301 of the main communal cemetery in Budapest. Despite this attempt to erase the memory of the Hungarian quest for freedom, brave Hungarians during the 1980's began putting flowers on their resting places to symbolize the continuing guidance of their example. Ultimately, the HSWP succumbed to popular will and permitted their resting places to be dignified with grave markers and a public funeral on June 16, 1989.

The Hungarian revolt of 1956 continued to be a symbol of the quest for self-rule and freedom into the twenty-first century. Demonstrations against the communist system in the spring of 1989 demanded that October 23 be made a national holiday, and on

Hungarians gather around a toppled statue of former Soviet dictator Joseph Stalin in Budapest on October 24, 1956—the day after the Hungarian government declared the nation to be a free republic. (AP/Wide World Photos)

October 23, 1989, the Hungarian government declared Hungary to be a free republic. The date is now Republic Day, a national holiday.

Further Reading

Békés, Csaba, ed. *The 1956 Hungarian Revolution: A History in Documents.* Herndon, Va.: Central European University Press/Books International, 2002. In 120 original documents from Soviet, American, and Hungarian official files, the complete story of the revolution is documented.

Liptak, Bela G. *A Testament to Revolution.* College Station: Texas A&M Press, 2001. A moving first-person, eyewitness account of a student activist caught up in the events of 1956, and his subsequent escape to freedom in the United States

Molnár, Miklós. *A Concise History of Hungary.* New York: Cambridge University Press, 2001. In this translation from the 1996 French original, Molnár places the 1956 revolution in the context of the long national struggle for independence. Lavishly illustrated, the book includes pictures of the 1989 funerals for the martyrs from the 1956-1958 era.

Gordon L. Bowen

See also Eisenhower Doctrine; Kennan, George F.; Khrushchev's visit to the United States; Lodge, Henry Cabot; Mindszenty, Cardinal József; Olympic Games of 1956; Radio Free Europe; Suez Crisis; Teller, Edward; Warsaw Pact.

■ Hydrogen bomb

Definition Powerful nuclear weapon that generates a large portion of its explosive power through nuclear fusion
Date First tested on March 1, 1954

Development of the hydrogen bomb raised the stakes in the nuclear weapons arm race, magnified tensions in the Cold War, and intensified public fear of thermonuclear war.

J. Robert Oppenheimer led the development of the atomic bomb, but he thought that creating a hydrogen bomb was both unlikely and unnecessary. His stance put him at odds with Edward Teller, who had pushed for the "super," a fusion bomb, since 1942. The "super" was given priority only after the Soviets tested their atomic bomb in 1949, because it was seen as a way to maintain American dominance of nuclear weapons and thereby limit Soviet adventurism.

The "super" championed by Teller would use a fission bomb to establish a detonation wave in liquid deuterium, a heavy isotope of hydrogen. Deuterium nuclei were expected to fuse into helium-3 nuclei or into tritium nuclei (the heaviest hydrogen isotope), and to release a huge amount of energy in the process. Polish mathematician Stanislaw Ulam completed a complex calculation in 1950 showing that the "super" could not be made to work, but he suggested an alternative two-stage device.

Bomb Design and Testing In the basic Ulam-Teller design, a fission bomb (the primary stage) is placed inside a heavy-walled, cylindrical tank, and a fusion package (the secondary stage) is placed beside it and aligned with the axis of the tank. The fusion package consists of three concentric cylinders: an outer jacket, a fusion fuel layer, and a uranium-235 or plutonium-239 core, called the "spark-plug."

Code named Ivy Mike, a Teller-Ulam configuration was tested for the first time on November 1, 1952. The fusion fuel was liquid deuterium, which must be kept below 23.57 Kelvins. The 10.4-megaton explosive yield was about twice the expected yield, and it obliterated Elugelab Island of the Eniwetok

Atoll in the South Pacific. In place of Elugelab, Ivy Mike left an underwater crater more than a mile wide and fifty yards deep. This ungainly design using liquid deuterium was weaponized and briefly placed in the stockpile.

The Soviet Union tested its own hydrogen bomb, Joe-4, on August 12, 1953. It was built of layers of fission and fusion fuel and had a 400-kiloton yield. The increasing pace of the arms race was evident when one considers that the Soviets were four years behind the Americans in testing an atomic bomb but only one year behind in testing a hydrogen bomb.

The first American test using lithium-deuteride was code named Castle Bravo and came on March 1, 1954. The design proved to be far more efficient than expected. The expected yield was 6 megatons, but the actual yield of 15 megatons made it the largest weapon ever tested by the Americans (the Soviet Union later tested a 50-megaton bomb). The wind changed shortly before the test, and the event should have been postponed; dangerous amounts of windborne radioactive dust fell on Marshallese Islanders

Hydrogen bomb test explosion in the Marshall Islands' Eniwetok Atoll in November, 1952. (U.S. Naval Photographic Center)

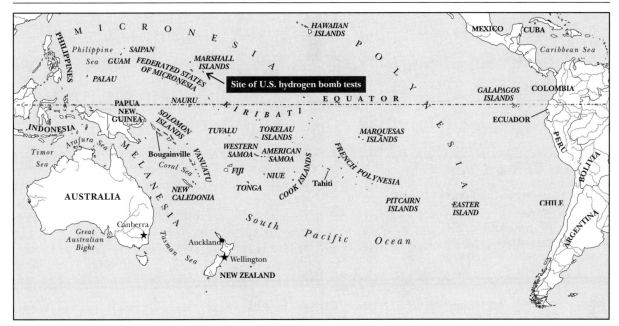

Site of U.S. hydrogen bomb tests

and on the twenty-three crewmen of the fishing boat *Fifth Lucky Dragon.* One member of the boat's crew later died from complications brought on by the radiation exposure. Testing nuclear weapons in the open atmosphere continued until the United States and the Soviet Union signed the Limited Test Ban Treaty in 1963, although a few other nations engaged in atmospheric testing after that time.

Impact When the Soviets deployed a long-range bomber capable of reaching the United States in 1955, American civil defense measures were pushed. Basements of public buildings were designated as fallout shelters and stocked with survival rations and Geiger counters. Schoolchildren were taught to "duck" under their desks and "cover" their necks with their hands if they saw the super-bright flash of a nuclear bomb. Near ground zero, this protective reaction would accomplish nothing, but far enough away from ground zero, it might reduce injuries.

After the Soviets obtained the bomb, the United States announced the doctrine of "massive retaliation" to deter the Soviets from using their bombs on American interests. Both nations engaged in an accelerating arms race of weapons and delivery capabilities in order to be able to bomb the other nation into oblivion. While most knew it would be insane to unleash the nuclear apocalypse, deterrence during this decade rested on the assumption that the other side was prepared to do exactly that, resulting in a global climate known as "the balance of terror." Ultimately, in spite of several threats to use nuclear weapons, the leaders of nuclear powers have always found other ways to resolve crises.

Further Reading

Ehrlich, Robert. *Waging Nuclear Peace: The Technology and Politics of Nuclear Weapons.* Albany: State University of New York Press, 1985. An excellent account of nuclear weapons and the arms race.

Herken, Gregg. *Brotherhood of the Bomb: The Tangled Lives and Loyalties of Robert Oppenheimer, Ernest Lawrence, and Edward Teller.* New York: Henry Holt, 2002. A compelling and authoritative account of three main characters in the development of nuclear weapons.

Morland, Howard. *The Secret That Exploded.* New York: Random House, 1981. An intriguing account of a reporter searching unclassified sources for the details of the design of the hydrogen bomb.

Rhodes, Richard. *Dark Sun: The Making of the Hydrogen Bomb.* New York: Simon & Schuster, 1995. An excellent popular-level treatment.

Charles W. Rogers

See also Atomic bomb; B-52 bomber; Bomb shelters; Civil defense programs; Cold War; DEW Line; Disarmament movement; Eisenhower, Dwight D.; Oppenheimer, J. Robert; Seaborg, Glenn; Teller, Edward.

I

■ *I Led Three Lives*

Identification Syndicated television series about a
double agent
Date Aired from 1953 to 1956
Original author Herbert A. Philbrick (1915-
1993)

Loosely based on the experiences of a real-life FBI agent, I
Led Three Lives *was an influential television series that
both reflected and contributed to the red scare paranoia of
the Cold War era.*

In 1952, Herbert A. Philbrick, a former agent of
the Federal Bureau of Investigation (FBI), published *I Led Three Lives,* an account of his nine years
as a double agent. Appearing at a time when the
United States was obsessed with Joseph McCarthy,
the Cold War, and the threat of world communism,
Philbrick's book about a patriotic FBI agent's daring
struggle against communist subversion quickly became a best-seller. The following year a dramatized television version of his experiences began being broadcast in syndication, with actor Richard
Carlson playing Philbrick. Over the three-season
life of the program, 117 episodes were made; those
broadcast during the first two seasons were taken
from Philbrick's book, and those of the final season were adapted from his unpublished notes.
Carlson played Philbrick under the latter's real
name, but other names used in the show were fictionalized.

In the context of the television show, Philbrick
was an advertising executive by day, a member of
the Communist Party by night, and an FBI agent.
Reflecting pervasive public fears of communist subversion, the show's themes revolved around stories
of sabotage plots, treason, espionage and infiltration of organizations, drug dealing, and insidious
propaganda. As an ostensibly loyal Communist Party
member, Philbrick found himself in the middle of
one kind of subversive plot or another every single
week but invariably managed to foil the plot and
emerge with his reputation for loyalty to the party
untainted. The sheer number and variety of communist plots in which Philbrick was involved strained
credibility, but the show was popular enough to last
three years, and reruns were broadcast into the
1960's.

A Typical Episode

In one episode of *I Led Three Lives,* Herbert Philbrick
is assigned by his Communist Party cell leader to
write a children's textbook on U.S. history that sub-
verts American values by presenting negative portrayals of George Washington, Abraham Lincoln,
and other great American leaders. What Philbrick
writes pleases his leaders greatly, but before the
books are printed, Philbrick sneaks into a printing
shop and resets the book's title page, adding a new
message of his own. Later, after the books have been
printed and distributed, Philbrick is at a cell meeting when a box of his books is delivered. The cell
members open the box and delightedly examine
copies of the book until Philbrick turns to the
book's title page and reads the message that he se-
cretly inserted. It states, in unequivocal terms, that
the book is a tool of communist propaganda, filled
with lies intended to undermine American values,
and names the communist leaders who are responsible; they include almost everyone but Philbrick
himself. Shaking with mock outrage, Philbrick demands to know how this disaster has happened, but
the other party members, fearing arrest, quickly
scatter.

Although virtually every communist plot in which
Philbrick is involved fails, his fellow insurgents never
seem to notice that Philbrick is usually the only communist cell member who escapes unscathed. As a
consequence, *I Led Three Lives* conveyed the unin-
tended message that communist agents must be stu-
pid, incompetent, or both.

Impact *I Led Three Lives* contributed to Cold War paranoia by repeatedly promoting the notion that no sector of American society—government, schools, churches, the military, industry—would be safe from communist subversion unless every citizen remained vigilant and reported suspicious activities to the FBI. FBI director J. Edgar Hoover was said to have been a strong supporter of the show, which he regarded as a public service program. In fact, the show actually moved some people to report neighbors and relatives to the FBI for expressing pacifist and even liberal sentiments. In this regard, the show got ordinary Americans to behave much like the youthful "Spies" in George Orwell's dystopian novel *Nineteen Eighty-Four* (1949).

I Led Three Lives also had international ramifications. Members of Great Britain's House of Commons debated the political implications of the show, and the Soviet government filed a protest against the show's broadcast in Mexico.

Further Reading

Britton, Wesley A. *Spy Television.* Westport, Conn.: Praeger, 2004. First book devoted to the history of the spy genre on television, tracing its roots back to radio dramas and supplying a rich trove of anecdotal material. Includes a brief but useful discussion of *I Led Three Lives* that makes a strong case for the series' seminal position in television history.

Philbrick, Herbert Arthur. *I Led Three Lives: Citizen, "Communist," Counterspy.* 1952. Washington, D.C.: Capitol Hill Press, 1972. Most recent edition of Philbrick's memoir about his double-agent days. The seventy-eight episodes of the television show's first two seasons are said to have been based on material contained in this book.

R. Kent Rasmussen

See also Communist Party of the U.S.A; Faulk, John Henry; Federal Bureau of Investigation; Rosenberg, Julius and Ethel; Television in the United States.

■ I Love Lucy

Identification Television situation comedy
Producer Desilu Productions
Date Aired from 1951 to 1957

I Love Lucy was the most successful television program during the 1950's and, through the production standards it established, became a model for future television situation comedies.

I Love Lucy began with the desire of comedian Lucille Ball to join her career with that of her husband, Cuban bandleader Desi Arnaz. Faced with the unwillingness of the Columbia Broadcasting System (CBS) and prospective sponsors to cast a non-American in a costarring role in a television sitcom, Lucy and Desi created a nightclub act and toured

Lucille Ball and Desi Arnaz as Lucy and Ricky Ricardo. (Arkent Archive)

during the summer of 1950. The tour was a huge success, and Lucy and Desi, believing they had proven themselves, began to develop their creative comedic antics for the new medium—television. CBS reluctantly agreed to finance a pilot starring the couple as Lucy and Ricky Ricardo.

The Premise Television during the 1950's sought to present a domestic ideal—the patriarchal family headed by the male breadwinner and kept orderly by the housewife—from which family values and appropriate behavior derived. Reflecting the home life of the Arnazes, the series featured Lucy and Ricky Ricardo, a young, struggling married couple who live in a brownstone apartment in Manhattan. He is an orchestra leader, and she is a housewife who is preoccupied with getting into show business. The zany talents of Lucille Ball seemed made to order in the premise of the series: Lucy launches endless efforts to get into the public arena and thus end her dependence upon her husband, only to be defeated by her own ineptitude and her inclination toward preposterous predicaments.

Lucy's ill-fated attempts to rebel against the male-dominated society of the 1950's—which always resulted with her return to the position of devoted housewife—actually served to undermine the domestic status quo. Moreover, despite the fact that Lucy's abrasiveness and wild physical humor were countered by her role as a devoted wife, the reality that Lucy was submerging her own professional self by playing a dutiful housewife added a satiric edge to the 1950's message of social conformity.

Within its central premise, *I Love Lucy* continued to enlarge its scope each season. The first year depicted the couple's adjustment to married life, with the help of Fred and Ethel Mertz (played by William Frawley and Vivian Vance), former vaudevillians who were regulars on the show as the Ricardos' landlords. During the second and third years, the birth of Little Ricky required Lucy and Desi to adjust to parenthood, a role that nonetheless

failed to stifle Lucy's ambitions; the fourth year saw the Ricardos and Mertzes on a tour to Hollywood; the fifth year featured a trip abroad; and the sixth and final year focused on family issues, ending with the Ricardos—and later, the Mertzes—following the 1950's trend and moving to the suburbs in Connecticut.

The Production Desi assembled the team of writers headed by Jess Oppenheimer and including Madelyn Pugh and Bob Carroll, Jr., who had been the creative team behind Lucy's three-year CBS radio sitcom (with Richard Denning), *My Favorite Husband*. Drawing on scenarios from the radio program, Lucy's routines and sketches used in the road tour, and escapades created by Lucy and Desi, the team set to work writing the first episodes and continued writing every episode for four years. In the fifth year, an additional writing team was added, and Desi took over producing after Oppenheimer took a job at the National Broadcasting Company (NBC). Three di-

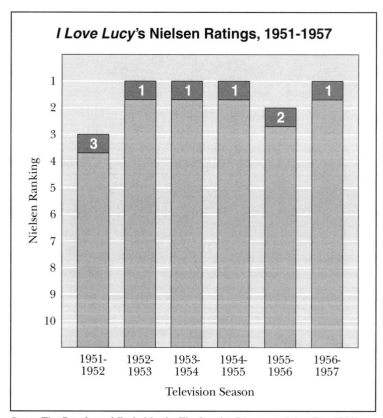

Source: Tim Brooks and Earle Marsh. *The Complete Directory to Prime Time TV Shows,* 1988.

rectors guided the show through its six years as a weekly series, and the few turnovers in personnel contributed to the consistency of the series.

Believing the series to be doomed to failure, CBS insisted that Lucy and Desi pay a larger percentage of the production costs and, in return, gave them complete ownership of the show. Lucy and Desi formed their own company, Desilu Productions, and resolved to shoot the series in film—an almost unprecedented practice in 1951, when most programs were shot live. They located a motion-picture sound stage large enough to accommodate a live audience and recruited Karl Freund, a German cinematographer and veteran of several prestigious American films, to assume control of film production. Freund devised a system for above-the-set lighting and strategically positioned three cameras in front of a live audience in order to combine the spontaneity of a live performance with the production values and relative permanency of film.

Impact   *I Love Lucy* debuted on Monday, October 15, 1951, to generally good reviews. The show climbed instantly to the top of the national ratings, and never ranked lower than third in popularity among all television programs. At the time of its final show, it was still the highest-rated program on television. *I Love Lucy* has remained enormously popular through its years of reruns.

Because of CBS's shortsighted decision to give Lucy and Desi total ownership of the show, they became the first millionaire television stars. Desilu Productions also expanded into production of other network and syndicated series. The decision to film the program rather than produce it live enabled it to be enjoyed for decades in syndication by television viewers.

Further Reading

Barreca, Regina. *They Used to Call Me Snow White . . . but I Drifted: Women's Strategic Use of Humor.* New York: Penguin, 1992. Explores differences between men and women with regard to their use of humor, their ideas of what is funny, and how they are perceived when telling jokes.

Horowitz, Susan. *Queens of Comedy: Lucille Ball, Phyllis Diller, Carol Burnett, Joan Rivers, and the New Generation of Funny Women.* London: Routledge, 1997. Details the impact female comedians have had on the predominantly masculine world of comedy.

Leibman, Nina C. *Living Room Lectures: The Fifties Family in Film and Television.* Austin: University of Texas Press, 1995. Analyzes many feature film and television comedies in order to redefine them as family melodramas concerned with appropriate values and behaviors.

Spigel, Lynn. *Make Room for TV: Television and the Family Ideal in Postwar America.* Chicago: University of Chicago Press, 1992. Focuses on the growth of television as a national medium as opposed to popular expectations for it.

Mary Hurd

See also   Gobel, George; *Honeymooners, The*; Latinos; *Leave It to Beaver*; Nielsen ratings; Television in the United States; Women and the roots of the feminist movement.

■ Immigration and Nationality Act of 1952

Identification   U.S. federal law governing foreign immigration and naturalization
Date   Signed into law on June 27, 1952

The Immigration and Nationality Act of 1952, which enacted new policies for immigration into the United States and for the acquisition of citizenship, adjusted the national quota formula of past immigration laws and reflected Cold War anticommunist sentiments.

Congress enacted the Immigration and Nationality Act, also known as the McCarran-Walter Act, over President Harry S. Truman's veto. The statute reformulated the national quota system of 1924. Under the new rules, half of immigrant visas were reserved for applicants with significant education, training, or experience. The remaining half were set aside for either relatives of United States citizens or permanent residents in the country.

Responding to Cold War sentiment, the law added to the list of those excluded from the United States by setting additional immigration and citizenship barriers based on association with the communist organizations or ideology. The statute strengthened government powers over aliens and naturalized citizens alike by establishing that association with subversive groups or advocacy of violent overthrow of government could result in deportation of legal resident aliens and the loss of United States nationality status of naturalized citizens.

Impact Although sections of the Immigration and Nationality Act were later rescinded or rewritten, the statute established the foundations of immigration law for more than fifty years, thus affecting demographic growth in the United States well into the twenty-first century.

Further Reading

Hutchinson, Edward Price. *Legislative History of American Immigration Policy, 1798-1965.* Philadelphia: University of Pennsylvania Press, 1981. Offers a thorough assessment of immigration policy from the nation's birth through the crucial years of the twentieth century.

Shanks, Cheryl. *Immigration and the Politics of American Sovereignty, 1890-1990.* Ann Arbor: University of Michigan Press, 2002. A definitive study of the relationship between politics and immigration law.

Pietro Lorenzini

See also Asian Americans; California's Alien Land Laws; Demographics of the United States; Immigration to the United States; Internal Security Act of 1950; Loyalty oaths; McCarthy, Joseph; Operation Wetback; Truman, Harry S.; United States Information Agency; War brides.

■ Immigration to Canada

During the 1950's, Canada pursued a policy of selective immigration, accepting migrants primarily from North America and Western Europe. Political and economic migrants fulfilled labor needs, increased the population, and eventually contributed to the country's ethnic diversity.

Immigration policy in Canada after World War II was tied closely to the country's labor needs, ethnic preferences, and humanitarian concerns. During the 1940's and 1950's, the Canadian government took special initiatives to entice and accommodate certain preferred immigrants, mainly British, American, Irish, and French. National legislation widened the admissible classes in 1950 in response to labor demands, and in fact, in 1951 Canada admitted small numbers of migrants from India, Pakistan, and Ceylon (Sri Lanka). On May 1, 1947, Prime Minister William L. Mackenzie King issued a doctrine to foster population growth in the country through immigration. During the same year, the Canadian government passed the Citizenship Act, which created Canadian citizenship as separate from British subject status.

Legal Barriers and Incentives With the close of World War II, Canada passed legislation that allowed displaced persons and refugees from Europe to enter the country. By 1952, the Enemy Aliens Act had been revoked, thus allowing free immigration from Germany and Italy. From the late 1940's, Canadian citizens could sponsor immigrants as long as employment for them was guaranteed in lumbering, mining, or agriculture. Most displaced persons immigrated to Canada under the sponsored labor plan, as domestic contract workers or under the special provision for family reunification. Under the sponsored labor plan, an immigrant signed a contract agreeing to work in farming, mining, railroad transportation, or domestic service for a period of two years. Between 1947 and 1953, about 165,700 persons came into Canada as displaced persons. Special programs accommodated specific ethnic groups, including

Hungarian refugees boarding a plane taking them to Canada. (Hulton Archive | by Getty Images)

Immigration to Canada, 1950-1959

Year	Foreign-born population	Canadian-born population	Total population	Foreign-born as percentage of total population	Total immigrants
1950	2,018,000	11,694,000	13,712,000	14.7	73,912
1951	2,060,000	11,949,000	14,009,000	14.7	194,391
1952	2,232,000	12,227,000	14,459,000	15.4	164,498
1953	2,329,000	12,516,000	14,845,000	15.7	168,868
1954	2,461,000	12,826,000	15,287,000	16.1	154,227
1955	2,547,000	13,151,000	15,698,000	16.2	109,946
1956	2,611,000	13,470,000	16,081,000	16.2	164,857
1957	2,783,000	13,806,000	16,589,000	16.8	282,164
1958	2,920,000	14,128,000	17,048,000	17.1	124,851
1959	2,980,000	14,462,000	17,442,000	17.1	106,928

Source: Dominion Bureau of Statistics, 1961.

the Netherland Farm Family Movement, begun by the national government in 1947. In 1951, the government also implemented the Assisted Passage Program, offering two-year loans to needy immigrants. Between 1951 and 1960, about 129,000 persons took advantage of this program.

The Canadian Immigration Act of 1952 was the major immigration legislation of the decade, the most significant policy change since 1910. The act limited immigration to Canada on the basis of nationality, lifestyle, worker suitability, and other discriminatory criteria. The act, however, was circumvented through the labor sponsorship program; for example, more than 90 percent of the Italians arriving in Canada came under this plan, mostly as dependent family members. Policy restrictions were relaxed in 1956-1957 to accommodate more than 37,000 Hungarians who sought refuge from revolution in their homeland. The deluge of Hungarians prompted the Canadian government to draw the distinction between political and economic applicants. The Suez Crisis of 1956 also brought a large number of British immigrants into Canada. In 1958, the Canadian government declared amnesty for illegal aliens in the country, and in response to the World Refugee Year (1959-1960), Canada relaxed its policies and broadened admissible classes to include persons of diverse non-European backgrounds, provided they offered needed skills.

Impact Immigrants during the 1950's concentrated in Canada's major urban centers, with Toronto the largest receiver (more than 50 percent), followed by Vancouver and Montreal. Immigration into the lightly settled areas of the country—Saskatchewan, Manitoba, the Maritimes, and the Northern Territories—was slight. Poor economic conditions in the Maritimes, for example, did not invite settlement by the foreign born.

Ontario was the only province to take an active role in immigration before 1960. The Ontario Placement Plan permitted skilled immigrants to enter as long as they fit specific labor roles for the province. Quebec was less receptive to immigrants because of concerns over maintenance of its French culture. Those who came to Quebec during this period were mostly Jews and Italians, who found homes in Montreal. British Columbia, particularly Vancouver, was second only to Ontario in settling immigrants during the 1950's. Alberta's oil and gas developments brought a flood of internal and international migrants, especially to the oil centers of Edmonton and Calgary. Manitoba and Saskatchewan received few migrants, mostly agricultural workers, from 1946 to 1955, and the sparsely settled Northern Territories received only a spattering of migrants. More than 1.5 million immigrants came to Canada during the 1950's, thus elevating the country's total population to about 14 million.

Subsequent Events Racial and ethnic restrictions against Africans, Asians, and Arabs through the 1950's gave way to more relaxed standards during the 1960's and 1970's. Discriminatory policies were largely removed in 1962, and from the 1960's forward Canada pursued a national "mosaic" policy. All immigrants into Canada in the period between 1949 and 1966 were overseen by the Ministry of Citizenship and Immigration. In addition to government programs, church and civic groups were active in receiving and integrating immigrants throughout the period.

Further Reading

Burnet, Jean, and Howard Palmer. *Coming Canadians: An Introduction to the History of Canada's Peoples.* Toronto: McClelland and Stewart, 1988. Summarizes settlement by indigenous peoples, Europeans, and non-Europeans.

Driedger, Leo, ed. *Multi-ethnic Canada: Identities and Inequalities.* Toronto: Oxford University Press, 1996. Covers a range of topics from multicultural regionalism to language and theories on ethnicity.

Hawkins, Freda. *Canada and Immigration.* 2d ed. Montreal: McGill-Queen's University Press, 1988. A history of immigration into Canada.

Kalbach, W. E., and W. McVey. *The Demographic Basis of Canadian Society.* 2d ed. Toronto: McGraw-Hill Ryerson, 1979. Addresses population growth and change through natural increase and migration.

Li, Peter S. *The Making of Post-War Canada.* Toronto: Oxford University Press, 1996. Addresses major social changes such as immigration, female labor, and reduced fertility since the war.

Ann M. Legreid

See also Business and the economy in Canada; Demographics of Canada; Immigration to the United States; Minorities in Canada; Religion in Canada; Urbanization in Canada; War brides.

■ Immigration to the United States

Immigration into the United States fostered population growth, satisfied labor needs, and contributed to the country's growing ethnic diversity. Immigration policy reflected labor needs, humanitarian concerns, and ethnic and racial preferences.

Throughout the history of the United States, immigration has fluctuated, responding to changing social, economic, and political conditions. Early immigration, from roughly 1820 to 1880, drew migrants predominantly from northern and western Europe; this was followed by a great deluge of new immigration, about 1880 to 1920, in which migrants hailed primarily from southern and eastern Europe. In contrast, the period between 1931 to 1960 showed a significant slowing of immigration. Only 4 million migrants entered the United States in this period, about 2.5 million of them arriving during the 1950's.

The immigrant tide was stemmed during the 1920's by new immigration laws, during the 1930's by the Great Depression, during the 1940's by World War II, and in general, by a drop in demand for cheap, unskilled labor in the American workplace. Between 1920 and 1960, Europe accounted for 60 percent of the immigrants into the United States, South and Central America 35 percent, and Asia 3 percent. From 1951 through 1960, more than 60 percent of the legal immigrants into the United States migrated from five countries: Germany (19 percent of the total), Canada (15 percent), Mexico (11.9 percent), the United Kingdom (7.8 percent), and Italy (7.4 percent).

Legal Barriers and Incentives Immigration policies have had a profound impact on the character and composition of immigration into the United States. The implementation of these policies during the 1950's was influenced in large degree by the country's labor needs and humanitarian impulses. They also reflected the country's need to court European allies during the first years of the Cold War. The Immigration Act of 1921 instituted a quota system that for the first time limited annual European immigration to 3 percent of the number of a nationality group in the United States, based on 1910 population figures. The migrant streams into the United States shifted from southern and eastern Europe to Canada, Mexico, and certain countries in western Europe. The 1921 act was followed in 1924 by the more restrictive Johnson-Reid Act, better known as the National Origins Act, which limited the annual number of immigrants from any nation to 2 percent of the U.S. population from that nation as of 1890. The intent was to maintain the ethnic composition of the American population by accepting assimilable blood lines. This national origins system remained the basis of American restrictionist policy up until 1965.

The quota acts of the 1920's had not restricted immigration from the Western Hemisphere. The door remained open to Mexican nationals and, in fact, Mexicans had been exempted from the acts' standard literacy testing, head taxes, and contract labor laws. The exemptions invited a heavy migration of Mexican workers into the country, most of them recruited by industry and agriculture as cheap, nonunionized labor. They concentrated in the American Southwest. The Mexican American population began to shift during the 1950's, pushing northward from the Southwest into the urban centers of the Midwest.

By 1940, there were large enclaves of Chinese, Filipino, and Japanese Americans, primarily in Hawaii and California. Repeal of the 1882 Chinese Exclusion Act in 1943 created an annual migration quota and, thus, opened the door to citizenship for foreign-born Chinese. The 1950's saw a marked increase in Chinese in the United States, and even greater numbers arrived during the 1960's and 1970's as the last of the discriminatory laws were brought down. The Chinese flowed into urban "Chinatowns" and into suburban communities.

World War II generated a heavy flow of refugees from war-torn Europe, and with the close of the war, immigration quickened in response to stability and economic prosperity. In 1945, President Harry S.

U.S. Border Patrol inspectors fingerprinting Mexican immigrants at a detention camp in El Centro, California, in 1951. Mexicans who entered the United States illegally were airlifted back to Mexico. (AP/Wide World Photos)

Sources of Immigration to the United States, 1950-1959

Year	Europe	Asia	Canada	Mexico	Other America	Africa	Australasia	All others	Total
1950	199,115	4,508	21,885	6,744	15,562	849	517	7	249,187
1951	149,545	7,149	25,880	6,153	15,598	845	527	20	205,717
1952	193,626	9,328	33,354	9,079	18,616	931	578	8	265,520
1953	82,352	8,231	36,283	17,183	24,184	989	782	430	170,434
1954	92,121	9,970	34,873	30,645	30,069	1,248	910	8,341	208,177
1955	110,591	10,935	32,435	43,702	34,299	1,203	1,028	3,597	237,790
1956	156,866	17,327	42,363	61,320	41,030	1,351	1,346	22	321,625
1957	169,625	20,008	46,354	49,321	38,485	1,600	1,458	16	326,867
1958	115,198	20,870	45,143	26,791	41,198	2,008	2,045	12	253,265
1959	138,191	25,259	34,599	22,909	35,553	1,992	2,162	21	260,686
Totals	1,407,230	133,585	353,169	273,847	294,594	13,016	11,353	12,474	3,397,051

Notes: Figures are for fiscal years ending on June 30. "Australasia" includes Australia, New Zealand, and Pacific Islands. "Other America" includes Caribbean, Central America, and South America.
Source: U.S. Department of Commerce, *Historical Statistics of the United States, Colonial Times to 1970.* Washington, D.C.: Bureau of the Census, 1975.

Truman encouraged immigration by using an executive order targeted toward displaced persons. With postwar prosperity, there were a series of initiatives by the federal government to link immigration policy to American labor needs, mainly in American industry. In addition, the War Brides Act of 1946 allowed a special migration of nonquota, foreign-born spouses and children of military personnel. About 120,000 entered the country under this act. The first Displaced Persons Act (1948) allowed up to 220,000 persons to enter the United States over a two-year period, with the stipulation that one-third of them be farmers. These individuals were required to have a guarantee of housing and employment from an individual or group sponsor. The second Displaced Persons Act (1950) maintained these quotas but was less restrictive and established a ceiling of 415,000 persons over a two-year period. The Refugee Relief Act of 1953 admitted 205,000 refugees as nonquota immigrants.

Displaced persons and refugees came to the United States in large numbers for more than a de-

cade after the war, most of them settling in major cities in the Northeast, Northwest, and West. Between 1937 and 1943, about 150,000 Jews fled Nazi Europe; following World War II, another 60,000 Jews came to the United States, most of them settling in New York City. Years after the war, Congress passed the Refugee Fair Share Law, which facilitated the admission of refugees still living in wartime refugee camps. American ethnic and religious organizations aided in the reception and integration of these displaced persons. While most Jews found homes in metropolitan New York, some were accommodated in suburban communities such as St. Louis Park in Minnesota.

Immigration and Nationality Act of 1952 The Immigration and Nationality Act of 1952, also known as the McCarran-Walter Act, was the most important immigration legislation during the 1950's; it also represented the first significant change in immigration policy since the quota acts of the 1920's. The 1952 act assembled all immigration laws into a unified code; certain liberalizing features, however, set it apart from earlier legislation. The provisions on national origin were maintained, while special-preference categories were created within the national-origin quotas. Special preferences were given to family members and immigrants with technical expertise. More specifically, the act gave 85 percent of the annual quota to northern and western Europe; it also allowed 150,000 annual migrants from the Eastern Hemisphere. Thus, admissible classes were broadened to include migrants from places outside Europe. Refugees from Southwest Asia as well as from communist and noncommunist countries could be admitted under the new law. The 1952 act lifted restrictions on Japanese immigration and established a small token quota for people from the "Asiatic Barred Zone" created in 1917.

Quotas also were established for the first time for colonial territories. These quotas, often racially motivated, were designed to limit the number of blacks from the British West Indies, who entered the United States by using the British quota. The parole clause in the act authorized the attorney general to study migrant groups on a case-by-case basis. This clause, for example, admitted more than 30,000 Hungarians in the period 1956-1958. Many Cubans fled the Batista regime during the early 1950's, established colonies in American cities, and lobbied for the rights and freedoms of their fellow Cuban citizens. More than 650,000 Cubans entered the United States following Fidel Castro's rise to power and the establishment of his communist regime in 1959-1960. The largest number settled in south Florida, where they built a vibrant economic and political community. Other legislation aided the flight and integration of persons from Asia and certain communist countries.

Impact Immigration during the 1950's meant the movement of human capital. Most immigrants sought economic opportunities, sold their labor, and integrated into society as both producers and consumers. These immigrants were generally young and unattached or newly married persons with small but growing families. They were primarily from the working class.

Immigration policy loosened during the 1950's in response to the needs of the postwar period. Annual quota limits were suspended as Congress allowed sizable refugee groups to enter, including Hungarians,

Yugoslavs, Chinese, and Dutch Indonesians. With the Cold War came the Internal Security (McCarran) Act of 1950, an act that required the deportation or exclusion of all aliens who had been members of the Communist Party. Ongoing concerns over national security prompted a full review of U.S. immigration law; policymakers decided it was time to update and recodify the legislation. By the late 1950's, the national origins policy looked archaic alongside the country's changing international relations.

However, public attitudes about foreign peoples were becoming more positive. World Refugee Year, 1959-1960, encouraged worldwide acceptance and accommodation of refugees. In the United States there was growing public sentiment for relaxing immigration controls so that refugees and migrants of more diverse backgrounds could enter the country. The existing laws were sharply criticized by President John F. Kennedy, and President Lyndon B. Johnson later pushed for wide-ranging reforms. The immigration reform movement culminated in the Immigration and Nationality Act of 1965, the Hart-Celler legislation, which completely abolished the national origins component. By the 1960's and 1970's, there was a broadening scope and acceptance of non-European immigrants in the United States, particularly those from Asia and Latin America. Clearly, the 1950's was a turning point in changing the face of immigration into America.

Further Reading

Borjas, George. *Friends or Strangers? The Impact of Immigration on the U.S. Economy.* New York: Basic Books, 1990. Finds that immigrants have not diminished wages and employment opportunities for natives.

Daniels, Roger. *Coming to America: A History of Immigration and Ethnicity in American Life.* New York: HarperPerennial, 1991. Covers the colonial period to the late twentieth century.

_____. *Guarding the Golden Door: American Immigrant Policy and Immigrants Since 1882.* New York: Hill and Wang, 2004. Addresses the inconsistencies and shortcomings of American immigration policy.

Gill, Richard T., Nathan Glazer, and Stephan Thernstrom. *Our Changing Population.* Englewood Cliffs, N.J.: Prentice-Hall, 1991. An examination of population changes from historical, sociological, and economic perspectives.

Muller, Thomas. *Immigrants and the American City.* New York: New York University Press, 1993. Examines social, political, and economic aspects of immigrants in the city.

Ann M. Legreid

See also Asian Americans; Bracero program; California's Alien Land Laws; Demographics of the United States; Hungarian revolt; Immigration and Nationality Act of 1952; Immigration to Canada; Latinos; Mexico; Operation Wetback; Urbanization in the United States; War brides.

■ "In God We Trust" on U.S. currency

The Event Phrase added to U.S. paper currency during the Cold War era
Date First appeared on dollar bills on July 25, 1957

The addition of the phrase "In God We Trust" to U.S. currency reflected the rising accommodation of religion in the public arena during the Cold War.

The rising tide of Cold War concerns with communism produced a form of civil religion during the 1950's referred to by some as "piety along the Potomac." In 1954, President Dwight D. Eisenhower expressed the sentiment of this renewed blending of religion and Americanism in stating, "Our government makes no sense unless it is founded on a deeply religious faith—and I don't care what it is." On Flag Day of 1954, as America was locked in a Cold War with "atheistic communism," the president signed legislation that added the phrase "one nation under God" to the Pledge of Allegiance. He was reassured in his action by the polls, which showed that 95 percent of the respondents declared themselves Protestants, Roman Catholics, or Jews, and 97 percent believed in God.

Two years later, the president approved a Joint Resolution of Congress that declared "In God We Trust" the national motto of the United States. In 1957, "In God We Trust" was first printed on the dollar bill, though this was not the first appearance of the phrase on American currency. During the dark days of the Civil War, when more Americans turned to religion for solace, Congress called for its inscription on the two-cent coin. Though its inclusion on other coins increased from then until 1957, and on higher-value bills until the early 1960's, its usage experienced interruptions prior to new legislation in 1956, which mandated its permanent inscription.

Impact While some objections to the phrase on American currency have arisen, it has been ignored by most. The Ninth Circuit Court of Appeals stated in 1970 that its use on currency is of ceremonial and patriotic character and does not constitute the government's sponsorship of a religious exercise. This position was confirmed in 1994 by the Tenth Circuit Court.

Further Reading

Gaustad, Edwin S. *Church and State in America.* New York: Oxford University Press, 1999. An excellent overview of the topic, especially addressed to elementary and middle school audiences.

Whitfield, Stephen J. *The Culture of the Cold War.* 2d ed. Baltimore: Johns Hopkins University Press, 1996. A foremost scholarly work covering a whole range of cultural issues prominent during the Cold War years.

Robert R. Mathisen

See also Cold War; Conservatism in U.S. politics; Pledge of Allegiance; Religion in the United States.

■ Inco strike

The Event Strike by workers of the International Nickel Company (Inco), one of the largest Canadian companies ever to have a strike
Date September-December, 1958

Inco employed fifteen thousand workers in Canada in 1958, making it one of the largest companies to go on strike that year. The Canadian District of the International Union of Mine, Mill and Smelter Workers represented the striking workers, and by mid-December, the union succeeded in getting them a 10 percent pay increase.

By January, 1958, unemployment in Canada had reached levels previously reached during the 1930's, with more than 600,000 unemployed workers. Unemployment was almost cut in half by July when the number of unemployed decreased to 286,000. However, the reduced unemployment cut did not curtail labor strikes in Canada during the summer and fall of 1958. The increases in the Canadian cost of living led some major industries to go on strike. The industries threatened by these strikes included railroads, shipping, brewing, and mining.

One of the largest companies to go on strike was the International Nickel Company in Sudbury, Ontario. This company employed fifteen thousand workers, and they were paid on average C$2.69 per hour, one of the highest wages in Canada. Nevertheless, the union that went on strike on September 24, 1958, demanded a 10 percent wage increase. The Canadian government made desperate attempts to try to avert the strike. Once enacted, the strike caused the Canadian government to take emergency action, and Provincial Minister of Labor Charles Daley made attempts at the start of the strike to intervene, calling for emergency action on the part of the province "in face of a walkout" of the company's employees. However, the union that represented many of the company's workers was unable to reach a labor agreement, and the strike lasted throughout the fall, not ending until mid-December. The strike had crippling effects on Sudbury's economy since Inco was its only large company.

Impact Many of the local churches in Sudbury conducted food drives to help feed the families of workers who were on strike that autumn. Finally, by mid-December, 1958, the workers represented by the Canadian District of the International Union of Mine, Mill and Smelter Workers reached an agreement with the management of Inco and received a 10 percent increase in their hourly wages, to an average of C$2.95 per hour.

Further Reading

Heron, Craig. *The Canadian Labour Movement: A Short History.* Rev. ed. Toronto: Lorimer, 1996. Details the impact of organized labor on Canadian industry and discusses the 1958 strike.

Story, Robert. "The Struggle for Job Ownership in the Canadian Steel Industry: An Historical Analysis." *Labour/Le Travail* 33 (Spring, 1994): 75-106. In its overview of the steel industry, the article provides context for the Inco strike.

Lloyd Johnson

See also Business and the economy in Canada; Steel mill closure; Steelworkers strike; Unions in Canada.

■ Income and wages in Canada

With the help of population increase and changes in the orientation of its economic sectors, Canada transformed itself into a modern industrialized country during the 1950's.

Canada's population grew rapidly during the 1950's, and this population growth arose from, and stimulated further growth in, job opportunities. The labor force increased at an average rate of 2.3 percent each year, so a rapid increase in the number of jobs was essential to provide employment for Canadian citizens. The birthrate, which dropped drastically during the Great Depression years, rebounded during the 1950's, rising from fewer than 20 per 1,000 inhabitants at the beginning of the decade to a peak of 26.8 per 1,000 in 1957.

Along with natural increase, Canada welcomed a large number of immigrants during the 1950's. Many were refugees from war-torn Europe, who sought the economic opportunities that Canada offered. Between 1852 and 1962, Canada welcomed 8,906,927 immigrants, but it also had experienced heavy emigration, primarily to the United States: 6,963,000 Canadians had moved away from the country. About one-half of the nearly nine million people who came to Canada during that period arrived shortly before World War I, but an equal number came after World War II. Most of them came from northwestern Europe, especially from Great Britain, but some came from the United States, seeking economic opportunities. Until the mid-1950's, immigrants had needed a sponsor in Canada, and this factor kept immigration numbers down somewhat. However, during the middle of the decade, the sponsor requirement was eliminated, and a flood of new immigrants arrived, often from parts of the world, such as the Caribbean, which hitherto had not sent many people to Canada.

Canadian Jobs During the 1950's, wage rates increased more than 80 percent, while the cost of living grew by only about 30 percent. Thus, Canadians enjoyed a strong improvement in their standard of living during the decade. This improvement was made possible by the growth of worker productivity, which increased at an average rate of 3.6 percent per year.

Although working Canadians enjoyed nearly full employment throughout most of the 1950's, the kind of employment they sought changed dramatically. Economies are divided occupationally into sectors: the primary sector, covering agriculture, forestry, mining, quarrying, fishing, and hunting; the secondary sector, comprising manufacturing and construction; and the tertiary sector, embracing a whole host of service-related businesses, including transportation, communication, retail and wholesale trade, finance, real estate, public administration, and education. In Canada during this decade, there was a dramatic shift in employment out of agriculture (which fell from 20 to 11 percent of employed persons) and into activities in the tertiary sector, often referred to as the "service sector." At the same time there was a significant reduction in subsistence farming, as many Canadians came to prefer both an urban setting and a steady job. Jobs in the secondary sector grew at about the same rate as the population, so that manufacturing jobs attracted the same percentage of Canadians at the end of the decade as they had in the beginning.

The biggest job growth during the 1950's was in the service sector, which rose from a little under 47 percent of jobs in 1951 to almost 56 percent ten years later. The startling growth of health care employment, especially in hospitals, played a major role in this increase: In the last half of the decade, employment in hospitals doubled. There was also a large increase in the number of teachers, as many of the new service sector jobs required greater education. Women holding jobs, especially those in the clerical field, increased significantly, while the number of women employed in agriculture increased as farms converted from "family farms" to business enterprises engaged in agriculture. Women, released from household duties by the many labor-saving household appliances, became the clerical staff of the new agricultural enterprises.

Job Benefits A major change related to wages was the rapid growth of unions. During the early part of the decade, there was sharp competition between industrial unions—affiliated with the Congress of Industrial Organizations (CIO) in the United States—and the more craft-oriented unions that belonged to the Trades and Labor Congress, which was linked to the American Federation of Labor (AFL) in the United States. The two Canadian groups merged in 1956 but continued to vie for membership. Regulation of labor disputes was the responsibility of the provincial governments, and the province of Ontario, where Canada's industrialized belt was located, created the Ontario Labor Relations Board in 1950 to adjudicate jurisdictional disputes. In 1951, Ontario passed laws establishing fair employment practices and requiring equal pay for men and women. Federal law, as well as that of most provinces, prohibited discrimination on the basis of race, color, religion, or national origin.

Other benefits guaranteed to workers included workers' compensation for those injured on the job or for those suffering long-term disability arising from conditions at work. Many union contracts made provisions for pensions for older workers, and many companies had mandatory retirement ages, often written into union contracts. Mandatory retirement also existed for salaried workers, but in the cases of scarce technical or administrative employees, it could be waived. Pension costs in Canada ran at about 5.6 percent of regular payroll payments, but in the case of higher-paid provincial and municipal employees, they ran at 6 to 7 percent of payroll.

Wages Paid Data collected by the Dominion Bureau of Statistics for 1959 showed that there were considerable discrepancies in the wages paid in different occupations. Mining, because of the risks associated with it, was the most highly paid, with an average weekly wage of a little over ninety dollars Canadian. Services earned the lowest wages, with an average weekly wage of a little under fifty dollars Canadian. Manufacturing and construction, the secondary sector, earned approximately seventy-five dollars Canadian per week, while public utility operating wages (many utilities were public corporations) were slightly under the mining wage, at eighty-seven dollars Canadian. Transportation (railroads were heavily unionized) occupations earned somewhat less, at seventy-nine dollars Canadian. Trade, wholesale and retail, came in at slightly under sixty-three dollars Canadian.

Unemployment Although by most reckonings Canada enjoyed full employment in the first half of the decade, unemployment rose noticeably in the latter half, from 3.6 percent to more than 6 percent. Unemployment as measured by claims for unemployment insurance hit 7 percent in 1958. There were sharp regional differences. In the Atlantic provinces, unemployment rose to more than 10 percent in 1958 and stayed there; by contrast, in the prairie provinces (Manitoba, Alberta, and Saskatchewan) it was less than 5 percent. In Ontario, Canada's most heavily industrialized province, it was slightly over 5 percent.

Canada had been providing unemployment insurance for those who worked for wages since 1940.

Both employee and employer contributed equal amounts to the fund, and the federal government added a sum equal to one-fifth of the other contributions. The amounts that could be paid out were limited and did not go at all to those earning more than a modest annual income. Some special provisions were made for "seasonal unemployment," a special problem for those employed in agriculture and forestry.

During the latter 1950's, when unemployment became a serious problem, both the federal government and the provincial governments began to implement economic stimulus measures. There was a substantial increase in public works spending, most notably on sewer and water systems for municipalities. Provincial governments provided the financing, under plans that enabled the municipalities to pay back the costs over an extended period of time. Since prior to this time few Canadian municipalities had either municipal water or sewer services, these projects both improved the quality of urban life and protected the environment.

The St. Lawrence Seaway was also completed during this time, making industrial transportation to the heartland markedly less expensive, thus boosting in particular firms located in Ontario. Pipeline constructed in this decade connected western provinces with Ontario, reducing the cost of gas and oil. The Canadian dollar's value fell below that of the U.S. dollar.

Impact Canada's economy was in many respects similar to that of its larger neighbor to the south. The principal difference was that Canada tended always to be a bit behind the United States; its industrial production, its wages and salaries, and its benefits tended to be a bit less than those enjoyed in the United States. Moreover, the full employment that had benefited Canadian workers early during the 1950's faded as the 1960's wore on, and although Canada continued to match and sometimes exceed U.S. productivity growth (as in the decade between 1974 and 1984), it remained behind the United States. In hours worked, Canadians were behind U.S. workers; few of them worked the full forty-hour week that was standard in the United States.

Further, as might be expected in a nation that stretches from the Atlantic to the Pacific Ocean, there were marked regional differences. The area that had the most difficulty providing employment for its people was the Atlantic region—Newfoundland, Prince Edward Island, Nova Scotia, and New Brunswick. Indeed, for Newfoundland during the 1950's, often the only source of jobs was the fisheries. As these were increasingly invaded by international fishing fleets, the position of workers in Newfoundland became ever more precarious, and the colder climate made self-sufficient agriculture almost impossible. Nova Scotia had coal mines, but these were not very competitive economically, and they experienced serious labor troubles. Prince Edward Island, which has valuable agricultural lands, survived mostly on the strength of its agricultural output.

Quebec, with a cultural focus different from most other parts of Canada, nevertheless began to depart from the agricultural foundation that had determined its character for three centuries. Although Quebec was less industrialized than its neighbor, Ontario, it began to share some of the characteristics of the Ontario economy. However, during the 1950's, before some of this transformation had taken place, Quebec's unemployment rate rose to almost 10 percent.

At the opposite end of the country, British Columbia, with its mild climate, nevertheless suffered from being so far from the heartland of Canada and from Ontario. Its unemployment rate was more variable, as many people sought opportunities there, including some job seekers from the United States. However, the transportation costs made successful business enterprise more problematic, and British Columbia during the decade still relied heavily on its forests, which, thanks to the climate, were extraordinarily productive.

Further Reading

Dominion Bureau of Statistics, Information Services Division. *Canada 1961: The Official Handbook of Present Conditions and Recent Progress*. Ottawa: Government Printer, 1961. Contains many useful statistics for the previous decade.

Faruqui, Umar, et al. "Differences in Productivity Growth: Canadian-U.S. Business Sectors, 1987-2000." *Monthly Labor Review* 126, no. 4 (April, 2003): 16-29. Discusses, though for a later period, the differences in labor productivity between the United States and Canada.

Peitchinis, Stephen G. *The Economics of Labour: Employment and Wages in Canada*. Toronto: McGraw-

Hill, 1965. Contains a vast amount of information, and even the technical parts are relatively easy to understand.

Rea, K. J. *The Prosperous Years: The Economic History of Ontario, 1939-1975.* Toronto: University of Toronto Press, 1985. Although focused on Ontario, it says much about Canada as a whole.

Nancy M. Gordon

See also AFL-CIO merger; Agriculture in Canada; Business and the economy in Canada; Gross national product of Canada; Gross national product of the United States; Health care systems in Canada; Inflation in Canada; Recession of 1957-1958; Unemployment in Canada; Unionism in Canada.

■ Income and wages in the United States

An unexpected decade of growing prosperity following World War II enabled Americans to improve their standard of living and take advantage of other material and cultural changes taking place. This growth in affluence was not even, nor did it solve all social ills.

Following the Allied victory in World War II, most economists and policymakers expected the Great Depression of the 1930's to reassert itself. Defense needs would fall to their previous levels, and many assumed that returning soldiers and laid-off war workers would swell the unemployment rolls, reducing demand for consumer goods in an uncertain economic environment. Accordingly, many of the economic strictures of the 1940's remained in place well past the end of World War II. Price controls on most items were lifted in 1946, but the Federal Reserve Board did not resume its monetary (money supply) powers until 1951; the top marginal tax rate of 94 percent would not be reduced until President Kennedy's tax cut of the early 1960's. The U.S. government remained determined to reinvoke its wartime power over the economy at a moment's notice.

As it turned out, however, such vigilance was not needed. Although consumer prices rose rapidly for a short time (increasing 8.5 percent in 1946 and 14.3 percent in 1947), the diversion of returning veterans into higher education via the G.I. Bill, along with pent-up demand for consumer goods, prevented a reassertion of the economic depression that had preceded the war.

The transition from a wartime economy driven by defense spending into a consumer economy driven by the needs and desires of individual consumers and families was surprisingly smooth, though not without its difficulties. The closing of many wartime factories was financially stressful for their owners and employees. The women, teenagers, and retirees who had staffed them found their jobs reassigned to returning soldiers and their own employment prospects limited.

A Growing Sense of Prosperity In virtually all measures of income, however, Americans became wealthier during the 1950's. Although defense spending had dropped precipitously during the late 1940's, from a high of $93 billion in 1945 to slightly under $30 billion in 1948, pent-up consumer demand fed growing automotive, housing, and consumer products industries. War workers who had earned high wages during the 1940's had found very little on which to spend their wages in an economy where gasoline, tires, nylons, and even butter and sugar were rationed. Those goods that were not rationed were often hard to find or not produced at all during the war. Drives to encourage war workers to buy savings bonds (in effect, to finance the war that paid their wages) meant that after the war, consumers held a great deal of cash with which to satisfy many long-standing wants and needs.

Median household income (that income which is greater than that earned by 50 percent of all households and less than that earned by the other 50 percent of all households) rose from $3,139 in 1950 to $5,417 in 1959. Even after adjusting for price inflation of 21 percent during the decade, the median family household increased its income 30 percent in ten years.

When broken down into specific types of households, the results all followed a common path of growth. White households saw their median income grow from $3,445 in 1950 to $5,643 ($4,664 after adjusting for inflation) in 1959—a real (inflation-adjusted) growth rate of 35 percent. African American households saw their median income grow from $1,869 in 1950 to $2,915 ($2,409 adjusted for inflation) in 1959 for a real growth of 29 percent. Female-headed households fared least well, seeing their median income grow from $1,992 in 1950 to $2,764 ($2,284 when adjusted for inflation) in 1959 for a real growth rate of less than 15 percent over the decade.

Income Transfers to Households Although the vast majority of household income continued to come from paid employment, transfer payments from the federal government to individual households grew during the 1950's. Most of these programs were "New Deal" programs started during President Franklin D. Roosevelt's administration. From 1950 to 1959, retirement program payments (Social Security) rose from $1.5 billion to $11.5 billion per year, while income maintenance programs (for example, Aid to Families with Dependent Children, or AFDC) grew from $2.4 billion per year to $3.4 billion. Likewise, payments for unemployment compensation rose from $1.5 billion to $2.9 billion per year during the decade. The only major transfer payment to decline during the 1950's was veterans' benefits, which fell from an annual payment of $7.7 billion per year in 1950 to $4.5 billion annually in 1959. It should be noted, however, that these figures reflect the eligibility standards of the programs as they were adminis-

tered during the 1950's. For example, AFDC at the time provided for the needs of the child(ren) living in a household but not of the parents, who were expected to support themselves. Likewise, Social Security as it existed during the 1950's did not cover either medical care (Medicare) or disabled people younger than retirement age. These programs were added and expanded after 1959.

Persistent Poverty Although nationwide, formal poverty statistics did not exist in the United States before 1959, poverty was considerably more pervasive during the 1950's than it was in later decades. Even after a decade of relatively peaceful prosperity, the poverty rate in 1959 was 22 percent of the population, compared with an average rate of 11 percent during the early twenty-first century. At the beginning of the 1950's, 35 percent of homes in the United States lacked indoor plumbing (defined as hot and cold running water, a bathtub or shower,

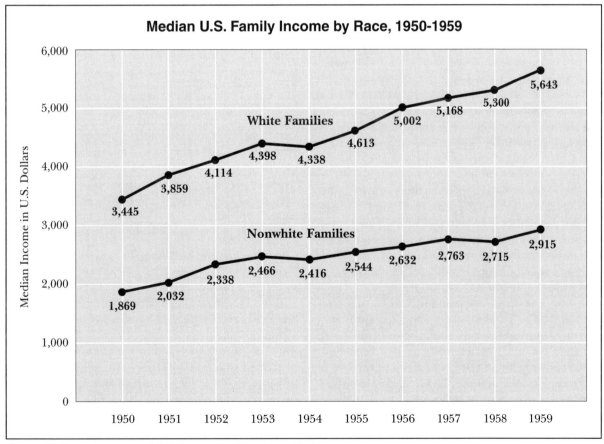

Source: U.S. Census Bureau, *Statistical Abstract of the United States,* 2003.

and a flush toilet); in ten states, more than half of the residents lacked indoor plumbing. By 1960, only 17 percent of homes lacked indoor plumbing, and in no state did less than half the homes have indoor plumbing.

Throughout the 1950's, large pockets of poverty pervaded the Appalachian mountains, the rural South, and inner-city slums in the large northern cities. In 1950, the five poorest states (in terms of the average income of their citizens) were Mississippi, Arkansas, Alabama, South Carolina, and Kentucky, with incomes 53 to 70 percent of the national average. By 1959, the five poorest states were Mississippi, Arkansas, South Carolina, Alabama, and West Virginia, with incomes ranging from 60 to 70 percent of the national average. Rural southern states were catching up with the rest of the nation, however slowly, but the region was also losing population, thus accounting for these poverty statistics.

During the 1950's, as during the 1940's, younger African Americans left the South in large numbers to pursue more attractive lives in the northern states. The large numbers of African Americans who left the region of their birth and their family ties attests that conditions for African American workers in the industrial cities of the North during the 1950's were better than those in the South.

Life on the Farm In the agricultural sector, including the southern states from which many African Americans fled, farm incomes were stagnant during the 1950's, after tripling during the 1940's. The value of farm products in 1950 was $13.2 billion. In 1959, it was $14.7 billion, or $12.1 billion after adjusting for inflation. Farm production was up during this period, as both labor and land productivity grew at a previously unknown rate, but the combination of high productivity and improvements in shipping and transportation resulted in a large surplus of farm products and lower profits.

During the 1950's, the number of farms and ranches in the United States shrank, as did the amount of land under cultivation and the number of people living on farms. Those farms that remained were 36 percent larger and more mechanized at the end of the decade than they had been in 1950. The distribution of income in agricultural areas increasingly favored those farmers with large investments in land and equipment. Farming was increasingly the province of those who could either afford tractors

and large tracts of land or, more frequently, those who had access to ample credit and were willing to assume substantial debt. Marginal farmers in the South and Midwest increasingly found their fortunes in the cities.

The Union Difference Once displaced farmers and other rural denizens reached the industrial cities of the North and Midwest, they discovered that about one-third of all jobs belonged to union members. Union membership had risen after the war and prospered in the large manufacturing plants of the 1950's. Increased demand for American goods in the rest of the world, fueled in part by the Marshall Plan for rebuilding Europe, prompted growth in heavy manufacturing. A record 32.5 percent of all jobs were union jobs in 1953—a proportion that would not be reached again during the twentieth century.

The record number of labor stoppages and strikes during the 1950's attests to the strength of labor unions during this time. In 1952 alone, a postwar-record 470 work stoppages at firms with more than one thousand employees took place, affecting more than 2.7 million workers. Union employees' wages generally exceeded nonunion employees' wages in similar jobs by 10 to 30 percent during the 1950's, but very often entire industries were unionized, providing very little in the way of nonunion wages to use for comparison. Conditions in large plants in the steel, coal, automotive, and other manufacturing plants of the day were as close to ideal for union organizing as they would ever be: a large population of workers performing standardized jobs for a single employer. The fact that many had prior and personal knowledge of work conditions during the 1930's also increased labor unions' popularity.

Consumerism and Its Critics The relative peace that followed the first years after World War II was not to last. The spread of communism in Europe and Asia and the U.S. response to North Korea's invasion of South Korea in 1950 resulted in increased military spending beginning during the early 1950's. Such military extravagance, in the face of a low probability of a direct attack on the United States, left some public figures questioning the direction the U.S. economy appeared to be heading. Now that basic human needs appeared to have been satisfied, the issue of what to do with the surplus generated by prosperity assumed greater importance.

One of the most vocal critics of the ways in which Americans were spending their incomes was economist John Kenneth Galbraith. Raised on a farm in Canada during the early twentieth century, Galbraith had been an economic adviser to President Franklin D. Roosevelt during the 1930's, in charge of wartime price controls during the 1940's, and a Harvard professor by the time he published *The Affluent Society* in 1958. In *The Affluent Society*, Galbraith asserted that private consumption in the United States was excessive while public consumption was inadequate. He criticized Americans' propensities to drive their modern cars (complete with the then-fashionable tail fins) over poorly maintained roads littered with billboards and commercial signs. The state of public education and services for the poor were singled out as worthy of Americans' income just as the perceived excesses of the domestic automobile and fashion industries were condemned as a waste of consumers' purchasing power.

Galbraith's *Affluent Society* would continue to influence public dialogue well into the 1980's, although he would later moderate some of his more contentious conclusions. His book was significant in that for the first time America was seen as being wealthy enough to ask important questions about the proper distribution between private and public consumption. These concerns probably would not have found a very wide audience twenty, or even ten, years prior to the decade. Higher wages and incomes during the 1950's, as well as the persistence of poverty, racial discrimination, and other social ills, would prove less amenable to rapid or easy solutions. The 1950's marked a turning point in Americans' economic well-being, but the problems of how to apply this higher income would remain in the decades ahead.

Impact The 1950's started off with a pleasant surprise and ended with the kinds of questions that could be asked only by a nation that was satisfied with the progress it had made in a decade. Far from seeing the return of the economic conditions of the 1930's that most had expected, the end of World War II ushered in the beginning of an era of increased prosperity and high demand for consumer goods, both in the United States and in the rest of the world. Incomes grew in most industries, and higher wages lured many African Americans and rural dwellers to the large cities of the Midwest and North. Once they arrived at their destinations, these workers found an increasingly unionized work environment in their new homes.

Rising wages and incomes did not address old social ills, however. African Americans still found their incomes lagging behind those of white Americans, and this gap did not narrow during the 1950's. Poor states in the rural South remained behind other states, and households headed by women saw their incomes grow at the slowest rate of all households. Farmers found that they needed to adopt the latest technology and expand their investment if they were to compete in the new agricultural marketplace. As a result, the portion of the population living on farms declined 40 percent during the 1950's while the amount of acreage farmed by the typical farmer increased by 36 percent.

Further Reading

Cohen, Elizabeth. *A Consumers' Republic: The Politics of Mass Consumption in Postwar America.* New York: Knopf, 2003. A good source for discerning economic trends during the late 1940's, 1950's, and early 1960's in the United States.

Daniel, Pete. *Lost Revolutions: The South in the 1950's.* Washington, D.C.: University of North Carolina Press for Smithsonian National Museum of American History, 2000. Cultural history of the American Southeast, focusing on the factors which would lead to its transformation in coming decades.

Finkelstein, Norman H. *The Way Things Never Were: The Truth About the "Good Old Days."* New York: Atheneum, 1999. A lighthearted account of the reality of the 1950's, including many of the things Americans might prefer not to remember as a nation, such as the limitations placed upon women and African Americans.

Galbraith, John Kenneth. *The Affluent Society.* Boston: Houghton Mifflin, 1998. Reprinted, with a new foreword, from the original 1958 classic. The author's premise seems dated in light of later conditions, but a worthy read for anyone interested in a contemporaneous commentary on the 1950's.

_____. *A Journey Through Economic Time: A Firsthand View.* Boston: Houghton Mifflin, 1994. A classic in economic history from a liberal point of view. Galbraith's writing style is readily accessible to most readers, whether or not they agree with his conclusions.

Harris, Seymour, ed. *American Economic History.* New York: Beard Group, 2002. A comprehensive account of the economic history of the United States from 1800 through the late 1950's.

Kallen, Stuart A., ed. *The 1950's.* San Diego, Calif.: Greenhaven Press, 2000. Debunks many of the myths that the 1950's were a time of conformity and striving for perfection.

Phalen, Richard C., ed. *How We Have Changed: America Since 1950.* New York: Pelican, 2003. A collection of interviews with forty-five journalists and public figures. Good source for first-person accounts of the experience of living during the 1950's and after.

Betsy A. Murphy

See also Affluence and the new consumerism; *Affluent Society, The*; African Americans; Agriculture in the United States; American Dream; Bracero program; Business and the economy in the United States; Chrysler autoworkers strike; Housing in the United States; Unemployment in the United States; Unionism in the United States.

■ Indian Act of 1951

Identification Revision of an 1876 Canadian law that defined and regulated the status of Canada's First Nations
Date Became law on September 4, 1951

The 1951 Indian Act opened a new era in Canadian federal Indian policy.

All effective Indian legislation in Canada is contained in the Indian Act of 1951. This legislation came about as a result of a growing realization that the original Indian Act, with its various amendments passed since its inception in 1876, had failed in its stated goals and not served the interests of Canada's aboriginal peoples. The original Indian Act had created an enduring nationwide framework for Indian policy.

The main purpose of the 1876 legislation was ultimate termination of indigenous societies, institutions, and culture though a process of civilization and assimilation into the dominant Anglo-European culture. In this aspect, Canada's Indian policy mirrored that of its American neighbor. Over the years, new amendments dealt continuous blows to sovereign rights and First People's cultural heritage. The federal government's Department of Indian Affairs assumed management and control of Indian reserves and property. Officials eventually lost sight of the proclaimed goal of assimilation without undo duress. In pursuit of the civilizing mission, edicts banned customs, dances, and ceremonies central to maintaining aboriginal peoples' traditional spirituality but deemed inconsistent with values of the dominant culture. Indian children were taken from their homelands and parents and were placed in industrial schools or church-operated boarding schools until the age of eighteen. Here, youngsters were deprived of their Indian identity and ancestral heritage, and many children suffered systematic abuses by the authorities. Indians who obtained a university education, those few who qualified for the franchise and citizenship, and children of Indian women and non-Indian men were among those who lost their legal standing and rights as Indians.

Policy Reversal The major revision in 1951 reversed many past policies. The authority of the government minister over the First People's bands and reserves was reduced largely to that of a supervisory role, and most cultural prohibitions were repealed. While local bands gained more self-control—such as the right to incorporate as municipalities and to elect officials—the new act stopped short of allowing them to establish their own forms of government. However, bands now had the authority to manage surrendered and reserve lands, control their own revenues, and administer bylaws. Prohibitions on forming political organizations, as well as raising and spending funds for political ends, were lifted, and the bands could fund lawsuits to advance land claims. Bands regained control over membership, and individuals who had lost their legal status as Indians could reclaim it. In a move toward lessening federal control and responsibility over Indian affairs, the act allowed for gradual integration of Amerindians into provincial programs that provided benefits such as education, child welfare, and social assistance.

Impact Some indigenous leaders were dissatisfied with the 1951 act since the goal of assimilation remained and some impediments to the full exercise of sovereignty continued. The past legacy of wrongs to aboriginal communities continued to be addressed via litigation over abuses that had transpired. Nevertheless, the new act was a step forward and foreshadowed ongoing government concessions in future decades on issues of sovereignty and land claims.

Further Reading

Cardinal, Harold. *The Unjust Society: The Tragedy of Canada's Indians.* Edmonton: Hurtig, 1969. A critical evaluation of Canadian federal Indian policy, including the 1951 act.

Dickason, Olive Patricia. *Canada's First Nations: A History of Founding Peoples from Earliest Times.* Toronto: McClelland & Stewart, 1992. Comprehensive overview of the experience of Canada's aboriginal peoples, including detailed treatment of federal Indian policy and Indian-government relations.

David A. Crain

See also Minorities in Canada; Native Americans; Racial discrimination.

■ Inflation in Canada

An increase in public expenditures on services such as health care helped drive inflation in Canada to new levels during the 1950's.

Canada's consumer price index during the 1950's was based on the year 1949, which based the index at 100. By 1952, it had already reached 116.5, driven largely by U.S. price increases that were substantially fueled by the Korean War. From 1952 through 1955, prices remained relatively stable, fluctuating around the level attained in 1952. In 1956, however, prices again began to climb, with average annual increases of around 3 percent, until the consumer price index reached 126.5 in 1959.

The major explanation for the resumption of inflation during the late 1950's was the large increase in public expenditures in those years. The sharp jump in unemployment in 1957-1958 spurred both the government and the Bank of Canada to adopt stimulus measures. The federal government, and most notably the provincial and municipal governments, gave generous pay increases to public employees. In addition, dramatic increases in health care also led to sharp cost increases.

The price increases, however, varied across different sectors of the economy. General wholesale prices actually fell during the period 1952-1955; they jumped sharply in 1956 and again in 1959. The prices of Canadian farm products fell throughout the 1950's. However, fully manufactured goods and nonresidential building materials recorded sharp increases during the late 1950's, after dropping or remaining steady during the early years of the decade. Shelter also recorded sharp increases.

Despite these increases, there was a greater increase in wages and salaries, especially in the public sector. Over the decade, price inflation averaged 30 percent; wages and salaries increased, on average, more than 80 percent, thus substantially increasing the standard of living of most ordinary Canadians.

Impact Since the majority of Canada's foreign trade was with the United States, Canada was strongly affected by economic developments in that country. Generally, the economy in Canada tended to track that of its southern neighbor, and it is not surprising, therefore, that inflation in the United States tended to be replicated in Canada. However, Canada is a resource-rich country, with a world-class farm sector and many of the raw materials required for industry, such as gas and oil, nickel, gold, and iron. Therefore, the Canadian economy is affected more by changes in commodity prices than is the United States.

Subsequent Events Canada was inevitably affected by the inflation that hurt the United States as a consequence of the Vietnam War and the subsequent oil price crises of the 1970's. Some important raw materials rose sharply in value in the subsequent decades: the value of iron ore produced in Ontario, for example, increased fourfold between 1960 and 1975. Nickel production in Ontario, a major producer of the mineral, rose in value from $278 million in 1960 to $811 million in 1975. The value of copper mined in Ontario rose threefold during the same period. At the same time, Canada continued to spend heavily on such consumer oriented items as health care; per-capita health care expenditures in Ontario rose threefold between 1960 and 1975.

Further Reading

Faruqui, Umar, et al. "Differences in Productivity Growth: Canadian-U.S. Business Sectors, 1987-2000." *Monthly Labor Review* 126, no. 4 (April, 2003): 16-29. Contains a useful graph charting the ratio of Canada's productivity growth relative to that of the United States.

Rea, K. J. *The Prosperous Years: The Economic History of Ontario, 1939-1975.* Toronto: University of Toronto Press, 1985. Although this account is restricted to Ontario, as the most economically advanced province Ontario gives a good indication of conditions elsewhere in Canada.

Nancy M. Gordon

See also Business and the economy in Canada; Gross national product of Canada; Gross national product of the United States; Income and wages in Canada; Inflation in the United States; International trade of Canada; Unemployment in Canada; Unionism in Canada.

■ Inflation in the United States

Price increases of the 1950's, coming primarily during the Korean War, did little harm to the U.S. economy and actually stimulated fruitful experiments with federal government macroeconomic policies.

During the 1950's, consumer prices in the United States increased by an average of about 2 percent per year. Price index estimates cannot accurately adjust for the normal improvement in the quality and variety of products. Very possibly such improvements offset much of the annual increase in prices. Thus, on the average, inflation was not a major problem during the decade. This was in contrast to the price instability of the 1940's, associated with World War II. Prices became much more stable after 1949.

Korean War Inflation However, the U.S. economy did sustain a sharp burst of inflation attending the Korean War, which broke out in mid-1950. Consumers, fearing a return to the shortages and rationing they had experienced during World War II, rushed to stock up on goods. Business firms tried to build up their inventories. Although federal government defense spending increased slowly, a rapid expansion in defense contracts encouraged a rise in business capital expenditures. Much of the increased spending was met by increased production, which rose by 20 percent from 1949 to 1952. However, prices went up about 10 percent over that period.

One reason inflation was not more severe was federal fiscal policy. Tax rates were increased in the latter part of 1950; consequently the federal government did not engage in large-scale deficit spending as it had done during the 1940's. Fiscal policy was aided by the reimposition of direct economic controls, which had been extensive during World War II. Under the Defense Production Act of September, 1950, a system of allocating scarce materials was set up, and in January, 1951, price controls were imposed.

Monetary Policy The Korean inflation reflected flaws in the monetary policies of the Federal Reserve Board. During World War II, the "Fed," as it was known, had maintained a program that supported the prices of publicly traded U.S. government bonds. This helped keep interest rates low and held down the government's expenditures to pay interest on its bonds. During the buying frenzy of 1950, many households and businesses borrowed from banks to finance their expenditures. Banks obtained lending funds by selling to the Fed some of the government bonds they had bought during the war. When the Fed bought these, it created additional money to pay for them. The public's money holdings increased by six billion dollars during 1950.

Federal Reserve officials were unhappy with this experience. Despite pressure from President Harry S. Truman and Treasury Secretary John Snyder, the Fed negotiated a declaration of independence for monetary policy, termed the "Accord" of March, 1951. Henceforth the Fed would have no commitment to support government bond prices. Interest rates were free to increase, and the Treasury paid the higher rates when it issued new bonds.

The Fed also imposed some direct restrictions on credit. It issued regulations setting minimum down payments and maximum maturities for consumer credit and for housing credit. Down payments for buying stocks on credit ("margin") were raised to 75 percent. With the end of hostilities in Korea in 1953, most of the direct controls were removed. The remainder of the decade was characterized by economic growth and relative stability. Price increases exceeded 2 percent only in 1957 and 1958, and then not by much.

Damage from Inflation Most people have little doubt that inflation makes them worse off. For the entire economy, however, this is questionable. Inflation is commonly the result of strong upward change in the demand for goods and services, enabling business firms to obtain higher prices. Mild inflation (as during the 1950's) tends to stimulate rather than to deter production. The same inflation that raises product prices also tends to raise wages. When production increases, it is doubtful if the society as a whole is made worse off.

However, there are always some households with relatively fixed incomes, and during the early 1950's, many households still held savings accounts and savings bonds with very low interest rates. Inflation reduced the value of such incomes and such assets. Further, federal income tax rates were steeply graduated on the basis of money income. Even if inflation raised prices and wages by the same proportion, higher tax liability would lower household real incomes.

Inflation tends to generate anxiety even among people who appear objectively to benefit from it. This is because most people do not understand the sources of the inflation and feel they are being victimized by a force out of their control. Such anxiety can lead to harmful scapegoating of business firms and labor unions and to political "remedies" such as price controls which may do more harm than good.

Impact During the 1950's, inflation was largely confined to the Korean War period of 1950-1953 and did little harm to the national economy. The price increases helped stimulate production in the short run and encouraged business capital expenditures in the long run. The initial failure of monetary policy led to beneficial reforms in the conduct of Federal Reserve monetary policies. The direct controls on prices, wages, and credit were quickly removed.

Subsequent Events After 1952, the United States enjoyed a sustained period of price stability. Not until the Vietnam War of the late 1960's and disturbances to the world petroleum markets of the 1970's did inflation again become a national economic problem. Success in avoiding inflation came largely from good management of monetary and fiscal policies in a buoyant atmosphere of business optimism.

Further Reading

Hickman, Bert G. *Growth and Stability of the Postwar Economy*. Washington, D.C.: Brookings Institution, 1960. Chapters 5 and 14 deal with the Korean inflation and subsequent events.

Stein, Herbert. *The Fiscal Revolution in America*. Chicago: University of Chicago Press, 1969. A policy insider gives a particularly good account of the liberation of monetary policy in chapter 10.

Vatter, Harold G. *The U.S. Economy in the 1950's*. New York: W. W. Norton, 1963. Condensed but readable; price developments are stressed in chapters 3 and 5.

Paul B. Trescott

See also Business and the economy in the United States; Economic Stabilization Agency; Recession of 1957-1958; Steel mill closure.

■ *Inherit the Wind*

Identification Dramatic work protesting attacks on free speech
Authors Jerome Lawrence (1915-2004) and Robert E. Lee (1918-1994)
Date First produced in January, 1955
Place Dallas, Texas

This dramatic re-creation was written to warn U.S. audiences against the repressive influence of demagogues such as Senator Joseph McCarthy.

Inherit the Wind was inspired by the 1925 trial of John Scopes, a Tennessee biology teacher, for breaking a state law by teaching the theory of evolution. The prosecutor in the case was William Jennings Bryan, and the defense attorney was Clarence Darrow. However, as the playwrights point out, *Inherit the Wind* is not history, but theater; the setting, the characters, and the events are all fictional.

All of the action of *Inherit the Wind* takes place in or outside the courthouse in Hillsboro, a small country town. When the play begins, Bert Cates has been jailed for teaching the theory of evolution. Even Rachel Brown, who loves him, does not understand why he felt compelled to break the law. Her father, the Reverend Jeremiah Brown, believes that Cates is a tool of the devil; the prosecutor, Matthew Harrison Brady (who resembles Bryan), sees the case as a battle between good and evil. When E. K. Hornbeck, a cynical newspaperman, announces that the atheistic Henry Drummond (surrogate for Darrow) is coming to defend Cates, Brown refers to Drummond as "Satan."

Act 2 starts with an emotional prayer meeting led by Brown. Brady ultimately suggests that the crowd disperse, quoting from Proverbs, "He that troubleth his own house . . . shall inherit the wind." At the trial, Brady has no trouble proving that Cates did teach the theory of evolution, and Drummond is not allowed to call scientists to testify for the defense. In desperation, Drummond calls Brady as an expert on the Bible; before long, Drummond has everyone laughing at Brady. However, the jury finds Cates guilty, and he is freed on bond, pending an appeal. Rachel has made her decision; the two leave Hillsboro together. Meanwhile, Brady dies. To Hornbeck's amazement, Drummond calls his antagonist a great man who, like Cates, had the right to search for God. The play ends with a reminder of the importance of freedom of speech and thought. A film version of the play appeared in 1960, starring Fredric March as Brady and Spencer Tracy as Drummond.

Impact During its long run on Broadway, *Inherit the Wind* reminded thousands of playgoers that the freedoms of speech and thought are basic to American democracy. The 1960 film version of the play, which became a classic in film history, continued to be attacked on occasion by religious fundamentalists, who argued that its presentation of evolution makes it unsuitable for public schools and libraries.

Further Reading

Benen, Steve. "Inherit the Myth?" *Church and State* 53, no. 7 (2000): 15. Argues that the 1960 film version of *Inherit the Wind* so altered facts that it must be judged an "inadequate reflection of history."

Larson, Edward J. *Summer for the Gods: The Scopes Trial and America's Continuing Debate over Science and Religion.* Cambridge, Mass.: Harvard University Press, 1998. Pulitzer Prize-winning book that presents a detailed account of the real-life trial and considers its influence.

Mosle, Sara. "Inherit the Zealots." *The New Yorker* 72, no. 4 (1996): 38-39. Reports the reactions of a group of New York City high school students to the play *Inherit the Wind* and then to a performance the next day, with their mentor Tony Randall in the role of Henry Drummond.

Rosemary M. Canfield Reisman

See also Conformity, culture of; Education in the United States; Film in the United States; McCarthy, Joseph; Religion in the United States; Theater in the United States.

■ Instant photography

The Event Introduction of the first instant-print camera

Manufacturer Polaroid Corporation

Date First marketed in November, 1948

The instant-print camera reinvented photography itself, altered a major industry, and invigorated the scientific community.

In 1947, before the Optical Society of America in New York City, Edwin Land made the first public demonstration of his instant-print photography. Using a large portrait camera, he took his own picture, which he developed in fifty seconds in a metal chamber attached to the back of the camera, producing an 8-by-10-inch sepia photograph. The technical community marveled at Land's innovation, proclaiming that his new invention was as revolutionary as the transition from wet plates to daylight-loading film. This new development was widely reported in the media, with the sepia self-portrait being reproduced in *The New York Times* and *Life* magazine. Although the publicity generated great public demand for the new invention, the first instant-print camera was not marketed until 1948.

The first Polaroid Land camera, the Model 95, was a large, four-pound folding camera. It used a film consisting of two rolls of negative emulsion and positive paper, together with pods of developing chemicals. After a picture was taken, a sixty-second wait was required before the picture could be removed from the camera back, the chemicals could be washed off, and a protective sealer could be manually painted over the image.

In 1950, a new orthochromatic film, which made black and white pictures, was introduced, and Land also added an automatic device for setting exposure time. Throughout the decade, the company released progressively faster film until, by 1960, development time had been reduced to ten seconds. Also during the 1950's, Polaroid expanded its range of cameras for both professional and amateur photographers. In 1958, taking the process even further, Land marketed a separate Polaroid back to fit conventional cameras.

Impact Like George Eastman before him, Edwin Land appealed more to the amateur photographer than to the professional when marketing his instant-print cameras. Although it should be noted that both Kodak and Polaroid made cameras for professional use, a large part of the output of both companies was directed toward the mass market. Eastman, with his first Kodak and the Brownie, had made photography a truly democratic art form. Land, while demonstrating Model 95 at the Royal Photographic

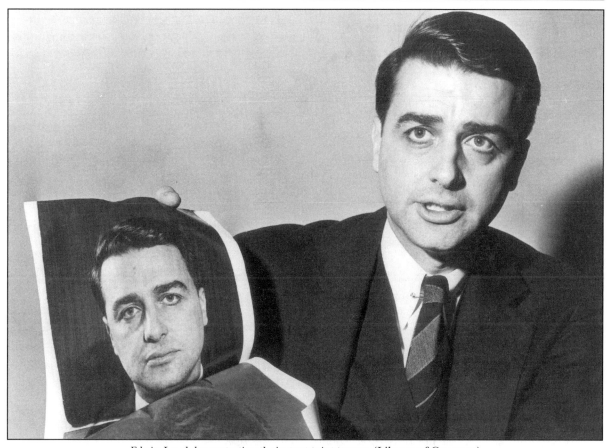

Edwin Land demonstrating the instant-print process. (Library of Congress)

Society in London in 1949, suggested that with his camera, the average amateur could become an aesthetic experimenter, developing creative ideas on the spot, just as a painter or sculptor would. By making it possible for photographers to observe their work and subject matter simultaneously and by removing most of the manipulative barriers between the photographer and the photograph, Land had made it possible for photography to be explored as an art.

Subsequent Events From the beginning, Land worked to develop a color film for his instant print camera. To help finance this research, Polaroid was listed on the New York Stock Exchange in 1957. The first Polacolor film appeared on the market in 1963, along with the Polaroid Land Automatic 100 camera, the first to take film packs rather than picture-rolls. Moreover, in 1972, with the introduction of the SX-70, Land finally made the camera he had visual-

ized during the early 1940's—one that truly made "one-step photography" possible.

Further Reading

Adams, Ansel. *Polaroid Land Photography.* Boston: New York Graphic Society, 1963. Adams demonstrated how instant photography can be a serious creative medium. Well illustrated throughout.

Innovation/Imagination: Fifty Years of Polaroid Photography. New York: Harry N. Abrams, 1999. Details the uses of and changes in Polaroid photography.

Olshaker, Mark. *The Instant Image.* New York: Stein and Day, 1978. A balanced and objective account of Polaroid's evolution.

Orvel, Miles. *American Photography.* New York: Oxford University Press, 2003. Examines the history of American photography in the context of its cultural impacts and its technological advancements.

LouAnn Faris Culley

See also Art movements; Inventions; Photography.

■ Institute of Pacific Relations

Identification Research organization created to
study Asian affairs
Date Founded in 1925

Founded by officials of the Young Men's Christian Associa-
tion (YMCA) to study Far East affairs, the Institute of Pa-
cific Relations (IPR) found itself a key target in the anti-
communist hysteria that swept America during the 1950's.

The purpose of the institute was to study Far East affairs. It was supported by funds from a number of
corporations and major foundations, and it published *Pacific Affairs*, a quarterly journal. One of
its most prominent members was Owen Lattimore,
who served as the editor of *Pacific Affairs* and whom
Republican senator Joseph R. McCarthy identified
in 1950 as the "top Russian espionage agent."

In the spring of 1950, when McCarthy first attacked Lattimore, the IPR was investigated by U.S.
Army Intelligence. Retired Brigadier General Elliott
R. Thorpe testified before a Senate subcommittee
that the IPR "contains within its membership highly
respectable citizens interested in the Pacific basin
and the furthering of peace in that part of the
world." The institute thought that was the end of the
controversy until a schoolteacher discovered some
discarded institute files. Although there was nothing
sinister about the files—the FBI reviewed them—the
schoolteacher believed he had uncovered evidence
of subversion and telephoned McCarthy's Washington, D.C., office, which then passed the files to the
Internal Security Subcommittee for further hearings.

Impact In July, 1951, the Senate's McClellan Committee, which investigated issues related to the Internal Security Act, began hearings on the communist
infiltration of the IPR and its seven semiautonomous
regional centers. The hearings ended in June of
1952 and were released in fifteen parts, with considerable material on the Chinese Communist Party.
The IPR was accused by the McClellan Committee of
being filled with Soviet agents and of placing communist propaganda in textbooks, among other
charges, and it was questioned about its ties with the
China lobby.

The institute's use as a propaganda front to influence U.S. policy in Asia was confirmed by the subcommittee's report (Senate Report 2050) issued

later in 1952. The IPR was unable to survive the relentless barrage of congressional criticism, and the
institute, discredited in the public view, was disbanded.

Further Reading

Akami, Tokomo. *Internationalizing the Pacific.* London: Routledge, 2001. Although focused primarily on the era before the 1950's, gives good background material to understand the importance
of the IPR.

Thomas, John. *Institute of Pacific Relations: Asian*
Scholars and American Politics. Seattle: University of
Washington Press, 1974. Describes the struggles
of the institute during the 1950's.

Martin J. Manning

See also Internal Security Act of 1950; Japan; Mc-
Carthy, Joseph; McClellan Committee.

■ Internal Security Act of 1950

Identification Federal legislation limiting
communist activity in the United States
Date Became law on September 22, 1950

The Internal Security Act, also known as the McCarran
Act, was one of the most controversial products of anticom-
munist hysteria in 1950's America.

By 1950, fear of international communism had swept
the United States as the result of a series of events, including the communist revolution in China, the Soviet Union's acquisition of a nuclear device, and accusations by Wisconsin senator Joseph McCarthy of
communist activity in the United States government. In response to perceived communist threats,
Senator Patrick McCarran introduced legislation in
late 1950 that would require members of the Communist Party of the U.S.A. and other "subversive" organizations to register with the attorney general, bar
members of these organizations from entering the
country, and permit the United States government
to deport or detain known or suspected communists.

The Internal Security Act passed easily through
both houses of Congress. However, President Harry
S. Truman vetoed the bill on September 22, 1950,
citing constitutional protections of free expression
and association and the reputation of the United
States as the standard-bearer for freedom in the
world. Congress overrode Truman's veto by large

margins (248 to 48 in the House, 57 to 10 in the Senate), however, and the act became law.

Impact The Internal Security Act was utilized infrequently during the early 1950's to restrict immigration and prosecute suspected communists. Subsequent court decisions weakened the law, and it was rarely used by the end of the decade. In 1969, a Supreme Court ruling protecting political speech not designed to incite "imminent lawless action" essentially nullified the act. Congress repealed it in 1990.

Further Reading

Fried, Albert. *McCarthyism: The Great American Red Scare.* New York: Oxford University Press, 1997. This documentary history of the McCarthy era examines the Internal Security Act from its passage to its eventual demise.

Schrecker, Ellen. *The Age of McCarthyism: A Brief History with Documents.* 2d ed. New York: Palgrave Macmillan, 2002. Contains numerous relevant primary source documents, including a list of "subversive" organizations and the text of Truman's veto.

Michael H. Burchett

See also Communist Party of the U.S.A.; *Dennis v. United States*; Espionage and Sabotage Act of 1954; Federal Bureau of Investigation; House Committee on Un-American Activities; Immigration and Nationality Act of 1952; Institute of Pacific Relations; Loyalty oaths; McCarthy, Joseph; Rosenberg, Julius and Ethel.

∎ International Business Machines Corporation

Identification American information-processing company

International Business Machines Corporation (IBM) became synonymous with "computer" during the 1950's, when it also joined the list of America's largest industrial corporations with sales of more than one billion dollars.

During World War II, scientists developed a more precise and faster way of calculating the data used to design and operate new weapons and decipher code: the digital electronic computer. By the mid-1950's, IBM had begun its revolution in computer technology and had amassed sixty thousand employees in two hundred offices throughout the world, fifteen hundred patents, and six thousand

different models of business machinery. The company's mainstays were the punch card, sorter, and tabulator machines. These machines automated business accounting systems and scientific calculations.

Products, Research, and Development Made from thousands of vacuum tubes in addition to a variety of IBM's electromechanical data-processing machines and punch cards, the first digital computers were mammoth, weighed a great deal, and occupied several rooms. In 1951, IBM's major competitor Remington Rand introduced the first of these computers for commercial use, the Universal Automatic UNIVAC computer. Nearly two years later, IBM countered with its IBM 701 data processor. Made up of a collection of refrigerator-sized cabinets, the 701 was IBM's first computer with internal, addressable memory. The IBM 702 followed a year later and used magnetic tape memory storage. In 1956, IBM was first to ship a computer hard drive, the IBM 305 Random Access Memory Accounting Machine (RAMAC). The size of two large refrigerators, the IBM 305 RAMAC had a 5-megabyte hard drive costing $10,000 per megabyte.

During the Cold War, the U.S. government pumped money into computer research. The Semi-Automatic Ground Environment (SAGE) was a massive air defense system unveiled in 1956. When fully deployed in 1963, the system consisted of twenty-one centers throughout North America, each with an IBM computer system containing more than 50,000 vacuum tubes, weighing 250 tons, and occupying one acre of floor space. The SAGE was the first large computer network to provide human-machine interaction in "real time." IBM's involvement with SAGE was an important factor leading to its domination of the computer industry.

Other notable achievements for IBM in research and development during this time included the IBM 608, the first all-transistor commercial calculator, in 1957; the development of FORTRAN (FORmula TRANslation), the most widely used scientific programming language, also in 1957; and the first fully automated production line for transistors, in 1959.

Corporate Culture and Monopoly The persona of IBM's founder, Thomas J. Watson, Sr., defined IBM's culture. Watson was famous for his speeches to employees, and his employees sang songs to IBM's greatness. Watson's admonition to "THINK" hung in every hallway of the company. Very early in his ca-

Woman operating an IBM computer during the mid-1950's. (Hulton Archive | by Getty Images)

reer, Watson promoted women to executive-level positions, and in 1953, he published the company's first equal-opportunity-policy letter. In 1952, Watson survived a 1952 antitrust lawsuit filed by the Justice Department. In 1956, IBM settled the case by signing a consent decree, requiring it to sell machines (as opposed to renting exclusively), to allow competitors into the punch card manufacturing business, and to make its patents available. Whether IBM was monopolist was a topic scrutinized by the U.S. government throughout IBM's history and into the 1980's. Watson transferred the title of president to his son Thomas J. Watson, Jr., in 1952, and his son became executive officer of the company in 1956.

Impact When the decade began, IBM had 30,261 employees and $266 million in revenue. By 1959, IBM had grown to 94,912 employees, had $1.3 billion in sales, and ranked thirty-second in *Fortune* magazine's "Directory of the 500 Largest Industrial Corporations," published in 1960. The company's

role in large government and military projects, its highly publicized computer designs, and its overall computer sales made IBM the undisputed leader in the electrical and mechanical industry of the 1950's.

Further Reading

Maney, Kevin. *The Maverick and His Machine: Thomas Watson, Sr., and the Making of IBM.* New York: J. Wiley & Sons, 2003. Explores the role of Watson in creating IBM and transforming the business world.

Tedlow, Richard S. *The Watson Dynasty: The Fiery Reign and Troubled Legacy of IBM's Founding Father and Son.* New York: HarperBusiness, 2003. Examines IBM and the role of its founders during the tenure of the Watson family between 1914 and 1971.

Sheri P. Woodburn

See also Business and the economy in the United States; Computers; ENIAC computer; FORTRAN; Transistors; UNIVAC computer.

■ International Geophysical Year

The Event Year of international scientific cooperation that provided a temporary thaw in the Cold War

Date July 1, 1957, to December 31, 1958

The International Geophysical Year (IGY) 1957-1958 continued a pre-Cold War tradition of international scientific cooperation, resulting in several significant discoveries.

The International Geophysical Year of 1957-1958 was the third major international effort at scientific cooperation of the modern era. The first was instigated by Karl Weyprecht, an officer in the Austro-Hungarian navy who explored the Arctic in 1871. In 1875, Weyprecht suggested the creation of an "International Polar Year" every fifty years, during which many nations would cooperate in polar research. The first successful International Polar Year took place in 1882-1883. Scientists from eleven countries (Austria, Germany, Sweden, Norway, Finland, Holland, the Soviet Union, the United States, Denmark, Great Britian, and France) joined efforts in establishing fourteen stations in the Arctic polar region (but none in Antarctica). The scientific results were presented at the International Polar Conference in Vienna, Austria, in 1884.

Fifty years later, in 1932-1933, during the Second International Polar Year, forty countries participated in gathering scientific observations related to meteorology, magnetism, aurora, and transmission of radio waves in the ionosphere. Lloyd Viel Berkner, who took part in the Second International Polar Year, proposed at the 1952 International Council of Scientific Unions that the third International Polar Year should be moved from 1982 to 1957, primarily because of the projected peak of solar activity in that year.

Broad International Participation Renamed the International Geophysical Year of 1957-1958, the third cooperative effort broadly expanded its focus and its international base, and, in fact, extended well beyond one year. During the preparation of this worldwide event, forty-six nations agreed formally to participate in this effort, and by December of 1958, more than seventy nations had actively participated in the scientific endeavor. For a period of eighteen months, thousands of scientists gathered data about the earth's interior, oceans, crust, and atmosphere, and the Sun's activity in relation to Earth. U.S. participation in the IGY included research projects in aurora and airglow, cosmic rays, geomagnetism, glaciology, gravity, the ionosphere, latitude and longitude determinations, meteorology, oceanography, seismology, solar activity, and rocket and satellite studies of the upper atmosphere.

During the IGY, twelve countries installed forty-eight bases in Antarctica. The United States built McMurdo, the largest of all American bases, located on the Ross Ice Shelf; the Amundsen-Scott base at the South Pole; and Byrd base in Mary Byrd Land. The Soviet Union constructed Vostok near the Geomagnetic South Pole, at the center of the East Antarctic Ice Sheet, and Mirny, named after a historic expedition ship. France constructed the Dumont d'Urville base in Adélie Land and the Charcot base about two hundred miles inland. This base was devoted to the study of glaciology, and three French glaciologists, including the famous Claude Lorius, spent the entire eighteen months making observations that changed the understanding of glaciology in the areas of ice movement, temperature, age, and mass balance.

Scientific Results The IGY is credited with two important discoveries: the identification of the Van Allen radiation belts and confirmation of the existence of a 64,000-kilometer-long, mid-oceanic ridge.

On October 4, 1957, the Soviet Union launched *Sputnik I*, the first artificial satellite to orbit Earth; on January 31, 1958, the United States launched *Explorer I*, the first successful American satellite. Based on the data received from the scientific instruments on these satellites, Fred Singer, Paul Kellogg, and the Soviet S. N. Vernov identified the magnetic radiation belts, located in a region above the equator and produced by cosmic radiation. They were named after James Van Allen, the principal investigator of the program.

The discovery of mid-oceanic ridges confirmed the theory of continental drift and provided the basis for the later development of plate tectonics. This discovery, produced by an extensive and coordinated sequence of oceanographic voyages, was accompanied by other substantial findings about the flow of deep ocean currents and the seasonal fluctuations of sea level. Scientists discovered that sea level is about one foot higher in the summer and the fall than in the spring and winter.

Nations Formally Participating in the International Geophysical Year

Argentina	Ireland
Australia	Israel
Austria	Italy
Belgium	Japan
Bolivia	Mexico
Brazil	Morocco
Bulgaria	Netherlands
Canada	New Zealand
Chile	Norway
China, People's	Pakistan
Republic of	Peru
Colombia	Philippines
Czechoslovakia	Poland
Denmark	Portugal
Finland	Romania
France	South Africa, Union of
German Democratic	Soviet Union
Republic	Spain
German Federal	Sweden
Republic	Switzerland
Great Britain	Tunisia
Greece	United States
Hungary	Uruguay
Iceland	Yugoslavia
India	

Scientists took advantage of the peak in solar activity in 1957—one of the reasons Berkner had suggested that the third international year be scheduled for that year—to study the lifetime of sunspots, their effects on seasonal weather, and their effects on radio communications and navigational systems. In the area of meteorology, nearly sixty weather stations were established in the Antarctic and the sub-Antarctic waters. These stations filled an enormous gap in the number of meteorological stations in the Southern Hemisphere. By launching balloons equipped with weather instruments capable of radioing back to Earth information on temperature, atmospheric pressure, humidity, winds, and structure of the atmosphere, these stations dramatically increased the ability to understand and predict weather patterns. Other meteorological stations were placed along three meridians, and these stations targeted atmospheric circulation and the jet streams.

Impact The IGY produced a wide range of cooperative scientific endeavors, many of which could never have been envisioned in a tense world where the Cold War had made international cooperation difficult or impossible. Resulting from the vision of Karl Weyprecht seventy-five years before, it reminded the scientific community of the vast potential of a collaborative quest for knowledge.

Further Reading

Eklund, Carl R., and Joan Beckman. *Antarctica: Polar Research and Discovery During the International Geophysical Year.* New York: Holt, Rinehart and Winston, 1963. A description of the extraordinary achievements of the IGY.

Fraser, Ronald. *Once Around the Sun: The Story of the International Geophysical Year, 1957-1958.* 2d ed. London: Hodder and Stoughton, 1959. Details the solar discoveries of the IGY.

Hyde, Margaret O. *Exploring Earth and Space.* New York: McGraw-Hill, 1958. Examines the the spatial and terrestrial exploration that occurred during the IGY.

Stuster, Jack. *Bold Endeavors: Lessons from Polar and Space Exploration.* Annapolis, Md.: Naval Institute Press, 1996. Takes a behavioral science perspective and examines how humans adjust and perform in long-term isolation, such as that found on spacecraft. Provides good context for several notable expeditions since the nineteenth century.

Wilson, J. Tuzo. *IGY, The Year of the New Moons.* New York: Alfred A. Knopf, 1961. A Canadian geophysicist explains the spatial discoveries of the IGY.

Denyse Lemaire

See also Antarctic Treaty of 1959; Astronomy; National Aeronautics and Space Administration; Science and technology; Space race; *Sputnik I*; Van Allen radiation belts.

■ International trade of Canada

Canada has long been one of the major trading partners of the United States, and its relationship with the United States has often uneasy, but generally the two countries have benefited.

The earliest instance of Canadian trade was probably in 1497, when John Cabot and his sons claimed the Grand Banks and Newfoundland for Great Britain during the reign of Henry VII. Samuel de Champlain established the first settlement in North America (Annapolis on Bay of Fundy) in 1604 but moved the settlement to Quebec in 1608 when he established French sovereignty over the St. Lawrence drainage basin. A growing conflict between French fur traders and missionaries and British settlers created tensions that became part of European dynastic struggles as more British settlements were founded along the Atlantic seaboard, beginning with Jamestown, Virginia, in 1607, and Plymouth, Massachusetts, in 1620. During the eighteenth century, tensions mounted between colonies and different economic interests as Britain and France, two major economic powers, developed full-fledged mercantilist trade and industrial policies to govern their overseas economic interests.

On July 1, 1867, Ontario, Quebec, New Brunswick, and Nova Scotia formed a new confederation, in part to ease trade among themselves and to offset negative effects of increased barriers to the U.S. market. Parliament adopted the first Canadian tariff legislation and raised protection in the Maritime colonies. In 1892, the Conservative minister of trade and commerce Richard Cartwright established the Trade Commissioner Service to promote Canadian exports, to find new export markets, to negotiate trade agreements, and to provide services to Canadian exporters. The 1913 Underwood Tariff in the United States lowered many American tariffs on imports from Canada.

World Wars Era World War I disrupted Canada's normal trade relations, as revenues were needed to engage in war and the government looked to an increasingly diverse range of taxes. During World War II, trade policy played a role subordinate to broader strategic and security concerns. The United States, Great Britain, and Canada worked closely together to structure postwar political and economic multilateral institutions, including institutions to address international trade and monetary problems. Between 1947 and 1948, Canada and the United States initiated, but did not conclude, negotiations toward a bilateral free trade agreement (FTA). The United States promoted necessary amendments to include FTAs in the General Agreement on Tariffs and Trade (GATT), with provisions governing regional agreements. On January 1, 1948, GATT was enacted by Canada, the United States, and Britain,

among others, on the basis of the Protocol of Provisional Application which, by its extensive grandfather provisions, allowed members to bring GATT into force without seeking specific enabling legislation.

Postwar Years The 1950's saw a relative openness of the U.S. market and continuing difficulty in accessing British, European, and other markets as a result of currency restrictions and balance-of-payments forces. These and other forms of protection led to growth of deeper Canada-U.S. trade and investment links. In 1950 and 1951, GATT held its third tariff negotiating conference in Torquay, England, which expanded membership to thirty-three nations. Canada invited members to hold the next round in Toronto the following year, but it was never held because of the failure of the United States to gain negotiating authority. Also in 1951, France, Germany, Italy, Belgium, Luxembourg, and the Netherlands agreed to establish a European Coal and Steel Community (ECSC) to help address problems of trade and industrialization among participants; the ruling Labour government in Britain nationalized the steel industry and kept it out of the ECSC.

On November 12, 1953, an exchange of notes established a Joint U.S.-Canadian Committee on Trade and Economic Affairs as a permanent mechanism to consider economic and trade problems important to relations between the two countries. The committee met once a year, with the site alternating between Ottawa and Washington, D.C. The first meeting was held in Washington on March 16, 1954; the second meeting took place in Ottawa on September 26, 1955. Throughout the 1950's, these meetings focused on topics such as domestic economic developments in both countries, Canadian concerns that U.S. trade programs would displace Canada's efforts in traditional world markets, U.S. private investment policies in Canada, U.S. surplus disposal policies, and certain trade restrictions on goods as diverse as magazines and fruits and vegetables.

In 1955, the United States successfully engineered an open-ended waiver from its GATT obligations for its quotas and other restrictions covering most of its agricultural sector; the result set a precedent that made it increasingly difficult to introduce discipline on world trade in agriculture. Canada was one of few countries that protested this development. When GATT held its fourth tariff negotiating conference in 1956, it consolidated the tariff schedules of its thirty-five members, including Canada. With the subsequent Review Session of Contracting Parties, GATT was placed on more permanent footing by an agreement that tariff bindings would no longer be time-bound.

In 1957, the Royal Commission on Canada's Economic Prospects, chaired by Walter Gordon, warned of Canada's increasing dependence on U.S. foreign investment. John Young's study for the commission emphasized the high cost of protection to the Canadian economy. That same year, there was a new Conservative government in Canada, under Prime Minister John Diefenbaker, which wanted to shift trade from the United States to Britain and the Commonwealth dominions, but it failed to take any concrete measures to bring this about.

In July, 1958, U.S. president Dwight D. Eisenhower and his secretary of state, John Foster Dulles, made an informal visit to Canada. In his address to the Canadian Houses of Parliament, the president spoke about U.S.-Canadian trade relations, discussing U.S. surplus wheat disposal policies, the imbalance in U.S.-Canada trade relations, and U.S. private investment in Canada. At the end, he reassured his audience that the United States would continue its reciprocal trade program.

In October, 1958, an international group of academic economists, led by Gottfried Haberler of Harvard University, submitted their report to GATT, *Trends in International Trade: Report by a Panel of Experts*, which provided an intellectual basis for a series of GATT initiatives. It recognized that GATT had reached the end of postwar reconstruction, that currencies were now convertible, and that it was time to address three major problems within the trading system: the organization of a new round with a mandate to tackle tariffs seriously on a horizontal rather than item-by-item basis, the mounting problem of trade in agriculture, and the emerging problem of developing countries. During the same year, the Diefenbaker government killed the Canadian-led Avro Arrow defense project and entered into Defense Production Sharing Arrangements (DPSAs) with the United States to meet Canadian defense and industrial objectives. At the end of the 1950's, after a decade of enthusiastic support for GATT, with often disappointing results, Canada exhibited a subtler approach to GATT membership on its own policy formation.

Ships loaded with Canadian grain for export in Quebec's Montreal Harbour, around 1950. Throughout the twentieth century, Canada was one of the world's leading producers of wheat, and during the early 1950's, it exported more wheat than the United States. (Hulton Archive | by Getty Images)

Impact The successful trade policies of the 1950's, initiated by the disruptions of World War II, put Canadian trade on a successful course that was maintained through succeeding decades, thanks to the support of bilateral agreements with new trading partners that diversified Canada's trade relations. Canada has historically benefited from its long-standing reliance on trade with other countries, particularly with the United States, the world's largest market. However, these close trade ties with the United States have also tied Canada to the ups and downs in the U.S. economy. Canada is also the largest trading partner of the United States—in both exports and imports. Canada's impact on U.S. markets is substantially greater than its impact on the global economy.

Subsequent Events In 1967, Paul and Ronald J. Wonnacott published their pioneering study of benefits of free trade between Canada and United States, *Free Trade Between the United States and Canada: The Potential Economic Effects.* In 1975, the Economic Council of Canada released the report *Looking Outward: A New Trade Strategy for Canada,* which recommended that Canada and the United States negotiate a bilateral free trade agreement. By the 1980's, a global recession hit Canada particularly hard, which led to a broad reevaluation of interventionist economic and industrial policies.

Throughout the 1990's, the United States and Canada expanded their FTA to include Mexico, beginning with implementation of the North American Free Trade Agreement (NAFTA), which entered into force in January, 1994, following protracted ratification procedures in the United States and Canada. In 1995, government leaders of members of Asia Pacific Economic Cooperation (APEC), including the United States, Canada, Japan, Australia, and members of the Association of South East Asian Nations (ASEAN), agreed to work toward a process of coordinating unilateral trade liberalization with a broad goal of achieving tariff-free trade for industrialized participants by the year 2010 and for developing participants by 2020.

Further Reading

Hart, Michael. *A Trading Nation: Canadian Trade Policy from Colonialism to Globalization.* Vancouver, B.C.: UBC Press, 2002. A scholarly, well-researched book; many readers will find the chronology, dating back to 1497, particularly useful.

Muirhead, B. W. *The Development of Postwar Canadian Trade Policy: The Failure of the Anglo-European Option.* Montreal: McGill-Queen's University Press, 1992. Focus is on the complex relationship between Canada and the British Commonwealth.

Stovel, John A. *Canada in the World Economy.* Cambridge, Mass.: Harvard University Press, 1959. A more general overview which places trade policy in context.

Martin J. Manning

See also Agriculture in Canada; Business and the economy in Canada; Canada and Great Britain; Canada and U.S. investments; Continentalism; Diefenbaker, John G.; Gross national product of Canada; Inflation in Canada; International trade of the United States.

■ International trade of the United States

During the 1950's, U.S. economic and trade policies were intimately tied to U.S. efforts both to minimize Soviet influence abroad and to protect its own interests in an increasingly free-market, interdependent world.

U.S. foreign trade and global economic policies have changed direction dramatically since the nation's founding. During the early days of the nation's history, government and business mostly concentrated on developing the domestic economy irrespective of what went on abroad. During the late eighteenth century, U.S. treasury secretary Alexander Hamilton advocated a protective tariff to encourage American industrial development, a stance the country largely followed. On July 31, 1789, a collection of customs revenue was established when the Tariff Act became effective. By the end of the War of 1812, Americans had witnessed the growth of a market economy over the previous twenty-five years, and a U.S. economy, based both on farming and on commerce, was firmly established.

The U.S. Civil War and its aftermath reinforced the economic disparities between the North and South in their labor forces and their industrial resources. The Spanish-American War in 1898 and World War I stimulated further economic development. World War I initially cost the United States government about $33 billion plus interest, but rather than hurting the domestic economy, the war effort strengthened and improved the United States' competitive position in the world. Farmers enjoyed boom years as agricultural prices rose, and the international market for their products expanded. Real wages for blue-collar workers increased modestly, and all sectors profited from the war.

An important turning point in U.S. trade policy came when the Underwood-Simmons Act of 1913 sharply lowered American tariffs from an average of 19.3 percent on dutiable and free imports under the Payne-Aldrich Tariff of 1895 to 9.1 percent in 1916, the year the U.S. Tariff Commission was created by an act of Congress as an independent, fact-finding agency of the U.S. government to study the effects of tariffs and other restraints to trade on the U.S. economy. When the Republicans returned to power in 1921, the Fordney-McCumber Tariff raised tariff rates again. In 1934, the first Reciprocal Trade Agreements Act (RTAA) was passed; it was later extended by further acts of Congress until all of the bills were superseded by the Trade Expansion Act of 1962. These acts provided authority for the U.S. president to reduce tariffs through both bilateral negotiations and multilateral negotiations under the General Agreement on Tariffs and Trade (GATT). GATT was finalized in Geneva, Switzerland, in 1947; it was the first successful postwar, multilateral codification of free trade principles. Also in 1947, the Marshall Plan was created to provide reconstruction assistance to European countries devastated by the war; among its guidelines were terms of renewed trade favorable to U.S. corporations.

Cold War Beginnings By 1950, the success of the Marshall Plan allowed Europeans to resume domestic production and trade with the United States on a greater basis than before the war. The Soviet Union, which rejected Marshall Plan funds, created an economic bloc that it closed to U.S. trade. The 1950's also experienced a relative openness of the U.S. market and continuing difficulty in accessing European and other markets as a result of currency restrictions, balance-of-payments measures, and other forms of protection that led to growth of deeper Canada-U.S. trade and investment links.

The postwar years of the 1950's began with two 1951 pieces of legislation: the Battle Act, also called the Mutual Defense Assistance Control Act, which allowed the president to prohibit exports of strategic goods to communist countries and to terminate aid to countries that did not go along with the American restrictions; and the Trade Agreements Extension Act of 1951, which renewed the president's authority to negotiate trade agreements under the RTAA with the stipulation that all tariff concessions previously granted by the RTAA to the Soviet Union and to other communist-bloc countries be withdrawn.

The third round of GATT trade negotiations was held in Torquay, Great Britain, in 1950-1951; it achieved 8,700 tariff cuts. In 1952, the Agreement on the Importation of Educational, Scientific, and Cultural Materials, also called the Florence Agreement, entered into force, followed two years later by the Agricultural Trade Development and Assistance Act of 1954, which promoted the foreign distribution of U.S. agricultural products.

For the incoming Dwight D. Eisenhower administration, there was concern that the United States was consistently running an export surplus that created an overly favorable balance of trade. For economic defense, trade controls focused on retarding the buildup of Soviet strength and assisting underdeveloped countries in order to counteract the appeal of the Soviet system. This approach manifested itself in the last year of President Harry S. Truman's administration as the allies of the United States became more restive, when the Korean War ended, with the restrictions imposed on them by the Battle Act.

When the Eisenhower administration came to office, a major reassessment of East-West trade policy was undertaken "to switch from discouraging to encouraging trade," as Secretary of State John Foster Dulles noted. President Eisenhower warned his senior advisers not to "forget that we are trying to induce the satellites to come over to our side by judicious use of trade." He believed that trade overtures could be used to drive a wedge between the Soviet Union and its satellites and that special trade exemptions should be continued for communist countries, such as Yugoslavia, that displayed a degree of independence from the Soviet Union. In 1953, as the U.S. economy slipped into a recession, Eisenhower's first priority was renewal of the RTAA, set to expire that June.

Relations with Canada On November 12, 1953, an exchange of notes established a Joint U.S.-Canadian Committee on Trade and Economic Affairs as a permanent mechanism to consider economic and trade problems important to relations between the two countries. The committee met once a year; the first meeting was held in Washington, D.C., on March 16,

1954, and the second meeting took place in Ottawa on September 26, 1955. Throughout the 1950's, these meetings focused on topics such as domestic economic developments in both countries, Canadian concerns that U.S. trade programs would displace Canada's efforts in traditional world markets, U.S. private investment policies in Canada, an apparent advocacy of a shift of 15 percent in trade away from the United States, U.S. surplus disposal policies, and certain trade restrictions on goods as diverse as magazines and agricultural produce. In July, 1958, President Eisenhower and Dulles made an informal visit to Canada. In his address to the Canadian Houses of Parliament, the president spoke about U.S.-Canadian trade relations, discussing U.S. surplus wheat disposal policies, the imbalance in U.S.-Canada trade relations, and U.S. private investment in Canada. At the end, he reassured his audience that the United States would continue its reciprocal trade program.

Study Commissions In September, 1953, the president obtained congressional approval to establish the Commission on Foreign Economic Policy, headed by Clarence Randall, to study all aspects of American trade policy and to recommend policy changes. These studies focused on issues such as an East-West trade policy coordinated with CoCom (Coordinating Committee for Multilateral Export Controls), strengthened strategic trade controls, and potential trade in peaceful goods, especially since the Soviet Union was a source of vital raw materials. President Eisenhower accepted the commission's findings and asked Congress for a three-year renewal of the RTAA in March, 1954; he was granted only one year. In September, 1954, Eisenhower established the Interagency Committee on Agricultural Surplus Disposal to coordinate the administration of Public Law 480. The committee, headed by Clarence Francis, consisted of officials from the Departments of Agriculture, Commerce, the Treasury, and State; the International Cooperation Administration; and the Bureau of the Budget.

Congressional and Presidential Proposals In 1955, the United States successfully engineered an open-ended waiver from its GATT obligations for its quota limits and other restrictions covering most of its agricultural sector; the result set a precedent that made it increasingly difficult to introduce discipline on world trade in agriculture. That same year, Congress

voted for a three-year renewal after lengthy debate and opposition from the textile industry, which was upset by rapidly expanding Japanese textile sales in the United States and by the U.S. government's sale of surplus American cotton in foreign markets at cut-rate prices. In 1957, congressional protectionists fought the president again when Eisenhower asked for the 1958 RTAA renewal to be extended five years; after a bitter fight, he got four years.

In his 1958 state of the union address, Eisenhower proposed extending the Trade Agreements Act with broadened renegotiating authority for five years. The president elaborated on his suggestion in his 1959 budget recommendations to Congress. He also proposed that Titles I and II of the Agricultural Trade Development and Assistance Act of 1954 be extended for one year and that authorization for sales of surplus agricultural commodities for foreign currencies be increased from $4 to $5.5 billion; Congress gave him a two-year extension and $7.5 billion. Eisenhower's proposals were discussed in January, 1958, in connection with legislation to extend the Reciprocal Trade Act. The president also recommended an extension of the Export Control Act, amendment of certain provisions pertaining to customs administration of the Tariff Act of 1930, and additions to the Antidumping Act of 1921.

On January 14, 1959, before the Senate Foreign Relations Committee, Dulles testified about the basic principles underlying U.S. foreign policy. For economic progress, he noted that "our trade and financial policies continue to promote recognition and positive use of the benefits of interdependence." A week later, the Committee on World Economic Practices, chaired by Harold Boeschenstein, submitted to the White House its report on a combined governmental and private enterprise program to counter the Sino-Soviet bloc offensive through an expanding Free World economic system. Section V dealt with trade and transportation.

Impact Following the Great Depression and World War II, the United States generally sought to reduce trade barriers and coordinate the world economic system. This commitment to free trade had both economic and political roots as the United States increasingly came to view open trade not only as a means of advancing its own economic interests but also as a key to building peaceful relations among nations.

Further Reading

Jackson, John H. *The World Trading System: Law and Policy of International Economic Relations.* 2d ed. Cambridge, Mass.: MIT Press, 1997. The broader discussion of the world trade system includes good background information on the 1950's trade situation.

Rothgeb, John M. *U.S. Trade Policy: Balancing Economic Dreams and Political Realities.* Washington, D.C.: Congressional Quarterly Press, 2001. Chapter 5 has a substantial discussion of 1950's trade policies, and the book's bibliography includes a good section on U.S. trade policy during the 1950's.

U.S. Department of State. *Foreign Relations of the United States.* Washington, D.C.: Office of the Historian, U.S. Department of State, 1983-1992. Serves as the official record of U.S. trade policy during the 1950's. Pertinent volumes include 1952-1954 (General: Economic and Political Matters), 1955-1957 (Foreign Economic Policy; Foreign Information Program), and 1958-1960 (Foreign Economic Policy). Essential to any study of U.S. trade policy in the 1950's as it provides time lines for major economic developments.

Martin J. Manning

See also Agriculture in the United States; Canada and U.S. investments; Food for Peace; Foreign policy of the United States; Gross national product of the United States; International trade of Canada; Japan; Latin America; Mexico.

■ Interracial marriage laws

Definition State laws banning interracial marriages with the goal of keeping the "races" separate and identifiable; such laws made a marriage that was legal in some states a criminal act in others

The existence and legal challenge of interracial marriage laws helped bring race relations and their inherent inequality to the forefront of the American conscience.

Laws preventing marriages between white and nonwhite people date back to the colonial period, appearing in colonial statutes in the late seventeenth century. In 1950, approximately thirty states still had such laws. While nearly all states of the South had such laws, many northern and western states also still carried them. No uniform definitions of what constituted a "white" or "nonwhite" person existed and

standards varied from state to state. Interracial marriage laws usually specifically banned marriage between a white person and a person of the opposite sex with at least one black great-grandparent.

While most such laws were specifically aimed at black-white couples, marriages between whites and other nonwhites such as Asians, Native Americans, and Hispanics were also affected by such laws, although enforcement in such cases tended to be less stringent. State laws varied considerably. On one extreme was Virginia, with a 1922 law that made being married itself a crime for black and white couples, regardless of where the marriage occurred. Other states simply refused to issue marriage licenses to couples of different races but did nothing officially against couples married in other states.

Fears and Underlying Values Interracial marriage laws reflected white society's fears of miscegenation and were specifically aimed at preventing sexual relationships between white women and black men. Sexual relationships between white men and nonwhite women were often tolerated if kept discreet and if such couples did not seek legal sanction. Many of the states with anti-interracial marriage laws also had laws that defined any sexual contact between black men and white women as rape, regardless of the circumstances. In a society that depended in part on easily definable categories of "race," children of such unions presented problems that laws against interracial marriage attempted to prevent.

The Beginning of the End The end of anti-interracial marriage laws began with the marriage of Richard Loving, who was white, and Mildred Jeter, who was black, in 1958. Unable to wed in their native Virginia, the couple wed in Washington, D.C. Upon their return to Virginia as a married couple, they were arrested and faced up to five years in prison for breaking the Virginia law. Under a plea, the couple agreed to leave the state and not return for twenty-five years. They then moved to Washington; in 1963, they began a court action against Virginia. Their suit eventually reached the U.S. Supreme Court, which ruled in 1967, in *Loving v. Virginia*, that state laws banning interracial marriages were unconstitutional. At the time, some sixteen states still had such laws; many states had been repealing them in the two decades before the Supreme Court ruling. By the end of the 1950's, an estimated 51,000 mixed black and white marriages existed in the

United States, compared to almost a half a million by the end of the twentieth century.

Impact Interracial marriage laws were but one form of overt racism that propelled America's race relations into the spotlight during the 1950's. Such laws could not prevent interracial marriages among committed couples, who traveled to states without such restrictions to marry. However, these laws did force interracial couples to choose their state of residence carefully and made travel in states with such laws problematic. Official disapproval of such marriages limited their acceptance, and the numbers of interracial marriages only began to swell after such laws were nullified by the Supreme Court, a milestone in the Civil Rights movement. During the late twentieth and early twenty-first century, the earlier existence of such laws and their eventual removal would serve as a legal precedent for Americans who sought to legalize same-sex marriages.

Further Reading

Gay, Kathlyn. *The Rainbow Effect: Interracial Families.* Danbury, Conn.: Grolier, 1987. Sociological study of interracial marriages, with emphasis on the children of such marriages and their complex racial identity.

McNamara, Robert P., Maria Tempenis, and Beth Walton. *Crossing the Line: Interracial Couples in the South.* Westport, Conn.: Greenwood Press, 1999. A scholarly sociological and historical study of interracial marriages.

Moran, Rachel F. *Interracial Intimacy: The Regulation of Race and Romance.* Chicago: University of Chicago Press, 2001. Argues that historically, laws against interracial marriage sought to buttress white privilege. Although such laws no longer exist, racism makes same-race marriages the norm, with Asian American men and African American women bearing the brunt of restricted marriage opportunities.

Robinson, Charles Frank, II. *Dangerous Liaisons: Sex and Love in the Segregated South.* Fayetteville: University of Arkansas Press, 2003. Scholarly study of interracial couples, often unmarried, in the American South throughout history.

Barry M. Stentiford

See also African Americans; Asian Americans; *Brown v. Board of Education*; Civil Rights Act of 1957; Civil Rights movement; Jewish Americans; Latinos; Racial discrimination.

■ Interstate highway system

Definition National system of limited access roads built to facilitate movement across the country
Date Enabling act passed in Congress on June 26, 1956

Interstate highways allowed much faster movement across the country, facilitated vacations, allowed the creation of suburbs, and helped devastate the inner cities.

The highway system of the United States developed slowly. By the 1920's, despite the invention of the automobile some twenty years prior, no system of well developed and paved roads had yet developed. It might take someone in an automobile five days to travel one hundred miles, and newspapers published guides to day trips that in today's automobiles would take less than two hours. Cars of that era had frequent breakdowns, and tires were touted if they lasted four thousand miles, while roads frequently were made of dirt. The 1920's saw some attention to these issues, and the first paved roads were made linking cities. These roads ran from town to town, and thus travelers encountered stoplights in each town through which they ventured. Moreover, the roads were not overly straight or direct, making vehicle trips time-consuming.

During the 1920's, the first attempt was made to create highways that would link major cities. In 1925, Congress passed the first legislation to create an interstate highway system across America. However, this system was slow to develop and was hindered by the Great Depression. The Works Progress Administration (WPA) helped complete some segments of the highways. One of the most famous routes developed was Route 66, immortalized in the Nat King Cole song "(Get Your Kicks On) Route 66." This road was not fully finished and paved, however, until 1938. The highways were used as travel routes by the many who migrated for jobs during the Great Depression, and those who could afford to used it for vacations during the 1920's and 1930's. The roads, however, were crumbling by the end of the 1940's, as little had been done to maintain them during World War II. The nation came to realize the need for a higher-capacity highway system that would serve the growing needs of a burgeoning population.

During the 1930's, President Franklin D. Roosevelt had called for national toll roads to be built to support greater traffic. In 1938, Congress had paid for a national study of the issue. This report held that toll roads would not be self-supporting but that a system of nontoll roads would be beneficial. This nontoll system was popularized by the General Motors Futurama display at the 1939 World's Fair, which suggested that fourteen-lane roads be built with radio beams separating the cars, and that cars should be able to travel up to 100 miles per hour.

Government Support The federal government was the impetus behind the creation of the interstate system, and President Dwight D. Eisenhower championed the cause. Eisenhower remembered being a young army officer moving his troops from one side of the United States to the other and the inordinate length of time involved in that trip. During World War II, he had also seen the wonderful German *Autobahn* system. His own negative experience with the American system and positive experience with a foreign system led him to believe that a new system of highways was sorely needed, and in his years before and during his presidency, he campaigned for a better highway system. Eisenhower believed that there was a huge amount of congestion caused by the lack of good highways and that many deaths and injuries resulted from the lack of good roads.

Eisenhower had advocates in his search for a better highway system. Among the congressmen who were vital in their support of the bill were Senator Albert Gore, Sr., and representatives George H. Fallon and Hale Boggs. There were also private individuals and cabinet officials who supported the program. These people included Francis V. DuPont and Charles Curtiss, who both worked for the Bureau of Public Roads, and Charles E. Wilson, secretary of defense, who formerly had been the leader of General Motors. Thus, President Eisenhower, cabinet officials, private individuals, and the U.S. Congress all were in favor of better interstate highways.

Factors Precipitating the Interstate System At the start of the 1950's, the U.S. interstate highway system was inadequate, largely as a result of the rise of the suburbs. After World War II, many Americans moved out of the cities to buy a suburban house with a backyard. However, most working-age Americans still needed to commute into the city for their jobs, a task that proved time-consuming on antiquated highways. However, if one could access a highway and drive fifty or sixty miles an hour to work, commute times could be cut in half, enabling people to live twice as far away from work. One of the first suburbs to be developed in the United States was Levittown, on Long Island, New York. Levittown and similar suburbs used mass-production techniques to cut costs, which made the suburbs even more affordable and available. Federal housing aid, in the form of low-cost mortgages, also made the suburbs accessible to Americans. Suburbia, therefore, was at the heart of an increased demand for the highways.

The postwar affluence in the United States and the population's concomitant love of cars played an important role in the rise of the highway system. In the years between 1945 and 1960, the per-capita income of the average American increased 20 percent, even accounting for inflation. Many people invested a portion of their surplus income in an automobile or in a second automobile. Moreover, the growing power of labor unions affected workers' salaries. Many unions managed to negotiate "escalator" clauses into their contracts so that their wages would grow every year of the contract, making life better for union members and decreasing the number of strikes. In the long run, this made some American industries less competitive, but it also increased the paychecks of many union workers, enabling their purchase of more automobiles.

Many believed that the poor road system also held back the national economy by hindering the transportation of goods. People also wanted to travel more on the roadways, and the 1950's saw the origination of theme parks, such as Disneyland, as national leisure destinations. Perhaps most important, the desire for better national defense led many to believe that American roads had to be improved. The 1950's experienced the height of the Cold War and widely held fears of an imminent Soviet attack. Eisenhower firmly believed that the United States needed good roads to move troops quickly. Others argued for a system of interstates to allow cities to be evacuated in the case of a nuclear attack.

The Interstate System Becomes Reality After considerable debate over the apportionment of the funding between the federal government and the states, as well as several congressional amendments, the National Interstate and Defense Highways Act of 1956 was passed on June 26, 1956, in the U.S. Congress. In the act, the interstate system was expanded to 41,000 miles, and to construct the network, $25 billion—or approximately 90 percent of the construction costs—was authorized for fiscal years 1957 through 1969. The other costs and upkeep of the system were left to the state governments, typically funded via an increase in taxes on such things as gasoline; it is a structure still in existence. The act commenced what would prove to be the biggest public works project in the nation's history.

Impact The interstate highway system had three main effects on America. The first was that it allowed the continuation and expansion of the suburbs. With highways, suburbs were able to expand, and people moved farther from city centers. The highways also cemented America as a car culture. Americans have used motor transportation for both business and pleasure purposes; had the interstate highway system not been built, a more effective mass transportation infrastructure would have to have been created. The interstate highway system also generally contributed to a decline of America's cities. Most of the middle and upper classes moved out to the suburbs, a process that devastated home values and led to a decline in both the revenues of the cities and the quality of the school systems, an unfortunate and unforeseen consequence of the interstate highway system.

Further Reading

Daniels, George H., and Mark H. Rose, eds. *Energy and Transport: Historical Perspectives on Policy Issues.* Beverly Hills, Calif.: Sage Publications, 1982. Examines historical components of energy and transportation issues.

Dilger, Robert Jay. *American Transportation Policy.* Westport, Conn.: Praeger, 2003. Examines why the United States has failed to develop a coordinated national transportation policy, focusing especially on political issues. It examines highways, railroads, and airports.

Kaszynski, William. *The American Highway: The History and Culture of Roads in the United States.* Jefferson, N.C.: McFarland, 2000. Provides a pictorial and analytical look at the development of the American highway system. Also explores the related development of roadside restaurants, hotels, and gas stations.

Lewis, Tom. *Divided Highways: Building the Interstate Highways, Transforming American Life.* New York: Penguin, 1999. This work discusses how the building of the American freeway system changed America, particularly by moving people who were in the highway's path, destroying their neighborhoods, and creating the suburbs.

Rose, Mark H. *Interstate: Express Highway Politics, 1939-1989.* Knoxville: University of Tennessee Press, 1990. Explores the political considerations and landscape that brought about the interstate highway system.

Scott A. Merriman

See also Automobiles and auto manufacturing; Chevrolet Corvette; Edsel; Eisenhower, Dwight D.; Ford Thunderbird; Holiday Inn; Levittown; Motels; Trans-Canada Highway; Volkswagen.

■ Invasion of the Body Snatchers

Identification Science-fiction film about the takeover of a California town by alien life-forms
Director Don Siegel (1912-1991)
Date Released in 1956

A provocative story line and relentless pacing made this low-budget film one of the best science-fiction and horror productions of the 1950's.

Based on a novel by Jack Finney, *Invasion of the Body Snatchers* opens as a hysterical Dr. Bennell (played by Kevin McCarthy) tries to convince police in San Francisco that his town of Santa Mira has been taken over by aliens. When another doctor agrees to listen, Bennell's story unfolds as a flashback.

Bennell notices that his patients complain of changes in loved ones so profound that they no longer seemed to be the same people. However, a day later, many assure Bennell that they had been mistaken. One night his friend finds a body in his house, a body that resembles him but that seems "unfinished." The film's characters realize that the residents of Santa Mira are being replaced by replicas growing in the giant pods of alien plants and that those so replaced are aiding the invasion. The process occurs while humans are sleeping, so Bennell struggles to stay awake and get word to the outside world.

Impact *Invasion of the Body Snatchers* alarming theme struck a chord with audiences, leading commentators to suggest that it played upon national anxieties that were emerging over external aggression and internal subversion and served as an apt metaphor for Cold War paranoia.

Further Reading

Biskind, Peter. "The Mind Managers: *Invasion of the Body Snatchers* and the Paranoid Style in American Movies." In *Seeing Is Believing: How Hollywood Taught Us to Stop Worrying and Love the Fifties.* Rev. ed. New York: Pantheon Books, 2000. Biskind interprets the film as reflecting the strained ideological atmosphere of the 1950's.

McCarthy, Kevin, and Ed Gorman, eds. *"They're Here . . . " "Invasion of the Body Snatchers": A Tribute.* New York: Berkley Boulevard Books, 1999. Co-edited by the star of the film, this volume includes essays and interviews with key figures from the film.

Grove Koger

See also Conformity, culture of; *Creature from the Black Lagoon*; *Day the Earth Stood Still, The*; Drive-in theaters; Film in the United States; Flying saucers; *Forbidden Planet*; *Thing from Another World, The*; War of the Worlds, The.

■ Inventions

Judged by the number of patents granted during the 1950's, the pace of invention, compared with preceding and succeeding decades, slowed slightly during the decade; however, the impact of the decade's inventions was great, as the inventions such as the hydrogen bomb and integrated circuitry demonstrate.

The countries that emerged from the horrors of World War II were not only politically and socially changed but also economically and technologically different. In particular, the United States had become the world's most powerful nation, and the development of the atomic bomb served as evidence of American technological and military superiority. The United States tried to maintain this position during the 1950's by developing even more powerful weapons, most notably the hydrogen bomb.

Because of the unexpectedly rapid creation of the Soviet atomic bomb, President Harry S. Truman, in 1950, authorized a project to make a thermonuclear weapon. Designed by physicist Edward Teller and Polish mathematician Stanislaw Ulam, the hydrogen bomb was tested successfully on an atoll in the Pacific Ocean in 1952. Not long after this test, the Soviet Union exploded a fusion weapon of its own, fomenting an arms race that led to inventions such as missiles that had a range of thousands of miles. To protect North America from nuclear-armed missiles, the U.S. Air Force set up a Distant Early Warning (DEW) system, a network of radar installations across Alaska and northern Canada. Richard Buckminster Fuller, famous for inventing the geodesic dome, devised fiberglass "radomes" to shield delicate radar technology from the Arctic winds and cold.

Although nuclear technologies helped fuel the Cold War, including the U.S. Navy's 1955 introduction of the world's first nuclear-powered submarine, the *Nautilus*, these technologies also had peaceful purposes, such as the nuclear power station opened at Shippingport, Pennsylvania, in 1957. This and other nuclear reactors built during the late 1950's depended on the fission of uranium 235. However, during this decade, a new kind of reactor—the fast breeder—was invented in which a mixture of fissionable plutonium 239 and nonfissionable uranium 238 created more fuel, or plutonium, than it used.

The computer was another example of a war-developed technology that subsequently was adapted for important new applications. In 1950, some of the same scientists who had developed the first electronic computer during the war joined with Princeton mathematician John von Neumann to build the first stored-program computer, the Electronic Discrete Variable Automatic Computer (EDVAC). The first commercial computer, the Universal Automatic Computer (UNIVAC), achieved fame when it correctly forecast Dwight D. Eisenhower's election in 1952 as president.

At this same time, Grace Murray Hopper, a mathematician who would later become a rear admiral in the U.S. Navy, revolutionized computer software by devising a system to translate programming codes into a language accessible to computers, and in 1959, she headed a team that developed COBOL (Common Business-Oriented Language), which became the most widely used software for businesses.

By the mid-1950's, the transistor, which was invented during the late 1940's, was being manufactured at an annual rate of many millions, and by 1959, transistor miniaturization had progressed sufficiently that a large number of them could be etched onto a thin slice of silicon. Jack S. Kilby, working for Texas Instruments, played an important role in the development of these integrated circuits, which would later make it possible to build smaller, faster, cheaper, and more versatile computers.

Charles H. Townes with his first maser in 1958. (AP/Wide World Photos)

The maser was another invention that grew out of World War II, in particular out of radar. Microwaves are radiations with wavelengths between infrared and short-wave radio, and in the postwar period, physicists investigated whether they could create coherent, monochromatic microwaves. In 1953, Columbia University physicist Charles H. Townes invented a gadget that produced an intense beam of pure microwaves. He called it a "maser" since it involved *m*icrowave *a*mplification by the *s*timulated *e*mission of *r*adiation. By the end of the decade, Theodore H. Maiman, working for Hughes Research Laboratories, had invented the laser, a device able to produce very pure, intense visible light. It would be adapted for such common commercial applications as supermarket price scanners and DVD players.

Consumer Electronics and Commercial Products After World War II, American consumers sought the creature comforts denied them during the conflict, and inventors answered these pent-up demands in

several ways. Some inventors improved radios, while others created new sound-recording and playback devices. Patrick Haggerty, president of Texas Instruments, was the force behind the introduction of the transistor radio in 1954. Other inventors and entrepreneurs were responsible for the introduction of high-fidelity, or "hi-fi," phonographs and recordings, which, by the end of the decade, were being offered in "stereo," since these recordings, when played on the proper equipment, provided listeners with wider-frequency, two-dimensional sounds. Similarly, inventors in the 1950's tried to improve television. The principal development of this period was color television. Although photomechanical color television had been developed in the 1940's, RCA (Radio Corporation of America) introduced an all-electronic color television system in 1953.

Early attempts to preserve television broadcasts depended on kinescope recordings—filming directly from the face of the television tube—but image quality was poor and sound needed to be recorded separately. During the 1950's, various individuals and companies worked on inventing a suitable videotape recorder. In 1952, Ray Dolby, who worked for the Ampex company, invented the basic electronic circuitry for videotape recording. Television networks were using Dolby's device by 1956, but it could only record black-and-white telecasts. During the late 1950's, Ampex and RCA agreed to develop recorders that could preserve both color and black-and-white telecasts.

American companies whose products were marketed to a specialized clientele used new inventions to improve and diversify their commercial offerings. For example, in 1955, International Business Machines Corporation (IBM) marketed a new typewriter, the Selectric, which, instead of type bars and a movable carriage had a sphere-shaped device that rotated to print characters. An even more significant office machine developed during this time was the photocopier. For years, Chester F. Carlson had been working on a machine that would use light, electricity, and a dry powder to make copies (because his process was liquidless, he called it "xerography" for "dry writing"). Carlson's discoveries and patents bore fruit in 1958, when the Xerox machine finally reached the market. Other commercial products that appeared in the 1950's include Superglue, an adhesive needing no air to dry, and Lycra, an elastic substance introduced by Dupont that could be stretched several times its length and still return to its original length when relaxed.

Medical Advancements The 1950's was also a time when medical discoveries and inventions significantly improved the health of Americans. For example, in 1955, Jonas Salk, a microbiologist, reported that his killed-virus vaccine was "80 to 90 percent effective" in preventing polio, a disease that had crippled many children. In 1957, Albert Sabin, a Polish-American microbiologist, introduced a live-virus vaccine that largely replaced the Salk vaccine because it could be taken orally and conferred greater immunity on its recipients.

Pharmaceutical companies introduced several new antibiotics in the 1950's, which helped cure many illnesses. However, a troubling trend emerged when several antibiotic-resistant microorganisms made appearances. In 1957, Gertrude Elion, the first woman inducted into the National Inventors Hall of Fame, synthesized a drug that helped solve the problem of the human body's rejection of transplanted tissues and organs. Other medical researchers developed such psychoactive drugs as Librium and Valium, while others worked to find a drug that would prevent pregnancy. In 1960, the federal Food and Drug Administration (FDA) reported that a birth control pill developed by researchers was safe for prolonged use as a contraceptive.

Transportation and Space Exploration During the postwar years Americans reignited their passion for the automobile and airplane, and inventors created new devices to increase the speed, efficiency, comfort, and aesthetic appeal of these modes of travel. Automobiles of the era were heavier and more powerful than their predecessors, but power steering and improved brakes made control of these vehicles nearly effortless. More than half of American cars after 1954 had automatic transmissions. Many automakers used "fins" to sell their product, and one patent in 1956 even had a large fin perched on the middle of the car's trunk.

During the 1950's, airplanes became the major transporters of people and mail over long distances. Boeing introduced the first successful commercial jet, the 707, in 1954. New military airplanes also appeared: For example, the North American F-86 Sabre Jet was extensively used in the Korean War, achieving supremacy over the Soviet MiG-15. The Boeing B-52 Stratofortress bomber began service in

1955, and in 1957, three of these eight-jet airplanes flew nonstop around the world. The Canadians built a revolutionary jet interceptor, the Avro Arrow, during the late 1950's. This plane, capable of speeds more than twice the speed of sound, was the first to make extensive use of various computer-controlled instruments. (The program to build the Avro Arrow was canceled, however, during John Diefenbaker's ministry.)

Although American inventors led the world in many fields in the 1950's, some areas, most notably spaceflight, were neglected. In 1957, when the Soviet Union launched *Sputnik I*, the first artificial satellite in space, many Americans were shocked. Public outrage forced President Eisenhower to establish the National Aeronautics and Space Administration (NASA) and to accelerate the U.S. space program. The first successful U.S. satellite, *Explorer I*, was launched on January 1, 1958, followed by *Vanguard I* on March 17, 1958. However, these efforts were inferior to continuing Soviet space accomplishments, and by the early 1960's, the Soviet Union was able to put the first human into orbit around Earth.

Impact American inventions in the 1950's had both negative and positive influences on developments in later decades. The hydrogen bomb, for example, led first to a nuclear arms race between the United States and the Soviet Union, and then to nuclear weapons proliferation, as other countries created their own bombs and missiles. These weapons became so numerous that they had the potential of destroying, many times over, all human life on the planet.

However, positive consequences of the decade's inventions were also in evidence during the later decades of the twentieth century. Building on medical and agricultural technologies invented in the 1950's, researchers of later decades devised other means of extending lives and improving the health of Americans. The foundation for the explosive growth of computers and biotechnology was also fashioned during the 1950's. Furthermore, it took Americans less than a decade to surpass the Soviet Union in the "space race," and by the end of the 1960's, as President John F. Kennedy had promised, Americans were walking on the moon.

On the whole, most Americans saw these accomplishments as progressive, but some critics began calling attention to the harm that some American technologies were causing to the environment. These critics also analyzed the psychological toll that accelerated technological development was exacting on the emotional and spiritual lives of many Americans. The complex interactions among science, technology, and society demonstrated to Americans that technological progress was not always matched by social, political, and cultural progress.

Further Reading

Brown, David E. *Inventing Modern America: From the Microwave to the Mouse.* Cambridge, Mass.: MIT Press, 2002. This beautifully illustrated account of thirty-five American inventors over the twentieth century emphasizes how their inventions have transformed the lives, work, and environments of American citizens.

Hillman, David, and David Gibbs. *Century Makers: One Hundred Clever Things We Take for Granted Which Have Changed Our Lives Over the Last One Hundred Years.* New York: Welcome Rain, 1999. Instead of analyzing such inventions as nuclear power and computers, the authors write about "humble" inventions that have changed daily life in small ways, such as paperclips, nylon stockings, and Superglue. They discuss these inventions chronologically, so that the thirteen inventions of the 1950's are readily accessible. Illustrated, with an index.

Van Dulken, Stephen. *American Inventions: A History of Curious, Extraordinary and Just Plain Useful Patents.* New York: New York University Press, 2004. Americans registered more than five million patents in the twentieth century, and the author analyzes this "exuberant world" of invention by selecting many patents that, in one way or another, helped create the American Dream.

Vare, Ethlie Ann, and Greg Ptacek. *Patently Female: From AZT to TV Dinners, Stories of Women Inventors and Their Breakthrough Ideas.* New York: John Wiley & Sons, 2002. This book, a sequel to the authors' *Mothers of Invention: From the Bra to the Bomb, Forgotten Women and Their Unforgettable Ideas* (1988), emphasizes inventions by women in the period from the 1950's to the end of the twentieth century.

Williams, Trevor I. *A Short History of Twentieth Century Technology.* New York: Oxford University Press, 1982. This book, which is thematically organized, emphasizes the first half of the twentieth century, but discussions of various technologies often extend into the 1950's.

Robert J. Paradowski

See also Aircraft design and development; Automobiles and auto manufacturing; Computers; Diamond synthesizing; DNA (deoxyribonucleic acid); Geodesic dome; Instant photography; Photovoltaic cell; Ribonucleic acid (RNA); Superconductivity research; Tranquilizer chlorpromazine; Transistors.

■ *Invisible Man*

Identification Novel exploring the invisibility of black life in twentieth century America
Author: Ralph Ellison (1914-1994)
Date Published in 1952

One of the most significant literary achievements of the and perhaps of the twentieth century, Ralph Ellison's Invisible Man *was the first book by an African American writer to win the National Book Award. It has been translated into fourteen languages and has never gone out of print.*

Ralph Ellison's 1952 novel *Invisible Man* was one of the most significant literary achievements of the decade, garnering for Ellison literary status unheard of for first-time novelists. The novel traces the life of an unnamed African American narrator as he migrates from an unfinished college education in the South to Harlem in New York City. There, after initial failure, he finds work as an orator and political operative for the Brotherhood, a radical organization that promises to create new opportunities for African Americans through political upheaval. When Ellison's narrator discovers that the Brotherhood seeks to use him and other black members in Harlem to create a violent revolution that will catapult the Brotherhood into power, he retreats to an underground hole in Harlem. There he becomes a writer instead of a speaker, writing the story that becomes *Invisible Man*. Significantly, in the epilogue to the book, the narrator promises to emerge from his hole to take on "a socially responsible role."

Critiquing American Life Encyclopedic in the scope of its literary and historical allusion (particularly to African American history and culture), *Invisible Man* quickly became the epic of African American life in twentieth century America. Few novels of the twentieth century explored American and African Ameri-

Ralph Ellison. (National Archives)

Ellison's *Invisible Man* ends with the haunting words, "Who knows but that, on the lower frequencies, I speak to you?" Since his novel was aimed at a multiracial audience, the ultimate meaning of invisibility cuts in many directions. Racial invisibility is only one dimension of human invisibility, Ellison argues, and when Americans see beyond illusion, they can recognize the possibility of American life.

Influences Though Ellison always denied that the Brotherhood was patterned on the Communist Party, many literary critics have linked the two together. Such speculation was fueled in part by Ellison's own involvement in the party during the 1940's. As a friend of Richard Wright, author of the ground-breaking *Native Son* (1940), Ellison not only wrote for leftist publications but also attended party meetings. Similarly, the college from which the narrator emerges was clearly patterned on Booker T. Washington's Tuskegee Institute, the school that Ellison attended for three years before heading north.

Impact *Invisible Man* was notable for addressing the ways in which the shifting social and political foundations of the United States during the 1940's played an important role in the formation of individual identity, whether that identity be related to a white or black "race." Ellison used the novel to dramatize and explore the social, psychic, and metaphysical dimensions of racism. Moreover, by using a wide range of African American cultural forms, such as blues music and folktales, Ellison brought to the forefront a multidimensional African American experience. The multiculturalism that became part of American life in the 1960's and 1970's was in many ways anticipated in *Invisible Man.*

Ellison's novel appeared four years before the bus boycotts in Montgomery, Alabama, and the beginning of the modern Civil Rights movement. Given the juxtaposition, it is difficult not to see Ellison as prophetic.

can life and history so fully or with such artistic integrity. Indeed, much of Ellison's critique of American life was summarized in the opening words of the narrative: "I am an invisible man." Much like Herman Melville's famous line, "Call me Ishmael," which opened *Moby Dick: Or, The Whale* (1851) a century before, Ellison's words lead the reader into much more than a story.

The text draws the reader into a world of horror, humor, and distortion, but still a world that is very recognizably American. The metaphor of invisibility catches the true nature of black life in a 1950's America. As American prosperity and technology promised a world of endless tranquillity and conformity, Ellison insists that readers examine those features of American life that they have been taught not to see. There in the shadows of American life one finds not the archetypal Negro or the reliable employee that Booker T. Washington had promised in his "Atlanta Exposition Address" (1895). Instead, there is a human being with all the complications, contradictions, and unexpected genius that American life has always promised. There in the shadows is an America that is "woven of many strands," as the narrator of *Invisible Man* observes.

Further Reading

Butler, Robert J. *The Critical Response to Ralph Ellison.* Westport, Conn.: Greenwood Press, 2000. Traces the critical reception of Ellison's work and includes the initial reviews of *Invisible Man.*

Callahan, John F. *Ralph Ellison's Invisible Man: A Casebook.* New York: Oxford University Press, 2004. Offers critical analysis of the novel.

Rice, H. William. *Ralph Ellison and the Politics of the Novel.* Lanham, Md.: Lexington Books, 2003. An examination of Ellison's work within the context of the tumultuous politics during the last half of the twentieth century.

H. William Rice

See also African Americans; Civil Rights movement; King, Martin Luther, Jr.; Literature in the United States; Montgomery bus boycott; Racial discrimination.

■ Isolationism

Definition Refusal of a nation to join international organizations and refusal to participate in international political life among the world's nations

The historical refusal of the United States to involve itself politically or militarily in other nations' affairs came under attack during the 1930's and 1940's, when the stance contributed materially to the ability and willingness of fascist powers to embark on the militarization and expansionist policies that led to World War II. This failure to prevent fascist aggression, coupled with postwar ideological tensions, led America to rethink its position, and the 1950's witnessed the country embarking on numerous treaties and alliances in the effort to curb perceived Soviet aggression during the Cold War.

Isolationism was the dominant feature of American foreign policy from the foundation of the nation in the late eighteenth century until World War II. George Washington declared that it was America's "true policy to steer clear of permanent alliances with any portion of the foreign world," and Thomas Jefferson argued for friendship with every nation, but "entangling alliances with none."

After World War I, President Woodrow Wilson attempted to induce the nation to adopt an internationalist stance, beginning with membership in the League of Nations. The Senate rejected the treaty, however, and Americans retreated back into an isolationist mode. Strong sentiment was directed toward refusing involvement in World War II, but the bombing of Pearl Harbor in 1941 changed that mentality overnight.

Multilateralism After World War II, contrary to what many observers predicted, Americans did not retreat to their previous isolationist mind-set and ac-

companying policies. Instead, they embraced their dominant role on the world stage by becoming a charter member of the United Nations (U.N.) in 1945, initiating the Truman Doctrine in 1947, effecting the Berlin Air Lift between 1948 and 1949, enacting the Marshall Plan and establishing the North American Treaty Organization (NATO) in 1949, and going to war in Korea in 1950, among many other policies.

In addition to the keystone American alliance of NATO, the 1950's brought other alliances, including the Southeast Asia Treaty Organization (SEATO), established in 1954. In 1956, the United States also pledged to cooperate with the Baghdad Pact (later called the Central Treaty Organization, or CENTO), formed for the defense of the Middle East. The Eisenhower Doctrine of 1957 committed the nation to intervene in the Middle East under certain circumstances, and in 1958, the United States intervened in Lebanon. Indeed, U.S. secretary of state John Foster Dulles was so eager for the United States to join alliances that he was sometimes accused of "pactomania." This type of eagerness was the polar opposite of isolationism, and it remained American policy for the duration of the Cold War.

Domestic Reception Although it is sometimes postulated that the American people had an isolationist mind-set during the 1950's, it is difficult to associate this alleged frame of mind with any important influence on American foreign policy or on the electoral behavior of voters. There was no clamor for candidates who wished to return to the anti-alliance policies of a previous age, and neither the Congress nor the executive branch could be categorized as isolationist during the period.

On the other hand, during the 1950's Canada was in a position different from that of its southern neighbor. Throughout its history, Canada was closely allied with its mother country, Great Britain, by sentiment and tradition. Moreover, Canada was a member of the British Commonwealth, which gave it an international role with many other nations around the world. Even if it wished, Canada was hardly in a position to become an isolationist state. Canada fought in World Wars I and II, joined the United Nations, joined NATO, fought in Korea, and in many other ways carried out the roles of a non-isolationist state.

Impact The emergence of an internationally involved United States in the post-World War II period and the corresponding support among the American people wrought a fundamental change in world affairs that continues unabated in the twenty-first century. Active American diplomacy backed by military force during the 1940's and 1950's fundamentally altered the landscape of international politics.

Further Reading

Adler, Selig. *The Isolationist Impulse: Its Twentieth-Century Reaction.* Toronto: Collier-Macmillan Canada, 1957. A readable survey of the isolationist mind-set and its consequences during the mid-twentieth century.

Chalberg, Robert W. *Isolationism: Opposing Viewpoints.* San Diego, Calif.: Greenhaven Press, 1995. A collection of writing that articulates a variety of views on isolationism, including those that favor such policies.

Kaplan, Lawrence. *NATO and the United States: The Enduring Alliance.* Rev. ed. New York: Twayne, 1994. Details the history of the organization, looking at key figures in its development such as John Foster Dulles, how it was received during the 1950's, and how its mission evolved as the Cold War ended.

Charles F. Bahmueller

See also Canada as a middle power; Cold War; Dulles, John Foster; Eisenhower Doctrine; Foreign policy of Canada; Lebanon occupation; North Atlantic Treaty Organization; Southeast Asia Treaty Organization; Suez Crisis; Truman Doctrine.

■ Israel

Identification Newly established Middle Eastern nation with a predominantly Jewish population that maintained a close relationship with the United States and its citizens

American and Canadian recognition and support during the 1950's was critical for the survival of the fledgling state of Israel.

On May 14, 1948, the state of Israel was established, ending the British mandate over Palestine and creating the first official Jewish homeland in nearly two thousand years. Immediately following the pullout of British troops, Israel was invaded by five Arab nations' armies, and the survival of the state was confirmed only after a bloody war for independence. David Ben-Gurion became the first prime minister.

President Harry S. Truman was a strong supporter of Israel, and upon its independence, the United States immediately proclaimed its recognition of the provisional government as the de facto, or "actual," authority of Israel. In January, 1949, the United States confirmed Israel's existence on a de jure, or "by right," basis. In May, 1949, Canada likewise recognized Israel on a de jure basis, following its de facto recognition the previous December.

U.S. and Canadian relations with Israel during the 1950's were often tempered by the need for oil purchased from the surrounding Arab states. Prime Minister Ben-Gurion made his first visit to the United States in 1951, but even this event was carried out privately and was afforded no official invitation. Ben-Gurion did not visit Canada until 1961, though Canada and Israel did exchange ambassadors in 1953.

U.S.-Israeli Relationship President Dwight D. Eisenhower continued the strong support of Israel followed his election in 1952. However, Eisenhower's policies regarding the Middle East reflected two major factors of the period—the West's growing need for Arab oil and the ongoing Cold War.

During the 1950's, the United States steadily increased its economic and military assistance to Israel, while at the same time attempting to balance its relations with the Arab countries. The Tripartite Declaration between the United States, Great Britain, and France stated that the West would attempt to demonstrate an evenhanded policy with respect to arms sales in the Middle East. The Baghdad Pact, an attempt by the United States to maintain bases in Iraq in exchange for armaments, was a result of the policy. Nevertheless, the Soviet Union took full advantage of Arab resentment of American policies toward Israel with the beginning of large-scale military assistance to Arab states in general and Egypt in particular. Israel hoped to turn this to its own advantage through a security agreement with the United States. However, this proposal for a security agreement was turned down by Secretary of State John Foster Dulles, a result of his hope that American relations with the Arab states would not further deteriorate. Moreover, Israel was assured that it would not be abandoned by the United States.

Jews in the United States and Canada provided enormous economic aid to the new state during this period. As well, the U.S. Export-Import Bank guaranteed a $100 million loan to support the Israeli economy. Additional grants and loans by 1960 provided an additional $65 million; all loans were eventually repaid.

Israeli policy toward its neighbors was at times frustrating to the United States. In particular, the British-French-Israeli invasion of Egypt following the closing of the Suez Canal by President Gamal Abdel Nassar in 1956 produced a strong U.S. response. Israel was told to halt its incursions and bring an end to the conflict or risk a cutoff of U.S. aid. The issue of whether the West would recognize Jerusalem as Israel's capital also created controversy. The United Nations supported an internationalization of the city, a solution resisted by Israelis. The

United States supported the U.N. proposal, sometimes stridently, before eventually dropping the issue. Overall, however, U.S.-Israeli relations during this period became increasingly cordial as Israel became one of the strongest proponents of U.S. policies.

Canadian-Israeli Relations As did their counterparts in the United States, Canadian Jews increasingly supported Israel with both economic and political aid. The primary difference, however, was that Canadian Jews never had the equivalent numbers or political power during these formative years. Canadian Jews often looked at themselves as "outsiders," a viewpoint not completely at odds with the rest of the population. Only with the Six-Day War in 1967 would Canadian Jews develop a consolidated network for support of Israel.

Each of the Canadian prime ministers during this period—Louis St. Laurent (1948-1957) and John Diefenbaker (1957-1963)—supported economic relations with Israel. During the 1956 Suez Crisis, Canada won international recognition for proposing the first U.N. peacekeeping force to "secure and supervise the cessation of hostilities" in the region. Lester Pearson, Canada's minister for external affairs, won the Nobel Peace Prize for his efforts to promote peace. Finally, the Canada-Israel Corporation, as well as other institutions, was established to encourage bilateral trade between Canada and Israel.

Impact The increasingly close relationship between Israel and the United States and Canada ensured the survival of the country during its early turbulent years. As a consequence, however, American relationships with most Middle Eastern Arab states deteriorated during this same period. A new generation of Arab youth developed both envy and hatred toward the West, a factor that proved an ongoing problem during the struggle against militant terrorism during the early twenty-first century.

Further Reading

Encyclopedia Judaica. Jerusalem, Israel: Keter, 1971. The section dealing with the United States includes significant discussion of relations between the two countries during Israel's formative years.

Gilbert, Martin. *Israel: A History.* New York: William Morrow, 1998. A complete history of the state of Israel. Covers the period from the formation of Zionism through the turbulent beginning of the modern state.

Schoenbaum, David. *The United States and the State of Israel.* New York: Oxford University Press, 1993. A detailed history of the evolution of relations between the two countries. In particular, the author describes the increasing interdependence between the two countries.

Shlaim, Avi. *The Iron Wall.* New York: W. W. Norton, 2001. Primarily a discussion of the history of Israeli-Arab relationships. However, the author does provide insight into American-Israeli relations during the 1950's.

Richard Adler

See also Bunche, Ralph; Canadian Labour Congress; Diefenbaker, John G.; Dulles, John Foster; Eisenhower, Dwight D.; Foreign policy of Canada; Foreign policy of the United States; Jewish Americans; Pearson, Lester B.; St. Laurent, Louis; Suez Crisis.

■ *I've Got a Secret*

Identification Television game show
Producers Mark Goodson, Bill Todman, and Allen Sherman
Dates Aired from 1952 to 1967 and in the summer of 1976

A pioneering television game show, I've Got a Secret *appealed to audiences' sense of sophistication by featuring the witty and spontaneous banter of an urbane celebrity panel dedicated to guessing contestants' secrets.*

I've Got a Secret, produced for CBS by game show impresarios Mark Goodson and Bill Todman, was

hosted by the genial and popular Garry Moore. Debuting on June 19, 1952, the show took off in its second season to become one of the decade's most highly rated programs.

The format was simple. With the contestant sitting next to the show's host, Moore, each of four celebrity panelists took thirty-second turns questioning about and then guessing a contestant's secret. Each half-hour episode used four contestants, one of whom was a celebrity. In one such episode, horror-film actor Boris Karloff—best known as the monster in *Frankenstein* (1931)—revealed that he was afraid of mice. Most contestants, however, were ordinary people.

The appeal of *I've Got a Secret* centered on the breezy repartee between Moore, the contestants, and the star panel, whose regulars included actors Jayne Meadows, Faye Emerson, and Betsy Palmer; former Miss America Bess Myerson; and funnymen Henry Morgan and Bill Cullen. Moore presided over the long-running show from 1952 to 1964, Steve Allen from 1964 to 1967, and Bill Cullen for a brief summer revival in 1976.

Impact *I've Got a Secret* was a consistent top-ten program during the 1950's. Most significantly, by attracting audiences with the sophisticated ad libs of its celebrity panelists rather than with huge prizes for competitors—as did programs such as *The $64,000 Question*—the show survived the quiz show scandals of 1958-1959.

Further Reading

Graham, Jefferson. *Come on Down! The TV Game Show Book.* New York: Abbeville Press, 1988. Explores the history of the genre.

Schwartz, David, et al. *The Ultimate TV Game Show Book.* New York: Checkmark Books, 1999. Contains trivia and facts about numerous television game shows and includes a summary of each program, rules of the game, air dates, hosts, celebrity guests, network affiliations, production companies, producers, and creators.

Chuck Berg

See also Linkletter, Art; Marx, Groucho; Television game shows; Television in the United States.

J

■ Japan

Identification East Asian nation with which the United States and Canada built new relationships after World War II

As the Allied occupation of Japan ended and the Korean War began, Japan used its new economic strength to forge special ties with North America and establish patterns of trade and political cooperation that paved the way for their economic and diplomatic relationships in subsequent decades.

When World War II ended in August, 1945, Japan effectively was under sole political and military control of General Douglas MacArthur, the Supreme Commander for the Allied Powers (SCAP). The headquarters and bureaucracy of SCAP governed all aspects of Japanese life and instigated many social and economic reforms in a radical attempt to democratize the country and stamp out all vestiges of militarism.

At the start of the 1950's, relations between Japan and America could be not characterized as warm but were certainly becoming more cordial. While there were still 115,000 American troops and more than five thousand civilian bureaucrats in Japan, these numbers were significantly lower than the force of 430,000 at the height of SCAP's command in 1945. Many of the early restrictions imposed by the Allied occupation—for example, censorship of the school curriculum, the mails, and the media, as well as limitations on travel both within and outside the country by Japanese nationals—were slowly being lifted.

The Korean War and Cold War However well the occupation succeeded in American eyes, less than six years after the end of World War II, the United States was once again involved in another armed conflict in Asia. On June 25, 1950, the Korean War began, a struggle that would last for the next three years. The Korean War, along with increasing tensions with the Soviet Union and China, drastically altered attitudes toward Japan held by American policymakers

and was the most significant incident in postwar Japanese-American relations. In 1951, the United States-Japan Security Treaty was signed, guaranteeing American protection of Japan in the event of war and allowing the United States to station permanent troops in the country. In 1952, the San Francisco Peace Treaty was signed, officially ending the war between Japan and the United States.

Race and Immigration Policy During the 1950's, though the U.S. government was prone to forgive much of the past because of Cold War expediency, for many Americans the legacy of Pearl Harbor and World War II still lingered. An element of distrust and racial animosity was common. For example, the Japanese Americans and Japanese Canadians who were detained in internment camps during World War II received no redress or compensation for lost property even though most were American or Canadian citizens. Prejudicial views were also seen in American immigration policy. Tens of thousands of Japanese women who married American servicemen during the occupation were not able to accompany their husbands who returned home. The 1952 McCarran-Walter Act, though abolishing the previous law of 1924 that essentially prohibited immigration and naturalization for Japanese, still set a theoretical quota of only eight hundred Japanese immigrants per year allowed to enter the United States. However, during the decade, many thousands of "non-quota" Japanese entered the country as war brides or, in some cases, as relatives of those already in the United States.

Economics A common stereotype of the 1950's was that Japan was a producer of cheap or shoddy manufactured goods. Unlike the situation in later decades, when Japanese automobiles and electronic equipment were considered among the best in the world, goods that carried the Japanese mark were assumed to be products of a poor, underdeveloped country. Though Japan struggled to rebuild its shattered infrastructure after the devastation of World

Members of a Japanese delegation presenting a petition to a U.N. assistant secretary-general appealing for Japan's admission to the United Nations in 1952. (AP/Wide World Photos)

War II, the Korean War more than anything else boosted Japan's recovery. American and United Nations forces that needed military supplies were provisioned by Japanese factories, which gained hard currency for Japan to pay for needed imports. Canada, finding an important customer for its abundant natural resources, strongly supported Japan's 1955 entry into the General Agreement on Tariffs and Trade (GATT), the main organization regulating international commerce. By the mid-1950's, Japan's economy was slowly recovering, and in 1955, a trade war between the United States and Japan arose over the importation of inexpensive cotton textiles.

Popular Culture In the arena of popular culture, the influence of Japan in 1950's North America was certainly noticeable. Science-fiction monster films were the first films from Japan to become major international box-office successes. *Godzilla* (first released with its Japanese title *Gojira*), a movie about a giant

reptile that destroys Tokyo, was first introduced in 1954 and spawned dozens of imitators and sequels. Godzilla was said to be awakened from his slumber by an explosion of an atom bomb, and such allusions played on all the Cold War fears and postwar guilt of 1950's America. Nonetheless, as pure entertainment, the Japanese monster-movie genre influenced a whole generation of American B-movies and even attracted the attention of some major American studios such as Columbia (which itself revamped and released the original Godzilla film).

Impact The 1950's legacy of Japan-North American relations cannot be overestimated. At the start of the twenty-first century, there were thousands of American soldiers stationed in Japan under the auspices of the security treaties of the 1950's. The patterns of trade and commerce begun during the 1950's continued in subsequent decades, despite Japan's status as the world's second-largest economy. While video games may have replaced Godzilla in the hearts of young consumers, science fiction and fantasy are still major staples of Japan's contribution to popular culture.

Further Reading

Dower, John W. *Embracing Defeat: Japan in the Wake of World War II.* New York: W. W. Norton, 1999. Often called the best history about Japan and its relations to the United States after World War II, this book won both the Pulitzer Prize and the National Book Award.

Eiji, Takemae. *Inside GHQ: The Allied Occupation of Japan and Its Legacy.* New York: Continuum, 2002. One of the most comprehensive books ever written on Japan's "American Interlude," coming from one of Japan's most important historians of the postwar era.

Neu, Charles. *The Troubled Encounter: The United States and Japan.* New York: John Wiley & Sons, 1975. A classic history of the misunderstandings that have often characterized Japanese-American political relations.

James Stanlaw

See also Asian Americans; California's Alien Land Laws; Dulles, John Foster; Immigration and Nationality Act of 1952; Institute of Pacific Relations; International trade of Canada; International trade of the United States; Korean War; MacArthur, Douglas; *Ugly American, The;* War brides.

■ Jazz

Definition Musical genre that retained its key features of improvisation and the juxtaposition of polyrhythm over harmony, while encompassing a growing range of musical forms and acquiring more complex cultural associations during the 1950's

During the 1950's, the world of jazz, which had been popular during the 1930's and 1940's, began to develop contrasting styles that spoke to diverse but smaller audiences, even as some of its more traditional and commercial performers continued to entertain through the new medium of television.

As the young people who had danced and courted to swing music of the "big band" era of the previous decade settled down to start families, they began to embrace the new technology of television, and programming tended to reflect their mainstream styles and tastes. Popular, jazz-influenced arrangements using standard "big band" instrumentation (saxophones, trumpets, trombones, piano, double bass, and drum set) were included in dance-entertainment programs. Situation comedies and variety programs also used this approach: *I Love Lucy* used theme music played by Desi Arnaz's orchestra, and viewers of *The Ed Sullivan Show* heard music from a pit orchestra. This situation was not ideal for the majority of jazz musicians, however, since television and movie productions hired a mere handful of players compared to the plentiful touring bands of the 1940's, and improvisation was restricted because the emphasis was on entertainment.

In less commercial environments and in the African American community, the experimentation and stylistic departures of the be-bop innovators continued unabated, especially in New York. Life was difficult for jazz players working in urban environments during the early 1950's. Heroin addiction, while almost unheard of in the sheltered suburbs, was endemic among jazz musicians during this period and damaged many of their careers. Moreover, an "underground" aspect tended to infiltrate the modern forms of jazz that were being played during the 1950's. Intellectuals, including poets such as Allen Ginsberg, embraced the music and composed "Beat" poetry inspired by the rhythms, phrases, and melodic convolutions of modern jazz. Some groups, such as the Modern Jazz Quartet and small groups led by pianist Dave Brubeck, became popular with college audiences. However, the majority of Americans were only vaguely familiar with these developments, if at all.

Differences in Styles Some of the characteristics of early be-bop, such as extremely fast tempos and aggressively dissonant harmonies, had already been tempered by the more minimalist approaches of trumpeter Miles Davis, pianist Thelonious Monk, and other artists. After the expanded vocabulary of be-bop was adopted by larger groups of musicians, those who favored a more relaxed sound came to be placed in the "cool" category. Along with Davis, alto saxophonist Lee Konitz, trumpet-vocalist Chet Baker, saxophonist Stan Getz, pianists John Lewis and Lennie Tristano, and vibraphonist Milt Jackson were early practitioners of this style. In 1952, baritone saxophonist Gerry Mulligan moved to California and formed a piano-less quartet with Chet Baker on trumpet, helping to create what became known as the "West Coast" school.

In contrast to the "cool" and "West Coast" styles, other musicians—including drummer Art Blakey, pianist Horace Silver, tenor saxophonists Hank Mobely and Sonny Rollins, organist Jimmy Smith, trumpeter Clifford Brown, and others—emphasized the music's African American elements. This approach to jazz included references to the gospel and rhythm-and-blues traditions, which were also at the core of rock and roll, which, by the mid-1950's, had largely displaced jazz as the most popular and commercially successful popular music genre. Players in this "hard bop" school emphasized the vocal textures, melodic inflections, and driving percussion shared with more popular forms of African American music. They retained some of the innovative practices and rhythmic intensity of the late 1940's be-bop players but rejected the more elitist trappings of modernism.

While categories such as "cool" and "hard bop" were useful in attempting to describe various trends and styles of jazz for music listeners, critics, and record companies, most of the musicians were profoundly individualistic, and the process of finding one's own distinctive voice remained an important value throughout this period.

Innovations, Crossovers, and Trends As previously established musicians such as Duke Ellington, Louis Armstrong, and Benny Goodman continued to mature within their own styles, important younger musicians emerged who defied categorization. Charlie Mingus, a double bassist, bandleader, and composer, played in almost all of the jazz styes available during the 1950's. His experiences ranged from accompanying Louis Armstrong to being part of a West Coast bop trio with vibraphonist Red Norvo and guitarist Tal Farlow, to creating his own modern styles as a leader of his own group later in the decade. Pianist Monk used displaced repetition and insistent dissonances woven into his highly original compositions and improvisations.

Although the small combo became a more typical instrumental configuration during the 1950's, a few of the earlier "big band" leaders, including Ellington, Stan Kenton, Count Basie, Woody Herman, and others, continued to tour and incorporated more modern elements in their music. Music promoters

such as Norman Granz, who continued his "Jazz at the Philharmonic" series until 1957, found that audiences enjoyed hearing jazz in concert settings that featured diverse artists. In 1954, the first annual Newport Jazz Festival was held, establishing a new and important venue for jazz musicians in the years to come.

Vocalists continued to straddle the popular and elite streams in jazz during the 1950's, even as the gulf was widening between these trends. While Frank Sinatra and other popular singers of the swing era stayed close to the style in which they had achieved fame, Ella Fitzgerald and Sarah Vaughn, building on the "scat," nontextual vocalizing begun in earlier decades by Armstrong and modernized during the late 1940's by Fitzgerald, often created improvised melodies that reflected the complexity and virtuosity of be-bop. There were also important "crossovers" from jazz into popular music. Nat King Cole, a brilliant jazz pianist, was making vocal recordings that were enormously popular and appeared regularly on television. The electric guitar, the dominant instrument of the popular but musically conservative rock genre, continued to develop as a voice in jazz. The drumless piano trio (piano, electric guitar, and double bass) became a standard configuration from the late 1940's through the 1950's and was utilized by Art Tatum, George Shearing, Oscar Peterson, Cole, and other pianists. Near the end of the 1950's, guitarist Wes Montgomery, who had developed a very fluid glissando technique that reinforced melodies with octave and other doublings, became very popular.

John Coltrane, who had played many innovative solos with Davis and other musicians throughout the 1950's, began to explore more modernist directions, playing with rapidly shifting harmonies such as his piece "Giant Steps," and extending modal playing with extended chromatic approaches. At the very end of the decade, saxophonist Ornette Coleman, trumpeter Don Cherry, and pianist Cecil Taylor extended the modernist trend even more and began to play the "free" jazz that would become very influential during the 1960's.

A facet of the jazz movement during the 1950's was the emergence of serious jazz criticism. *Jazz: Its Evolution and Essence,* a book by French composer André Hodeir, who applied formal analysis and an aesthetic vocabulary borrowed from European art, was published in French in 1954 and in English in

Jazz singer Billie Holiday performing in Los Angeles in 1952. (Hulton Archive I by Getty Images)

1956. In 1958, a new periodical, *Jazz Review*, appeared, with Gunther Schuller's analysis of a Sonny Rollins solo. These and similar publications enhanced the interest in jazz among elite circles during this time and paralleled an increase in artistic cross-fertilization between the two great musical traditions. In 1957, Schuller used the term "Third Stream" to describe the conscious blending of modern jazz and Western classical music. Schuller, along with John Lewis, Jimmy Giuffre, Kenton, and others, continued to experiment in this area, and many of their efforts were well received.

Long-playing Albums In comparison to the relatively brief 45-rpm record, which was the mainstay of rock-and-roll music marketed to young people, the $33\frac{1}{3}$-rpm, long-playing record became the primary delivery vehicle for jazz artists and marked important moments in the music's development. Often,

these LP (long-playing) records were organized around a concept or theme. In 1956, vocalist Fitzgerald began working on a series of highly successful albums. Each LP was developed as a "songbook" that featured a great American songwriter. After a group of pieces that trumpeter Davis had recorded in earlier years was released in 1949 on an LP titled *Birth of the Cool*, jazz fans eagerly awaited subsequent Davis albums, which often included collaborations with arranger Gil Evans and resulted in classic LPs such as *Miles Ahead* (1957) and *Porgy and Bess* (1958). In another landmark album, *Kind of Blue* (1959), Davis applied modal techniques and contrasted his own solo style with those of tenor saxophonist Coltrane, pianist Bill Evans, and alto saxophonist Adderly, bringing leading exponents of the "hard bop" and "cool" styles together in the same creative environment. Another very influential album, *Time Out*, was recorded in 1959 by the Dave Brubeck Quartet. It featured each piece in a different time signature, including the famous "Take Five" by alto saxophonist Paul Desmond.

Social and Political Commentary Jazz musicians continued to be in the vanguard of racial integration during the 1950's, and many of them, both black and white, spoke out against ongoing segregation and mistreatment of African Americans. In terms of demeanor, the younger musicians rejected the more comedic and self-effacing mannerisms of preceding generations. Musicians continued to experience harassment and racial profiling—Davis was beaten by police just outside a club where he was working in New York—but they were more openly defiant in the face of such treatment. Composer and bassist Mingus incorporated feelings about racial injustice in pieces such as "Haitian Fight Song." Armstrong expressed his bitterness about segregation in his beloved New Orleans and criticized President Eisenhower for moving too slowly on civil rights.

Jazz even played a role in the Cold War. During the previous decade's struggle against fascism, Americans had been surprised and pleased to find that for many of their European allies, jazz was associated with democracy and freedom of expression. In the public relations battle between the major powers of the 1950's, Marxist critics pointed to continued racial segregation and inequities within the United States as proof of the failure of capitalism. The State Department responded by sponsoring tours that sent well-known jazz artists abroad in the role of cultural ambassadors, including Armstrong, Ellington, Brubeck, and others.

Impact By the end of the 1950's, much of the emergent jazz clearly reflected an increasingly diverse and challenging alternative to popular culture, even though a nostalgia-driven version of its older styles maintained a foothold in mass media and continued to influence larger audiences. This set the stage for further fragmentation and diversification in later decades. The development of serious jazz criticism and the use of jazz in representing the American overseas marked the global recognition of jazz as an important American art-music genre.

Further Reading

Collier, James Lincoln. *Jazz: The American Theme Song.* New York: Oxford University Press, 1993. Organized by theme, explores social and aesthetic issues.

Enstice, Wayne, and Paul Rubin. *Jazz Spoken Here: Conversations with Twenty-two Musicians.* Baton Rouge: Louisiana State University Press, 1992. Transcripts based on radio interviews of well-known musicians, most of whom were active during the 1950's.

Gioia, Ted. *The History of Jazz.* New York: Oxford University Press, 1997. Thoughtful overview, with a great deal of information about jazz during the 1950's, arranged by concept rather than strict chronology.

Goldberg, Joe. *Jazz Masters of the Fifties.* Cambridge, Mass.: Da Capo Press, 1988. Includes detailed information about the activities of key jazz artists during the 1950's.

Gottlieb, Robert, ed. *Reading Jazz.* New York: Vintage Books, 1999. Organized into three sections: autobiography, reportage, and criticism, with pieces in each section arranged chronologically.

Shipton, Alyn. *A New History of Jazz.* London: Continuum, 2001. Comprehensive work, organized by jazz style.

Walser, Robert, ed. *Keeping Time: Readings in Jazz History.* New York: Oxford University Press, 1999. Narratives, articles, and essays, preceded by extensive editorial commentary, illustrating key issues and figures in different time periods.

John Myers

See also Beat generation; Belafonte, Harry; Brubeck, Dave; Civil Rights movement; Cole, Nat King; Fitzgerald, Ella; Long-playing records; Music; Newport Jazz Festival; Peterson, Oscar; Rock and roll.

■ Jewish Americans

Identification Americans of Jewish descent from many countries of origin

After the destruction of major Jewish European centers during World War II, America became home to one of the largest, richest, and most important Jewish communities in the world. The decline of anti-Semitism, a generational movement from tradesmen to professionals, and a geographic movement from inner cities to the new suburbs led to the assimilation of Jews and their subsequent contributions to many institutions of North American society.

Before the cost of assimilation and loss of Jewish identity became problems for American Jews, the goal of entering American life as accepted and participating citizens was a major motivation during the 1950's. The most popular Jewish professions in 1950 were medicine, law, dentistry, and teaching, but there were barriers to admission in professional schools. After the anti-Semitism of the World War II years, the landmark *Brown v. Board of Education of Topeka* Supreme Court decision in 1954 revoked the tradition that "separate" was "equal" in matters of civil and minority rights. The following years saw an explosion of openings in universities and a decline of most Jewish quotas. During America's growing prosperity, high school diplomas did not satisfy Jewish families: Many assumed that every Jew who wanted a college education could achieve it. By 1955, 62 percent of American Jews of college age were attending college. At only 3 percent of the American population, they made up about 7.5 percent of the total college population.

Move to the Suburbs During the 1950's, the widespread trend of moving to the suburbs had important impacts on Jews in the United States. Jews reflected the widespread desire to start over after the war, but for them, this dispersion of population to the suburbs removed them from the crowded, inner-city environment in which religious and family ties were paramount. This meant a change of values from the importance of belonging to a traditional Jewish community to a new acceptance of mobility (both social and geographical) and the pursuit of individual happiness. However, the first waves of Jewish movement to the suburbs reflected a certain desire to retain old ties while testing new ones.

During the 1950's and early 1960's, Jews tended to settle in suburban areas that were close to the dense urban communities from which they came. This pattern held in most of the large cities where the Jews were concentrated: New York, Baltimore, Philadelphia, Boston, Newark, Miami, and Washington, D.C. There were also smaller Jewish population islands in Los Angeles, Chicago, Detroit, Cleveland, Pittsburgh, San Francisco, and St. Louis. In those early days, the suburbs themselves were mixed in population, and for the first time in the United States, Jews lived among non-Jews. The younger the suburbanites, the greater the significance of this cross-cultural contact and the sooner they experienced a loosening of ethnic ties.

This movement took place almost in one generation, and by the time the next generation had grown up, the relocation into suburbia extended even farther out, reaching towns where Jews were the smallest of minorities. This geographic shift mirrored a cultural shift, and assimilation advanced rapidly, largely as a result of the attractiveness of American culture and the breakdown of institutionalized anti-Semitism.

The Canadian Jewish experience did not match this model, partly because the Canadian Jews were really a postwar phenomenon, with about half of them arriving after 1945. They mostly settled in two areas: Montreal, with about 100,000 Jews, and Toronto, with some 120,000. Winnipeg and Vancouver also had small Jewish populations of about 15,000 each. From the beginning, Canadians held an ideal of cultural "pluralism" rather than cultural "assimilation," even in the top tiers of government.

Synagogues in the Suburbs Americans were turning to religion in growing numbers in the postwar era. Jews paralleled this movement by building and attending synagogues, which in turn came to play an important symbolic role. As they moved into the suburbs, the synagogues served as a kind of monument to their ethnic identity, as well as a physical sign that they had arrived.

However, these synagogues and the organizations they supported were not the same as those of an earlier time. They were often spare, modern buildings that fit well into the suburban landscape; one, Temple Beth Shalom in Elkins Park, Pennsylvania, was designed by the quintessentially American architect Frank Lloyd Wright. As handsome and meaningful to the Jews as these synagogues were, they were at first infrequently attended. In order to gain membership, some of them became a kind of secularized community center featuring social events, lectures, Israeli fund drives, and clubs. Unlike their immigrant forebears, Jews no longer felt they needed the confines of an exclusively Jewish institution. Uneven attendance at the synagogues during the 1950's reflected their ambivalence during a time when they were torn by two opposing values: integration into United States society and survival as a distinctive group. Alternatively, Jews in Canada did not need to join synagogues to achieve status as a community. Zionism, the Yiddish language, theater, and press were never regarded by Canadian Jews as alien to their Canadian identity. Jews there were respectable Canadians in a country that valued and safeguarded ethnic differences, even in the public schools.

In its religious practices, the suburban synagogue blurred differences among Jewish denominations. Usually Reform or Conservative in name, the religion often drifted into a mix of Reform laxity regarding religious observation at home and Conservative ceremonies, Hebrew reading, and chanting at the services.

One popular program synagogues established in the United States was children's education. Offered on a part-time basis, and usually employing immigrants or aging scholars as teachers, the classes taught Hebrew language, Tanach (the Hebrew Bible), and modern Jewish history. These schools became enclaves of Jewish cultural life rather than a means to assimilation. However, even nonobserving parents sent their children to these schools, perhaps out of a reluctance to give up their Judaism completely. Between 1950 and 1960, enrollment in Jewish education increased by more than 131 percent, and the synagogues moved toward becoming child-centered.

Emergence of Zionism After its establishment in 1948, the state of Israel became an important focus of Jewish life in the United States as well as a cause around which Jews united. Historically, Jewish nationalism had never been divorced from the religious tradition, and supporting the state of Israel appealed to the many American Jews who had abandoned the rites of traditional worship. It was a way of maintaining their ties to Judaism. This support was repeatedly endorsed by congressional resolutions and was applauded by Americans of all faiths except for those who were anti-Semitic. Publicly, Zionism was considered consistent with American values, and many thought the movement to establish a state of Israel among hostile people in rugged terrain paralleled the early movement to settle the American frontier.

Jewish women were in the vanguard in promoting this kind of benign, middle-class Zionism. Always strong partners, they were no longer silent ones, and they created a powerful Zionism in American life by organizing Hadassah, the Women's Zionist Organization of America, which became one of the largest and most powerful Jewish organizations in the world. Many women joined the Zionist movement

to help Palestinian Jews build schools and hospitals, drain swamps, plant forests, and rescue European refugees from horrible fates. By the time the facts of Jewish persecutions and displacement became widely known after World War II, synagogues, Jewish community centers, religious schools, and virtually the entire international Jewish community espoused the Zionist cause. Ideological struggles between Orthodox religious Jews and those who sought social and economic reform were muted publicly. In pursuit of the goals of rehabilitating and saving the lives of their fellow Jews, Jewish organizations in the United States raised more funds than had ever been raised for such purposes by any private group in history.

The idea fit well with the values of a middle-class community, for fellow Jews were not only reclaiming the land under real physical hardship, but they were also forming a unique culture. Israelis were creating modern literature, art, and music, and the renaissance of Hebrew culture was internationally recognized and discussed.

Marriage and Childbearing An important change in the lifestyles of Jews during the 1950's was directly related to their pattern of secular education and the timing of their marriages. By proportionately spending more years in school than their forebears or their peer groups in the United States, Jews started to marry later, and these later marriages had an influence on their fertility rate. Despite the fact that world Jews had lost more than six million of their people during the war years, there was no organized community effort to enhance their numbers. The U.S. Census of 1957 stated baldly that Jews in the United States did not participate in the postwar baby boom as much as Roman Catholics and Protestants. The reasons for this low birthrate were closely tied to the situation of the Jews during the 1950's. The realization that large families would be an impediment to financial and social success and required lengthy educational tenures for professional careers did not encourage high fertility. Moreover, the variables associated with high fertility in the United States such as poverty, contraceptive ignorance, and rural residence were almost unknown among Jews of childbearing years.

This desire to succeed in the United States also encouraged intermarriage. University experience and professional careers brought Jews into intimate social contact with non-Jews, the same people who had been their schoolmates in the suburbs. Although in 1957 the census reported that 94 percent of Jews were married to people of the same religion, young Jews started dating members of other religions during the 1950's.

Impact Rapid economic growth, public acceptance of religious and cultural pluralism, educational achievements, and the overwhelming determination to succeed in their new country contributed to the rise to prominence of American Jews in the decade of the 1950's. It led the way for Jews to reach unprecedented heights in the following decade, when they headed some of the most important branches of the federal government, and in the following decades when they ascended to many positions of corporate power and college presidencies. However, despite, or because of, their rapid entry into the mainstream of American life, the Jews in the United States ignored their falling birthrate and did not consider what costs their success would have in the years ahead. Their lives were going too well to worry, but their falling numbers left their heritage and identity as a unique group more vulnerable during the last half of the century.

Further Reading

Dinnerstein, Leonard. *Antisemitism in America.* New York: Oxford University Press, 1995. This first comprehensive history of Anti-Semitism in the United States won the 1995 Social and Behavioral Sciences Prize from the SBS Research Institute in Tucson, Arizona. It provides a complex narrative of the history of this prejudice.

Heilman, Samuel C. *Portrait of American Jews: The Last Half of the Twentieth Century.* Seattle: University of Washington Press, 1995. A book packed with statistics and useful information including a first chapter titled "Starting Over: Acculturation and Suburbia, the Jews of the 1950's."

Howe, Irving. *World of Our Fathers.* New York: Harcourt Brace Jovanovich, 1976. A classic account of the journey of the Jews from the *shtetl* to life in the United States. Section 4, titled "Dispersion," is a fascinating account of Jewish contributions in the arts and intellectual life of the 1950's.

Sachar, Howard. *A History of Jews in America.* New York: Vintage, 1993. Provides major accounts of the Jewish encounter in the United States in the last half of the twentieth century, including the

struggle for acceptance and the ambivalence of assimilation.

Sheila Golburgh Johnson

See also Immigration to Canada; Immigration to the United States; Israel; Religion in Canada; Religion in the United States; Urbanization in the United States; Uris, Leon; Wouk, Herman.

■ John Birch Society

Identification Ultraconservative anticommunist organization
Date Founded on December, 9, 1958

During the late 1950's, the John Birch Society brought national attention to conservative politics and a so-called communist conspiracy in the federal government and subsequently became the largest and best known anticommunist organization in the United States during the 1960's.

The John Birch Society was founded by businessman Robert Welch in Indianapolis, Indiana. Welch was motivated by his belief that there was an international communist conspiracy that had become increasingly successful during the Cold War. Welch's creation of the society marked the culmination of his increased interest and involvement in conservative politics. In 1950, Welch was an unsuccessful candidate for lieutenant governor of Massachusetts in the Republican primary. In 1952, he supported the candidacy of Senator Robert A. Taft for the Republican Party's presidential nomination and made twenty-five radio speeches on behalf of Taft. He was bitterly disappointed when the convention instead nominated General Dwight D. Eisenhower. Later, Welch asserted that the nomination was stolen from Taft by communists and "one-worlders" who had picked Eisenhower.

Welch was also a loyal supporter of Senator Joseph R. McCarthy, who claimed that communists in the federal government were responsible for American foreign policy failures. He addressed several state gatherings of groups called "Friends of Senator Joseph McCarthy" during the 1950's. Moreover, Welch began to write and publish conservative books and articles. In 1952, he published *May God Forgive Us*, which was Welch's analysis of President Harry S. Truman's dismissal of General Douglas MacArthur during the Korean conflict. In 1954, he published *The Life of John Birch: In the Story of One American Boy, the Ordeal of His Age.* Finally, in 1956,

Welch began publishing *One Man's Opinion*, a magazine that was published irregularly. When he started the John Birch Society, the publication's name was changed to *American Opinion* and became the official publication of the John Birch Society.

Robert Welch eventually concluded that the many anticommunist groups in the United States were ineffective because they relied on democratic procedures to get things done, and he decided that the communist menace could be challenged only by an authoritarian organization. In December, 1958, Welch met with eleven business friends in Indianapolis. For two days, Welch delivered a monologue on the advancement of communism and outlined the goals and organizational structure of a group designed to fight the menace in the United States. He named the organization after Captain John Birch, an army intelligence officer and Baptist missionary who was killed by Chinese communist guerrillas ten days after the end of World War II. Welch considered John Birch to be the first casualty of World War III, the war between the free world and the communist-bloc nations.

Impact The John Birch Society initially operated through small chapters of twelve to fifteen persons each. Welch sent the chapters monthly instructions, telling them which projects they should undertake to fight communism. Although at the end of the 1950's the John Birch Society was a small, obscure organization with a membership of a mere few thousand, it received its first national publicity in 1960, when Welch published *The Politician*, a book charging that President Eisenhower was a dedicated, conscious agent of the communist conspiracy. The society grew rapidly during the 1960's and reached an estimated membership of eighty thousand by the mid-1960's.

Further Reading

Broyes, J. Allen. *The John Birch Society: Anatomy of a Protest.* Boston: Beacon Press, 1966. An early study of the organization.

George, John, and Laird Wilcox. *American Extremists.* Amherst, N.Y.: Prometheus Books, 1996. An examination of various extremist groups. It includes a chapter on the John Birch Society.

William V. Moore

See also Communist Party of the U.S.A.; Conservatism in U.S. politics; Hungarian revolt; Loyalty oaths; McCarthy, Joseph; Red Monday.

■ Johns, Jasper

Identification American artist
Born May 15, 1930; Augusta, Georgia

With his paintings of recognizable objects, Jasper Johns was the first influential American artist during the 1950's to move away from abstract expressionism. As a result, he became one of the leading proponents of pop art.

Jasper Johns, Jr., was the son of Jasper Johns, Sr., and Jean Riley Johns. He grew up primarily in South Carolina, where he began to draw by the time he was three. After graduating from high school in 1947, Johns attended the University of South Carolina. He left college after three semesters and moved to New York City to pursue a career as an artist. Johns took classes at the Parsons School of Design, and by taking the time to visit various museums and galleries, he became acquainted with the works of Pablo Picasso, Jackson Pollock, Hans Hofmann, and Isamu Noguchi. During the early 1950's, he served in the U.S. Army and was stationed in Japan and at Fort Jackson, South Carolina. After being discharged from the Army in 1953, Johns moved back to New York.

Rise of a Pop Artist In 1954, Johns met fellow artist Robert Rauschenberg. The two artists became good friends, and they used each other as sounding boards for their various creative ideas. They experimented with adding "found" objects to their art, and they worked together designing window displays for Tiffany's department store. Johns realized that he wanted his art to incorporate everyday items with the techniques that had grown out of abstract expressionism. Unsatisfied with the art that he already had created, Johns destroyed most of his completed paintings. In a dream, he saw himself painting the American flag. Out of this vision Johns was inspired to paint his first flag. It was his intention to paint "things the mind already knows" in such a way as to make the viewer see them in a totally new way. He became primarily concerned with the craft of his painting and the way in which he could present things that everybody would instantly recognize. Since there was a simplicity to his subject matter, the creative process itself took on greater meaning.

In 1955, Johns painted *Target with Plaster Casts*. This work would be the first in a series of target paintings. He also painted his first arabic numerals during this year. On January 20, 1958, his first one-person show opened at the Leo Castelli Gallery in New York City. This exhibition became the talk of the art world. It garnered critical acclaim, but there was also much discussion among artists and critics alike concerning the propriety of using ordinary images as subject matter. The controversy did not deter the director of the Museum of Modern Art from purchasing three pieces for the museum. In a bold statement to the art community, Johns's *Target with Faces* was used on the cover of the January, 1958, issue of *ARTnews* magazine. Johns had established himself as an American artist who could not be ignored.

Impact Johns helped to move art away from the predominant abstract expressionism of the late 1940's and early 1950's by including "concrete" items in his paintings such as flags, targets, maps, and numerals. Through his efforts and those of Rauschenberg, the foundation was laid for the rise of such art movements as pop art and minimalism. In subsequent years, although Johns continued to paint "things the mind already knows," he also branched out into sculpture and printmaking.

Further Reading

Johns, Jasper. *Jasper Johns: Writings, Sketchbook Notes, Interviews.* Edited by Kirk Varnedoe. New York: Museum of Modern Art, 1996. An important collection that exposes the artist through his own public and private thoughts.

Johnston, Jill. *Jasper Johns: Privileged Information.* New York: Thames and Hudson, 1996. An intimate and analytical portrait of the artist and the man.

Jeffry Jensen

See also Abstract expressionism; Art movements; Guggenheim Museum; Pollock, Jackson; Rauschenberg, Robert.

■ Jorgensen, Christine

Identification First widely publicized transsexual
Born May 30, 1926; New York, New York
Died May 3, 1989; San Clemente, California

After Christine Jorgensen's much-publicized male-to-female transsexual surgery, she became a public speaker, performer, and role model. Her change both provoked and challenged ideas about sex and gender, as well as opening up once-taboo areas of discussion.

In 1926, a male child named George William Jorgensen, Jr., was born in New York to George and Florence Davis Hansen Jorgensen, immigrants from Denmark. A slender, blond boy, he always felt awkward and uncomfortable; he was attracted to men but rejected the idea that he was homosexual. In 1945, he was drafted into the U.S. Army, in which he served as a clerk, and in late 1946 he was honorably discharged. Meanwhile, he read widely about physiology, especially hormonal problems, and enrolled in the Manhattan Medical and Dental Assistant's School. There, he experimented with self-administered estrogen injections and learned that surgeons were performing sex-change operations in Europe.

In May, 1950, Jorgensen traveled to Copenhagen, Denmark, where, in 1951 and 1952, Dr. Christian Hamburger performed the first two of Jorgensen's three operations at the city's Danish State Hospital. The final surgery was performed in the United States in 1954. Jorgensen took the name Christine in honor of Hamburger.

Although not the first surgical transsexual, Jorgensen became the most publicized. Vast coverage worldwide began with a headline in the *New York Post* on December 1, 1952: "Ex-G.I. Becomes Blonde Beauty: Operation Transforms Bronx Youth." When she could not avoid the scandalous publicity, she decided to profit from it and shape it into something more educational and respectable. She sold her life story to *American Weekly Magazine* for twenty thousand dollars and released a spoken record, *Christine Jorgensen Revealed.*

Attractive, photogenic, and charming, Jorgensen became a celebrity. Although she would have preferred to be known as a photographer and filmmaker, she achieved fame and satisfaction as a speaker and performer. She appeared on talk shows and on the college lecture circuit; a stage act, in which she sang and did impersonations, drew audiences in places such as Las Vegas and Havana, Cuba. She was banned from using women's public toilets in Washington, D.C., but was named "Woman of the Year" for 1953 by the Scandinavian Societies of Greater New York. Her autobiography was published in 1967, and a mediocre movie based on it, called *The Christine Jorgensen Story,* appeared in 1970. Jorgensen died of bladder and lung cancer, on May 3, 1989.

Impact Jorgensen became a role model for many; applications for transsexual surgery skyrocketed

Christine Jorgensen aboard the ocean liner Andrea Doria *during her return voyage to the United States in September, 1954.* (AP/Wide World Photos)

as her story became public. She stressed the differences among homosexuality, transvestism, and transsexuality, opening awareness of topics that had previously only been snickered at, if discussed at all.

Additionally, though Jorgensen was not a feminist, her story helped promote feminism by undercutting the idea that anatomy is destiny. As an event that took place after the relative freedom women experienced while men were fighting in World War II and before the sexual revolution of the 1960's, the publicity about Jorgensen brought gender issues to the fore when many wanted to push them aside. The publicity emphasized Jorgensen's military service, which in reality was one that was short and uneventful; this focus seemed in part due to the perceived irony and anxiety about homosexuality in the military, an issue that proved persistent in later decades. Jorgensen's story also helped increase public respect for the sciences: The public was in awe of medical science that could change a man into a woman.

Further Reading

Ingrassia, Michele. "In 1952, She Was a Scandal." *Newsday,* May 5, 1989. This article, which served as an obituary after Jorgensen's death, is widely available online and is an excellent recapitulation of Jorgensen's life.

Jorgensen, Christine. *Christine Jorgensen: A Personal Autobiography.* Rev. ed. San Francisco: Cleis Press, 2001. A reprint of Jorgensen's autobiography with a new introduction by gay and lesbian historian Susan Stryker.

Bernadette Lynn Bosky

See also Homosexuality and gay rights; Kinsey Report; Sex and sex education; Women and the roots of the feminist movement.

K

■ Kazan, Elia

Identification American film and theater director
Born September 7, 1909; Constantinople, Turkey
Died September 28, 2003; Manhattan, New York

During the 1950's, Elia Kazan was one of the most honored directors of the theater and of film, although he became controversial after his appearance before the House Committee on Un-American Activities (HUAC), when he provided the committee with names of suspected communist sympathizers in Hollywood.

When Elia Kazan was four years old, he and his Greek parents emigrated to the United States, settling in New York City. He graduated from Williams College and studied drama at Yale University. He joined the Group Theater in 1932 and directed his first play in 1935; by the 1940's, Kazan had become an established director on Broadway. He made several documentaries during the 1930's and began directing feature films in 1945 with *A Tree Grows in Brooklyn.* He won his first Academy Award for *Gentleman's Agreement* in 1947. In that same year he cofounded the Actors Studio, the birthplace of "the Method" style of acting.

However, it was during the 1950's when Kazan flourished even more as a film director. After directing *Panic in the Streets* (1950), he adapted to the screen Tennessee Williams's play *A Streetcar Named Desire*, which he had directed in 1947 on Broadway. Kazan cast Marlon Brando, one of the Actors Studio's most famous students, as the film's lead, an appearance that made Brando a star. The next two films Kazan directed also featured Brando, *Viva Zapata!* (1952) and *On the Waterfront* (1954). The later film became an American classic and

showcased more Actors Studio alumni: Eva Marie Saint, Rod Steiger, Karl Malden, and Lee J. Cobb.

Critics of *On the Waterfront* have written that it reflected a defense of Kazan's own 1952 testimony before the HUAC, in which he admitted his membership in the Communist Party but also named eight other members, an act many felt was a betrayal of friendship to save his own career. His experience before the HUAC highlights one of the most contentious episodes of the 1950's: the communist witchhunts that devastated the entertainment world. Like many others in the business, Kazan found himself caught up in the communist hysteria generated by the Cold War. Many students of film eventually came

Film director Elia Kazan on the set of Panic in the Streets *in 1950.* (Hulton Archive | by Getty Images)

to judge his performance before the committee as a lapse in moral judgment and to regard Kazan's politics separately from his talent as a director, which remains highly regarded.

Kazan's next film was a 1955 adaptation of John Steinbeck's novel *East of Eden* (1952), and it tapped into the youth rebellion movement of the mid-1950's. The director again starred a young actor, James Dean, who, like Brando, would become an idol of the period. Kazan followed this success with *Baby Doll* (1956), a film that made a star out of Carol Baker, and *A Face in the Crowd* (1957), a movie about the rapid rise of an unknown actor to television stardom.

Throughout the 1950's Kazan also continued to direct a series of Broadway plays, such as Williams's *Camino Real* (pr. 1953) and *Cat on a Hot Tin Roof*, Robert Anderson's *Tea and Sympathy* (pr. 1953), and William Inge's *The Dark at the Top of the Stairs* (pr. 1957).

Impact Kazan's impact on theater and American cinema of the 1950's was substantial. Although his film career ran from 1942 to 1976, his most notable successes came during the 1950's, when he was noted especially for his direction of the plays of Arthur Miller and Tennessee Williams. However, his testimony before the HUAC plagued him for the rest of his life and colored his reputation within Hollywood. Despite his past, Kazan was honored time and again, not only for his film work but also for his theater direction, winning a total of three Tony Awards. In 1963, he was named codirector of the Repertory Theater of Lincoln Center for the Performing Arts. In 1983, he was given a Life Achievement award at the Kennedy Center, and in 1999, he accepted a lifetime achievement award from the Academy of Motion Pictures Arts and Sciences.

Further Reading

Kazan, Elia. *Elia Kazan: A Life.* New York: Alfred Knopf, 1988. Kazan's autobiography.

Michaels, Lloyd. *Elia Kazan: A Guide to References and Resources.* Boston: G. K. Hall, 1985. An annotated bibliography of the books, articles, and reviews about Kazan's film work.

Pauly, Thomas H. *An American Odyssey: Elia Kazan and American Culture.* Philadelphia: Temple University Press, 1983. A wide-ranging study of the impact of Kazan's work on American culture.

Charles L. P. Silet

See also Academy Awards; Actors Studio; Brando, Marlon; Film in the United States; House Committee on Un-American Activities; Miller, Arthur; *On the Waterfront*; *Streetcar Named Desire, A*; Theater in the United States; Williams, Tennessee.

■ Kefauver, Estes

Identification American politician
Born July 26, 1903; Madisonville, Tennessee
Died August 10, 1963; Bethesda, Maryland

As a United States senator, Kefauver made headlines as chair of a congressional subcommittee on organized crime. In 1956, he was chosen as Adlai Stevenson's candidate for vice president.

Carey Estes Kefauver was the second son of Robert Cooke Kefauver and Phredonia Estes. Kefauver transformed himself from rural farm boy to respected, urbane politician. Despite his driving ambition and knack for self-promotion, Kefauver remained a man of honesty and integrity. As a boy, Kefauver dreamed of becoming a lawyer. In 1920, he enrolled at the University of Tennessee at Knoxville. A mediocre student, he excelled in sports, edited the school newspaper, and was elected president of the student body. Later, he earned a law degree from Yale University and began practicing law in Chattanooga, Tennessee. After years of hard work, Kefauver became a respected corporate lawyer.

Politician and Reformer In 1938, Kefauver made his first bid for political office when he ran unsuccessfully for the Tennessee state senate. After his defeat, the governor appointed him state commissioner of finance and taxation. In the summer of 1939, Kefauver entered national politics and won a seat in Congress. As a "New Deal Democrat," Kefauver supported President Franklin D. Roosevelt's administration and gained a reputation as a congressional reformer; he coauthored a book on the ills of Congress.

Kefauver served nearly ten years in the House of Representatives. His colleagues labeled him a "southern liberal" because of his support of labor and some civil rights legislation. He supported the anti-poll-tax law but opposed the Fair Employment Practices Commission and the federal antilynching law. Kefauver believed these laws threatened civil liberties. Furthermore, he did not want to anger his southern colleagues or constituents.

In 1948, Kefauver ran for the U.S. Senate. During the campaign, he wore a coonskin cap in response to a party boss's accusation that Kefauver was a "pet coon." The "Davy Crockett" image also reinforced Kefauver's Americanism after opponents accused him of being soft on communism.

As a senator, Kefauver made a name for himself as a dedicated crime fighter. In 1950, he introduced Senate Resolution 202 calling for an investigation of organized crime in the United States. A congressional subcommittee was formed and became known as the Kefauver Committee. The committee held hearings in fourteen major cities and questioned politicians, law enforcement officials, and gangsters. In the end, the committee concluded that a nationwide organized crime syndicate existed and was linked to public officials, but the committee publicized rather than eradicated crime. In 1951, the Kefauver Committee held televised hearings, enthralling the American public. As a result, Kefauver became a nationally known political figure.

Kefauver sought the Democratic presidential nomination in 1952 and 1956. Both times, he was passed over in favor of Adlai Stevenson. Despite his disappointment, Kefauver toed the party line and campaigned for Stevenson. At the 1956 Democratic national convention, Stevenson allowed the delegates to choose his vice presidential running mate. Kefauver won a place on the ticket, narrowly beating Massachusetts senator John F. Kennedy. The Stevenson-Kefauver team lost the election to Republicans Dwight D. Eisenhower and Richard M. Nixon.

Following the 1956 election, Kefauver returned to the Senate. In 1957, he became the chairman of the Senate Antitrust and Monopoly Subcommittee. He also continued to sponsor bills to protect the rights of the people. His last major accomplishment was the passage of the Kefauver-Harris Drug Act, which protected Americans from potentially harmful drugs.

Kefauver died suddenly of a heart attack in 1963. His colleagues eulogized him as an honest politician.

Impact Estes Kefauver was an effective politician who failed to achieve his presidential aspirations. As a congressman, however, he successfully brought nationwide attention to criminal activities and championed the cause of the people. Kefauver was also one of the first southern congressmen to support civil rights legislation.

Further Reading

Gorman, Joseph Bruce. *Kefauver: A Political Biography.* New York: Oxford University Press, 1971. This work is a favorable biography of Estes Kefauver and his career in Congress.

Kefauver, Estes. *Crime in America.* Garden City, N.Y.: Doubleday, 1951. This work is Estes Kefauver's own account of the activities of the Senate Crime Investigating Committee. It includes colorful stories of organized crime figures and a detailed explanation of the committee's recommendations.

Rhonda Smith

Estes Kefauver (right) and Adlai Stevenson in April, 1956, when both politicians were campaigning for the Democratic Party's presidential nomination. After Stevenson won the nomination at the party's summer convention, Kefauver accepted the vice presidential nomination. (AP/Wide World Photos)

See also Celler-Kefauver Act of 1950; Civil Rights Act of 1957; Elections in the United States, 1952; Elections in the United States, 1956; Federal Bureau of Investigation; Kefauver Committee; Organized crime; Stevenson, Adlai; Teamsters union.

■ Kefauver Committee

Identification Congressional committee established to investigate organized crime in the United States
Date Operated from 1950 to 1951

The Kefauver Committee exposed a link between organized crime and public officials and bolstered Senator Estes Kefauver's career.

The Kefauver Committee was the brainchild of its namesake, Senator Estes Kefauver. A Tennessee congressman since 1939, Kefauver became interested in crime after serving as chairman of a House of Representative judiciary subcommittee. After joining the Senate in 1949, Kefauver decided to make crime a congressional issue. In 1950, he introduced Senate Resolution 202, which called for an investigation of crime in interstate commerce. Kefauver's action resulted in the formation of the Senate Crime Committee, which soon became known as the Kefauver Committee.

The committee included three Democrats and two Republicans, all members of either the Senate Judiciary or Commerce committees. They included Kefauver, Herbert R. O'Conor of Maryland, Lester C. Hunt of Wyoming, Alexander Wiley of Wisconsin, and Charles W. Tobey of New Hampshire. Kefauver served as chairman from May 10, 1950, to May 1, 1952. When he stepped down as chairman, he chose O'Conor as his replacement.

The Kefauver Committee had three responsibilities: to determine if a link existed between organized crime and interstate commerce; to determine and investigate people, firms, and corporations involved; and to determine if any of these interstate criminal operations violated federal or state laws. The committee held hearings in fourteen major cities including Miami, New York, Kansas City, and Chicago. Kefauver and his associates questioned politicians, law enforcement officials, and criminals. Some eight hundred witnesses testified before the committee, including an assortment of racketeers, gamblers, bookies, and alleged crime bosses, some left over from famed gangster Al Capone's criminal organization.

Televised Hearings In 1951, the Kefauver Committee hearings were televised. The medium was new, and the committee was only the fifth congressional committee to be broadcast. Kefauver's hearings caused a nationwide sensation as the American public tuned in to see government officials confront sleazy crime lords. The Kefauver Committee provided more drama than any regular television program. Some 200,000 to 300,000 people watched the committee hearings; businesses suffered, and theaters and hotels went vacant. Even housewives did daily chores in front of the television. Some merchants bought televisions and broadcast the hearings to draw customers back into their stores.

The televised hearings also promoted Estes Kefauver's career. While he investigated stereotypical villains such as James "Smiling Jimmy" Sullivan, Carlos "Little Big Man" Marcello, and the "Five Iron Men," the Tennessee senator was likened to a knight in shining armor. Television transformed the ostensibly dull, gangly Kefauver into a nationally known crime fighter. He was soon recognized as a potential candidate for the 1952 presidential election.

Impact In the end, the committee concluded that there was a nationwide organized crime syndicate with ties to political officials. The committtee drew up twenty-two recommendations including the establishment of a an independent federal crime commission operating from the executive branch. Other suggestions included the creation of a racket squad in the Justice Department, harsher penalities for narcotic producers and smugglers, and immigration reform to make it easier for the government to deport criminals.

The Kefauver Committee publicized, rather than eradicated, crime. Few new crimes or criminals were discovered. Few new questions were asked. The committee did, however, draw public attention to organized crime and aided local officials in the fight against corruption. The committee affected its chairman more than it did crime. Very few of the committee's suggestions were enacted into the law. Perhaps more than anything else, the Kefauver Committee hearings exemplified the power of television.

Further Reading

Kefauver, Estes. *Crime in America.* Garden City, N.Y.: Doubleday, 1951. Kefauver's own account of the activities of the Senate Crime Investigating Committee. It includes colorful stories of organized crime figures and a detailed explanation of the committee's recommendations.

Moore, William Howard. *The Kefauver Committee and the Politics of Crime, 1950-1952*. Columbia: University of Missouri Press, 1974. This work is a critical examination of Estes Kefauver and his crime committee. Kefauver is portrayed as a self-serving, exploiting politician who exaggerated the power of the criminal underworld.

Woodiwiss, Michael. *Organized Crime and American Power: A History*. Toronto: University of Toronto Press, 2001. Explores the history of organized crime in the United States by emphasizing the connections between criminals and government officials.

Rhonda Smith

See also AFL-CIO merger; Army-McCarthy hearings; Kefauver, Estes; *On the Waterfront*; Organized crime.

■ Kelly, Grace

Identification American film actor who became the princess of Monaco

Born November 12, 1929; Philadelphia, Pennsylvania

Died September 14, 1982; principality of Monaco

Hollywood films catapulted Grace Kelly to stardom and served as a prelude to her role as the princess of Monaco. Her union with Prince Rainier III produced an heir to the throne and thus ensured the continuance of an independent principality.

Grace Patricia Kelly was born the third of four children to John and Margaret Kelly. Her father built the family fortune as a bricklayer and rose to prominence in Philadelphia's social circles. Grace Kelly had an early desire to be an actor, and after graduating from high school in 1947, she followed her acting dreams to New York City. She worked briefly as a model, graduated from the American Academy of Dramatic Arts, and did a short stint in television before moving to California to pursue a film career.

Kelly's first film role, in *Fourteen Hours* (1951), was followed by a larger role as Amy Kane in *High Noon* (1952), where she shared the screen with Gary Cooper and Lloyd Bridges. Kelly appeared with Clark Gable and Ava Gardner in the 1953 African drama *Mogambo*. She rose to greater prominence with her role opposite James Stewart in Alfred Hitchcock's thriller *Rear Window* (1954). She did a second Hitchcock film, *Dial M for Murder* (1954), opposite Ray Milland, and her next film, *The Country Girl* (1954), earned her a best-actress Oscar. She starred in two

Prince Rainier III and Grace Kelly acknowledge cheering crowds while riding in an open car from their wedding ceremony in Monte Carlo's Cathedral of Saint Nicholas. (AP/Wide World Photos)

more films in 1954, *Green Fire* and *The Bridges at Toko-Ri*. She costarred with Cary Grant in Hitchcock's *To Catch a Thief* (1955), and in 1956 she filmed *The Swan* as well as *High Society*, the last of her Hollywood films. Kelly's work with Hitchcock assured her a place among the legends of Hollywood. Hitchcock tried repeatedly and unsuccessfully to duplicate the Kelly persona in other women actors.

In 1955, Kelly traveled to France for the Cannes Film Festival and the showing of *The Country Girl*. It was at the film festival that she met Prince Rainier of Monaco, her future husband. Grace and her family sailed to Monaco for the wedding on board the USS *Constitution*. "The Wedding of the Century" was held on April 18, 1956, at the Cathedral of Saint Nicholas in Monte Carlo. Because Kelly had broken her contract with the studio, the couple allowed a film of their wedding to be released as a movie in the United States.

Kelly's marriage to Rainier produced three children: Princess Caroline (b. 1957), Prince Albert (b. 1958), and Princess Stephanie (b. 1965). Princess Grace relinquished her acting career, although she later aided in the production of at least two films. She also served as the president of the Red Cross of Monaco, supported the arts, championed breastfeeding, and raised funds for developing countries.

Impact Beauty, elegance, and sensuality were Grace Kelly's trademarks on the screen. As Princess Grace, she is remembered as a beloved wife and mother, philanthropist, and goodwill ambassador. On September 13, 1982, Princess Grace and her daughter, Stephanie, were involved in a car crash on a mountain road above Monaco, the same stretch of roadway featured in the film *To Catch a Thief*. Princess Grace apparently suffered a stroke while driving. She died of her injuries the following day, while Stephanie was badly injured but survived. The princess's funeral was held at the Cathedral of Saint Nicholas, where her body was interred.

Further Reading

Curtis, Jenny, and Francine Hornberger, eds. *Grace Kelly: A Life in Pictures*. New York: Barnes and Noble Books, 1998. Chronicles Kelly's life from childhood until her death with more than 120 photographs.

Englund, Steven. *Grace of Monaco*. New York: Doubleday, 1984. A biography highlighting her contributions to the principality.

Wayne, Jane Ellen, et al. *The Golden Girls of MGM: Greta Garbo, Joan Crawford, Lana Turner, Judy Garland, Ava Gardner, Grace Kelly, and Others*. New York: Avalon, 2004. Explores Metro-Goldwyn-Mayer's female stars of Hollywood's golden age by using photographs and essays that detail the stars' filmographies.

Ann M. Legreid

See also Academy Awards; Fashions and clothing; Film in the United States; Hairstyles; Hitchcock films.

■ Kennan, George F.

Identification American diplomat, foreign policy planner, and historian
Born February 16, 1904; Milwaukee, Wisconsin

The 1950's witnessed George Kennan's rejection of his "containment theory" when he instead promoted American disengagement with the Soviet Union.

George Frost Kennan began his career in the U.S. Foreign Service with assignments in Switzerland, Germany, and the Soviet Union. After the establishment of United States-Soviet diplomatic relations in 1933, he was stationed in Moscow for several years.

As director of the U.S. State Department's planning staff, Kennan published his famous "X article"—initially anonymous, signed only with an "X" and titled "The Sources of Soviet Conduct"—in the July, 1947, issue of *Foreign Affairs*. In it, he argued that Soviet expansionism should be checked by a policy of containment backed by military force. The notion of containment became the basis of U.S. foreign policy toward the Soviet Union in the decades that followed. In 1952, he was appointed American ambassador in Moscow but was soon ousted when the Soviets declared him *persona non grata*.

In 1953, Kennan retired from the Foreign Service to write on Soviet-American relations, European diplomacy, and his memoirs while also acting as a member of the Institute for Advanced Study in Princeton, New Jersey. Perturbed by the increasingly military orientation of U.S. foreign policy, he became the leading critic of U.S. Cold War policies during the 1950's. In 1957, he caused a small sensation when he called for the mutual withdrawal of U.S. and Soviet forces from Germany and the unification and neutralization of East and West Germany.

Impact As architect of the containment policy toward the Soviet Union, Kennan left a deep imprint upon U.S. foreign policy in the postwar era. His role in Cold War politics cemented his legacy as a leading historian and American diplomat.

Further Reading

Kennan, George F. *Memoirs, 1925-1950; Memoirs, 1950-1963.* 2 vols. Boston: Little, Brown, 1967; 1972. Kennan's autobiography.

Mayers, David. *George Kennan and the Dilemmas of U.S. Foreign Policy.* New York: Oxford University Press, 1989. A well-informed, critical-intellectual biography.

George P. Blum

See also Acheson, Dean; Cold War; Dulles, John Foster; Foreign policy of the United States; Geneva Summit Conference; Germany's postwar occupation; Hungarian revolt; Marshall, George C.; North Atlantic Treaty Organization; Truman Doctrine; Warsaw Pact.

■ Kennedy, John F.

Identification U.S. senator from Massachusetts and future president of the United States
Born May 29, 1917; Brookline, Massachusetts
Died November 22, 1963; Dallas, Texas

During the 1950's, John F. Kennedy established himself as a young star of the Democratic Party and readied his platform for his candidacy for the 1960 presidential election.

At the beginning of the 1950's, John F. Kennedy was a young congressman from Massachusetts. Having won election to the U.S. House of Representatives in 1946, he began his career representing a working-class area of Boston, Massachusetts. An outspoken anticommunist, he was a proponent of federal social programs at home. His anticommunism caused some tension with members of his political party. Although a Democrat, Kennedy attacked President Harry S. Truman's administration, saying the president's foreign policy contributed to the victory of the Chinese communists in 1949. Distancing himself from the liberal wing of his party, Kennedy made several comments designed to differentiate his politics from those of the Roosevelt and Truman administrations. This stance later haunted him when he sought support for the 1960 Democratic presidential nomination: Prominent Democrats such as President

Truman and Eleanor Roosevelt opposed Kennedy's nomination.

Elected to the Senate in 1952 with the financial backing of his family, Kennedy moved to establish his credentials as a rising star in the Democratic Party. As a young senator, he was regarded as one of the most eligible bachelors in Washington, D.C., a status that ended when he wed Jacqueline Bouvier in 1953. He also began to assemble the staff that would assist him in his quest for the presidency later in the decade. It was at this time that Theodore Sorensen, a key aide during Kennedy's White House years, joined his staff.

Kennedy's Senate career was not without controversy, however. The Kennedy family's friendship with Senator Joseph McCarthy caused embarrassment. When many were beginning to question the propriety of McCarthy's congressional anticommunist hearings, Kennedy's younger brother Robert went to work for McCarthy's Senate committee investigating communist influence in American life. When McCarthy's political fortunes took a downward turn in 1954, the Senate, without Senator Kennedy's vote, passed a resolution of censure against the Wisconsin Republican. While Kennedy claimed illness prevented him from casting a vote on the censure resolution, critics saw this as an excuse for avoiding a personally difficult vote against his colleague.

As the saga surrounding McCarthy reached its dramatic high point, Kennedy's popular book *Profiles in Courage* (1956) appeared in print. Critics claimed that Kennedy had not shown much political courage during the McCarthy episode, and this charge would haunt him throughout the remaining years of the decade. However, the publication of the Pulitzer Prize-winning book was an enormously popular step, and it provided him with additional press exposure. By 1956, he was being considered for the vice presidential nomination. Although he did not receive the vice presidential nod, his bid for the nomination enhanced his standing as a rising star in Democratic Party politics.

Setting a Presidential Platform By the late 1950's, Kennedy was a national political figure. Taking several steps to bolster his credentials as a possible contender for the 1960 Democratic nomination, he began to speak publicly on international affairs and to publish articles setting forth his views on the policy

Senator John F. Kennedy, standing with his wife, Jacqueline, thanks his supporters after learning that he has won reelection in the November, 1958, election. (AP/Wide World Photos)

debates of the time. Calling for greater defense spending, he criticized the Eisenhower administration as complacent and lacking in imagination. He began to speak of a "missile gap," or an alleged advantage the Soviet Union had acquired in intercontinental ballistic missile technology. Although subsequent information confirmed that there was no missile gap, the issue resonated with voters concerned that the Soviet launch of the *Sputnik* satellite had revealed a glaring weakness in American space and defense technology. He also began to speak on whether the United States should be more involved in Asian affairs. On this score, he said the United States had a responsibility to meet the Soviet challenge throughout the world.

Realizing the connection between economic strength and military influence, Kennedy criticized the Eisenhower administration for tolerating slow economic growth. Although his public speeches on this subject were helpful to him politically, his primary area of interest remained foreign policy. Indeed, Kennedy's passion for foreign policy stood in contrast to his comments on civil rights. While he did support new measures to bring about equality under the law for the country's African American citizens, this was not a passionate issue for him. However, it would become perhaps one of the central domestic issues of the Kennedy presidency.

Impact Kennedy's warnings regarding the "missile gap" pointed to his presidency of the 1960's. His aggressive campaign rhetoric during the 1950's continued throughout his time as president. Although his views changed as he moved from being simply another Massachusetts politician to a national political figure, his basic anticommunism remained in place. As a congressman, as a senator, and later as president, he displayed a more substantial interest in foreign as opposed to domestic policy. Nevertheless, he did change American domestic politics in fundamental ways. Not only was he the first Roman Catholic elected as president of the United States, but he was also the first candidate to successfully exploit the new technologies of television and modern campaigning. The Kennedy senatorial victories in 1952 and 1958 were harbingers of his 1960 presidential campaign and of a new style of running for office.

Further Reading

Bernstein, Irving. *Promises Kept: The New Frontier of John F. Kennedy.* New York: Oxford University Press, 1991. This is a favorable interpretation of the Kennedy administration.

Matthews, Christopher. *Kennedy and Nixon: The Rivalry That Shaped Postwar America.* New York: Simon & Schuster, 1996. This is a study of the competition between Kennedy and Nixon during the 1950's.

Reeves, Thomas. *A Question of Character: A Life of John F. Kennedy.* New York: Free Press, 1991. This study presents a harsh critique of Kennedy's personality and leadership traits.

Michael E. Meagher

See also Cold War; Eisenhower, Dwight D.; Gallup polls; Hoover, J. Edgar; Lodge, Henry Cabot; McCarthy, Joseph; Meany, George; Nixon, Richard M.; *Profiles in Courage*; *Sputnik I*.

■ Kerouac, Jack

Identification American writer
Born March 22, 1922; Lowell, Massachusetts
Died October 21, 1969; St. Petersburg, Florida

Jack Kerouac is best known as the voice of the Beat generation, the hip youth culture of the 1950's.

Jack (Jean-Louis) Kerouac was born in Lowell, Massachusetts, where he grew up in a tight-knit French-Canadian community. A high school football star, Kerouac won a full scholarship to Columbia University. There he met a circle of writers, which included Allen Ginsberg, William Burroughs, Lawrence Ferlinghetti, and Neal Cassady. This group became known as the Beat writers. The term "Beat" has been attributed to Jack Kerouac and has been defined variously as tired or disillusioned or as an abbreviation of "beatific" or saintly. In reaction to the conservatism of the Cold War era, the Beats experimented with a free lifestyle characterized by restless traveling; writing in a spontaneous, stream-of-consciousness style; and abuse of drugs, sex, and alcohol.

During the late 1940's, while working on the manuscript of his first novel, *The Town and the City* (1950), Kerouac took a series of road trips across the country from New York to San Francisco with Neal Cassady. These trips became the basis for the novel *On the Road* (1957), and Cassady's lifestyle and charisma became the model for the character of Dean Moriarty, while Kerouac became narrator Sal Paradise.

In 1950, Kerouac published *The Town and the City* and began work on several different drafts of *On the Road*. He continued to travel, hitchhiking across America to visit his friends among the Beat writers, who later became characters in his novels. He wrote a series of autobiographical novels through the early and mid-1950's, while looking for a publisher for *On the Road*.

Kerouac published *On the Road* in 1957. The book was an immediate success, establishing Kerouac's reputation as an important American writer. He continued to publish novels, poetry, and nonfiction for the next ten years, including *Doctor Sax* (1959), *Maggie Cassidy* (1959), *Visions of Gerard* (1963), and *Vanity of Duluoz* (1968), written about his youth in Lowell. Other works included *The Subterraneans* (1958), *The Dharma Bums* (1958), *Mexico City Blues* (1959), and *Desolation Angels* (1965), the last of which detailed his travels and adventures of the Beat generation.

Fame was difficult for Kerouac to handle. He was both hailed and criticized as the representative of the irresponsible Beat generation. However, Kerouac was a complicated man, a disillusioned romantic, and a Roman Catholic, who lived much of his life with his mother. He grew increasingly alienated from the youth culture that embraced his books. He died in Florida in 1969 of complications of alcoholism. He was only forty-seven years old.

Impact Jack Kerouac has a place in the canon of American literature as an important writer whose philosophy is sometimes compared to those of Henry Thoreau and Walt Whitman. The spontaneous prose style of *On the Road* is studied by literary critics and scholars. He is considered the voice of the Beat generation and the youth of the 1950's. He is also studied as the voice of working-class, French-Canadian Lowell, Massachusetts.

Further Reading

Charters, Ann, ed. *Jack Kerouac: Selected Letters, 1940-1956*. New York: Viking, 1995. A primary source edited by a prominent Kerouac biographer, scholar, and critic. Letters are linked by brief commentary by the editor.

Miles, Barry. *Jack Kerouac, King of the Beats: A Portrait*. New York: Henry Holt, 1998. A portrait of Kerouac from the youthful era of *On the Road* to his disillusionment of the 1960's. Explores the contradictions in Kerouac's character.

Theado, Matt. *Understanding Jack Kerouac*. Columbia: University of South Carolina Press, 2001. A book-by-book approach to the Kerouac canon. Presents a framework for understanding Kerouac's themes and writing techniques.

Susan Butterworth

See also Beat generation; Burroughs, William; Corso, Gregory; Ferlinghetti, Lawrence; Ginsberg, Allen; *Naked Lunch*; *On the Road*; Poetry; Rexroth, Kenneth; San Francisco Renaissance; Youth culture and the generation gap.

■ Khrushchev's visit to the United States

The Event Soviet leader Nikita Khrushchev traveled across the United States and conferred with President Dwight D. Eisenhower at Camp David

Date September 15-27, 1959

Khrushchev's visit opened the door to better American-Soviet relations and to progress on disarmament.

Khrushchev landed outside Washington, D.C., on September 15, 1959, less than three years after the Soviet suppression of the Hungarian revolt. Hungarian refugees organized a reception of silence by the public lining the parkway coming into the city and later by the crowds assembled in the streets of New York.

On September 17, Khrushchev addressed the Economic Club in New York. Before his remarks, Khrushchev engaged in thirty minutes of banter with his audience but then had to read through his long speech, already published in Moscow, with consecutive interpretation. Alcohol flowed in the audience, resulting in catcalls, and some attendees began to walk out to catch the last suburban trains so they could get home. At what was already a late hour, the organizers arranged a panel to question Khrushchev. The first question critiqued Soviet impediments to free dissemination of information via government acts such as jamming of foreign broadcasts and banning the free sale of Western newspapers. Khrushchev, already tired from the time difference from Moscow, reacted badly, saying that he would fly home if he was not welcome in the United States. Henry Cabot Lodge, the president's designated host on Khrushchev's tour, conceived the idea of rebutting Khrushchev's assertions while introducing him in each city. Khrushchev clearly did not find Lodge's debating strategy pleasing.

In a speech to the United Nations in New York, Khrushchev advocated general and complete disarmament, a proposal that evoked a skeptical U.S. press reaction.

Reception in California In Los Angeles, Khrushchev was shown a somewhat risqué filming of a cancan dance and took offense, walking out of the studio with his wife, Nina, on his arm. At lunch, he exchanged comments about the Soviet Union's Greek Orthodox heritage with Twentieth Century-Fox film studio president Spyros Skouras, who represented the Christian point of view against Khrushchev's atheism. Khrushchev also expressed a desire to visit Disneyland, but his own security chief disapproved the visit because ensuring Khrushchev's security in the amusement park would be virtually impossible. It gave Khrushchev the opportunity, however, to imply that U.S. authorities were keeping him from contact with ordinary Americans even in a place so innocent of strategic importance as Disneyland.

Soviet premier Nikita Khrushchev (right) jokes with Americans in Coon Rapids, Iowa, in September, 1959. (AP/Wide World Photos)

On the evening of September 19, Khrushchev attended a reception at which his host, among others, was Mayor Norris Paulson of Los Angeles. Paulson criticized Khrushchev's remark that "we shall bury you." Khrushchev reacted negatively.

At a crucial private meeting in Lodge's hotel room in Los Angeles, Llewellyn Thompson, U.S. ambassador to the Soviet Union, persuaded Lodge to moderate his introductions and alter the tone of his confrontational hosting. Khrushchev was warmly greeted by Californians at stops on the Los Angeles-San Francisco rail trip. Harry Bridges, the head of the Longshoremen's Union of the Pacific Coast, arranged to give Khrushchev a warm and enthusiastic reception in the streets and in the union's hiring hall when Khrushchev reached San Francisco. Khrushchev also met with U.S. Trade Union leaders and visited an IBM computer factory. The visits to San Francisco made an excellent impression, partly because of the beauty of the city, seen by Khrushchev from a ship cruising the bay on a sparkling blue day, and partly because this portion of his trip balanced the previously contentious atmosphere of the visit.

Final Days In Iowa, Khrushchev visited advanced agriculture-related laboratories at Iowa State University and the farm of Roswell Garst, an innovator in the development of hybrid corn. At Garst farm many of the more than five hundred journalists covering the visit crowded in, and Khrushchev at one point threw a clod of manure at one of them.

In Pittsburgh, the reception of Khrushchev was cordial. Khrushchev spoke at the University of Pittsburgh and visited the Mesta Steel Plant. On September 24, Khrushchev returned to Washington, D.C., where he met with U.S. business and commercial leaders, visited the Beltsville experimental agricultural station, addressed the U.S. public on television, and held talks with President Eisenhower at Camp David. The visit ended with both sides warmly anticipating Eisenhower's planned return visit to the Soviet Union, which later was aborted when Soviet antiaircraft batteries shot down an American U-2 spy plane in central Russia on May 1, 1960.

Impact Khrushchev's visit marked the first time a top Soviet leader set foot on U.S. soil, and the visit occurred at the height of the Cold War. His unpredictability, temper, and wit characterized the visit and proved to Americans that he was a shrewd opponent in ongoing international tensions.

Further Reading

Kharlamov, M., and O. Vadeyev, eds. *Face to Face with America: The Story of N. S. Khrushchev's Visit to the USA.* Honolulu: University Press of the Pacific, 2002. Paperback reprint. Collection of articles by Soviet journalists who accompanied Khrushchev on his trip. First published in Moscow in 1960.
Khrushchev in America. New York: Crosscurrents Press, 1960. Provides full texts of speeches made by Khrushchev during his visit.
Taubman, William. *Khrushchev: The Man and His Era.* New York: W. W. Norton, 2003. An award-winning biography that draws on historical archives opened in the Soviet Union during the early twenty-first century.

Nathaniel Davis

See also Cold War; Eisenhower, Dwight D.; Elizabeth II's visit to North America; Hungarian revolt; Nixon's "Checkers" speech; Nixon's "kitchen debate"; U-2 spy planes.

■ King, Martin Luther, Jr.

Definition African American civil rights leader
Born January 15, 1929; Atlanta, Georgia
Died April 4, 1968; Memphis, Tennessee

Thrust into leadership of the Montgomery, Alabama, bus boycott in 1955, King emerged as the both the primary leader and the personification of the national Civil Rights movement.

Martin Luther King, Jr., was born into a comfortable, middle-class Georgia family. Both his father and his maternal grandfather had been active in the National Association for the Advancement of Colored People (NAACP) and local voter registration drives for African Americans, and both men had been recognized as leaders of Atlanta's black community. However, no one could have predicted that Martin Luther King, Jr., would fulfill the role he established for himself during the mid- to late 1950's and 1960's. During a public career that lasted only thirteen years, he, more than any other individual, crystallized the moral power of the Civil Rights movement. In the process he transformed American politics.

Public Career A graduate of Atlanta's Morehouse College, King also earned a bachelor's degree in divinity from Crozer Theological Seminary in Chester,

Martin Luther King, Jr., received a kiss from his wife, Coretta Scott King, after scoring a legal victory in court during the Montgomery bus boycott in March, 1956. (AP/Wide World Photos)

Pennsylvania, and a doctorate in theology from Boston University. In late 1955, he was only twenty-six years old and had been the pastor of Dexter Avenue Baptist Church in Montgomery, Alabama, for less than two years when Rosa Parks, a local woman, started a revolution by refusing to abide by a segregation law that required she give up her seat on a public bus to a white man. When Parks was arrested, her show of defiance touched a nerve. African Americans, who had long objected to Montgomery's segregation laws, launched a citywide bus boycott, organized the Montgomery Improvement Association, and made King their spokesman.

During the long boycott that ensued, King developed a practical philosophy of direct confrontation of unjust laws and nonviolent resistance to authorities that attempted to enforce such laws. Throughout his public career, he repeatedly insisted that black Americans were merely demanding the rights they should already have received as American citizens.

After a boycott of twelve months, the Montgomery Improvement Association forced the city of Montgomery to desegregate its public buses. The successful campaign marked the beginning of the end of officially enforced racial segregation in the South, but much work remained to be done. African Americans, particularly those in the South, were still disfranchised, relegated to inferior schools, segregated in other forms of public accommodations, and unable to compete for well-paying jobs. Through the coming years, King turned his attention to those and other issues, all the time employing the tactics of nonviolent mass protest that had worked so well in Montgomery.

To mobilize African Americans and organize new protest movements, King oversaw the creation of the Southern Christian Leadership Conference (SCLC) in 1957. King was elected its first president and held the position until his death in 1968. The SCLC quickly became one of the nation's preeminent civil rights organizations.

Impact Many Americans regarded King as the leader of the Civil Rights movement after Montgomery and until his death in 1968. However, such a view is complicated, as King himself would have acknowledged. The movement never had a single leader; moreover, leaders of mass movements can do little without the thousands of men and women who carry out the movements' work. Throughout most of the 1960's, King and the SCLC led notable campaigns in Alabama, Georgia, Illinois, Tennessee, and Washington, D.C., until King was struck down by an assassin in Memphis, Tennessee, in 1968.

Further Reading

Abernathy, Donzaleigh. *Partners to History: Martin Luther King, Jr., Ralph David Abernathy, and the Civil Rights Movement.* New York: Crown, 2003. Inside view of the Civil Rights movement, written by the daughter of King's closest associate, Ralph Abernathy.

Branch, Taylor. *Parting the Waters: America in the King Years, 1954-1963.* New York: Simon & Schuster, 1988. Prizewinning history of the Civil Rights movement, with considerable attention to King's role.

Fairclough, Adam. *To Redeem the Soul of America: The Southern Christian Leadership Conference and Martin Luther King, Jr.* Athens: University of Georgia Press, 2001. Thorough examination of the Civil

Rights movement that explores the SCLC's internal structure and its role in shaping civil rights policy.

Todd Moye

See also African Americans; Belafonte, Harry; Civil Rights movement; Federal Bureau of Investigation; Graham, Billy; *Invisible Man*; Montgomery bus boycott; Parker, Suzy; Racial discrimination; Southern Christian Leadership Conference.

■ Kingston Trio

Identification Folk music group
Date Formed in 1957

The Kingston Trio led a folk music revival that paved the way for the protest singers who emerged during the 1960's.

In 1957, three young men—Bob Shane, Nick Reynolds, and Dave Guard—emerged from the local San Francisco music scene. Dressed in trademark button-down shirts and singing in three-part harmony, the Kingston Trio had a clean-cut, collegiate image that appealed to the American public. Their version of the Appalachian murder ballad "Tom Dooley" put them on the map, going to number one on the charts and earning the trio their first Grammy Award in 1958. The following year they won another Grammy for their album *The Kingston Trio at Large*.

Unlike the pop acts they followed, the Kingston Trio sold more long-playing records (LPs) than singles. In their first four years, they cut ten albums. At one point *Billboard* magazine listed four of their albums in the Top Ten, an accomplishment unmatched into the early twenty-first century.

Impact The music industry took note not only of the appeal of the Kingston Trio's combination of traditional, gospel, calypso, and folk genres, but also of the willingness of the record-buying public to purchase LPs rather than singles. The Kingston Trio fostered people's interest in folk music and laid the foundation for the emergence during the 1960's of people such as Joan Baez and Bob Dylan, but the trio also changed the industry's approach to making records and marketing their musical groups.

Further Reading

Blake, Benjamin. *Kingston Trio on Record*. Naperville, Ill.: Kingston Korner, 1986. A comprehensive compendium of interviews, pictures, and commentaries on songs and albums.

Unterberger, Richie, and Mark Brend. *Turn! Turn! Turn! The Sixties Folk Rock Revolution*. San Francisco: Backbeat Books, 2002. Includes discussion of the rise of folk-rock during the 1950's.

Lacy Schutz

See also Belafonte, Harry; Long-playing records; Music; Rock and roll; San Francisco Renaissance; Youth culture and the generation gap.

Bob Shane, Dave Guard, and Nick Reynolds. (Arkent Archive)

■ Kinsey Report

Identification Two-volume report on the sexual
behavior of Americans
Author Alfred C. Kinsey (1894-1956)
Date First volume published in 1948; second
volume published in 1953

*This controversial study had an important impact on the
sexual mores of the 1950's and set the stage for the sexual
revolution of the 1960's.*

The Kinsey Report was issued in two volumes: The
first, *Sexual Behavior in the Human Male*, was published in 1947 and the second, *Sexual Behavior in the
Human Female*, was issued in 1953. The reports took
their name from their principal author, Alfred C.
Kinsey, a Harvard-trained biologist and Indiana University professor. With financial support from the
Rockefeller Foundation, Kinsey's research team interviewed tens of thousands of Americans, and in
turn compiled "sexual histories," which revealed
that a high percentage of both sexes had a wide variety of sexual experiences outside the bounds of marriage. Conventional moralists were outraged at his
first volume's finding that startlingly high numbers
of American men masturbated and engaged in homosexual activities.

While Kinsey's opponents were likely most of-
fended at the study's findings, they concentrated on
attacking his methodology. For twenty years, Kinsey's
research had exposed the defects of conventional biology's attempts to classify insects theoretically without looking at them. Kinsey personally examined
more than 100,000 gall wasps to demonstrate the
fallacy of biology's conventional approaches to research. When his interest turned to sex research, he
applied the same methodology to its study, making
it clear that he was conducting biological research
and not conducting a public opinion poll. Critics
seemed to misunderstand Kinsey's distinction, however, and insisted that Kinsey's research did not conform to accepted public opinion polling practices, a
point that Kinsey could not deny but considered ir-
relevant to his research.

The furor over *Sexual Behavior in the Human Male*
had subsided somewhat by 1953, when Kinsey published his second volume, on female sexual behavior. This volume reported high levels of female mas-
turbation, lesbianism, and extramarital sex. While
the results were broadly similar to the first volume,

moralists were even more outraged at these revelations about the "fairer sex." Reacting politically, the
Rockefeller Foundation discontinued funding for
any further Kinsey research.

Impact Critics claim that Kinsey's allegedly non-
mainstream sexual preferences and his ideological
stance toward nontraditional forms of sexuality
might have skewed his research. Nonetheless, his reports likely helped facilitate the nascent feminist
and gay rights movements, public discussion of
cross-gender and transsexual issues (such as the controversial Christine Jorgensen case), a greater public acceptance of "risqué" magazines (such as *Playboy*), and attacks on censorship (such as the U.S.
Supreme Court case of *Roth v. the United States*).
Kinsey's efforts spurred the field of sexology and
acted as an important precedent to the sexual revolution of the 1960's.

Further Reading

Gathorne-Hardy, Jonathan. *Sex the Measure of All
Things: A Life of Alfred C. Kinsey.* Bloomington: Indiana University Press, 2000. Details Kinsey's life
while also serving as a sharp critique of James H.
Jones's work (see below).
Jones, James H. *Alfred C. Kinsey: A Public/Private Life.*
New York: Norton, 1997. This remarkable biography reveals that Kinsey engaged in bisexual activities throughout his life and is further categorized by Jones as a "voyeur" and a "masochist,"
even though Jones supports Kinsey's conclusions
in terms of the limits of his methodology.
Stanley, Liz. *Sex Surveyed, 1949-1994: From Mass-
Observation's Little Kinsey to the National Survey and
the Hite Reports.* London: Taylor & Francis, 1995.
Takes a feminist stance in discussing sex research
through several decades.

Richard L. Wilson

See also Birth control; Censorship; Homosexuality
and gay rights; *Playboy*; *Roth v. United States*; Sex and
sex education; Women and the roots of the feminist movement; Youth culture and the generation
gap.

■ Kline, Franz

Identification Abstract expressionist painter
Born May 23, 1910; Wilkes-Barre, Pennsylvania
Died May 13, 1962; New York, New York

Kline helped created one of the most important painting forms of the 1950's, abstract expressionism, which is considered by critics to be the first style unique to America.

Franz Kline studied illustration in Boston and London during the 1930's and settled in New York by 1939. He became part of a circle known as the New York School, which included Jackson Pollock, Willem de Kooning, Mark Rothko, and Arshile Gorky. Kline's first one-man show in 1950 established him as an influential figure in the art movement known as abstract expressionism.

Kline is best known for his large black and white abstract paintings, which consist of powerful strokes made with large brushes. The effect produced was one of action and physical impact, and his works have been likened to grids or Oriental calligraphy. Kline reduced abstract art to its most elemental: black, white, line, and geometric form.

Impact During the 1950's, the works of de Kooning, Pollock, Kline, and others challenged the aesthetic establishment and led abstract expressionism to a popularity that was international in scope. For Kline, the subject of his art emerged both from his personal experiences and from the very act of making a painting. Social realism and cubism proved important to his inspiration.

Kline was a personable man with an accessible style. His work influenced his peers and subsequent American abstract painters. Throughout the decade, he mounted seven one-artist shows in New York and showed his work at important international shows. He won a special award at the Venice Biennale in 1960. Kline died in New York in 1962.

Further Reading

Gaugh, Harry F. *The Vital Gesture: Franz Kline.* New York: Abbeville Press, 1985. In-depth monograph covering the full scope of Kline's work.

Sylvester, David. *Interviews with American Artists.* New Haven, Conn.: Yale University Press, 2001. Includes interviews with Franz Kline and artists in his circle.

Susan Butterworth

See also Abstract expressionism; Art movements; de Kooning, Willem; Guggenheim Museum; Motherwell, Robert; Pollock, Jackson.

■ *Kon-Tiki*

Identification Firsthand account of a trans-Pacific voyage in a primitive vessel
Author Thor Heyerdahl (1914-2002)
Date Published in the United States in 1950

Heyerdahl's vivid account of his courageous voyage became a best-seller and sparked a debate about the peopling of the Pacific islands.

While conducting research in the South Pacific, Norwegian Thor Heyerdahl came to believe that, contrary to accepted theory, the inhabitants of the Pacific islands had migrated westward from the coast of South America. He demonstrated the possibility of such a migration by sailing a primitive raft (named *Kon-Tiki* after a legendary Polynesian leader) with five crewmen from Peru to the Tuamotu islands in French Polynesia in 1947.

Heyerdahl published *Kon-Tiki: Across the Pacific by Raft,* an account of his voyage, in Norway in 1948 and

Thor Heyerdahl with a model of Kon-Tiki *in 1950.* (Hulton Archive | by Getty Images)

in the United States in 1950. The book was an immediate success. It recounted the 101-day, 4,300-mile journey in vivid prose that captured the imaginations of reviewers and readers alike. Public interest was intensified by excerpts in magazines such as *Life* and by a 1951 film (also called *Kon-Tiki*) that won an Academy Award for best documentary.

Despite public acclaim, however, few anthropologists accepted Heyerdahl's theories, citing archaeological evidence that the Pacific's inhabitants had migrated eastward from Southeast Asia.

Impact Although Heyerdahl's conclusions were debunked by professional scholars, his attempt to demonstrate links between early South American and Polynesian cultures raised public interest in history and archaeology and prompted scientific debate about diffusionist theories.

In 2004, a team of Norwegian scientists that included Heyerdahl's grandson Olav Heyerdahl made plans to reenact Heyerdahl's voyage in 2005.

Further Reading

Conniff, Richard. "Kon Artist?" *Smithsonian* 33, no. 4 (July, 2002): 26-27. Article casting doubt on Heyerdahl's veracity as an anthropologist.

Harmon, Melissa Burdick. "Across the Ocean on a Wooden Raft." *Biography* 6, no. 7 (July, 2002): 82-85. Illustrated account of Heyerdahl's life.

Heyerdahl, Thor, and Christopher Ralling. *Kon-Tiki Man: An Illustrated Biography of Thor Heyerdahl.* San Francisco: Chronicle Books, 1991. A profusely illustrated biography issued in conjunction with a television series about Heyerdahl.

Grove Koger

See also Archaeology; Book publishing; *Life*; Literature in the United States.

■ Kono, Tommy

Identification Japanese American weight lifter and bodybuilder
Born June 27, 1930; Sacramento, California

From the Japanese American internment camps of World War II, Tommy Kono emerged to become the leading American weight lifter through the Olympic Games of 1952, 1956, and 1960.

Tommy (Tamio) Kono was born the fourth son of a Japanese American family that was planning to emigrate from California to Japan when the Great De-

pression intervened. In late 1941, as the Depression eased, Japan's attack on Pearl Harbor occurred, and the Kono family was interned until December, 1945, at the Tule Lake Relocation Center. Tommy Kono, however, was young enough to ignore the social and cultural ramifications of the internment and enjoy his early teenage years.

Meanwhile, at the age of eleven—like many other American boys—he sent a postcard to the famous bodybuilder Charles Atlas but could not afford Atlas's mail-order course. When Kono was about fourteen years old, a friend gave him a barbell, and Kono began his weight-lifting career. Four years later, in March of 1948, he accompanied a friend to the Northern California Amateur Athletic Union (AAU) championships and decided to enter the competition. Though he finished second in a group of only two, he loved the mental and physical discipline the sport demanded and began to craft what would be a fifteen-year international career.

Kono eventually ranked second in Olympic weight-lifting medals won by an American, taking gold in the lightweight snatch at the 1952 Helsinki Olympics and gold in the light-heavyweight clean-and-jerk at the 1956 Melbourne Olympics. At the Rome Olympic Games in 1960, in what he considered a disappointing performance, he won only a silver medal.

During a career spanning the years 1948-1965, he won six world titles, along with several victories in the Pan-American Games and numerous national championships. He also set twenty-six world records in four weight divisions. Although bodybuilding was not his chief focus, he also won one Mr. World title and Mr. Universe titles three times.

Impact Tommy Kono was both the most successful American weight lifter of the 1950's and one of the most prominent Japanese American athletes in history. After his retirement from competition, he returned to his home in Hawaii but continued his involvement in the sport. He has coached the Mexican, West German, and United States national weight-lifting teams and has also written a book on weight lifting.

Further Reading

Gaines, Charles. *Yours in Perfect Manhood, Charles Atlas: The Most Effective Fitness Program Ever Devised.* New York: Simon & Schuster, 1982. Conventional biography of the bodybuilding icon whose magazine advertisements helped to inspire Kono's career.

Hess, Tyler. "Interview with Tommy Kono." *Power Athletes Magazine* 1 (2003). Typical of most Kono interviews, this one discusses how Kono overcame adversity and some of his lifting theory; however, its contains nothing that reveals the man behind the public persona.

Kono, Tommy. *Weightlifting, Olympic Style.* Aiea, Hawaii: Author, n.d. Kono's self-published book is difficult to find except by mail order, but many passages from it, as well as commentaries by other weightlifters, are available on the Internet.

Oila, Dennis. "Olympic Flashback." *Honolulu Star-Bulletin*, September 30, 2000. Story in which Kono comments on the contemporary controversies about drug use in his sport.

Daniel J. Fuller

See also Asian Americans; Olympic Games of 1952; Olympic Games of 1956; Sports.

■ Korean War

The Event Military conflict between communist and noncommunist forces in Korea
Date June 25, 1950-July 27, 1953

A coalition involving the United States and its allies under a United National Command prevented communist-led North Korea from taking over South Korea, thus permitting South Korea to become a prosperous and democratic country.

The Korean War was the first war in which an international organization played a major role. After North Korean troops invaded South Korea on June 25, 1950, the United Nations (U.N.) condemned the invasion and requested member countries to come to the assistance of South Korea. Sixteen countries responded by sending troops, while forty-one countries sent food, equipment, and other supplies. Because the United States paid for 90 percent of the costs of the war, President Harry S. Truman chose the commanders and made major decisions on strategy. China sent troops to fight with the North Koreans, and the Soviet Union provided substantial amounts of military equipment.

The war was costly in numbers of casualties, military expenditures, and destruction of property. The U.N. and South Korean forces, at their greatest strength, consisted of more than one million troops, including about 590,000 South Koreans and about 480,000 Americans. During the three years of fighting, approximately 1,600,000 communist troops and about 580,000 troops from the United Nations and South Korea were killed, seriously wounded, or reported missing. About 1.4 million Americans fought in the war, and more than 35,000 died in combat, with an additional 103,000 wounded and missing. Probably at least one million Korean civilians were killed, and several million more became refugees. The United States spent some $67 billion on the war, substantially increasing the deficit and the national debt.

The North Korean Invasion The conflict grew out of the artificial division of Korea at the end of World War II. After expelling the Japanese, who had controlled Korea since 1895, the United States and the Soviet Union divided Korea into two occupation zones at approximately the thirty-eighth parallel. In 1947, the U.N. General Assembly called for free elections to unify the country, but the Soviets refused to permit elections in the North. In the spring of 1948, the South Koreans elected a national assembly, which soon established the government of the Republic of Korea. Syngman Rhee, a long-standing Korean nationalist, was elected president. On September 9, the Korean Communist Party created the People's Republic of Korea. Kim Il Sung, who was trained militarily in the Soviet Union, became the country's first premier.

Both governments claimed to exercise sovereignty over all of Korea, and between 1948 and 1950, their troops had several struggles along the thirty-eighth parallel. The political situation was especially unstable in South Korea, where leftist forces engaged in guerrilla activities. Kim Il Sung, with Soviet assistance, built up a large military force. The Soviet Union viewed North Korea as part of its security zone in Northeast Asia, and Soviet leaders therefore provided the country with a large arsenal of military equipment. The United States did not provide South Korea with comparable assistance because it feared that Syngman Rhee might be tempted to attack North Korea. At the time, American officials minimized the strategic importance of the Korean peninsula. In January, 1950, Secretary of State Dean Acheson publicly stated in a speech to the National Press Association that the peninsula was outside America's defense perimeter.

In the spring of 1950, Kim went to Moscow and Beijing in an attempt to persuade Soviet leader Joseph Stalin and Chinese leader Mao Zedong to approve an invasion of South Korea. Both leaders feared that an attack might expand into a wider war without significantly advancing their national interests. However, Kim insisted that his forces could conquer South Korea within a few days. After Stalin unenthusiastically agreed to provide tanks and other military equipment, Mao Zedong had no choice but to go along.

The North Korean army had about 135,000 well-trained troops that were supported by Soviet airplanes, heavy artillery, and tanks. The South Korean army had about 95,000 poorly trained troops and very few airplanes or tanks. Because of their superior strength, combined with the advantages of a surprise attack, the North Koreans achieved a smashing success. Within three days of the attack, they had captured the capital city of Seoul and continued to advance southward. Without foreign intervention, the South Korean government had no chance of survival.

The United States Enters the War At the time of the invasion, the Truman administration was firmly and publicly committed to a foreign policy of "containment," or preventing the further expansion of communism. Influenced by Cold War confrontations, U.S. officials assumed that the impetus behind the invasion likely was coming from the Soviet Union, and they believed that the credibility of the U.S. government was at stake. In addition, revelations about the subversive activities of alleged spies Karl Fuchs and Alger Hiss were already being exploited by anticommunist zealots, most notably Senator Joseph McCarthy of Wisconsin. A significant number of Americans blamed the recent "loss of China" on liberals and Democrats. For these reasons, Truman and his advisers quickly assumed that they had no real choice other than military intervention.

The Truman administration called for an emergency meeting of the U.N. Security Council, which met on June 25, 1950, and voted nine to none to approve a resolution calling for a cease-fire and a withdrawal of North Korean forces. On June 27, the Security Council passed a second resolution, requesting countries to assist South Korea "to repel the armed attack and restore international peace and security in the area." The Soviet delegate would have

vetoed the two resolutions, except that the Soviet government was boycotting the Security Council to protest the refusal of the United Nations to replace the Nationalist Chinese government on Taiwan with the People's Republic of China. The Soviet delegate later returned to the Security Council in August to attempt to veto the two resolutions, but the council held that a veto could only be legally exercised at the same time that the resolutions were passed.

The same day that the second U.N. resolution was approved, President Truman ordered U.S. air and naval forces to support South Korean troops. On July 1, a U.S. task force of 403 men flew from Japan to Pusan at the southeastern tip of Korea. Americans fought their first battle with the North Koreans on July 5 at Osan, thirty miles south of Seoul. Two days later, the Security Council voted in favor of a unified command in Korea, under a commander to be chosen by the United States. The next day, Truman designated General Douglas MacArthur for the position. MacArthur would direct operations from his Japanese headquarters. For the field commander in Korea, Truman appointed Lieutenant General Walton "Bulldog" Walker of the U.S. Eighth Army, then on occupation duty in Japan.

Early Combat Many of the U.S. soldiers first deployed to Korea were young and undertrained, and most of their officers had limited combat experience. In the last week of July, 1950, a confused situation resulted in the tragic incident at the railroad overpass near No Gun Ri, not far from Yongdong. As the North Koreans occupied the region, huge numbers of South Korean civilians fled for their lives. Military intelligence reported that enemy soldiers were sometimes posing as refugees, and frightened young American soldiers had a difficult time distinguishing between civilian refugees and the enemy. During July 26-29, an uncertain number of American soldiers fired at civilians who were inside the No Gun Ri overpass. The soldiers likely believed they had received small arms fire from the location of the overpass. South Korean sources reported that about 250 civilians were killed, while most American sources claimed that no more than 100 were killed.

The initial U.S. intervention did little to slow the North Koreans from advancing south. By August 2, they had taken all of South Korea except for an eighty-mile defense perimeter around the southeastern port of Pusan. By then, however, the cumula-

North Korean refugees fleeing from Pyongyang across the city's badly damaged bridge to escape advancing Chinese troops in December, 1950. (AP/Wide World Photos)

The Inchon Landing The conflict dramatically changed when General MacArthur personally directed an amphibious landing at Inchon, only twenty-five miles south of Seoul. The Joint Chiefs of Staff (JCS) and most military strategists had opposed the operation as unwise. The major problem was that tides of thirty feet required ships to land precisely at high tide to escape entrapment in mud. In addition, a formidable seawall protected the city. MacArthur, who was known for his self-confidence and willingness to take risks, argued that conditions would assure the element of surprise that was essential to the success of the landing. The JCS reluctantly deferred to his judgment.

On September 15, 1950, the Inchon landing was almost as successful as MacArthur had predicted. After landing, allied forces began to sweep eastward across the peninsula. On September 26, the X corps, commanded by Major General Edward Almond, captured Seoul. While allied planes attacked North Korean supply lines leading to the Pusan Perimeter, General Walker's Eighth Army fought its way out of the perimeter and inflicted heavy losses on the enemy. On September 28, Generals Walker and Almond joined forces near Seoul. By then, most of the North Korean armies had retreated north of the thirty-eighth parallel. Since the U.N. forces had successfully accomplished the objectives of the U.N. resolutions, the U.N. Command might have simply declared victory. Instead MacArthur broadcast a demand for the North Koreans to surrender, which they ignored.

U.N. Forces Invade North Korea Delighted by the success of the Inchon landing, Truman and his strategic advisers decided to change the war's objective from liberating the South to "rolling back" commu-

tive growth of American troops, airplanes, and tanks was making it possible for General Walker to halt further North Korean advances. As North Korea tried to break through the Pusan Perimeter in scattered attacks, Walker reacted by sending in reserves who were protected by U.S. planes. In early August, the allies successfully counterattacked after the North Koreans crossed the Naktonk River. Walker's forces again halted desperate efforts of the enemy to cross the perimeter in late August and early September. The two armies appeared to be deadlocked.

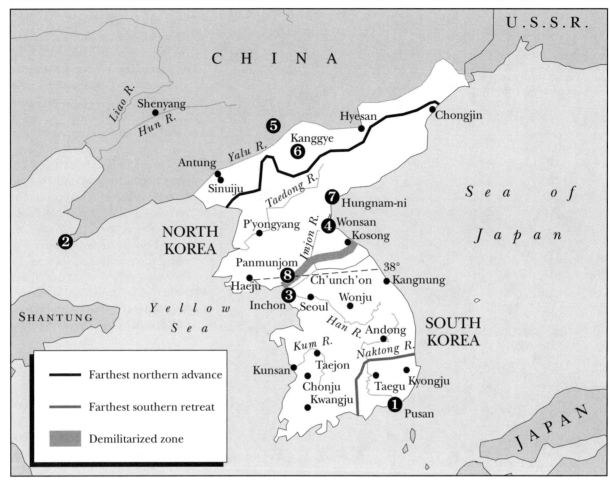

(1) Main U.N. base. (2) Russian-Chinese naval installation. (3) Sept. 15, 1950, U.N. forces land. (4) Oct. 26, 1950, U.N. forces land. (5) Nov. 26, 1950, Chinese attack. (6) Dec., 1950, Battle of the Reservoir. (7) Dec. 9, 1950, U.N. forces evacuate. (8) July 27, 1953, armistice signed.

nism and uniting the Korean peninsula under a noncommunist government. The majority of the American public agreed with this change in policy; both *Life* magazine and *The New Republic* endorsed attacking North Korea. On October 7, a few days after U.N. troops crossed the thirty-eighth parallel, the General Assembly endorsed the establishment of a "unified, independent, and democratic" government of Korea. The Chinese government responded with warnings that it could not "stand idly by" and allow the overthrow of North Korea. Experts disagreed about whether the warnings should be taken seriously.

On October 15, President Truman and General MacArthur held a strategy conference at Wake Island. MacArthur dismissed China's warnings and predicted that the war would soon be over. He also apologized to the president for a message that he had sent to the Veterans of Foreign Wars, in which he had proposed policy changes without getting advance approval. Truman declared that he was delighted with the conference. Accepting MacArthur's judgment, he authorized U.N. troops to continue to move northward. On October 20, the capital city of Pyongyang was captured. On October 26, the allied advance reached Chosan on the Yalu River border with China. At this time army intelligence began to report that Chinese soldiers were fighting alongside the North Koreans.

During the next month, about 300,000 Chinese "volunteers" gradually crossed into North Korea. Based on faulty intelligence that greatly underestimated Chinese infiltration, MacArthur and other allied commanders continued to be optimistic about the prospects of a quick victory. Allied war planes bombed North Korean forces while allied warships bombarded North Korean port cities. After heavy fighting, the Chinese troops unexpectedly withdrew, perhaps in order to give the allies a false sense of security. MacArthur ordered a major advance to begin on November 24. He predicted with confidence that the war would be over by Christmas, 1950.

Retreat and Stalemate On November 26, the North Korean and Chinese troops counterattacked in massive "human waves," supported by large numbers of Soviet planes and tanks. The allies were taken by surprise and forced to retreat in bitter winter conditions. MacArthur observed that it had become "an entirely new war." Within a week, communist forces had driven a wedge between the Eighth Army in the west and the X Corps in the east. Stunned by the offensive, Truman, on November 30, refused in a press conference to rule out the use of atomic weapons, and he even suggested that the decision rested with the field commander. The comment created great dismay among European allies, and British prime minister Clement Attlee flew to Washington for reassurance that the U.S. would not use atomic weapons or attack China. Truman, in an effort to calm European fears, stated that he did not intend to use atomic weapons and promised to inform the Europeans of any change in policy.

Soldiers of the Eighth Army were forced to withdraw more than three hundred miles, which is the longest retreat in U.S. military history. On December 4, the allies were forced to begin their withdrawal from Pyongyang. In the port city of Hungnam, about 105,000 U.S. and South Korean troops had to be evacuated. On January 4, 1951, communist troops again occupied Seoul. The allies no longer hoped to unite Korea, but they returned to their original objective of preserving an independent South Korea.

After General Walker was killed in a jeep accident, General Matthew Ridgway replaced him as commander of the Eighth Army, and the X Corps was also merged under his command. Because of his eminent career as a combat officer, Ridgway was extremely popular with the troops. His approach concentrated on improving morale, insisting on strict discipline, and inflicting heavy casualties on the enemy. He adopted a "meat grinder" tactic, aggressively searching out the enemy troops and then striking them repeatedly with artillery and tanks. In mid-January, U.N. forces were finally able to stop the Chinese advance, and on January 25, they begin a counteroffensive called Operation Thunderbolt. When advancing, Ridgway insisted on moving slowly enough to make certain that all enemy forces in an area were effectively eliminated.

Beginning on February 21, Ridgway launched Operation Killer, which was soon followed by Operation Ripper. In March, the allies marched triumphantly into Seoul. On April 22, the Chinese launched their greatest military offensive of the war, capturing Seoul for the third time. This time, however, the Chinese took heavy casualties and were overextended. By May, U.N. forces managed to establish a new defensive line, the Line Wyoming, which was somewhat north of the thirty-eighth parallel: At its center, it reached almost to the heavily defended region called the "iron triangle" (Pyonggang-Kumhwa-Chorwon). As the allies brought in more heavy artillery and air support, the Chinese had no realistic chance of breaking through the line.

Although fighting would continue for two more years, neither side would make any significant advances. There were, nevertheless, many fierce battles for strategic positions. During this period, which is characterized as the Battle for the Hills, thousands of soldiers died in a region called the Punchbowl. The most famous of the battles included Bloody Ridge, Heartbreak Ridge, Old Baldy, Finger Ridge, and Pork Chop Ridge. All the while, the United States inflicted massive bombing attacks on North Korea, devastating to irrigation dams, hydroelectric plants, and most cities. Immense numbers of Korean civilians died from the bombing raids.

The Truman-MacArthur Controversy Shortly before the Chinese intervention, the American public had every reason to believe that the war was going well and that the "boys" would soon be returning home. The humiliating retreat of allied forces initiated a great debate about the U.S. role in the world. A large percentage of Americans simply could not understand how underdeveloped Asian countries could humiliate the wealthiest and most powerful country in the world. Such frustrations encouraged many people to listen to right-wing critics who insisted the

Truman administration was not sufficiently committed to the anticommunist cause.

Even after the Chinese intervention, General MacArthur continued to oppose anything short of total victory. He argued that extending the war into China would pave the way to ending communism in Asia. He advocated bombing the bases in Manchuria, blockading the Chinese coast, and utilizing Nationalist Chinese soldiers in Korea. The proposed plan was contrary to Truman's policies, and almost all officers and strategists agreed that the plan was impractical. In interviews with the press, MacArthur continued to contradict official policies without obtaining approval from government leaders, and he strongly challenged the notion of limited warfare in a letter to Republican congressman Joseph Martin. After Martin read the letter on the floor of the House on April 11, Truman relieved MacArthur of all his commands and appointed Ridgway to take his place.

The dismissal of MacArthur was cheered in Europe, but it was highly unpopular with the American public. Returning to his native country for the first time after fifteen years, General MacArthur received a hero's welcome. In a joint declaration before Congress, he defended his plan for escalating the war. While politely applauding the aging general, the majority of the members of Congress remained unconvinced that his proposals would lead to victory. In subsequent Senate hearings, almost no military strategists defended the idea of attacking China, and General Omar Bradley of the Joint Chiefs of Staff warned that it would put the United States "in the wrong war, at the wrong place, at the wrong time, and with the wrong enemy." Even Republican senators conceded that MacArthur had exceeded his authority by challenging the president's foreign policies and that the president had the constitutional power to appoint and remove military commanders.

Many military officers, nevertheless, shared MacArthur's frustrations about fighting for limited objectives. General Ridgway wanted to act more aggressively, and he privately complained that the instructions of the JCS were frequently unhelpful. However, Ridgway, unlike his predecessor, was a team player who was always careful not to make any public statements inconsistent with official policies. In fact, Ridgway was highly critical of MacArthur's cavalier disregard for the orders from Truman and the JCS, and he believed that MacArthur should have been fired as early as August of 1950.

Prisoners of War When the war began, none of the participating countries had ratified the Geneva Convention Relative to the Treatment of Prisoners of War of 1949. Nevertheless, within a month, the United States, North Korea, and South Korea stated that they would apply the guidelines of the convention. These guidelines stated that the captors were required to treat prisoners of war (POWs) humanely and not to allow the coercion of military information. However, neither side fully honored its commitments in this regard.

The North Koreans had no organized system for keeping war prisoners. During the first months of the war, the North Korean People's Army simply moved the POWs to rear areas and subjected them to death marches. From April of 1951, the Chinese Communist Forces (CCF) took charge of most of the American POWs. Ignoring the Geneva Convention, the Chinese physically abused the prisoners and subjected them to "brainwashing" techniques. Although some of the POWs signed peace petitions and made anti-American statements, few, if any, provided their interrogators with information of any value. A total of 7,245 U.S. soldiers were taken as prisoners, and of these, 2,806 died in captivity.

The U.N. forces held more than 150,000 North Korean and Chinese POWs, whose treatment was a matter of considerable controversy. Critics, including British observers, alleged that U.S. guards were racially biased and looked upon the POWs as "Asian cattle." This was especially true in the camp on Koje-do, a small island off the southern coast of Korea. The camp contained thousands of dedicated communists who strongly objected to the American policy of screening prisoners to find out their political backgrounds. The Americans adopted the policy because in prisoner repatriation, they did not want to send large numbers of men to their deaths, as had happened during World War II in the case of Eastern European prisoners who had been sent to the Soviet Union.

The Chinese and North Koreans looked upon the POWs as active combatants. Some of them allegedly had surrendered intentionally to U.N. troops to disrupt the camps. Beginning in the summer of 1951, militant prisoners at Koje-do murdered U.S. Army guards. In early 1952, attempts to screen prisoners resulted in the deaths of more than eighty prisoners. On May 7, the commandant of the island, Brigadier-General Francis Dodd, made the mistake of meeting with a group of prisoners to discuss their grievances. Dodd was taken as a hostage, and he was released only after he and his temporary replacement agreed to stop the screening process. The incident attracted great consternation among the American public.

The Long Truce Talks From the outbreak of the war, European members of the U.N. coalition put pressure on the Truman administration to seek a compromise settlement. By March, 1951, Truman had decided to announce that the U.N. Command was ready to enter into negotiations. General MacArthur, however, undermined the peace initiative by giving the enemy an ultimatum. When MacArthur was no longer an obstacle, the governments of the United States and the Soviet Union agreed in June to begin negotiations toward a cease-fire. The talks began on July 10 in Kaesong and then moved to Panmunjom. The talks would continue in an on-again-off-again manner for the next two years.

The first issue of disagreements was about whether the demarcation line would be the thirty-eighth parallel or the defensive line at the time of the cease-fire. After the two sides agreed on a compromise solution to the border issue, they quickly deadlocked over the more difficult issue of prisoner exchange. The U.N. Command insisted that prisoners of both sides be allowed to choose whether or not they would return to their homelands. Approximately one-third of the North Korean and Chinese captives did not wish to be repatriated. Both the United States and the communists considered the issue to be a matter of principle, and both also were concerned with its propaganda value. On October 8, 1952, the U.N. Command adjourned the talks, stating that they would not resume until the communists were ready to offer helpful suggestions for resolving the repatriation issue.

The war was a major issue of the presidential election of 1952. Dwight D. Eisenhower announced that if elected, he would travel to Korea to promote an end to the fighting. Shortly after winning the election, he visited Korea, but with little effect. Only six weeks after Eisenhower became president, Soviet dictator Joseph Stalin died, and the new leaders of the Kremlin were more flexible about a settlement. On March 28, communist negotiators accepted an earlier offer by the U.N. Command to exchange sick and wounded prisoners, a move that allowed talks to resume. Between April 20 and May 3, in an operation called Lit-

tle Switch, the U.N. Command returned 6,670 sick and wounded prisoners, while it received 684 prisoners in return, including 149 Americans.

As the two sides drew closer to an agreement, South Korean president Syngman Rhee, who still hoped to unite all of Korea under his leadership, sabotaged the talks by releasing about 25,000 North Korean prisoners who reportedly desired to stay in South Korea. The Chinese and North Korean governments were so furious that they launched a military offensive against South Korean units. U.S. negotiators promised to restrain Rhee, and they also began discussing a defense alliance with Rhee in order to encourage him to agree to a truce based on the territorial status quo.

Determined to reach a settlement, President Eisenhower and his senior advisers seriously considered using tactical nuclear weapons as a way of getting the other side to make concessions. Secretary of State John Foster Dulles used diplomatic channels to warn the Chinese government about the nuclear threat. In subsequent years, Dulles and Eisenhower would claim that this warning was a critical factor in making the armistice possible. Skeptical historians, however, have noted that the warning about nuclear weapons was never given as a firm ultimatum. There is considerable evidence, moreover, that Mao Zedong had earlier expected the United States to use nuclear weapons, and such a threat had never appeared to moderate his behavior. Rather than the threat of nuclear weapons, it seems more likely that peace occurred because all parties to the conflict had simply decided that a continuation of fighting was not in their interests.

An End to Hostilities On June 4, 1953, the Chinese and North Korean negotiators at Panmunjom agreed to allow voluntary repatriations, with both sides having an opportunity to try to persuade defectors to return home. The exchanges were to be under the supervision of a Neutral Nations Repatriation Commission (NNRC), which was composed of representatives from Sweden, Switzerland, India, Poland, and Czechoslovakia. With this contentious issue out of the way, the two sides were able to agree on the few remaining issues, including the location of the border separating the two Koreas.

On July 27, 1953, representatives of the various countries signed an armistice that ended the fighting. The truce recognized a demilitarized zone

Troops of the First U.S. Cavalry Division land at Pohang on the east coast of Korea on July 19, 1950, in the first combat amphibious operation since World War II. (AP/Wide World Photos)

(DMZ) two and one-half miles wide to divide North and South Korea. Both sides agreed not to enlarge their military strength. A Military Armistice Commission, with representatives from each side, was established to enforce the terms of the truce. In September, 1953, the U.N. Command and the communist countries exchanged the remaining 88,559 prisoners. Among those refusing to return home were 14,222 Chinese, 7,582 North Koreans, 325 South Koreans, and 21 Americans. The truce provided for a future conference that was supposed to work out a final settlement. In 1954, representatives of the countries participating in the war, along with the Soviet Union, met for this purpose, but the conference failed because each of the Korean states refused to recognize the legitimacy of the other.

Impact The Korean War made the thirty-eighth parallel a permanent division between North and South Korea, and it intensified the mutual animosities and tensions of the two regimes. While the truce meant an end to the fighting, it did not actually mean an end to the war. Officially, a state of war continued into the twenty-first century, and the border between the two countries remained one of the most heavily militarized and dangerous locations in the world. In the fifty years following the truce, numerous persons have been killed on both sides of the DMZ.

From an economic perspective, the war helped give South Korea access to Western markets, stimulating an impressive record of economic growth. In contrast, both the war and the truce tended to isolate North Korea from external influences, promoting an authoritarian political system and a very impoverished standard of living for its citizens.

As a result of the Korean War, Asia became a much more important region of concern in international relations. It was during the war that the United States began to provide France with substantial assistance to fight the nationalist-communist insurgency in Vietnam, a commitment that grew and expanded after the French left Vietnam in 1954. The war also resulted in the U.S. policy of defending Taiwan from attack by the People's Republic of China. In addition, it hastened the signing of the Japanese peace treaty and led to the formation of the Southeast Asia Treaty Organization (SEATO). In Europe, the war had the effect of strengthening the military forces of the North Atlantic Treaty Organization (NATO). Although the Korean conflict exacerbated Cold War tensions, some historians have suggested that it helped motivate policymakers not to allow future differences to escalate into a third world war.

On the U.S. domestic scene, the Korean War helped fuel the anticommunist hysteria known as the "second red scare." The war required a doubling of the budget for military and related expenditures, and it led to a bipartisan consensus on the need for better preparedness for possible conflicts in the future. Critics argued that the expenditures promoted the growth of a "military-industrial complex." Unquestionably the war enhanced the powers of the office of the president, contributing to the so-called imperial presidency. One far-reaching aspect of this trend was Truman's conviction that the commander in chief possessed constitutional authority to conduct a large-scale "police action." Thus, he decided it was unnecessary to ask Congress to formally approve participation in what became a major international war. Dissatisfaction with this precedent would eventually result in passage of the controversial War Powers Act of 1973, which attempted to limit the president's prerogatives for waging war without congressional authorization.

Further Reading

Blair, Clay. *The Forgotten War: America in Korea, 1950-1953*. New York: Times Books, 1987. A highly detailed and lively popular account of the conflict, critical of both MacArthur and Truman.

Catchpole, Brian. *The Korean War, 1950-1953*. New York: Carroll & Graf, 2000. A narrative that is generally favorable toward American policies during the conflict.

Clark, Eugene, and Thomas Fleming. *Secrets of Inchon*. New York: Putnam, 2002. Discusses the debates and many logistical problems associated with the daring operation.

Dorr, Robert, and Warren Thompson. *Korean Air War*. Chicago: Motorbooks, 2003. An interesting account of an important aspect of the war, combining narration with oral history interviews.

Goncharov, Sergi, John Lewis, and Xue Litai. *Uncertain Partners: Stalin, Mao, and the Korean War*. Stanford, Calif.: Stanford University Press, 1993. A scholarly book that focuses on the differences among communist leaders, especially the extreme reluctance of Stalin and Mao to allow Kim Il Sung to order the 1950 invasion.

Granfield, Linda, ed. *Korea: Veterans Tell Their Stories of the War, 1950-1953*. New York: Houghton Mifflin Company, 2001. A valuable collection recording the firsthand experiences of thirty-two participants.

Hanley, Chalres, Sang-Hun Choe, and Martha Mendoza. *The Bridge at No Gun Ri: A Hidden Nightmare from the Korean War*. New York: Henry Holland, 2001. Summarizes interviews of more than 150 participants in the tragic shooting of civilians in July, 1950.

Jian, Chen. *China's Road to the Korean War: The Making of the Sino-American Confrontation*. New York: Columbia University Press, 1994. A scholarly work that emphasizes Mao's revolutionary ideology. Jian argues that Mao decided to intervene even before U.N. forces crossed the thirty-eighth parallel.

Kaufman, Burton. *The Korean Conflict*. Westport, Conn.: Greenwood Press, 1999. A succinct guide that is readable, interesting, and balanced. It includes major documents, biographical summaries, and a long annotated bibliography.

Spiller, Harry, ed. *American POWs in Korea: Sixteen Personal Accounts*. Jefferson, N.C.: McFarland, 1998. Memoirs that tell about brutal treatment and terrible conditions.

Stueck, William. *The Korean War: An International History*. Princeton, N.J.: Princeton University Press, 1997. Comprehensive study from an international perspective, utilizing archives from several countries.

_____. *Rethinking the Korean War: A New Diplomatic and Strategic History*. Princeton, N.J.: Princeton University Press, 2002. Well-written short synthesis by an outstanding scholar of the war.

Thomas Tandy Lewis

See also Acheson, Dean; China; Cold War; Foreign policy of Canada; Foreign policy of the United States; Formosa Resolution; Isolationism; Japan; MacArthur, Douglas; Marshall, George C.; Ridgway, Matthew B.; Truman, Harry S.; Truman Doctrine.

■ Kovacs, Ernie

Identification American television writer and entertainer
Born January 23, 1919; Trenton, New Jersey
Died January 13, 1962; Beverly Hills, California

Ernie Kovacs was one of the first performers to see the unique comedic possibilities in the television medium, and he used innovative video and photography techniques to develop popular, if unorthodox, programs during the 1950's.

Ernie Kovacs was born to Mary Chebonick and Andrew J. Kovacs, a Hungarian-born policeman and bootlegger. In 1941, he got an announcing job with a Trenton, New Jersey, radio station and began displaying the wit and irreverence for which he would later become famous.

In 1949, Kovacs's success as host of a cooking show on Philadelphia television station WPTZ inspired the station to give him a morning show, *Three to Get Ready.* In it, he created new characters, such as the creepy Uncle Gruesome and Percy Dovetonsils, an effeminate but heterosexual avantgarde poet. He was noted more for his visual imagination, and with the assistance of WPTZ engineer Karl Weger, he pioneered new visual tricks with special effects photography.

In 1952, Kovacs moved to national television with the NBC network. In September of 1954, he married Edie Adams, a singer on several of his shows. They had one child and remained married until his death. In January, 1957, Kovacs put on perhaps his most successful show, a thirty-minute program that used no dialogue and was performed in pantomime; it became known as "the silent show."

Kovacs was always more a critical than a popular success. During the late 1950's, he decided to abandon the frenetic world of television to become a writer and actor. His one novel, *Zoomar* (1957), a sardonic look at show business, amused readers but was considered a minor contribution to the literary world. Kovacs's distinctive appearance—with his thick mustache and omnipresent cigar—limited his movie roles, though he gave a memorable performance as the cynical Cuban police captain Segura in the 1959 film adaptation of Graham Greene's 1958 novel *Our Man in Havana.*

Impact Kovacs expanded the visual range of the television studio with his use of video and photography and used numerous techniques previously considered off limits, including dialogue with the camera crew and audiences and forays into the studio

Comedian Ernie Kovacs and his wife, Edie Adams, strike poses inside an amusement park ride that reflect the zaniness of Kovacs's television performances. (Hulton Archive | by Getty Images)

corridor. He was perhaps best known for his skits involving the Nairobi Trio, which used a bit of performance art by depicting three people, dressed in formal clothing worn over gorilla suits, who play chamber music.

Further Reading
Rico, Diana. *Kovacsland: Biography of Ernie Kovacs.* San Diego, Calif.: Harcourt Brace, 1990. A biography of Kovacs that also details his influence on subsequent television programming.
Walley, David. *The Ernie Kovacs Phile.* New York: Simon & Schuster, 1987. A revision and expansion of Kovacs's 1975 biography, *Nothing in Moderation.*
                                        Arthur D. Hlavaty
See also Freberg, Stan; Lehrer, Tom; Television in the United States; *Tonight Show.*

■ Kramer, Jack

Identification American tennis player
Born August 1, 1921; Las Vegas, Nevada

Jack Kramer was the most prominent amateur American tennis player from 1940 to 1947 and a professional player from 1948 to 1954. During the 1950's, he was chief promoter of the men's professional tennis tour.

Jack Kramer won many U.S. national championships as an amateur, including the boys' singles at age fifteen and the adult U.S. National Championship Doubles titles in 1940, 1941, 1943, and 1947. In 1947, he also won the U.S. National singles and the British singles and doubles titles. He was the leading player for the U.S. Davis Cup team that won in 1946 and 1947. Kramer was a powerful player with a big serve and an excellent volley. In late 1947, he turned professional, and he won the U.S. Professional singles tournament in 1948 and 1949, and the pro doubles in 1949.

During the early 1950's, his chief opponents on the traveling tour included Bobby Riggs, Pancho Gonzáles, Pancho Segura, and Frank Sedgman; against all he had a significant winning percentage. He retired as a pro player in 1954 but continued as the American pro tour's chief organizer and promoter through the 1950's and well into the 1960's.

Impact Jack Kramer's influence as a player and promoter of the professional tour during the 1950's was a major influence in the development of modern-day "open tennis." He was inducted into the International Tennis Hall of Fame in 1968.

Further Reading
Gillmeister, Heines. *Tennis: A Cultural History.* New York: University Press, 1998. The world evolution of tennis from the Middle Ages to the modern game of the twentieth century.
Kramer, Jack. *The Game: My Forty Years in Tennis.* New York: Putnam, 1979. Jack Kramer's autobiography.
                                        Alan P. Peterson
See also Connolly, Maureen; Gibbs, Althea; Gonzáles, Pancho; Sports; Tennis.

■ Kroc, Ray

Identification Head of the McDonald's Corporation
Born October 5, 1902; Oak Park, Illinois
Died January 14, 1984; San Diego, California

Ray Kroc expanded the McDonald's hamburger restaurants into the biggest and most successful fast-food chain in the United States.

A high school dropout, Ray Kroc spent the greater portion of his life working odd jobs ranging from ambulance driver at the age of fifteen to milkshake mixer salesman, before joining the McDonald's Corporation at the age of fifty-two. Prior to his career with McDonald's, Kroc had sold the hamburger chain his own line of milkshake makers, Multimix, that had, in part, been key to McDonald's fast-food production success. Threatened by growing competition from big mixer makers such as Hamilton Beach, Kroc decided to approach the owners of McDonald's, Maurice (Mac) and Richard (Dick) McDonald, to ask them to take him on as director of franchise sales in 1954. The brothers agreed.

Impact Kroc is responsible for making McDonald's a household name and a synonym for what people consider American fast food. In his position at McDonald's, Kroc standardized quality control across franchises to ensure repeat business and the company's reputation. His efforts produced huge dividends as McDonald's continued to expand to more than two hundred franchises by the end of the 1950's. Kroc's fast-food operational standards helped popularize drive-in restaurants during the 1950's, thus helping make the hamburger and fast food distinctive traits of American culture.

Subsequent Events In 1961, after an eroding relationship with the McDonald brothers, Kroc bought them out for more than two million dollars and went on to expand McDonald's to six continents with more than fifteen thousand stores. He stepped down as chief executive of McDonald's in 1968 but continued to remain active in the company's affairs.

Further Reading

Kroc, Ray, with Robert Anderson. *Grinding It Out: The Making of McDonald's.* Chicago: Contemporary Books, 1977. The story of McDonald's from Kroc himself.

Love, John. *McDonald's: Behind the Arches.* Rev. ed. New York: Bantam, 1995. Presents the history of the hamburger empire.

Michael J. Garcia

See also Affluence and the new consumerism; Fast-food restaurants; McDonald's restaurants.

■ Ku Klux Klan

Identification Primarily southern white supremacist organization

Date Founded in 1865

The Ku Klux Klan, or KKK as it is well known, was revitalized during the 1950's in response to the U.S. Supreme Court's 1954 decision that "separate but equal" public schools were unconstitutional.

Formed during the winter of 1865-1866 as a social organization, the Ku Klux Klan soon developed into a secret society fostering white supremacy. Six Civil War veterans of the Confederate army met in Pulaski, Tennessee, in an atmosphere permeated by the Union's efforts at Reconstruction of the defeated South. The new movement spread to other southern states, where under cover of night, members wearing white hooded robes and riding on horseback would wreak violence on African Americans and their sympathizers. When Reconstruction ended in 1887, political power shifted back to whites in the South, and Klan membership dwindled.

During the early twentieth century, an influx of millions of European immigrants into the United States prompted a Klan resurgence. In addition to African Americans, the Klan persecuted Roman Catholics, Jews, and members of labor unions—many of whom had predominantly immigrant memberships. By the late 1920's, the national exposure of the violence and internal corruption shrank the Klan a second time.

Revival The 1930's, 1940's, and early 1950's saw a skeletal, dormant Klan. However, the Supreme Court's 1954 *Brown v. Board of Education* ruling against public school segregation sparked renewed Klan growth and activity. Eldon Edwards, a painter at an Atlanta auto body plant, reactivated the Klan in Georgia, and his group soon had branches in nine southern states. Meanwhile, other new white supremacist groups sprang up in response to the court's desegregation decision. Among these were the American States Rights Association, the National Association for the Advancement of White People (NAAWP), and most notably, the White Citizens' Councils. The meetings of the councils often became private KKK meetings after the groups' moderate members left the meetings.

When African Americans attempted to integrate various southern institutions, the Klan often responded in force. For example, the Montgomery Bus Boycott that began in late 1955 brought the Klan out in support of city officials. Autherine J. Lucy's at-

Hooded Ku Klux Klan members attempting to intimidate African Americans during the Montgomery, Alabama, bus boycott in late 1956. (AP/Wide World Photos)

tempt to enroll at the University of Alabama in 1956 was greeted by Klan members under the leadership of a fired disc jockey named Ace Carter. Lucy gave up her effort after three days of picketing and verbal harassment.

Violence, always an ingredient of Klan activity, increased during the 1950's. Stonings, burnings, and shootings continued, now supplemented by the use of explosives. The dynamiting of larger buildings, such as churches, synagogues, schools, and a YWCA, has been attributed mainly to other disruptive agencies. However, thirty racially motivated home bombings reported by the American Friends Service Committee in 1959 were almost exclusively Klan-related.

Impact The resurgence of the Ku Klux Klan and like-minded organizations reminded Americans of the 1950's that the nation's deep-seated racist tendencies would not disappear without a struggle. Klan acts of violence against minorities and their sympathizers had the paradoxical effect of helping to unite the country against racism. Sporadic Klan violence toward African Americans continued into the 1960's. However, the Klan gradually lost support.

Further Reading

Chalmers, David M. *Hooded Americanism: The History of the Ku Klux Klan.* 3d ed. Durham, N.C.: Duke University Press, 1987. Solid, scholarly history of the Klan that has gone through several editions.

Katz, William Loren. *The Invisible Empire: The Ku Klux Klan Impact on History.* Washington, D.C.: Open Hand, 1986. Sociological study of Klan activities.

Lester, J. C., and D. L. Wilson. *Ku Klux Klan: Its Origin, Growth, and Disbandment.* Reprint. New York: Da Capo Press, 1973. Comprehensive history of the Klan.

Wade, Wyn. *The Fiery Cross: The Ku Klux Klan in America.* New York: Oxford University Press, 1998. Although primarily a discussion of the Ku Klux Klan, this book also discusses the role of the White Citizens' Councils in the prosegregation movement.

Jim Heaney

See also African Americans; *Brown v. Board of Education*; Civil Rights movement; Racial discrimination; School desegregation; White Citizens' Councils.

■ *Kukla, Fran and Ollie*

Identification Children's television series featuring puppets and a live host
Date Aired from 1948 to 1957
Place Originated at WBKW, Chicago, Illinois

The award-winning artistry of puppeteer Burr Tillstrom and the unscripted dialogue between puppets and host Fran Allison made this show popular with children and adults and influenced the next generation of puppet shows, including Sesame Street *and* The Muppets.

On *Kukla, Fran and Ollie*, the hands behind the curtain belonged to Burr Tillstrom, but center stage belonged to Kukla, a boyish clown who exuded goodness in his dealings with Fran and Oliver J. Dragon, or Ollie. Ollie, whose "one prehensile tooth" was often the focus of conversation, displayed a shy affection for Fran. Several other Kuklapolitans shared their own "histories" and everyday experiences with the audience. According to Tillstrom, each puppet represented a facet of human behavior.

Impact *Kukla, Fran and Ollie* emphasized social values, but no children appeared as audience or performers. Unrehearsed, surprisingly candid reflections on the day's events provided opportunities for solving problems and mending relationships among performers and often became topics for discussion among viewers after their evening visits with the Kuklapolitans. With a modest budget and simple technology, it was the first network program televised in 1949, capturing the attention of a wide audience until its stage went dark in 1957.

Further Reading

Marling, Karal Ann. *As Seen on TV: The Visual Culture of Everyday Life in the 1950's.* Cambridge, Mass.: Harvard University Press, 1996. This book provides a social commentary on the early days of television and its influence on the decade's popular culture.

Thummin, Janet. *Small Screens, Big Ideas: Television in the 1950's.* London: I. B. Tauris, 2001. Explores the way in which television prompted and reflected social change and values in postwar America and Great Britain. Includes many illustrations and photographs.

Gale M. Thompson

See also *Captain Kangaroo; Howdy Doody Show; Mickey Mouse Club;* Television for children.

L

■ *Lady Chatterley's Lover*

The Event U.S. federal court's overturning of censorship bans on D. H. Lawrence's 1928 novel

Date Book released in unexpurgated form in the United States on July 21, 1959

The federal court ruling holding that D. H. Lawrence's novel was not obscene signaled the end to government censorship of sexual content in artistic expression.

D. H. Lawrence's novel *Lady Chatterley's Lover* was banned in Europe, the United States, and Canada after its publication in Italy in 1928. However, copies were circulated and smuggled throughout Europe and the United States. Although mild by later standards, the novel's four-letter words and somewhat graphic description of sexual acts were clearly illegal at the time.

The issue came to a head in the United States early in 1959 when Grove Press published a paperback edition and sold it through the mail. The postmaster general banned its sale, and the matter immediately came to federal court. On July 21, 1959, Judge Frederick van Pelt Bryan in the U.S. District Court of New York ruled that the novel was not obscene and was a work of art.

Impact This court ruling, which was never appealed to the U.S. Supreme Court, assured that artistic expression would not be held hostage to conventional attitudes about sex and religion. It paved the way for free expression without censorship, that would be established during the 1960's and subsequent decades.

Meanwhile, during the late 1950's, the New American Library published the novel in Canada, where it met charges of obscenity and was also banned. In 1960, a judge in Montreal upheld the censorship; his decision was overturned in June, 1962, by the Supreme Court of Canada. In a 5-4 decision, the court ruled that the book could be legally bought and sold throughout Canada.

Further Reading

Miscellaneous Items Concerning the Lawsuits Connected with the Grove Press Edition of "Lady Chatterley's Lover." New York: Grove Press, 1959. A collection of materials concerning the actual court case and other matters, including newspaper editorials and statements by others involved.

Pilditch, Jan. *The Critical Response to D. H. Lawrence.* Westport, Conn.: Greenwood, 2001. Traces significant events in Lawrence's life and presents critical analyses of his work.

Widmer, Kingsley. *Defiant Desire: Some Dialectical Legacies of D. H. Lawrence.* Carbondale: Southern Illi-

Author D. H. Lawrence. (Courtesy of District of Columbia Public Library)

nois University Press, 1992. In Chapter 5 of this critical work, the author discusses Lawrence's problems with censorship, as well as the problems confronting his works after his death.

Carl Singleton

See also Censorship; *Lolita*; *Peyton Place*; *Roth v. United States*; Supreme Court decisions, U.S.

■ LaLanne, Jack

Identification American fitness expert and television personality
Born September 26, 1914; San Francisco, California

Jack LaLanne opened the first American health club in 1936 and was the host of the first televised exercise program, which premiered in 1952 and stayed on the air for thirty-four years.

When Jack LaLanne was a teenager, his mother took him to a lecture by a physical therapist and nutritionist who claimed his life had been saved by exercise and a change in diet. The lecture had a great impact on LaLanne's life, and he pledged to eat properly and get active. LaLanne went into business for himself at the age of eighteen, selling health foods and opening the nation's first health club in 1936 in Oakland, California. His health clubs grew nationwide to nearly one hundred, all of which he would later sell to Bally Total Fitness

After being turned down by the television networks in 1950, LaLanne produced his own weekly exercise program and sold it to nearly two hundred individual stations. Dressed in a black jumpsuit, he led housewives in a thirty-minute program of sit-ups, push-ups, and jumping jacks to the accompaniment of organ music.

LaLanne also performed outrageous stunts to show off his physical prowess. On his fortieth birthday in 1954, for example, he swam the length of the San Francisco Golden Gate Bridge, and the following year, he swam from Alcatraz Island to Fisherman's Wharf in San Francisco wearing handcuffs He also received much publicity in 1956, when he performed more than one thousand push-ups and chin-ups on the popular television show *You Asked for It.*

Impact LaLanne developed the basic approach to physical fitness and nutrition used in many health clubs in subsequent decades. By the early 1950's, he

made full use of the new medium of television and encouraged millions of people, particularly housewives, to work out at home.

Further Reading
Rose, Marla Matzer. *Muscle Beach: Where the Best Bodies in the World Started a Fitness Revolution.* New York: St. Martin's Press, 2001. Chronicles the beginnings of a private enclave of fitness and muscle building in Santa Monica, California, and its early participants, including LaLanne.
Whorton, J. *Crusaders for Fitness.* Princeton, N.J.: Princeton University Press, 1982. A good description of the early health and fitness crusaders.

Mary McElroy

See also Fads; Health care systems in the United States; Television in the United States.

■ Landrum-Griffin Act of 1959

Identification Federal labor legislation that amended the National Labor Relations Act (NLRA) of 1947
Date Passed on September 14, 1959

The Landrum-Griffin Act of 1959 extended the NLRA to encompass the internal affairs of labor unions and to make the unions more democratic by requiring them to increase members' rights.

The official name of the Landrum-Griffin Act was the Labor-Management Reporting and Disclosure Act. During the 1950's, corruption was found in labor unions, and members' rights were not protected. Senate hearings uncovered instances of numerous improper activities in labor unions, including collusion between employers and union officials, the use of violence by labor leaders, and the personal use of union funds by union leaders. The Landrum-Griffin Act resulted in several reforms, including better control over union funds and a requirement that financial records be retained and that periodic reports be made to the federal government.

The act's reforms were numerous. Secondary boycotting and picketing of companies that recognized other unions were restricted by the act. The law also outlawed "hot cargo" provisions in collective bargaining (when a neutral employer and a union voluntarily agree that the neutral employer will refuse to deliver union-designated "hot cargo" to another employer with whom the union has a conflict). Regarding arbitration, the act authorized states to process cases that fall outside the domain of the National Labor Relations Board. The influence of the Cold War was also evident in the act: Former members of the Communist Party and former convicts were prevented from holding a union office for a period of five years after resigning their Communist Party membership or being released from prison.

Bill of Rights The Landrum-Griffin Act also allowed union members to be protected against abuses by a bill of rights, which included guarantees of freedom of speech and elections. Unions must inform their members about provisions of the act. Union members have equal rights to nominate candidates for union office, vote in union elections, and participate in meetings. They may also meet with other union members and express opinions on labor matters. Unions may impose assessments against members and raise dues only if the action is approved by democratic procedures. Also, unions must give members a full and fair hearing of any charges against them.

Impact The Landrum-Griffin Act helped democratize labor unions and led to better control over the finances of unions in an era when organized crime played a troublesome role in labor relations. However, the act was not without controversy and was not universally supported. Labor unions opposed the act because their leaders felt that it strengthened what they considered the antilabor provisions of the NLRA. In subsequent decades, the office of the secretary of labor enforced certain provisions of the act and delegated authority to the Office of Labor-Management Standards of the Department of Labor's Employment Standards Administration.

Further Reading

Bellace, Janice R., Alan D. Berkowitz, and Bruce D. Van Dusen. *The Landrum-Griffin Act: Twenty Years of Federal Protection of Union Members' Rights.* Philadelphia: University of Pennsylvania, 1979. This book outlines the many benefits of the act.

Lee, R. Alton. *Eisenhower and Landrum-Griffin: A Study in Labor-Management Politics.* Lexington: University Press of Kentucky, 1990. This scholarly work deals with the politics of getting the act passed in 1959.

Lichtenstein, Nelson. *State of the Union: A Century of American Labor.* Princeton, N.J.: Princeton University Press, 2002. Chronicles the rise and decline of American labor unions, examining the 1950's as an era of increased membership and political activity.

McLaughlin, Doris B, and Anita L. Schoomaker. *The Landrum-Griffin Act and Union Democracy.* Ann Arbor: University of Michigan Press, 1979. This volume highlights the ways that the act has led to better union representation of members.

Dale L. Flesher

See also AFL-CIO merger; Communist Party of the U.S.A.; Eisenhower, Dwight D.; Hoffa, Jimmy; Meany, George; Organized crime; Steelworkers strike; Teamsters union; Unionism in the United States.

■ Larsen's perfect game

The Event World Series game pitched by Don Larsen
Date October 8, 1956
Place Yankee Stadium, Bronx, New York

Don Larsen's perfect game helped the New York Yankees to win the 1956 World Series against the Brooklyn Dodgers and became permanently entrenched in baseball lore.

In the long history of Major League Baseball, only seventeen perfect games—in which all twenty-seven players are retired in order without reaching first base safely—had been pitched through early 2004. In 1956, Don Larsen of the New York Yankees achieved this feat under the intense pressure of the fifth game of the 1956 World Series against the crosstown rival Brooklyn Dodgers.

Larsen was a talented pitcher, although he lacked the discipline or control to win consistently. On October 8, however, Larsen was magnificent. Using a no-windup delivery and pinpoint control of his curves, fastballs, and sliders, Larsen struck out seven batters and completely frustrated the Dodgers. Centerfielder Mickey Mantle contributed to the 2-0 victory by hitting a home run and making a difficult backhanded catch of a line drive hit by Gil Hodges. When Larsen struck out pinch-hitter Dale Mitchell to end the two-hour-and-nine-minute game, catcher Yogi Berra ran out and jumped into Larsen's arms as 64,519 fans cheered themselves hoarse. Larsen had achieved baseball immortality.

Impact The World Series contests between the New York Yankees and the Brooklyn Dodgers during the

Catcher Yogi Berra jumps into pitcher Don Larsen's arms after Larsen strikes out the last Dodgers batter to complete the first perfect game in World Series history. (AP/Wide World Photos)

1950's attracted the interest of baseball fans across the nation as well as those in New York, the nation's largest market. Larsen's startling feat against the National League's best team became a permanent part of baseball lore. It also added to the fabled history of the New York Yankees.

Further Reading

Buckley, James, Jr. *Perfect: The Inside Story of Baseball's Sixteen Perfect Games.* Chicago: Triumph Book, 2002. A lively account of these remarkable games.

Kahn, Roger. *The Era, 1947-1957: When the Yankees, the Giants, and the Dodgers Ruled the World.* Lincoln: University of Nebraska Press, 2002. A celebration of the decade when the Yankees, Giants, and Dodgers dominated baseball.

Shaw, Mark, and Don Larsen. *The Perfect Yankee.* Champaign, Ill.: Sagamore Publishing, 1996. Don Larsen tells his story in his own words.

M. Philip Lucas

See also Banks, Ernie; Baseball; Berra, Yogi; Dodgers and Giants relocation; Mantle, Mickey; New York Yankees; Stengel, Casey.

■ *Lassie*

Identification Television series about a heroic female dog
Producers Robert Maxwell et al.
Date Aired from 1954 to 1971

Lassie *represented classic 1950's values such as family, community service, and courage, which Americans embraced in the post-World War II and Korean War era.*

September 12, 1954, marked the beginning of a new series, *Lassie*, on CBS. British writer Eric Knight created the canine character of Lassie in a 1938 short story, and during the 1940's and 1950's, several films and one radio show featured Lassie.

The television program was set in rural America. More than five hundred episodes were produced, first in black and white and later in color. Shows depicted Lassie as a loyal companion to the families who owned her. Initially, Lassie was the pet of Jeff Miller (played by Tommy Rettig), who lived on a farm with his mother and grandfather. Episodes focused on the relationship between Jeff and Lassie and their interactions with people and nature, where they often encountered danger. Lassie routinely rescued both humans and animals. In 1958, the Martin family acquired Lassie as a pet for orphaned Timmy (Jon Provost).

Program themes emphasized friendship, bravery, perseverance, and sacrifice and touched on 1950's social concerns. Jeff's father was a war casualty, and episodes often dealt with veterans' issues and addressed racism toward Japanese Americans. *Lassie* also won two Emmy Awards.

Impact *Lassie* was a sentimental favorite that appealed to urban audiences who were nostalgic for America's rural past. Collies became a popular dog breed in the United States during the 1950's, and *Lassie* products—including Halloween costumes, children's and comic books, and watches—were marketed widely. Lassie became a staple in entertainment programming for decades following the debut of the original show.

Further Reading

American Kennel Club Museum of the Dog. *Lassie: A Collie and Her Influence*. St. Louis, Mo.: Dog Museum, 1993. A catalog published when Lassie was inducted into the American Kennel Club's Hall of Fame.

Collins, Ace. *Lassie: A Dog's Life, the First Fifty Years*. New York: Penguin Books, 1993. Provides a comprehensive account of the dogs who played Lassie and the people involved in the television series and films.

Elizabeth D. Schafer

See also Emmy Awards; Film in the United States; *Kukla, Fran and Ollie*; Television for children; Television in the United States.

■ Latin America

Identification The mostly Spanish- and Portuguese-speaking nations south of Canada and the United States, including the nations of Central America, South America, and the Caribbean

During the 1950's, U.S. officials increasingly recognized that Latin America's geographical proximity and economic potential made the region strategically important to U.S. foreign policy goals, and as such, the region became an important front in Cold War politics.

The United States wielded enormous military, political, and economic power in Latin America during the 1950's. The country gave military aid to dictators who were willing to fight the spread of communism in the region. Many Latin Americans protested against American involvement in Latin American politics and economics. Toward the end of the decade, the United States began to use economic aid to ease poverty and to improve its image in the region. Meanwhile, the rising level of poverty in Latin America drew huge numbers of Latinos to the United States in search of jobs; the Cuban revolution in 1959 contributed to this migration. The immigrants became a vital source of labor for the U.S. economy and introduced cultural influences to many parts of the United States during the decade.

U.S. Support of Dictators After the Korean War began in 1950, the United States became concerned that communism might spread into Latin Amer-

ica, an understandable concern. The region was suffering from poverty, social alienation, and political oppression—all problems that communism addressed. The United States wanted democracy to take root in the region, yet, it used its influence and financial aid to prop up military juntas and dictatorships that professed anticommunist ideas.

The most notorious rulers to receive U.S. aid during the decade included Rafael Trujillo of the Dominican Republic, Fulgencio Batista of Cuba, Marcos Pérez Jiménez of Venezuela, Anastasio Somoza and his son Luis in Nicaragua, Getúlio Vargas of Brazil, and Alfredo Stroessner of Paraguay. These and other Latin American dictators quickly swore loyalty to the anticommunist campaign. They promised to ban communism from their shores and told their diplomats to vote with the United States on Cold War issues within such organizations as the United Nations, Pan-American Conferences, and the Organization of American States.

Repeatedly, the United States used military aid to prop up dictators even as they replaced one another by means of revolts or rigged elections. Dictators suppressed most forms of dissent, and no communist-influenced governments came to power during the 1950's. However, in 1959, after several years of civil strife and a lengthy guerilla war, Fidel Castro toppled Batista's dictatorship in Cuba. Although the revolt was not communist inspired, Castro would declare Cuba a communist state in 1961.

Rise of Latin American Nationalism Nationalism is a desire to assert the interests of one's own nation by breaking away from unwarranted foreign interference. Anti-Americanism became a popular basis of patriotic rhetoric among elected officials' speeches and in street protests in Latin America. "Yankee go home" became a popular way of expressing a dislike of the United States during the 1950's.

There were many reasons why Latin American protesters focused their anger on the United States. The United States was the main foreign influence in Latin American affairs, and many Latin Americans did not like U.S. support of dictators. They also held a pent-up anger toward the United States' record in previous decades of using military force in the region. Moreover, Latin Americans were irritated because U.S. companies in the region paid low wages and did not reinvest profits in countries where they operated. Many Latin Americans were angered even more when the Central Intelligence Agency (CIA) ousted a noncommunist government in Guatemala in 1954. They saw the action as a blatant effort to protect U.S. business interests there.

The United States also tried to protect American farmers and industries from Latin American imports; subsidies on U.S. cotton and quotas on U.S. mineral imports hurt the economies of several Latin American countries. Panama was perturbed about American control of the Panama Canal Zone. A vocal and militant minority of Puerto Ricans wanted complete political independence for their country. The United States raised the ire of its neighbors even more when the U.S. Marshall Plan pumped massive sums of money and other aid into postwar Europe. However, the United States refused to create a similar aid program in Latin America.

U.S. Aid for Economic and Social Development The United States was not fully sensitive to the severity

of anti-American feeling in the region through most of the decade. U.S. awareness grew after Vice President Richard M. Nixon took a tour of several South American countries in 1958. Nixon made the trip to show U.S. support for the region's anticommunist governments. Zealous anti-American crowds met him throughout his travels, and in Caracas, Venezuela, he endured riots and insults and was nearly killed by a mob. The glaring display of anger and disrespect toward a major U.S. leader was a diplomatic blow for the North Americans.

President Dwight D. Eisenhower was spurred into action after witnessing Nixon's angry reception. He sent his brother Milton Eisenhower, a renowned educator, and John Foster Dulles, the secretary of state, to the region in 1959. They asked for advice from Latino political leaders in the United States on ways to improve U.S. relations in the region. These contacts suggested that U.S. policy focus on taking steps to support social and economic growth in the region.

Flag-waving Ecuadorian children greet U.S. vice president Richard M. Nixon on his arrival in Quito during his 1958 tour of Latin America. (AP/Wide World Photos)

American officials knew that mending the negative image of the United States would be difficult. In fact, during the same year that Eisenhower sent his brother and Dulles to Latin America, anti-American riots in the Panama Canal Zone led to attacks on American property, the deaths of three American soldiers and twenty Panamanian rioters, and the burning of the United States flag.

In the final days of the decade, the United States tried to improve its relations in the region. The country put together international price agreements on farm products and minerals. Such accords would assist Latin American exports to foreign markets. Overdependent on one-product economies, these countries had been pressing for such protective actions for years. The United States also increased its share of funding of the Pan-American Highway, a cooperative project that linked Western Hemisphere nations with 16,000 miles of roads and promoted cultural and economic ties.

The United States also withdrew its objection to a new lending agency, the Inter-American Development Bank (IDB). Moreover, the country provided most of the startup funds for the bank. The IDB began giving low-interest loans and grants to countries in the region in 1959. Significantly, the IDB stipulated that its money could not go to the military. Funds had to aid economic and social development in order to raise the living standards of the region's citizens.

Latin American Emigration to the United States Emigration from Latin America to the United States increased rapidly during the decade. The primary "push" factors were a growth in Latin America's population and a sharp increase in poverty in the region. Latin America's population increased by a phenomenal 23.5 percent during the 1950's. Most of this growth was taking place in rural areas. At the same time, Latin countries were trying to expand their manufacturing base, but the industrial focus created more jobs in the city than it did in the countryside. Job seekers from poor rural areas moved to cities in huge numbers. The majority of them ended up working in low-wage menial jobs or went unemployed. Large shantytowns, filled with poor rural emigrants in desperate need of work, grew up around the cities.

The main "pull" factor for Latin Americans' immigration to the United States was a growth in job opportunities there. The country was undergoing a postwar economic expansion. Migrant workers from Latin America's shantytowns and countryside supplied supplemental labor for the expansion. American workers already had taken the better paying jobs, but the low wages offered by U.S. employers seemed opulent by Latin American standards.

Jobs drew hundreds of thousands of Latino immigrants to the United States during the 1950's. They came mainly from Puerto Rico, Cuba, and Mexico, the countries bordering the United States. Puerto Ricans emigrated with less red tape than other groups, as Puerto Rico's political status shifted from U.S. protectorate to U.S. commonwealth in 1952. Immigration to Canada was negligible. The paucity of migration there was a reflection of geographical distance as well as fewer job opportunities.

Impact U.S. support of dictators through military aid aroused harsh criticism from Latin America's universities, its middle class, and labor unions. The critics had three arguments. First, armies absorbed aid that was badly needed for economic progress. Second, military aid reinforced the grip of dictators and made it possible for them to be even less responsive to rightful complaints of the people. Finally, supporting Latin dictators might serve the United States' anticommunist stance, but in the long term, such support put at risk the U.S. goal of friendship with its neighbors.

Despite these arguments, the overriding concern of the United States was to hold back communism at its borders. U.S. policies helped to achieve this objective, and communism did not gain popular support in any Latin American country during the 1950's. Even in Cuba, communists played a minor role in the removal of Batista.

The population of Latin American immigrants living in the United States grew rapidly during the 1950's. The newcomers brought with them the Spanish language and different preferences for food and music. Their destinations followed geographical patterns already set by Latin American immigrants before them. Puerto Ricans immigrated to northeastern cities, mainly to New York City. This primarily urban group found work in factories and mills in the region. Cubans immigrated to Florida, primarily to localities in the Miami and Tampa areas. A large-scale Cuban immigration occurred in 1959, immediately after Castro took power. He expelled most of his country's upper and middle classes. Many of these of people started businesses in Florida. Mexicans made up the largest group of immigrants. They moved into mainly rural areas of the American Southwest. Many of them became itinerant agricultural laborers and followed seasonal harvests as far north as Washington State and Michigan. This group also moved to cities, especially to Los Angeles, where they found jobs as gardeners, house cleaners, and daily laborers. Although the immigrants introduced numerous positive cultural and economic aspects to the United States, their presence was not always welcome, and the 1950's witnessed a growing xenophobia that culminated in programs such as Operation Wetback.

Subsequent Events The United States continued to give priority to fighting communism until the former Soviet Union's demise in 1991. It established military missions in almost every Latin American nation and large-scale provision of military assistance to most of them. The buildup of armaments led to a wasteful arms race in the region. Moreover, American ambassadors became intimate friends of dictators and acquaintances of generals, damaging further the image of the United States in the region.

Further Reading

Eisenhower, Milton S. *The Wine Is Bitter: The United States and Latin America.* Garden City, N.Y.: Doubleday, 1963. The author was the president's brother and close adviser on Latin American affairs. His book deals with U.S. and Latin American affairs during the 1950's and 1960's.

Hamil, Hugh. *Caudillos: Dictators in Spanish America.* Norman: University of Oklahoma Press, 1992. This volume examines dictators and their politics in Latin America from the nineteenth century to the late twentieth century.

Kryzanek, Michael. *U.S.-Latin America Relations.* Westport, Conn.: Praeger Publishers, 1996. Analysis of the key events and controversies that have shaped American-Latin American relations.

Ward, John. *Latin America: Development and Conflict Since 1945.* New York: Routledge, 1997. This volume discusses economic history and expansion as well as social, political, and environmental issues since 1945.

Williamson, Edwin. *The Penguin History of Latin America.* New York: Penguin Books, 1999. Background

to the social and economic conditions of Latin America during the 1950's.

Richard A. Crooker

See also Bracero program; Castro, Fidel; Cuban Revolution; Eisenhower Doctrine; Foreign policy of the United States; Guatemala invasion; International trade of the United States; Mexico; Nixon's Latin America tour; Operation Wetback; Organization of American States; Puerto Rico as a commonwealth; United Fruit Company.

■ Latinos

Definition Persons of Latin American descent living in the United States

Awareness of their own status as minorities and an increase in Spanish-speaking groups migrating to the United States led Latinos to a more visible presence in education, government, and the arts.

Although Latinos entered the United States prior to the 1950's, it was not until World War II and the years following that they began coming in great numbers. Economic incentives and political upheaval in Latin American countries were typically the "push" factors that prompted Latinos to choose the United States as a destination. For example, since a large portion of the American labor force was lost to the military during World War II, the governments of the United States and Mexico negotiated an agreement called the Mexican Farm Labor Supply Program in July of 1942 to bring Mexican farmworkers to the United States. Day laborers, or "braceros," were encouraged through various programs to enter the United States through December of 1964 and formed an important presence in American agriculture during the 1940's and 1950's.

After the Spanish-American War of 1898, when Spain ceded Puerto Rico to the United States, Puerto Ricans began coming to the United States. The largest migration, however, occurred after World War II. They migrated during this time mainly for economic reasons. By 1940, there were close to forty thousand Puerto Ricans in New York City alone, but the community tripled in size by 1950. Puerto Ricans began moving in significant numbers to Connecticut, New Jersey, Pennsylvania, Illinois, and Massachusetts.

Cuban settlements existed in Tampa, Florida, as early as the latter part of the nineteenth century.

Most Cubans migrated to Key West and Ybor City to work in the tobacco- and sugarcane-growing sectors; others arrived and then left with each political turmoil in Cuba. In 1950, there were more than 29,000 Cuban-born people living in the United States; nearly 8,000 of them lived in Florida. However, the largest migration to the United States by Cubans occurred after Fidel Castro took power in January, 1959, after overthrowing Fulgencio Batista's government. Cuban relations with the United States soon began to deteriorate. Castro confiscated property belonging to U.S. companies and established close ties with the Soviet Union. Waves of Cuban immigrants began arriving on American shores and continued to come to Florida, New York, New Jersey, and cities such as Chicago, Atlanta, and Los Angeles in subsequent decades.

Growing Visibility During the 1950's, the visibility of Latinos and their achievements began getting noticed by American society. It was a decade that found Latinos earning unprecedented positions in education, entertainment, sports, and government sectors.

Latinos faced a host of issues in the educational arena during the decade. These issues included continued school segregation, the struggle for bilingual education, and inclusion in higher education; Latino participation in higher education was very limited before the 1950's.

The *Brown v. Board of Education* Supreme Court decision of 1954 paved the way for the Civil Rights movement. Segregation in public schools was ruled unconstitutional, but Latinos continued to remain in segregated schools for years to come and were subjected to subtle forms of racism within educational institutions. For example, throughout the Southwest, many legal rulings banning segregation of Latino students were simply ignored, often based on prevalent views held by the social majority that nonwhites were inferior and "culturally deficient." In 1950, representatives from the League of United Latin American Citizens (LULAC) appeared before the Texas State Board of Education to address a list of twenty cities still practicing segregation. The board proposed a policy statement on the illegality of segregation but allowed individual districts to handle the complaints. It created a bureaucracy in which few grievances actually reached the state commissioner of education: Between 1950 and 1957, only

Puerto Rican actor José Ferrer, the first Latino to win an Academy Award for acting, got the award for his portrayal of the long-nosed French poet Cyrano de Bergerac. (AP/Wide World Photos)

nine school districts were brought to the commissioner although hundreds were practicing segregation throughout Texas.

Another reason for the continued practice of segregation among Latinos was the notion that the Spanish language was inferior to English. Politicians continued to use this to retain segregation, and bilingualism was criticized as being "un-American" and an obstacle for learning. Latino students often were held back for several years until they learned English, a practice that caused many of them to drop out of school as they became older than their classmates. Many educators supported the idea of intensive English instruction without maintaining Spanish instruction during the 1950's and early 1960's, and bilingual programs did not exist prior to the 1960's. Latinos were also funneled into vocational programs. This practice tended to maintain the unequal division of power and status in the labor force and set young Latinos on a course for low-paying jobs.

Film and Television Presence The television and movie industries began showcasing Latinos during the 1950's. Puerto Rican actor José Ferrer became the first Latino to win the Academy Award for best actor for his role in *Cyrano de Bergerac* (1950). Ferrer had a lengthy career as an actor, director, and producer; during the 1950's, he starred in films such as *Moulin Rouge* (1952), *The Caine Mutiny* (1954), and *The Great Man* (1957). In 1952, actor Anthony Quinn became the first Mexican American to win the Academy Award for best actor in his role as the brother of Mexican revolutionary Emiliano Zapata in the 1952 film *Viva Zapata!* Quinn was born in Mexico to Irish Mexican parents. He went on to win his second Academy Award for *Lust for Life* (1956) with his role as Vincent Van Gogh. Quinn appeared in more than one hundred films and acted in English, Spanish, and Italian.

In 1958, Américo Paredes, a folklorist, published *With His Pistol in His Hands: A Border Ballad and Its Hero.* This landmark study of the folk ballad became an important model for Chicano scholarship for more than twenty years. His book was also the first Chicano work to become the basis for a film, the television movie *The Ballad of Gregorio Cortez* (1982), which became a landmark in the history of Chicano culture.

Television's first Spanish-language program in the United States, *Buscando Estrellas* (looking for stars) started in 1951. Broadcast from San Antonio, Texas, this program was produced and hosted by José Pérez del Río. It was a weekly talent-search program that visited Texas towns on a rotating basis. Pérez del Río also produced *Cine en Español* between 1956 and 1961, a show that featured old films from Spain, Mexico, and Argentina.

I Love Lucy was introduced to television in 1952, the first television comedy to feature a Latino as a star. Cuban-born Desi Arnaz and his wife, Lucille Ball, brought a different twist to the Latin-lover and dumb-wife stereotypes. Audiences were captivated by a mixed marriage between an Anglo and a Latino who played and sang Afro-Cuban music. The show ran for nine years and enjoyed a long life in syndication.

In 1955, KCOR-TV became the first Spanish-language television station in the United States and broadcast from San Antonio, Texas. Moreover, Chita Rivera became the first Latina dancer featured in a television variety show. She later appeared in the *Gary Moore Show, The Ed Sullivan Show, The Arthur Godfrey Show, The Sid Caesar Show,* and others. She was the first Latina star dancer on Broadway when she was selected for a part in *Guys and Dolls* in 1952. Alongside Rita Moreno, she received fame and a Tony nomination for *West Side Story* (1957), a Broadway play that ran for 732 performances.

Even though Latinos had begun to have an influence on film and other media during the 1950's, it was not until 1969 that the actor Ricardo Montalbán became the president of Nosotros, a Hollywood-based organization of Latino actors. This organization was developed to bring forth a more positive portrayal of Latinos in film and television and to make the film industry more integrated.

Performing Arts Mexican immigrant José Limón became the first Latino professional modern dancer. Raised in Los Angeles, he began touring with his dance company around the United States. Some of his most recognized works include *Danza de la muerte* (Dance of Death), *La Malinche,* and *The Moor's Pavane.* In 1950, he received an award from *Dance* magazine for outstanding achievement in modern dance choreography, giving him the first recognition of a Latino in dance.

In 1953, Chilean-born Lupe Serrano became the first Latina ballerina principal dancer of the American Ballet Theater. At the age of eighteen, she toured with Alicia Alonso, the Cuban ballerina and later performed with the Ballet Folklórico de México. Serrano came from a performing arts background: Her father was a Spanish Argentine musician. She acquired fame throughout the United States and abroad and retired in 1971.

In music, Lalo Guerrero composed "Pancho López" a satiric version of "Davy Crockett." This 1956 song is considered the first crossover Latino hit played nationally. Mainly expressing the sentiments of the working class, Guerrero's songs were known for their humorous approach to subjects.

Born of Hungarian parents in Mexico City, Jorge Mester became the youngest teacher-conductor at the Juilliard School of Music in 1957 at the age of twenty-two. He also conducted the Juilliard Opera Theater for six years. Also in 1957, Carlos Chávez, the leading composer of classical music in Mexico, had the world premiere of *The Visitors* at Columbia University in New York. As a composer, he was mostly self-taught, and he completed his first symphony at the age of nineteen. Chávez served as director of the National Fine Arts Institute in Mexico from 1947 to 1952.

In 1958, Ritchie Valens became the first Mexican American rock star. Born Ricardo Valenzuela, Valens became famous with his hits "Come On, Let's Go," "La Bamba," and "Donna." He was the first Mexican American to be featured on television's *American Bandstand*. He died in a plane crash in 1959 at the height of his career.

Literature In 1958, novelist Floyd Salas became the first Latino to receive a Rockefeller grant. He was sent to the prestigious Centro Mexicano de Escritores in Mexico City, where he studied creative writing. His novels, based on his experiences as a creative writing instructor in the San Francisco Bay Area and his participation in various campus movements, included *What Now My Love?* (1970) and *State of Emergency* (1996). His first novel, *Tattoo the Wicked Cross*, was published in 1967. He received praise for this novel dealing with the brutalities found in juvenile jails.

In 1959, José Antonio Villarreal published what later was considered as the first Chicano novel, *Pocho*, a coming-of-age novel about a young Mexican in an immigrant family in Depression-era California. It also was the first novel by a Latino American writer released by a major U.S. publisher, Doubleday.

Sports The first Latino professional baseball player in the United States was Orestes (Minnie) Miñoso in 1951. The Cuban-born Miñoso stole thirty-one bases, the most in one season. In 1948, he began playing with the New York Cubans of the Negro League, and once the color barrier was eliminated, he signed with the Cleveland Indians. He had played for four decades by the time he served as a designated hitter for the Chicago White Sox in 1976. Alfonso (Chico) Carrasquel became the first Latino to be selected to the all-star game in 1951. Carrasquel served as the opening player for his shortstop position. In 1954, Roberto (Beto) Avila was the first Latino to win a batting championship in professional baseball. The Mexican-born Avila batted .341, drove in sixty-seven runs and scored 112 with fifteen home runs.

In 1956, Luis Aparicio became the first Latino rookie of the year in American professional baseball history. While playing for Baltimore, he drove in fifty-six runs, scored sixty-nine runs, and led the league in stolen bases. In 1984, he was inducted into the Baseball Hall of Fame.

In boxing, José Luis "Chegüi" Torres became the first Latino to win a medal in the Olympics. He won a silver medal in the light middleweight boxing division for the United States. In 1965, he won the middleweight championship as a professional boxer and was also the winner of the middleweight championship in 1966.

Catherine Machado was the first American Latina to compete on the U.S. Winter Olympic team in 1956. She was a senior figure skater and finished eighth in the overall competition of women's singles. In 1958, she went on to win the World Professional Figure Skating Championship in England. She was the first Latina to earn such an accomplishment. She later joined the Ice Capades.

Government Latinos also made their mark within government institutions during the 1950's. In 1951, President Harry S. Truman appointed the first Latino to the U.S. Court of Appeals for the Second Circuit. Mexican American and New York-born Harold R. Medina, Sr., was a graduate of Princeton University in New Jersey and received his law degree from Columbia University Law School. His most famous case was the Cramer treason case during World War II. He won the case on appeal to the U.S. Supreme Court. Also in 1951, Adam Díaz became the first Mexican American to serve on the Phoenix, Arizona, city council. In 1954, Dr. Héctor García Pérez was the first Latino appointed to the Democratic National Committee. Later, in 1956, Henry B. González became the first Mexican American to be elected to the Texas state senate in 110 years. His first elected office was that of city councilman in 1953. In 1957, Raymond Telles was elected mayor of El Paso, Texas. His campaign minimized racial and ethnic differences, and he received a large part of the white vote. He had served as El Paso county clerk since 1948.

Hernández v. Texas was the first Mexican American discrimination case to reach the Supreme Court. The 1954 suit claimed that Pete Hernández, a convicted murderer, had been denied equal protection under the law because he had faced a jury with no Mexican Americans. Despite having a Mexican American population of 14 percent, Jackson County, Texas, had not chosen a Mexican American juror in twenty-five years. The Court ruling was the first to recognize Latinos as a separate class of people who suffered discrimination in the United States. Previously, Latinos were not recognized as a separate, minority class but simply as "white." The decision paved the way for Latinos to use legal ways to defend themselves from discrimination in the United States. In addition, this was also the first case before the U.S. Supreme Court that was argued by Mexican American attorneys, Carlos Cadena and Gus García.

A group of Puerto Rican nationalists, who wanted Puerto Rico's independence from the United States, attacked the U.S. Congress in 1954. This was considered one of the first political terrorist attacks committed against the United States. Lolita Lebrón was the leader of the attack in which five congressmen were shot. Lebrón and her followers were tried, and she spent twenty-five years in jail. Her crime, however, made her a martyr and hero of the independence movement.

In 1959, The Mexican American Political Association (MAPA) was founded in California. It was the first Mexican American civil rights organization to acknowledge racism as the main problem confronting Latinos.

Impact The 1950's opened the door for Latinos in the United States within many areas, despite ongoing racism and discrimination. It was a decade of searching, discovering, and defining an identity within the United States.

Further Reading

Augenbraum, Harold, and Ilan Stavans, eds. *Growing Up Latino: Memoirs and Stories.* Boston: Houghton Mifflin, 1993. The foreword in this anthology summarizes Latino culture and literature in the United States.

Kanellos, Nicolás. *Hispanic Firsts: Five Hundred Years of Extraordinary Achievement.* New York: Visible Ink Press, 1997. This readable book presents the contributions and achievements of Latinos in the United States through five centuries.

Olson, James S., and Judith E. Olson. *Cuban Americans: From Trauma to Triumph.* New York: Twayne, 1995. Chapter 4 is dedicated exclusively to Cuban America during the 1950's.

Stavans, Ilan. *Latino U.S.A.: A Cartoon History.* New York: Basic Books, 2000. This book, made up entirely of cartoons, is a historical view of major Latino groups in the United States from the Conquest to the twenty-first century.

José A. Carmona

See also Bracero program; *Brown v. Board of Education*; Civil Rights movement; Film in the United States; Gonzáles, Pancho; *Hernández v. Texas*; *I Love Lucy*; Immigration to the United States; Interracial marriage laws; Operation Wetback; *Pocho*; Puerto Rican nationalist attack on Congress; Racial discrimination; Valens, Ritchie.

■ *Leave It to Beaver*

Identification Television comedy series
Date Aired from 1957 to 1963

Later considered a sentimental idealization of the American family during the 1950's, Leave it to Beaver *was, within television conventions of its decade, an attempt at a realistic depiction of childhood and child-parent relationships.*

Only moderately successful in its original run, *Leave It to Beaver* achieved popularity only in syndication. Subsequently considered a major pop-culture mani-

The stars of Leave It to Beaver *were Jerry Mathers (left) as the Beaver and Tony Dow (right) as his older brother, Wally Cleaver.* (Arkent Archive)

festation of the 1950's, it was never in the top-twenty ratings of the time. Featuring the Cleaver family—father Ward, mother June, and sons Wally and "Beaver" (Theodore)—in the small town of Mayfield, the series focused on the younger brother, Beaver, and his day-to-day struggles to understand the world and cope with its complexities. The scripts were often based on the writers' experiences with their own children, and although problems were always sorted out easily and quickly, a definite sense of realism pervaded the subject matter, if not the happy endings, of most episodes. The troubles Beaver confronted were typical of any childhood: facing bullies, wearing embarrassing clothes, losing something valuable, and misunderstanding adults. Furthermore, in contrast to many television children, Beaver was neither precocious nor articulate beyond his years. His understanding and verbal skills were always age-appropriate, and his parents were occasionally shown to be fallible, losing their temper or expecting too much of him.

Impact However sanitized the show's depiction of family life during the 1950's seemed to be to later audiences, its touches of realism distinguished it among more raucous, more farcical contemporary series and perhaps ensured its popularity with later generations.

Further Reading
Elliott, Michael. *The Day Before Yesterday.* New York: Simon & Schuster, 1996. Cogent explanation for the cultural context of *Leave It to Beaver*'s popularity in syndication.
Stark, Steven D. *Glued to the Set.* New York: Free Press, 1997. Chapter 15 is an excellent appraisal of *Leave It to Beaver,* and the other chapters provide context.

Thomas Du Bose

See also *Adventures of Ozzie and Harriet, The;* American Dream; Baby boomers; Conformity, culture of; *Father Knows Best; I Love Lucy; Kukla, Fran and Ollie;* Nielsen ratings; Television for children; Television in the United States.

■ **Lebanon occupation**

The Event Deployment of U.S. Marines to Lebanon to stabilize a rebel uprising
Date July-September, 1958

The U.S. invasion of Lebanon was the first test of the 1957 Eisenhower Doctrine, a Cold War treatise that asserted the right of the United States to assist Middle Eastern countries against armed aggression from any country controlled by international communism.

During the 1950's, Lebanon was one of the most Western-oriented and modernized states in the Middle East. Its women had the vote and its capital, Beirut, was a cosmopolitan economic center of both the Middle East and Mediterranean. Lebanon was an anomaly in the Arab world in many ways. Its society and government were remarkable examples of multicultural pluralism as evidenced by Muslims and Christians living together peacefully.

An agreement known as the National Pact stipulated that members of Lebanon's Chamber of Deputies, elected for four-year terms, were proportionally represented by both religion and region to reflect the nation's 1932 census. Furthermore, the president was required to be a Maronite Christian, representing the largest Christian sect in Lebanon; the prime minister a Sunni Muslim, representing the second largest Muslim sect; and the speaker of the Chamber a Shia Muslim, representing the largest Muslim sect. Nevertheless, Christians, despite no longer being the majority in population, held the majority of the wealth and positions of power and tended to espouse Western perspectives.

In contrast, many Lebanese Muslims and Druze (a religious group considered to be Muslim but which includes elements of paganism and Christianity) identified more with their Arab heritage. They were outraged when the Maronite Christian president Camille Shamun did not break off diplomatic ties with France and Britain when they, along with Israel, invaded Egypt in 1956 during the Suez Crisis. Then, in 1957, rumored Western interference in the Chamber of Deputies election raised further fears about the country's autonomy. By 1958, Egypt's President Gamal Abdel Nasser had become wildly popular to many in the Arab world. Arab communities hoped that Egypt's uniting with Syria to form the United Arab Republic in early 1958 heralded the formation of a unified state strong enough to counteract interference from their former colonial rulers as well as perceived threats from Israel.

Eager to see their country join the new republic, Muslim and Druze rebels began a civil war to oust President Shamun. Although Shamun's six-year term of office was almost up, rebels feared he would try illegally to succeed himself instead of stepping down. These fears were based upon the results of the disputed 1957 election, when Shamun's followers gained enough seats in the Chamber of Deputies to win a possible vote to overturn the constitution's prohibition on second presidential terms. Tensions continued to mount when an anti-Shamun editor of an opposition newspaper was assassinated. On July 14, the Iraqi monarchy was overthrown, and the entire pro-Western royal family was executed. In Lebanon, some radio stations began broadcasting forecasts that Shamun was next in line to be killed.

American Marines Arrive General Fuad Shihab, commander of the Lebanese army, refused to obey presidential orders to attack the rebels because he believed that many in the army would mutiny or desert if he ordered them into action. Reflecting the pluralism of the rest of Lebanon's government, the army was made up of mostly Christian officers and Muslim regulars. Helpless to oppose the rebels and believing the independence of Lebanon to be threatened, President Shamun summoned the American, British, and French ambassadors to ask for their nations' assistance in quelling the rebellion; he claimed it was being supplied with Soviet arms by the Syrians. He also invoked the Eisenhower Doctrine, a policy pledging American support to defend any government threatened by communist subversion, which Lebanon had endorsed the year before.

Ten hours later, the U.S. responded by mobilizing the Sixth Fleet to prevent an invasion by Syria. On July 16, five thousand Marines initiated an unopposed landing on the beaches of Beirut, wading ashore through beach umbrellas and sunbathers. Troops remained until the presidential succession was settled. Shamun did not seek reelection, and on July 31, General Shihab, widely admired for his levelheaded handling of the military situation, was elected president. By the time of Shihab's inauguration on September 23, the situation had stabilized, and U.S. forces began their departure. During the three months of U.S involvement, American forces did not engage in active combat. Only one U.S. battle death occurred, and U.S. troops inflicted no civilian casualties.

Impact The Lebanon invasion proved to the world how quickly U.S. troops could be mobilized in the event of a foreign policy crisis. American policy makers responded to the pleas of Lebanon's president with alacrity, arguably more in reaction to the revolution then developing in Iraq than to the rebellion in Lebanon. However, some diplomats also warned that a U.S. troop presence in the region would instigate a second Suez crisis or a war with the Soviet Union. While U.S. resolve was not tested in action, the U.S. military proved to allies such as Turkey and Iran that the United States could act quickly to support its allies in the event of a threatened communist insurrection. However, U.S. support for President Shamun, in combination with increasing economic and military aid to Israel, further alienated Arab nationalists.

Subsequent Events In all, between two thousand and four thousand lives were lost during the Lebanese civil war. President Shihab attempted to reunite Lebanon by instituting reforms favorable to Muslims and other minorities. Although an uneasy peace was maintained for some years, underlying internal and external tensions exacerbated by the influx of Palestinian refugees led to a bloody civil war in 1975 and the chaos that was to follow.

Further Reading

Alin, Erika G. *The United States and the 1958 Lebanon Crisis: American Intervention in the Middle East.* Lanham, Md.: University Press of America, 1994. Details the U.S. invasion, its aftermath, and consequences for U.S. Middle East policy.

Gordon, David C. *The Republic of Lebanon: Nation in Jeopardy.* Boulder, Colo.: Westview Press, 1983. Survey of Lebanon's history, economy, social structure, and politics, and French, British, Palestinian, Israeli, and American interventions and influences.

Hahn, Peter L. *Caught in the Middle East: U.S. Policy Toward the Arab-Israeli Conflict, 1945-1961.* Chapel Hill: University of North Carolina Press, 2004. Details the strategic, diplomatic, political, and cultural factors that influenced American policies in the Middle East during the 1950's.

Picard, Elizabeth. *Lebanon: A Shattered Country: Myths and Realities of the Wars in Lebanon.* Translated by Franklin Philip. New York: Holmes and Meier, 1996. Lucid explanation of factors that transformed a prosperous, peaceful, multiethnic society into a combat zone.

Yaqub, Salim. *Containing Arab Nationalism: The Eisenhower Doctrine and the Middle East.* Chapel Hill:

University of North Carolina Press, 2004. Uses recently declassified Egyptian, British, and American archival sources to examine Eisenhower's efforts to counter Nasser's appeal throughout the Arab Middle East.

Sue Tarjan

See also Acheson, Dean; Cold War; Eisenhower, Dwight D.; Eisenhower Doctrine; Foreign policy of the United States; Isolationism; Israel; Lodge, Henry Cabot; Suez Crisis.

■ Lehrer, Tom

Identification American satirical singer and songwriter
Born April 9, 1928; New York, New York

During the 1950's, Tom Lehrer developed a devoted following for performances and recordings of his sophisticated satirical songs.

As a boy, Tom Lehrer began learning classical piano, but his tastes ran more toward musical theater, and he was soon playing show tunes. After entering Harvard to study mathematics at the age of fifteen, he began performing his own satirical songs at college parties. His association with the prestigious institution, where he continued as a graduate student, inspired such songs as "Fight Fiercely, Harvard" and "Bright College Days" and gave him an audience ready to appreciate his sophisticated, often topical humor. He recorded and released his first album, *Songs by Tom Lehrer*, in 1953 and his second studio album, *More of Tom Lehrer*, in 1959.

Impact Though Lehrer's liberal politics often colored his songwriting, he was never counted among the great political humorists of his time. Many of his best-known songs, such as "Poisoning Pigeons in the Park" and "The Masochism Tango," are simply clever parodies of the style and content of popular mid-twentieth century music. Others, however—such as "The Old Dope Peddler" and "We Will All Go Together When We Go" (about the threat of nuclear war)—are more topical and pointed.

Lehrer continued to record and perform until the mid-1960's, after which he retired from the stage to teach college math and musical theater. His records, however, remained popular enough that a review of his songs from the 1950's, *Tomfoolery*, had a successful run in London and New York during the early 1980's. In 2000, Rhino Records released a compact-disc box set of Lehrer's complete recorded works.

Further Reading
Bernstein, Jeremy. "Tom Lehrer: Having Fun." *The American Scholar* 53 (1984): 295-302. Interview and retrospective article.
Lehrer, Tom. "In His Own Words: On Life, Lyrics, and Liberals." *Washington Post*, January 3, 1982: E1. Lehrer discusses the sociopolitical content of his music.

Janet E. Gardner

See also Freberg, Stan; Kovacs, Ernie; *MAD*; Music; Sahl, Mort.

■ Levittown

Identification Mass-produced suburban American housing development
Manufacturer William Levitt
Date First Levittown opened in 1947

William Levitt's introduction of mass production techniques to housing construction made single-family dwellings affordable for millions of Americans and contributed to the growth of suburbs around the nation.

When William Levitt appeared on the cover of *Time* magazine on July 13, 1950, his Levittown suburban housing projects in New York, New Jersey, and Pennsylvania had been under way for several years. By marrying mass production techniques to housing construction, Levitt revolutionized the suburban real estate market. Levitt, who learned his construction techniques as a Navy SeaBee during World War II, recognized the opportunity the postwar housing shortage presented. Cities had been generating suburbs for generations, as builders first followed rail lines and later highways, but developers' traditional construction required skilled craftsmen. With a few exceptions, such as planned communities such as that of Greenbelt, Maryland, suburban development targeted the upper middle class. Levitt turned housing construction into an assembly line process and, as a result, made the single-family home available to average working Americans.

Beginning in 1947, with a simple two-bedroom Cape Cod design erected on a concrete slab foundation, Levitt's first suburb was built on a former potato field on Long Island. The floor plan focused on

Levittown, New York, during the mid-1950's. (Hulton Archive | by Getty Images)

economies in building rather than convenience for the eventual inhabitants. The bathroom and the kitchen, for example, were placed back to back to require only one waste stack for the plumbing. The poured concrete slab floor eliminated the need for skilled masons. The second floor was left unfinished as an expansion attic available for conversion to additional living space when the home owner needed it.

Levitt organized his construction crews so each worker focused on only a handful of tasks, such as painting wood trim or laying shingles, and thus ensured that labor turnover could never constitute a problem. While architectural critics bemoaned the homogeneity of Levittowns and the copycat developments that followed, thousands of ordinary Americans took advantage of low prices and Veterans Administration financing. Where critics saw a monotonous raw landscape carpeted with boxlike houses,

buyers saw the promise of the good life in the suburbs in an affordable, easy-to-maintain home.

The first Levittown development featured only one design, a Cape Cod oriented toward the street. In 1949, Levitt introduced a variation on the basic floor plan, which he called the Ranch, and flipped the plan so the living room faced the backyard. This emphasized the home as a retreat from the larger world. The family was facing inward, away from the troubles and uncertainties of the Cold War and its threats. By 1951, a third variation, also a Ranch, incorporated more architectural details such as a split roof to make the house appear less mass produced and a living room picture window to bring in more light.

Impact The communities Levitt built, beginning with the original Levittown on Long Island, greatly influenced American housing development, and during the 1950's, suburban communities were built throughout the country. The success of Levittown encouraged other developers to target the lower middle class as potential home buyers.

Further Reading

Duany, Andres, et al. *Suburban Nation: The Rise of Sprawl and the Decline of the American Dream.* New York: North Point Press, 2001. A history and critique of national suburban development.

Jackson, Keith. *Crabgrass Frontier: The Suburbanization of the United States.* New York: Oxford University Press, 1987. Considered a classic in the field of urban and suburban studies, this book is thought provoking and accessible to the general reader.

Kelly, Barbara M. *Expanding the American Dream: Building and Rebuilding Levittown.* Albany: State University of New York Press, 1993. A comprehensive history of the first Levittown community on Long Island, detailing both its construction and evolution over time.

Nancy Farm Mannikko

See also Affluence and the new consumerism; American Dream; Architecture; Baby boomers; Conformity, culture of; Demographics of the United States; Housing in the United States; Interstate highway system; Urbanization in the United States.

■ Lewis, Jerry Lee

Identification American rock-and-roll musician
Born September 29, 1935; Ferriday, Louisiana

An early contributor to rock and roll, Jerry Lee Lewis helped the genre grow beyond its country roots.

In 1949, Jerry Lee Lewis's parents mortgaged their house in 1949 to buy young Lewis a piano, and he began playing with a local country-western band. In 1950, Lewis studied music at a fundamentalist school in Waxahachie, Texas, only to be expelled for playing a boogie-woogie version of a spiritual.

In 1956, Lewis and his father sold thirty-three dozen eggs to finance a trip to Memphis and an audition at Sun Records. When "Whole Lotta Shakin' Goin' On" was released in 1957, some radio stations banned it because of its suggestive lyrics. That December, Lewis joined Elvis Presley and Carl Perkins in an impromptu Sun recording session.

After Lewis performed on television's *The Steve Al-*

Jerry Lee Lewis in 1957. (AP/Wide World Photos)

len Show, sales of "Whole Lotta Shakin' Goin' On" took off, eventually amounting to six million copies. Hits such as "Great Balls of Fire" and "Breathless" followed.

In late 1957, Lewis married his thirteen-year-old second cousin, Myra Gale Brown, while still married to his second wife. American churches condemned him, and the outrage of the British press ended a tour of Great Britain in 1958. The resulting scandal took years for Lewis to overcome. (These events inspired the 1989 film *Great Balls of Fire*, with Dennis Quaid playing Lewis).

Impact Despite Lewis's legal, marital, and medical problems, his career thrived, and he was inducted into the Rock and Roll Hall of Fame in 1986. His colorful, tawdry personal life made him the first in a long line of rock-and-roll wild men. By blending rock, country, gospel, and blues, Lewis demonstrated the insignificance of musical boundaries.

Further Reading

Lewis, Jerry Lee, and Charles White. *Whole Lotta Shakin' Going On: The Life and Times of Jerry Lee*

Lewis. New York: Hyperion Press, 1994. Lewis's candid autobiography.

Tosches, Nick. *Hellfire: The Jerry Lee Lewis Story.* New York: Delacorte Press, 1982. Novelistic treatment of Lewis's life and considered one of rock's best biographies.

Michael Adams

See also Berry, Chuck; Domino, Fats; Haley, Bill; Holly, Buddy; Little Richard; Music; Presley, Elvis; Rock and roll.

■ Lewis, John L.

Identification American labor leader
Born February 12, 1880; Lucas, Iowa
Died July 11, 1969; Alexandria, Virginia

As president of the United Mine Workers union, John L. Lewis was one of the most prominent and controversial figures during a period when the labor movement had its strongest influence in American life.

John Llewellyn Lewis was the son of an immigrant Welsh coal miner and a devout Mormon mother. He completed ten years of schooling before joining his father as a coal miner at age sixteen. In 1907, he married Myrta Edith Bell, the well-educated daughter of a local doctor. The following year, he settled with his wife in the mining town of Panama, Illinois. He was soon elected president of the United Mine Workers (UMW) Local 1475. In 1911, he left the mines to become a union organizer for the American Federation of Labor (AFL). He retained his ties to the UMW, however, and was a close ally of its president, John White. In 1920, he was elected president of the United Mine Workers Union, a post that he would hold for forty years.

In 1935, Lewis, along with seven other labor leaders, formed the Congress of Industrial Organization (CIO) for the purpose of organizing workers in the mass-production industries. During the founding convention in 1938, he was elected its first president. After disagreements with President Franklin D. Roosevelt over war policy and other matters, he endorsed Wendell Wilkie, the Republican presidential candidate, for the election in 1940. When the union membership failed to follow his lead and Roosevelt was reelected, Lewis resigned as president of the CIO and took the UMW out of the CIO. Through the rest of the decade, Lewis led miners on several strikes and work stoppages.

Years of Repose During the 1950's, coal production declined substantially as cleaner and more convenient fuels replaced it. The market for coal was increasingly confined to public utility and industrial users. Lewis realized that improved technology and labor-saving machinery were necessary to keep coal competitive and maintain high wages and benefits. Accordingly, the union continued to obtain income and benefit increases throughout the 1950's, but union membership declined to half the level of the preceding decade.

Lewis struggled during the 1950's to bring about labor unity. He sought to return the UMW to the AFL and in turn, merge the AFL and CIO so that labor would speak with one voice. Leaders of the other unions, while favoring a merger in principle, would not cooperate with Lewis to bring it about, preferring instead to initiate a change through by their own efforts

Impact Lewis did not have a broad political or social agenda: His focus was on the improvement of wages, benefits, and working conditions for miners. In this endeavor, he excelled, but his abrasive and uncompromising stand as champion of the coal miners, while endearing him to his union membership, rendered him an ugly stereotype of an irascible union leader especially to many outside the labor movement.

Further Reading

Dubofsky, Melvyn, and Warren Van Tine. *John L. Lewis: A Biography.* New York: Quadrangle/New York Times Books, 1977. A thorough account of Lewis as a union leader.

Zieger, Robert H. *John L. Lewis: Labor Leader.* Boston: Twayne, 1988. A short analytical biography.

Gilbert T. Cave

See also AFL-CIO merger; Income and wages in the United States; Meany, George; Unionism in the United States.

■ Liberalism in U.S. politics

Definition Political ideology stressing social, political, and economic equality, aiming to secure and expand individual freedom and civil rights

Evolving from early Western political thought that taught that the purpose of government is to safeguard individual rights, American liberalism focused on securing and expanding civil rights for individuals during the 1950's.

Liberals have traditionally believed in the virtue of individuality and in the respect for the uniqueness and dignity of each person in society. They tend to be vigorous defenders of individuals or groups who have been discriminated against, such as members of racial minorities, women, and the poor, and demand that everyone have the same opportunities to improve their lives. They generally oppose most governmental restrictions on freedom of expression and focus on the virtue of the individual. According to this view, protection of and respect for the uniqueness and dignity of each person in society should be the goal of government. According to liberals, individuality can best be protected by prohibiting government from interfering with any exercise of the fundamental constitutional freedoms: free speech, press, religion, assembly, association, and privacy.

Both liberals and conservatives share many fundamental values and assumptions. However, conservatives stress economic rights, while liberals stress civil rights and liberties. Liberals tend to believe in the basic human goodness of individuals, while conservatives less readily attribute antisocial behavior to environmental factors, contending instead that there are always those in society who place themselves ahead of general societal welfare. Conservatives have fewer qualms than liberals about disparities in wealth or privilege and look to the past and conventional institutions—family and church especially—for guidance in meeting the challenges of the present.

Cold War Liberalism Although democracy is not one of liberalism's core principles, it is the only political system under which its principles can exist. A liberal democracy demands regular free and fair elections in which all adults are permitted to vote. American liberalism of the Cold War era was an immediate outgrowth of President Franklin D. Roosevelt's New Deal and the Progressive era of the early twentieth century. Its major positions included support for a domestic economy based on a balance of power between labor (in the form of organized labor unions) and management, a foreign policy focused on curtailing communist activity of the Soviet Union and its allies, and support for the continuation and expansion of New Deal social welfare programs such as Social Security.

Cold War liberalism developed at a time when most African Americans were politically and economically disenfranchised. The overwhelming majority of American voters were white. President Harry S. Truman appointed the Committee on Civil Rights in 1946, which recommended a series of changes, including a permanent Fair Employment Practices Commission, the creation of a Civil Rights Commission, desegregation of the armed forces, abolition of the poll tax, and support for integrated housing. President Truman became the first U.S. president to address a national meeting of the National Association for the Advancement of Colored People (NAACP), pledging to close the gap between black and white citizens. Although he ordered the desegregation of the armed forces in 1948, it was not until after the end of the Korean War in 1953 that integration actually took place.

Brown v. Board of Education Attorney and later U.S. Supreme Court justice Thurgood Marshall led the landmark 1954 fight for integration in the public schools, arguing that segregation by definition represented a denial of equality. The Supreme Court agreed in a unanimous and concise opinion by Chief Justice Earl Warren. In so doing, the Warren court abandoned a long-standing constitutional precedent and precipitated a revolution in public education. Marshall and others predicted that within less than one decade, all segregated schools would disappear, with other forms of mandated segregation to follow. The ruling, however, was not enforced immediately, in part because President Dwight D. Eisenhower disliked the decision in *Brown*. He believed that changing racial customs by force should be avoided and that the government should not interfere in local racial situations. As a result, he initially did little to make desegregation in the nation's schools a reality.

The 1954 decision in *Brown* left open the question of how and when desegregation would be accomplished. In a follow-up decision in 1955 (referred to as *Brown II*), the Supreme Court called for implementation of school desegregation "with all deliberate speed." Recognizing that compliance would be more difficult to achieve in the South than in other sections of the country, the Court left it to federal judges to apply the ruling while considering the circumstances surrounding race relations within their respective jurisdictions. Some of the Court's critics called for the impeachment of the chief justice and accused the Court of "meddling" in state and local affairs. Others called for militant noncompliance with the Court's directive.

In one of the most dramatic efforts to resist the Court's desegregation decisions, Arkansas governor Orval Faubus called out the National Guard in 1957 to prevent nine African American students from entering Little Rock Central High School. After the guard was withdrawn, an angry mob of whites continued to harass the students. Eisenhower sent federal troops into Little Rock to quell the violence and enforce the court-ordered desegregation.

The voices of average citizens were being raised. In 1955, Rosa Parks, a Montgomery, Alabama, seamstress, refused to abide by regulations that required African American riders to give up their bus seats to white riders. The bus boycott that resulted represented the assertion of the power of social forces already in place. Black institutions were prepared to mobilize their resources. Students at Greenboro's North Carolina A&T University began the sit-in movement, triggering similar demonstrations in fifty-four cities in nine states within eight weeks. The Student Non-Violent Coordinating Committee (SNCC) was founded in 1960, and the student phase of the Civil Rights movement had begun.

Impact Liberalism during the 1950's represented a transition between the New Deal policies of commitment to social welfare during the Depression and the John F. Kennedy presidential administration's attempt at social self-determination and activism. *Brown* spearheaded the Civil Rights movement, which ultimately culminated in legislative, judicial, and administrative attempts aimed at achieving racial equality. It was followed by controversies surrounding issues of mandatory school busing to achieve racial integration and affirmative action guidelines aimed at rectifying past injustices. Other significant public policy issues related to equality and equal treatment involved the rights of various ethnic groups, women, and the poor.

Further Reading

Baradat, Leon P. *Political Ideologies: Their Origins and Impact.* 8th ed. Upper Saddle River, N.J.: Prentice-Hall, 2003. A supplemental college text introducing basic concepts of political ideologies.

Chafe, William H., ed. *The Achievement of American Liberalism.* New York: Columbia University Press, 2003. This series of essays written by various au-

thors focuses on liberalism in its historical and social context.

Magstadt, Thomas M. *Understanding Politics: Ideas, Institutions, and Issues.* 6th ed. Belmont, Calif.: Wadsworth/Thomson, 2003. A basic college text introducing fundamental concepts.

Marcia J. Weiss

See also Civil Rights movement; Commission on Civil Rights; Conservatism in U.S. politics; Eisenhower, Dwight D.; Elections in the United States, 1952; Elections in the United States, 1956; Faulk, John Henry; McCarthy, Mary; Morse, Wayne; National Association for the Advancement of Colored People; Powell, Adam Clayton, Jr.; Stevenson, Adlai; Truman, Harry S.; Twenty-second Amendment; Warren, Earl.

■ Life

Identification General interest and news magazine
Publisher Henry R. Luce (1898-1967)
Date Published from 1936 to 1972

With its high-circulation figures, advertising revenues, and sophisticated visual designs, Life *was the flagship of Henry R. Luce's publishing empire and a dominant force in the American media of the 1950's.*

During the 1930's and 1940's, *Life* magazine offered a popular medley of serious news photography, trick photographs and visual stunts, "girly" pin-ups in bathing suits, and sensational tabloid images of suicides and murder victims. During the 1950's, however, it became a more serious and sometimes a more pretentious magazine. Thanks to *Life*'s advertisers and its impressive circulation statistics during that decade, its editors had the resources to help fulfill their magazine's original 1936 prospectus: "To see life; to see the world; to eyewitness great events; to watch the faces of the poor and the gestures of the proud." To achieve this goal, *Life* commissioned brilliant photoessays by some of the best photographers of its time, including Dorothea Lange, Ansel Adams, Margaret Bourke-White, W. Eugene Smith, and Henri Cartier-Bresson. The "proud" were ably represented by images of presidents and statesmen and volumes of Sir Winston Churchill's prose. However, the poor and the obscure were part of *Life* too: Lange's Mormon and Irish farmers and Smith's nurse-midwife and the villagers in his photoessay about a desolate Spanish hamlet.

Prosperity and Family Values In its special editions and feature stories that appeared frequently during the 1950's, *Life* offered bravura displays of full-page color images on subjects such as religion, history, and art. Americans, *Life* implied, had the leisure and the interest to learn about such subjects, and it provided them with affordable and easily accessible introductions to these topics. As for the United States itself, it was the subject of annual special issues, usually appearing in early January, which were vigorously optimistic. With titles such as "America's Assets" (1951) and "The American and His Economy" (1953), the special issues extolled the nation's prosperity and its new suburban way of life. All the clichés about the 1950's as an American golden age of optimism and security were depicted in *Life* during this decade, but they were especially prominent in the special issues.

Some of *Life*'s important advertisers included the manufacturers of the appliances and processed foods used in America's new suburban kitchens; consequently, the magazine had a keen interest in family values. Its viewpoint, whether expressed openly or by innuendo, was conservative but moderately so. White, middle-class nuclear families, preferably with cute children, were prominently featured in the magazine's lifestyle feature stories and special issues. Men were portrayed as breadwinners, but "working wives" and mothers were acceptable, albeit with caveats. The magazine did not frequently mention, much less advocate, "feminist" issues such as child care. However, it approved of married women working to buy household goods for themselves and their families, since this helped to expand the nation's "booming" consumer economy. The ideal situation, *Life* insinuated, was for a family to be affluent enough to hire servants to care for the children while the mother pursued a professional or business career.

Political Bent Because of *Life*'s popularity and influence, its editors often spoke as if they had a mission to show Americans how to see themselves, their nation, and the world. Frequently didactic, *Life* did not hesitate to tell its audience what to think about art, history, world politics, and other topics that came to the editors' attention.

In the area of national politics, *Life*, like other magazines published by Luce, was staunchly conservative and Republican, though usually less openly biased than its sibling, *Time*. The conflicts and confrontations over school integration following the 1954 *Brown v. Board of Education* Supreme Court ruling, however, made it more supportive of civil rights, and by the mid-1950's, the magazine was publishing photoessays clearly but discreetly criticizing segregation.

Impact Throughout the decade, *Life* dominated the national, general-interest mass media, and it was considered more successful than such competitors as *Look*, *Colliers*, and the *Saturday Evening Post*. However, it could maintain this dominance only as long as its true rival, television, was confined to small screens and black-and-white images. When that medium became more sophisticated, *Life*'s advertising revenues plummeted, and it suspended publication as a weekly magazine in 1972.

Further Reading
Baughman, James. *Henry R. Luce and the Rise of the American News Media.* Boston: Twayne, 1987. Covers *Life* and its publisher-creator in the context of their times.

Doss, Erika, ed. *Looking at "Life" Magazine.* Washington, D.C.: Smithsonian Institution Press, 2001. Thirteen essays examine how *Life* helped shape national identity.

Edey, Maitland, ed. *Great Photographic Essays from "Life."* Boston: New York Graphic Society, 1978. An excellent selection of *Life*'s photojournalism.

Kozol, Wendy. *Life's America: Family and Nation in Postwar Photojournalism.* Philadelphia: Temple University Press, 1994. A very good analysis of *Life*'s vision of domesticity.

Jarod Kearney

See also Famous Artists School; Hairstyles; *Kon-tiki*; *Look*; News magazines; *Reader's Digest*; *Sports Illustrated*.

■ Linkletter, Art

Identification Canadian radio and television personality
Born July 17, 1912; Moose Jaw, Saskatchewan, Canada

Art Linkletter pioneered the information-entertainment format for daytime television during the 1950's and hosted some of the longest-running series in broadcast history.

Born Arthur Gordon Kelly, Art Linkletter earned fame as a radio broadcaster, television personality, producer, author, lecturer, film adviser, and businessman during a career that has spanned almost seventy years. Abandoned by his natural parents at the door of a local church in Moose Jaw, Canada, he was adopted by a traveling minister and his wife; they eventually settled in California. He attended San Diego State College, where he studied linguistics and drama and competed on the football, handball, and swimming teams. He found work as a radio announcer for KGB in San Diego, and following graduation, he became the station's principal announcer.

Linkletter appeared on hundreds of radio programs during the 1930's and turned to Hollywood, in 1942 for new roles in the entertainment industry. He acted in the films *People are Funny* in 1946 and in *Champagne for Caesar* in 1950. In Hollywood, he teamed up with John Guedal to create the radio broadcasts *House Party* and *People Are Funny*, both of which he adapted to television during the 1950's. He was emcee of several television series, including *Life with Linkletter* (1950-1952), *House Party* (1952-1969), and *People Are Funny* (1954-1961), *The Art Linkletter Show* (1963), *Hollywood Talent Scouts* (1965-1966), and *Kids Say the Darndest Things* (1998-2000). His work on television included many guest appearances, including *Wagon Train*, *What's My Line?*, *General Electric Theater*, *I've Got a Secret*, and *Zane Grey Theater*. Linkletter also played himself in many television series and episodes, including *Hollywood Goes to Bat* (1950), *Screen Snapshots: Hollywood's Great Entertainers* (1953), and *Disneyland* (1959).

Art Linkletter and his wife in 1954. (Hulton Archive | by Getty Images)

Impact Linkletter is best known for his straight-man role as an interviewer of elementary school children, and his book *Kids Say the Darndest Things* (1957) was an instant success and ranks as one of the most successful best-sellers in American publishing history. *The Secret World of Kids* (1959) was followed by more than twenty books. He has delighted and inspired audiences throughout a prolific speaking and writing career. He is the recipient of three Emmy Awards, including the Lifetime Achievement Award by the Daytime Emmys, which he received in 2003. Moreover, he holds a Grammy Award and ten honorary doctorates.

Subsequent Events Linkletter was propelled into the antidrug campaign following the drug-related suicide of his daughter, Diane, in 1969. He served on the President's National Advisory Council for Drug Abuse Prevention. President Ronald Reagan appointed him ambassador to Australia during the 1980's.

Further Reading

Linkletter, Art. *I Didn't Do It Alone*. Ottawa, Ill.: Caroline House, 1980. An autobiography as told to George Bishop.

_____. *Kids Say the Darndest Things*. Englewood Cliffs, N.J.: Prentice-Hall, 1957. Quotes from children with some autobiographical material.

Ann M. Legreid

See also Disneyland; Emmy Awards; Film in the United States; *I've Got a Secret*; Radio; Television in the United States.

■ Literature in Canada

During the 1950's, Canadian writers produced works of high quality that not only had Canadian settings and characters but also explored universal issues.

During the early decades of the twentieth century, most Canadian fiction writers catered to the popular taste for mysteries, thrillers, sentimental love stories, and historical romances, many of which did not even use Canadian settings. However, there were some who believed that Canadian readers were ready for more substantial fare. One of these was Thomas Head Raddall, who received two Governor General's Literary Awards during the 1940's, one for a collection of short stories and the other for a history. Though Raddall was admired for his meticulously researched historical novels, most of them set in Nova Scotia, during the 1950's, he published three contemporary romances that were far superior to most of the previous works in the romance genre. In *The Nymph and the Lamp* (1950), Raddall used the Maritime Provinces setting so effectively and presented the inner struggles of his characters so realistically that some critics have called the book his finest work.

Another Nova Scotian, Hugh MacLennan, was also determined to write novels that were not only realistic but wholly Canadian. In *Each Man's Son* (1951), for example, he looked at the way a Puritan heritage and the bleak natural environment affected the residents of a Cape Breton mining village.

Canadian fiction written in French also reflected this new emphasis on realism. Having established her reputation with *Bonheur d'occasion* (1945; *The Tin Flute*, 1947), which was set in working-class Montreal, Gabrielle Roy continued to write novels about ordinary Canadians. *La Petite poule d'eau* (1950; *Where Nests the Water Hen*, 1950) described frontier life in northern Manitoba; *Alexandre Chenevert* (1955; *The Cashier*, 1955) was the portrait of a lonely Montreal bank teller; and *Rue Deschambault* (1955; *Street of Riches*, 1957), which won both the Governor General's Literary Award for Fiction and the Prix Duvernay award, was the story of a young girl who, like the author, spent her formative years in suburban Winnipeg, Manitoba.

The Quest for Meaning In addition to their insistence on realistic settings and characters, the fiction writers of the 1950's were preoccupied with moral and spiritual issues. One of the few Canadian writers who had become well known internationally during the 1920's and 1930's was Morley Callaghan, a native of Toronto, Ontario, who was a friend of the American writer Ernest Hemingway when they were both employed at the same newspaper, the *Toronto Daily Star.* After a sojourn in Paris with Hemingway, Gertrude Stein, F. Scott Fitzgerald, and their circle of American expatriate writers, Callaghan returned to Toronto and during the 1930's, produced a series of successful novels about spiritual crises, sin, and redemption. After a fallow period during the 1940's, Callaghan published the work that many consider his masterpiece, *The Loved and the Lost* (1951). The book won the Governor General's Literary Award for Fiction and was set in urban Montreal. Its protagonist is a woman who refuses to recognize the social barriers between white and black, rich and poor, and the novel shows how her stubborn innocence leads to her being crushed by society.

Another writer who produced her finest work during the decade was Ethel Wilson. Wilson was born in South Africa, but after being orphaned at the age of ten, she went to live with her maternal grandmother in Vancouver, British Columbia, which became her permanent home. She began writing late; her first story was published in 1937, her first novel, *Hetty Dorval*, in 1947. Of the novels she published in the following decade, *The Swamp Angel* (1954) is now the best known. On one level, it is the story of a woman who flees from an unhappy marriage to make a new life for herself in the wilderness; more profoundly, however, it deals with the relationships between individuals and other human beings, with nature, and with God. Wilson was also important in the development of Canadian fiction because as one of the finest stylists Canada produced, she was an important influence on her contemporaries and on the generations that followed.

Diversity and Cultural Independence Other writers of the 1950's were using very different approaches to Canadian subject matter. Robertson Davies published the Salterton trilogy, which included the novels *Tempest-Tost* (1951), *Leaven of Malice* (1954), and *A Mixture of Frailties* (1958). In these comedies of manners, set in small-town Ontario, Davies satirized the provincial narrow-mindedness and hypocrisy that he believed kept the inhabitants from attaining moral grandeur.

Mordecai Richler, another satirist, published his first novel, *The Acrobats*, in 1954. Three more soon followed, including *The Apprenticeship of Duddy Kravitz* (1959), a hilarious coming-of-age story about a young Jewish Canadian man attempting to find his way out of the Montreal ghetto and into the ranks of successful businessmen.

Richler once commented that by being both a Jew and a Canadian, he was doubly an outsider. Works such as his and those of Adele Wiseman, whose book *The Sacrifice* (1956) drew upon her Jewish Ukrainian heritage, reminded Canadians of their ethnic diversity. In both his nonfiction and his fiction, Farley Mowat demonstrated his concern not only for endangered animals but also for the endangered tribal peoples of the northern wilderness.

Most Canadian writers, however, remained outsiders on the literary scene, little read by people in other countries. That began to change in 1949, when the Royal Commission on National Development in the Arts, Letters, and Sciences was established and charged with furthering the development of an independent cultural tradition in Canada. The establishment of a National Library followed, and in 1957, the Canada Council for the Encouragement of the Arts, Letters, Humanities, and Social Sciences was formed. With financial help from the Canada Council, a number of new literary magazines were founded. Now there were new outlets for poetry and short fiction. In Quebec, a literary group called L'Hexagone started several literary magazines and published volumes of poetry. L'Hexagone became a central force in the French Canadian poetic renaissance.

Poetry Triumphant Canadian poetry in English was long established before the 1950's. E. J. Pratt, the most important of the earlier poets, was typical in his use of traditional forms. In 1952, for example, he published *Toward the Last Spike*, a long narrative poem in blank verse about the building of the transcontinental railroad.

However, the newer poets who appeared during the 1950's often used traditional forms in unusual ways. For example, the 1957 winner of the Governor General's Literary Award for Poetry was *The Boatman*, by Jay Macpherson, a collection of lyrics linked by a very modern symbolic pattern. The 1958 award went to *A Suit of Nettles* by James Reaney, twelve eclogues modeled on the sixteenth century

Shepheard's Calendar by the English poet Edmund Spenser but set in Stratford, Ontario, and including, among other things, a summary of Canadian history. The sonnets in *The Stunted Strong* (1954), by Fred Cogswell featured ordinary people from New Brunswick, and most of the poems in *The Cruising Auk* (1959) by George Johnston, though written in formal patterns, featured a cast of Canadian village eccentrics. The poet Wilfred Watson, who won a Governor General's Literary Award in 1955 for his first book, *Friday's Child*, was also highly inventive in his use of traditional forms, themes, and symbols in poems of religious illumination and apocalyptic visions.

Writers also varied as to how they used Canadian materials. In *Trio* (1954), a volume he co-authored along with Gael Turnbull and the existentialist poet Phyllis Webb, Eli Mandel filled Ontario and Saskatchewan with characters from classical mythology and the Bible. Douglas LePan, who focused on the unpopulated wilderness in his first book, *The Wounded Prince* (1948), used a European setting for his second publication, *The Net and the Sword* (1953), though the characters were soldiers from Canada. That volume, which won a Governor General's Literary Award, was a brilliant example of the new free verse form at its best.

Impact During the 1950's, Canadian writers made progress in their efforts to establish a rich cultural tradition that was not dependent on Europe or the United States. They began to write fiction and poetry that was not tailored merely for popular consumption; they experimented with form and subject matter; and they helped found new literary magazines, in which new writers could try their skill. Their efforts were aided immeasurably when the Royal Commission on National Development in the Arts, Letters, and Sciences recommended the establishment of a National Library and the formation of the Canada Council for the Encouragement of the Arts, Letters, Humanities, and Social Sciences.

At the beginning of the decade, Canada was already the home of many good poets, and their numbers increased each year. The 1950's marked a significant development in fiction, too, as novelists outside of the lucrative mainstream began to be more widely read. As more magazines appeared, more short stories were published, though that genre was still not popular, and it was a decade or two before authors would see their short fiction as collections on the shelves of book stores.

Although there was a good deal of talk about searching for a Canadian identity, during the 1950's, it was becoming clear that Canada, like its southern neighbor, was a nation that benefited from its very diversity. Writers were realizing that Canada's two languages, its regional distinctions, and the varied ethnic backgrounds and long-standing traditions of its people made its literature more interesting. Moreover, it was obvious that these differences would not impede any reader's grasp of human issues and universal themes. At mid-century, Canadians learned to accept themselves. Now it was necessary for the rest of the world to learn what literary treasures Canada possessed.

Further Reading

Atwood, Margaret Eleanor. *Survival: A Thematic Guide to Canadian Literature*. Toronto: Anansi, 1972. Argues that the primary preoccupations of Canadian writers have been "survival and victims." Controversial when published, this book has had a major influence on Canadians' views of themselves.

Blodgett, E. D. *Five-Part Invention: A History of Literary History in Canada*. Toronto: University of Toronto Press, 2002. Looks at Canadian literature as representing various ethnic and cultural groups and speculates as to why it continues to be fragmented.

Keith, W. J. *Canadian Literature in English*. London: Longman, 1985. Traces the development of Canadian literature by genre. Includes useful chronology and brief notes on individual authors.

Klinck, Carl F., ed. *Literary History of Canada: Canadian Literature in English*. 2d ed. 3 vols. Toronto: University of Toronto Press, 1976. Incorporates essays by a number of major scholars, including a well-known "conclusion" by Northrop Frye.

Meyer, Bruce, and Brian O'Riordan. *In Their Words: Interviews with Fourteen Canadian Writers*. Toronto: Anansi, 1984. Since ten of the writers interviewed had works published during the 1950's, this volume would be a good starting point for any student of the decade.

Rosemary M. Canfield Reisman

See also Book publishing; Canadian Broadcasting Corporation; Film in Canada; *Maclean's*; Minorities in Canada; Roy, Gabrielle; Theater in Canada.

■ Literature in the United States

The literature of the 1950's not only preserved traditional literary forms but also reflected a spiritually nuanced quest for personal identity and moral justice in an economically prosperous decade, which was often perceived to be authoritarian, conformist, and materialistic.

Delmore Schwartz, whose Bollinger Prize-winning *Summer Knowledge* (1959) combined his old and new poems, complained that 1950's poetry was generally as insignificant as a quiet sunny day in a park. However, the 1950's witnessed both the consolidation of work by older writers and new directions in work by younger authors. The consolidation of established traditions was evident in editions of collected or selected poems by poets such as Carl Sandburg (1950), William Carlos Williams (1950, 1951), Marianne Moore (1951), Archibald MacLeish (1952), Wallace Stevens (1954), Robert Frost (1955), Amy Lowell (1955), Theodore Roethke (1957), Richard Wilbur (1957), and Stanley Kunitz (1958). Most of these volumes won national awards, most often the Pulitzer Prize, and most of their authors continued as presences throughout the decade. At the same time, the spontaneous open form of Charles Olson's *In Cold Hell, in Thicket* (1953) revised the traditional sense of a poem's structural closure, while the sonnet sequence of John Berryman's *Homage to Mistress Bradstreet* (1956) altered the traditional understanding of American literary origins.

Fiction Like 1950's poetry, the fiction of the decade also is considered to be fundamentally conservative in disposition, neither experimental in form nor antagonistic to the decade's conformist social mentality. Certain best-sellers of the decade might encourage such an impression—for example, Henry Morton Robinson's *The Cardinal* (1950), Thomas B. Costain's *The Silver Chalice* (1952), and Catherine Marshall's *A Man Called Peter* (1951). A sense of the traditional cast of the period's fiction also might be suggested by the commercial appeal of conventionally told stories that were stronger on plot than on character, especially romances by Frances Parkinson Keyes and Frank Yerby.

The old-fashioned technique prevails in Edna Ferber's *Giant* (1952) and *Ice Palace* (1958) as well as in James Michener's *The Bridges of Toko-Ri* (1953), *Sayonara* (1954), and *Hawaii* (1959)—each book immensely popular during the decade. Besides John P. Marquand's *Melville Goodwin, U.S.A.* (1951), a traditional novel of manners, readers also relished the time-honored method of James Gould Cozzens's account of contesting emotion and reason in *By Love Possessed* (1957), Edwin O'Connor's portrait of an flawed Irish-American big-city boss in *The Last Hurrah* (1956), and John O'Hara's depiction of ruthless personal goals in *Ten North Frederick* (1955) and *From the Terrace* (1958).

Traditional fiction or poetry, nevertheless, often achieves more than simply meeting prevailing expectations. John Hersey's novels *The Wall* (1950), *The Marmot Drive* (1953), *A Single Pebble* (1956), and *The War Lover* (1959) exhibit predictable fictional techniques, but they also express deep humanitarian concerns that critique rather than reinforce various American postwar attitudes. Sometimes, as well, the conventional manner of widely read fiction—for instance, Herman Wouk's Pulitzer Prize-winning *The Caine Mutiny* (1951), Sloan Wilson's *The Man in the Gray Flannel Suit* (1955), and Leon Uris's *Exodus* (1958)—registers submerged reservations about authority and conformity, two key issues during the decade.

Featuring poor and elderly people defying institutional control in his works, John Updike developed the theme of dignity achieved through resistance in his debut novel, *The Poorhouse Fair* (1959), and in his short-story collection *The Same Door* (1959). Resistance to social convention also emerges in Truman Capote's *The Grass Harp* (1951), the reminiscences of misfits living in a tree house. The transgressive naïveté of the aptly named Holly Golightly in Capote's *Breakfast at Tiffany's: A Short Novel and Three Stories* (1958) is a slighter version of the defiance of gender norms by an aging actress who undertakes a desperate affair with a gigolo in Tennessee Williams's *The Roman Spring of Mrs. Stone* (1950).

Williams's best play of the 1950's, the Pulitzer Prize-winning *Cat on a Hot Tin Roof* (pr. 1955), highlights the failure of marriage to mitigate human loneliness. Moreover, loneliness and the pain of self-awareness are treated with unusual candor in William Inge's plays *Come Back, Little Sheba* (pr. 1950), *Picnic* (pr. 1953), *Bus Stop* (pr. 1955), and *The Dark at the Top of the Stairs* (pr. 1957). *Picnic* ends with its heroine, Madge, defying family and community standards as she leaves town in search of a more au-

thentic personal identity in an undefined and risky urbane future.

Older generations of poets were productive during this decade. William Carlos Williams, for instance, added significantly to his five-book project, *Patterson* (1946-1958), a Walt Whitman-like sweeping meditation on the productive interaction of humanity and technology as represented in one New Jersey city. Williams's sympathetic contemporary Ezra Pound likewise expanded his own ongoing, multidecade *Cantos* project, which freely juxtaposed diverse, often esoteric cultural and historical elements into a moral assessment of postwar experience. Pound's and Williams's liberated verse forms influenced many poets, including Gwendolyn Brooks's lyrical children's book *Bronzeville Boys and Girls* (1956). Like Pound and Williams at this stage of their careers, Brooks rejected the notion of art for art's sake. For these poets, art was affected by and had an effect upon the real world.

As these examples indicate, America during the 1950's was hardly the world later nostalgically imagined as Happy Days. Fiction writers and poets of the decade were aware of the problems of postwar conformity and acquisitiveness that were identified in David Riesman's *The Lonely Crowd* (1950), John Kenneth Galbraith's *The Affluent Society* (1958), William H. Whyte's *The Organization Man* (1956), and Vance Packard's widely read *The Status Seekers* (1959). They also encountered Ayn Rand's *Atlas Shrugged* (1957), a blunt top-ten best-seller that promoted individual self-interest over social altruism. While it is true that issues concerning women's rights, poverty, sexual identity, and racism would be more pointedly addressed during the 1960's, these subjects were by no means neglected in 1950's fiction and poetry, which mingled traditional literary techniques and the need for social revision.

Social Experience and Calls for Reform Ralph Ellison's *Invisible Man* (1952), arguably one of the most important novels of the 1950's, treated the decade's search for identity specifically in light of African American experience. The irregular and painful coming-of-age experiences of its nameless narrator represent the plight of his race. Replete with black folk tales and musical traditions, this novel is as powerfully poignant in its angry indictment of American culture as it is compellingly instructive in its canny manipulation of American literary traditions.

A strong case for a collectivist black effort is made in *Iron City* (1951), Lloyd Brown's story of an African American wrongly accused of murder. Transforming southern black schools is the subject of W. E. B. Du Bois's *Mansart Builds a School* (1959), a sequel to his *The Ordeal of Mansart* (1957). Du Bois relies on character types to highlight the setbacks and advances made by African Americans after the Civil War. *Youngblood* (1954), by university professor John O. Killens, reveals how poor white Georgians and their black peers share the same deprivations; the book argues that they should be allies rather than racial antagonists. In *The Outsider* (1953) and *The Long Dream* (1958), both written in France with little notice in the United States, expatriate Richard Wright added a philosophical overview to his ongoing critique of racism.

Greater impact was made by *A Raisin in the Sun* (pr. 1959), Lorraine Hansberry's successful play about an impoverished African American family suddenly put into crisis by an unexpected insurance

Richard Wright, one of the first African American writers to gain national attention. (Library of Congress)

benefit. Similarly popular were James Baldwin's *Go Tell It on the Mountain* (1953) and *Giovanni's Room* (1956), novels that highlight issues of racial and sexual identity. Gender issues, underscored by a profound sense of the connection between human loneliness and unfulfilled desires, define Carson McCullers's story of tangled love affairs among three people in *The Ballad of the Sad Café* (1951). Problems related to racial and gender identity are also addressed in Brooks's well-received *Maud Martha* (1953), while the struggles of economically deprived women in working-class environments are depicted in Tillie Olsen's short stories published during the 1950's and collected in *Tell Me a Riddle* (1961). Even Grace Metalious's sensationalistic two-year best-seller, *Peyton Place* (1956), candidly addressed female sexuality and highlighted contemporary patterns of victimization regarding gender and social class.

Besides Olsen, who was the daughter of Russian émigrés, other Jewish American voices emerged during the 1950's. Grace Paley, also the daughter of Russian Jewish emigrants, tellingly renders characters through their speech in the short fiction collected in *The Little Disturbances of Man: Stories of Men and Women in Love* (1959). A funny but pointed contest between a graduate student and his fiancé's distinctly Jewish expectations informs Philip Roth's *Goodbye Columbus* (1959), a self-conscious and skeptical engagement of the recurrent 1950's search-for-identity theme.

More serious is Saul Bellow's emphasis on the process of self-discovery through reason. Resistance to expectations characterizes the protagonist of Bellow's *The Adventures of Augie March* (1953), a study of the precarious nature of identity formation in a world of contradictory meanings. Death in *Seize the Day* (1956) ironically leads to a somewhat improved sense of life, whereas an agitated protagonist's search of identity in Bellow's *Henderson the Rain King* (1959) yields only uncertainty because the world and the self are unavoidably defined by antagonistic forces.

A stronger sense of certainty about the underlying meaning of life surfaces in Bernard Malamud's *The Natural* (1952), the story of how a baseball player's life is schematized along deep mythic patterns. In both *The Assistant* (1957) and *The Magic Barrel* (1958), Malamud specifically depicts Jewish experience, defined by biblical undercurrents, to suggest the slow but steady eventuation of a moral destiny.

Moral Justice and the American Dream Moral issues pervade John Steinbeck's fiction, including the story of loneliness resolved by a child adoption in *Burning Bright* (1950). The family saga in Steinbeck's *East of Eden* (1952), a contemporary version of the Old Testament account of Cain and Abel, instructively features the moral complexities of human behavior. *Sweet Thursday* (1954) offers another Steinbeck study in loneliness that is alleviated by human commitment.

Like Steinbeck, particularly in his earlier work, Nelson Algren mingles a naturalistic and a Marxist moralistic point of view in his stories of people struggling for survival at the low end of the American socioeconomic grid, particularly in the urban settings celebrated in his *Chicago* (1951). Algren's *A Walk on the Wild Side* (1956), a work flawed by exaggerated characterization, implicitly questions middle-class conformist standards by featuring the unconventional lives of French Quarter denizens in 1930's New Orleans. Impoverished inner-city neighborhoods provide the setting for *Let No Man Write My Epitaph* (1958), Willard Motley's study of the tragic toll paid by the economically disadvantaged.

The underside of the American Dream, specifically its negative impact on individualism and its inverse effect even on the economically successful, is exposed in Budd Schulberg's novel *The Disenchanted* (1950) and short-story collection *Some Faces in the Crowd* (1953). The emptiness of the so-called good life in suburbia is highlighted in John Cheever's stories in *The Enormous Radio, and Other Stories* (1953).

In *Birth of a Hero* (1951), *The Prospect Before Us* (1954), *The Man Who Was Not with It* (1956), and *The Optimist* (1959), Herbert Gold similarly undercuts the 1950's emphasis on material acquisition as a measure of personal success and instead urges a deeper self-awareness as a means to a realization of personal identity. Norman Mailer's harsher and pessimistic critique of Cold War America in *Barbary Shore* (1951) and *The Deer Park* (1955) highlights the troubling alliance of political oppression, capitalistic excess, and personal self-indulgence.

The human costs of factory industrialization, especially in the Detroit auto district, prove to be spiritually and artistically depleting for displaced Gertie Nevels in Harriette Arnow's *The Dollmaker* (1954). The plight of impoverished Latino coal miners, whose union activities stir fears of communism, is the subject of Philip Stevenson's *Morning, Noon, and Night* (1954) and *Out of the Dust* (1956). Both books were published under the pseudonym Lars Lawrence because Stevenson, a social activist, became a blacklisted screenwriter after he refused to cooperate with the House Committee on Un-American Activities.

The fact that not even the U.S. State Department was exempt from Senator Joseph McCarthy's witch-hunt for communists provides the subject of *The Survivor* (1958), Carl Marzani's personally informed documentation of political purges facilitated by Cold War hysteria. Arthur Miller's play *The Crucible* (1953) uses the Salem witch scare to emphasize the tragic dehumanization of McCarthyism, a theme also evident in the case Miller makes for individual integrity in his portrait of Brooklyn dockworkers in *A View from the Bridge* (1956). University professors appear in *The Searching Light* (1955), Martha Dodd's fictional study of the dire career consequences for anyone who resists loyalty oaths or other intimidat-

Norman Mailer. (Library of Congress)

ing McCarthyist efforts to control thought. A satiric treatment of this problem appears in Mary McCarthy's *The Groves of Academe* (1952), a politically ambiguous novel in which a professor's false claim of being persecuted because of his communist beliefs succeeds in saving his job, which had actually been cut because of budgetary constraints.

Elementary and high school children dominated several coming-of-age novels touching on moral principles and the American dream. The relationship between experience and belief is addressed in James Agee's *The Morning Watch* (1951), a short work depicting a day in the life of a twelve-year-old Tennessee boy who struggles with competing religious and secular influences on his emerging sense of self. Agee's posthumously published *A Death in the Family* (1957), an account of three children's reactions to the sudden death of their father, won a Pulitzer Prize and was converted by Tad Mosel into the Pulitzer Prize-winning play *All the Way Home* (1961). Less humanistic narratives of young men cut off from families and subsequently adrift in a depraved world of conflicted gender identity appear in James Purdy's short stories in *Color of Darkness* (1957). Purdy's *Malcolm* (1959) recounts the morally estranging experiences of a fifteen-year-old youth searching for his father.

By far the most surprising 1950's coming-of-age novel was J. D. Salinger's *The Catcher in the Rye* (1951), which did not become a hit at the time of its publication but would remain in print and eventually achieve cult status among later young readers. Holden Caulfield, the novel's lonely sixteen-year-old narrator, effects a cynical posture toward the hypocrisies of his middle-class upbringing. However, for all his self-protective attitudes in the course of his two-day misadventure in New York City, Holden is at heart compassionate, emotionally needy, and spiritually famished as he clings to the last vestiges of childhood innocence and the only principled identity he knows. Various kinds of loss, particularly as experienced by children, also inform Salinger's *Nine Stories* (1953).

The Material World and Mystery A still more fundamental loss during the decade's pursuit of material prosperity—the attrition of a deep regard for the mystery of being—informs Flannery O'Connor's novel *Wise Blood* (1952) and her short-fiction collection *A Good Man Is Hard to Find* (1955). O'Connor relies on such narrative devices as grotesque characters, peculiar imagery, and startling violence to jolt readers out of comforting illusions and their egotistical attachment to the physical world. The character of Hazel Motes in *Wise Blood* represents the unenlightened reader when he maintains that the senses and the material world constitute all there is to know. Even the human awareness of selfhood is an illusion for O'Connor. Precisely what mystery lies behind the veil of the world is less clear in O'Connor's fiction, which suggests a mystery so deep, so beyond human understanding, that even conventional religious recognition of it does not come close to identifying it.

A similar sense of mystery, augmented by Pound's and William Carlos Williams's social definition of poetry and their seeming improvisational manner, is conveyed in the innovative experiments of such Beat poets as Allen Ginsberg and Lawrence Ferlinghetti. In *Pictures of the Gone World* (1955) and *A Coney Island of the Mind* (1958), Ferlinghetti, a member of the San Francisco Renaissance, features everyday experience as the primary business of the artist. Ginsberg's populist and antiformalist *Howl* (1956) occasioned a failed obscenity trial. Ginsberg's uninhibited language, radical politics, and alternative lifestyle paralleled the rebel-without-a-cause sensibility of 1950's youth. Ginsberg dramatically resisted anything, even thoughts, that might repress self-expression. In his romantic quest for true self-identity, Ginsberg combined the claims of the body, 1950's politics, and an Eastern-nuanced mysticism.

Another distinctive poetic voice trailing clouds of a romantic sensibility while questing for personal identity surfaced in Theodore Roethke's *Praise to the End!* (1951), *The Waking* (1953), *The Exorcism* (1957), and *Words for the Wind* (1958). Attempting both to penetrate a Freudian terrain deep beneath consciousness and to recover a child-eyed sense of wonder, Roethke produced a highly personal verse celebrating a pantheistic universe. "The Waking," commonly anthologized, celebrates an ebullient faith-empowered spontaneity found only when conscious self-direction yields to the unconscious and nature as two mysterious but allied eternal and life-affirming forces.

Also influenced by seventeenth century metaphysical poets and likewise intimating a sacred dimension behind natural beauty, Richard Wilbur emerged as a major figure in *Ceremony* (1950), *Things of This Word* (1956), and *Poems* (1957). Wilbur's Romantic recognition of the mystical undercurrent of nature is not as purely emotional as that of Roethke's. In poems such as "The Death of a Toad" and "In the Field," for example, spiritual awareness requires close rational attention to scientific detail. In *Riprap* (1959), Gary Snyder likewise insists on an informed awareness of nature as critical to a mystical sense of the sacramental relationship between humanity and environment.

A related but much vaguer intimation of Transcendentalist metaphysics informs poet Howard Nemerov's circuitous language and reality in *Guide to the Ruins* (1950), *The Salt Garden* (1955), *Small Moment* (1957), and *Mirrors and Windows* (1958). Presenting the human mind as peculiarly positioned between the world and idea, Nemerov reprises Whitman's understanding of language as the weblike link between mind and nature. W. S. Merwin relies more on mythic and totemic properties to suggest the mysterious bond between humanity and nature. In *A Mask for Janus* (1952), *The Dancing Bears* (1954), and *Green with Beasts* (1956), Merwin hints at dimly perceived primal linkages relating the mind to the world.

Some undefined otherness deep within nature is also evident in Marianne Moore's *Collected Poems* (1951) and in her protégée Elizabeth Bishop's Pulitzer Prize-winning *Poems: North and South—A Cold Spring* (1955). Bishop's surprising combination of apparently unrelated images implies an unfamiliar reality lurking beneath the seemingly firm but unstable superficial meanings of daily lives. A harsher understanding, specifically the insignificance of humanity in relation to the alien indifference of nature's life-force, informs Robinson Jeffers's *Hunger Field, and Other Poems* (1954).

A Sense of Place and the Human Spirit The very material world critiqued by O'Connor and others is cherished by Ernest Hemingway, who details the late-in-life experiences of war veteran Richard Cantwell in *Across the River and into the Trees* (1950). This novel's title, drawn from Civil War general Stonewall Jackson's dying words, suggests an ironically courageous affirmation of the physical world despite the fate of human mortality. This affirmation registers still more forcefully in Hemingway's biblically nuanced *The Old Man and the Sea* (1952), the Pulitzer Prize-winning and commercially popular story of Santiago's dogged determination to

catch a marlin far from the safety of shore. Santiago has little to show for his life-threatening struggle with the big fish other than the self-respect that comes from the mastery of personal emotions and fishing skills. Hemingway, who celebrated the endurance of the human spirit against life's crushing disappointments, received the Nobel Prize in Literature in 1954.

Hemingway's southern contemporary William Faulkner was awarded the Nobel Prize in Literature in 1949 for his depiction of a changing South where human determination, both admirable and ignoble, resists life's adversities. Following *Collected Short Stories of William Faulkner* (1950), Faulkner published *Requiem for a Nun* (1951), a sequel to *Sanctuary* (1931) that highlights the lure of evil, the consequences of human will, and the subsequent guilt associated with self-awareness. In *The Town* (1957) and *The Mansion* (1959), Faulkner concluded his Snopes family trilogy, which commenced with *The Hamlet* (1940). *The Mansion* tells of two men responding to hostile social environments, one through murder and the other through commerce, while the reader is left to arrive at a moral perspective in a world in which people struggle to prevail. Ambiguity also characterizes Faulkner's Pulitzer Prize-winning *A Fable* (1954), in which biblical allusions to Christian redemption do not parallel the plot's outcome in this novel about thirteen French pacifists who refuse to fight Germans during World War I.

Mississippi-born Eudora Welty shares Faulkner's sense of place, a deep appreciation of southern culture both as a physical and as a psychological setting that bears testimony to the abiding human spirit. The humanely comic family narrative of a hotelkeeper in Welty's *The Ponder Heart* (1954) and the varied short stories of *The Bride of the Innisfallen, and Other Stories* (1955) suggest some underlying reality, akin to light itself, that informs any given present moment. This belief explains Welty's reliance on mythological and fairy-tale patterns in much of her fiction.

In his novels *World Enough and Time: A Romantic Novel* (1950), *Band of Angels* (1955), and *The Cave* (1959), Robert Penn Warren observes the ambiguity of human motives, the illusion of egotism, the tortured path to self-awareness, and a phoenixlike hope despite life's obstacles. Faulkner's influence registers in *Lie Down in Darkness* (1951), William Styron's story of Peyton Loftis's tragic flight from

William Faulkner (left) presents fellow American novelist John Dos Passos the American Academy and National Institute of Arts and Letters gold medal award for fiction in May, 1957, as institute president and critic Malcolm Cowley looks on. (AP/Wide World Photos)

Virginia to New York in search of a new sense of place and a personal cohesiveness in a world of confusing moral standards.

Self-alienation, rather than the dogged human spirit and a sense of place, became an emerging theme for various poets of the 1950's, who were inclined toward a new confessional mode that would develop further in the following decade. To a significant degree, Ginsberg's and Roethke's quests for both an authentic self and a sacral awareness was confessional. Alternating perspectives in James Merrill's *First Poems* (1951) and *The Country of a Thousand Years of Peace* (1959) anticipate his confessional verse to come. Especially noteworthy in terms of the rise of the confessional mode are Robert Lowell's *Life Studies* (1959) and his student W. D. Snodgrass's first book *Heart's Needle* (1959). Emphasizing personal crises, these irony-tinged poems not only are less emotionally radical but also are more overtly intimate than is Roethke's esoteric and metaphysical example.

Self, more than place, also matters in Styron's *The Long March* (1952), a study of defiance of authority. By resisting an unreasonable command of his colonel, a marine captain defines his sense of personal identity during the Korean War. Conflict with officers during World War II also occurs in the most popular book of 1951, James Jones's National Book Award-winning *From Here to Eternity.* A uncompromising private and a more accommodating sergeant arrive at different outcomes in their mutual struggle to maintain a sense of respectable self-definition in a dehumanizing and class-segregated army. However, that which appeared to be bold in Jones's narrative candor seemed far less impressive in his *Some Came Running* (1957) and *The Pistol* (1959).

Spontaneous prose, designed to convey an open-ended quest for self-identity, made Beat author Jack Kerouac's *On the Road* (1957) a cult favorite among readers. This same style and theme, in conjunction with a critique of 1950's middle-class values, informed Kerouac's less appealing *The Dharma Bums*

(1958) and *The Subterraneans* (1958). Unusual, too, are the seemingly unstructured interconnecting narratives in William Goyen's *The House of Breath* (1950) and *In a Farther Country: A Romance* (1955), both lyrically rather than linearly registering the deepest unfulfilled longings of the human heart.

William S. Burroughs—in a more radical departure from the properties of the novel as a form in *The Naked Lunch* (1959; republished as *Naked Lunch*, 1962)—rejected the values of the decade through a drug-addict's weirdly absurd perceptions represented in jumbled blocks of prose. Likewise presenting multiple perspectives that never resolve into "the truth," William Gaddis's *The Recognitions* (1955) implies the elusiveness of reality in any absolute sense.

Another challenge to a traditional understanding of reality, including the idea of novel writing itself, emerged in John Barth's *The Floating Opera* (1956) and *The End of the Road* (1958). Both works, critically defined as antinovels, insist that fiction cannot reflect the world other than to suggest that one's sense of reality and of the self is actually as fictional as novels are. Reality and fiction, in short, are merely constructions of one's language of the mind. A related insistence that reality is only a figment of the mind occurs in Vladimir Nabokov's *Lolita* (1955) and *Pnin* (1957), two more rogue novels featuring peculiar points of view. *Lolita* was a top-ten best-seller because of its sensationalist account of a pedophile's obsession with a twelve-year-old nymphet, but it is doubtful that most readers of this thoroughly nonerotic and cryptically satiric book ventured very far into the unreliable narrator's pun-ridden, chess-game text.

Short Fiction and the Pulps The 1950's was as receptive to the short story as it was to the novel. Print media from the decade ranged from *The New Yorker, The Atlantic Monthly, Harper's Magazine, Story, Esquire, The Saturday Evening Post,* and *Colliers,* to a wide variety of women's magazines. Lifestyle changes, especially an increase in television viewing, would eventually curtail the decade's abundant commercial marketplace for short stories. From the 1960's onward, short fiction would increasingly be consigned to small and little read university-based literary journals. During the 1950's, however, the short story was the form of choice of writers such as Tillie Olsen and Grace Paley. Paul Bowles in *The Delicate Prey, and Other Stories* (1950) and Peter Taylor in *Happy Families Are All*

Alike (1959) excelled in this literary form. Some critics maintain that the talents of novelists Flannery O'Connor, Eudora Welty, Truman Capote, John Cheever, and especially John O'Hara, among others, were best exhibited in short fiction.

Opportunities to publish short fiction in pulp magazines specializing in Westerns, mystery stories, and science fiction were also abundant. The Western genre included the prolific Louis L'Amour. The mystery genre ranged from Mickey Spillane's tough-guy *My Gun Is Quick* (1950), Jim Thompson's noirish *The Killer Inside Me* (1952), and Ross Macdonald's hard-boiled *Find a Victim* (1954), to Mignon Eberhart's woman-in-peril stories collected in *Deadly Is the Diamond* (1955).

Harlem black detectives were featured in Chester Himes's *Couché dans le pain* (1959; *The Crazy Kill,* 1959) and *The Real Cool Killers* (1959). In the suspense category, William March (William Campbell) published *The Bad Seed* (1954), a story of an eight-year-old murderer that cast an atavistic and Freudian shadow over the 1950's image of blithe domesticity. The science-fiction genre attained what would later be called its golden age, a time when exaggerated space-opera action gave way to a more ambitious and respectable management of plot, character, and prediction. Science fiction during this era ranged from hard-science stories by Robert Heinlein and Isaac Asimov to lighter fare by Clifford D. Simak and Ray Bradbury. Jack Finney's *The Body Snatchers* (1955), reflecting the paranoia of the McCarthy era, became a classic and was adapted to film several times. Such 1950's science fiction reflected the deepest anxieties of the decade.

Nonfiction Several nonfiction books of the decade deserve attention. Especially noteworthy were autobiographies such as novelist Ellen Glasgow's posthumous *The Woman Within* (1954) and playwright Hart Moss's *Act One: An Autobiography* (1959). In *Advertisements for Myself* (1959), Norman Mailer fashioned an experimental form of social critique that mingled fiction and nonfiction. Immensely popular at the time of its publication and also decades later, *Profiles in Courage* (1956) recounted individual acts of moral valor in highly readable episodes ghostwritten for John F. Kennedy.

Perhaps the most stunning nonfiction work of the period was Rachel Carson's two-year best-seller, *The Sea Around Us* (1951), a compelling and eloquent revelation of the place of the oceans in human life. It won a National Book Award, was widely translated, and was followed by Carson's *The Edge of the Sea* (1955).

Impact A survey of 1950's poetry and fiction reveals a multifaceted collective enterprise. Many of these works mingle traditional forms and reformist topics as they anxiously address a concern about personal identity and moral justice. For many of the decade's authors, meaningful selfhood and a just society were threatened, first, by an economic prosperity that fostered a dehumanizing materialistic sensibility and, second, by a Cold War politics of national security that fostered a conformist sensibility concerning authority. In short, these writings registered concerns about superficial lives defined by accumulated status symbols, both always vulnerable to nuclear annihilation. Even those authors who exhibited a profound sense of regional place tended in one way or another to ask: Is human life in this time of increasing affluence and technology as good as it gets? Expressing doubts, some sought a spiritual resonance or detected a deep sense of mystery behind material existence. These authors expressed a Romantic-age valuation of a spiritualized inner self that resists its dehumanizing disempowerment in an acquisitive culture shaped by commercial and techno-political power. At the same time, other authors rejected any sense of an abiding spiritual undercurrent. They ironically depicted an alienated "dangling man," existentially caught between the end of traditional values and the open-ended choices in a world devoid of any firm moral guidance.

The fact that *The Search for Bridey Murphy* (1956), Morey Bernstein's dubious case-study proof of reincarnation, seized the reading public's imagination suggests a curious cultural ambivalence. On the one hand, it indicates an unrecognized desire for a transcendent relationship to 1950's material definition of existence; on the other hand, it indicates a desire for a permanent connection to the material world. A similar divided sensibility underlies the success of Norman Vincent Peale's *The Power of Positive Thinking* (1952) and Bishop Fulton J. Sheen's *Life Is Worth Living* (1953-1957), which value physical existence precisely in terms of spiritual meaning. Therefore, in the anxious culture of the 1950's, the conformist Man in the Gray Flannel Suit, who hoped to find fulfillment through material prosperity, lived uncomfortably next door to the Rebel Without a Cause, who insisted on a more authentic life, whatever that elusive authenticity might be.

Further Reading

Galloway, David D. *The Absurd Hero in American Fiction.* Austin: University of Texas Press, 1970. Considers hope in writings by Bellow, Salinger, Mailer, Styron, and Updike.

Gery, John. *Nuclear Annihilation and Contemporary American Poetry: Ways of Nothingness.* Gainesville: University Press of Florida, 1996. Interprets poems responding to the Cold War.

Hendler, Jane. *Best Sellers and Their Film Adaptations in Postwar America: "From Here to Eternity," "Sayonara," "Giant," "Auntie Mame," "Peyton Place."* New York: Peter Lang, 2001. Examines film adaptations of novels during the 1950's, focusing primarily on the portrayal of gender identity and conflict.

Hilfer, Tony. *American Fiction Since 1940.* New York: Longman, 1992. Surveys developments in African American, southern, Jewish American, and meta-fictional stories, among other topics.

Schaub, Thomas Hill. *American Fiction in the Cold War.* Madison: University of Wisconsin Press, 1991. Considers the relationship between literature and political developments of the era.

Tuttleton, James W. *The Novel of Manners in America.* Chapel Hill: University of North Carolina Press, 1972. Examines the longevity of a traditional form of the novel.

Wood, Ruth Pirsig. *Lolita in Peyton Place.* New York: Garland, 1995. Reviews novels, from highbrow to lowbrow, in terms of moral issues.

William J. Scheick

See also Bellow, Saul; Burroughs, William; *Catcher in the Rye, The*; Corso, Gregory; *Fahrenheit 451*; Hemingway, Ernest; *Lolita*; McCarthy, Mary; Michener, James; *Peyton Place*; Pound, Ezra; Steinbeck, John; Uris, Leon; Wilson, Edmund; Yerby, Frank.

■ Little Richard

Identification African American singer and a founder of rock-and-roll music
Born December 5, 1932; Macon, Georgia

Little Richard helped undermine racial barriers by bringing his exuberant rock music to a young, white audience.

Born Richard Wayne Penniman, Little Richard grew up in the southern Bible Belt, where he loved the lively gospel music of the Pentecostal and similar churches. He began singing and playing piano in local nightclubs, perfecting his electrifying stage presence and blending gospel and blues music.

In 1955, Speciality Records recorded Little Richard's "Tutti Frutti," which eventually sold three million copies. In 1956 and 1957, he toured successfully, recorded fourteen hit songs, and appeared in three films. His hits included "Rip It Up," "Lucille," "Jenny, Jenny," and "Long Tall Sally." At the height of his fame, Richard retired and became a preacher. When he later returned to rock, musical tastes had changed, and he did not match his earlier successes.

Impact Little Richard's explosive singing and dancing style later influenced such entertainers as James Brown and Michael Jackson and made rock music as much about performance as about music. His recordings became emblematic of the wildness and unpredictability of rock and roll during the era. After the 1950's, Richard drew big concert crowds all over the world. He appeared often on television and in several films. He was inducted into the Rock and Roll Hall of Fame in 1986 and received a Lifetime Achievement Grammy Award in 1993.

Further Reading

Ward, Ed, Geoffrey Stokes, and Ken Tucker. *Rock of Ages: The Rolling Stone History of Rock & Roll.* Englewood Cliffs, N.J.: Rolling Stone Press/Prentice-Hall, 1986. A survey that places Little Richard in rock-and-roll history.

White, Charles. *The Life and Times of Little Richard: The Authorised Biography.* New York: Omnibus Press, 2003. A lively biography based on interviews with Little Richard and his friends.

Martha E. Pemberton

See also Berry, Chuck; Boone, Pat; Dance, popular; Diddley, Bo; Domino, Fats; Freed, Alan; Lewis, Jerry Lee; Music; Presley, Elvis; Rock and roll.

▪ Little Rock school desegregation crisis

The Event Crisis in federal-state relations arising from the refusal of Arkansas state officials to comply with a court order to allow African American students to enroll in Little Rock's Central High School

Date 1957-1959
Place Little Rock, Arkansas

The widely publicized events in Little Rock made school desegregation a nationally recognized issue and gave momentum to the early Civil Rights movement.

On May 17, 1954, in the case of *Brown v. Board of Education*, the U.S. Supreme Court ruled that racially segregated public schools were illegal. The court issued a second ruling on the case one year later, ordering local school boards to desegregate "with all deliberate speed." One of the first and most widely publicized tests of the new federal position on school segregation came in Little Rock, Arkansas.

At first, it appeared as if Little Rock schools would quietly follow the orders of the Supreme Court. On May 22, 1954, the Little Rock school board announced that it would comply with the Supreme Court order as soon as the Court established a method and a schedule for desegregation. In May 1955, the school board voted to adopt a policy of gradual desegregation to start in 1957. Under the plan devised by School Superintendent Virgil Blossom, the city would first integrate the city's Central High School and then gradually integrate lower grades.

The Crisis Erupts The crisis broke out in 1957, the year that the school board had hoped to manage the quiet enrollment of a few African American pupils to white schools. Seventeen students were selected to be the first to break down the racial lines, but only nine of them decided to pursue enrollment. Shortly before the beginning of the school year, on August 27, the Little Rock's Mother's League sought an injunction to halt integration. The injunction was granted by Pulaski County chancellor Murray Reed, but it was rejected three days later by federal district judge Ronald Davies.

The enrollment of the African American students might have proceeded in a relatively peaceful manner if the Arkansas governor Orval Faubus had not used the event for political advantage. Faubus was searching for political support to win a third term in office, and he decided to appeal to white constituents who were eager to preserve segregation. Governor Faubus declared that he would not be able to maintain order if Central High School were integrated, and on September 2, he ordered the state's National Guard to surround the school. His stand

Federal troops stand guard in front of Little Rock's Central High School. (Library of Congress)

drew public attention to the situation and attracted white segregationist mobs to the streets. The next day, Judge Davies ordered that the integration of Central High should continue.

The National Association for the Advancement of Colored People (NAACP), under the local leadership of Daisy Bates, organized the nine African American students to arrive in a group. They were met by National Guardsmen who turned them away with bayonets. One of the students arrived after the others and was confronted by screaming segregationists. Television, which occupied a central place in most American homes by 1957, broadcast the scenes from Little Rock around the nation. On September 20, Judge Davies ruled that Governor Faubus had used the National Guard to prevent integration and forbade the guard's employment in this way. Faubus then replaced the guard with local police. The nine black students entered Central High School through a side door on September 23. As they made their way into the school, an unruly mob

of more than one thousand people massed on the streets outside.

Federal Intervention President Dwight D. Eisenhower met with Governor Faubus on September 14. The president believed that the governor had agreed to allow school integration to continue. It soon became evident that Governor Faubus had no such intention.

Alarmed by the developments in his city, on September 24, Little Rock mayor Woodrow Mann asked President Eisenhower for federal troops to maintain order. Eisenhower responded by sending one thousand troops of the 101st Airborne Division and placing the Arkansas National Guard under federal control. The troops then escorted the nine students to the school each day. Some Americans were shocked to see that military protection was needed to protect the basic rights of citizens. Others were disturbed at what they believed was a federal military occupation of a state, reviving historical memories of the military occupation of the South during the era of Reconstruction in the years following the Civil War.

Years of Struggle The struggle continued even after the mobs in front of Central High returned to their homes and jobs. On February 8, 1958, after several angry confrontations with white students, one of the nine, Minnijean Brown, was suspended for the rest of the year. Shortly after, the school board asked the federal court for a delay of the integration order until the concept of "all deliberate speed" was defined. The delay was granted in June and reversed in August. In the meantime, the first African American student graduated from Central High in May.

Upon the opening of the 1958-1959 school year, Governor Faubus ordered Little Rock public schools closed, and white students enrolled in private schools and in other districts. On September 27, 1958, Little Rock residents voted on school integration and overwhelmingly rejected it. However, on June 18, 1959, a federal court declared that Little Rock's public school closing was unconstitutional. Little Rock schools opened one month early for the 1959-1960 school year and enrolled both African American and white students.

Impact The Little Rock crisis was the first major test of the federal government's determination to enforce the Supreme Court's *Brown* decision. President Eisenhower's willingness to use troops for school desegregation was controversial, but it marked the beginning of the U.S. government's commitment to desegregated schools. Little Rock was also the beginning of a series of struggles over school desegregation that continued for several decades across the nation. The event proved to be one of the defining events during the early Civil Rights movement.

Further Reading

Counts, Ira Wilmer. *A Life Is More than a Moment: The Desegregation of Little Rock's Central High.* Bloomington: Indiana University Press, 1999. Provides essays and photographs concerning the events at Central High.

Huckaby, Elizabeth. *Crisis at Central High: Little Rock, 1957-1958.* Baton Rouge: Louisiana State University Press, 1980. The crisis as recounted by one of the original African American students.

Kirk, John A. *Redefining the Color Line: Black Activism in Little Rock, Arkansas, 1940-1970.* Gainesville: University Press of Florida, 2002. Draws on the oral histories of important grassroots civil rights activists who shaped the critical events in Little Rock.

Carl L. Bankston III

See also African Americans; *Bolling v. Sharpe*; *Brown v. Board of Education*; Civil Rights movement; Eisenhower, Dwight D.; Faubus, Orval; National Association for the Advancement of Colored People; Racial discrimination; School desegregation; Southern Manifesto; Supreme Court decisions, U.S.; White Citizens' Councils.

■ Lodge, Henry Cabot

Identification U.S. ambassador to the United Nations from 1953 to 1960
Born July 5, 1902; Nahant, Massachusetts
Died February 27, 1985; Beverly, Massachusetts

Henry Cabot Lodge helped formulate U.S. domestic and foreign policies during the 1950's as political adviser to President Dwight D. Eisenhower and as a member of Eisenhower's cabinet.

The patrician grandson and namesake of a powerful Massachusetts Republican senator, Henry Cabot Lodge was a journalist and state legislator before he gained election to the same U.S. Senate seat in 1936. Reelected in 1942, he resigned to serve in World War II, rising to the rank of lieutenant colonel. A prewar isolationist, Lodge returned to the Senate in 1947 and became an ardent postwar internationalist, who supported the Marshall Plan and the North Atlantic Treaty Organization (NATO). In 1952, he chaired the successful campaign of presidential candidate Dwight D. Eisenhower but lost his own bid for reelection to Democrat John F. Kennedy. Eisenhower then named Lodge as the second U.S. permanent representative to the United Nations (U.N.), a post Lodge occupied from January, 1953, to September, 1960.

Impact Lodge was a gifted speaker, and he used his diplomacy to help wage the Cold War against the Soviet Union within the United Nations during the 1950's. At the United Nations, he was clever and effective in publicizing the U.S. case against the Soviet Union on many issues, ranging from the Hungarian revolt in October, 1956, to the U-2 spy plane incident in May, 1960. His influence on U.S.

policy derived from his close relationship and regular personal contacts with Eisenhower. At first, Lodge faithfully endorsed the anticommunist policies of Secretary of State John Foster Dulles, but he later became a champion of nonalignment and decolonization.

After losing in his bid to be vice president as Richard M. Nixon's running mate in 1960, Lodge twice served as ambassador to South Vietnam, silencing mainstream Republican criticism of Democratic policies escalating the Second Indochina War. However, in 1968, he was one of the "Wise Men" who helped persuade President Lyndon B. Johnson to deescalate the war.

Further Reading

Finger, Seymour Maxwell. *Your Man at the UN: People, Politics, and Bureaucracy in Making Foreign Policy.* New York: New York University Press, 1980. Describes Lodge's performance as proof for his thesis that "a determined individual, enjoying the confidence of the president and backed by a competent staff, can exert policy leadership."

Lodge, Henry Cabot. *The Storm Has Many Eyes: A Personal Narrative.* New York: W. W. Norton, 1973. Lodge's autobiography.

James I. Matray

See also Cold War; Dulles, John Foster; Eisenhower, Dwight D.; Elections in the United States, 1952; Guatemala invasion; Hungarian revolt; Lebanon occupation; North Atlantic Treaty Organization; U-2 spy planes; United Nations.

■ *Lolita*

Identification Controversial novel about a middle-aged man's obsession with a young girl
Author Vladimir Nabokov (1899-1977)
Date Published in France in 1955 and in the United States in 1958

Although attacked by censors, Lolita *was hailed by critics as a literary masterpiece and purchased by many readers.*

The theme of the novel *Lolita* had occurred to Russian-born writer Vladimir Nabokov during the mid-1930's, but it was only in 1946—a year after he became an American citizen—that he began work on the novel. Even then he was dissatisfied and would have burned his notes if not for the intervention of his wife.

Vladimir Nabokov. (Alfred Appel, Jr./Maclean Dameron)

Lolita purports to be the confessions of Humbert Humbert, a European émigré who harbors a passion for what he calls "nymphets," girls approaching their teenage years. Humbert marries widow Charlotte Haze in order to be near her twelve-year-old daughter, Lolita. When Charlotte is killed in an automobile accident, Humbert takes Lolita on a phantasmagoric road trip across the United States.

Nabokov was unable to find an American publisher willing to handle a novel with such a daring theme and so turned to Paris-based Olympia Press, a firm specializing in experimental and sexually explicit works in English. The novel appeared in France in 1955 and in the United States in 1958. Critics praised the novel for its verbal inventiveness and its pathos, but in both countries, government officials attempted to ban it. Perhaps expecting a more salacious work, American readers made *Lolita* a bestseller.

Impact The publication of *Lolita* in the United States made available a major literary work, while its successful legal defense advanced the cause of intellectual freedom. At the turn of the twenty-first century, literary critics consistently listed *Lolita* as one of the most significant novels of the century.

Further Reading

Olsen, Lance. *"Lolita": A Janus Text*. New York: Twayne, 1995. A detailed analysis placing the novel in its literary and historical context.

Pifer, Ellen, ed. *Vladimir Nabokov's "Lolita": A Casebook*. New York: Oxford University Press, 2002. Includes an interview with Nabokov and essays on the novel and its cultural impact.

Grove Koger

See also Book publishing; Censorship; *Lady Chatterley's Lover*; Literature in the United States; *Peyton Place*.

∎ *The Lone Ranger*

Identification Popular television Western series based on a radio program

Producer Jack Chertok (1906-1995)

Date Aired from 1949 to 1961

This Western, aimed at children, centered on a heroic former Texas Ranger who reflected conservative 1950's values such as justice, fair play, and honesty.

Created during the 1930's by George W. Trendle, *The Lone Ranger* was a successful radio series and two movie serials before moving to television in 1949. Unlike other Westerns, such as *The Roy Rogers Show* and *The Gene Autry Show*, it ran in prime time. In each episode the Lone Ranger and his faithful Native American companion, Tonto, defeated Old West outlaws and rode away to the sound of Gioachino Rossini's *William Tell Overture*. During the televised series' run, Clayton Moore played the Lone Ranger (except in one season when John Hart took the role), while Jay Silverheels was always Tonto.

According to the series' backstory, the Lone Ranger was originally John Reid, a Texas Ranger whose

posse was ambushed by the Butch Cavendish gang and left to die. Although the other Rangers perished, Reid was rescued by Tonto, who had been saved by Reid years before. Donning a mask made from a Ranger vest, Reid was told by Tonto he was now the "Lone Ranger." Known as "Kemo Sabe" ("faithful friend" or "trusty scout") to Tonto, the Lone Ranger befriended a wild stallion he named Silver and, exclaiming "Hi-Yo Silver," repeatedly and successfully hunted down the Cavendish gang.

Impact The Lone Ranger espoused a fair-play code, that influenced the moral values of post-World War II children. According to creator Trendle, the Lone Ranger never smoked, used profanity, or drank. His grammar was as perfect as his aim, he never shot to kill, and he always demonstrated respect for law

Clayton Moore (left) as the Lone Ranger and Jay Silverheels (right) as his faithful partner, Tonto. (Arkent Archive)

and order. Such mores sat well with 1950's conservative families and helped the program become ABC's earliest success in the nascent television age.

Further Reading

Aaker, Everett. *Television Western Players of the Fifties: A Biographical Encyclopedia of All Regular Cast Members in Western Series, 1949-1959.* Jefferson, N.C.: McFarland, 1997. Collection of brief biographies of television actors, including those on *The Lone Ranger.*

Moore, Clayton. *I Was That Masked Man.* Dallas: Taylor, 1998. Moore's memoirs of his career as the Lone Ranger, among other life details.

Spigel, Lynn. *Make Room for TV: Television and the Family Ideal in Postwar America.* Chicago: University of Chicago Press, 1992. Focuses on the growth of television as a national medium as opposed to popular expectations for it.

Thummin, Janet. *Small Screens, Big Ideas: Television in the 1950's.* London: I. B. Tauris, 2001. Explores the way in which television prompted social change in postwar America and Britain. Includes many illustrations and photographs.

Charlie Sweet

See also *Captain Video; Cisco Kid, The;* Comic books; *Davy Crockett; Gunsmoke;* Mutual Broadcasting System scandal; *Sergeant Preston of the Yukon; Sky King;* Television for children; Television Westerns.

■ The Lonely Crowd

Identification Book on changes in American society during the 1950's
Author David Riesman (1909-2002)
Date Published in 1950

The Lonely Crowd *provided illuminating insights into the new American character that emerged during the prosperous, consumer-driven era after World War II.*

The Lonely Crowd: A Study of the Changing American Character records what David Riesman perceived to be revolutionary changes in American character that were occurring during the 1950's. It is one of a number of books written by theorists as diverse as Hannah Arendt and John Kenneth Galbraith at that time on the topic of social and national psyche. Riesman's theoretical contribution to this discussion was his model of the tripartite social character and his provocative suggestion that the American character was moving from "inner" to "other" direct-

edness. A typical modern American's source of life-direction and value would not be internalized ideals, parental influence, or traditions; rather its source would be friends, acquaintances, and presciently, the mass media. Riesman argued that Americans were coming to adjust their behavior to the perceived expectations of important others whose approval they sought.

Impact Riesman's thesis struck a chord with the American public, with *The Lonely Crowd* selling more than one million copies. It provided a vocabulary through which Americans could understand the changes of value they were undergoing, and it provided a diagnosis of the causes of those changes. It accomplished all of this without the trappings of sociological jargon. To Riesman's chagrin, the book was often read by critics and admirers as an indictment against modern American conformity and the country's individualist nineteenth century predecessors. However, Riesman noted that all societies require some form of behavioral conformity from their members. The ability to get along well with others is what is appropriate for members of an advanced consumer society.

Further Reading

Bellah, Robert, et al. *Habits of the Heart: Individualism and Commitment in America.* Berkeley: University of California Press, 1996. A study of religious and civic commitment in modern American society.

Sennett, Richard. *The Corrosion of Character: The Personal Consequences of Work in the New Capitalism.* New York: W. W. Norton, 2000. Sennett chronicles the effects of modern "flexible" capitalism on the lives of workers.

Edward W. Maine

See also *Affluent Society, The;* American Dream; Business and the economy in Canada; Communications in the United States; Conformity, culture of; Mills, C. Wright; News magazines; *Organization Man, The;* Urbanization in the United States.

■ Long Day's Journey into Night

Identification Play about members of a theatrical family confronting their lives as they realize that the youngest son has contracted tuberculosis and the mother is sliding back into drug addiction
Author Eugene O'Neill (1888-1953)
Date First produced in the United States in 1956

An autobiographical examination of Eugene O'Neill's troubled family life, Long Day's Journey into Night tackled issues of alienation, isolation, and the inability to communicate—themes that resonated with 1950's audiences striving for the American Dream and struggling with the uncertainties of the Cold War era.

Long Day's Journey into Night takes place in 1912 in the Connecticut summer house of the tumultuous Tyrone family. During one day and night, the members of this intense and conflicted family reminisce, fight, drink, apologize, joke, and slowly and painfully face the deepest truths about their hopes, dreams, failures, and fears. The artistry and emotional impact of the play and its timeless exploration of family relationships and individual aspirations made it a classic American drama.

Impact The play, considered by many critics to be one of the greatest American dramas of the twentieth century, was withheld at its author's request from publication or production until after his death. The 1956 production posthumously placed Eugene O'Neill back in the first rank of American dramatists. It also won for O'Neill his fourth (and posthumous) Pulitzer Prize and made O'Neill a theatrical contemporary to the new generation of serious dramatists, such as Tennessee Williams, Arthur Miller, and William Inge. Sidney Lumet's 1962 film version with Katharine Hepburn brought the play to an audience of millions.

Further Reading

Bogard, Travis. *Contour in Time: The Plays of Eugene O'Neill.* Rev. ed. New York: Oxford University Press, 1988. The standard one-volume study of O'Neill's full career, it has a strong biographical orientation and is excellent at placing the plays in their intellectual contexts.

Manheim, Michael. "The Stature of *Long Day's Journey into Night.*" In *The Cambridge Companion to Eugene O'Neill,* edited by Michael Manheim. Cambridge, England: Cambridge University Press, 1998. A detailed yet accessible reading of the play, full of sharp insights about both form and content.

Roger J. Stilling

See also American Dream; Film in the United States; Literature in the United States; Miller, Arthur; Nobel Prizes; Theater in the United States; Williams, Tennessee.

■ Long-playing records

Definition Twelve-inch vinyl sound disc played at a speed of 33⅓ revolutions per minute

Date Introduced in June, 1948

Long-playing records contributed to the expansion of musical styles and repertoire and the growth of the music industry during the 1950's.

Prior to the introduction of long-playing records (LPs), commercial recordings were ten- or twelve-inch discs made of a composite of materials, including shellac, and played at a speed of 78 revolutions per minute (rpm). These discs played for three to five minutes per side, produced a great deal of surface noise, wore out quickly, and shattered easily. Longer musical works, especially classical pieces, had to be recorded over several discs, which were sold in sets as record "albums." In June of 1948, Columbia Records introduced a long-playing disk that could play up to thirty minutes on each side. Columbia achieved this by slowing the speed of the record to 33⅓ rpm and increasing the number of grooves per inch impressed on the disc, marketed as "microgrooves." The new discs were made of vinyl, which was more durable, and produced sound more faithfully than shellac 78s.

Before launching LPs, Columbia management met with its main competitor, RCA Victor, and offered to share the technology and set standards for the new records. RCA refused, and Columbia began selling LPs after contracting with Philco to sell relatively inexpensive record players. In 1949, RCA countered with a seven-inch, 45-rpm disc, allowing the same 3-5 minute playing time as 78-rpm records. At first, neither the LP nor the 45 format was quickly adopted by the public, which held off investing in either one with their proprietary players, and sales fell from previous highs set in 1946 and 1947. Gradually, however, record companies produced both LPs and 45s, players were made that could play at several speeds, and by 1955, record sales began climbing above previous levels.

Impact The concurrent development and use of magnetic tape for sound recording led to LPs affecting the repertoire of available music. Tape recorders allowed the capture and editing of performances at a relatively low cost. Small recording studios and independent record labels emerged and captured new markets ahead of the bigger labels. The recorded classical repertoire greatly expanded from a limited set of favorites to include Renaissance and Baroque music, more obscure Classic and Romantic works, and contemporary experimental music. Recordings of Broadway musicals were among the first big LP sellers, promoting the growth of the genre during the 1950's. Additionally, jazz musicians were free to improvise beyond the three to five minutes of a 78, better capturing the free-form experience of live jazz. Single 45-rpm records became the standard for popular music as record companies supplied radio stations and millions of juke boxes with them. Home listeners, especially the burgeoning teenage market, bought 45s of hit songs and often ended up buying the LP albums from which the hit singles originated. In all, the combination of technology and social trends helped the U.S. recording industry grow from $151 million in 1951 to $514 million in 1959.

The introduction of LPs spurred interest in developing high-fidelity (hi-fi) sound systems, especially with the advent of stereo recordings in 1957. Dissatisfied with commercially available equipment, hi-fi enthusiasts built component systems from kits and parts from other electronic applications in pursuit of a concert hall experience in the home. The movement engendered hi-fi clubs and magazines such as *High Fidelity*.

Further Reading

Day, Timothy. *A Century of Recorded Music: Listening to Musical History.* New Haven, Conn.: Yale University Press, 2000. Discusses the effect of recording technology, including LPs, on the style and repertoire of classical music.

Millard, Andre. *America on Record: A History of Recorded Sound.* Cambridge, England: Cambridge University Press, 2003. An engaging history of sound recording and its musical and cultural impact.

Sanjek, Russell. *Pennies from Heaven: The American Popular Music Business in the Twentieth Century.* New York: Da Capo Press, 1996. Detailed study of the business of the recording industry.

Paul Orkiszewski

See also Belafonte, Harry; Broadway musicals; Brubeck, Dave; Fitzgerald, Ella; Jazz; Kingston Trio; Music; Rock and roll.

■ *Look*

Identification General interest photo magazine
Publisher Gardner A. Cowles, Jr. (1903-1985)
Date Published biweekly from 1937 to 1971

After beginning as a "sensational," tabloid-style magazine, Look became a sedate rival to Life, with its emphasis on lifestyle photoessays and articles that advocated moderate solutions to social problems.

Like its popular competitor, *Life, Look* magazine provided its readers during the 1950's with a simplified, optimistic vision of reality as seen from a middle-class American perspective. Published every two weeks, *Look* did not attempt to compete with *Life*'s, or television's, coverage of hard, topical news. Instead, it concentrated on feature stories, social trends, and generalized articles, mainly about how "typical" Americans lived, worked, and spent their leisure time in suburbs and small- to medium-sized towns. The magazine stressed that America was changing, and these changes could be visualized and conceptualized by its editors in photo-essays about subjects such as suburban housewives, convenience foods, and "labor-saving gadgets" and appliances, which mimicked the messages of the magazine's advertisers.

Prosperity and Problems The United States, as depicted on *Look*'s pages, was a stable, prosperous nation changing rapidly for the better as cheap energy, easy credit, and its industries' increasing productivity enabled white, working- and middle-class citizens to buy homes in the suburbs and fill their driveways with second and third cars. *Look* not only reassured its readers of their nation's social and economic progress, but also highlighted inspirational aspects of life with a biweekly column by Dr. Norman Vincent Peale, the best-selling author of *The Power of Positive Thinking*.

While *Life* depicted American optimism more fervently, *Look* was more sensitive to America's problems of the decade, such as the treatment of minorities, declining urban environments, rising divorce rates, and women who were discontented despite their shiny new kitchens and appliances. *Look*'s editors acknowledged that these difficulties existed by responding to them with representations of American individuals or groups who had discovered reasonable, common-sense solutions. Or, as the magazine's editors said in a 1956 photo-essay on changing gender relationships among American men and women, "we specialize in happy endings."

Impact *Look* promoted and articulated middle-class America's values during the 1950's, especially its optimism. The magazine's editors acknowledged that America had problems, but they sought to solve these issues with good will and reason.

Further Reading

Baughman, James L. *The Republic of Mass Culture: Journalism, Filmmaking, and Broadcasting in America Since 1941.* 2d ed. Baltimore: Johns Hopkins University Press, 1997. Explores how the advent of television affected the content of rival media, including magazines.

Rosten, Leo, ed. *The Look Book.* Foreword by Gardner Cowles. New York: H. N. Abrams, 1975. Details how the magazine's editors and publisher envisioned their magazine.

Suburbia: The Good Life in Our Exploding Utopia, by the Editors of "Look" Magazine. New York: Cowles Educational, 1968. *Look*'s analysis of one of its favorite subjects.

Jarod Kearney

See also Affluence and the new consumerism; Famous Artists School; Hairstyles; Home appliances; *Life*; News magazines; Peale, Norman Vincent; *Reader's Digest.*

■ *Look Back in Anger*

Identification British play set in northern England
Author John Osborne (1929-1994)
Date Opened on May 8, 1956
Place The Royal Court Theatre, London

John Osborne's Look Back in Anger *was hailed by theater critics as being an influential drama. Its realism and critique of social issues influenced the development of modern British and American theater, and its themes of alienation and frustration spoke to groups of disenfranchised people in both countries.*

John Osborne submitted the script of his play in response to an advertisement, placed by George Devine, in *The Stage,* a British theater weekly. Devine was looking for new scripts for his English Stage Company. The play was notable for its blunt language and realistic portrayal of everyday life, which was in sharp contrast to the contemporary and popular light comedies. It was the first "kitchen sink"

drama—a term that refers to the depiction of gritty working-class realities—and focused on Jimmy Porter, the quintessential angry young man of the period, who rails against Great Britain's class system and the complacency of its population. Kenneth Tynan, the influential drama critic for the English newspaper the *Observer,* called it a totally original play of a new generation, while *The Evening Standard* described it as a self-pitying snivel.

After a tour to Moscow, the play opened at the Lyceum Theatre in New York in October, 1957, enjoyed great success, and ran for 407 performances. Brooks Atkinson, an American critic, praised it as "the most vivid British play of the decade." The following year, Tony Richardson adapted and directed it as a film starring Richard Burton as Jimmy Porter and Claire Bloom as Alison.

Impact The play was hailed, especially in Great Britain where class divisions were more entrenched, as giving voice to a frustrated and disenfranchised audience, a young generation that had grown up during World War II and continued to find itself within a conservative, class-bound world dominated by the prewar generation. In the United States, the play's impact and critical reception was felt most directly within New York City. In both countries, many saw the play as an indictment of the contemporary political and cultural establishment. The play indirectly gave rise to the phrase "angry young man" to the English language and sparked an "angry young man" literary movement in Britain.

Further Reading

Gilleman, Luc M. *John Osborne: Vituperative Artist.* New York: Routledge, 2002. Provides criticism and analysis of Osborne's life and works, including *Look Back in Anger.*

Osborne, John. *Almost a Gentleman: An Autobiography, 1955-1966.* London: Faber & Faber, 1991. Osborne's life and inspirations in his own words.

Susan E. Hamilton

See also Film in the United States; Literature in the United States; Theater in the United States; Youth culture and the generation gap.

■ "Louie Louie"

Identification Popular dance song first recorded by Richard Berry and the Pharaohs
Date Recorded in 1956; released in 1957

"Louie Louie" was released to modest success in 1957 but later became a rock-and-roll classic because of its allegedly obscene lyrics.

The inspiration and beat for "Louie Louie" come from "El Loco Cha Cha," a song by Rene Touzet. Richard Berry created lyrics that told the tale of a homesick Jamaican sailor pining for his island lover. He pours out his troubles to Louie, the bartender, as the latter pours him drinks.

The original 45-single was recorded by Flip Records in 1956 and released in 1957. "Louie Louie" was the B-side to Berry's cover of "You Are My Sunshine." The catchy song with the calypso beat was a modest success in the Los Angeles area, where it was recorded. Berry sold publishing rights to the song for $750.

Impact Although the song debuted during the 1950's, it found its greatest success several years later when, in 1963, Jack Ely and the Kingsmen recorded the version that made it a rock-and-roll standard. A rival version by Paul Revere and the Raiders vied for dominance on the *Billboard* chart, but the Kingsmen eventually triumphed. Contributing to the popularity of the Kingsmen's version were its unintelligible lyrics, an unintentional by-product of inferior recording techniques. As a result, rumors started that the words were obscene, leading to a spike in sales by eager teenagers, a Federal Bureau of Investigation (FBI) investigation, and a ban on radio airplay of the song by the state of Indiana, which only further ensured its success.

Further Reading

Marsh, Dave. *Louie Louie.* New York: Hyperion, 1993. Chronicles the song's time frame and gives a definitive history.

Propes, Steve, and Galen Gart. *L.A. R&B Vocal Groups: 1945 to 1965.* Winter Haven, Fla.: Big Nickel, 2003. Richly detailed account of the environment that inspired "Louie Louie's" creation.

Sue Tarjan

See also Censorship; Dance, popular; Music; Radio; Rock and roll; Youth culture and the generation gap.

■ Loyalty oaths

Definition Political tests mandated for employment in state and local governments and educational institutions

Mandated loyalty oaths became points of conflict between those who believed the oaths were necessary for the security of the United States and those who believed that they were violations of civil liberties.

Loyalty oaths were a part of the wave of anticommunist measures that followed World War II, beginning with the loyalty program in the federal government designed to oust from federal service those disloyal to the United States. Scrutiny of federal employees was intense, and thousands of people were fired. During the late 1940's and early 1950's, local and state governments followed the federal government's lead by investigating their own employees' associations and by passing various laws and policies requiring loyalty oaths. These policies typically included an oath of loyalty to the government and a denial of membership in any organization dedicated to the overthrow of the state or federal government. Fear of communism fueled the movement. Loyalty oaths were so popular with some state politicians that they even were part of the process of obtaining a fishing license in New York and obtaining a professional wrestling license in Indiana.

Educational Institutions Leaders of anticommunist interest groups were particularly concerned, however, that communists would have influence over the minds of young people. As such, loyalty oaths were used primarily to root out communism from schools and universities. For instance, the Regents of the University of California required the signing of loyalty oaths for employment in the university. Faculty members were given two months to sign the oaths in the spring of 1950, or they faced removal from their positions.

Fierce controversy accompanied this mandate, especially at the University of California at Berkeley and at the University of California at Los Angeles (UCLA). Some professors refused to take the oaths on the grounds of academic freedom, and thirty-one were fired. Most signed the oaths reluctantly and kept their jobs. The controversy destroyed professional relationships and friendships. The oaths stifled dissent and led to teachers' fears of broaching controversial topics. Not only public universities were affected: In Colorado, employees of private colleges were also required to take the oaths, on the ground that the institutions received certain tax advantages from the state. At Colorado College in Colorado Springs, although many employees protested vehemently, all ended up signing the oaths.

Debate was most intense at the college level, where there was a strong tradition of academic freedom and the protection of tenure, but teachers at all levels were fired if they refused to take the oaths. Opponents contested loyalty oaths in state courts. California's supreme court ruled them unconstitutional in 1952, but the U.S. Supreme Court reversed that decision and, in most cases, upheld states' rights to screen out subversives.

Impact Loyalty oaths caused anxiety and personal trauma to employees while doing little to secure the United States against its enemies. Some people lost their jobs because they refused to take the oaths. Many anguished over the decision but ultimately signed. Most historians agree that persons who wished to overthrow the United States government would have had no problem signing false oaths at the time.

Further Reading

Diggins, John Patrick. *The Proud Decades: America in War and Peace, 1941-1960.* New York: W. W. Norton, 1988. Briefly covers the loyalty oaths in the larger context of McCarthyism.

Schrecker, Ellen. *The Age of McCarthyism: A Brief History with Documents.* 2d ed. New York: Palgrave Macmillan, 2001. Traces the course of anticommunist furor in the United States.

Bonnie L. Ford

See also Army-McCarthy hearings; Cold War; Conformity, culture of; Espionage and Sabotage Act of 1954; Federal Bureau of Investigation; Hoover, J. Edgar; House Committee on Un-American Activities; Internal Security Act of 1950; John Birch Society; McCarthy, Joseph.

MacArthur, Douglas

Identification U.S. commander of United Nations forces at the beginning of the Korean War
Born January 26, 1880; Little Rock, Arkansas
Died April 5, 1964; Washington, D.C.

As commander of the United Nations (U.N.) forces in Korea, Douglas MacArthur wanted to expand the war in the hope of winning a decisive victory, and his dismissal in 1951 ignited one of the greatest controversies of the decade.

Douglas MacArthur was one of the most controversial military commanders in U.S. history. He was a charismatic leader with a majestic countenance and outstanding oratorical abilities. Adept at public relations, he became known for his trademarks of a corncob pipe, a rumpled military cap, an open collar, and sunglasses. Although few people questioned his heroism, his firm convictions and great confidence caused many to view him as arrogant and dogmatic. While he demanded strict obedience from his own subordinates, he often resented and sometimes disregarded the authority of his civilian commanders. Critics argued that he tended to underestimate the enemy and was willing to take excessive risks that might have had disastrous consequences.

A Remarkable Career The son of General Arthur MacArthur, a Civil War hero and military governor of the Philippine Islands, Douglas MacArthur graduated from West Point first in his class in 1903. During World War I, he demonstrated great courage in battle and was promoted to the rank of general. Between the world wars, he was superintendent of West Point and then served as army chief of staff for five years. As commander of U.S. troops in the Philippine Islands in 1941, he was criticized for failing to prepare adequately for the Japanese attack, but he skillfully directed the offensive that culminated in the retaking of the Philippines. Promoted to commander of U.S. Army forces in the Pacific, he accepted Japan's formal surrender aboard the battleship USS *Missouri* in 1945.

President Harry S. Truman appointed MacArthur to direct the occupation of Japan as supreme commander for the Allied Powers, a position he held until his dismissal in 1951. Even his critics concede that he helped promote economic reconstruction and successfully oversaw the establishment of a democratic political system. Public opinion polls indicated that he was the second-most respected man in the United States, behind General Dwight D. Eisenhower. In 1948, many Republicans wanted their party to nominate MacArthur for president. However, after he allowed his name to be placed on primary ballots, his candidacy fizzled because of a lack of organization. His partisan activities in 1948 soured his relations with President Truman and other Democratic officials. Given his advanced age, it appeared that his career was coming to an end.

The Korean War In June, 1950, the unexpected outbreak of the Korean War quickly propelled MacArthur back into the limelight. Recognizing his prestige and knowledge of Asia, President Truman, on July 9, reluctantly appointed the seventy-year-old general as commander of the American-led coalition of U.N. forces. MacArthur directed the operations from his headquarters in Tokyo. Meanwhile, the North Koreans were rapidly occupying all of South Korea, but they were finally stopped at the perimeter around the port of Pusan. On September 15, MacArthur successfully executed a risky amphibious operation at the port of Inchon, two hundred miles behind North Korean lines. Catching the North Koreans by surprise, the operation enabled U.N. forces to break their supply lines and push them far north of the Thirty-eighth parallel.

Within a month, U.N. troops began to approach the Yalu River, which formed the border between China and North Korea. China sent signals that it would intervene if the U.N. offensive continued. At the Wake Island planning conference, MacArthur confidently told President Truman that the Chinese were bluffing. The prediction turned out to be mistaken. On November 24, some 300,000 Chinese soldiers attacked U.N. forces in North Korea. By December, the U.N. army had been driven below the Thirty-eighth parallel. MacArthur wanted to respond by bombing China, using air bases on Taiwan, and bringing Nationalist soldiers of Taiwan into the war. Truman vetoed such policies, which he feared might result in a third world war.

MacArthur's militant statements in speeches and letters contradicted the limited war measures and objectives of the Truman administration. European allies complained that his comments were creating confusion and anxiety about American intentions. Senator Joseph McCarthy and other Republicans quoted him when denouncing the administration. In March, 1951, MacArthur presented China with an ultimatum, undermining Truman's attempts to negotiate a peace settlement. Then the Republican leader of the House of Representatives, Joseph Martin, publicly read MacArthur's intemperate letter declaring that there was "no substitute for victory." President Truman, finally deciding that MacArthur's insubordination was intolerable, relieved the general of his command on April 11, 1951.

Impact In the short-term, Truman's dismissal of MacArthur unleashed a storm of outrage. When the general returned to the United States, he was welcomed as a hero everywhere he went. In New York City, millions of people enthusiastically participated in his ticker-tape parade. His "Old Soldiers Never Die" speech before Congress is still recognized as a historic event. However, when the Senate held hearings to review the conduct of the war, almost all military leaders agreed that his proposed policies were excessively expensive and highly risky. Although MacArthur gave a rousing keynote speech at the Republican national convention in 1952, the majority of observers viewed him as a romantic figure of the past. The next year, the Eisenhower administration ignored MacArthur's views and negotiated a truce in Korea.

General Douglas MacArthur speaking in Chicago in April, 1951, shortly after being dismissed from his command in Korea. It was his first visit to the United States in fourteen years. (National Archives)

For many years, anticommunists and opponents of appeasement would continue to invoke MacArthur's memory. The fallout of the Truman-MacArthur controversy sometimes motivated political leaders to take hard-line positions in opposing communist advances. However, as the United States became bogged down in the Vietnam War during the 1960's, the public increasingly looked upon the Korean settlement in a more favorable light. By the end of the Cold War, few historians were still arguing that the United States should have risked a war with the Soviet Union in an attempt to reunite the Korean peninsula. However, in subsequent military conflicts, a significant number of Americans continued to share MacArthur's disdain for the idea of fighting a limited war instead of using all means available and seeking an unambiguous victory.

Further Reading

Clayton, James D. *Years of MacArthur: Triumph and Disaster, 1945-1964.* Boston: Houghton Mifflin, 1985. The third volume of a detailed and very scholarly biography.

Leary, William, ed. *MacArthur and the American Century: A Reader.* Lincoln: University of Nebraska Press, 2001. A collection of interesting essays by outstanding historians.

MacArthur, Douglas. *Reminiscences.* New York: McGraw, 1964. Relying primarily on MacArthur's speeches, the book gives insight into his character, ideas, and personal egoism.

Weintraub, Stanley. *MacArthur's War: Korea and the Unmaking of an American Hero.* New York: Free Press, 2000. Presents highly unfavorable interpretations of MacArthur and his ideas about extending the war.

Thomas Tandy Lewis

See also Bradley, Omar; Cold War; Gunther, John; Japan; Korean War; Pearson, Drew; Ridgway, Matthew B.; Truman, Harry S.; United Nations.

■ McCarthy, Joseph

Identification Red-baiting U.S. senator
Born November 14, 1908; Grand Chute, Wisconsin
Died May 2, 1957; Bethesda, Maryland

Joseph McCarthy, a Republican senator from Wisconsin, conducted an investigation of government officials that came to symbolize anticommunist hysteria in 1950's America.

Prior to the 1950's, Joseph McCarthy was an obscure politician with a mediocre record. Born the fifth of nine children in a community of Irish farmers, McCarthy attended college and law school at Marquette University, receiving a law degree in 1935. His early career as a lawyer was unsuccessful, prompting him to dabble in gambling and politics to supplement his meager earnings. He won his first political office, a circuit court judgeship, in 1939 by switching parties and falsifying both his and his opponent's ages, drawing a reprimand from the Wisconsin supreme court. After serving in World War II, he was elected to the U.S. Senate in 1946 in a wave of postwar patriotism.

McCarthy's early record in the Senate was lackluster, notable primarily for his heavy drinking and shady financial dealings. The turning point came in February of 1950, when McCarthy, seeking an issue to obscure his questionable activities, volunteered to join his Republican colleagues on a circuit of cross-country campaign speeches. Party leaders assigned McCarthy a series of obscure speaking engagements, beginning with an address to a group of Republican women in Wheeling, West Virginia, on February 9. It was there that McCarthy first raised the issue of a communist conspiracy in the United States government, holding aloft a piece of paper that he claimed contained the names of 205 State Department employees known to be members of the Communist Party. McCarthy repeated the claim in subsequent speeches, varying the number of alleged conspirators to suit his audience.

Anticommunist Fervor The response to McCarthy's allegations was immediate and dramatic. Postwar fears of the Soviet Union and international communism prompted many people to accept his allegations at face value. Several Democratic senators lost their seats in the 1950 election for daring to question McCarthy's claims, further enhancing his fearsome reputation and establishing him as a rising star in the Republican Party. Popular support for his anticommunist crusade grew, helping reelect him to the Senate in 1952 and contributing to Republican Dwight D. Eisenhower's defeat of Adlai Stevenson—whom McCarthy had accused of being soft on communism—in the presidential election. Following his reelection, McCarthy was made chairman of the Senate Permanent Subcommittee on Government Operations.

McCarthy used the subcommittee to broaden his investigation of alleged communist activity in the U.S. government. Although a Republican administration was now in office, McCarthy continued to level accusations of a communist conspiracy at work within the highest levels of government. As his skilled manipulation of the media continued to win him popular support, McCarthy intensified his hunt for communist conspirators. He called numerous government employees before his subcommittee, grilling them about their alleged communist activities with little regard for civility or due process. His investigations were typically conducted on the basis of little or no tangible evidence and often amounted to little more than character assassination. Many who refused to cooperate with the investigations saw their careers destroyed when McCarthy leaked derogatory information about them to employers and the public.

To the majority of U.S. citizens, "McCarthyism," as the crusade against communism came to be called, was a heroic struggle against an evil institution. However, to a growing minority of Americans familiar with McCarthy and his ruthless tactics, he represented a commitment to intimidation and coerced conformity that was in itself anti-American. By questioning the patriotism of his critics, McCarthy managed to intimidate even his Republican colleagues in Congress while enhancing his image as a populist crusader and further obscured ongoing allegations of his drunkenness, graft, and corruption.

Political Demise The Republican leadership, desperate to exploit public fear of communism, grudgingly supported McCarthy during the early 1950's, but McCarthy soon jeopardized that support by leveling specious accusations against prominent Republicans, at one point even suggesting that Eisenhower himself was "soft" on communism. In mid-1954, allegations by McCarthy that the U.S. Army had knowingly employed a communist sympathizer culminated in a series of nationally televised hearings before his investigative subcommittee. For the first time, the public was exposed to the inner work-

ings of McCarthyism, and many were appalled at the strong-arm tactics of McCarthy and his chief counsel, Roy Cohn.

When evidence surfaced that McCarthy and Cohn had sought favors for a staff member recently inducted into the Army, McCarthy responded with accusations against an associate of Army counsel Joseph Welch. Welch then angrily confronted McCarthy, accusing him of having "no sense of decency." Visibly defeated, McCarthy quickly brought his investigation of the Army to a close. The Senate voted to censure him in December of 1954, and he faded into obscurity. He died at Bethesda Naval Hospital on May 2, 1957, of liver disease brought on by years of alcohol abuse.

Impact By capitalizing on public fears of communism, Joseph McCarthy helped the Republican Party reclaim both Congress and the presidency in 1953, but his subsequent downfall also contributed to the

Senator Joseph R. McCarthy surrounded by autograph-seeking high school students while dining in a Washington, D.C., restaurant in April, 1950. (AP/Wide World Photos)

Republicans' loss of Congress in the midterm elections of 1954. His purging of experts on communism and communist countries from sensitive government positions exerted a lasting effect upon American foreign policy, prompting some historians to blame McCarthyism for the later defeat of U.S. forces in Vietnam. The most lasting effect of McCarthyism, however, was the creation of a new style of politics that would combine old-fashioned demagoguery with skilled manipulation of information through the use of modern media.

Subsequent Events Little evidence exists to indicate that McCarthy was successful in eliminating communist activity from government institutions. Government documents declassified in 1995 reveal that a handful of the people McCarthy investigated were indeed communist operatives but also indicate that McCarthy seriously overestimated the extent of communist activity in the government, raising speculation that his limited success in ferreting out communist agents was largely accidental.

Further Reading

Ranville, Michael. *To Strike at a King: The Turning Point in the McCarthy Witch-Hunts.* Ann Arbor, Mich.: Momentum Books, 1997. A case study of an Air Force officer who fell victim to the excesses of McCarthyism.

Reeves, Thomas C. *The Life and Times of Joe McCarthy: A Biography.* Lanham, Md.: Madison Books, 1997. A detailed account of McCarthy's life and career.

Schrecker, Ellen. *Many Are the Crimes: Maccarthyism in America.* New York: Little, Brown, 1998. A comprehensive history of McCarthyism and its impact upon American society.

Michael H. Burchett

See also Army-McCarthy hearings; Censorship; Cold War; Communist Party of the U.S.A.; Conservatism in U.S. politics; Faulk, John Henry; Federal Bureau of Investigation; Hoover, J. Edgar; House Committee on Un-American Activities; Internal Security Act of 1950; Loyalty oaths; Miller, Arthur; Murrow, Edward R.; Rosenberg, Julius and Ethel.

■ McCarthy, Mary

Identification American novelist, essayist, and critic
Born June 21, 1912; Seattle, Washington
Died October 25, 1989; New York, New York

Through her acclaimed literary works and unconventional lifestyle, Mary McCarthy became for many during the 1950's a leading model of the liberated American woman fashioning a distinguished career on her own terms.

Mary Therese McCarthy was the eldest of four children of a Seattle banker. Orphaned at six, she was consigned, along with her three brothers, to the cruel, arbitrary discipline of elderly relatives. The experience left her embittered but determined to survive. She did so not least because of a deep interest in literature that allowed a certain escape from a grim existence. Following graduation from Vassar College in 1933, she launched her literary career as drama critic and book reviewer for literary journals in New York City. In 1942, she published her first work of fiction, *The Company She Keeps*, a well-received collection of short stories based on people she had known. Her first novel, *Oasis*, appeared in 1949.

By 1950, McCarthy was recognized as a promising young author and critic. During the remainder of the decade, she would publish two novels, another volume of short stories, a book of theater criticism, two art books on Renaissance Italy, and in 1957, her masterpiece, the autobiographical *Memories of a Catholic Girlhood.* Most of these works carried her distinctive literary stamp, namely, a smooth and beautiful style that used wit and scathing satire to target the many hypocrisies, rigid ideologies, and repressive social conventions she observed in contemporary America. By the end of the decade, McCarthy's probing social commentary and criticism in a variety of literary genres lifted her to the first rank of American writers.

Impact Over a literary career that spanned nearly a half-century, McCarthy published some twenty-eight volumes of fiction and nonfiction. However, her later literary reputation has tended to be overshadowed by the public image of her private life. Many see in her an attractive, brilliant, and exciting American woman who managed in her time to forge a unique feminine identity. Her free-spirited way of life involved multiple marriages and affairs, and sometimes bitter controversies with literary adversaries who felt the sharp lash of her satire. In sum, while McCarthy was less read in later decades than in earlier ones, she continued to be applauded as a trailblazer for women aspiring to bolder, less traditional roles in life.

Further Reading

Bennett, Joy, and Gabriella Hochman, eds. *Mary Mc-Carthy: An Annotated Bibliography.* New York: Taylor & Francis, 1992. Provides a list of McCarthy's publications in order as well as review articles, general criticism, book reviews, essays, theater reviews, short stories, and novels.

McKiernan, Frances. *Seeing Mary Plain: A Life of Mary McCarthy.* New York: W. W. Norton, 2000. A full, lively biography based on excerpts from McCarthy's writings and on extensive interviews with McCarthy's admirers and critics.

Donald Sullivan

See also Liberalism in U.S. politics; Literature in the United States; Women and the roots of the feminist movement.

■ McClellan Committee

Identification U.S. Senate Select Committee on Improper Activities in the Labor or Management Field, created to investigate union corruption
Date Operated from 1957 to 1959

The McClellan Committee made headlines by exposing union corruption, particularly in the Teamsters Union. It exposed criminal control of various unions and advanced the political careers of several of its members, including John F. Kennedy, Robert F. Kennedy, and Barry Goldwater.

From 1957 to 1959, the U.S. Senate's Select Committee on Improper Activities in the Labor or Management Field (commonly known as the McClellan Committee) conducted highly publicized hearings into union corruption and America's underworld. The committee involved a number of personalities who later would play a major role in American political life.

The committee made headlines with its investigations of the Teamsters Union and the dramatic confrontation between Chief Counsel Robert F. Kennedy and Teamsters president James Hoffa. The committee brought dozens of organized crime figures into the spotlight even though few of the infamous figures answered any questions.

The committee began its hearings on February 26, 1957, and heard more than fifteen hundred witnesses. Its chair was Senator John L. McClellan from Arkansas. McClellan was a member of the powerful southern bloc in the Senate and a strong conservative. Other members of the committee included first-term Massachusetts senator John F. Kennedy (considered prolabor) and second-term Arizona senator Barry Goldwater (considered antilabor).

Throughout the summer of 1957, the committee focused its attention on Teamsters president David Beck. Evidence of corruption within the Teamsters was so overwhelming that Beck did not seek reelection to the group's presidency that year.

In addition to union officials, the committee investigated numerous underworld figures, including Tony Accardo and Sam Giancana from Chicago. Most of the alleged gangsters simply plead the Fifth Amendment and refused to say anything at all.

The highlight of the hearings was the explosive confrontations between Teamsters president Jimmy Hoffa and Robert F. Kennedy. A series of dramatic exchanges took place, which ended with Hoffa repeatedly stating that he did not remember events or individuals. The confrontations made national news as newspapers, magazines, and television gave the hearings extensive coverage.

In the summer of 1957, Hoffa was arrested and charged with attempts to bribe a committee member to leak information. On July 19, in a trial in Washington, D.C., a jury acquitted him following a sensational trial. In spite of the verdict, evidence continued to mount that the Teamsters were closely tied to organized crime and infested with corruption.

On December 5, 1957, the AFL-CIO expelled the Teamsters Union from the organization. While the ouster increased suspicion of the Teamsters, it ultimately allowed them to expand without any connection to the AFL-CIO.

The McClellan Committee was in session for three years. During that time it also investigated antiunion activities by certain large companies and the actions of more radical unions, including the United Autoworkers. Neither of these investigations generated the publicity or controversy of the Teamsters confrontations.

Impact The McClellan Committee was a publicity bonanza for several of the participants. Some, such as the Teamsters and organized crime figures, did not enjoy the spotlight but many of the political figures did. Senator John F. Kennedy was overwhelmingly reelected to the Senate in 1958 and went on to win the American presidency. One of Kennedy's first cabinet appointments was his brother Robert as attorney general. The new attorney general focused his attention on the same figures he had confronted as a staff member for the McClellan Committee.

Further Reading

Kennedy, Robert F. *The Enemy Within: The McClellan Committee's Crusade Against Jimmy Hoffa and Corrupt Labor Unions.* Reprint. Cambridge, Mass.: Da Capo Press, 1994. First published in 1960, this book gives Kennedy's account of the hearings.

Moldea, Dan E. *The Hoffa Wars: Teamsters, Rebels, Politicians, and the Mob.* Putnam Pub Group, 1978. A popular account of the rise and fall of Hoffa.

Witwer, David. *Corruption and Reform in the Teamsters Union.* Champaign: University of Illinois Press, 2003. Chronicles the history of lawmakers' efforts to stop corruption within the Teamsters Union and includes a good discussion of the McClellan Committee.

Charles C. Howard

See also AFL-CIO merger; Congress, U.S.; Hoffa, Jimmy; Institute of Pacific Relations; Kennedy, John F.; Meany, George; Organized crime; Teamsters union.

■ McDonald's restaurants

Identification American fast-food hamburger chain restaurant

McDonald's institutionalized the American fast-food industry during the 1950's, creating in the hamburger not only a significant characteristic of American culture but also a symbol of American influence abroad.

McDonald's hamburger restaurant chain was the brainchild of two brothers, Maurice (Mac) and Richard (Dick) McDonald. The McDonald brothers opened their first restaurant, a modest food stand, in 1937, near Pasadena, California. While the stand was a moderately successful venture, the brothers decided to expand their business by moving it to San

A McDonald's restaurant during the mid-1950's, when hamburgers cost only fifteen cents. (Hulton Archive | by Getty Images)

Bernardino, California, some forty miles away. Mac and Dick saw in the sprawling mobile growth of the greater Los Angeles area a potential for greater success in the fast-food business and decided to capitalize on the momentum.

A marked departure from the typical hamburger establishment of the time, McDonald's featured large look-in windows, stainless steel walls, and a prominent slanted roof. Inside, the kitchen was entirely exposed so that customers could see the food preparations. A key to success was a limited nine-item menu, an assembly-line food operation using a limited number of employees, and a walk-up self-service window. The approach competed with the prevalent carhops and extensive menus of the day. The MacDonald brothers' new concept became a hit and marked the beginning of the 1950's American love affair with hamburger drive-ins. As newer mechanized food preparation improvements were installed, profits quadrupled. By the early 1950's, the McDonald brothers had expanded their business to fifteen franchises.

The McDonald's success story was in large part a response to the demographic dynamics of post-World War II America. With some ten million returning military veterans eligible for G.I. Bill housing loan benefits, the United States began to experience urban sprawl, particularly in states such as California. By the early 1950's, new suburban communities began to emerge across the country. This urban growth was complemented in large measure by the growing postwar baby boom, which accounted for twenty-five million births between 1945 and 1953. These two events—along with an increasing automobile-oriented, mobile society—created an enduring relationship between drive-in restaurants such as McDonald's and suburban America. Young parents saw fast-food chains as places for quick, cheap, convenient meals that not only met the family budget but also lent themselves nicely to an expanding "on the go" lifestyle.

In 1954, the McDonald brothers hired Ray Kroc to take over franchising operations. Kroc was a visionary who believed that expansion of the business relied on using greater mechanized operational efficiencies and standardizing quality-control measures. By 1960, Kroc had established 228 franchises. At odds with Mac and Dick over management decisions, Kroc bought out the McDonald brothers and took full control of the company for more than two

million dollars in 1961, eventually taking the company public in 1965. By the early 1970's, McDonald's had become the largest fast-food chain in the United States, going international during the late 1970's and expanding to more than fifteen thousand restaurants worldwide by the mid-1990's.

Impact By the end of the 1950's, McDonald's had established itself as a "trade name" synonymous with fast food, despite the long list of copy-cat hamburger chains that followed and still compete with McDonald's today. The restaurant's legacy is not merely in its Americanization of the hamburger. The name "McDonald's" has become a hallmark of Americanism globally. Now, with restaurants on six continents, McDonald's golden arches are as recognizable overseas as the Stars and Stripes.

Further Reading

Love, John. *McDonald's: Behind the Arches.* Rev. ed. New York: Bantam, 1995. Presents the history of the hamburger empire.

McDonald, Ronald L. *The Complete Hamburger: The History of America's Favorite Sandwich.* Secaucus, N.J.: Carol, 1997. The nephew of the original McDonald brothers gives a personal account of the restaurant's success.

Michael J. Garcia

See also Affluence and the new consumerism; Fast-food restaurants; Kroc, Ray.

■ Mackinac Bridge

The Event Opening of the first bridge to connect Michigan's upper and lower peninsulas, which are separated by the strait linking Lake Michigan and Lake Huron

Date Opened on November 1, 1957

Place Straits of Mackinac, Michigan

Spanning a five-mile stretch, the Mackinac (pronounced MA-ki-naw) Bridge became the longest suspension bridge in the Western Hemisphere and was one of the most significant design and engineering achievements of the twentieth century when it opened in 1957.

In 1888, Cornelius Vanderbilt proposed that a bridge be built to join Michigan's upper and lower peninsulas. Lack of adequate ferry service isolated the upper peninsula, intensifying economic, social, and cultural problems of its residents. Skeptics argued that it was impossible to build a structure over the Mackinac Straits because the bedrock in the area would not support the weight, nor would a bridge be able to withstand the region's harsh weather.

In 1950, the Mackinac Bridge Authority convinced the state legislature that building a bridge was possible. Construction began on May 7, 1954. David B. Steinman created the cutting-edge design, which included stiffened trusses and an open-grid roadway. More than one million tons of concrete, five million rivets, and 42,000 miles of steel cable were used. Upon completion, the bridge's main span measured 3,800 feet, and its towers soared to 552 feet.

Impact Connecting Mackinac City and St. Ignace, the Mackinac Bridge increased business and tourist traffic to the upper peninsula. Ferry service, which had an average waiting time of nineteen hours, was eliminated. Crossing by car took only minutes. The bridge's innovative design became the model for future long-span suspension bridges.

Further Reading

Rubin, Lawrence A. *Bridging the Straits: The Story of Mighty Mac.* Detroit: Wayne State University Press, 1985. The story of the physical, political, and engineering challenges the builders of the Mackinac Bridge faced.

_____. *Mighty Mac: The Official Picture History of the Mackinac Bridge.* 1958. Reprint. Detroit: Wayne State University Press, 1986. A visual chronology of the construction of the Mackinac Bridge.

Steinman, David B., with John T. Nevill. *Miracle Bridge at Mackinac.* Reprint. Detroit: Wayne State University Press, 1989. A firsthand account of the construction of the Mackinac Bridge by its designer.

Pegge Bochynski

See also Architecture; Interstate highway system; Trans-Canada Highway.

■ *Maclean's*

Identification Canadian magazine focused on the country's affairs and world news
Publisher John Bayne Maclean
Date Began publication as *The Business Magazine* in 1905; name changed to *Maclean's* in 1911

Maclean's, a biweekly magazine, showcased the work of some of Canada's finest journalists, authors, and essayists during the 1950's and continued its role in promoting a unique and newly modern Canadian identity.

Maclean's magazine evolved from an obscure business journal that Toronto, Ontario, journalist and entrepreneur Lieutenant Colonel John Bayne Maclean purchased in 1905. Later that year, Maclean began monthly publication of *The Business Magazine,* a digest of articles compiled from American, British, and Canadian periodicals. The magazine, which changed its name to *Maclean's* in 1911, grew rapidly, incorporating original articles and short stories from Canadian writers and developing a reputation for hard-hitting stories on issues relevant to Canada and its citizens. The dramatic financial success of *Maclean's* magazine was stifled by the Great Depression during the 1930's, but the magazine continued to enhance its journalistic reputation by publishing stories of the struggles of ordinary Canadians. Although the magazine tended to present a conservative view of Canadian life in its early years, its editorial slant had moderated somewhat by mid-century as a result of the influence of editor in chief Arthur Irwin.

Creative Peak Irwin, who worked for *Maclean's* from 1925 through 1950 as associate editor and editor in chief, was responsible for amassing a pool of young talent that would compose the core of the magazine's writing and editorial staff during the 1950's. A fervent nationalist, Irwin believed that *Maclean's* should define and represent a distinctively Canadian identity. Nevertheless, he refused to subscribe to the Anglocentric viewpoint of many Canadian nationalists and often published editorials advocating bilingualism and greater cooperation and understanding between the nation's French and British subcultures.

Irwin retired in 1950, turning editorship of the magazine over to Ralph Allen. Under Allen, *Maclean's* underwent a creative renaissance, publishing a diverse assortment of art and literary criticism, social commentary, political gossip, illustrations, and photography by a variety of contributors, including Canadian writers such as Pierre Berton, June Callwood, and Sydney Katz. The magazine developed a reputation for featuring contributions from Canada's foremost novelists, historians, diplomats, scientists, and educators, yet the depth and diversity of stories from its staff of journalists remained its chief asset. Even its most embarrassing moment of the decade—the premature and erroneous prediction of a Liberal Party victory in the federal elections of 1957—proved favorable for the magazine after the editorial staff issued a witty and humble apology.

As chief editor, Allen continued to emphasize the bilingualism and biculturalism that his predecessor Irwin so strongly advocated, establishing his position early in 1950 with an editorial suggesting that the Canadian Broadcasting Corporation should broadcast English and French lessons. Allen also used his editorial forum to promote neutral names for national holidays and bilingual education for civil servants. Some critics have suggested that Allen's choice of stories also reflected a bias toward his vision of a nationalistic but bicultural Canada.

Impact *Maclean's* magazine served both as a reflection and a determinant of Canadian culture during the 1950's, documenting a critical period in the development of Canada as a nation. Following Irwin's example, Allen and his staff transformed *Maclean's* into a magazine by and for Canadians that reflected the sophistication and diversity of modern Canada. The magazine continued to build upon this success in subsequent decades, becoming a weekly news magazine during the 1960's. The magazine remained in publication in print and online at the start of the twenty-first century.

Further Reading

Chalmers, Floyd S. *A Gentleman of the Press; The Story of Colonel John Bayne Maclean.* Toronto: Doubleday, 1969. Biography of the magazine's founder and publisher.

Mackenzie, David. *Arthur Irwin: A Biography.* Toronto: University of Toronto Press 1993. Biography of *Maclean's* editor discusses how Irwin assembled the bevy of talent that fueled the magazine's success during the 1950's.

Michael H. Burchett

See also Canadian Broadcasting Corporation; Communications in Canada; Literature in Canada.

■ McLuhan, Marshall

Identification Canadian scholar and communications theorist
Born July 21, 1911; Edmonton, Alberta, Canada
Died December 31, 1980; Toronto, Ontario, Canada

The insights of Marshall McLuhan regarding the impact of both television and an expanding global media network fundamentally changed the way in which people of the 1950's understood technology and communications.

Marshall McLuhan's attempts to understand why language affects hearers and readers differently led to his predictions during the 1950's that television would produce a new way of thinking and a new kind of global community. He argued that an acoustical, intuitional, and tribal sensibility would supplant the visual, linear, and rational thought patterns of older literate people. His experiments proved that students learn more from a lecture shown on television than from one presented on radio, in print, or by live delivery. McLuhan noted that because television makes the mind create a picture from a single, fast-moving point of light, viewers become involved on an unconscious level, and attitudes and values change. While spectators at a boxing match cheer the aggressor, experiments showed that television viewers typically empathized with the aggressor's victim. McLuhan predicted that television would curb war and turn politics into a branch of show business.

McLuhan's proclamation that "the medium is the message" emphasized that the form of a communications medium matters more than its content. He argued that media subliminally alter the ways senses influence the mind: Literate minds, dominated by one sense—sight—cultivate detachment while multisensory, "tribal" minds crave emotional involvement. To his followers, McLuhan's theories helped explain the era's generation gap and the growing interest in sex, drugs, and loud music.

Impact McLuhan influenced business executives, advertisers, literary critics, and educators. He promoted interdisciplinary studies and multimedia teaching aids, advanced the reader-response school of literary criticism, helped advertisers achieve subliminal effects, and championed software over hardware. Many of his predictions came true, including the rise of the Internet and videocassettes, the decline of literacy, and the proliferation of microelectronics and telephony.

Further Reading

Benedetti, Paul, and Nancy Dettart, eds. *Forward Through the Rearview Mirror.* Scarborough, Ont.: Prentice-Hall Canada, 1997. Explores McLuhan's life and work in the context of the information age by using short prose passages, biographical text, interviews, letters, and dialogues by McLuhan. Vividly illustrated.

Zingrone, Frank, and Eric McLuhan, eds. *Essential McLuhan*. Toronto: Anansi, 1995. A compilation of McLuhan's main ideas and predictions.

John L. McLean

See also Advertising; Communications in the United States; Computers; Famous Artists School; Television in Canada; Television in the United States; Youth culture and the generation gap.

■ *MAD*

Identification Satirical magazine
Publisher William M. Gaines (1922-1992)
Date First published in 1952

Originally a satirical comic book, MAD *responded to censorship and marketing pressures in 1955 by becoming a magazine and turning its focus to sophisticated parodies and satires on many facets of American pop culture.*

MAD began in October, 1952, with the publication of the first volume of a ten-cent comic book called *Tales Calculated to Drive You Mad*. The first issue was thirty-two pages long and aimed for the teenager and young-adult market but did not talk down to its readership. A total of twenty-three similar issues would eventually be produced. The comic books presented illustrated parodies of other comic book stalwarts such as superheroes, Archie, and Micky Mouse, as well as films and other cultural touchstones. Stories tended to ridicule the divergence between reality and life as portrayed in comics and films.

Each issue contained four stories, all in color. The stories were written by Harvey Kurtzman and illustrated by artists such as Bill Elder, Jack Davis, John Severin, and Wally Wood. Their style followed a general pattern, with an opening panel crammed with the main characters, visual jokes, and enough small background detail to allow a reader to notice something new even after several readings. Many of the earlier volumes also contained a one-page written humorous piece, usually by Jerry DeFuccio.

Publisher William Gaines, along with Kurtzman, started *Tales Calculated to Drive You Mad* after censorship had ruined his earlier horror comic line. However, comic books in general became the target for various groups concerned with a rise in juvenile delinquency. Following U.S. Senate hearings on the problem in 1955, the comic book industry adopted a strict code of what could be published. As a result, comic books as a literary form in the United States quickly became harmless pulp aimed at mcuh younger audiences. Compliance with the Comics Code, although theoretically voluntary, killed *Tales Calculated to Drive You Mad*: Newsdealers would not sell a comic that did not carry the seal of the Comics Code Authority. For Gaines to bring *Tales Calculated to Drive You Mad* in line with the Comics Code would have betrayed its very reason for existence. To avoid the code and reach a broader market, Gaines reworked his concept and, in 1955, debuted his new *MAD* magazine.

MAD **Magazine** The new *MAD* magazine, although illustrated in black and white, contained a more varied assortment of features in order to justify its higher price of twenty-five cents. The lack of advertising in the magazine allowed *MAD* to ridicule potentially lucrative advertisers. From cars to cigarettes to entertainment, *MAD* skewered mass consumerism without fear of reprisal in the form of lost advertising revenue. In addition to satires of popular films, other features parodied diverse aspects of American mass culture, such as eating out, the suburbs, and increasingly, television.

Kurtzman left with most of the magazine's artists shortly after the change in format when Hugh Hefner hired him for his new humor magazine *Trump*, but Gaines was able to recruit excellent writers and artists such as Don Martin, George Woodbridge, Mort Drucker, Norman Mingo, Kelly Freas, Bob Clarke, and Dave Berg, and kept the quality high. Most of Gaines's staff were unknown at the time but would be the cornerstone of the magazine's later success. Except for celebrity contributors such as Sid Caesar, Tom Lehrer, and Ernie Kovacs, writers received no bylines during the early years. Gaines compensated his talent by paying promptly and at higher rates than most of the industry. In return, Gaines acquired sole rights to republish material in compilations without further compensating artists and writers.

Although *MAD* came from a slightly left-of-center stance in that it mocked most consistently what would later be called "The Establishment," it tended to be apolitical and made fun of public figures from across the political spectrum. A noticeable early departure from Gaines's ideal of ignoring politics came with the comic book's satirical attack on Senator Joseph McCarthy at a time when few others dared to challenge him openly.

The magazine adopted as its mascot an image of a young man with a missing front tooth and slightly misaligned eyes, who wore a vacant expression of pleasure. The mascot, named Alfred E. Neuman by *MAD*, had been used in advertising for decades. His image bore the motto "What—Me Worry?" which would often be used as a not-very-subtle poke at anyone who thought all was right in modern society.

Impact *MAD* magazine reached a zenith during the 1950's and early 1960's, when it occupied an otherwise empty niche in the market. *MAD*'s satires of American culture during the height of the Cold War kept alive a healthy criticism of modern life at a time when anything criticizing American culture tended to be seen as subversive. Although often overlooked in its impact on American culture, the magazine's influence can best be measured by how mainstream its form of humor had become by the 1980's. Besides obvious copycat magazines such as *Cracked, Crazy,* and *Sick*, other magazines such as *Playboy, National Lampoon,* and *Spy* owed much to *MAD*'s pioneering efforts. Television, so often a target of *MAD*, adopted much of *MAD*'s style of humor, with such influence most strongly evident in shows such as *Saturday Night Live* and *The Simpsons*. *MAD*'s success dulled the magazine's sharp edge by the mid-1970's, when it no longer stood alone in its style of criticizing modern American life.

Further Reading

Otfinoski, Steven. *William Gaines: Mad Man (Made in America)*. Vero Beach, Fla.: Rourke Book Company, 1993. A biography of the founder and longtime guiding force behind *MAD*.

Reidelbach, Maria. *Completely Mad: A History of the Comic Book and Magazine*. New York: Little, Brown, 1991. A largely uncritical history of *MAD*, focusing on Gaines and business aspects of the magazine.

"The Usual Gang of Idiots." *MAD About the Fifties*. Boston: Little, Brown, 1999. A collection of material from the comic book and magazine during the 1950's, plus a brief history of the company.

Wright, Bradford W. *Comic Book Nation: The Transformation of Youth Culture in America*. Baltimore: Johns Hopkins University Press, 2001. Scholarly account of the rise of the comic book during the 1930's, through its retrenchment in the face of governmental pressure during the 1950's, to its state at the end of the twentieth century.

Barry M. Stentiford

See also Capp, Al; Censorship; Comic books; Gaines, William M.; Lehrer, Tom; *Peanuts*; *Playboy*; *Pogo*; Sahl, Mort; Youth culture and the generation gap.

■ *The Man in the Gray Flannel Suit*

Identification Novel about American conformity and consumerism
Author Sloan Wilson (1920-2003)
Date Published in 1955

The Man in the Gray Flannel Suit used a literary form, the novel, to comment on the complacency and conformity of many Americans during the 1950's and argued that life continues to be just as fraught with problems and mistakes as in prior decades and one should take responsibility for one's own choices.

One of the best-selling novels of the 1950's was Sloan Wilson's *The Man in the Gray Flannel Suit*. It never received the critical acclaim of the works of Ralph Ellison or Saul Bellow, but it resonated with average readers who were increasingly aware of the bland conformity of the age. In a decade of relative peace and prosperity, Wilson insisted that something might be missing, something that could not be fathomed by considering yearly income or the square footage of one's home or the type of car one drives. On the level of the popular novel, Wilson presented a critique of American culture similar to that which was emerging from the underground and from Beat literary figures such as Allen Ginsberg and Jack Kerouac.

Wilson's novel focuses upon the awakening of Tom Rath, who came home from World War II to pursue the American Dream. He and his wife, Betsy, live with their three children in the suburbs, and like so many Americans, they have almost enough to be happy, almost enough to pay their bills. As Rath seeks a higher-paying job, he must complete a single sentence on the employment application: "The most significant thing about me is. . . " Though Rath gets the job, the unfinished sentence foreshadows Rath's confrontation with himself: He must decide if he really wants to become a company man, unearth dormant memories of a brutal war experience, and acknowledge an illegitimate child he fathered in Europe. Together, Tom and Betsy discover that beneath the calm exterior of mid-1950's conformity and gray flannel suits, the chaos of human life waits for everyone. It is not to be escaped even among the upwardly mobile in tranquil suburbs.

Impact *The Man in the Gray Flannel Suit* was made into a successful film starring Gregory Peck and Jennifer Jones in 1956. Wilson wrote many other novels, but none was as influential as *The Man in the Gray Flannel Suit.* He received little attention from literary critics at the time, though the novel is frequently discussed in studies of American culture and American business.

Further Reading

Halberstam, David. *The Fifties.* New York: Ballantine Books, 1994. Chapter 35 analyzes the impact of Wilson's novel.

Korda, Michael. *Making the List: A Cultural History of the American Bestseller, 1900-1999.* New York: Barnes and Noble Books, 2001. Korda devotes a chapter to each decade, within which he surveys important books and how they shaped collective dreams, fears, and experiences.

H. William Rice

See also Advertising; American Dream; Beat generation; Censorship; Conformity, culture of; Mills, C. Wright; *Organization Man, The*; Youth culture and the generation gap.

■ *The Man with the Golden Arm*

Identification Film about drug addiction starring Frank Sinatra
Director Otto Preminger (1906-1986)
Date Premiered on December 14, 1955.

The Man with the Golden Arm *was the first major Hollywood film to tackle the subject of drug addiction, which was still a taboo subject for American films during the 1950's. Its release defied censorship codes of the time while its success signaled moviegoers' growing interest in serious, adult film themes.*

As the film opens, Frankie Machine (played by Frank Sinatra) has sworn off drugs while serving a jail sentence. He returns to his home in a Chicago

Frank Sinatra as drug addict Frankie Machine with costar Kim Novak, who played Molly. (Museum of Modern Art, Film Stills Archive)

slum, determined to make a living as a jazz drummer—the film's title refers to Frankie's skill as a talented jazz drummer and not to his shooting heroin into his arm. Unfortunately, Frankie drifts back to his occupation as a poker dealer and his addiction to gambling, which also proves to be a return to his narcotics addiction.

With the emotional support of Molly (Kim Novak), a woman with a heart of gold, Frankie kicks his heroin habit cold turkey in the film's most harrowing scenes. The picture concludes with Frankie and Molly preparing to build their future together. The critics extolled the film, lauding Sinatra for giving a performance of raw power under Preminger's strong direction.

Impact Preminger was well aware that the regulations of the industry's censorship code forbade any depiction of narcotics addiction in a movie. He decided to challenge the embargo on dealing with drugs in a film because he staunchly maintained that *The Man with the Golden Arm* was a film of depth and purpose. In essence, the film is really a cautionary tale about the perils inherent in experimenting with drugs. Nevertheless, the industry censors at the time upheld the code's ban against this controversial topic and denied to *The Man with the Golden Arm* the film industry's official seal of approval. Preminger decided to release the film without the industry's seal, and *The Man with the Golden Arm* played to large audiences throughout the country. Thus Preminger almost singlehandedly broke the ban on the portrayal of drug addiction as a legitimate topic for motion pictures during the 1950's.

Further Reading

Preminger, Otto. *Preminger: An Autobiography.* Garden City, N.Y.: Doubleday, 1977. A highly personalized account of the director's life and the making of controversial films such as *The Man with the Golden Arm.*

Ringgold, Gene, and Clifford McCarty. *The Films of Frank Sinatra.* Rev. ed. New York: Carol, 1993. A well-illustrated survey of Sinatra's films, with background material on *The Man with the Golden Arm.*

Gene D. Phillips

See also Censorship; Film in the United States; Sinatra, Frank.

■ Mantle, Mickey

Identification American baseball player
Born October 20, 1931; Spavinaw, Oklahoma
Died August 13, 1995; Dallas, Texas

Nicknamed the "Commerce Comet," Mickey Mantle helped lead the New York Yankees to seven American League pennants and five World Series titles between 1951 and 1959.

Mickey Mantle grew up in a family with a passion for baseball. His father, Elvin, had played semiprofessional baseball and named his son after Mickey Cochrane, a catcher for the Detroit Tigers. Mantle's father trained him to bat from both sides of the plate, and by his senior year at Commerce High School, Mantle's skills as a switch-hitter had attracted major league scouts. He signed a contract with the New York Yankees, and after playing two years in the minor leagues, he was promoted in 1951 to the major league. Over the next eighteen seasons, Mantle established himself as the greatest switch-hitter in baseball history, accumulating 536 home runs, 1,509 runs batted in, and a .298 lifetime batting average.

The Yankees were the team of the decade during the 1950's. They played in eight of the decade's ten World Series and won six titles. As one of the key players on the 1950's-era Yankees, Mantle appeared in every all-star game from 1952 to 1959, won two American League Most Valuable Player (MVP) Awards (1956 and 1957), and won the triple crown for batting in 1956. As a sign of his hitting prowess and popularity with the American public, Mantle was elected to the Baseball Hall of Fame in his first year of eligibility in 1974.

Mantle's success on the baseball diamond did not follow him off the field. Drinking and marital problems along with failed business ventures plagued his private life. In June, 1995, Mantle was hospitalized as a result of liver complications. He died in Dallas, Texas, two months after receiving a liver transplant.

Impact Mantle's prowess with a bat made him one of the most recognized baseball players of the 1950's. His "tape measure" home runs helped his team win five World Series titles during the 1950's, solidifying the New York Yankees position as the team of the decade and marking him as one of baseball's greatest hitters.

Yankees star Mickey Mantle poses with Milwaukee Braves star Hank Aaron before a charity game in New York in May, 1958. (AP/Wide World Photos)

Further Reading

Falkner, David. *The Last Hero: The Life of Mickey Mantle.* New York: Simon & Schuster, 1995. A good, balanced biography.

Liederman, Bill, and Maury Allen, eds. *Our Mickey: Cherished Memories of an American Icon.* Chicago: Triumph Books, 2004. A list of notable figures from baseball contribute stories and memories about Mantle.

Mark R. Ellis

See also Baseball; Berra, Yogi; DiMaggio, Joe; Larsen's perfect game; Mays, Willie; New York Yankees; Snider, Duke; Stengel, Casey.

■ Marciano, Rocky

Identification Heavyweight boxing champion
Born September 1, 1923; Brockton, Massachusetts
Died August 31, 1969; near Newton, Iowa

The only heavyweight boxing champion to retire without a defeat, Rocky Marciano holds the record as the heavyweight champion to go the longest time being undefeated.

Known during his boxing career as Rocky Marciano, the "Brockton Blockbuster" was christened Rocco Francis Marchegiano. Although Marciano had a brief whirl at becoming a professional baseball player with the Chicago Cubs organization, he decided that his talents were better suited for boxing. Making his professional debut in 1947, Marciano reeled off thirty-seven consecutive victories, thirty-two by knockout, before facing his boyhood idol and former heavyweight boxing champion of the world, Joe Louis, on October 26, 1951. After overcoming his reluctance to inflict any punishment on the aging "Brown Bomber," Marciano knocked Louis out in the eighth round. Facing the top heavyweight contenders in his next four bouts, Marciano ran his record to forty-two wins, no losses, and thirty-seven knockouts.

On September 23, 1952, Marciano faced world heavyweight champion Jersey Joe Walcott for the title. It was a grueling match, which many experts regard as the greatest heavyweight championship fight ever. Marciano was knocked down in the first round and could barely see out of his swollen left eye at the end of the twelfth round. Losing the fight on all the scorecards, Marciano delivered a devastating right cross to the jaw of Walcott in the thirteenth round, dropping the champion into a heap on the canvas. After Walcott was counted out, Marciano was crowned the new heavyweight champion of the world. It took several minutes to revive Walcott.

Title Defenses Marciano defended his heavyweight title six times. The first was a rematch with Walcott on May 15, 1953. Marciano knocked out the old warrior in the first round. On September 4, 1953, Marciano was matched against top heavyweight contender Roland LaStarza. Marciano hammered on LaStarza's body and biceps until the challenger could barely lift up his arms. Marciano won by a knockout in the eleventh round. In 1954, Marciano defended his title on two memorable occasions against a former heavyweight champion, Ezzard Charles. The first match ended with Marciano winning a close decision. In their second bout, Charles split Marciano's nose open in the sixth round, and the bleeding was unstoppable. Knowing that the fight might be stopped at any time, Marciano knocked Charles out in the ninth round to retain his title.

On May 16, 1955, Marciano stopped challenger Don Cockell in the ninth round. Marciano fought his last bout on September 21, 1955, knocking out Archie Moore in the ninth round. Marciano retired undefeated on April 27, 1956, with a record of forty-nine wins, no losses, and forty-three knockouts.

Impact In all of sports, Marciano is a prime example of toughness, power, heart, and grit. Although not possessing the greatest skills for a heavyweight boxing champion, he was one of the greatest champions of all time, retiring without a defeat. After retirement, Marciano hosted a weekly boxing program on television. He died in a plane crash in Iowa in 1969.

Further Reading

Skehan, Everett M. *Rocky Marciano.* London: Robson Book, 1999. Captivating biography of Marciano.

Sullivan, Russell. *Rocky Marciano: The Rock of His Times.* Urbana: University of Illinois Press, 2002. Paints a complete portrait of an American sports legend.

Suster, Gerald. *Champions of the Ring: The Lives and Times of Boxing's Heavyweight Heroes.* New York: Robson Book, 1996. Examines the illustrious boxing career of Marciano.

Alvin K. Benson

See also Patterson, Floyd; Robinson, Sugar Ray; Sports; Walcott, Jersey Joe.

Rocky Marciano (right) punches challenger Archie Moore in the fifth round of a heavyweight title fight in New York's Yankee Stadium in September, 1955. (AP/ Wide World Photos)

■ Marshall, George C.

Identification American general and statesman
Born December 31, 1880; Uniontown, Pennsylvania
Died October 16, 1959; Washington, D.C.

George C. Marshall was chief of staff of the U.S. Army and Franklin D. Roosevelt's most trusted adviser during World War II; he acted as secretary of state and secretary of defense during the early 1950's.

George C. Marshall grew up in Western Pennsylvania in modest circumstances. He graduated from the Virginia Military Institute in 1901 and was commissioned in the infantry. He served in various troop and training commands and graduated first in his class at the staff college at Fort Leavenworth. Selected for the first group of officers sent to France in 1917, Marshall quickly established a reputation as a brilliant staff officer. He planned the complex movement of the U.S. Army in preparation for the Meuse-Argonne Offensive in 1918.

Marshall held a series of training and teaching assignments during the 1920's and 1930's, the most important being the five years he spent as assistant commandant of the Infantry School. On September 1, 1939, he was chosen to be the chief of staff of the army. Marshall planned and supervised the transition of the army from 200,000 men to more than eight million. He, more than anyone else, shaped both the transition of American's industrial might to fight the war and the strategy followed by the armed forces. President Roosevelt considered him to be indispensable. Marshall was promoted to general of the army in December, 1944. He stepped down as chief of staff in November, 1945 (he was succeeded by General Dwight D. Eisenhower), and accepted President Harry S. Truman's assignment to negotiate an end to the civil war in China. The mission failed, although Marshall was able to achieve a temporary cease-fire. (During the early 1950's, he was savagely attacked for having lost China to the communists.)

Marshall was appointed secretary of state on January 21, 1947, and began the arduous task of building an alliance—the North Atlantic Treaty Organization (NATO)—to stop the spread of communism and rebuild Europe. The Plan for European Recovery, known as the Marshall Plan, was immensely successful. In early 1949, Marshall left the State Department, and after a short tenure as head of the

American Red Cross, he returned to the Truman administration as secretary of defense on September 30, 1950. Although he only served until September of 1951, Marshall was able to reorganize the Defense Department and begin the rebuilding of American military power. Marshall retired from public service on September 1, 1951, and he was awarded the Nobel Peace Prize in 1953.

Impact Marshall was the "organizer of victory" during World War II. He, more than anyone else, was responsible for America's success. As secretary of state, he inaugurated the Marshall Plan, which shaped the postwar world and helped lay the foundations for America's diplomatic relations with Europe during the 1950's. Returning to the military as secretary of defense, he used his formidable organizational skills to create a postwar military that could fight Cold War aggression in several locales.

Further Reading

Cray, Ed. *General of the Army: George C. Marshall, Soldier and Statesman.* New York: W. W. Norton, 1990. A very readable and comprehensive study of Marshall's life and influence.

Pogue, Forrest. *George C. Marshall.* 4 vols. New York: Viking Press, 1963-1987. The definitive work on Marshall's life, indispensable for understanding the man.

Stoler, Mark. *George C. Marshall: Soldier-Statesman of the American Century.* Boston: Twayne, 1989. A shorter and excellent study of Marshall's life.

J. W. Thacker

See also Bradley, Omar; Cold War; Eisenhower, Dwight D.; Kennan, George F.; Korean War; Nobel Prizes; Truman, Harry S.; Truman Doctrine.

■ Martin and Lewis

Identification Popular comedy acting team

Dean Martin
Born June 7, 1917; Steubenville, Ohio
Died December 25, 1995; Beverly Hills, California

Jerry Lewis
Born March 16, 1926; Newark, New Jersey

Dean Martin and Jerry Lewis were among the first comedy teams to move from nightclubs to television and movie stardom and were one of the most popular comedy teams of the early 1950's.

Dean Martin (left) and Jerry Lewis in 1953. (AP/Wide World Photos)

Born Joseph Levitch, Jerry Lewis was the son of entertainers. At the age of five, he joined his parents' act, playing the "borscht belt" in the Catskills. He had little success during his early show business years, however, and held a variety of jobs. Dean Martin, born Dino Crocetti, had a much different kind of background. He was the son of Italian immigrants. His early life included jobs as a coal miner, clerk, and even a boxer. Entering the entertainment industry as a singer in speakeasies, he changed his name to Dean Martini, then Martin.

Success came to Martin and Lewis when they first met each other in March of 1946. They were introduced on a street corner in New York City and by coincidence were both booked into the Havana Club. They became an informal team in July, when each was playing the 500 Club in Atlantic City, and legally became a team in 1947. Lewis played the slapstick comedian, while Martin was the straight man with the husky, baritone voice.

From 1950 to 1955, Martin and Lewis rotated with other entertainers on television's *The Colgate Comedy Hour.* After they made sixteen films, they broke up in 1956. Each went on to star in numerous films, while Martin essentially played himself in a series of television programs. Lewis's television success was associated primarily with the Muscular Dystrophy Telethon, which he began hosting on Labor Day, 1966.

Impact The two performers were among the most popular entertainers during the early to mid-1950's and helped fuel the success of television in its first decade.

Further Reading

Levy, Shawn. *King of Comedy: The Art and Life of Jerry Lewis.* New York: St. Martin's Press, 1997. A thorough biography of Lewis.

Schoell, William. *Martini Man: The Life of Dean Martin.* Lanham, Md.: Rowman & Littlefield, 2003. Explores Martin's career-defining partnership with Jerry Lewis, among many other details of his life.

Richard Adler

See also Berle, Milton; Davis, Sammy, Jr.; Film in the United States; Sinatra, Frank; Sullivan, Ed; Television in the United States.

■ Marx, Groucho

Identification Comedy film star best known during the 1950's as the host of a radio and television quiz show
Born October 2, 1890; New York City, New York
Died August 19, 1977; Los Angeles, California

Groucho Marx's television show, You Bet Your Life *(1950-1961) was among the first programs to push the limits of television censors and enjoyed wide success during the decade.*

Born Julius Marx, Groucho Marx was the oldest of five brothers who formed one of the great comedy teams of the vaudeville era. The comic antics and mannerisms of each brother resulted in the brothers becoming one of the great comedy teams of the period. Though each brother developed his own persona, Groucho Marx in particular became known for a leering smile and comments with clear underlying sexual connotations.

The Marx brothers' popularity was waning when, in 1947, Groucho Marx became host of a radio program, *You Bet Your Life,* on which contestants were

Groucho Marx during the mid-1950's. (Hulton Archive | by Getty Images)

asked a series of questions to win money. In 1950, the program moved to television, on which Marx's style helped him reconnect with audiences and made the show the greatest success in his long career. Audiences liked his irreverence for authority, his one-line jokes and sexual innuendos, and his humorous banter with contestants. Marx was also liberal in his political leanings. His critical remarks about politics and his alleged friendships with communist sympathizers led to investigations by the Federal Bureau of Investigation.

Impact With his slouching walk, omnipresent cigar, and mustache, Marx was among the most recognizable Hollywood figures during the 1950's. His television program during this decade helped entrench the popularity of comedy and game shows for first-generation television viewers and cemented his legendary status in American culture.

Further Reading

Kanfer, Stefan. *Groucho: The Life and Times of Julius Henry Marx.* New York: Knopf, 2001. Documents

the rise of the Marx Brothers and explores the insecurities and sadness in Groucho's life.

Louvish, Simon. *Monkey Business: The Lives and Legends of the Marx Brothers.* New York: St. Martin's Press, 2001. A biography of the Marx brothers.

Richard Adler

See also Berle, Milton; *I've Got a Secret*; Radio; Television game shows.

■ Mathias, Bob

Identification American track-and-field athlete
Born November 17, 1930; Tulare, California

The winner of Olympic medals in the decathlon in the 1948 and 1952 Games, Bob Mathias inspired a "boy wonder" story that captured the imagination of sports fans in the United States.

At the age of seventeen, Robert "Bob" Mathias surprisingly qualified at the 1948 U.S. Olympic trials in the decathlon while he was still a Tulare, California, high school student—even though he had never before competed in the event. Decathlon participants compete in the 100-meter sprint, long jump, shot put, high jump, 110-meter hurdles, discus, pole vault, javelin, and 400- and 1,500-meter runs. At the 1948 Olympic Games in London, England, Mathias won the decathlon and became the youngest man ever to win a gold medal in track and field. He also won the 1948 Sullivan Award as the nation's top amateur athlete.

In 1949, Mathias enrolled at Stanford University, where he starred in both track and football, playing the fullback position. He won Amateur Athletic Union (AAU) decathlon titles in 1949 and 1950, setting a world record in 1950. In 1951, he led Stanford to a Pacific Coast Conference football title and a Rose Bowl appearance. He won the 1952 AAU Nationals and Olympic trials with a second decathlon record, posting lifetime bests in eight of the ten events. Mathias earned another Olympic gold medal at Helsinki, Finland, in 1952, breaking the decathlon world record. He returned to the United States to play football that fall.

After graduating from Stanford in 1953, Mathias enlisted in the U.S. Marine Corps. He starred in a movie about his own life, *The Bob Mathias Story*, in 1954 and won the 1956 interservice decathlon.

Impact A four-time national champion, three-time world record holder, and two-time Olympic champion in the decathlon, Mathias was considered the greatest all-around athlete during the early 1950's and elevated the status of the decathlon in sports fans' eyes. He subsequently pursued a movie and television career, served four terms in the U.S. House of Representatives as a Republican, and directed the U.S. Olympic Training Center. He was elected to the the U.S. National Track and Field Hall of Fame in 1974 and to the U.S. Olympic Hall of Fame in 1983.

Further Reading

Mathias, Bob, with Bob Mendes. *A Twentieth Century Odyssey*. Champaign, Ill.: Sports, 2000. Mathias's own candid autobiography.

Terrence, Chris. *Bob Mathias: Across the Fields of Gold*. Lenexa, Kans.: Addax, 2000. Provides a good account of Mathias's life and information about his teams and important figures in his life. Includes numerous family photos.

David L. Porter

See also Bowden, Don; Connolly, Olga; Oerter, Al; Olympic Games of 1952; Sports.

■ *Maverick*

Identification Western television series
Creator Roy Huggins (1914-2002)
Date Aired from 1957 to 1962

Making its debut on television at a time when Westerns dominated network programming, Maverick *brought something new to the genre: adult humor and an ability to laugh at the Western form itself.*

When ABC introduced *Maverick* on Sunday evenings in September, 1957, the program was merely the latest of scores of Western series that television offered during the 1950's. The show was conceived as a relatively standard Western, starring James Garner as Bret Maverick, a professional card player who wanders the West. However, it soon became evident that Garner, a newcomer to television, brought an easy, wry sense of humor to the role that should be exploited. Scripts were then written to emphasize humorous situations, and Bret Maverick soon emerged as the first television Western antihero—a character who preferred talking his way out of trouble to fighting and who was not above running. Meanwhile, he charmed both leading ladies and audiences with his winning smile, glib talking, and

folksy wisdom he had learned from his "pappy." *Maverick* developed into a Western in which comparatively little shooting or fighting occurred.

As the show developed, it occasionally verged into deliberate satire by taking on other, established Westerns. One of its most famous episodes, titled "Gun Shy," was a parody of the popular *Gunsmoke* series, in which James Arness played a rugged frontier marshal who opened every episode by drawing his gun to shoot an outlaw. In a takeoff from *Gunsmoke*'s opening scene, Maverick appears in the role of the outlaw involved in a shootout with a tough lawman. The lawman draws and shoots at Maverick but misses. Afterward, Maverick explains that he stood too far away to be hit by a pistol shot; the point he makes is valid, but it surprised audiences of the 1950's who were not accustomed to questioning the conventions of television Westerns.

Several months into *Maverick*'s first season, its producers realized that the show's production schedule could not keep up with its broadcast schedule, so they

James Garner's portrayal of the irreverent gambler Bret Maverick introduced adult wit to television Westerns. (Arkent Archive)

introduced a second actor, Jack Kelly, to play Bret's brother Bart in episodes that would be separately produced. Thereafter, episodes tended to alternate between Bret and Bart, with both characters appearing together in occasional episodes. In 1960, Garner left the show in a contract dispute and British actor Roger Moore was introduced as cousin Beau Maverick

Impact By challenging the conventions of the standard Western program, *Maverick* helped to pave the way toward more creative television programming during the 1960's. *Maverick* itself remained on the air until July, 1962, but was never quite the same after the departure of Garner, who went on to a distinguished career in both television and films.

Subsequent Events In 1974, Garner recaptured the flavor of the original *Maverick* in an unrelated series, *The Rockford Files* (1974-1980), in which he played a contemporary private investigator whose attitude and behavior were similar to those of Bret Maverick. While his new show was still running, an attempt was made to re-create *Maverick* itself in a new series called *Young Maverick*, whose title character was supposed to be a cousin of Bret Maverick. That show was launched in late 1979 but lasted only a few months. Two years later, after he was finished with *The Rockford Files*, Garner himself returned as the title character in another series called *Bret Maverick*. That show lasted a full year but failed to match the charm and novelty of the original show.

Further Reading

Aaker, Everett. *Television Western Players of the Fifties: A Biographical Encyclopedia of All Regular Cast Members in Western Series, 1949-1959.* Jefferson, N.C.: McFarland, 1997. Contains brief biographies of about three hundred actors who had regular parts in 1950's Western series, including *Maverick*.

Bianculli, David. *Dictionary of Teleliteracy: Television's Five Hundred Biggest Hits, Misses, and Events.* New York: Continuum Publishing, 1996.

Robertson, Ed. *Maverick: Legend of the West.* Los Angeles: Pomegranate Press, 1994. History of the television series—including its later revivals—that includes detailed cast lists and plot summaries of every episode.

Strait, Raymond. *James Garner.* New York: St. Martin's Press, 1985. Full-length biography of Garner through the early 1980's that focuses on his television and film work.

Yoggy, Gary A. *Riding the Video Range: The Rise and Fall of the Western on Television.* Jefferson, N.C.: McFarland, 1995. Seven-hundred-page survey of the history of television Westerns, with attention to more than 150 individual programs, including *Maverick*.

R. Kent Rasmussen

See also *Cisco Kid, The; Sky King; Lone Ranger, The;* Television in the United States; Television Westerns.

■ Mays, Willie

Identification African American baseball player
Born May 6, 1931; Westfield, Alabama

Willie Mays was one of the most dominating baseball players of his day and perhaps the best center fielder ever to play the game. His artistic play and success on the field helped to foster public acceptance of racial integration in Major League Baseball.

Born in Alabama, one of the most segregated areas of the South, Willie Howard Mays grew up with his father and two female cousins. At the age of sixteen, he began playing baseball in the Negro Leagues, just as Jackie Robinson was breaking the color barrier in Major League Baseball by playing for the Brooklyn Dodgers. Mays himself later signed with the Dodgers' crosstown rivals, the New York Giants.

When a twenty-year-old Mays with a .477 batting average was promoted from the minor leagues to the New York Giants in 1951, he was reluctant. In his first twenty-five plate appearances in the majors, he had only one hit. He was ready to quit until his manager persuaded him to stay. Mays responded with twenty home runs and earned the league's Rookie of the Year Award.

Mays proceeded to exceed expectations and set standards for achievement few players have ever matched. He is among the top-ten leaders in home runs and nearly every other offensive category. In 1954, he won the first of his two National League Most Valuable Player Awards, and between the years 1951 and 1959, he had a batting average of .308.

Impact Mays was a complete player, who could hit, run, field, throw, and steal bases. Although he batted for both average and power, he was particularly known for his colorful waist-level "basket" catches—which he developed to make his fielding more inter-

During the 1954 World Series, Willie Mays made one of the most memorable catches in baseball history, while running full speed toward the centerfield wall. (AP/Wide World Photos)

esting to spectators. Perhaps the most memorable event of Mays's career was a spectacular catch that he made during the 1954 World Series; the catch was immortalized in snapshots and film clips and remains one of the most enduring images of athletic prowess during the 1950's. In more than a century of Major League Baseball, Mays's 660 career home runs have been exceeded only by Babe Ruth, Henry Aaron, and his godson, Barry Bonds.

Further Reading

Einstein, Charles. *Willie's Time.* Philadelphia: J. P. Lippincott, 1979. One of a number of books by Einstein devoted to Mays.

Honig, Donald. *Mays, Mantle and Snider: A Celebration.* New York: Random House, 1990. A comparison of the three greatest outfielders of the 1950's.

David W. Madden

See also Baseball; Campanella, Roy; Dodgers and Giants relocation; Mantle, Mickey; New York Yankees; Snider, Duke; Thomson, Bobby.

■ Meany, George

Identification President of the AFL-CIO
Born August 16, 1894; New York, New York
Died January 10, 1980; Washington, D.C.

George Meany was responsible for uniting the two most powerful labor unions in the United States into one major union, the AFL-CIO, in 1955.

George Meany grew up in the Bronx, quit school at the age of sixteen, and became a plumber's apprentice. Shortly thereafter, he joined the local plumber's union and thus began his long career in union politics.

Meany's rise in the American Federation of Labor (AFL) was consistent. In 1922, he was elected business manager for his plumber's local, became active in the New York City Building Trades Council and, in 1932, was elected one of the vice presidents of the New York Federation of Labor. Using his union position, Meany became active politically in New York and in the New Deal era of President Franklin D. Roosevelt. By 1940, he moved further up the union ladder, becoming secretary-treasurer of the AFL. Working vigorously to help the working person in World War II and after, he fought against the 1947 Taft-Hartley Act, which mandated certain labor-management relations. He was a rabid anticommunist in and outside the union movement as evidenced by his attack on the World Federation of Trade Unions in 1945. Strongly supporting President Harry S. Truman's foreign policy of containment, Meany remained vocal in his support of American foreign policy thereafter, especially during the Korean and Vietnam Wars. It was, however, during the 1950's that Meany made his most important contributions.

After his 1947 clash with United Mine Workers of America leader John L. Lewis at the AFL convention, Meany was considered a potential successor to William Green as president of the union. In 1952, his chance came, and he was elected president of the AFL. Realizing the opportune moment that existed, Meany worked with the Congress of Industrial Organizations (CIO) leaders to affect a unification. By December, 1955, a joint convention met, the AFL-CIO was created, and Meany became its first president, a position he kept until 1979, only one year before his death.

Throughout his union presidency, Meany controlled the union and made it a politically powerful group. He cleared the union of all criminal elements by expelling both the Longshoreman's and Teamsters' unions. He also fought hard for the minimum wage, better working conditions for his workers, and civil rights. However, he remained particularly vocal in his anticommunism. He developed close relationships with Presidents John F. Kennedy and Lyndon B. Johnson, and he strongly endorsed not only their foreign policies but also their economic programs. It was not until the presidency of Richard M. Nixon that he began openly to oppose U.S. foreign policy, particularly toward China and the Soviet Union. Although he later regretted his unswerving support of the Vietnam War, he was close to Johnson, but his relationship with Jimmy Carter was somewhat distant. As a result of his efforts, the American labor movement changed. By 1979, old and in ill health, Meany turned over the AFL-CIO to Lane Kirkland. He died one year later.

Impact Meany's impact on the American labor movement was important. He not only breached the divide between the AFL and CIO, but he also made labor's voice heard by U.S. presidents beginning with Dwight D. Eisenhower and within the halls of Congress as well. Organized labor owes much to the gruff, cigar-smoking George Meany.

Further Reading
Robinson, Archie. *George Meany and His Times: A Biography.* New York: Simon & Schuster, 1981.
Zieger, Robert. "George Meany: Labor's Organization Man." In *Labor Leaders in America,* edited by Melvin Dubofsky and Warren Van Tine. Urbana: University of Illinois Press, 1987.

Michael V. Namorato

See also AFL-CIO merger; Cold War; Eisenhower, Dwight D.; Hoffa, Jimmy; Landrum-Griffin Act of 1959; Lewis, John L.; McClellan Committee; Nixon, Richard M.; Steelworkers strike; Unemployment in the United States; Unionism in the United States.

■ Medicine

The 1950's was an important period in the therapeutic revolution that transformed the practice of modern medicine, enabling physicians to control diseases, such as polio and tuberculosis, that once caused extensive debility and death throughout the world, as well as gain insight into the causes and treatments of several medical problems.

After World War II, the medical professions made almost unbelievable progress in combating diseases that once caused high rates of morbidity and mortality in many parts of the world. During the 1950's alone, doctors and medical researchers successfully proved that penicillin and streptomycin were invaluable antibiotics. They showed that cortisone was capable of relieving the painful joints and swelling associated with arthritis, one of the oldest diseases known to humankind. Early in the decade, investigators in England and the United States showed that there was a link between smoking and lung cancer. In 1952, mental health specialists began using chlorpromazine to treat schizophrenia. In 1955, two major achievements occurred: The National Foundation for Infantile Paralysis (NFIP) publicized the success of the Salk polio vaccine, and surgeons Walton Lillehei and John Kirklin successfully performed open-heart surgeries.

Streptomycin and Tuberculosis Tuberculosis, one of the oldest-known human diseases, is caused by mycobacterium tuberculosis. The lungs are the most common site for the disease, although the infection can attack other organs such as the lymph nodes, bones, gastrointestinal tract, kidneys, skin, and meninges. Pulmonary tuberculosis, its most common form, is associated with a severe cough and blood-stained sputum. Since the victim loses weight and appears to be wasting away, pulmonary tuberculosis once was known as consumption. Until the early twentieth century, this disease caused chronically poor health and death for thousands of Americans, especially city dwellers. As the century unfolded, the incidence of tuberculosis showed signs of declining; historians of medicine cited improved environment and better diet as the reasons. More important, the discovery of streptomycin, an antibacterial substance contained in soil mold, revolutionized the treatment of the disease and allowed the medical community to control tuberculosis.

Selman A. Waksman, a Russian immigrant studying microorganisms in soils, discovered a source of streptomycin. He continued his research, and after earning a doctorate in biochemistry, Waksman joined the faculty at Rutgers University, where he eventually became one of world's leading authorities in soil biology.

At the time that Waksman was conducting his investigations, one of the major challenges facing the medical community was finding a substance that could control tuberculosis. In their tests involving streptomycin, Waksman and his colleagues identified mycobacterium tuberculosis as a bacterium that streptomycin could inhibit. Along with William Feldman of the Mayo Foundation and others, Waksman was able to continue his research when they injected guinea pigs with human tubercule bacilli. For fifty-four days, investigators injected the animals until they exhausted their supply of streptomycin. The guinea pigs injected with the antibiotic showed only small amounts of tuberculosis in their tissues when they were examined microscopically. Feldman and his associates were anxious to use the antibiotic on human subjects, although Waksman was reluctant to undertake a project of that nature.

After additional studies using streptomycin on laboratory animals, Rutgers University and Waksman arranged for the pharmaceutical firm Merck and Company to conduct research on the antibiotic, since Merck could perform these studies more quickly and more efficiently at their laboratories. This investigation clearly showed that a major killer disease could be controlled. In November, 1950, the medical community announced that streptomycin, in combination with recently discovered PAS (para-aminosalicylic acid), drastically increased the survival rate for victims of tuberculosis. In 1952, Waksman received the Nobel Prize for his discovery of streptomycin.

Penicillin and Cortisone During the 1950's, penicillin was not a new drug. In 1929, Sir Alexander Fleming had accidentally discovered this antibacterial substance when he was growing colonies of bacteria on culture plates. During the 1930's and 1940's, other scientists conducted investigations proving that penicillin was a drug with great potential. In 1945, Fleming shared the Nobel Prize with Howard Florey and Ernst Chain for their work with penicillin. During the 1950's, researchers found that penicillin was more effective than sulfonamides, or sulfur drugs, in treating many infectious diseases. Pneumonia, scarlet fever, puerperal sepsis, common varieties of meningitis, and rheumatic fever all responded favorably to this antibiotic. Even more significantly, researchers found that the two major sexually transmitted diseases, syphilis and gonorrhea, responded more favorably to penicillin than to any therapeutic previously used.

One of the world's oldest known diseases, arthritis, is any condition of the joints, limbs, or spine involving inflammation or structural change. Although scientists had isolated cortisone from beef adrenal glands during the 1930's, little interest was shown in it because of the difficulties involved in obtaining large quantities of the steroid hormone cortisone. In some respects, its usefulness was accidentally discovered.

During the mid- to late 1940's, Philip Showalter Hench of the Mayo Clinic observed that one of his older physician patients had made an interesting discovery. When the older man was stricken with jaundice, his arthritic pain and swelling seemed to diminish. Hench believed that his friend was observing more than a mere oddity and looked for an explanation. Next, he observed that one of his pregnant patients had experienced a remission of her arthritis. Hench wanted to find the mysterious substance that seemed to cause arthritis to go into remission.

Around the same time that Hench and his colleague Edward Kendall searched for the unknown substance, Hans Selye of Toronto's McGill University and his staff were attempting to determine the exact functions of the hormone secreted by the adrenal glands. Military intelligence had discovered that large shipments of adrenal glands from Argentine beef were being shipped to Nazi Germany. Since it was wartime, researchers were anxious to understand that country's interest in the beef adrenals. Rumors held that German pilots injected with cortisone were able to fly at altitudes of more than 40,000 feet. The U.S. Air Force communicated with laboratories in Canada and the United States that were studying the adrenal gland hormones.

In 1949, Hench was able to report that cortisone could diminish arthritic pain and swelling. News of his findings caused both lay and medical persons to believe that cortisone was a miracle drug. Many patients who had been literally crippled and laid prostrate by arthritis were able to overcome their invalidism and to resume their earlier lifestyles. In 1950, Philip S. Hench and Edward Kendall, professor of physiological chemistry at the Mayo Clinic, shared a Nobel Prize for their work with cortisone.

Smoking and Lung Cancer During the early 1950's, when it seemed as though the medical community was winning the battle with tuberculosis, lung cancer was replacing that disease as a leading cause of death. Defined at that time as a malignant tumor, cancer was one of the most feared diseases.

In 1950, British researchers Sir Richard Doll and Bradford Hill released the findings of their study of 709 subjects, which indicated that there was a link between smoking and lung cancer. Around the same time, Ernst Wynder and Evarts Graham were observing 684 cases of Americans diagnosed with lung cancer. In both countries, the doctors used a case-control method whereby they compared cancer patients to subjects without the disease, or control patients. Both research teams found a connection between smoking and lung cancer.

The identification of smoking as a health hazard associated with cancer of the lungs was an important milestone of the decade since it indicated the connections between lifestyles and diseases. The public became aware that one could choose not to smoke and by so doing, would decrease one's chances for developing lung cancer.

Mental Illness During the 1950's, the medical community also made significant inroads in treating mental illness. Schizophrenia—an incurable, chronic, and disabling brain disorder found all around the world—posed a challenge for psychiatrists and others in the field of mental health. In 1952, Parisian surgeon Henri Laborit was searching for a way to lower the anxiety level of his patients awaiting surgery. He discovered that chlorpromazine reduced their fears considerably.

Even though the use of chemotherapy in psychiatric patients was unacceptable to some members of the profession, a Parisian psychiatrist, Pierre Deniker, heard about Laborit's observation and tried chlorpromazine on some of his mentally ill patients. He found that the drug appeared to reduce their bizarre behaviors.

Around the same time that Deniker and Laborit were concluding that chlorpromazine had great potential, Canadian psychiatrist Heinz Lehmann was looking for a better therapy for his schizophrenic patients. In May of 1953, he administered chlorpromazine. Lehmann soon observed that many of his patients appeared to be symptom-free. He was convinced that the drug had forced the disease into remission.

As investigators in France and Canada agreed that they had found a possible miracle drug, Ameri-

can drug company Smith Kline was hoping to market a new product. In 1952, the company bought the rights to chlorpromazine from Rhone-Paulenc, a European company. Originally, Smith Kline wanted to market the drug as an antivomiting medication. However, when the company learned of the drug's effectiveness in treating schizophrenia, it tried to persuade medical schools to test the medication on psychiatric patients, an effort that failed. Still determined to market the drug, Smith Kline invited Deniker to sell the product to the American psychiatric community. Promising to save state governments expenses associated with running asylums for the mentally ill, Deniker persuaded mental health professionals at some public hospitals to test the drug on some of their severely affected patients. The results were unbelievably promising. In 1954, the Food and Drug Administration approved the use of chlorpromazine. The drug was a success, and it allowed many people who would have otherwise remained institutionalized to return to the community.

Polio and the Salk Vaccine Polio, also known as infantile paralysis, is caused by a virus that usually affects the anterior horn cells of the spinal cord and the gray matter of the brain stem and cortex. This viral infection is spread by feces and travels the contaminated hands-mouth route. Even healthy children were at higher risk for the disease during the warmer months of the year during the early 1950's.

Polio was a relatively new disease in the United States at midcentury; the first identifiable epidemic of polio occurred in Vermont in 1896, affecting 183 persons. The illness became well known after World War II, when more than thirty thousand people fell victim in 1950 alone. Two years later, eyewitnesses described American hospitals as resembling wartime field hospitals. However, the wounded were not soldiers, but children, many of them in iron lungs, an apparatus that allowed them to breathe after the virus damaged cells in their brains and spinal cords.

During the mid-1940's, Jonas Salk agreed to head a research project for the National Foundation for Infantile Paralysis. Through repetitive laboratory studies, Salk confirmed that polio resulted from three viruses. He was finally able to develop a formalin-killed vaccine against all three strains of the disease. Convinced that he was ready to test it, he adminis-

Dr. Jonas Salk in his University of Pittsburgh bacteriology laboratory in 1954. (AP/Wide World Photos)

tered it to a group of children, including his own three sons. Afterward, Salk notified the NFIP that he was encouraged by the test results but was cautious about undertaking studies of large numbers of children at that time.

In view of the devastating outbreak of polio in 1952, the NFIP disagreed with Salk. In January of 1953, the organization voted to proceed with a mass trial study. In 1954, 1.8 million school-age children took part in the polio vaccine study. It was the largest single clinical test in history. The results were impressive as the vaccine caused the children to develop antibodies against all strains of the disease. Not one child contracted the disease after being vaccinated. Early in 1955, when the NFIP revealed these findings, church bells and factory sirens sounded all over America. By May 7, 1955, four million doses of the Salk Vaccine had been dispensed throughout the United States.

Open Heart Surgery The most anatomically complex organ of the human body, the heart is the site of a variety of abnormalities. Before the mid-1950's, surgeons attempting to correct defects in the heart relied on closed heart surgery, using their fingers and knives to guide them to the sites in need of repair.

In 1955, surgeons Walton Lillehei of the University of Minnesota and John Kirklin of the Mayo Clinic successfully performed open-heart surgeries in which they opened up hearts in order to correct the defects within the organs. However, before they could perform successful procedures inside hearts, they had to find a means to disconnect the heart while mechanically allowing the blood to circulate since reconstructing parts of this complex organ could be time-consuming.

In 1953, surgeon John Gibbon was able to perform the heart's function with a heart-lung machine. Some historians of medicine concluded that the heart pump enabled cardiac surgery to become the most sophisticated of all surgical specialties. Moreover, surgeons performing open-heart procedures had a positive effect on all surgical specialties since their patients required the use of intensive care facilities during their recovery.

Impact Scientists in the medical community played a vital role in creating a healthier nation, especially during the decade of the 1950's. Hand in hand with medical research, however, was the post-World War II affluence in the United States, which created a higher standard of living for the nation. An improved economy and living standards helped foster a healthier nation.

Medical progress made during the 1950's led researchers to the discovery of a range of new antibiotics, including oxytetracycline, nystatin, and erythromycin. Similarly, since cortisone appeared to encourage the body to heal itself, researchers discovered that steroids could be effective in treating many disorders, including Addison's disease, blood disorders, cancer, epilepsy, gastrointestinal diseases, male infertility, and neurological disorders.

Moreover, the optimism generated by medical progress during the post-World War II era and the need to take advantage of its possibilities led to the creation of the Department of Health, Education, and Welfare in 1953. It was America's first national health agency since the demise of the National Board of Health in 1883.

Further Reading

Dubos, Rene, and Jean Dubos. *The White Plague.* New Brunswick, N.J.: Rutgers University Press, 1952. A very readable account of the scientific community's struggle with tuberculosis.

Duffy, John. *From Humors to Medical Science.* Urbana: University of Illinois Press, 1993. An interesting account of how the medical profession developed and functioned from colonial times to the last decade of the twentieth century.

Le Fanu, James. *The Rise and Fall of Modern Medicine.* New York: Carroll and Graf, 1999. An examination of how the medical community managed to overcome major challenges, only to find that there are always new challenges emerging.

Spink, Wesley W. *Infectious Diseases: Prevention and Treatment in the Nineteenth and Twentieth Centuries.* Minneapolis: University of Minnesota Press, 1978.

A very detailed account of how the medical community managed to gain control over life threatening diseases.

Betty L. Plummer

See also Asian flu epidemic; Birth control; Cancer; Health care systems in Canada; Health care systems in the United States; Human growth hormone; Polio; Science and technology; Smoking and tobacco; Tranquilizer chlorpromazine.

■ Mercury space program

Identification First U.S. manned space program; also known as Project Mercury

Date Officially started October 7, 1958; ended May 16, 1963, with the recovery of the last Mercury spacecraft

The Mercury space program provided the basic groundwork, training, and knowledge needed for future manned space flights.

Early developments that eventually led to Project Mercury began during World War I, when President Woodrow Wilson formed the National Advisory Committee on Aeronautics (NACA) so that the United States could be a leader in advanced military aviation. During World War II, numerous advances were made in military aviation, including oxygen-breathing systems and pressure suits. German research on jet- and rocket-propelled aircraft during that war was both impressive and frightening. When Germany surrendered, both the United States and the Soviet Union took German engineers, their documentation, and their knowledge back to their respective countries. After World War II, the United States and the Soviet Union entered into the Cold War as political, ideological, and military enemies in a race to develop advanced weaponry. The space race initially began as an attempt to secure military superiority.

Interest in rocket and space flight had existed for a long time, but the early to mid-1950's saw a surge in publicity and public interest. For the United States, the real impetus came with the general perception that the Soviet Union's space program was more advanced. On October 4, 1957, the Soviet Union launched *Sputnik I*, the first artificial satellite. The United States responded by supplying more funds for missile development and a manned space program. The space race became a matter of national pride and a validation of the American way of life, as well as a response to national security concerns. The United States launched its first satellite, *Explorer 1*, on January 31, 1958, and the *Vanguard I* went into orbit in March, 1958.

In 1958, President Dwight D. Eisenhower suggested that the exploration and development of space should fall under civilian, rather than military authority, except for matters involving national security. Congress agreed and NACA became the basis for the National Aeronautics and Space Administration (NASA) in July, 1958. NASA became operational on October 1, 1958, and Project Mercury was begun less than one week later.

The seven astronauts chosen for Project Mercury were announced in April, 1959. The "Mercury Seven" were Lieutenant Colonel John Hershel Glenn, Jr., from the Marine Corps; Lieutenant Commanders Walter Marty "Wally" Schirra, Jr., and Alan Bartlett Shepard, Jr., and Lieutenant Malcolm Scott Carpenter from the Navy. Captains Donald Kent "Deke"

Slayton, Leroy Gordon Cooper, Jr., and Virgil I. "Gus" Grissom from the Air Force were assigned to duty as NASA test pilots and Mercury astronauts. These men were portrayed as average Americans, and the public quickly developed an overwhelming interest in all the details of their lives. The astronauts became celebrities and heroes and helped ignite the interest of the American public in space exploration.

The objectives of Project Mercury were to put a manned spacecraft in orbit around Earth, study human ability to function in space, and recover both the person and spacecraft safely. Project Mercury made six manned flights from 1961 to 1963 and supplied invaluable information and experience for the scientists and engineers who worked on future space exploration projects, especially the Gemini and Apollo programs.

Impact Originally conceived to reestablish American technological supremacy in the eyes of the na-

Project Mercury engineers assembling space capsules. (Library of Congress)

tions of the world, Project Mercury also captured the imagination of the public. Shaken and alarmed by the early success of the Soviet program, Americans needed to prove that their educational system, technology, scientists, engineers, and weapons were equal or superior to those of the Soviet Union. The public demanded that the space program be accelerated, and the government responded.

Although not as impressive overall as the Soviet Union's Vostok manned space program—which had heavier spacecrafts, longer and more flights, sent the first woman into space, and held all the internationally recognized manned space flight records—Project Mercury was a success in its own right. In less than five years, manned space flight was achieved. During these flights, extremely important information was gathered on the physical and psychological effects of space travel on the human body. Additionally, twenty-five scientific experiments in areas such as earth observations, photography, and radiation were successfully completed.

Although Project Mercury produced fewer than fifty-four hours of manned space flight, the knowledge gained from the construction of the spacecraft and the infrastructure necessary to support the program provided the basis for NASA's future space program.

Subsequent Events Alan Shepard became the first American in space on May 5, 1961. Gus Grissom was next in space on July 21, 1961. John Glenn became the first American to fly in Earth's orbit on February 20, 1962. He was in orbit for four and one-half hours. M. Scott Carpenter was the second American in orbit on May 24, 1962. He made three orbits of the earth. Wally Schirra lifted off on October 3, 1962, and made six orbits of the earth. L. Gordon Cooper piloted the last Mercury flight on May 15, 1963. His mission was the longest, with a twenty-two-orbit flight that lasted thirty-four hours. Deke Slayton never flew on Project Mercury because of a minor heart problem. Of the Mercury Seven astronauts, three later flew Gemini spacecraft, three were on Apollo crews, and one worked on the Apollo-Soyuz Test Project in 1975.

Further Reading

Catchpole, John. *Project Mercury: NASA's First Manned Space Programme*. Chichester, United Kingdom: Springer-Praxis, 2001. An extremely detailed book covering all aspects of Project Mercury, ar-ranged in sections describing the origin, equipment, organizations, and people involved.

Crouch, Tom D. *Aiming for the Stars: The Dreamers and Doers of the Space Age*. Washington, D.C.: Smithsonian Institution Press, 1999. An integrated account of the history of space exploration, focusing on the people who played major roles.

Walsh, Patrick J. *Echoes Among the Stars: A Short History of the U.S. Space Program*. Armonk, N.Y.: M. E. Sharpe, 2000. A brief introductory history discussing the importance of the space program in terms of the scientific, social, and cultural context.

Virginia Hodges

See also Cold War; Eisenhower, Dwight D.; *Explorer I*; National Aeronautics and Space Administration; National Defense Education Act of 1958; Science and technology; Space race; *Sputnik I*.

■ Mexico

Identification Latin American nation immediately to the south of the United States

Important economic and political changes took place in Mexico after World War II, and relations between the two nations became more cooperative and friendly during those developments.

Miguel Alemán Valdes was elected president of Mexico in July, 1946, in the most orderly election in Mexican history. He was also the first civilian to become president since the overthrow and murder of President Francisco I. Madero in 1913. The candidate whom Alemán defeated did not mount the usual armed challenge to the election, and a loyal opposition developed. Soon after taking office, Alemán reaffirmed Mexico's friendship with the United States. He and President Harry S. Truman met to promote increased bilateral cooperation, and in 1947, Mexico signed the Inter-American Treaty of Reciprocal Assistance, also known as the Treaty of Rio de Janeiro. Mexico favored the treaty because it tied Mexico to the United States in a mutual security pact.

Mexico and the United States cooperated in several areas. The United States spent millions of dollars to eradicate hoof-and-mouth disease among cattle in northern Mexico. In 1951, a new bracero program accord replaced the original agreement of 1942 and permitted Mexican laborers to enter the

United States to work primarily in the Southwest. The laborers were assured of minimum wages and working conditions. Mexico agreed to the renewal only after the United States guaranteed penalties for American farmers who used illegal laborers. In the United States, farm labor unions continued to oppose the treaty because they believed that Mexican laborers lowered farm wages. Congress finally passed the treaty, and it was signed in Mexico City.

Alemán Administration While Alemán was in office, the United States played a major role in achieving social and economic stability in Mexico. Alemán was the first president to emphasize industrialization, welcoming private enterprise and foreign capital. Most of the foreign capital came from the United States, and the bulk of Mexican exports went to the United States. The United States also played a major role in the stabilization of the peso.

In 1947, Mexico and the United States entered into a currency stabilization pact, which was supplemented by further agreements after Alemán left office. Alemán devalued the peso in 1948 and again in 1949 to encourage tourism and foreign sales. The United States added 25 million dollars to its contribution to the stabilization fund. The agreement on stabilization of the peso was extended to 1953, and the U.S. Monetary Stabilization Fund agreed to buy up to fifty million pesos to keep Mexico's currency at the pegged value, 6.5 to 1 U.S. dollar.

By 1951, the economy of Mexico had become more or less stable. The stability agreement on the peso and an influx of United States capital were the major reasons, but dollars came from many sources, both official and private. A major source of dollars was the money sent home by the laborers, or braceros, working abroad. Furthermore, by the terms of an agreement on the compensation claims for nationalization of the Mexican Eagle Oil company property confiscated in 1938, the United States provided PEMEX, the Mexican national oil company, with capital and drilling technology.

Ruiz Cortines Administration Throughout the twentieth century, Mexican presidents were very powerful and were able to select their successors. President Alemán Valdes chose one of his portages, Adolfo Ruiz Cortines, as his successor in 1952. According to government figures, Ruiz Cortines was elected by one of the largest electoral majorities in Mexican history.

President Ruiz Cortines followed the Good Neighbor Policy of his predecessor with little change. The United States continued to provide development credits and loans to Mexico, and the migrant workers agreement was extended. The illegal labor problem gradually declined. In 1951, Ruiz Cortines and Eisenhower and Prime Minister Louis Stephen St. Laurent of Canada met in White Sulfur Springs, West Virginia, in a three-day conference that had no agenda. The meeting was held for the heads of government to get to know one another better and to discuss informally matters of common concern. No agreements were reached, but all three participants said the meetings were valuable.

During this period, the United States was committed to helping its southern neighbor in its economic development efforts. Presidents Dwight D. Eisenhower and Ruiz Cortines inaugurated a joint irrigation and hydroelectric project on the Rio Grande River, the Falcon Dam. It was located about two hundred miles from the mouth of the river and served a dual purpose: irrigation and flood control and generation of electricity. The project had been agreed upon in the 1944 river treaty.

In 1954, United States assistance included U.S. Import-Export Bank credits totaling 65 million dollars for railroad projects, a U.S. Import-Export Bank loan of 4 million dollars for the Oviachic Lake irrigation dam, and more than 1 million dollars for telegraph and telephone facilities. The United States also provided major financial assistance to construct and improve the Mexican railroad system. The largest loan, made in 1954, was 61 million dollars for new railroads. Another credit for 28.6 million dollars was made to the Mexican National Railways for purchase of American-made locomotives and rolling stock and for construction and track equipment.

Some problems continued to exist in relations between Mexico and the United States, but none was serious. One of the controversies concerned American-owned shrimp boats that fished in Mexican waters or used Mexican ports for refueling or during bad weather. Many shrimp boat owners refused to abide by the terms of a proposed bilateral agreement. The problem continued but caused no major problems.

Another issue was the ownership of borderlands in Mexico. An expropriation decree, which prohibited foreign ownership of land within 100 kilometers of the border or 50 kilometers of the coast, was

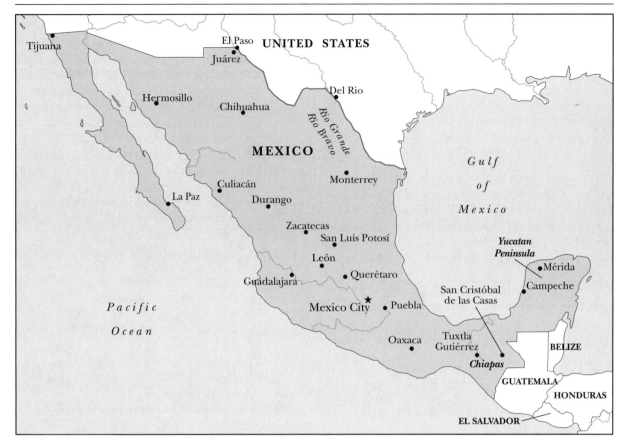

signed by Ruiz Contines in 1958. The largest property affected was the nearly 650,000-acre Cananea ranch owned by American citizens. A compensation value was fixed by an appraisal, and the money was placed in escrow until all the former owners agreed upon apportionment of the money.

The bracero farm labor agreement signed in 1951 during the Alemán Valdes administration came up for renewal during the Ruiz Cortines administration. The U.S. Farm Labor Act had authorized Mexican seasonal farm labor to work in the United States. Mexico favored the continuation of the bracero program, which helped with unemployment problems in Mexico. The Mexican minister of labor insisted that the new agreement contain welfare provisions and guarantee that payment for braceros be equal to that for American citizens. American farmers in need of seasonal laborers supported the program. However, the United States labor movement criticized the program. In spite of labor opposition and the lack of Mexican agreement, a bill for continued recruitment of Mexican labor

was passed by Congress and signed by President Eisenhower in March of 1954. The bill permitted recruitment of Mexican laborers at six border points and guaranteed pay not less than the prevailing wages received by American farmworkers.

Shortly after the bill was passed, Mexico and the United States signed a two-year extension of the labor recruitment accord that had expired two months previously. Changes in the new agreement provided for continued border recruitment and occupational insurance at the workers' expense. Mexican laborers who quit before the expiration of their contract had to pay part of their return fare. The U.S. Congress refused to make the agreement permanent.

However, illegal laborers caused problems with the bracero agreements. Illegal laborers could be used to create a labor surplus and reduce wages. As a result of pressure from U.S. labor unions, Congress instituted a program called Operation Wetback to end illegal labor migration from Mexico. The border patrol intercepted Mexicans entering illegally and deported them. The United States Immigration Commission stated in its 1954 year-end report that illegal entries had been reduced by more than 86 percent during that year.

The year 1954 also saw devaluation of the peso. The monetary agreement designed in 1947 to help stabilize the peso was extended through 1957, and the United States made 75 million dollars available for peso stabilization between 1955 and 1957.

Several natural disasters occurred during the Ruiz Cortines administration; an earthquake in southern Mexico, flooding in the Rio Grande Valley above the Falcon Dam, and devastation in the Yucatán Peninsula and on the Gulf Coast from Hurricane Janet. The United States responded with money and supplies. After Hurricane Janet, helicopters from the U.S. carrier *Saipan* rescued survivors and provided doctors and medicine.

López Mateos Administration New issues arose after 1958, when Adolfo López Mateos followed Ruiz Cortines. The Cuban Revolution initiated by Fidel Castro caused some disagreement between Mexico and the United States. López Mateos maintained neutrality in the United States-Cuban dispute; it did not see any need to reexamine it policy until the missile crisis of 1962.

Under López Mateos, the Mexican government wanted to play a larger role in world affairs. Mexico moved to establish better and closer relations with world powers other than the United States. It was particularly interested in the development of markets outside the United States since the country was again industrializing and wanted to broaden its economic support. López Mateos also planned to make Mexico a major leader in the Latin American Free Trade Association (LAFTA). Mexico reassured the European Market that there was no economic protectionism planned in Latin America.

Mexico's move to play a larger role in world affairs did not interrupt its good relations with the United States. In 1959, early in his administration, López Mateos met with President Eisenhower in Acapulco and later that year in Washington, D.C. In a joint statement, the two presidents agreed to cooperate and consult to protect the cotton interests of both countries; cotton was a major Mexican export. Both countries also pledged to solve the pollution problem caused by lead and zinc. In addition, they agreed to set up an irradiation program to solve a parasitic screw-worm health problem, and they agreed to build the 100 million-dollar Diablo Dam on the Rio Grande River near Del Rio, about 100 miles upstream from the Falcon Dam. In 1960, the two presidents met midway on the international bridge at Del Rio to announce the Amistad Dam project about ten miles upstream that was to supplement the Diablo Dam in controlling the Rio Grande.

Impact The 1950's ended with excellent relations between Mexico and the United States. Cooperation was characteristic, and no major problems had arisen during the decade. Mexico received financial and economic assistance for its economic development programs, while the United States became the most important trading partner of Mexico in both imports and exports. Although Mexico supported United States foreign policy during the Cold War, it refused to be drawn further into that conflict by the United States. For example, during the Korean War, the United States wanted to include Mexico in an anticommunist defense program and offered it military aid in exchange for support. Mexico rebuffed the United States proposal but remained committed to mutual defense of the hemisphere.

Further Reading

Hofstadter, Dan, ed. *Mexico 1946-1973.* New York: Facts on File, 1974. Detailed account of developments in Mexico from 1946 to 1973.

Keen, Benjamin, and Keith Haynes. *A History of Latin America.* Vol. 2. *Independence to the Present.* Boston: Houghton, Mifflin, 2000. This is a good textbook, brief and readable, with a bibliography for each chapter and a glossary of Spanish words.

Meyer, Michael C., and William L. Sherman. *The Course of Mexican History.* 5th ed. New York: Oxford University Press, 1995. A highly readable, general history by two leading scholars of Mexican history. Includes a bibliography after each chapter.

Smith, Peter. "Mexico Since 1946." In *Latin America Since 1930: Mexico, Central America and the Caribbean.* Vol. 3 in *The Cambridge History of Latin America.* Edited by Leslie Bethel. New York: Cambridge University Press, 1990. This is one of the highly recognized histories of Latin America, with each chapter written by an expert in the field.

Robert D. Talbott

See also Agriculture in the United States; Bracero program; Cuban Revolution; Guatemala invasion; Immigration to the United States; International trade of the United States; Latin America; Operation Wetback; *Pocho*; United Fruit Company.

■ Michener, James

Identification American novelist
Born February 3, 1907; New York City
Died October 16, 1997; Austin, Texas

During the 1950's, James Michener introduced his readers to cultures throughout the world in a string of popular epic historical novels.

James Michener is best known as the author of epic historical novels such as *Tales of the South Pacific* (1947), *Hawaii* (1959), and *Alaska* (1988). His extensive research, which involved living in, and learning the history of, the cultures about which he wrote, is evident in all of his writing. The winner of the 1948 Pulitzer Prize for *Tales of the South Pacific*, Michener continued to write until shortly before his death.

Michener's 1992 autobiography, *The World Is My Home*, tells of his curiosity about the world's people and their diverse cultures. His novels are the result of his intense study of these people and cultures.

During his tour of duty in the U.S. Navy during World War II, Michener was stationed in the South Pacific, where he worked as a naval historian writing reports about the various islands. Based on this experience, he wrote *Tales of the South Pacific*, which was later adapted by musical collaborators Richard Rodgers and Oscar Hammerstein II into the long-running musical *South Pacific*. The play remained popular from its 1949 debut throughout the 1950's and was made into a movie in 1958.

Though Michener's *Tales of the South Pacific* won a Pulitzer Prize, the book never achieved best-seller status. However, after its adaptation as a play and film, Michener's novels became popular successes during the 1950's. With the earnings from *Tales of the South Pacific*, Michener was able to become a full-time writer. During the 1950's alone, he published ten books, including both fiction and nonfiction. These books include *Return to Paradise* (1951), *The Bridges at Toko-Ri* (1953), *Sayonara* (1954), *The Bridge at Andau* (1954), and *Hawaii* (1959).

Michener published his epic novel *Hawaii* in 1959—the same year in which Hawaii was admitted to the union. With *Hawaii*, Michener established his most popular formula: long, sweeping narratives that encompass the whole history of a place and the people who have lived there and shaped its story.

Impact Michener continued to enlighten his readers about the world's diverse cultures throughout the 1950's until his death in 1997. During the 1950's and into the 1960's, Michener often used the South Pacific and the Far East as the settings for his novels and nonfiction works alike.

During most of the 1950's, Michener lived in Hawaii, where he became politically active. A self-proclaimed political liberal, he was always keenly interested in politics and was an outspoken critic of McCarthyism during the decade. He also reported on the Korean War, focusing on communist activities in Korea, the Soviet Union, and China. In 1956, Michener helped Hungarian freedom fighters in their quest for a sanctuary. His activities led to his appointment to several advisory boards in Washington, D.C. In 1957, he became a member of the U.S. State Department advisory committee on the arts. These political activities during the 1950's led him to an unsuccessful run for Congress during the early 1960's.

Michener's epic novels sold millions of copies worldwide throughout the decades following the 1950's and established him as one of the twentieth century's most prolific and popular authors.

Further Reading

Hayes, John. *James A. Michener: A Biography*. New York: Bobbs-Merrill, 1984. As a colleague of Michener, Hayes was granted permission by the author to write this biography and enjoyed full access to Michener's private collection of papers. The biography is considered by many to be an accurate portrayal of the author's life and work.

Michener, James A. *The World Is My Home*. New York: Random House, 1992. Michener's own memoir, which gives readers an in-depth view of the extraordinary life and experiences of an author who was known for being an intensely private man.

Kimberley M. Holloway

See also Broadway musicals; Literature in the United States; Theater in the United States.

■ Mickey Mouse Club

Identification Children's television series
Producer Walt Disney Company
Date Aired from 1955 to 1959

Walt Disney's early venture into children's afternoon television programming captured the imagination of the nation's children and became a 1950's cultural phenomenon.

The *Mickey Mouse Club* debuted as a half-hour show on October 3, 1955, on the ABC network and aired 360 episodes during its four-year run. The show was Walt Disney's first attempt at Disney-branded television programming and featured a cast of preteen boys and girls and two adult hosts, Jimmy Dodd and Roy Williams. Disney insisted that the program be cast with "regular kids," so his staff searched for talent in the local schools. The show's young stars—who were called "Mouseketeers," included Annette Funicello, Bobby Burgess, Darlene Gillespie, Don Grady, Cubby O'Brien, and Karen Pendleton.

The show's unvarying routine began with a roll call and included musical numbers, classic Disney cartoons, and serialized adventures such as *Spin and Marty* and *The Hardy Boys*, starring Tim Considine and Tommy Kirk. Each day of the week featured a particular theme, such as "Talent Round-Up Day." Disney attempted to revive the show in 1977 and again in 1989, but subsequent shows never achieved the popularity of its first incarnation, although the last version produced such future stars as Britney Spears, Justin Timberlake, and Christina Aguilera.

Impact This show, which was expanded to a full hour during its last two seasons, had an indelible impact on American culture. The *Mickey Mouse Club* is a cultural touchstone for a generation whose anthem is the Mickey Mouse Club theme and whose uniform includes a pair of mouse ears.

Further Reading

Bowles, Jerry G. *Forever Hold Your Banner High! The Story of the "Mickey Mouse Club" and What Happened to the Mouseketeers.* New York: Doubleday, 1976. A "where are they now?" look at the stars of the *Mickey Mouse Club.*
Santoli, Lorraine. *Official "Mickey Mouse Club" Book.* Los Angeles: Disney Editions, 1995. A nostalgic look at the *Mickey Mouse Club*, including its history, interviews with its stars, and backstage stories.

Mary Virginia Davis

See also *Captain Kangaroo; Davy Crockett;* Disneyland; *Howdy Doody Show;* Nielsen ratings; Television for children; Television in the United States.

■ Military conscription

Definition Compulsory military enrollment, also known as the draft

From 1940 until 1973, the United States depended on a combination of voluntary recruitment and conscription to fill its military. Although the numbers of men drafted during wartime dwarfed those of peacetime, during the 1950's, Cold War tensions prompted more than one million American men to be called to military duty, and several thousand draft evasion cases were investigated.

The United States traditionally relied on volunteers for its military. During the Civil War, the Confederate and Union governments attempted to use conscription to fill their armies. The experiment was a failure as a result of widespread opposition and the contempt that volunteers felt toward conscripts. Conscription ended when the Confederacy surrendered.

The United States did not conscript again until 1917, when the nation entered World War I. In this second attempt at conscription, the government developed the basic system that would be used again from 1940 until the end of conscription in 1973. Under the system known as Selective Service, local civilians were appointed to draft boards, which determined a young man's physical condition, his role in the economy, and his obligations to support family before deciding whether he would be forced to enter the military. The government stopped conscription when the World War I ended in late 1918 and did not draft again until 1940, when the nation began its first peacetime draft as part of its preparations prior to entering World War II.

Peacetime Conscription Following the end of World War II, the country debated the future of conscription. Many Americans called for universal military training, in which all able-bodied men would perform military training, be released to civilian life, and then be subject to recall in a war. Others called for universal military service, which would require all adult free men to remain on active service for a period of years. Although the army still depended on large formations of foot soldiers, it feared that equipping and training the great masses of men who would become eligible each year would leave insufficient funds for higher-echelon training or equipping more specialized units.

The Army believed that men trained for short periods and then released to civilian pursuits would be little better than raw recruits when recalled for war. On June 24, 1948, Congress passed a new Selective Service Act. The new act made men between the ages of eighteen and twenty-six years liable for up to twenty-one months of active service with five years following as an individual reservist with a liability for recall in the event of war. The period in the reserve could be reduced to three years if the soldiers joined and maintained good standing in the National Guard or a unit of what was then called the Organized Reserve Corps, later renamed the Army Reserve.

The Korean War Between the end of World War II in 1945 and the outbreak of the war in Korea in 1950,

the United States decreased its ground forces and only 300,000 men were drafted. The outbreak of war in Korea drastically changed the scale of the draft. Originally, reservists and National Guardsmen were called to active service to fill out the active army for the war, but the government increasingly sought to use Selective Service instead of the reserve components to ensure manned troops. In June of 1951, Congress passed the Universal Military Training and Service Act, which in theory obligated all adult men to perform military service. However, the crisis of the war in Korea delayed the implementation of the full implications of the act. Instead, Selective Service boards deferred many draft-age men, taking in only the numbers needed by the army.

Post-Korean War Conscription Following the ceasefire and the end of the war in Korea in July, 1953, the draft continued in reduced form. American society had reached a consensus on mandatory military service, but the military did not need the massive

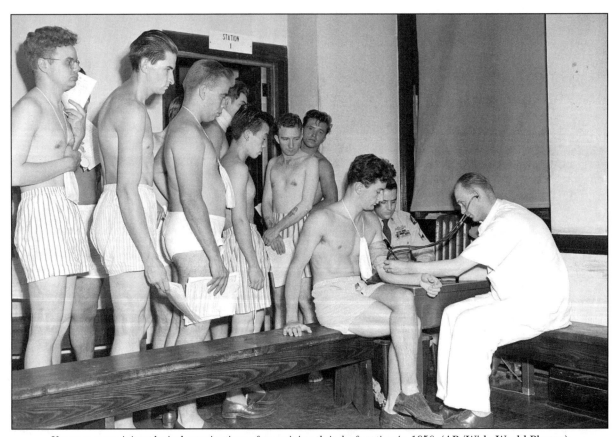

Young men receiving physical examinations after receiving their draft notices in 1950. (AP/Wide World Photos)

numbers that could theoretically be raised by this method. A variety of programs allowed many young men to avoid military service. If a man got his draft notice, he could still avoid service in the army by enlisting in one of the other branches. Air Force and Navy recruiters found their offices deluged with young men who had gotten their draft notices. Volunteers for the Air Force and Navy served longer periods on active service but usually ate chow-hall food instead of field rations and enjoyed the benefits of indoor plumbing.

In 1955, in response to shortcomings in the existing draft law, Congress amended the law to lower the number of obligatory years from eight to six. However, under the new law, soldiers leaving active service before the completion of six years were required to join reserve units and train regularly or face recall into active service. Up to a quarter of a million men between ages seventeen and eighteen and a half could join the reserves and serve only six months on active duty followed by seven and a half years in the reserves.

Impact During the 1950's, a generation of young men served in the military or took steps such as early marriage and having children to avoid it. Other young men voluntarily served eight years in the National Guard or the reserves and avoided the draft.

Further Reading

Chambers, Robert Whiteclay II. *To Raise an Army: The Draft Comes to Modern America.* New York: Free Press, 1987. Solid background in the history of conscription in the United States. The creation of an acceptable conscription system in 1917 and the draft for World War II fills the bulk of the work.

Davis, James Warren. *Little Groups of Neighbors: The Selective Service System.* Chicago: Markham, 1968. A largely celebratory study of civilians who ran the Selective Service—those who decided who would serve and who would not.

Flynn, George Q. *The Draft, 1940-1973.* Lawrence: University of Kansas Press, 1993. Scholarly history of the draft. Argues that the draft stemmed from political desires rather than military needs and was accepted by most Americans until the Vietnam War ended public support.

Stearn, Frederick M. *The Citizen Army: Key to Defense in the Atomic Age.* New York: St. Martin's Press, 1957.

Contemporary study focusing on obligatory military service as a cornerstone of American unity in the face of the communist threat.

Barry M. Stentiford

See also Cold War; Korean War; Veterans organizations.

■ Military-industrial complex

Definition Term coined by President Dwight D. Eisenhower to describe the conjunction of the U.S. military establishment and the civilian arms industry

For the first time in its history, the United States maintained a large peacetime military force following World War II, and its associated expenditures on weaponry represented an important part of the nation's economy.

In World War II, the United States became the "arsenal of democracy" with industry and the labor force dedicated to the war effort, and defense expenditures became almost as large as the civilian component of the economy. After the war ended in 1945, a demobilization of the military and a retooling of the economy to civilian pursuits began, with some industries such as aircraft manufacturing being severely curtailed. This disarmament was halted by the onset of the Cold War during the late 1940's, and a military force numbering in the millions was deployed at home and abroad.

In 1947, the U.S. Army and Navy were absorbed into a new Department of Defense, which also included a separate Air Force, and each of these services began to compete for defense dollars. After the outbreak of the Korean War in 1950, defense expenditures quickly grew to become the largest part of the federal government's budget, and this continued after the war ended in 1953. The hydrogen bomb joined the atomic bomb in the nation's arsenal in 1954, part of an arms race with the Soviet Union that spurred development of a variety of expensive nuclear weapons systems, including B-52 strategic bombers, intermediate range and intercontinental ballistic missiles, and missile-launching Polaris submarines.

During the 1950's, the line between industry and the armed forces blurred as never before in peacetime. The majority of money spent on research and development in the United States came from the defense budget, the electronics and aerospace industries were primarily in the service of the Pentagon, and by 1959, hundreds of retired military and naval officers were employed by defense contractors. Under President Dwight D. Eisenhower, the civilian leadership of the defense department was recruited largely from business. His three secretaries of defense, for example, included a former president of General Motors, a former president of Proctor and Gamble, and a former investment banker. Congressmen from every state were interested in attracting military construction and defense spending, providing a sympathetic ear to the lobbying of the arms industry.

Impact National defense spending represented more than half of the federal budget from 1951 through 1961 and in some years reached two-thirds. This financial backing placed in the hands of the military-industrial complex an enormous amount of political and economic power. In his 1961 farewell address, President Eisenhower coined the term "military-industrial complex," and while he accepted it as a necessity, he cautioned against it being granted unwarranted influence, a warning that seemed all the more significant because it came from one of the nation's most admired military leaders. In the years to follow, an unpopular war in Vietnam and the subsequent decline in the share of the federal budget devoted to defense left the military-industrial complex a diminished but still potent force in the corridors of power.

Further Reading

Hooks, Gregory. *Forging the Military-Industrial Complex: World War II's Battle of the Potomoc.* Urbana: University of Illinois, 1991. A study of how World War II laid the foundations of the military-industrial complex.

Walker, Gregg, David Bella, and Steven Sprecher, eds. *The Military-Industrial Complex: Eisenhower's Warning Three Decades Later.* New York: Peter Lang, 1992. A collection of essays addressing the historic, economic, and political aspects of the military-industrial complex.

Lawrence W. Haapanen

See also B-52 bomber; Boeing 707; Business and the economy in the United States; Cold War; Eisenhower, Dwight D.; Hydrogen bomb; Korean War; Mills, C. Wright; Polaris missiles; Science and technology.

■ Miller, Arthur

Identification American playwright, political figure, and husband of Marilyn Monroe
Born October 17, 1915; New York City

Arthur Miller made a name for himself during the 1950's by opposing McCarthyism and by his surprising marriage to film star Marilyn Monroe.

When the 1950's began, Arthur Miller had recently become one of the most popular and respected playwrights in the United States, thanks to the success of his play *Death of a Salesman*, produced in 1949. That play established Miller as a serious writer of dramas that explored the connections between individuals and society.

Miller was also a long-time advocate of radical and communist causes, the support of which became dangerous during the late 1940's and 1950's because of the attacks made on them by Senator Joseph McCarthy and the House Committee on Un-American Activities (HUAC).

Responding to these attacks, in 1950, Miller wrote an adaptation of Henrik Ibsen's *An Enemy of the People*, an 1882 play about the persecution of individuals for holding unpopular views. In response to the arrest of Ethel and Julius Rosenberg on charges of spying for the Soviet Union, Miller wrote *The Crucible* (pr. 1953). This play depicted the 1692 witch trials in Salem, Massachusetts, drawing implicit parallels between the witch-hunts of 1692 and the investigations of left-wing individuals during the 1950's, which also were referred to as "witch-hunts."

Miller himself was caught up in the political attacks of his day. In 1954, his contract to write a screenplay about juvenile delinquency was cancelled because studio executives considered him to be too closely associated with communists. In 1956, he was summoned before HUAC and asked to provide the names of those who had attended communist-sponsored meetings. Miller refused to name names and was cited for contempt of Congress. He was convicted, fined, and given a suspended jail term, but the conviction was overturned on appeal.

The issue of informing is a central concern of Miller's 1955 one-act play, *A View from the Bridge*, which is sometimes seen as an indictment of his friend, director Elia Kazan. Unlike Miller, Kazan did name names. He then defended his actions in his popular movie *On the Waterfront* (1954), in which a longshoreman who informs on corrupt union leaders is portrayed as heroic. In contrast, in Miller's play, also about a longshoreman, the central character's decision to turn informer is seen as villainous.

After *A View from the Bridge,* Miller did not finish another play until the mid-1960's. Some critics have attributed this dry spell to his political ordeal with HUAC. Others point to his relationship with Marilyn Monroe, whom Miller married in 1956, much to the surprise of those who wondered what a serious, intellectual playwright could have in common with a Hollywood starlet. During the marriage, which lasted until 1961, Miller spent much of his time on location with his actor wife, subordinating his own career to hers and becoming known less as a respected playwright than as Marilyn Monroe's husband.

Even when Miller returned to playwriting during the 1960's, he did not completely win back his reputation. His serious social dramas were seen as old-fashioned. However, he began to return to favor at the end of the twentieth century.

Playwright Arthur Miller and Marilyn Monroe about three weeks after their June 29, 1956, marriage. (Hulton Archive | by Getty Images)

Impact In the first half of the decade, through both his plays and his refusal to name names, Miller gained importance as one of the few individuals who dared to stand up to the attacks on unpopular viewpoints and political activity. In the second half of the decade, he became known more for his marriage to Marilyn Monroe.

Further Reading

Bigsby, Christopher, ed. *The Cambridge Companion to Arthur Miller.* Cambridge, England: Cambridge University Press, 1997. A collection of essays on Miller's plays.

Gottfried, Martin. *Arthur Miller: His Life and Work.* Cambridge, Mass.: Da Capo Press, 2003. A good full-length biography.

Moss, Leonard. *Arthur Miller.* Rev. ed. Boston: Twayne, 1980. Brief discussion of Miller's life and extended analyses of his plays. Includes a 1979 interview with Miller.

Sheldon Goldfarb

See also Communist Party of the U.S.A.; House Committee on Un-American Activities; Kazan, Elia; McCarthy, Joseph; Monroe, Marilyn; *On the Waterfront*; Rosenberg, Julius and Ethel; Theater in the United States.

■ Mills, C. Wright

Identification American sociologist, author, and social critic

Born August 28, 1916; Waco, Texas

Died March 20, 1962; West Nyack, New York

C. Wright Mills maintained in his writings that increasingly affluent Americans led lives deprived of real power and meaning. This thesis addressed a widespread middle-class anxiety. His view that the real control of society was held by a "power elite" became a prevailing theme of the post-Marxian Left.

The son of an insurance executive, C. Wright Mills spent his youth in Texas. He received his masters degree in sociology from the University of Texas and went to Wisconsin for his doctoral work. Although Mills spent most of his adult life elsewhere, his flamboyant dress, large size, and abrasive manner seemed to forever brand him a Texan.

After a short stint at the University of Maryland, Mills taught at Columbia University in 1945 and remained there through the rest of his career. While

Mills's early writings pertained to sociological theory, his books concerning class differences (what he called "social stratification") most influenced popular culture. Foremost among these were *White Collar: The American Middle Classes* (1951) and *The Power Elite* (1956).

Themes in Mills's Writings To Mills, social classes differed both in prestige and in power to influence society's decisions. Like socialist philosopher Karl Marx, Mills saw stark differences between a controlling class of oppressors and everyone else. However, he described a type of oppression distinctly different from that of Marx. Marx predicted that monopolistic capitalists would increasingly impoverish the masses of people. Mills's analysis, in contrast, suggested that the white-collar middle class was more numerous and more affluent than ever before but was deficient in both power and joy. Unlike the small entrepreneur of an earlier America, the white-collar worker neither owned his own business nor controlled his own product. A minute part of a giant organization, this worker's economic contributions were fragmented into routine, repetitive efforts. His opinions counting for little, the white-collar worker suffered not from poverty but from meaninglessness.

A "power elite" held the real control in society. This elite consisted not of Marx's rich capitalists but of a trinity of military commanders, managing directors of huge corporations, and nonelected political advisers. This elite generally functioned behind the scenes, and its members had similar backgrounds and enjoyed a unity of interest in retaining power. The elite made the big decisions of society such as initiating a war or an economic policy. The elite believed that public support could be secured later by manipulating the media.

Impact Certain themes in Mills's writings fit the temper of the times. His characterization of a newly affluent but powerless middle class reflected an anxiety highlighted by several other 1950-era writers. Even President Dwight D. Eisenhower expressed dismay over the unrestrained influence of the military-industrial complex nourished by Cold War fears.

More controversial was Mills's characterization of an enduring power elite. The political Left, disillusioned by events that discredited Marxism, welcomed Mills's revised views of the oppressors. Liberal critics, however, maintained that controlling

democratic coalitions were not concentrated in any fixed power elite but tended to shift with events and the times.

Mills's final writings during the early 1960's grew more blatantly political as he tried to rally intellectual support for the "people's revolution" in Cuba led by Fidel Castro. Felled by a heart attack in 1962, Mills did not live to see his influence upon protesting Vietnam-era students rallying against a seemingly intransigent, power-elitist "establishment."

Further Reading

Halberstam, David. *The Fifties.* New York: Villard Books, 1993. Chapter 35 highlights Mills's influence within this decade.

Horowitz, David. *C. Wright Mills: An American Utopian.* New York: The Free Press, 1983. A comprehensive account of the life and works of Mills.

Thomas E. DeWolfe

See also Affluence and the new consumerism; *Affluent Society, The*; Castro, Fidel; Communist Party of the U.S.A.; Conformity, culture of; *Lonely Crowd, The*; *Man in the Gray Flannel Suit, The*; Military-industrial complex; *Organization Man, The*; Packard, Vance.

■ Mindszenty, Cardinal József

Identification Hungarian churchman and resolute opponent of communist rule in Hungary

Born March 28, 1892; Csehimindszenti, Austro-Hungarian Empire

Died May 6, 1975; Vienna, Austria

Cardinal József Mindszenty became, especially in the United States during the 1950's, a living symbol of heroic resistance to communist tyranny in Eastern Europe.

József Mindszenty was the eldest of four children of a Hungarian farmer. As a Roman Catholic bishop during World War II, Mindszenty was jailed for condemning the Nazi treatment of Hungary's Jews. A few years later, in 1948, Mindszenty, now a cardinal, was arrested by the new communist regime in Hungary because of his bitter opposition to the state taking over the Catholic schools. Drugged and tortured in captivity, Mindszenty finally confessed to charges of treason and conspiracy and was sentenced to life imprisonment. He was freed during a student revolt in 1956 but his freedom lasted only four days. He was granted asylum in the American embassy in Budapest but only in 1971, after some fifteen years in the embassy, was he allowed to leave the country. However, long before his death in 1975, Cardinal Mindszenty had become a source of inspiration far beyond his native land.

Impact During the 1950's, while the Soviet Union tightened its grip on Eastern Europe, several American Christian groups were vehement in their condemnation of the "Red Menace." To some of them, the very existence of Christianity in Eastern Europe was at stake. For many American Christians, especially Catholics, Cardinal Mindszenty came to personify the valiant resistance of the besieged Christian churches of Eastern Europe to atheistic Marxism. In 1958, an American Catholic couple, Fred and Phyllis Schlafly, established the Cardinal Mindszenty Foundation. Its purpose, in the spirit of its namesake, was to counter Soviet values and influences wherever they could be confronted. The Mindszenty Foundation became a significant fund-raiser, publisher, and clearing house for anticommunist activities.

In 1974, the Schlaflys were instrumental in bringing the old cardinal to the United States, where he received a hero's welcome in several cities. In his speeches and sermons, he continued to assail the Soviet system in all its forms.

Further Reading

Közi-Horváth, József. *Cardinal Mindszenty: Confessor and Martyr of Our Time.* London: Aid to the Church in Need, 1979. Details the life and times of Mindszenty.

Vecsey, Joseph, and Phyllis Schlafly. *Mindszenty the Man.* St. Louis, Mo.: Cardinal Mindszenty Foundation, 1972. Views Mindszenty as a martyr for religious and political freedom against communist tyranny and, as such, a powerful inspiration to anticommunist movements in the United States, especially during the 1950's.

Donald Sullivan

See also Army-McCarthy hearings; Cold War; Foreign policy of the United States; Hungarian revolt.

■ Minorities in Canada

The 1950's witnessed important changes in the socioeconomic status of several of Canada's minority groups, although inequalities and racism continued to exist.

Canada was a multiethnic and multicultural society during the 1950's. The status of minority communi-

ties during that decade is better understood with a brief overview of the historical context for Canada's dual national heritage and increasingly multicultural makeup.

English speakers from the British Isles occupied the position of Canada's dominant culture. The large French Canadian minority, Canada's other so-called founding culture, followed in importance, influence, and numbers. Canada's indigenous groups, the Inuit and Amerindians, who occupied the land for many millennia prior to European contact, later would use the term "First Nations" to define themselves. Other minorities who were also part of the ethnic scene during the 1950's were non-Anglo Europeans, African Canadians, and Asians.

Dual European Heritage Canada was not founded on a single cultural and linguistic heritage. Although Great Britain conquered French Canada during the early 1760's, and English speakers eventually outnumbered francophones, by the early nineteenth century, British rule failed to assimilate the large French minority concentrated primarily in Quebec. French Canadians, motivated by *la survivance* (cultural survival), clung to their language, Roman Catholic faith, customs, and special institutions. A high birthrate—sometimes called "the revenge of the cradle"—kept the percentage of French Canadians high in spite of continuing immigration from the British Isles. Anglo political leaders were eventually forced to accept the "French fact." When Canada gained self-rule from Britain in 1867 and organized a confederation of five provinces, Quebec agreed to join only after it was granted sole control over its educational system and cultural affairs. Throughout the years that followed, Quebec jealously guarded and asserted its separate identity.

During the 1950's, French Canadians accounted for more than 30 percent of Canada's population and resided primarily in the central and eastern regions. In Quebec, Canada's second-largest province, they constituted 82 percent of the inhabitants. The biggest concentration of French speakers outside of Quebec were the Acadians in nearby New Brunswick with 38.3 percent of that province's total population. Ontario's portion of francophones was 10.4 percent. Scattered throughout the western provinces and northern territories were small pockets of French Canadians. Isolated in a sea of English speakers,

An Inuit woman holding a split and smoked salmon, around 1950. (Hulton Archive | by Getty Images)

their ethnicity, including their primary use of French, was on the wane.

Government-promoted Immigration The ethnic makeup of the population did not change much through most of the nineteenth century as Canada attracted relatively few immigrants. Wanting to develop the sparsely western prairie regions, Canadian government officials assiduously promoted immigration toward the end of this century. From this time until World War I, Canada received a steady flow of immigrants that transformed the country. Although the newcomers included English speakers from the British Isles and the United States, the most significant influx was from central, southern, and eastern Europe. Germans and Slavs (mainly Ukrainians) were the most numerous of the non-Anglo European groups. Jews also arrived in fairly significant numbers and settled mainly in large urban centers. In time, Anglo Canadians became a minority in the Prairie provinces. Here the so-called New Cana-

dians, many of whom were peasants, settled both in rural areas and in urban centers such as Winnipeg, Manitoba, where they formed tight-knit communities in the neighborhoods of that city's north end. The same pattern occurred in large cities to the east such as Toronto and Montreal. By 1951, after several generations, these groups had largely lost the use of their native languages and become English speakers.

A strong Asian presence was evident on the West Coast, mainly in the Vancouver area, where Chinese and some Japanese immigrants came in the nineteenth century as laborers. Other "visible minorities" included the Inuit, residing in the Arctic, and the indigenous First Nations, located largely on reserves in remote nonurban environments north of settled arable areas. Another minority, Canadians of African descent, were mostly descendants of slaves who accompanied the Loyalist migration to Nova Scotia after the Revolutionary War and persons smuggled through the pre-Civil War Underground Railroad system from the United States into urban areas of southeastern Ontario.

Postwar Immigration After World War II, Canada experienced another immigration surge. Although this wave was not as large as the great influx around the turn of the twentieth century, it did exert an impact on the nation's ethnic composition. Data from the federal censuses of 1951 and 1961 reveal the trends unfolding during the decade. Canadians with a British Isles origin remained the largest segment of the population but declined from 47.9 percent of the total in 1951 to 43.8 percent in 1961. French Canadians generally maintained their position with figures of 30.8 percent in 1951 and 30.4 percent in 1961. Residents with ethnic ties to other parts of Europe increased from 18.3 percent in 1951 to 22.6 percent in 1961. Within this group, Germans formed the highest percentage of immigrants, followed by Ukrainians, Scandinavians, Dutch, Poles, and Jews.

Among noticeable patterns as the decade progressed was a dramatic jump in numbers of persons coming from southern and eastern Europe, such as Italians, Portuguese, Greeks, and to some extent, Ukrainians and Yugoslavs. These newcomers settled in major metropolitan centers such as Toronto and Montreal and enriched the fabric of life there. Toronto, once a bastion of staid puritanism and Anglo culture, was transforming into a more lively, interesting, and dynamic cosmopolitan center. Although still relatively few in number, Asians were on the increase in the period between the two censuses. Indians and Inuit were only 1.2 percent in 1951, but the Inuit held their numbers, and the First Nations outstripped national population growth throughout the decade.

Socioeconomic and Political Inequalities Following 1945, the phrase "two founding nations" increasingly came into use, partly as a conciliatory gesture to French Canadians. If this acknowledgment of the important role of francophones in the nation's history also implied equality in terms of affluence and power, the facts did not support it. On one hand, Quebec was experiencing a process of steady modernization, urbanization, and economic change that contradicted old stereotypes of the province as a backward, rural, peasant society under the thumb of the clergy. Nonetheless, the Quebeçois still faced inequalities. Statistical studies showed that in spite of the ongoing economic change, French Canadians were under-represented in the higher-earning occupations in proportion to their numbers while English Canadians, who made up a mere 14 percent of the province's total residents, were over-represented in such occupations. French Canadians were gradually moving into more modern jobs but not into the positions that controlled those jobs. Moreover, figures showed that with the passage of time, this comparative disadvantage of French Canadians was actually widening. In 1951, French Canadians were even more under-represented in professional and financial jobs than they were in 1931 and in 1961, they were at a greater occupational disadvantage than in 1941.

Montreal, the largest Canadian city at that time, had long been a bastion of the Anglo financial elite, and their institutions were very prominent there. Native French speakers, who totaled 64 percent of the city's population in 1951, frequently could not find sales clerks in English-owned department stores such as Hudson Bay or Eaton's who would assist them in French.

On the political scene, Quebec's government under Maurice Duplessis and his Union Nationale party made use of traditional French Canadian conservative nationalism. Duplessis was an outspoken critic of strong central governmental powers and championed provincial rights as a means to defend Quebec's unique cultural heritage, language, and institutions.

The socioeconomic positions of other minorities, such as the New Canadians of Europe, were improving. For example, Ukrainians gradually moved away from agriculture, although many (35.3 percent) in 1951 were still in this sector. The number of laborers and unskilled workers had dropped by more than half since 1931, and by the 1950's, more were working in manufacturing and construction. In Winnipeg, where the non-British population of the city was around 60 percent by the end of the 1950's, New Canadians were moving into prestigious occupations such as law and medicine, once the almost exclusive reserves of Anglo Saxons. At the same time, they were gradually relocating out of the ethnic ghettos in the north end. Winnipeg's tradition of discriminating against foreigners was also abating. The political monopoly of the British elite was also broken in 1956, with the election of the city's first non-Anglo-Saxon mayor, Stephan Juba, a Ukrainian who won reelection to many terms.

Responding to Racism Some groups continued to experience racism and blatant discrimination in spite of the assumption of many Canadians that their country was free from prejudice. This was especially true of the so-called visible minorities, such as the indigenous First Nations, African Canadians, and Asian Canadians. Most Canadian provinces enacted legislation prohibiting racial and religious discrimination in employment and housing. However, old racist practices and attitudes were slow to change. African Canadians often found that persistent, strong organizational efforts were necessary to fight for enforcement of their legal rights. Japanese Canadians—many of whom had been victimized during World War II through forced relocation, deprivation of civil rights, and enormous economic loses from sales of their property without consent—finally had their right to vote restored in 1949. However, a Canadian federal judge who considered the matter of compensating members of this group for property losses made a ruling in 1950 that amounted to the inconsequential sum of fifty-two dollars per person.

Canada's indigenous peoples, subjected since the late nineteenth century to a policy of cultural genocide and deprivation of self-rule under the federal government's Indian Act of 1876, received some relief when the act underwent a revision in 1951.

Boarding schools to which Indian children were herded by force to "unlearn" their culture were closed and the indigenous communities were given some control over their own affairs. Paternalism in federal dealings with the First Nations did not cease, however, and the First Nations people continued to struggle with poverty, disease, and other social problems. Nevertheless, the indigenous bands slowly were beginning to organize in defense of their interests. For example, a regional organization, the Federation of Saskatchewan Indians, appeared at the end of the 1950's.

Impact During the 1950's, some significant developments and changes in regard to minorities were beginning to appear in Canada. These new trends would find expression in the years ahead in fuller and more potent manners. Changing patterns in ethnic composition of the population as a result of shifting immigration patterns foreshadowed the arrival in much greater numbers over the next twenty years of southern and eastern Europeans, people from Commonwealth nations in Asia and the Caribbean, and various other developing countries. The nascent organizational activities among the First Nations and black Canadians evident during this decade took off during the militant 1960's. Finally, Quebec's defensive nationalism and rising challenge to Canadian federalism was a prelude to the upsurge of radical militancy in that province during the 1960's and the coming to power of a separatist movement during the 1970's.

Further Reading

Day, Richard J. F. *Multiculturalism and the History of Canadian Diversity.* Toronto: University of Toronto Press, 2000. Traces the evolution of Canadian policy toward ethnic, racial, and religious minorities from colonial times to the present.

Kalbach, Madeline A., and Warren E. Kalbach. "Demographic Overview of Ethnic Origin Groups in Canada." In *Race and Ethnic Relations in Canada*, edited by Peter S. Li. Don Mills, Ont.: Oxford University Press, 1999. Touches on ethnic origins, immigration, population distribution, urbanization, and characteristics of Canada's ethnic groups. Supplemented with useful data and charts for various time periods.

Lupul, Manoly R. *A Heritage in Transition: Essays on the History of Ukrainians in Canada.* Toronto: McClelland & Stewart, 1982. Articles on historical aspects, political participation, and economic status of Ukranian Canadians.

Porter, John. *The Verticle Mosaic: An Analysis of Social Class and Power in Canada.* Toronto: University of Toronto Press, 1973. This well-known study includes information on the relative socioeconomic position of Anglo Canadian elites and ethnic minorities using much data from the 1951 and 1961 federal censuses.

Winks, Robin W. *The Blacks in Canada: A History.* 2d ed. Montreal: McGill-Queen's University Press, 1997. The major study to date on the experience of one of Canada's "visible minorities."

David A. Crain

See also Canadian regionalism; Demographics of Canada; Diefenbaker, John G.; Education in Canada; Immigration to Canada; Indian Act of 1951; Literature in Canada; Native Americans; O'Ree, Willie; Racial discrimination.

■ Miss America pageants

Identification Annual beauty competition for women
Date Begun in 1921

America's oldest beauty pageant, the Miss America pageant is a cultural institution as well as a reflection of women's role in American society. The 1950's saw the pageant reach a mass audience and gain even greater popularity with the advent of televised pageants.

The Miss America pageant was founded in 1921 as means of stretching the Atlantic City, New Jersey, tourist season beyond the traditional close of the season on Labor Day. The first pageant had seven contestants from beach cities along the East Coast and offered a first prize of one hundred dollars. The pageant grew throughout the decade but shut down in 1927, in response to growing charges that it was immoral. However, it resumed in 1933, as Atlantic City business leaders attempted to give the Depression-era economy a boost. In 1935, a talent competition was added. In 1941, Lenora Slaughter became pageant director and brought greater respectability to the contest by offering college scholarships to winners and involving the contestants in war-bond sales.

The Pageant Thrives In 1950, pageant officials decided to postdate the winner's title, and the tradition of selecting a Miss America for the following cal-

Finalists in the September, 1954, pageant that selected the Miss America of 1955. The eventual winner was Lee Meriwether, Miss California (second from the left). (AP/Wide World Photos)

endar year was introduced. In September of 1950, Yolanda Betbeze was crowned Miss America of 1951 and promptly caused an uproar by refusing to model swimsuits, announcing that she was an opera singer, not a pin-up girl. Slaughter supported Betbeze, causing a major sponsor, Catalina Swimwear, to withdraw its support and establish the rival Miss USA and Miss Universe pageants, which were based entirely on contestants' physical appearance and required their contestants to wear the sponsoring companies' swimwear. Meanwhile, Slaughter continued to push for more scholarship money for the Miss America pageant. By 1953, the amount had increased to such an extent that the Miss America organization became the largest scholarship foundation for women in the world.

The pageant became a household name in 1954, when it was televised for the first time, airing live on September 11 to an audience of twenty-seven million viewers, nearly 40 percent of the television viewing audience. The following year, Bert Parks began

a quarter-century tenure as the host of the program. He became a national icon in the process and introduced his trademark song, "There She Is, Miss America." By 1958, the television viewing audience had reached sixty million people, and the telecast was expanded to two full hours. In 1959, the contest was aired for the first time in its entirety and every state in the union was represented.

Impact During the 1950's, most of the country shared the idealized version of American womanhood put forth by the Miss America pageant. The televising of the contest raised it to new heights of popularity and caused a whole generation of young girls to aspire to the title. At the time, it was one of the few ways young women could achieve the American Dream of success. The pageant also embodied the contradictions of the American view of the female role, glorifying both modesty and sexuality and simultaneously promoting both traditional womanhood and independence.

Miss Americas, 1951-1960

Year	Winner	Home state
1951	Yolande Betbeze	Alabama
1952	Colleen Hutchins	Utah
1953	Neva Jane Langley	Georgia
1954	Evelyn Ay	Pennsylvania
1955	Lee Meriwether	California
1956	Sharon Kay Ritchie	Colorado
1957	Marian McKnight	South Carolina
1958	Marilyn Van Derber	Colorado
1959	Mary Ann Mobley	Mississippi
1960	Lynda Lee Mead	Mississippi

Note: There was no Miss America 1950. The first year of the decade marked the beginning of the practice of postdating titles, so in the fall of 1950, that year's winner was crowned "Miss America 1951." Similarly, Miss America 1960 was crowned in 1959.

Further Reading

Banet-Weiser, Sarah. *Most Beautiful Girl in the World: Beauty Pageants and National Identity.* Berkeley: University of California Press, 1999. A cultural analysis of beauty pageants.

Bivans, Ann Marie. *Miss America: In Pursuit of the Crown: The Complete Guide to the Miss America Pageant.* New York: Master Media, 1997. Thoroughly researched history of the pageant with photos.

Mary Virginia Davis

See also American Dream; Barbie dolls; Fashions and clothing; Parker, Suzy; Women and the roots of the feminist movement.

■ Monroe, Marilyn

Identification American film actor and symbol of female glamour

Born June 1, 1926; Los Angeles, California

Died August 5, 1962; Los Angeles, California

Marilyn Monroe's performance in 1953's Gentlemen Prefer Blondes *established her as a successful comedian with a combination of sex appeal and timing. Her* overt sexuality challenged the prudish norms of the 1950's.

Marilyn Monroe took her first screen test in 1946 but made the majority of her films during the 1950's. Out of the twenty-nine films she completed, twenty-four were released in that decade, including *All About Eve* (1950), *Let's Make It Legal* (1951), *Niagara* (1953), *How to Marry a Millionaire* (1953), *River of No Return* (1954), *There's No Business Like Show Business* (1954), *The Seven Year Itch* (1955), *Bus Stop* (1956), and *Some Like It Hot* (1959).

Monroe regarded her acting career seriously. Although her career began with a shaky start during the mid-1940's as a contract actor playing bit parts with little control over her choice of scripts. Through her talent, genuine sex appeal, persistence, professional training, and a magnetic screen presence, she was able to improve her career. By the 1950's, she was given the opportunity to appear in more challenging roles. Monroe received the Henrietta Award for Most Promising Personality of the Year in 1951, *Photoplay*'s award for "fastest rising star" in 1952, and in 1953, the *Redbook* award for Best Young Box Office Personality. In 1953, after her appearance in three successful films, *Niagara, Gentlemen Prefer Blondes*, and *How to Marry a Millionaire*, she became a box office star, and in 1954, she received *Photoplay*'s best-actress-of-the-year award for her roles in these films. Together, the films grossed for Twentieth Century-Fox Studios more than twenty-five million dollars—a huge sum in that era.

Professional Achievements Monroe's biggest break came under the direction of Howard Hawks in the musical comedy, *Gentlemen Prefer Blondes*. Monroe was chosen for this film after receiving rave reviews for her previous successful role in the comedy *Monkey Business* (1952), also directed by Hawks. In *Gentlemen Prefer Blondes*, she played the naïve, sexy nightclub singer, Lorelei Lee. She was able to take novelist Anita Loos's character and breathe her own life into her, radiating complete innocence with a natural sense of timing, making her character wonderfully funny. The film included the first scene ever to be filmed in Cinema Scope, as the polished and sleek Monroe danced and sang "Diamonds Are a Girl's Best Friend" in a strapless, shocking-pink gown. This scene showcased her ability to captivate an audience, and it became one of the most popular scenes in film history. Throughout the film, Monroe achieved the perfect balance of sex and humor, and the film world took notice.

Despite the fact that Monroe's upfront sexuality often clashed with the prudish morals of the 1950's, her films were extremely successful with male and female audience members alike, and in 1954, she was chosen by the Hollywood Foreign Press as the World Film Favorite. Her career as a sex goddess was launched and several more successful films followed. She was picked as best foreign actress of 1958 and received the Crystal Star in France as well. Her most successful film, however, was *Some Like It Hot* (1959), directed by Billy Wilder, for which she won

the Golden Globe Award in 1960 for best actress in a comedy or musical.

Monroe received $100,000 plus 10 percent of the profits for her last films; however, more important to her was that after forming her own Marilyn Monroe Productions, Inc., in 1955, Monroe successfully challenged the Hollywood studio system to gain more control over her film career: She won the right to reject scripts and choose her own directors, to make four films in seven years, and to be free to make one film during that time period for another studio. Her efforts made a major impact on the film industry, especially for the rights of women in the prefeminist era.

During the early 1960's, Monroe appeared in two more films, *Let's Make Love* (1960) and *The Misfits* (1961), which was the last film that she completed. She did not finish her last film, *Something's Got to Give* (1962). In 1962, shortly before her death, she was awarded the Golden Globe for the World's Most Popular Star.

Personal Life On January 14, 1954, Monroe married the baseball icon, Joe DiMaggio. It was the second marriage for both. They divorced on October 4, 1954. She was married again on June 29, 1956, to the Pulitzer Prize-winning playwright Arthur Miller. Miller wrote the film script for *The Misfits*, which starred Monroe and Clark Gable. The couple divorced in January of 1960. Monroe died on August 5, 1962, at the age of thirty-six of an overdose of prescription drugs, leaving an estate worth 1.6 million dollars.

During the filming of The Seven Year Itch *in 1954, Marilyn Monroe stood over a sidewalk grating with an updraft and struck one of the most famous poses in show business history.* (AP/Wide World Photos)

Impact Monroe was one of the most popular film actors of the 1950's and became a cultural icon of the twentieth century. She personified Hollywood glamour and combined alluring sex appeal with an innocence and vulnerability. In subseqent decades, Monroe remained a potent sex goddess in the eyes of many, and in 1995, her picture was featured on a thirty-two-cent U.S. postage stamp as a Legend of Hollywood. She was also voted by *People* magazine in 1999 as the Sexiest Woman of the Twentieth Century.

Further Reading

Baty, S. Paige. *American Monroe: The Making of a Body Politic.* Los Angeles: University of California Press, 1995. Examines the way in which popular icons are made and remade in public consciousness, using Monroe as its primary example.

Clayton, Marie. *Marilyn Monroe: Unseen Archives.* New York: Barnes & Noble, 2003. Archived photographs are used to tell Monroe's biography.

Spoto, Donald. *Marilyn Monroe: The Biography.* Lanham, Md.: Rowman & Littlefield, 2003. A competent and often engaging biography.

Garlena A. Bauer

See also DiMaggio, Joe; Fashions and clothing; Film in the United States; *Gentlemen Prefer Blondes*; House Committee on Un-American Activities; Miller, Arthur; *Playboy*; Women and the roots of the feminist movement.

■ Montgomery bus boycott

The Event Successful mass-based effort to abolish racial segregation in public transportation
Date December 1, 1955, to December 21, 1956

The Montgomery bus boycott signaled a shift from legal battles to nonviolent direct action within the Civil Rights movement. The event precipitated the emergence of Martin Luther King, Jr., as a national leader.

The Montgomery bus boycott began on December 1, 1955, following the arrest of Rosa Parks, a seamstress, for refusing to surrender her seat on a bus to a white man when ordered to do so by the driver. However, the community response to this arrest was built on many years of activism and preparation. Parks was a member of the local branch of the National Association for the Advancement of Colored People (NAACP) headed by E. D. Nixon. She had attended interracial organizing workshops at the Highlander Folk School in Tennessee. Nixon had tried twice in the prior year to get community support for victims of similar bus segregation arrests but failed because of class frictions within the black community. Parks, with her working-class job and respectable middle-class demeanor, was an ideal focus for protest. After she was released on bail, organizing began.

Nixon and a group of women faculty at all-black Alabama State College called for a one-day boycott of city buses on Monday, December 5, followed by a mass meeting at Holt Street Baptist Church. Local ministers Ralph Abernathy, Robert Graetz, and Martin Luther King, Jr., were part of the planning, and a new group called the Montgomery Improvement Association (MIA) was created. King, a minister relatively unknown in the community, was chosen as president. At the mass meeting, he delivered an electrifying speech that united the community behind a continued boycott. As Nixon often expressed it later: "We picked a number out of a hat and got Moses."

MIA demands initially called only for greater courtesy from drivers, the hiring of black drivers on predominantly black routes, and a clarification of segregated seating arrangements; it did not urge total desegregation. However, negotiations with the city and the privately owned bus company were unsuccessful. In turn, to facilitate an ongoing boycott, carpooling arrangements used cars made available by middle-class supporters. By the beginning of 1956, the carpool system was strained but still working, and the bus service told city commissioners that it was facing bankruptcy.

Opposition Escalates In January, 1956, Montgomery police commissioner Clyde Sellers attended a rally of the local White Citizens' Council and assured a crowd of twelve hundred people that he would never trade his "Southern birthright for a few hundred Negro votes." He joined the council, as did Montgomery's two other city commissioners. Sellers maintained that the boycott was succeeding only because of the intimidation of what he called "Negro goon squads." On January 22, the *Montgomery Advertiser* carried a false story planted by Sellers saying that the boycott had been settled. However, King received advance notice of the story from Minneapolis reporter Carl T. Rowan and saw to it that the story was refuted in every pulpit in the community. The boycott continued.

Fred Gray, a young black lawyer who had been involved in the Parks case from the beginning, announced an MIA-backed suit in the federal courts challenging the legality of bus segregation. Montgomery police began harassing and arresting carpool drivers; King was arrested for alleged speeding on January 26, but he was released after a large crowd of his supporters gathered at the jail. The following Tuesday, King's house was bombed. On February 1, a bomb exploded in Nixon's yard. Gray's draft deferment was revoked, and a grand jury charged him with barratry—a legal term for the persistent incitement of litigation, a charge often leveled against civil rights lawyers during the 1950's.

Boycott leaders were arrested in late February, and many others arrived at the sheriff's office voluntarily. They created such a joyous atmosphere that the sheriff had to shout "This is no vaudeville show!" King was arrested soon after, and his four-day trial in March was covered by reporters from across the United States and the world. He was sentenced to a $500 fine but vowed that the boycott would continue.

The NAACP, which had long favored court litigation over mass action, announced that its legal staff would handle the MIA's appeals and the federal bus desegregation suit. On June 1, Alabama attorney general John Patterson obtained a court order banning most NAACP activities in the state on the grounds that the organization was "organizing, supporting, and financing an illegal boycott by Negro residents of Montgomery."

Victory Despite Setbacks On June 4, a panel of three federal judges ruled in favor of the MIA's suit against bus segregation. Although segregation laws would remain in place until the U.S. Supreme Court ruled on the city and state appeal, victory became likely. The MIA raised $120,000 and safely placed it in banks outside Alabama. New station wagons purchased by the MIA eased the burden on private car owners. King addressed the NAACP convention in San Francisco and testified before the platform committee of the Democratic convention.

On August 25, dynamite exploded in the front yard of Robert Graetz, a white Lutheran minister serving a black congregation who was a strong boycott supporter. The mayor of Montgomery accused him of bombing his own house. The city petitioned a state court for an injunction banning the MIA carpool. On November 13, the injunction was granted, and the state imposed a fifteen-thousand-dollar fine on the MIA. That same day, the U.S. Supreme Court affirmed the lower court judgement that Montgomery bus segregation was unconstitutional. Boycott supporters continued to walk until notice was served on city officials on December 20, 1956. King

boarded a city bus the next day. Reporters took his picture in a front seat next to the white community leader Glenn Smiley. Shotgun snipers fired at integrated buses, and there were more bombings, but the violence gradually diminished. In January, 1957, King met with other leaders in Atlanta to form the Southern Christian Leadership Conference to promote the lessons of the boycott.

Impact The success of the boycott directed international attention to the Civil Rights movement and to Martin Luther King, Jr.; inspired similar movements in hundreds of communities; and established the efficacy of nonviolent direct action as an American political tool.

Further Reading
Branch, Taylor. "First Trombone" and "The Montgomery Bus Boycott" in *Parting the Waters: America in the King Years, 1954-1963*. New York: Simon & Schuster, 1988. An excellent account of the boycott and its origins.

Burns, Stewart, ed. *Daybreak of Freedom: The Montgomery Bus Boycott*. Chapel Hill: University of North Carolina Press, 2003. Uses original source documents to chronicle the boycott and discuss its impact.

Fields, Uriah J. *Inside the Montgomery Bus Boycott: My Personal Story*. New York: America House, 2002. An account of the boycott told by the original secretary to the Montgomery Improvement Association.

Leventhal, Willy S., ed. *The Children Coming On . . . A Retrospective of the Montgomery Bus Boycott*. Montgomery, Ala.: Black Belt Press, 1998. Participants of the boycott reminisce about their experiences.

J. Quinn Brisben

See also Civil Rights movement; King, Martin Luther, Jr.; National Association for the Advancement of Colored People; *National Association for the Advancement of Colored People v. Alabama*; Parks, Rosa; Racial discrimination; Rowan, Carl T.; Southern Christian Leadership Conference; White Citizens' Councils.

■ Morse, Wayne

Identification U.S. senator from Oregon (1945-1969)

Born October 20, 1900; near Madison, Wisconsin

Died July 22, 1974; Portland, Oregon

While serving in the U.S. Senate during the 1950's, Wayne Morse was a leader on a number of issues, including civil rights, and a vocal opponent of Senator Joseph McCarthy's communist witch-hunts.

Wayne Morse graduated from the University of Wisconsin in 1923 and then studied law at the University of Minnesota and Columbia University. In 1929, he became an assistant professor of law at the University of Oregon. He gained recognition as an arbitrator in labor disputes and served on the National War Labor Board from 1942 until 1944.

Morse was elected to the United States Senate in 1944. A liberal Republican, he became a target of Senator Joseph McCarthy's attack on communists in the federal government. Morse's popularity among Oregon voters allowed him to survive McCarthy's claims that he was a communist. He was one of six senators who signed the 1950 Declaration of Conscience, which attacked McCarthy's abuse of power. He also supported civil rights for African Americans, working particularly to end segregation in Washington, D.C.

In 1952, Morse refused to support Dwight D. Eisenhower, the Republican presidential nominee, in order to protest the selection of conservative California senator Richard M. Nixon as Eisenhower's running mate. Morse left the Republican Party in 1953, becoming an independent. He was reelected to the Senate in 1956 as a Democrat, the only senator at the time to change parties and be reelected.

Impact As a senator, Morse exemplified the term "political maverick," opposing the views of the president of his party and his party's majority in the Senate, while promising to serve no master but his own conscience.

Further Reading

Drukman, Mason. *Wayne Morse: A Political Biography.* Portland: Oregon Historical Society Press, 1997. This biography is a detailed examination of the personal and public aspects of Morse's life.

Wilkins, Lee. *Wayne Morse: A Bio-bibliography.* Westport, Conn.: Greenwood Press, 1985. Includes a biography as well as a bibliography of works by and about Morse.

John David Rausch, Jr.

See also Civil Rights movement; Cold War; Eisenhower, Dwight D.; Elections in the United States, 1952; Liberalism in U.S. politics; McCarthy, Joseph; Tidelands oil controversy.

■ Motels

Definition Public lodging establishments, usually on or near busy thoroughfares, catering primarily to automobile travelers

Economic prosperity, improvements in the automobile, and new highway construction created a boom in interstate travel during the 1950's, resulting in increased demand for inexpensive, standardized roadside lodging.

At the beginning of the 1950's, the American motel industry was still in its infancy. The development of highway systems during the early twentieth century brought about demand for overnight lodging to accommodate long-distance automobile travelers; however, by mid-century, finding suitable lodging was still a difficult task for motorists. Many urban hotels had deteriorated or were located in neighborhoods that were dangerous or inconvenient to travelers on the new highway systems, while the motor courts and motels that dotted the landscape around the new roads often varied in cleanliness, room size, and amenities offered as a result of a lack of industry standards. Motel patronage also posed special problems for families; motels typically charged extra for children and often were located inconveniently to restaurants and family-friendly recreational facilities. Some loose federations of motels, such as Travelodge and Best Western, existed prior to the 1950's, but they were primarily referral networks with no control over the quality of their member motels.

Birth of Motel Chains In the summer of 1951, real estate developer Kemmons Wilson and his family embarked on a vacation from their hometown of Memphis, Tennessee, to Washington, D.C. Astonished by the inconsistent quality of the motels he encountered and annoyed at surcharges that often doubled the price of a stay, Wilson resolved to establish his own chain of motels. Each of these "Holiday Inns" (named for a popular 1942 movie) would offer standard-sized rooms with air conditioning and television, restaurants, and swimming pools. The motels would be designed and operated with families in mind; children, he insisted, would stay for free.

The first Holiday Inn opened in Memphis on August 1, 1952. Although the motel was an instant success, Wilson initially struggled in his efforts to sell Holiday Inn franchises. However, business boomed during the late 1950's as the growth of the interstate highway system created even greater demand for construction of new motels. Having incorporated his business, Wilson was able to secure enough capital to purchase prime locations adjacent to the newly constructed highways for his Holiday Inns. He developed a reputation for his ability to choose sites for new motels; he insisted that each site be highly visible and located on the side of the highway heading into a city, so that incoming motorists would not have to make left turns. His system was so effective that many of his competitors simply opened new motels next to freshly constructed Holiday Inns. By the end of the decade, Wilson had nearly attained his initial goal of opening four hundred Holiday Inns nationwide.

Impact The success of Holiday Inns inspired a number of competitors to enter the burgeoning motel industry during the 1950's. In 1954, the first Ramada Inn opened in Flagstaff, Arizona, and the first Howard Johnson's Motor Lodge began operation in Savannah, Georgia. These chains and others enjoyed tremendous advantages over private motel owners, many of whom lacked the capital to move their operations to the new highways. As a result, business steadily dwindled for the old colorful roadside motels, forcing many to close. It was, perhaps, symbolic of the decline of independent motels that the off-highway Bates Motel was the setting of the 1960 horror classic *Psycho*.

Further Reading

Halberstam, David. *The Fifties*. New York: Villard Books, 1993. Discusses in detail the economic and cultural trends that led to the development of motel chains during the 1950's, including an entire chapter on Kemmons Wilson and the creation of Holiday Inns.

Jakle, J. A., et al. *The Motel in America*. Baltimore: Johns Hopkins University Press, 1996. A comprehensive history of the motel industry, with emphasis upon the impact of motels on American popular culture.

A Florida motel in 1952. (Hulton Archive | by Getty Images)

Witzel, Michael K. *The American Motel.* Osceola, Wis.: Motorbooks International, 2000. A popular history of the American motel. Contains numerous photos and illustrations as well as detailed narrative of the early history of the motel industry.

Michael H. Burchett

See also Affluence and the new consumerism; Architecture; Automobiles and auto manufacturing; Holiday Inn; Interstate highway system.

■ Motherwell, Robert

Identification American artist
Born January 24, 1915; Aberdeen, Washington
Died July 16, 1991; Provincetown, Massachusetts

Robert Motherwell joined with other abstract expressionist artists during the 1950's to create works of art that emphasized the process of painting as well as emotional truth and authenticity of feeling. As a group, the abstract expressionists shifted the focus of the international art world to a wholly new form unique to American artists.

Although Robert Motherwell studied literature, psychology, and philosophy, he decided to become an artist after seeing modern paintings on a trip to France during the late 1930's. During the following decade, he befriended American artists Jackson Pollock and Lee Krasner and moved to New York City, where he became a key member of the new artistic movement known as abstract expressionism.

Forsaking realistic imagery, Motherwell and his fellow abstract expressionists drew upon their unconscious minds through spontaneous painted gestures, making their paintings actual documents of what they came to think of as spiritual quests.

In 1949, Motherwell began what would become his most famous series of paintings, *Elegies to the Spanish Republic.* Completed more than two decades later and including more than 140 large, predominantly black-and-white works, the series cataloged Motherwell's reaction to the Spanish Civil War of 1936-1939, in which Spain's elected government had been overthrown. His more intimate series *Je T'aime* (1954-1958) chronicled the failure of his second marriage.

Although Motherwell continued to produce paintings and prints, only his late series *The Hollow Men* matched the intensity of his earlier works.

Impact Through his paintings and writings, Motherwell helped shift the attention of art critics, collectors, dealers, and fellow artists from France to the United States, helping to establish abstract expressionism as a form unique to America.

Further Reading
Caws, Mary Ann, and Robert Motherwell. *Robert Motherwell: What Art Holds.* New York: Columbia University Press, 1996. An inventive biography featuring interviews with Motherwell and a number of reproductions.
Motherwell, Robert. *The Collected Writings of Robert Motherwell.* New York: Oxford University Press, 1992. Essays, interview, and letters illuminating Motherwell's formative influences and his artistic philosophy.

Grove Koger

See also Abstract expressionism; Art movements; de Kooning, Willem; Famous Artists School; Guggenheim Museum; Kline, Franz; Pollock, Jackson; Rauschenberg, Robert.

■ Motorcycle gangs

Definition Violent clubs of male motorcycle riders

During the 1950's, the violence and structured organization of motorcycle gangs were not well understood by the general public or law-enforcement agencies, which meant that the gangs were able to expand exponentially late in the decade.

The first working motorcycle appeared during the 1880's, but American motorcycle manufacturing did not begin until the early twentieth century with the establishment of the Harley-Davidson Motor Company and Hendee Manufacturing (developer of the Indian motorcycle). Both companies initially prospered, and in 1908, Harley-Davidsons were purchased by the Detroit Police Department, with other police units soon following Detroit's lead.

During World Wars I and II, motorcycles were supplied to the military, and soldiers were taught to ride and repair them. After each war, returned servicemen often purchased their own motorcycles and formed clubs. Some of these motorcycle clubs served benign social functions, but others were "outlaw clubs," identified by fear-inspiring names such as the "Booze Fighters" and "Satan's Sinners."

Club gatherings or rallies had been a feature of the motorcycle club scene since the 1930's, but a major change in public perception of these gatherings occurred after the Hollister Riot of 1947. This motorcycle club invasion of a small California town was later dramatized in the move *The Wild One* (1954), starring Marlon Brando. Brando's character was typical of media and Hollywood views that motorcycle gangs were merely another form of counterculture movements.

During the 1950's, there generally was little understanding of the violent paramilitary underpinnings to many of these groups, and it was not until the mid-1960's when the general public became educated about the antisocial brutality of motorcycle gang members. In 1964, an alleged gang rape of two California teenagers by cyclists was extensively reported in the media. The following year, Thomas Lynch, the attorney general of California, published a damming report documenting the activities of the Hells Angels.

Hells Angels Several notorious motorcycle gangs had their genesis during the 1950's, but the Hells Angels was the most infamous of these groups. Various independent clubs, each of them operating under the name Hells Angels, established themselves in California during the 1940's. The name allegedly was borrowed from the military and the first club members most likely were retired military personnel. Ralph "Sonny" Barger, for example, who was responsible for unifying and organizing Hells Angels, was discharged from the military during the mid-1950's. By 1957, in company with several like-minded young men, he formed Hells Angels Oakland. A year later, Barger was the chapter president and began to establish dominancy over Hells Angels Berdoo (the San Bernadino chapter, formerly known as the Booze Fighters, established in 1948), Hells Angels Frisco (established in 1954), and Hells Angels North Sacramento (which collapsed under pressure in 1957).

Impact The dangerous nature of motorcycle gangs was not altogether appreciated during the 1950's, which meant that law enforcement was slow to infiltrate the gangs. As a result, gangs were able to establish their dominance in organized crime. In later years, they became extremely powerful in North America and around the world.

Further Reading

Lavigne, Yves. *Hells Angels: Into the Abyss.* Toronto: HarperCollins, 1996. This publication documents law-breaking activities of motorcycle gangs during the late twentieth century with some attention paid to events of the 1950's.

Osgerby, Bill. "Sleazy Rider: Exploitation, 'Otherness,' and Transgression in the 1960's Biker Movie." *Journal of Popular Film and Television* 31, no. 3 (2003): 98-108. An account of 1960's motorcycle gang films, with some references to earlier films and gang history.

Wood, John. "Hell's Angels and the Illusion of the Counterculture." *The Journal of Popular Culture* 37, no. 2 (2003): 336-351. A discussion of media fascination with and misinterpretation of Hells Angels' practices.

Susan J. Wurtzburg

See also Brando, Marlon; Film in the United States; Organized crime; Veterans organizations; *Wild One, The.*

■ Mr. Potato Head

Identification Toy using a potato as a head
Manufacturer Hasbro, Inc.
Date Entered the market in 1952

Mr. Potato Head was the first toy to be advertised on network television and the first major toy success for Hasbro, Inc.

The original Mr. Potato Head was created by George Lerner and did not have a body—buyers had to supply their own potatoes. It consisted of plastic pieces such as eyes, ears, noses, hats, and mustaches. The pieces had push pins that could be stuck into any piece of fruit or vegetable to create an endless variety of funny faces. Lerner sold his idea to Hassenfeld Brothers (later known as Hasbro), and on May 1, 1952, in Pawtucket, Rhode Island, Mr. Potato Head was born.

America was introduced to Mr. Potato Head through a television advertisement stating that he was the most wonderful friend a child could have. Mr. Potato Head was joined by Mrs. Potato Head in 1953, and they quickly became one of the hottest couples of the 1950's. Mirroring the times, they became conspicuous consumers with their own convertible, boat, trailer, airplane, and locomotive. In 1964, a hard plastic potato "body" was included with the set to replace the need for a real potato.

Impact By using the new medium of television, Mr. Potato Head became a cultural icon of the 1950's. It secured Hasbro's place as a major player in the toy industry. The toy has served as an ambassador for many causes, including antismoking, physical fitness, and voting. In 1995, he had a starring role in the movie *Toy Story*, and by 2003, more than fifty million Mr. Potato Heads had been sold.

Further Reading

King, Gil. *Mr. Potato Head: Celebrating Fifty Years of One Sweet Potato.* Philadelphia: Running Press, 2002. A small book about the life of Mr. Potato Head.

Wulffson, Don L. *Toys! Amazing Stories Behind Some Great Inventions.* New York: Henry Holt, 2000. Includes a chapter titled "Mr. Potato Head."

Joy M. Gambill

See also Advertising; Affluence and the new consumerism; Baby boomers; Fads; Silly Putty; Television in the United States.

■ Murrow, Edward R.

Identification American news broadcaster
Born April 25, 1908; Greensboro, North Carolina
Died April 27, 1965; Pawling, New York

Edward R. Murrow pioneered the development of broadcast news and documentary production.

Raised in Washington State, Edward R. Murrow entered broadcasting in 1935 when he was hired by CBS. In 1937, he was sent to London to organize the radio network's European news operation. As World War II began, Murrow was already a premier correspondent. He recruited a team of reporters stationed across Europe, and "Murrow's Boys" became widely recognized for their performances and professionalism.

Following the war, Murrow returned to the states and assumed a prominent position in CBS's television news division. Through the 1950's, he hosted two influential programs. *See It Now* featured hard-hitting documentaries on often controversial subjects, as when Murrow investigated Senator Joseph McCarthy in 1953. *Person to Person* was a more relaxed interview program that took CBS cameras into the homes of politicians, actors, scientists, and other celebrities as Murrow posed questions from his studio easy chair.

Murrow's style was by turns inspirational and conversational, which contributed to his appeal even when addressing complex or contentious subjects.

Edward R. Murrow, sitting next to a picture of actor Marilyn Monroe, who was to be the subject of one of his Person to Person *interview programs in 1955.* (Hulton Archive | by Getty Images)

Disillusioned by television's declining commitment to the high standards he espoused, Murrow left CBS in 1961 to head the U.S. Information Agency.

Impact Murrow set a standard for journalistic integrity in broadcasting that remained a benchmark in the profession. He trained, or provided an example for, most of the first generation of television news people who dominated the airwaves during the 1950's and in many cases, beyond.

Further Reading

Cloud, Stanley, and Lynn Olsen. *The Murrow Boys: Pioneers on the Front Lines of Broadcast Journalism.* New York: Houghton Mifflin, 1996. Addresses the influence of Murrow and those he recruited on broadcast news through the rise of television during the 1950's.

Sperber, A. M. *Murrow: His Life and Times.* New York: Freundlich Books, 1986. A comprehensive biography of Murrow.

John C. Hajduk

See also Army-McCarthy hearings; Communications in the United States; McCarthy, Joseph; Radio; Television in the United States; United States Information Agency.

■ Music

During the 1950's, popular music and the music industry in general continued its evolution from an artist-oriented, performance-based medium to a more commercial, producer-driven product. New technology and changes within the music industry paved the way for country, jazz, and rhythm and blues to emerge from the nightclubs and concert halls and reach wider audiences. As interest in the new styles of music grew, hybrids emerged in the form of rockabilly, doo-wop, and ultimately, rock and roll.

Many of the significant changes that occurred in the music industry during the 1950's had roots in the previous decade. Traditional big band music was already on the way out. Part of the decline was due to economics; concert halls and other venues realized that it was cheaper to hire a small band than an entire orchestra. A 1942-1943 strike by the American Federation of Musicians over royalties forced record companies to turn to the only nonunion members of the bands—the singers. Focus shifted from the stage to the recording studio, and musical decisions that had been up to the bandleaders and musicians now fell to record company executives, specifically, the Artists and Repertoire (A&R) representatives. The most notable of these was Mitch Miller, who became head of the A&R department at Columbia Records in 1950. A musician in his own right, Mitchell had an approach to recording that emphasized production rather than performance and influenced such later greats as Phil Spector and Berry Gordy, Jr.

At the start of the 1950's, popular music reflected the upbeat mood of the post-World War II era. It was happy music for the middle class, and artists such as Pat Boone, Frank Sinatra, and Mantovani dominated the airwaves. Musical genres fell into three classifications: country (also called country-western, or "hillbilly music"), rhythm and blues (R&B, also called "race music" or "Negro music"), and the more mainstream "popular" music. Popular music dominated the airwaves, record sales, and concert venues in a still-segregated society.

The Publishing Companies A dispute between the two major songwriting publishing companies, the American Society of Composers and Publishers (ASCAP) and Broadcast Music Incorporated (BMI), brought significant change to the musical landscape during the 1940's and early 1950's. ASCAP, formed in 1914, was the more powerful of the two entities and licensed most of the popular music created by professional songwriters. Recorded music had to be licensed for radio airplay, with established fees based on stations' advertising revenue. ASCAP oversaw the collection of royalties for each time a licensed song was performed. As prerecorded music became more popular, radio stations balked at paying higher royalties because they felt they were providing free publicity for the artists. BMI was formed in late 1939, in part to give radio stations an alternative source of music. With its focus on singer-songwriters who performed their own material, BMI increased exposure for artists and music previously unknown by mainstream listeners.

When ASCAP instituted a 100 percent increase in royalty fees, many radio stations responded by refusing to play its music. The BMI artists benefited with increased airtime and higher record sales for songs that would otherwise not have been played on the radio. This led to the increase visibility of jazz, country, and R&B and later, the burgeoning genre known as rock and roll.

The Labels In 1945, the major American record labels were Decca, RCA, Capitol, Metro-Goldwyn-Mayer, Mercury, and Columbia, known collectively as "the Big Six." The invention of magnetic tape recording led to a decrease in the cost of making records and the emergence of smaller studios. By the early 1950's, there were more than four hundred labels. The smaller labels were more open to new artists and genres, and which gave country, R&B, jazz, and rock-and-roll musicians the chance to get into the studio and onto the airwaves. Three of the most influential of the new labels were Sun, Atlantic, and Chess.

Recording pioneer Sam Phillips opened the Memphis Recording Service in 1950. His motto was "We record anything, anywhere, anytime." The Memphis Recording Service was one of the first places African American performers could go to record their songs. Demos by legendary blues artists such as Muddy Waters and Howlin' Wolf were created and sold to independent labels across the country. Phillips used the proceeds from these recordings to establish his own label, Sun Records, in 1953. Phillips and Sun Records would go on to launch the careers of Jerry Lee Lewis, Johnny Cash, B. B. King, and Elvis Presley, and produced more rock-and-roll records than any other label of the period.

In 1947, Ahmet Ertegun and Herb Abramson founded Atlantic Records in New York City. Ertegun orchestrated a switch from jazz to R&B after a trip to the American South. After touring nightclubs in many cities, he realized his smooth urban jazz was not selling because the young people could not dance to it. A hands-on executive, Ertegun produced or coproduced most of the songs released on his new label. Atlantic was also one of the first of the independent labels to provide a serious challenge to the Big Six for airplay and would become home to such legendary R&B performers as Ray Charles, Lavern Baker, and the Drifters.

Like Sun and Atlantic, Chess Records also provided African American artists the chance to get into the studio. Chicago nightclub owners Leonard and Phil Chess bought shares in Aristocrat Records in 1947. By 1950, the label was renamed after the brothers and was releasing records by such blues legends as Willie Dixon, Muddy Waters, and slide guitarist Robert Nighthawk. Through the first part of the decade, the Chess brothers continued to record and give exposure to many blues artists but knew they needed something different if they were to cross over into mainstream recording. It was Muddy Waters who would solve the problem by bringing a young Chuck Berry to meet Leonard Chess in 1955.

Chuck Berry proved to be the Atlantic Records "breakthrough" artist—one of the first African American performers to cross over to mainstream listeners when his song "Maybellene" reached number 5 on the *Billboard* charts. Berry would go on to have many singles reach the pop and R&B charts simultaneously: "Johnny B. Goode," "Sweet Little Sixteen," and "Almost Grown."

Radio Format Changes Radio formats changed as drama- and comedy-format programs migrated to television, and stations turned to prerecorded music to fill airtime. The first all-transistor radio became available in 1955, replacing the expensive console radios, and music suddenly became portable. People who had previously been unable to afford a radio could now own one at a relatively inexpensive price. At the same time, automakers began offering AM radios as standard equipment in new cars, and by the end of the decade, FM radio was becoming available on the luxury models.

By 1951, radio stations began to specialize in particular forms of music. That year, Todd Storz and Bill Stewart created the concept known as Top 40 for an Omaha, Nebraska, radio station. This format repeated the same forty songs throughout the day, imitating the way patrons utilized jukeboxes in diners and nightclubs. By 1957, the most popular disc jockeys (DJs) were receiving up to seventy-five new records per week. This led to accusations that DJs were being paid to play particular records, and the subsequent payola scandals of the 1960's.

Music and Race During the first part of the century, many African Americans from the South moved to northern cities such as Chicago and Detroit to take advantage of an increase in industrial jobs. By the 1950's, the average wage for African Americans was four times higher than it had been during the previous decade. With this newfound prosperity came disposable income, and a new market segment for the music industry was born.

Before 1954, African American audiences typically listened to white artists, but white audiences seldom listened to African American performers. Artists such as Johnny Mathis and Nat King Cole were the exceptions. Both had broken the color barrier, but the songs they recorded were the same safe, homogenized popular music being performed by their white counterparts. Nat King Cole would ultimately come under fire during the mid-1950's when he declared himself outside the Civil Rights movement and continued to play "whites-only" venues in the South. Stung by this criticism, he later joined the National Association for the Advancement of Colored People (NAACP) and participated in the boycott of segregated venues.

Radio station WDIA in Memphis, Tennessee, was the first U.S. radio station to switch to an "all-R&B" play list. This station also featured the first African American announcer, Nat D. Williams, a former schoolteacher. Other stations quickly followed suit, and by the mid-1950's, there were twenty-one stations with similar formats. In addition, hundreds of stations across the country started devoting regular airtime to programs featuring R&B music.

R&B also gave many white teenagers their first exposure to African American culture. Music stores in white neighborhoods did not stock R&B, so white fans began patronizing African American-owned record stores and nightclubs. Segregationists believed that R&B music would lead to race mixing and miscegenation and that exposing white teenagers to "Negro music" could result only in immorality and juvenile delinquency. There was concern in the African American community as well, but for a different reason. Much of the early blues music had an earthy quality to it, and civil rights leaders feared that the white audiences would look at sly, suggestive songs such as "Work With Me, Annie," by Hank Ballard and the Midnighters, and the Dominoes' "Sixty Minute Man" and think that a preoccupation with sex and good times was a key to African American culture.

Backlash against R&B's explicit lyrics and sexually charged performances increased, and by 1954, artists and record companies voluntarily began toning down the suggestive nature of their music. It was a matter of self-preservation; in order to continue to make inroads into the previously white-dominated markets, the music and performances had to resemble more closely those of their white counterparts.

Ultimately, R&B's newfound success proved to be a mixed blessing for African American performers and songwriters. On one hand, their music was finally crossing the color lines, and they were getting recording contracts and creating hit songs. On the other hand, many white artists and producers were taking advantage of the African American cultural heritage by taking R&B songs, stripping away the song's "soul" by re-recording them, and as the songs climbed record charts, overshadowing the original recordings and their artists.

Crossover and Cover Artists During the early days of the music industry, there was little mixing among the genres. For example, country music artists recorded country music songs, which were purchased by country music fans. Popular music arguably had an assembly line feel to it. Songwriters created the music as part of a "stable" of talent, which was often attached to the major record labels. The completed songs were turned over to the label A&R representatives, who in turn, gave them to the most suitable recording artists. The artists, also under contact to the recording label, then recorded the songs, often without being asked their opinions. The singers seldom wrote their own songs but rather performed "interpretations" of songs written by professional songwriters.

Columbia's Mitch Miller is credited with establishing the first crossover artists. Miller arranged for the popular artists on his label to cover songs from other genres. For example, Frankie Laine released a cover version of the theme song to the film *High Noon* (1952), beating country artist Tex Ritter (who had recorded it for the film released in 1952) to the punch and garnering a top-five single in the process. Tony Bennett and Jo Stafford covered the country songs "Cold, Cold Heart" and "Jambalaya" respectively, and the crossover artist was born.

Similar cross-pollination occurred between popular music and R&B. African American R&B artists were recording and selling but could not match the sales numbers emanating from white pop artists' covers of their songs. For example, two of Little Richard's staple tunes, "Tutti Frutti" and "Long Tall Sally," were first made popular by Pat Boone, and a subsequent Boone cover of "Ain't That a Shame" outsold Fats Domino's original version.

Jazz The early big band music of the 1930's and 1940's was divided into two styles: "sweet," typified by Glenn Miller and Guy Lombardo, which was a safer, less improvisational, sound; and "swing" or "hot," which featured hard-driving rhythms and solo improvisation from artists such as Count Basie and Duke Ellington. It was from this tradition that "bop" or "be-bop" evolved. During the after-hour jam sessions in the nightclubs, soloists would abandon the melody and improvise based on the chord structure. Famous names from this genre included Charlie Parker and John Birks "Dizzy" Gillespie.

Two new types of jazz music emerged during the 1950's. One was the evolution of be-bop, the other, a reaction to it. "Hard bop" (also known as post-bop, funky jazz, and soul jazz) was played by pianist Horace Silver, tenor saxophonist Cannonball Adderly, drummer and bandleader Art Blakey, and trumpeter Clifford Brown. Hard bop retained the driving qualities of traditional bebop but mixed it with other genres such as funk, gospel, and blues. Drummers were no longer "just keeping time"; their roles within the bands grew to the more "conversational" style used by other musicians.

At the same time, Miles Davis and arranger Gil Evans established a band whose music had a more or-

Jazz pianist Count Basie in 1950. (AP/Wide World Photos)

chestral sound. This heralded the "cool" style of jazz (also known as "West Coast jazz"), in which the harsh edges of bop were softened and the arrangements became important once again. Davis himself was a controversial figure, and his music was frequently overshadowed by his extravagant lifestyle. Other important artists included trumpeter Chet Baker, baritone saxophonist Gerry Mulligan, and tenor saxophonist Stan Getz.

When jazz musician Dave Brubeck appeared on the cover of *Time* magazine in 1954, it signaled that jazz was reaching the mainstream. However, his appearance created controversy because the magazine chose a white artist to be the first jazz musician to appear on its cover. Brubeck himself claimed to be embarrassed by the honor, because so many of the genre's founders were African Americans.

Folk Music American folk music was born in the Great Depression. By the 1950's, folk songs from that era were giving way to protest music. Some groups adapted traditional songs, while others strove to re-create the traditional sounds and stay true to the original music. Nostalgia was one of folk music's draws. It also provided a contrast to rock and roll and big bands. However, whereas folk music originally sprung from rural areas, the newer folk sounds were emerging from college campuses.

Throughout the 1940's and early 1950's, much of folk music was tainted by the specter of communism. The Almanac Singers were an important folk group during the early 1940's and included singers Pete Seeger and Woody Guthrie, two artists who would continue to influence the genre for several decades. The Almanac Singers were forced to disband in 1943, in part as a result of their connections with leftist political organizations and the American Communist Party.

Another controversial folk music group was the Weavers, which consisted of Lee Hays, Pete Seeger, Ronnie Gilbert, and Fred Hellerman. The Weavers formed in 1949 and popularized folk music, creating the hits "Tzena Tzena Tzena," "Goodnight Irene" (a cover of Leadbelly's song), "So Long (It's Been Good to Know Ya)" written by Guthrie, and "On Top of Old Smokey." Because of their alleged communist ties, this group was also forced to disband during the early 1950's, but reunited in 1955 with a successful concert at Carnegie Hall.

Folk music did not find broad popular success until the end of the decade with Harry Belafonte's "Jamaica Farewell," the Tarriers' "Banana Boat Song" (also covered by Belafonte), and the widely popular "Tom Dooley" by the Kingston Trio. However, it would not be until the 1960's that folk music would finally move into the true mainstream.

Country Country-western music got its start during the early part of the twentieth century in the rural southern United States, evolving from the musical traditions of immigrants from Ireland, Scotland, and England. As the century progressed, these traditions gave rise to string-based dance music of "western swing;" the highs and lows of steel guitar "honky-tonk," and "hillbilly boogie," which was honky-tonk with a dance beat. Popular artists of the time included Jimmie Rodgers and the Carter Family, who could be heard by country music fans during broadcasts from the Grand Ole Opry, which had been carried by WSN in Nashville, Tennessee, since 1925.

When record companies were looking for the next big thing to replace big band music, country music was an alternative. Once written off as "hillbilly music," the genre required songwriters such as Hank Williams to bring it to popularity. Tony Bennett reluctantly recorded Williams's "Cold, Cold Heart" in 1951, bringing the country legend's music to a whole new audience. Williams only enjoyed four years of success; his drinking and erratic lifestyle led to his death on New Year's Day, 1953, when he was found dead in the back of a car. The last song he released was "I'll Never Get Out of This World Alive."

As the color and genre lines began to blur during the 1950's, country music moved more toward the mainstream, incorporating pop production techniques that smoothed out the traditional "hillbilly" sound. Nashville became known as "Music City, USA," and the "Nashville Sound" evolved as a way to bring country music to a larger audience. Musician Chet Atkins (who was also the head of RCA Records Country division) created a smooth commercial sound, which had its roots in the country music tradition but without the rough edges of honky-tonk music. Patsy Cline, Jim Reeves, and Conway Twitty were some of the important artists that emerged from this tradition.

Rhythm and Blues Like country music, R&B also emerged from the southern part of the United States. A blending of gospel and blues, R&B featured the blues narrative style melded with gospel's hand clapping and call-and-response style. W. C. Handy and Robert Johnson were important progenitors. Subgenres emerging from R&B included the percussive, piano-based "boogie-woogie"; "blues shouters," or singers who called out the lyrics in order to be heard over the band; and up-tempo, horn-driven "jump blues."

Chicago-style blues emerged during the 1940's and 1950's, when northern musicians took the southern sounds of their Delta forbearers, amplified them, then added drums, bass, and keyboards for a fuller sound. "(I'm Your) Hoochie Coochie Man," written by Willy Dixon and recorded by Muddy Waters, was a prime example of Chicago blues. By the end of the decade, a subgenre known as West Side blues had emerged, which was simply Chicago blues with a horn section.

R&B played such an important role in the birth of rock and roll that it is difficult to say where one genre

ends and the other begins. A distinction along color lines might be easy to make, and for a long time, record companies, radio stations, and the listeners themselves did just that. *Billboard* magazine began using the term "R&B" in 1949, though what it described varied from region to region. For some experts, R&B is what emerged during the mid- to late 1950's, when the early blues artists began to tone down the rough edges and sexual content of their music. It was similar to "jump blues" but with the emphasis on the arrangement as opposed to improvisation.

Doo-wop also emerged from this tradition during the mid-1950's, featuring vocal-based harmonies, in which the sound was more important than the words. In most cases, the voices were the instruments, and doo-wop groups consisted of a lead vocalist, backed by a first tenor or "falsetto," a second tenor, a baritone, and a bass. Though traditionally believed to have begun on street corners, singing for spare change, many of the young singers got their start in church groups and high schools. The doo-wop genre is rife with "one-hit-wonders," but some of the more enduring groups included Frankie Lymon and the Teenagers, the Five Satins, and the Chords.

Rockabilly and Elvis Presley An important progenitor of rock and roll, rockabilly came into its own during the 1950's. With a thumping bass line, screaming guitar, and uninhibited lead vocals, rockabilly was the cultural child of hillbilly boogie but with an R&B feel. Although Sam Phillips of Sun Records gave many African American artists their first opportunities to record demos, many venues and markets still would not play their music. Phillips knew the key to success would be finding a white performer who could sing the blues.

Elvis Presley, a poor white boy from Tupelo, Mississippi, wandered into the Memphis Recording Service in 1953. Presley recorded two songs on a ten-inch acetate—"My Happiness" and "That's When Your Heartaches Begin," both originally by the Ink Spots. Phillips saw nothing remarkable in the polite young man, who returned a few times before being given the opportunity to record a demo in the summer of 1954. The session went badly, even after the addition of guitarist Scotty Moore and stand-up bass player Bill Black. However, when Presley picked up a guitar and strummed out a stripped-down version of an old blues song by Arthur Crudup, something in the sound struck Phillips's ear and the trio quickly recorded the tune. "That's All Right, Mama," backed with country standard "Blue Moon of Kentucky," became Presley's first single, released on July 19, 1954.

Radio stations did not know what to do with Presley's new record. It was "too black," "too country," "too ragged," and, according to one station in Presley's hometown, "a bunch of crap." However, the audiences loved it and it became an ultimate crossover record—an R&B song sung by a white artist and purchased by country music fans.

Presley would go on to record five singles for Phillips at Sun Records, before moving to RCA under the management of Colonel Tom Parker in 1956, when his contract was sold for $35,000. By the end of the decade, Presley had numerous hit records, including "Hound Dog" and "Don't Be Cruel."

Other rockabilly artists on Sun Records included Carl Perkins, Johnny Cash (later a country artist), and Jerry Lee Lewis. Though Presley's version was more famous, Carl Perkins's recording of the song he penned, "Blue Suede Shoes," hit the country, pop, and R&B charts at the same time in 1956. Presley would accomplish the same feat in 1957 with "Heartbreak Hotel."

Rock and Roll For many established artists from other genres, rock and roll signaled the end of their broad successes: By 1956, 68 percent of the music on the radio was rock and roll, and by the end of 1957, rock and roll accounted for nearly every top-ten single. Howver, the genre was not without its critics. Religious groups and civic leaders decried it as "the devil's music," claiming it made young people act and dance in sexually suggestive ways and would

Rock star Elvis Presley (right) and pianist Liberace switch instruments during an impromptu jam session at Las Vegas's Riviera Hotel in November, 1956. (AP/Wide World Photos)

lead to a dramatic increase in juvenile delinquency throughout the country.

Newspapers such as *The New York Times* were filled with horror stories about the violence and sexual depravity that occurred at rock-and-roll concerts. Promoters were appalled that audience members did not remain quietly in their seats; instead, they jumped, stood, screamed, shrieked and, worst of all, danced. When critics were not citing the dangers of rock and roll, they were decrying it as trash. Even Frank Sinatra called it written by "cretinous goons" and containing "sly, lewd . . . dirty lyrics."

Alan Freed was one of the first mainstream DJs who played R&B for a predominantly white audience and is credited with coining the phrase "rock and roll" to help eliminate the stigma of R&B for white listeners. Freed's nickname was "Moondog," after his signature tune, "Moondog Boogie." His first live concert revue was the Moondog's Rock and Roll Party and Coronation Ball in Cleveland in 1952, an event made notable when six thousand fans crashed the gates to enter the venue that already held an audience of ten thousand in attendance to see top black acts perform.

Bill Haley, another rock-and-roll pioneer, started out playing country music, but frustrated with his lack of success, he started experimenting with R&B. His group, then called the Saddlemen, recorded "Rocket 88" and "Rock the Joint," both of which sold well in his native Philadelphia. Their major-label debut on Decca, recorded as Bill Haley and the Comets, was "Rock Around the Clock." Initially, the song spent one week on the *Billboard* charts, reached number 23, then disappeared. Not until the song was used during the opening credits of the movie *Blackboard Jungle* (1955) did it become a breakout hit.

New Orleans also proved to be a starting point for many rock-and-roll pioneers. Legendary pianist Fats Domino sold nearly as many records as Elvis Presley, including hits such as "Ain't That a Shame," "I'm Walkin'," and "Blue Monday."

Teen Idols and Star Makers Teen idols were not strictly a 1950's phenomenon; young girls had screamed for Sinatra and Johnnie Ray during the 1940's. However, as the recording companies and A&R representatives gained increasing control over the music industry, they were able to use their control to create stars. This phenomenon was fueled in part by the major labels' desire to cash in on the rock-and-roll success stories from the smaller labels.

The emergence of a new teen culture during the decade also introduced a new generation who no longer listened to the same music as their parents, and the traditional "easy listening" artists grew marginalized since their recordings tended toward Broadway musicals and film soundtracks. Teenagers had their own money, and the new 45-rpm records were affordable. Teenage consumers were more likely to relate to songs sung by their contemporaries, as opposed to songs by crooners from their parents' generation.

Producers and A&R reps hoping to mimic Presley's success plucked young singers from obscurity and made them into stars. When the first wave of rock-and-roll singers faltered as a result of the untimely deaths of Buddy Holly and Ritchie Valens in 1959, military service (Elvis Presley), and scandal (Jerry Lee Lewis and Chuck Berry), record companies were ready with their own crop of white, clean-cut, all-American boys to take their places in the hearts of teenage girls. The industry put all their muscle behind these new heart throbs: Promotions, radio airplay, and appearances on television's *American Bandstand* all combined to create instant teen idols. These wholesome young men provided parents with a welcome alternative to the more suspect beats of R&B and rock and roll. For example, Philadelphia musical entrepreneurs Peter DeAngelis and Bob Marcucci founded Chancellor Records during the late 1950's. The duo is credited for discovering a handsome young man sitting on a stoop in his neighborhood. He was given singing and poise lessons and was molded into the teen idol known as Fabian. Frankie Avalon was another of their protégés—he produced six top-ten hits between 1958 and 1960 and went on to star in a number of popular beach films with Annette Funicello in the following decade.

Not all teen idols came prepackaged. Singer-songwriter Paul Anka first hit the charts in 1957 at age fifteen with "Diana." His songs reflected the simple but poignant issues important to teenagers. Other Anka hits included "You Are My Destiny," "Lonely Boy," "Put Your Head on My Shoulder," and "Puppy Love." Ricky Nelson, of television's *The Adventures of Ozzie and Harriet* was able to parlay his television role into a successful recording career.

A dark side to the careers of these young stars was that all the power remained with the record companies, and the contracts were seldom to the artist's advantage. They took young, impressionable children, promised them fame and fortune, and made them into stars, all the while pocketing the profits. This is especially true of some of the R&B pioneers such as Chuck Berry and Little Richard, whose records continued to sell for decades. Because of their contracts, they did not own the rights to the recordings, and despite good sales of their music, they were unable to make a profit.

Impact Not until the British Invasion of the mid-1960's would popular music undergo the same level of changes it experienced during the 1950's. The music of the 1950's proved a pivotal influence to the popular artists of the following decade, however. Members of both the Beatles and the Rolling Stones, along with guitar legend Eric Clapton, cite artists such as Presley, Berry, and Buddy Holly as their musical influences.

Further Reading

Altschuler, Glenn C. *All Shook Up: How Rock 'n' Roll Changed America.* New York: Oxford University Press, 2003. This accessible overview of the birth of rock and roll shows how the new musical genre affected race relations, sexuality, and generational conflict.

Asirvatham, Sandy. *American Mosaic: African American Contributions: The History of Jazz.* Philadelphia: Chelsea House, 2003. A history of jazz music during the twentieth century, with an emphasis on contributions by African American artists.

Bacon, Tony, ed. *Echo and Twang: Classic Guitar Music of the 1950's.* San Francisco: Backbeat Books, 1996. A collection of essays on changes within the music industry during the 1950's.

Escott, Colin. *Roadkill on the Three-Chord Highway: Art and Trash in American Popular Music.* New York: Routledge, 2002. Profiles of some of the early pioneers of country, rockabilly, and rock and roll.

Friedlander, Paul. *Rock and Roll: A Social History.* Boulder, Colo.: Westview Press, 1996. A history of the first thirty years of the rock-and-roll era as it related to changes in society.

Gribin, Anthony J., Andrew M. Schiff, and Matthew M. Schiff. *The Complete Book of Doo-Wop.* Iola, Wis.: Krause, 2000. An extensive history of doo-wop music from the 1950's to the early 1970's, including song lists and sheet music covers.

Helander, Brock. *The Rockin' Fifties: The People Who Made the Music.* New York: Schirmer Books, 1998. An overview of the roots of rock and roll and the subgenres that made up the musical landscape during the 1950's.

Hochman, Steve, ed. *Popular Musicians.* 3 vols. Pasadena, Calif.: Salem Press, 1999. Encyclopedic reference work on late twentieth century musicians, with numerous articles on individuals and bands of the 1950's.

Kempton, Arthur. *Boogaloo: The Quintessence of American Popular Music.* Pantheon Books, 2003. The history of African American contributions to the music industry.

Sieling, Peter. *North American Folklore: Folk Music.* Broomall, Pa.: Mason Crest, 2003. A brief overview of the folk music genre.

Wolf, Kurt. *Country Music: The Rough Guide.* Penguin Books, 2000. A detailed history of country music and how it evolved throughout the twentieth century.

P. S. Ramsey

See also *American Bandstand*; Belafonte, Harry; Berry, Chuck; Brubeck, Dave; Cole, Nat King; Domino, Fats; Fitzgerald, Ella; Jazz; Kingston Trio; Long-playing records; Presley, Elvis; Rock and roll; Sinatra, Frank; *Your Hit Parade.*

■ Mutual Broadcasting System scandal

The Event Radio executives accused of illegal activities
Date 1958-1959

The Mutual Broadcasting System scandal, involving financial and ethical improprieties of network executives, was one of several high-profile scandals that plagued the broadcast industry during the late 1950's.

The Mutual Broadcasting System (MBS) was established in 1934 as a joint venture among several large East Coast radio stations. Unlike a traditional broadcasting network in which programming was sold to subscribing affiliates, the MBS operated as a cooperative in which each affiliate held an equal share in the network and shared programming and operational costs. Moreover, unlike previous attempts at establishing broadcasting cooperatives, MBS built a successful network that competed with the giants of early network radio—NBC and CBS. Some of the most popular radio programs of the 1930's and 1940's, such as *The Lone Ranger, The Shadow,* and *Amos and Andy* were broadcast on MBS.

The culture of mutual ownership that characterized the network in its early years began to unravel in the postwar era as the initial partners sold their shares in the cooperative. By 1950, one company, General Tire and Rubber, owned the majority of the network's stock. The company was reorganized into a more traditional network, producing programming and distributing it to affiliates for a fee. Mutual's ratings, always a distant fourth to those of its major competitors, declined steadily during the 1950's as several of its popular programs went off the air.

Scandal Throughout the 1950's, ownership of MBS passed through a series of large corporations. In 1958, the struggling network was purchased by Hal Roach Studios, a subsidiary of the Scranton Corporation. Alexander Guterma, controlling stockholder in the Scranton Corporation, soon assumed the presidency of the network. During his term as president, Guterma was indicted on a variety of fraud charges and securities offenses, including failure to report stock transactions to the Securities and Exchange Commission (SEC). Guterma resigned from Mutual in February, 1959, and sold his shares in the network to its chief executive, Hal Roach, Jr.

The scandal intensified in September, 1959, after a federal grand jury charged that Guterma, Roach, and another Mutual official accepted $750,000 from high-level officials of the Dominican Republic in exchange for the promise that Mutual would broadcast political propaganda disguised as news on behalf of the Dominican government. Whether the network ever actually broadcast such propaganda is uncertain; however, the scandal exacerbated the network's already precarious financial state. The Mutual Broadcasting System declared bankruptcy in 1959 and was purchased by the 3M company in 1960.

Impact The Guterma scandal and resultant financial difficulties were the final episodes in the steady decline of the Mutual Broadcasting System during the 1950's. The network that had once exemplified cooperative ownership of the airwaves had become a corporate subsidiary, its financial and organizational instability rendered vulnerable to corrupt management that had not only committed financial

indiscretions but also compromised the network's integrity by accepting bribes to broadcast propaganda for a foreign country. This incident, along with the "payola" and quiz show scandals, weakened public confidence in the broadcast industry as a whole during the late 1950's.

Subsequent Events Guterma was convicted of securities fraud and in 1960 was sentenced to a three-year prison term. He died in 1977. The Mutual Broadcasting System continued to operate into the 1990's, but never fully regained its former prestige. In 1999, the network was purchase by CBS/Viacom and ceased operating under the Mutual name.

Further Reading

Brooks, John. *The Go-Go Years: The Drama and Crashing Finale of Wall Street's Bullish Sixties.* New York: Wiley, 1999. Provides some information on Guterma and the impact of his activities upon the U.S. stock market.

Hillard, Robert L. *The Broadcast Century and Beyond: A Biography of American Broadcasting.* 3d ed. Boston: Focal Press, 2001. An informal history of the broadcast industry that traces the early development of the Mutual Broadcasting System.

Michael H. Burchett

See also *Amos and Andy;* Communications in the United States; *Lone Ranger, The;* Radio; Television game shows; Television in the United States; Top 40 radio.

■ *My Fair Lady*

Identification Broadway musical about an English speech professor who transforms a Cockney flower girl into an aristocratic lady
Date Premiered on March 15, 1956
Place Mark Hellinger Theatre, New York City
Authors Book and lyrics by Alan Jay Lerner, music by Frederick Loewe

This musical adaptation of a play by George Bernard Shaw set a record as the longest-running musical in the history of the American musical theater to its time.

Alan Jay Lerner and Frederick Loewe's musical version of George Bernard Shaw's play *Pygmalion* (pr. 1914) focuses on the relationship of Henry Higgins, an egotistical speech teacher (played by Rex Harrison), and Eliza Doolittle (Julie Andrews), the cockney flower girl whom he transforms on a bet into the

Julie Andrews as Eliza Doolittle and Rex Harrison as Henry Higgins during a performance of My Fair Lady *at New York's Mark Hellinger Theater in 1956.* (AP/Wide World Photos)

script of the screen version of *Pygmalion* (1938). In the film, Shaw allowed the ending of his play, in which the estranged couple do not kiss and make up at the final curtain, to be altered so that Eliza and Henry are clearly reconciled before the final fade-out. It is this latter ending that Lerner incorporated into his script for the stage production of *My Fair Lady.* This happy resolution to the plot does not do violence to Shaw's play, as some critics have charged, since the original ending of *Pygmalion* was arguably ambiguous and did not close off entirely the possibility of an eventual reunion between Henry and Eliza.

Impact *My Fair Lady* was a milestone in the American musical theater during the 1950's. Lerner's sophisticated libretto set a new standard for a musical play and the musical was punctuated with a singable score and several sumptuous production numbers. The show won nine Tony Awards for 1956, and its 2,717 performances between 1956 and 1962 established it as one of the longest-running shows in Broadway history.

Further Reading

Flinn, Denny. *Musical! A Grand Tour.* New York: Schirmer Books, 1997. A very readable account of the musicals that have influenced the development of this genre in the United States.

Ganzl, Kurt. *The Musical: A Chronicle.* Boston: Northeastern University Press, 1997. A historical study of the American musical theater, highlighted by hallmark musicals over the years.

Gene D. Phillips

See also Broadway musicals; Rodgers and Hammerstein musicals; Theater in the United States.

belle of a society ball. Initially called *Lady Liza,* the musical finally took its title from the lyrics of an old nursery rhyme: "London Bridge is falling down, my fair lady." The title of Shaw's play in turn is a reference to a classical myth that tells the story of an ancient king of Cyprus who fell in love with the statue of a beautiful maiden, which he had carved out of ivory and which Aphrodite then brought to life in answer to his prayer.

During the 1930's, Shaw himself worked on the

N

■ *Naked Lunch*

Identification Controversial American novel
Author William Burroughs (1914-1997)
Date Published in France in 1959; published as
The Naked Lunch in the United States in 1962

The French publication of Naked Lunch *in 1959 gave the novel an underground reputation in the United States and established Burroughs as a major avant-garde writer.*

The American writer William Burroughs began writing the notes and letters that would become *Naked Lunch* while living in the Moroccan city of Tangier in North Africa. He was visited there during the 1950's by fellow Beat writers Jack Kerouac and Allen Ginsberg, who were so impressed by the powerful yet disordered pages that Burroughs had accumulated in his tiny apartment that they helped assemble them into a book

Burroughs had struggled for years with an addiction to morphine, and on one level, his novel recreates the disjointed and disorienting experiences of withdrawal. On another level, the narrator's travails in a seedy underworld reflect a more universal condition of addiction and psychological control. Set in the sordid world of Interzone (which combined aspects of Tangier, Central America, and the American South), the bleakly funny novel seemed to mock accepted standards of conduct and literary composition.

Naked Lunch (whose title was supplied by Kerouac) was published in 1959 by Olympia Press, a Parisian firm specializing in experimental and sexually explicit books in English. Although the novel did not appear in the United States until 1962, the early publication of several chapters in literary journals sparked controversy and legal action.

Impact Pioneering avant-garde compositional techniques and an extreme explicitness, *Naked Lunch* ushered in a new era in American literature. The book was the subject of an important 1965 obscenity trial following its U.S. publication.

Further Reading

Caveney, Graham. *Gentleman Junkie: The Life and Legacy of William S. Burroughs.* Boston: Little, Brown, 1998. Inventive and profusely illustrated biography reflecting Burroughs's compositional techniques.

Goodman, Michael Barry. *Contemporary Literary Censorship: The Case History of Burroughs's "Naked Lunch."* Metuchen, N.J.: Scarecrow Press, 1981. Detailed study of the book's composition and publication as well as the censorship battles that followed.

Skerl, Jennie. *William S. Burroughs.* Boston: Twayne, 1985. Discusses the composition and content of *Naked Lunch* within the context of Burroughs's total body of work.

Grove Koger

See also Beat generation; Book publishing; Burroughs, William; Censorship; Ginsberg, Allen; Kerouac, Jack; Literature in the United States; *On the Road.*

■ National Aeronautics and Space Administration

Identification Federal agency responsible for the U.S. space program
Date Established in 1958

The National Aeronautics and Space Administration (NASA) unified America's fragmented space program into a single agency for aeronautics and space research, which included the development of rocket propulsion, Earth satellites, lunar and planetary space probes, and the manned spaceflight program.

NASA emerged from several developments after World War II. During the war, Germany completed the development of the V-2 rocket under the leadership of Wernher von Braun and began production of about six hundred rockets per month. It launched its first tactical, bomb-carrying V-2 toward London on September 9, 1944. At the end of the war, von

Braun surrendered to the U.S. Army, and 127 German rocket scientists were selected for relocation in the United States. After a series of research projects with captured V-2 rockets at the White Sands Missile Test Range in New Mexico, the German scientists were relocated to the Army's Redstone Arsenal in Huntsville, Alabama, in the spring of 1950. Meanwhile, U.S. scientists were beginning to organize their own space efforts.

International Geophysical Year and *Sputnik* After the war, American scientists under the leadership of James Van Allen formed the Upper Atmosphere Research Panel to advise the Army Ordinance Department on the development of scientific programs to fly on the V-2 rockets. At Van Allen's home in 1950, a group of scientists proposed an international campaign to gather data about the earth. This led to the formation of a committee in 1953 to plan the International Geophysical Year (IGY), which was set to begin in July of 1957, at the beginning of a period of maximum solar activity. On July 29, 1955, the Eisenhower administration announced its plans to launch several small Earth satellites as part of the U.S. contribution to IGY research. In September of 1956, the Soviet Union announced similar plans to place scientific satellites into orbit.

During this same period of time, the United States and the Soviet Union each decided to build intercontinental ballistic missiles (ICBMs) to deliver atomic bombs. These actions, along with the IGY decision, effectively opened the space age, leading to the development of the technology, equipment, and worldwide tracking facilities needed to launch and operate scientific satellites and space probes.

In October of 1957, the world was shocked by the successful launch of the 183-pound *Sputnik I* satellite

German American rocket scientist Wernher von Braun. (Hulton Archive | by Getty Images)

into orbit by the Soviet Union, followed by the half-ton *Sputnik II* on November 3, which carried a live dog into orbit. On December 3, 1957, the United States attempted to launch its first satellite from Cape Canaveral, Florida, but the Navy's Viking rocket failed at liftoff, and its three-pound *Vanguard I* satellite fell to the ground. Finally, on January 31, 1958, von Braun's Juno rocket was used successfully to launch the thirty-one-pound *Explorer I* satellite into orbit. In spite of its small size, *Explorer I* included an eleven-pound scientific package designed by Van Allen, which led to the first important discovery of the Space Age: belts of intense radiation circling the earth.

The Birth of NASA The launch of both *Sputnik* satellites led to intense pressure in Congress and across the United States to develop a more vigorous space program that could match the apparent Soviet goal of placing humans into orbit. President Dwight D. Eisenhower responded with a decision to form a single agency to consolidate the various space programs, with a goal of launching an American into space. Three candidates were considered for this assignment: the Department of Defense, the Atomic Energy Commission (AEC), and the National Advisory Committee for Aeronautics (NACA). With its Huntsville and Navy programs, the Department of Defense had the most experience with missile programs, but Eisenhower wanted to avoid the implications of extending the military into space. The AEC was a newer agency with little rocket experience. NACA, with several decades of experience in designing aircraft, seemed to be best qualified for the job.

After due consideration, the Eisenhower administration recommended that Congress assign America's space program to NACA. Congress quickly passed the bill to accomplish this, and Eisenhower signed it on July 29, 1958, with NACA's name officially changed to the National Aeronautics and Space Administration. All of NACA's facilities were transferred to NASA, including eight thousand employees and the X-15 rocket aircraft program. Several military programs were also transferred to NASA, including Air Force programs on rocket propulsion and lunar probes, the Ames Aeronautical Laboratory at Moffett field in California, the Army Ballistic Missile Agency (ABMA) in Huntsville, the Lewis Flight Propulsion Laboratory in Cleveland, and the

Navy's Project Vanguard. NASA began operations on October 1, 1958, with Keith Glennan, a former member of the AEC, appointed as head of NASA, and Hugh Dryden, former director of NACA, as deputy chief administrator.

Impact A week after NASA began operations, Glennan announced the start of Project Mercury, America's first manned space program. In April of 1959, the first group of seven astronauts was announced. By 1959, NASA had attempted thirty-seven satellite launches, but only about a dozen reached orbit. Work began on increasing the size and reliability of booster rockets. Finally, on May 5, 1961, Alan Shepard became America's first human in space on a suborbital Mercury flight, one month after the Soviets had launched Yuri Gagarin into humankind's first orbit around the earth. NASA then began to plan an accelerated program of earth satellites, planetary probes, and lunar missions. On May 25, 1961, President John F. Kennedy announced the U.S. intention to land a man on the moon, culminating in the *Apollo 11* landing eight years later and America's undisputed space leadership.

Further Reading

Bilstein, Roger E. *Orders of Magnitude: A History of the NACA and NASA, 1915-1990.* Washington, D.C.: NASA Scientific and Information Division, 1989. This 150-page book in the NASA History Series is comprehensive and well illustrated.

Lewis, Richard S. *Appointment on the Moon: The Inside Story of America's Space Venture.* New York: Viking Press, 1968. A popular account of America's space program including sixty NASA photos.

McNamara, Bernard. *Into the Final Frontier: The Human Exploration of Space.* New York: Harcourt College, 2001. A complete history of manned space flight with hundreds of illustrations.

Naugle, John E. *First Among Equals.* Washington, D.C.: NASA Scientific and Information Division, 1991. This 120-page book in the NASA History Series traces the origins of NASA and the process for selecting space experiments.

Joseph L. Spradley

See also Aircraft design and development; Astronomy; *Explorer I*; International Geophysical Year; Mercury space program; National Defense Education Act of 1958; Science and technology; Space race; *Sputnik I*; Van Allen radiation belts.

■ National Association for the Advancement of Colored People

Identification Organization founded to fight racism in the United States and strive for equal rights for African Americans
Date Established in 1909

The National Association for the Advancement of Colored People (NAACP) took the lead both in the courts and in the streets to desegregate U.S. schools, an effort which also helped desegregate other public facilities. At the same time, the NAACP fought racial discrimination throughout society—for example, in salary discrepancies, in hiring practices, and within the military.

A group of white and African American men and women formed the NAACP in 1909, when they realized that they needed a strong organization to fight repression and injustice. As the twentieth century progressed, the NAACP built a series of legal victories to reform the "separate but equal" premise of American education and, later, to lay the foundation to overturn segregation.

During the 1950's, the NAACP's strong leadership led a diverse group to several legal victories. Executive directors Walter White and Roy Wilkins headed the group, while the chief lobbyist, Clarence Mitchell II, served as a strong force for change in the U.S. Congress. The group's chief attorney, Thurgood Marshall, aided by his diverse staff of lawyers, counted numerous victories in the courts.

Commitment to Desegregation By the early 1950's, a series of school desegregation cases emanating from Washington, D.C., South Carolina, Delaware, and Kansas reached the U.S. Supreme Court. The Court decided to combine the cases because the issues were essentially the same: denial of access to nearer white schools to African American children who, consequently, had to travel incon-

venient distances to black schools. The lead case was that of Linda Brown, a seven-year-old girl from Topeka, Kansas, who lived three short blocks from a white school but several miles from the district black school, which she had to attend. The landmark *Brown v. Board of Education* (1954) became the NAACP's lead case.

Leading the NAACP legal team was Marshall, who later became the first African American Supreme Court justice. He gathered a team of attorneys and argued that he had precedent on his side, while the opposing counsel argued the precedent of the Court's *Plessy v. Ferguson* decision—an 1896 case that had originally legalized the separate-but-equal practice. Marshall, however, did not argue the *Brown* case; Robert Carter did, while Marshall argued one of the included companion cases.

On May 17, 1954, the Supreme Court rendered its decision in the *Brown* case and ruled that states must desegregate schools." The decision spurred a backlash of racial violence throughout the southern

NAACP executive secretary Roy Wilkins addressing the platform committee of the Democratic Party during the party's August, 1956, national convention. (AP/Wide World Photos)

states, with governors gaining popularity with the white voters by refusing to desegregate schools. While the battle to desegregate schools continued, with the NAACP fighting in courts to get the *Brown* decision actually implemented in all states, the group continued to bring suit against public and, later, private agencies that refused to desegregate their facilities.

Legal Challenges and Victories Meanwhile, southern states erupted in a reaction of violent frustration. When Emmett Till, a fourteen-year-old boy, was viciously murdered in the summer of 1955 for daring to speak discourteously to a white woman, the NAACP field secretary in Mississippi, Medgar Evers, protected witnesses by moving them out of the state and keeping them safe after they testified against the white defendants, who subsequently were not convicted by the all-white jury. This was the first time that African Americans testified in court against white people.

People active in the Montgomery, Alabama, chapter of the NAACP formed a coalition and called themselves the Montgomery Improvement Association (later the Southern Christian Leadership Conference) to integrate the public bus system. Rosa Parks, an NAACP youth adviser in Montgomery, was arrested for refusing to relinquish her seat on a bus. The case was heard in the Supreme Court, which ruled that Montgomery had to integrate the buses.

These victories swelled the ranks of the NAACP throughout the country. In Little Rock, Arkansas, in 1957, Daisy Bates, an NAACP worker, recruited a group of students who would be willing to integrate the city's Central High School. Eventually, despite the resistance of Governor Orval Faubus, the school did open to nine black students, who ultimately had to be protected by federal troops as they entered the school. This was the first time that the U.S. government forces intervened to protect integration.

While the major battles in court netted the most publicity, the NAACP also took on cases brought to their attention by African Americans related to discrimination in housing, restaurants, stores, and jobs.

Impact During the 1950's, the NAACP successfully desegregated schools and, in many cities, public buses, movie theaters, and shops. Its victories opened up job opportunities to African Americans that had, until then, been denied them. In subsequent decades, the NAACP continued to focus on policy advocacy, civil rights, economic empowerment, education, political empowerment, criminal justice, the legal system, and health issues.

Subsequent events Throughout the 1960's, the NAACP continued waging the legal war and lending support to the demonstrations that resulted in President Lyndon B. Johnson's leading Congress to enact in 1964 the Civil Rights Act and, in 1965, the Voting Rights Act. Affirmative action programs launched during the 1970's helped African Americans make up some of the historical inequities in college admission and jobs.

Further Reading

Branch, Taylor. *Parting the Waters: America in the King Years, 1954-63.* New York: Simon & Schuster, 1988. Branch's Pulitzer Prize-winning history discusses the Civil Rights movement while focusing on Martin Luther King's role in the events that changed the United States.

Carson, Clayborne, David Garrow, Bill Kovach, and Carol Polsgrove. *Reporting Civil Rights: Part I, American Journalism, 1941-1963.* New York: Library of America, 2003. A compendium of news accounts about civil rights issues.

Greenberg, Jack. *Crusaders in the Courts: How a Dedicated Band of Lawyers Fought for the Civil Rights Revolution.* New York: Basic Books, 1994. One of the attorneys who helped litigate cases for the NAACP discusses how it was done.

Tracy E. Miller

See also African Americans; *Bolling v. Sharpe, Brown v. Board of Education;* Civil Rights movement; Ku Klux Klan; Little Rock school desegregation crisis; Montgomery bus boycott; Racial discrimination; Supreme Court decisions, U.S.

■ *National Association for the Advancement of Colored People v. Alabama*

Identification U.S. Supreme Court decision on freedom of association
Date Decided on June 30, 1958

The U.S. Supreme Court explicitly recognized that a freedom of association was implied in the First Amendment's guarantee of free expression and free assembly and was an "inseparable aspect" of the liberty guaranteed by the Fourteenth Amendment.

The case originated when the National Association for the Advancement of Colored People (NAACP) appealed a contempt order after the association refused to provide the state of Alabama with a state-law-mandated list of NAACP members. The U.S. Supreme Court ruled that requiring disclosure of membership in an advocacy organization would effectively deny the constitutional rights of the members to free speech. The Court held that there was a "close nexus" between the freedoms of speech and assembly. It also noted that revealing membership in a controversial organization had resulted in economic and social reprisals so hostile as to effectively interfere with the rights to free speech and assembly.

Impact This Court decision was the first to link a right to privacy to the right to free association. The Court held for the first time that a constitutional right to associate freely with others was a basic liberty guaranteed under the due process clause of the Fourteenth Amendment.

Further Reading

Fellman, David. *The Constitutional Right of Association.* Chicago: University of Chicago Press, 1963. Brief but rather dense discussion of the small number of cases concerning the First Amendment right to assembly.

Perry, Michael J. *We the People: The Fourteenth Amendment and the Supreme Court.* New York: Oxford University Press, 1999. Details the Court's history of rulings regarding the Fourteenth Amendment.

Woods, Jeff. "Designed to Harass: The Act Ten Controversy in Arkansas." *Arkansas Historical Quarterly* 56, no. 4 (1997): 443-460. Examination of state law requiring state employees to list all organizational affiliations in the aftermath of *NAACP v. Alabama.*

Lisa M. Sardinia

See also African Americans; Montgomery bus boycott; National Association for the Advancement of Colored People; Supreme Court decisions, U.S.; Warren, Earl.

■ National Defense Education Act of 1958

Identification U.S. federal law enacted to promote educational development in science and mathematics

Date Signed into law on September 2, 1958

The National Defense Education Act (NDEA) was passed in response to the Soviet launch of Sputnik I *and was designed to encourage a new generation of mathematicians and scientists in the nation's quest for Cold War military supremacy.*

One of the most significant acts of legislation in the history of American education occurred in 1958, when the U.S. Congress and President Dwight D. Eisenhower authorized Public Law 85-864, the National Defense Education Act. This act provided millions of dollars to all sectors of American education to improve instruction in those school subject areas considered crucial to national defense and security.

National Security and Education During the World War II years, world society witnessed the introduction of long-range missiles and nuclear bomb technology. After World War II, world politics evolved into what was termed by Great Britain's Prime Minister Winston Churchill a "cold war" and a resulting "iron curtain" of political and geographic division and security defense tension between democratic and communist nations. In 1957, the Soviet Union, the chief rival of the United States in the Cold War, successfully orbited its space satellite, *Sputnik.* The combination of this Soviet space success, prior U.S. space failures, and Cold War tensions created a security crisis within American society. Some critics blamed the weakness of American students in mathematics and science as a cause of society's insecurities. The impetus of the *Sputnik* threat resulted in the creation of the NDEA.

Funding Specifically, the NDEA provided monetary aid to many levels of the United States' public and private educational systems. The main subject areas receiving most of the funding were mathematics and sciences; however, areas such as modern foreign languages, technical education, geography, English as a second language, counseling, school libraries, and educational media centers also received significant sums of money. Elementary and secondary schools benefited from federal control and support for improvement to curriculum, instruction, administration, programs, and personnel. Colleges and universities received significant funding for low-interest student loans amounting to $47.5 million for fiscal year 1959, $75 million for 1960, $82.5 million for 1961, and $90 million for 1962. The United States Commission of Education was directed to provide whatever funds were necessary during the years 1963-1966 to allow students in the program to complete their education.

Several important and specific directives within the law called for colleges and universities to target for loans students who were strong in science, mathematics, engineering, and modern foreign languages as well as those who might become elementary and secondary teachers. Elementary and secondary schools received millions of dollars for science equipment and laboratory supervisors. Similar amounts went to colleges for graduate student scholarships for those who would become college teachers. Other specifics of the act included millions of dollars for secondary school guidance counselors to test and identify gifted students, additional millions for audiovisual media purchases, and $60 million for vocational training of technicians. All recipients of funds were required to file affidavits of loyalty to the United States government.

Impact The passing of the NDEA signaled both American Cold War insecurities and officials' overt linking of education with military prowess. It is considered one of the most valuable and comprehensive pieces of education legislation ever sponsored by the federal government. Its positive educational benefit to society as a whole has affected many generations of American students and global development in technology.

Further Reading

Divine, Robert A. *The Sputnik Challenge: Eisenhower's Response to the Soviet Satellite.* New York: Oxford University Press, 1993. Details the technological crises spurred by *Sputnik*'s launch and the response of United States scientists.

Roman, Peter J. *Eisenhower and the Missile Gap.* Ithaca, N.Y.: Cornell University Press, 1995. Provides background and discussion on the United States government and the space race.

Williams, Gurney. "*Sputnik*: The Little Sphere That Changed the World." *Popular Mechanics* 164 (October, 1987): 59-61. Chronicles Soviet satellite and rocket technology development.

Alan P. Peterson

See also Atomic bomb; Cold War; Education in the United States; Eisenhower, Dwight D.; Mercury space program; National Aeronautics and Space Administration; Science and technology; Space race; *Sputnik I.*

■ Native Americans

Definition Members of the aboriginal peoples of the Western Hemisphere, who are also known as American Indians and the First Nations, or First Peoples, of Canada

During the 1950's, Native Americans faced both further losses of their lands and further erosion of their cultures through land seizure and federal programs meant to relocate and acculturate them in urban areas. The decade also saw the end of federal responsibility to social services for native communities.

During the 1950's, Native Americans experienced substantial attempts by the U.S. government to remove their collective land bases and to assimilate them into mainstream culture. By 1961, pressure was building among Native Americans to assert their own "self-determination," a movement which continued in subsequent decades. The 1953 termination policy, which divided tribal property among tribe members—a move that made them subject to taxation—and relocated Native Americans to cities for jobs, was a contemporary expression of some of the same assumptions that created government-led dislocation and acculturation of tribes during the nineteenth and early twentieth centuries.

The Depression-era Indian New Deal, legislated as the Indian Reorganization Act in 1934 and led by Bureau of Indian Affairs (BIA) commissioner John Collier, was an effort to restore Indian culture and heritage. It abandoned the land allotment system, approved new land for reservations, provided special funding for education, and established procedures for self-government, among other things. During the late 1940's and early 1950's, however, this movement aimed at liberalizing relations between Native American tribes and the U.S. government was stymied by new policies of "termination," which were meant to control Native American land and economic bases, as well as tribal identities.

Collier's policies increased Native American birthrates, improved health measures, and increased land bases, but native people still remained desperately poor compared to middle-class American standards. Arguments began to win favor that rapid assimilation demanded forceful elimination of tribalism and tribal lands. Proponents of termination policy assumed that obliteration of native identity both would propel native peoples out of poverty and

Members of the Iroquois Confederacy during their first annual pilgrimage to New York City in 1952. (AP/Wide World Photos)

would end their dependent or "ward" status with the federal government that the BIA had created. This consensus was built during the late 1940's and reached the peak of its political expression in a wave of terminations enacted by the government during the early 1950's. The 1953 House Concurrent Resolution 108, a resolution passed in the U.S. House of Representatives and the Senate, provided broad support for a new Indian policy as well as a withdrawal of U.S. governmental supervision of Indian nations.

By the 1950's, the economic rationale of allotment had become obsolete. Small-scale farming dissolved into the reality of large-scale, global agribusiness, and most Americans lived and worked in cities. Advocates of termination and relocation saw themselves generally as modernists and realists, promoting the eradication of native land, identity, and cultures for the Indians' own good, to ease the native communities' transition into the modern industrial economy.

Under termination, land and resources were purchased from tribes, and the proceeds were distributed to individual members, who found themselves temporarily enriched in cash but suddenly deprived of land and community. Through various legal devices, much of the purchased land was then transferred into the private sector, often through lease for a specific purpose, such as logging or mineral exploration, or outright sale. Some tribes disappeared altogether as organized communities. Their members moved to other places, particularly cities.

Political momentum toward termination accelerated as Dwight D. Eisenhower assumed the presidency in 1953. Eisenhower appointed Glenn L. Emmons as commissioner of Indian affairs. Between 1953 and 1962, Congress passed legislation terminating federal recognition and services to dozens of native nations and tribes. Congress sometimes held up claims payments until the native tribe or nation in question also agreed to termination proceedings, thereby obliterating both past and present land bases. In 1963, for example, the Claims Commission awarded the Kalispel people three million dollars, an award that was held by Congress (under legislation passed at the behest of Idaho senator Frank Church) until they agreed to termination. Sometimes, the pitch was different, but no less subtle.

Klamath and Menominee Experiences The Klamath people, who held title to one million acres of prime timber land in Oregon, were enticed into terminating their rights after BIA agents promised them per-capita payments of fifty thousand dollars. Only afterward did the Klamaths learn painfully that "going private" can be expensive: They found themselves paying rent, utilities, health care costs, and taxes that they had never faced before. Following their termination in 1953, the Klamath people lost more than 880,000 acres of ponderosa pine, 90,000 acres of which was quickly sold to Crown Zellerbach, a timber company. Most of the rest of their land was incorporated into two national forests; both were later heavily logged. Payments for the land to individual Klamaths were soon spent. Now landless, the Klamaths scattered, and many experienced alcoholism, poverty, death by suicide, increased incarceration rates, increased infant mortality, and decreased life spans. This was a far cry from their economic status before 1953, when Klamaths earned 93 percent of the national median income.

The Menominees of Wisconsin shared ownership of property valued at thirty-four million dollars when their termination bill was enacted in 1953. By 1961, each member of the former tribe had become the owner of one hundred shares of stock and a negotiable bond valued at three thousand dollars, issued in the name of Menominee Enterprises, Inc. (MEI), a private enterprise that held the former tribe's land and businesses. Governmentally, the Menominee Nation had become Menominee County, the smallest (in terms of population) and poorest (in terms of cash income) in Wisconsin.

As a county, Menominee had to raise taxes to pay for its share of services, including welfare, health services, and utilities. The only taxable property owner in the county was MEI, which was forced to raise the funds to pay its tax bill by restructuring: Stockholders had to buy their homes and the property on which they had been built. Most of the Menominees had little savings except for their three-thousand-dollar bonds, which were then transferred to MEI to make the required residential purchases. Many Menominees faced private-sector health costs, property taxes, and other expenses with no more money than they had possessed before termination. Unemployment rose to levels that most of the United States had known only during the Depression of the 1930's. By 1965, health indicators in

Menominee County indicated that tuberculosis afflicted nearly 35 percent of the population, and infant mortality was three times the national average. Termination, like allotment, had been an abject failure at anything other than alienating Indian land.

Opponents of Termination Many of termination's opponents were Native American traditionalists, who believed that distinct cultures and land bases should be maintained. During the renaissance of native activism during the 1960's, they were joined in their opposition efforts by the young, urbanized children of older Native American generations. Between 1953 and 1972, more than 100,000 Native Americans moved to urban areas; by 1980, about half of the Native Americans in the United States lived in cities. Young Native Americans raised in urban areas during the 1960's began to reverse relocation's effects. College-educated tribal members, as well as veterans of the Vietnam War or those who had served terms in state and federal prisons, began to return to reservations by the 1970's. Most important, in realizing that termination had proven to be an abject failure, Congress effectively repealed legal authorization for the policy in 1968.

Industrial Land Development Native American lands that remained intact after the early termination years subsequently were targeted for energy and industrial development. The Kinzua Dam and the St. Lawrence Seaway are but two examples of the development of native lands for industrial purposes during this era.

The construction of the Kinzua Dam flooded one-third of the Allegheny Seneca reservation: Nine thousand acres of Seneca reservation land were lost, requiring the removal of about 160 families, or about 600 people, from the valley in which many of them had lived for several generations. Plans to build this giant flood-control project to protect the growing city of Pittsburgh surfaced as early as 1908. For two decades, the U.S. Army Corps of Engineers studied the plan without informing the Native Americans living on the land that it would be flooded once the project became active.

In August, 1941, the Allegheny Reservoir Project was authorized by Congress. World War II intervened, so the project was not officially enacted until 1956. The dam was to be constructed at the Kinzua narrows along the Allegheny River near the southern part of New York State's border with Pennsylvania. The Seneca reservation was twelve miles downstream. The dam, which cost $125 million, flooded all Seneca land below 1,365 feet in elevation, including the entire Cornplanter Tract, land that held special economic and historic value to the Seneca people.

The Senecas, who had fought proposals to build a dam since 1927 using the 1794 Canandaigua Treaty as a defense, were told by the federal courts in 1958 that the "plenary power" of Congress allowed it to abrogate treaties unilaterally. The U.S. Supreme Court validated that point of view in June, 1959, by denying the Senecas a writ of *certiorari*. In 1984, the Seneca Nation of Indians declared September 24 "Removal Day" in observance of resistance to the Kinzua Dam.

While the St. Lawrence Seaway brought prosperity to the urban areas and industries that grew along its route, Native American peoples, mainly Mohawk communities, were devastated. The destruction of the Mohawk lands and resources was not a new development, however. As early as 1834, Mohawk chiefs told Canadian officials that structures built to channel the flow of the St. Lawrence River near Barnhart Island were destroying important fish spawning grounds. Environmental degradation in the Mohawk communities of Akwesasne and Kahnawake took a quantum leap after the late 1950's, however, when the St. Lawrence Seaway created bountiful cheap power. Access to power attracted heavy industry, which in turn polluted large segments of the river.

The Akwesasne area also was home to many wildlife trappers before construction of the seaway devastated trapping areas and wetlands. To speed the melting of ice in the spring, for example, the level of the river is raised and dropped very quickly so that air pockets caught in the water will pulverize the ice. The swirling, crushing action of water, ice, and air consequently floods muskrat and beaver hutches, killing their inhabitants. The animals drowned in masses, destroying the traditional trapping industry in the area.

Impact The 1950's was a devastating period for the Native Americans of both the United States and Canada. Government pressures on their lands increased, and the U.S. government attempted to withdraw from its historical responsibilities for Native American welfare.

Further Reading

Alfred, Gerald R. *Heeding the Voices of Our Ancestors: Kahnawake Mohawk Politics and the Rise of Native Nationalism.* Toronto: Oxford University Press, 1995. Covers the roots of self-determination, which in some cases began during the 1950's.

Bilharz, Joy A. *The Allegheny Senecas and Kinzua Dam: Forced Relocation Through Two Generations.* Lincoln: University of Nebraska Press, 1998. A detailed account of the Seneca resistance to construction of the Kinzua Dam.

Cohen, Felix. "Americanizing the White Man." *The American Scholar* 21, no. 2 (1952). Cohen makes an early case for Native American influence on American mainstream life.

_____. *Legal Conscience: Selected Papers of Felix S. Cohen.* Edited by Lucy Kramer Cohen. New Haven, Conn.: Yale University Press, 1960. Generally considered the best collection of Cohen's writings.

_____. *Readings in Jurisprudence and Legal Philosophy.* Boston: Little, Brown, 1951. Lays out Cohen's objections to termination and much more on his legal philosophy.

Hauptman, Laurence M. *The Iroquois Struggle for Survival: World War II to Red Power.* Syracuse, N.Y.: Syracuse University Press, 1986. Chronicles Iroquois struggles with New York state's dam-builders, as well as other issues.

Levitan, Sar A. *Big Brother's Indian Programs—with Reservations.* New York: McGraw-Hill, 1971. A critical examination of termination policies.

Wilson, Edmund. *Apologies to the Iroquois.* New York: Vintage Books, 1960. An erudite account of problems faced by the Iroquois during the 1950's.

Bruce E. Johansen

See also Alaska statehood; Archaeology; Demographics of Canada; Demographics of the United States; Indian Act of 1951; Minorities in Canada; Racial discrimination; Television Westerns; Wilson, Edmund.

■ Natural disasters

The decade of the 1950's was one of North America's worst for severe floods, northeasters, blizzards, hurricanes, tornadoes, summer heat waves, and droughts. However, the region did not experience serious volcanic eruptions, and it was nearly unscathed by earthquakes and landslides.

The most serious natural disasters cause extensive human injury and loss of life. They destroy or damage homes, businesses, and crops. They also wipe out expensive infrastructure (for example, sewers, streets, schools, hospitals, banks, and water supply and electricity networks). Such calamities are unwanted reminders of the merciless power of nature. The direct causes of most natural disasters are geological events, such as earthquakes and landslides, and weather-related incidents, such as floods and tornadoes.

Geological Disasters Earthquakes and earthquake-induced landslides and rockslides were the main disasters in the geological category during the 1950's; North America has active volcanoes stretching from Northern California to Alaska, but no volcanic eruption resulted in major loss of property and human deaths during the decade. Geological hazards are concentrated in the western one-third of the continent. This area forms the mountainous edge of the North America Plate, a large moving section of Earth's rocky outer layer. The plate is involved in a slow tectonic (mountain-building) interaction with neighboring plates to the west—the Pacific, Juan de Fuca, and Eurasia plates. As the plates grind against one another, they snap along geologic faults to produce earthquakes. The quakes vary in magnitude (M). On the Richter scale, which measures motion that an earthquake causes, M7.1 is detectable by recording devices over the whole world. Earthquakes along the continent's western rim are among the strongest in the world and include the San Francisco 1906 and Anchorage 1964 earthquakes, which had magnitudes of 8.3 and 9.2 respectively.

Earthquakes in western North America occurred over a wide geographical area during the 1950's. Four temblors qualified as major disasters for the damage and human suffering they caused. The most deadly was the M9.1 Andreanof Islands earthquake of 1957. The Andreanof Islands are located off the coast of Alaska and are part of the Aleutian Islands chain. The islands sit immediately north of the Aleutian Trench, a deep chasm where the Pacific Plate descends beneath the edges of the Eurasia and North America plates. At the epicenter (the point at Earth's surface directly above the origin of the quake), the earthquake killed no one and caused minimal damage. However, a tsunami, or seismic sea wave, continued far beyond the margins of the North America and Eurasia plates to Hawaii, where it destroyed two villages and inflicted five million

dollars in property damage on Oahu and Kauai islands. The 1952 M7.3 Kern County, California, earthquake was the largest tremor since the San Francisco shock of 1906. However, the population density of Kern County was low, so that the quake claimed only twelve lives and caused roughly sixty million dollars in property damage.

Earthquakes also caused two deadly land movements during the 1950's. The 1959 Hebgen Lake earthquake, the largest quake ever to strike in Montana, was one of these. It caused the Rockies' Madison Canyon landslide, the deadliest landslide disaster during the decade. The tremor jarred rock, soil, and trees loose from the south wall of the canyon; twenty-eight people camping in the canyon perished, but only seven bodies were ever recovered from beneath the massive slide. The second deadly landslide started by an earthquake took place in Lituya Bay, Alaska, in 1958. A massive rock slide at the head of the bay caused water to surge across the bay and up the opposite side; five people died.

Weather-Related Disasters Because of the slow movement of tectonic plates, geological disasters occur much less frequently than weather-related disasters do. The entire continent of North America is vulnerable to weather incidents due largely to its location in the northern middle latitudes. This zone spans the latitudes 35 degrees to 55 degrees and is a battlefront between polar and tropical air masses. The conflicting air masses give rise to middle-latitude cyclonic storms and severe thunderstorms. The continent is also open to outbreaks of frigid polar air from the north and tropical heat waves from the south. The continental midsection and the U.S. southeast coast are prone to hurricanes (or their storm remnants) that enter from the south. Moreover, each year, middle-latitude cyclones, thunderstorms, and hurricanes initiate several hundred tornadoes on the continent.

Cold dense air moving in from the north initiates middle-latitude cyclonic storms. Meteorologists call the leading edge of a cold air mass a cold front. The cold front pushes against warm moist air from the south. The cold air is denser and heavier than warm air, so the warm air spirals upward as the cold air pushes against it. As the warm air rises, it cools and forms clouds. Eventually a complex frontal storm develops. Most of these storms are not natural hazards. They are intense low-pressure cells. Strong winds blow into their centers, bringing energy and moisture that sustains them. Hundreds of middle-latitude cyclones occur in North America each year. Most of them are relatively harmless and are necessary to supply water to crops, wildlife, and people. Sometimes the storms are severe enough to bring disastrous results to human life and property. The storms form in three general areas: northern Pacific Ocean, Great Plains, and Gulf Coast. Guided by a polar front jet stream, the storms take a generally eastward track from their origins. The storms cause floods, blizzards, and northeasters on the continent.

Two types of middle-latitude cyclones initiate rain-fed floods: the fierce thundershower, which is of short duration and produces a flash flood, and the prolonged, widespread rain which, through sheer volume of water, creates extensive flooding over entire watersheds. The most devastating rain-caused flood during the 1950's was of the latter type. The flood took place in the Kansas and Neosho river basins in July, 1951. High rainfall from a series of large cyclonic storms soaked soils in eastern Kansas. Excess runoff flooded the Kansas and Neosho Rivers—sixty lives were lost. The deluge hit Kansas City especially hard. Damage to property cost 800 million dollars, making this flood the thirteenth-most-costly deluge of the twentieth century.

Blizzards and Ice Storms Heavy snows during the winter delay the possibility of flooding until spring or early summer. A warm moist wind or warm days with heavy rains cause rapid snowmelt and torrential runoff levels. A disastrous snow-fed flood caused the Red River flood of May 18, 1950. The Red River flows north from North Dakota and Minnesota in the United States into Lake Winnipeg in Manitoba, Canada. During the previous winter, a series of middle-latitude cyclones dumped huge amounts of snow in the river's drainage basin. A rapid snowmelt in the spring caused the river to flood. Floodwaters forced

U.S. Earthquakes with Magnitude 7.0 or Greater During the 1950's

Date	Location	Magnitude
July 21, 1952	Kern County, California	7.3
January 5, 1953	Near Islands, Alaska	7.1
December 16, 1954	Dixie Valley-Fairview Peak, Nevada	7.1
March 9, 1957	Andreanof Islands, Alaska	9.1
March 9, 1957	Fox Islands, Alaska	7.1
March 12, 1957	Andreanof Islands, Alaska	7.0
March 14, 1957	Andreanof Islands, Alaska	7.1
March 16, 1957	Andreanof Islands, Alaska	7.0
April 7, 1958	Huslia, Alaska	7.3
July 10, 1958	Lituya Bay, Alaska	7.7
August 18, 1959	Hebgen Lake, Montana	7.3

Source: United States Geological Survey.

100,000 people in southern Manitoba to flee the area, and the torrent destroyed five thousand homes and buildings. The deluge was one of the greatest natural disasters in Canadian history.

In winter, the middle section of the continent is subject to outbursts of cold arctic air. The cold air, when it occurs in association with a middle-latitude cyclone, can generate blizzards in the continent's midsection and on the East Coast. Under certain conditions, the same frigid air can trigger severe ice storms. Three major blizzards stood out during the 1950's; all of them were northeasters—middle-latitude cyclones that bring very cold temperatures and heavy snows to the East Coast. The first northeaster occurred on February 2, 1951, and became one of the continent's greatest ice storms of record. It spread an icy glaze from Texas to Pennsylvania, killed twenty-five people, and injured five hundred more. Tennessee suffered 100 million dollars in damaged property and interruptions in utilities from seven to ten days.

The second major northeaster occurred February 14-17, 1958. Journalists billed this northeaster the great snowstorm of the century. Snow fell on twenty-two eastern states, and areas from Maryland to New Hampshire accumulated more than thirty inches. After the snowfall ended, intense cold and high winds persisted, prolonging the effects of the blizzard. The storm claimed hundreds of lives and caused seventy million dollars in property damage. The decade's third disastrous blizzard was in St. John, Newfoundland, on February 16, 1959. Frigid winds blowing from the northwest created snowdrifts seven meters (27 feet) high. Motorists spent the night in strangers' homes along roads after snowdrifts buried their stalled cars. Six people died, and the storm left seventy thousand residents without electricity, telephone service, or transportation.

Hurricanes, Tornadoes, and Windstorms Hurricanes are tropical cyclones that form in the Atlantic Ocean, usually between June and November. During these months, oceans evaporate prodigious amounts of heat energy and moisture into the air, making it lighter. The lightweight air rises, causing a low-surface pressure to develop. A steady moist wind blows to "fill" the low pressure, but it also heats up, rises, cools, and creates dark, moisture-laden clouds and convective rainstorms over the ocean. Within a week or two, these storms combine to create a massive tropical storm. Once wind speeds exceed 73 miles per hour (116 km per hour), the storm is officially considered a tropical cyclone or hurricane. Thunder, lightning, hail, and tornadoes accompany them.

Eighteen hurricanes hit U.S. shores during the 1950's. Four of the storms rank among the twenty deadliest hurricanes ever to strike the country. Hurricane Audrey reached land near the Texas-Louisiana border in 1957 and ranks sixth, with 390 deaths. Diane, which made landfall in North Carolina in 1955, ranks as the thirteenth deadliest hurricane with 184 deaths. Hazel, which struck the Carolina border in 1954, ranks seventeenth with ninety-five deaths. Finally, Carol made landfall in Maine in 1954 and ranks nineteenth among the top twenty killer hurricanes with sixty deaths.

Hazel is the most-remembered hurricane in Canada. The storm had already caused ninety-five deaths and wielded 1.5 billion dollars in property damage in the United States. Hazel's remnants reintensified after merging with a low-pressure system over southern Ontario. The storm caused eighty-

one additional deaths there. It also caused more than 100 million dollars in added damages. Similarly, U.S. citizens remember Hurricane Diane less for its landfall in North Carolina than for the flooding and 714 million dollars in damage it caused in the northeast states.

The dark funnel clouds and trainlike roar of tornadoes strike terror in anyone who is in their path. Tornadoes form in the spring and summer in the plains and lowlands that separate the Rocky Mountains from the Appalachian Mountains. A clash of polar and tropical air streams sets up atmospheric conditions for localized outbreaks (swarms) of tornadoes from Texas to Florida and Louisiana to Ontario. The United States experiences more than 90 percent of the world's tornadoes each year. About seven hundred to one thousand twisters occur in the United States annually. Canada has many fewer, averaging only eighty tornadoes per year.

Meteorologists rank each year according to how many deaths occurred as a result of tornadoes. Four of the ten deadliest years since 1950 occurred during the 1950's: 1952 had 230 deaths, 1953 had 519 deaths, 1957 had 193 deaths, and 1955 had 129 deaths. The year 1952 was particularly horrific as most of the tornadoes occurred in a two-day period, March 21-22. Swarms of twisters spread death and destruction over Tennessee, Missouri, Mississippi, and Alabama. The swarms killed 208 people and injured more than 1,000 people. The year 1953 became a record year for deaths (519) from tornadoes. Twisters struck Waco, Texas, causing 119 deaths, and Flint, Michigan, causing 115 deaths; both rank among the ten deadliest tornadoes on record. A third tornado struck Worcester, Massachusetts; it caused 94 deaths.

Windstorms occur when an invasion of cold, dense polar air over North America brings with it high pressure. The rapid rise in pressure can initiate disastrous, high-speed winds. Wind-caused disasters typically occur in two instances: in mountainous areas where cold air descends canyon lands; and along the front edge of an advancing cold air mass, called a cold front. On May 15, 1952, a major wind-related disaster took place in the Wasatch Mountains in Utah. The mountains make a picturesque backdrop for the Salt Lake City-Ogden urban area. However, when there is a high-pressure center over Wyoming and a low-pressure center over Arizona, strong winds rush down the mountain canyons into these cities

Assumption College in the aftermath of the June 10, 1953, tornado that swept through Worcester, Massachusetts, leaving ninety-four people dead. (AP/Wide World Photos)

below. Winds damaged an estimated one million dollars worth of buildings, utility lines, and orchards in the area. The windstorm damaged airplanes at Hill Air Force Base. Wind speeds reached 82 miles per hour with gusts to 95 miles per hour. A rapidly advancing cold front caused another major wind disaster on June 20, 1959. Most of a Canadian fishing fleet sank in the Gulf of St. Lawrence, New Brunswick, as a result. A cold front approaching from the west generated a sudden gale that sank twenty-two salmon-fishing boats. Thirty fishermen died, making this the worst natural disaster to ever hit the Gulf.

A Decade of Summer Heat Waves and Drought Summer temperatures soared dramatically in the second half of the decade. The summer of 1955 had one of the worst heat waves on record in the U.S. Northeast. Americans in the large industrial cities endured hot, humid air in July and August. Temperatures were 4 or more degrees Fahrenheit (F)—or 2 degrees Cel-

sius (C)—above normal. The West Coast was not immune; Los Angeles had temperatures above 100 degrees F (38 degrees C) for eight straight days in late summer. The prolonged heat wave caused numerous health issues among elderly people and asthma suffers. The western United States continued to have torrid conditions to the end of the decade. In Yuma, Arizona, the mercury soared past the century mark every day in July, 1959. Temperatures in Pocatello, Idaho, were greater than 90 degrees F (32 degrees C) for nineteen consecutive days during the same month.

In the American West, several years of drought compounded the misery of the summer heat waves. Dryness first was felt in the southwestern United States in 1950 and spread to Oklahoma, Kansas, and Nebraska by 1953. The drought peaked in 1956, when it covered a ten-state area west of the Mississippi. It reached from the Midwest to the Great Plains and southward into New Mexico and Texas.

The drought devastated the West's agriculture, which depended heavily on rain for grain cultivation and livestock grazing.

Disaster Relief and Meteorological Innovations By the 1950's, the United States and Canada had already developed ad hoc relief systems of local government and private agencies to deal with such disasters. As much as they were able to, local governments, the Red Cross, community and church organizations, and family members and friends helped victims deal with financial and social needs in the aftermaths of disasters. National governments provided a small amount of aid to help rebuild homes and infrastructure.

Also during the decade, the two countries worked to upgrade and increase the number of weather and seismic stations. Radio stations began broadcasting an early warning system for emergencies. Communities in tornado- and hurricane-prone areas maintained sirens in town centers to warn of approaching storms. Scientists developed the first generation of computer models for forecasting weather and storm runoff. Engineers designed and built safer structures with the aid of more accurate geologic and hydrologic maps. The Teletype machine, which was essentially a typewriter that received and printed messages carried by telegraph or telephone, distributed weather data. Trained meteorologists used this data to predict three-day forecasts. Weather maps would not be readily available until the mid-1960's, but the first national network of radar became operational in the United States and Canada during the late 1950's. The network produced black-and-white images that helped detect light precipitation and was an unprecedented tool for short-term forecasting. However, the images only covered radiuses of a few tens of miles surrounding each radar station. Nevertheless, Teletype and radar systems provided enough timely information for television stations to begin including daily weather reports in their news shows.

Impact The natural disasters that the United States and Canada witnessed during the decade could have been worse. Geological events were not numerous; there were only two major earthquakes and two major earthquake-induced land movements. Although there were volcanic eruptions, none registered as a catastrophic event. Moreover, Canada escaped the summer heat waves, tornadoes, and hurricanes be-

cause of its northern location. Nevertheless, North America as a whole endured some of the worst hurricanes, northeasters, tornadoes, floods, heat waves, droughts, and blizzards on record.

Further Reading

Amdahl, Gary. *Disaster Response: GIS for Public Safety.* Redlands, Calif.: ESRI Press, 2001. An illustrated guide to using geographic information systems (GIS) to aid in responding to natural disasters.

Bryant, E. A. *Natural Hazards.* New York: Cambridge University Press, 1991. An excellent primer on a wide range of climatic and geological hazards.

Ludlum, David M. *The American Weather Book.* Boston: Houghton Mifflin, 1982. Ludlum's book lists extreme U.S. weather and weather-related phenomena for each day of the year up to the date of the book's publication.

Newsom, Lesley. *Devastation! The World's Worst Natural Disasters.* New York: DK, 1998. Covers several natural disasters during the 1950's.

Platt, Rutherford H., ed. *Disasters and Democracy: The Politics of Extreme Natural Events.* Washington, D.C.: Island Press, 1999. Addresses the political response to natural disasters.

Zebrowski, Ernest, Jr. *Perils of a Restless Planet: Scientific Perspectives on Natural Disasters.* New York: Cambridge University Press, 1997. Tracks scientists' work through history in their attempts to forecast natural disasters more accurately.

Richard A. Crooker

See also Farm subsidies; Mexico; Small Business Administration.

■ Natural resources

Population growth and increasing urbanization during the 1950's placed new stresses on natural resources although the long-term impact of these stresses would not be realized for some time.

Rebounding from the economic dislocations of the Great Depression of the 1930's and growing consumer demands derived from wartime scarcity during the 1940's, the American economy underwent a massive growth spurt during the 1950's. Growth liberalism, as it was called, was a driving force for both political parties as all leaders accepted that economic growth was a fundamental principle of American life. This policy helped to improve the material life of many Americans during the 1950's but at some cost. One major component of economic growth during the decade was the increased demand for nonrenewable and renewable resources, as well as changing patterns of land use. The exploitation of natural resources also imposed long-term costs such as air and water pollution and global warming. Rarely heard were the voices that questioned the long-term environmental impact of economic growth.

Economic and Population Growth Economic growth was bound up with Cold War ideology during the 1950's. People saw a rapidly growing American economy as a sign of strength and as evidence of the superiority of capitalism as opposed to communism. The perceived need for a strong defense posture contributed to the creation of military hardware as well as leading to the despoliation of the environment through weapons testing.

Economic growth was also fueled by an increased demand for consumer goods, housing, and military production. Many people held the optimistic view that science and technology were "cure-alls" that could overcome all obstacles and believed that increased industrial production resulting from this technological sophistication would lead to a better life for all Americans. Technological advances made it easier to extract natural resources from the earth and to increase agricultural production. As more American families owned automobiles, it became easier to commute to work from greater distances, a development that was coupled with a demand for housing to produce the growth of suburbia.

Population growth during the decade also helped foster increased resource consumption. The increasingly large and more affluent population demanded more and better consumer goods and housing, as well as increasing the demand for energy for their growing mobility. The impact of the baby boom generation began to be felt during the decade of the 1950's in a variety of ways. Young parents, for example, desired larger homes to accommodate their growing families.

The primary approach to the use of natural resources during the 1950's was one dating back to the colonial era. People perceived natural resources as a bounty to be used and gave little thought to the possible exhaustion of various resources. There was an awareness of the extinction of some species, but few

commentators connected this issue to a broader approach to the environment. Dating from the early twentieth century there was some awareness of the need to conserve resources so that they would be available in the future. Even the utilitarian conservation approach concentrated on the use of natural resources, rather than preservation, and gave no thought to the potential environmental impact imposed by the consumption of natural resources.

Economic growth was not cost free. Natural resources such as coal, oil, and metallic ores had to be extracted from the earth. Land had to be intensively cultivated to feed the growing population, and this demand for increased agricultural productivity often led to increased use of irrigation to make unproductive land productive and a greater reliance on chemical fertilizers and pesticides. The demand for increased agricultural production received further impetus as land once used for farming was developed for suburban growth, shopping centers, and highways. Even renewable resources such as water, timber, and fisheries were further exploited to keep up with the demand for goods emanating from the growing population. By 1950, the California sardine industry, for example, was nearly ruined by harvesting pressure, and other fisheries, such as the Newfoundland Banks, would feel the same pressure during the decade.

Coal Use Natural resources fall into two broad categories: nonrenewable and renewable resources. Nonrenewable resources are those that are used up by consumption and cannot be replenished. Examples include various carbon-based fuels such as coal, oil, and gas as well as metallic ores. Renewable resources such as timber, when used wisely, are not exhausted by consumption. However, over-exploitation makes it difficult, if not impossible, to replenish these resources and they, too, can become scarce or used up.

At the beginning of the 1950's, coal was still the primary energy source for much of the American economy and a heating source for many American households. The development of the American coal industry dated from the nineteenth century, and coal remained a labor-intensive industry through the end of World War II. From the late 1940's onward, technology increasingly was applied to coal production, and the amount of coal that the industry could bring to market increased. During most of the 1950's, both anthracite and bituminous coal were mined primarily in the eastern United States, especially Pennsylvania, West Virginia, and Kentucky, as well as in the Midwest, most notably in Illinois. Although some small-scale operators ran open pit mines, most eastern coal mining was carried out underground during the decade. Some experimentation was being carried out with massive surface mining using drag lines in southern Indiana, but this form of mining tended to be more characteristic of the emerging mining operations in states such as Wyoming than of eastern mines.

Underground coal mining was not as destructive of the environment as surface mining, but it created its own set of problems. Abandoned mines could cave in, leading to unexpected sinkholes. The coal that remained in these mines could catch fire and produce long-term underground fires, which could produce surface fires or subsidence as mine tunnels collapsed. The most notable of these fires began in 1962 in Centralia, Pennsylvania, when a surface garbage dump fire caught a coal seam in a mine abandoned during the 1950's. The fire continued for decades and made the town nearly unlivable through the production of noxious gases and land subsidence.

Underground mining often produced large impoundments of water pumped from the mines. Coal companies usually dammed the narrow valleys in states such as Kentucky and West Virginia to receive the contaminated water from the mines. Some of the dams were poorly constructed and floods occurred, damaging communities that were downstream. Even when this did not happen, the water was contaminated by mineral waste, which often leached into the water sources of nearby homes.

Surface mining, particularly when carried out on a large scale, irreparably scarred the landscape. Surface mining destroyed the existing ground cover and left behind lakes filled with a noxious brew of water and chemicals. It generally fostered erosion in areas near the surface mines.

Bituminous, or soft, coal burns with a greasy smoke that fouls the air, and the burning of both bituminous coal and anthracite, or hard coal, can produce atmospheric pollution such as sulfur dioxide or nitrogen oxides as well as the release of the "greenhouse" gas, carbon dioxide, into the atmosphere. While anthracite is "cleaner" than bituminous coal, it is also more expensive to mine and is not suitable for all uses; thus, many power companies relied on soft coal.

By the twenty-first century, much of North America's coal was mined in the western United States and Canada; production shifted from the East as coal reserves there became exhausted. This depletion was becoming more apparent beginning during the 1950's, when reserves in places such as Pennsylvania became exhausted. Although coal is in finite supply, the United States and Canada continued to have adequate supplies of coal in the twenty-first century because of the large coal reserves of both countries and because of a substitution of other carbon-based energy sources that began during the 1950's.

During the 1950's, individuals might have complained when their houses collapsed because of subsidence, and voices were raised to condemn floods produced by mine water, but generally the political strength of the coal companies coupled with a demand for cheap energy stilled any criticism. Coal fueled American industrial growth in the first half of the twentieth century and helped power American railroads. However, a transition began during the 1950's that would lead to the diminution of coal as an energy source. In some cases industry would begin to utilize oil and natural gas as cleaner and more efficient sources of energy. Coal, however, remained an important source of power for many power companies in subsequent decades.

Oil and Gas Use The importance of oil and natural gas as energy sources increased throughout the twentieth century. Both could be used as an energy source for industry and homes either directly or to generate electric power. The dramatic increase in the number of cars during the 1950's increased the demand for gasoline production. During the decade, some railroads began to retire their coal-powered steam locomotives in favor of diesel engines. Oil also served as the feedstock for the petrochemical industry. The turn to the use of plastics and synthetic fibers, for example, in this era added to the demand for oil. The new "miracle fabrics," such as nylon and rayon, began to be widely used and fostered a demand for other synthetic fibers.

Oil and gas, like coal, are carbon based and are in finite supply. Because oil was harder to find than coal, oil and gas exploration was big business during the 1950's and even earlier. Oil and gas production in the United States was centered in Oklahoma, Texas, Louisiana, and California, although wells were drilled elsewhere in the country, such as offshore in the Gulf of Mexico and in western Canada. During the decade, American energy companies also began to turn to Middle Eastern countries for oil. Although some people thought that oil would be the fuel of the future because it was nearly inexhaustible, not everyone was convinced. In 1956, M. King Hubbert, a geophysicist with Shell Oil Company, examined American oil consumption and American oil reserves and estimated that the amount of oil that could be discovered and produced by conventional means was between 150 and 200 billion barrels. Even his optimistic estimate indicated that American oil production would peak during the early 1970's; the actual peak year was 1970. Hubbert had many critics who decried his estimates and advocated increased reliance on oil.

Initially considered of little value, natural gas proved to be an important energy source by the 1950's. Environmentally cleaner than either of the other two fossil fuels, coal and oil, natural gas promised to be a clean, efficient fuel. Natural gas wells had to be drilled deeper than oil wells, and natural gas proved to be in more limited supply than oil. Nonetheless, natural gas would be utilized increasingly for electric energy generation and home and business heating during the decade.

The growth of automobile use during the 1950's increased the demand for gasoline, which is produced from oil. Cheap gasoline was a hallmark of American life in the decade and helped to foster the growth of individual mobility that Americans would come to take for granted. Combined with automobile use, other demands for energy increased oil consumption. Oil and natural gas began to replace coal as the fuel in some electric power plants, industry, and home heating. At the time, the substitution of one hydrocarbon for another was considered a cleaner energy use. Because oil and gas were also hydrocarbons, however, burning them produced many of the same long-term problems of atmospheric pollution and global warming as did the burning of coal.

Energy production was not the only use for oil, however. The growth of the American petrochemical industry relied upon oil for its feedstocks. Hydrocarbons were used for cleaning solvents, for synthetics, and particularly for plastics. Plastics began to

replace other materials such as wood and metal during the decade. The use of plastics would prove to be a two-edged sword over time. Their use in automobiles, for example, decreased the vehicles' weight and thus helped to improve mileage, thereby decreasing the demand for gasoline. However, the increased use of plastics would impose increasing demands for oil.

Metals Use The growth of industry during the 1950's increased the demand for metals such as lead, iron, and copper, which always had been mainstays of industrial development. Iron ore, for example, continued to be mined in the Mesabi Range in Minnesota. The demand for lighter and stronger materials also increased the demand for bauxite, or aluminum ore, and titanium, among others. Aluminum refining proved to be an energy-intensive process, requiring large amounts of electric power to carry out the smelting process. In general, the mining and smelting of metallic ores imposed environmental damage. For example, the mining and smelting of copper ore near Copper Hill, Tennessee, reduced the surrounding area by the 1950's to a virtual moonscape totally denuded of vegetation and subject to erosion.

The advent of the nuclear age during World War II also stimulated a demand for uranium ore. During the 1950's, some energy planners dreamed of using atomic energy to power America. Atomic energy was cited as clean, efficient, problem-free, and nearly inexhaustible. The difficulties of nuclear waste disposal would be realized only in the future, but it soon became evident that nuclear power would not replace fossil fuels. Nuclear power plants were expensive to construct and produced a potentially deadly side effect in their spent radioactive fuel rods. Uranium had another use: weapons production. The military demands for uranium production escalated during the decade as the United States engaged in an arms race with the Soviet Union. Uranium mining in the Rocky Mountains, especially in Colorado, would, however, produce the same problems of tailings and waste disposal as mining did elsewhere. Moreover, some of the waste would be radioactive. Uranium refining also was a major consumer of electrical energy, both in the Northwest, as evidenced with the Hanford nuclear plant in Washington State, and in the Southeast, with the uranium production at Oak Ridge, Tennessee.

Oil rigs in Huntington Beach, in Southern California, one of the most important oil-producing regions of the United States during the 1950's. (AP/Wide World Photos)

Water Use The 1950's witnessed increased dam construction throughout the United States and Canada, and hydroelectric power helped to power energy production sites in places such as Hanford and Oak Ridge. Nonetheless, hydroelectric power was surpassed by fossil fuels as an energy source during the 1950's. The large lakes, such as Lake Mead, Las Vegas, created from the Colorado River also helped with flood control and provided recreational opportunities.

In some parts of the country, artificial lakes also served another important purpose: a water source for irrigation. Irrigation was not a factor with the Tennessee Valley Authority lakes in the Southeast, but in California and the arid Great Plains and Southwest, irrigation was essential for agricultural success.

As populations grew, an increasing demand for food and other agricultural products, such as cotton, required that arid land be put under cultiva-

tion. Conservation advocate John Wesley Powell had warned of the potential environmental hazards of farming the plains in the nineteenth century, and the Dust Bowl plight of the 1930's illustrated the problem. Nonetheless, irrigation was used in the central valley of California to increase food production and began to be used in the Southwest to raise cotton as well as to support the suburban growth of cities such as Phoenix. Suburbia in the Southwest would demand beautiful green lawns in what was essentially a desert. Lawn irrigation became a major consumer of water as suburban areas grew. In some areas, such as Southern California, irrigation water derived from diverted surface water from other areas. For many areas on the Great Plains, surface water diversion was not possible because of the low rainfall levels, and deep wells that tapped underground aquifers began to be used extensively during the 1950's to address this problem. While surface water is a renewable resource, underground water is essentially nonrenewable, so the "water-mining" that intensified during the 1950's would have long-term consequences for sustainability. Plains farmers began to tap the Ogallala aquifer that stretched from Texas to Nebraska, which produced more water than the Mississippi River carried to the Gulf of Mexico in two hundred years. Starting during the 1950's, farmers on the plains began to mine the Ogallala aquifer at rates that exceeded its ability to replenish itself.

Extensive use of irrigation had long-term consequences that had not been foreseen. Irrigation water that travels in surface canals evaporates at a high rate and seeps into the ground, where irrigation ditches are unlined. Soil that has too much water applied to it becomes waterlogged and incapable of agricultural production. In other cases, irrigation water contains various minerals such as sodium chloride, or salt. Extensive use of irrigation without proper drainage can cause the salinization of the soil, which decreases agricultural productivity. Although this latter process was not yet a problem during the 1950's, by the 1960's the impact of long-term irrigation would cause previously productive land to be productive no longer, as in the case of the Imperial Valley of California.

Water was also used increasingly during the 1950's for recreation and waste disposal. Recreational use was often combined with other uses. Some cities and industries continued to rely upon nearby streams for the disposal of their waste. This use had an impact on downstream communities as water quality was degraded.

Throughout the country's history, water was often considered the ultimate renewable resource. Blessed with abundant supplies of water, most Americans took water for granted, and during the 1950's, an increased reliance on technological solutions caused many people to think that the desert could be made to bloom or that science would step in eventually and solve water issues. Throughout the decade, few people regarded water as a potentially finite resource. Although there was some concern for water pollution, water continued to be seen as an inexhaustible resource, and few people paid any attention to a potential need for water conservation.

Timber Use In many ways the growth of American society was fueled by the use of wood. Although wood use was surpassed by coal use in the nineteenth

century, wood had been the fuel of choice in early America: American houses were framed of wood, furniture built of wood, and paper generated by wood. By World War II, much of the eastern forests in the United States, and to a lesser extent in Canada, had been cut, leaving behind barren landscapes. During the 1950's, some of these landscapes were gradually being reforested. In the American West, however, the picture was different, as timber companies turned to western forests to supply the expanding demand for wood products at home and abroad. Although plastic and metal were replacing wood in some uses during the era, wood—especially plywood based on pine—continued to be the mainstay of the booming housing industry. Timber companies began to intensify their timber use on federal lands in the West. This timber was obtained at low cost, and its harvest began to leave tracts denuded of cover in the West. Although a few private owners had already begun a pattern of planting trees after cutting, the U.S. government did not require timber companies to do so on federal lands during this period. Even when trees were planted, they were usually the same type, often pine, such that forest diversity was lost.

Land Use As Americans moved westward in the nineteenth century, land was seen as a resource to be used for agriculture or to have its bounty, both above or below ground, harvested. In the twentieth century, the United States came to be an increasingly urban nation with more and more people living in or near cities. In the years after World War II, spurred by demand fueled by larger incomes, improved mobility from automobiles, and cheaper construction, many Americans moved to the suburbs. The 1950's became the era of suburban growth as rings of residential communities and shopping malls began to encircle American cities. Suburbia increased the demand for wood, asphalt, and brick for construction and indirectly for gasoline for transportation. The growth of suburbia also began a change in how land was used.

The demand for cheap housing led many developers to begin to build on cleared agricultural land near American cities. Because of improvements in agricultural productivity, less land was needed for agriculture, and many landowners sold out to developers in order to earn quick profits. The growth of residential suburbs necessitated the growth of highways to serve these suburbs, taking away even more land. Once enough people had moved to the suburbs, retail businesses followed. Shopping malls that served as magnets for the surrounding residential areas and were served by burgeoning highway systems became increasingly commonplace in 1950's America. The early malls were sprawling affairs that required large tracts of land for malls themselves and for their adjoining parking lots.

The move outward from American cities that accelerated during the 1950's was a path taken by industry as well. Seeking room for expansion and cheaper land prices, many industries began to move to the suburbs or beyond during the 1950's. In some cases this led to the conversion of prime agricultural land to other uses. Starting during the late 1950's, in St. Louis County, Missouri, for example, the "Gumbo Bottoms" area—a highly productive truck farming locale—began to be converted into small industrial parks. In this case, residential construction leap-frogged the industrial parks to even more rural St. Charles County, thus creating a boom in residential construction that would change the face of the county by 1980. This same process of outward movement would occur throughout the country.

As people moved out from the cities, they also sought recreational opportunities. In some cases this led to the construction of public parks. In other cases the demand for recreational opportunities led to commercial development. Perhaps the most famous of these commercial recreational centers emerged when the Walt Disney Company began to clear California orange groves and build Disneyland, which opened in 1955. These new recreational centers imposed heavy demands on the land for construction as well as highways to serve them.

The move to suburbia imposed considerable costs that went beyond taking land out of cultivation. Construction created a demand for natural resources of all sorts. Longer travel times by private car increased the demand for oil products. Subdivisions and shopping malls had an insatiable demand for water for drinking, waste treatment, and irrigation. Suburbs in the Southwest imposed stringent water demands as each house had a yard that had to be watered in an arid climate.

The development paths and land uses begun during the 1950's would change the American landscape in dramatic fashion. This new form of urban development would continue to impose enormous resource costs on the American environment, although the true nature of the costs would not be known for some time.

Impact During the 1950's, Americans lived much better than ever before, largely aided by the increase in the exploitation of the natural environment. It is unfair to criticize policymakers or the general citizenry for some of the side effects of this exploitation, which were neither recognized nor understood for several more decades. However, it is fair to say that most Americans continued to accept unquestioningly that all natural resources were inexhaustible during the 1950's and to use these resources with scant regard for the future. Moreover, some aspects of air and water pollution were becoming highly visible during the decade, although industry and government tended to ignore the issues.

The material standard of living for Americans increased dramatically during the decade of the 1950's. Some social critics condemned what they saw as the increased materialism of American society, but few questioned the ever-increasing exploitation of the natural environment. Other critics, such as M. King Hubbert in the oil industry, pointed out that most natural resources were finite. Still other figures, such as Aldo Leopold, David Brower, and Sigurd Olson, questioned what development was doing to the natural environment. However, vocal criticism was often not heard. Rachel Carson would prove to be another important advocate for conservationism; her 1951 best-selling book, *The Sea Around Us*, called attention to the delicate processes and life-forms of the ocean, while her 1962 book *Silent Spring* attacked the impact of pesticide and herbicide use.

The 1950's was arguably the last decade of unimpeded natural resource exploitation. Starting during the 1960's, American society would begin to pay the costs of the use of the environment that occurred during the 1950's and would gradually be forced to acknowledge that natural resources are finite.

Further Reading

Caudill, Harry M. *Night Comes to the Cumberlands*. Boston: Little, Brown, 1962. Details the devastating impact of coal mining on the Cumberland plateau.

Collins, Robert P. *More: The Politics of Economic Growth in Postwar America*. New York: Oxford University Press, 2000. A discussion of growth liberalism.

Deffeyes, Kenneth S. *Hubbert's Peak.* Princeton, N.J.: Princeton University Press, 2001. Explores the oil industry and the impending oil shortage.

Hays, Samuel P. *Beauty, Health, and Permanence.* Cambridge, England: Cambridge University Press, 1987. A useful account of environmental politics from 1955 to 1985.

Jackson, Kenneth T. *Crabgrass Frontier.* New York: Oxford University Press, 1985. Details the growth of suburbia.

Merchant, Carolyn. *Reinventing Eden.* New York: Routledge, 2003. Examines various intellectual reactions to nature.

Power, Thomas Michael. *Lost Landscapes and Failed Economies.* Washington, D.C.: Island Press, 1996. Treatment of the politics and economics of land use, especially mineral extraction, agriculture, and timber.

Reisner, Marc. *Cadillac Desert.* Rev. ed. New York: Penguin Books, 1993. Examines water resources in the American West.

Samuelson, Robert J. *The Good Life and Its Discontents.* New York: Random House, 1995. Discussion of the optimism of the 1950's and what it produced.

Scheffer, Victor B. *The Shaping of Environmentalism in America.* Seattle: University of Washington Press, 1991. Chronicles the development of various environmental problems traceable back to the 1950's and society's response.

Steinberg, Ted. *Down to Earth.* New York: Oxford University Press, 2002. A wide-ranging treatment of American environmental history that includes topics such as the West in the twentieth century and the impact of consumer society.

John M. Theilmann

See also Affluence and the new consumerism; Agriculture in the United States; Air pollution; Antarctic Treaty of 1959; Atomic Energy Act of 1954; Science and technology; *Sea Around Us, The*; Urbanization in the United States; Water pollution.

■ *Nautilus,* USS

Identification First American nuclear-powered submarine
Date Launched on January 21, 1954

The Nautilus *demonstrated the utility of nuclear-powered submarines as part of America's nuclear deterrence during the Cold War.*

Submarine warfare played a significant role during World War II, but submarines of that era were limited by fuel capacity in their capability to remain at sea and stay submerged for extended periods. Indeed, many scholars argue that submarines prior to the *Nautilus* were only submersible craft able to go beneath the ocean surface for limited periods. A nuclear submarine, however, would be limited in its ability to remain on duty only by the supply of consumables—air, water, and food—that its stores could carry. Fuel no longer would be as limiting a factor; nuclear submarines could remain submerged for weeks, even months at a time.

After World War II, with the introduction of atomic weaponry into military strategy, the United States and the Soviet Union entered into a Cold War competition that lasted more than four decades. During this time, strategic defense centered around the concept of "Mutual Assured Destruction," which meant the development of nuclear stockpiles so vast that neither side would be able to withstand a nuclear exchange. The American nuclear deterrent involved a triad of strategic bombers, land-based missiles, and submarine-based missiles. While bombers and land-based missiles were vulnerable to attack, nuclear missiles aboard submarines at depth could evade detection by the Soviets.

Perhaps the greatest proponent of a nuclear navy was Hyman G. Rickover. His dogged determination overcame considerable resistance to the nuclear submarine concept, and, on January 21, 1954, the *Nautilus* entered sea trials. The submarine was commissioned on September 30, 1954.

Constructed by the Electric Boat Division of General Dynamics Corporation at Groton, Connecticut, the *Nautilus* was 320 feet long, had a beam of 28 feet, a draft of 26 feet, and a displacement of 2,975 tons when surfaced. The *Nautilus* was armed with six twenty-one-inch torpedo tubes. The basic shape of the *Nautilus* shared much in common with German U-boats. Later nuclear submarines would take on a much more hydrodynamic shape.

Perhaps the *Nautilus*'s most notable achievement came in 1958, when its crew sailed completely underneath the Arctic ice pack on route to the North Pole, broadcasting from that location the brief recognition code "*Nautilus* 90 North." The *Nautilus* passed from the Pacific to the Atlantic Ocean under the ice pack.

The USS Nautilus *entering New York Harbor in 1956.* (Hulton Archive | by Getty Images)

Impact The *Nautilus* never actually carried nuclear missiles, as it was essentially a proof-of-concept vessel. It was followed by the Skipjack- and Thresher-class nuclear submarines; the first ballistic missile-equipped nuclear submarine, the USS *George Washington*, entered military service in 1960. Many improved classes of weapons-laden nuclear submarines followed. The ability of nuclear submarines to move nuclear weapons about the world, largely without detection, proved to be a critical aspect of American nuclear deterrence.

The *Nautilus* was decommissioned in 1980 and became a National Historic Landmark available for public viewing in Groton, Connecticut.

Further Reading

Anderson, William R. *Nautilus 90 North.* Cleveland: World Publishing Company, 1959. A first-person account of life aboard the USS *Nautilus.*

Craven, John Pina. *The Silent War: The Cold War Battle Beneath the Sea.* New York: Simon & Schuster, 2001. An insider's story of participation in underwater intelligence missions during the Cold War, detailing the innovative high technology and bold seafaring the United States employed against the

Soviet Union in the battle for nuclear and military supremacy.

Polmar, Norman. *Rickover.* New York: Simon & Schuster, 1982. A thorough biography of the greatest proponent of the nuclear navy.

David G. Fisher

See also Atomic bomb; Atomic Energy Act of 1954; *Bennington* explosion; Hydrogen bomb; Polaris missiles; *Savannah*; Science and technology.

■ New York Yankees

Identification Professional baseball team

The New York Yankees dominated baseball during the 1950's, setting numerous records and boasting several nationally adored players.

From 1921 through 1949, the New York Yankees established themselves as the most successful team in the history of Major League Baseball by winning sixteen American League pennants and twelve World Series titles. An even higher level of domination was reached during the 1950's as the Yankees won an amazing eight pennants and six World Series championships in ten seasons.

Team Accomplishments In 1950, the Yankees, hoping to repeat champion status, faced the Philadelphia Phillies in the World Series. The series opened with three one-run games, but the Yankees won them all and then completed a 4-0 sweep, claiming their thirteenth championship. A historic World Series opened in 1951 with Joe DiMaggio playing in his last season, and Mickey Mantle and Willie Mays playing in their first. The Yankees faced their crosstown rivals, the New York Giants, who claimed the National League pennant by winning a playoff game with the Brooklyn Dodgers on the strength of Bobby Thomson's three home runs in the bottom of the ninth inning. Giant magic failed in the series, however, as the Yankees won in six games. The Yankees beat their other crosstown rival, the Dodgers, in the 1952 and 1953 World Series, winning in seven and six games, respectively.

The 1953 championship was the Yankees' fourth World Series in a row and capped an incredible run of fifteen titles in sixteen series appearances. In 1954, the Yankees won the most games of any year in the decade—103—but lost the pennant to the Cleveland Indians. In the next season, the Yankees and Dodgers faced off for the third time in four years. However, the Dodgers claimed the championship in seven games, winning their first World Series title. The same two teams met again in the 1956 series, with the Yankees—capped by pitcher Don Larsen's perfect game in game five—claiming the championship in seven games. After six straight years of a World Series dominated by New York teams, a new city, Milwaukee, faced off against the Yankees in the 1957 and 1958 series. The Milwaukee Braves, led by Warren Spahn and Henry Aaron, won the 1957 title in seven games, while the Yanks claimed the championship in 1958, becoming the second team to win a World Series after falling behind three games to one. A 79-75 record in 1959 closed the Yankees' winning era, the only dim spot in a stellar decade.

Individual Achievements The most notable accomplishments by Yankee players during the 1950's included Don Larsen's perfect World Series game (the only such game in series history), Allie Reynolds's two no-hitters in 1951, and Mickey Mantle's triple crown (first in batting average, home runs, and runs batted in) in 1956. Most valuable player awards were won by Phil Rizzuto (1950), Yogi Berra (1951, 1954,

1955), and Mickey Mantle (1956, 1957); the Cy Young Award was won by Bob Turley in 1958.

Impact The Yankees' success caused baseball fever among the American public during the 1950's, and the team's persistence, prosperity, and staying power both reflected and bolstered America's postwar idealism. The popularity of baseball increased immensely because a star-filled team in America's biggest city dominated the game during the dawning of the television age. Many of the team's players later were inducted into the Baseball Hall of Fame, including Mickey Mantle, Joe DiMaggio, and Yogi Berra.

Further Reading

Fromer, Harvey, and Paul O'Neil. *A Yankee Century: A Celebration of the First Hundred Years of Baseball's Greatest Team.* New York: Berkley Publishing Group, 2002. Presents a thorough history of team's seasons and achievements.

Kahn, Roger. *The Era, 1947-1957: When the Yankees, the Giants, and the Dodgers Ruled the World.* Lincoln: University of Nebraska Press, 2002. The golden era of New York baseball is described in rich detail.

Paul J. Chara, Jr.

See also Banks, Ernie; Baseball; Berra, Yogi; DiMaggio, Joe; Larsen's perfect game; Mantle, Mickey; Mays, Willie; Robinson, Jackie; Snider, Duke; Stengel, Casey; Thomson, Bobby.

■ Newport Jazz Festival

The Event Two-day festival that brought together leading jazz musicians
Date July 17-18, 1954
Place Newport, Rhode Island

The success of the Newport Jazz Festival proved that jazz could draw large crowds with corporate sponsorship and a strong public relations approach.

In 1950, George Wein opened the jazz club Storyville in Boston, Massachusetts, and it soon became one of the leading jazz clubs in the United States. Through trial and error, Wein learned how to earn the trust of the great African American jazz players. For his club to stay in business, he knew that he would have to book noted jazz musicians. Over the ten-year life of the club, Wein booked every major jazz artist of the day, including Duke Ellington,

Louis Armstrong, Ella Fitzgerald, Charlie Parker, Miles Davis, Thelonious Monk, Oscar Peterson, and Billie Holiday. However, Storyville closed in 1960 because the leading jazz acts had become too big to play in clubs.

In 1953, after conversations with wealthy jazz supporters in Newport, Rhode Island, Wein was asked if he could organize a jazz festival. Newport had a population of approximately 35,000 residents and had a reputation as being a vacation spot for rich Americans. The board of governors of the Newport Casino voted unanimously that the casino could be used for a festival. By April, 1954, Wein was hard at work getting commitments to perform from a variety of remarkable jazz musicians. On April 29, 1954, the charter for the Jazz Festival of Newport, Rhode Island, Inc., was filed with the state. The corporation was chartered to carry out a number of activities for charitable purposes only, including putting on music festivals, raising funds for music scholarships, and holding music competitions.

The inaugural festival was held on the casino grounds in mid-July, but the Newport business community was not sufficiently prepared to handle the thousands of fans who invaded the area. On July 17, 1954, the *Providence Journal* stated that "Newport jazz fans jammed hotels, cleaned out kitchens, slept on beaches." Moreover, it was difficult for African Americans who attended the festival to find anyplace to stay. For all the headaches and inadequate planning, however, the first Newport Jazz Festival was a ringing success. Thousands of enthusiastic jazz fans paid as little as three dollars to attend the groundbreaking two-day event and to hear a variety of jazz styles. Such jazz traditionalist acts as Pee Wee Russell, Eddie Condon, Bobby Hackett, and Ella Fitzgerald shared the stage with the modernist lineup of Dizzy Gillespie, Oscar Peterson, Lee Konitz, and Gerry Mulligan. Stan Kenton served as master of ceremonies and during his opening comments noted that the festival was making history and that the United States "has taken jazz for granted. Europe has recently held several jazz festivals, for abroad they recognize jazz as a distinct form of music."

Impact Because of the success of the 1954 Newport Jazz Festival, other corporate-sponsored jazz events took place thereafter. Wein produced a jazz festival in 1958 at the World's Fair in Brussels, Belgium. By

Ray Charles performing at the Newport Jazz Festival in 1958. (Hulton Archive | by Getty Images)

the early 1960's, Wein was organizing festivals in such cities as Boston, Philadelphia, Buffalo, and Toronto. By 1957, the Newport Jazz Festival had become so popular that the crowds had grown to more than forty thousand.

Subsequent Events With the addition of popular music acts such as Chuck Berry, Ray Charles, Jethro Tull, and Sly and the Family Stone to the performance roster during the 1960's, the festival expanded its fan base. In 1972, the festival moved to New York, but in 1981, it moved back to Newport without giving up its ties to New York. The Japanese Victor Corporation became its sponsor in 1984, and the name was changed to the JVC Jazz Festival New York. Through the extraordinary efforts of George Wein and others, the wedding of music festivals and corporate sponsorship made it possible for large numbers of fans from around the world to see top-notch musical acts in person.

Further Reading

Goldblatt, Burt. *Newport Jazz Festival.* New York: Dial Press, 1977. Provides a year-by-year detailed history of the festival.

Wein, George, with Nate Chinen. *Myself Among Others.* Cambridge, Mass.: Da Capo Press, 2003. The autobiography of the founder of the festival.

Jeffry Jensen

See also Brubeck, Dave; Fitzgerald, Ella; Jazz; Music; Peterson, Oscar.

■ News magazines

Definition Weekly magazines that focused on major news makers, news events, and cultural trends

During the 1950's, news magazines enjoyed a surge in popularity as their coverage of the major events and news makers of the decade offered readers longer and more introspective stories, segmented news sections, and opinion columns.

News magazines give readers an alternative to the fast-paced news gathering of other media. The main goals of news magazines are to offer more information and a variety of expert viewpoints on the biggest stories of any particular time period. There have been a number of such magazines published, particularly since the 1980's. However, much earlier, three American magazines distinguished themselves: *Time, Newsweek,* and *U.S. News & World Report.* Although arguably, none of these is the oldest (*The Nation* first appeared in 1865), all have proven popular through subscription and store sales, and all three use sections (for example, "Science," "Business," and "Entertainment") to format the news and feature popular regular columns.

Background Business manager Henry Luce and editor Briton Hadden launched *Time* magazine in 1923. The format was considered the first of its kind—a general interest news magazine aimed at a national audience. In 1928, they introduced *Time*'s first-ever "Man of the Year," aviator Charles Lindberg. Time-Life, Inc., was organized in 1961 and led to ventures in other magazine publishing (including *Life* magazine), book publishing, radio, and television. *Newsweek,* which called itself "The Magazine of News Significance," was founded by Thomas J. C. Martyn, a former foreign editor at *Time,* and was first published in 1933. Like *Time, Newsweek* focused on the hard news of the day, as well as scientific and medical research. *U.S. News & World Report* followed in 1948, when journalist David Lawrence merged his weekly newspaper the *United States News* with his weekly magazine the *World Report.*

Format and Coverage During the 1950's, the three magazines' popularity increased as they became accepted alternatives to other media. The circulation leader, *Time,* was selling 400,000 copies a week by the late 1950's. During that time period, all three averaged about one hundred published pages a week.

The magazines used regular columns to engage loyal readers. Some of the columns that were prominent during the 1950's continued as part of the magazines' pages fifty years later: "Washington Whispers" in *U.S. News & World Report*; "Milestones" and "People" in *Time*; and "Newsmakers" and "Perspective" in *Newsweek.*

The magazines relied on the big headlines and the major events and trends of the era to guide content. All three focused on communism and the influence of Senator Joseph McCarthy's congressional hearings; national and international politics, particularly the Cold War and the Soviet Union; atomic and hydrogen weapons development and the space program; and the events leading up to and including the Korean War.

Covers *Newsweek* and *Time* covers often featured a photograph or illustration of a person important to the primary news event of the week, accompanied by one related headline and sometimes one or two unrelated "teaser" headlines. Both maintained heavy coverage of political and social world events as well as the people who were strongly associated with those events.

During the 1950's, *Time*'s covers featured Soviet leaders Joseph Stalin and Nikita Khrushchev, General Douglas MacArthur, presidents Harry S. Truman and Dwight D. Eisenhower, the Reverend Martin Luther King, Jr., Lyndon B. Johnson, Vice President Richard M. Nixon, and McCarthy. The magazine's "Man of the Year" choices in this decade included Winston S. Churchill, "G.I. Joe" (U.S. soldier composite), Secretary of State John Foster Dulles, and French leader Charles De Gaulle.

Other notable figures who appeared on *Time* covers included architect Edward Stone, actor Grace Kelly, test pilot Bill Bridgeman, heart specialist Dr. Irvine Page, International Business Machines Corporation's (IBM) Thomas J. Watson, Jr., and Antarctic explorer Paul Siple. *Time* did not always choose a person for the cover, however. On April 12, 1954, for example, its cover showed a hydrogen bomb test explosion over the Pacific Ocean with the simple headline, "H-Bomb over the Pacific." The magazine also had covers not associated with politics or international relations.

Likewise, *Newsweek* often used its cover to focus on the major news makers of the period, including Churchill, Eisenhower, Dulles, and military commanders and communist leaders. However, through-

out the 1950's, *Newsweek* covers also featured the Panama Canal, a U.S. tank, "Smokey Bear," singer Perry Como, actor Yul Brynner, and the B-52 bomber airplane.

U.S. News & World Report placed less emphasis on the photographs of news makers than on strong headlines and bold illustrations. Some of the featured topics included atom bombs, the rising cost of defense, the Cold War, communism, McCarthyism, a shaky stock market, and the space program. The headlines were often questions, such as "Why Go to

Time's "Man of the Year"

Since 1927, the editors of *Time* magazine have designated a person, group of people, or even a concept, "Man of the Year." A more apt title might be "newsmaker of the year," as the basis of the award is the impact that the awardee had upon world history and culture during the previous year. The fact that the impact of the newsmaker need not be meritorious is evident in the magazine's selection of Adolf Hitler and Joseph Stalin as recipients during the late 1930's.

Year	Recipient	Reason
1950	American Fighting-Man	Troops deployed in the Korea War.
1951	Mohammed Mossadegh	Iranian premier responsible for nationalizing Iran's oil industry.
1952	Queen Elizabeth II	Crowned monarch of Great Britain.
1953	Konrad Adenauer	Chancellor of the German Federal Republic (West Germany) who presided over the country's difficult postwar reconstruction.
1954	John Foster Dulles	U.S. secretary of state who helped coordinate the Western nations' resistance to the apparent threat of the Soviet bloc.
1955	Harlow Curtice	President of General Motors who helped lead American industrial expansion and the growth of the U.S. economy.
1956	Hungarian Freedom Fighter	All those persons who resisted Soviet domination during the Hungarian revolt.
1957	Nikita Khrushchev	First secretary of the Communist Party of the Soviet Union, presided over the launch of the first Earth-orbiting satellites and a period of general Soviet ascendancy.
1958	Charles de Gaulle	Premier and president-elect of France who averted civil war while presiding over the transition from the Fourth Republic to the Fifth Republic.
1959	Dwight D. Eisenhower	President of the United States who worked for world peace by traveling throughout Europe, Asia, Africa, and the Middle East.

the Moon? Stunt or Gain for Science?" and "Why Fear Russia?"

Subsequent Events The magazines' circulations, which peaked during the 1980's, leveled off by the mid-1990's. Statistics from 2002 listed *Time*'s circulation at 4.1 million, with *Newsweek* at 3.2 million and *U.S. News* at 2.3 million. In 2003, the average number of pages was ninety for *Time* and eighty for *Newsweek* and *U.S. News & World Report*.

By the late 1990's, the covers of all three magazines looked similar, with a single dominant photograph, usually of a person, and one or two short headlines. During this period, all were still covering the news, but the emphasis on celebrity often took precedent over major national or international news events.

Further Reading

Parry-Giles, Shawn J. *The Rhetorical Presidency, Propaganda, and the Cold War, 1945-1955*. Westport, Conn.: Praeger, 2002. Takes an analytical view of presidents Truman and Eisenhower, the use of propaganda, and the news.

Schneirov, Matthew. *The Dream of a New Social Order: Popular Magazines in America*. New York: Columbia University Press, 1994. Although an examination of the rise of *McClure's, Cosmopolitan*, and *Munsey's* in particular, nonetheless explores how magazines in general became the first national mass medium and expressed a new American culture based on the dream of a better future.

Sherri Ward Massey

See also Advertising; Book publishing; *Life*; *Look*; *Maclean's*; Newspapers in the United States; Nixon, Richard M.; *Reader's Digest*.

■ Newspapers in Canada

During the mid-1950's, daily newspaper circulation peaked in Canada at an average of one paper per household, with many households also receiving weekly newspapers and tabloids. In addition to the national news and local news, often published in provincial editions, Canadian daily newspapers included more international news than newspapers in other nations, including the United States.

Historians claim that from the eighteenth century into the twenty-first century, the Canadian public was among the best informed in the world, thanks to a proliferation of newspapers. The first Canadian newspaper was the Halifax *Gazette* in 1752, followed by the *Quebec Gazette*, founded in 1764 by former Philadelphia publishers William Brown and Thomas Gilmore. Other newspapers quickly followed in Nova Scotia, Upper Canada, and Ontario. The oldest surviving newspaper is the *Montreal Gazette*, first published in 1787. The first successful West Coast newspapers were the *British Colonist, Victoria Gazette*, and *The Standard*, founded in 1858. The Kingston *Whig-Standard* is the longest continuously published newspaper, first published in 1834.

Linking Party, Press, and Church Most nineteenth century newspapers were associated with political parties or churches, a tradition continued through the 1950's. *The Examiner*, the Victoria *Times*, and the Toronto *Globe* were Liberal Party newspapers; *The Leader* was Liberal Conservative; and *The Toronto Colonist* and Victoria *Colonist* were Conservative. *The Christian Guardian* was Methodist, while the *St. John Freeman* was Roman Catholic and Liberal in its approach. During the 1950's, the leading Conservative newspapers in Toronto, Canada's largest city, were the *Telegram* and the consolidated *Globe and Mail*; the Liberal newspaper was the *Star*.

Canadian newspapers were commercial ventures with a social purpose, serving either as adjuncts to a political party or as vehicles for disseminating moral, instructional, or educational messages. Party patronage and subsidies cushioned market forces. The press-party association continued until about 1960, when newspapers no longer identified themselves as Liberal or Conservative. However, this move did not free the press of political bias. Newly hired news reporters and editors tended to be increasingly liberal and leftist. A 1985 survey found most Canadian reporters to be more ideologically liberal and leftist than U.S. reporters.

The golden age of Canadian newspapers was the sixty years from Canadian Confederation until the 1930's Great Depression. Newspapers used their influence to promote social order, domestic harmony, modernity, and a belief in Canadian cultural and social superiority. This emphasis continued until the 1960's, when newspapers finally abandoned public service in order to emphasize profit.

In spite of liberal ideological leanings, Canadian newspapers remained a bastion of traditionalism during this era. Women were relegated to the women's sections of the newspapers until the 1970's, and few women entered management before the end of the century. Most newspapers employed few nonwhite employees until the 1990's, even in cities such as Toronto with significantly large and growing post-World War II immigrant and nonwhite populations. Newspapers during the 1950's exhibited racial bias, especially in linking race to crime. Unions successfully penetrated this traditionalism from the 1930's through the 1950's. In 1957, the Toronto *Star* was recognized as the most thoroughly unionized newspaper in North America.

The economic boom at the turn of the twentieth century brought new, big-business newspapers using modern production methods and a popular writing style, including "penny press" papers such as the *Montreal Star* and the *Toronto Telegram*. Some of these papers became political forces in their own right later in the century, capable of acting against parties and politicians; some focused on human-interest features and entertainment; and some promoted commercial and industrial ventures, such as railroad schemes and public policy agendas. Even with the rise of radio and television, the press remained as the political agenda-setter for Canadian politics through the 1950's.

Consolidation and the Profit Motive Throughout the twentieth century, the newspaper industry saw periods of bankruptcy, predatory marketing, mergers, and consolidation. Thomson Newspapers became Canada's first modern newspaper chain in 1931, followed by the Southam Group and Toronto Sun Publishing. Following World War II and throughout the 1950's, there was political concern about the concentration of newspaper ownership and lessening competition, but the press survived the criticism and remained unregulated. Renewed concerns during the 1970's were also fruitless.

To ensure economic survival, many newspapers turned to "yellow journalism." News turned away from truth and merely highlighted what someone— a quotable source—claimed was the truth. If it made a good story, it went to print. By the 1950's, pundits claimed the news comprised whatever journalists could get away with. Bribes to promote or squash stories were commonplace. Some editors admonished reporters to take only bribes they could eat or drink. There was no serious discussion of ethics, however, until the 1960's. New journalists brought their personal ethics into their careers, but there was little industry-sponsored effort to promote ethics during this era. Pressures from television journalism reduced unethical practices.

Impact The 1950's marked the end of the Canadian newspapers' leadership not only in Canadian politics and public policy but also in the educational realm of morality and public order. Pundits in subsequent decades bemoaned this loss and encouraged a newspaper revival. Newspaper readership dropped by more than one-quarter after the 1950's, and television emerged as the public's primary source of news and information.

Further Reading
Desbarats, Peter. *Guide to Canadian News Media.* Toronto: Harcourt Brace, 1996. Excellent review of Canadian newspaper and mass media history, development, economics, ethics, and interaction with politics.

Fethering, George. *The Rise of the Canadian Newspaper.* Toronto: Oxford University Press, 1990. Details Canadian newspaper history as part of the series *Perspectives on Canadian Culture.*

Kesterton, Wilfred. *A History of Journalism in Canada.* Toronto: McClelland and Stewart, 1967. A classic text and first historical account of the subject.

Komorous, Hana, ed. *Canadian Newspapers: The Record of Our Past, the Mirror of Our Time: Proceedings of the Second National Newspapers Colloquium, Vancouver B.C., June 11, 1987.* Ottawa: Canadian Library Association, 1989. Gives an insider perspective to the newspaper industry via essays and academic studies.

Miller, John. *Yesterday's News: Why Canada's Daily Newspapers Are Failing Us.* Halifax, N.S.: Fernwood, 1998. Discusses the concern with the shift to profit from public service and suggests ways to overcome press industry inertia to develop new reporting and publishing priorities.

Picard, Robert G., ed. *Press Concentration and Monopoly: New Perspectives on Newspaper Ownership and Operation.* Norwood, N.J.: Ablex, 1988. Examines Canadian and American newspaper ownership, press monopolies, economic aspects, and journalistic history.

Rutherford, Paul. *The Making of the Canadian Media.* Toronto: McGraw-Hill, 1978. A basic text that examines the history and impact of Canadian newspapers, among other media.

Gordon Neal Diem

See also Bell's swim across Lake Ontario; Canadian Broadcasting Corporation; Communications in Canada; Education in Canada; *Maclean's*; Newspapers in the United States; Religion in Canada; Television in Canada; Urbanization in Canada.

■ Newspapers in the United States

Despite growing competition from television, newspapers remained most Americans' main source of hard news, and they enjoyed high circulation numbers and strong advertising support during the 1950's.

The period between 1950 and 1959 arguably is one of the least studied eras in American newspaper history. This is not because newspapers were not thriving; indeed, they were. Television rapidly was becoming a part of Americans' everyday lives, but it was still considered primarily a source of entertainment. During the 1950's, both the total number of cities with daily papers and the total circulation of dailies steadily increased.

Two turmoil-filled decades bookend the 1950's. Newspapers often thrive in readership during major wars or times of great political or social conflict. During the 1940's, newspapers reported the battles and victories of World War II, while during the 1960's, the headlines were filled with news of political and social upheaval. The changes in news coverage, technology, and ownership, however, that occurred during the 1950's set the pace for the future of newspapers and prove the importance of the decade in newspaper history.

Historical Background How free should the press be? Where is a newspaper's loyalty when the United States is at war? What responsibility does the press hold for finding the truth? These arguments began for American newspapers long before the 1950's and even long before the United States was a nation. In 1690, printer Benjamin Harris first published *Publick Occurrences Both Foreign and Domestick* in Boston without the publishing license required in the colonies. Over the years, many newspapers were published as propaganda pieces or political public relations tools. From those early days to the mid-nineteenth century, the owners controlled the newspapers' content.

Some newspapers openly supported particular political parties or politicians and often published one-sided reports. Many took sides on political and social issues and trumpeted large, biased headlines. Newspapers of the early nineteenth century earned more readership and credibility thanks to competition, better printing methods, and the innovation of journalism's publishing giants. Three New York newspapers led the way: the *New York Tribune* (Horace Greeley), *The New York Times* (Henry Raymond), and the *New York Herald* (James Gordon Bennett). Their contributions made way for the sensationalism and intense competition of the so-called golden age of newspaper publishing during the late nineteenth century. The newspapers of Joseph Pulitzer and William Randolph Hearst aggressively covered the news of the day and attracted millions of readers.

Postwar Changes Newspapers had recently adjusted to the competition brought by FM radio during the 1940's when television arrived. The first decade of a new form of mass media is always a period of adjustment. New media typically gain part of their growth from established media, at least during the early years. In 1946, there were six television stations in the United States; in 1970, there were nine hundred. By 1952, more than 34 percent of American homes had at least one black-and-white television. That figure would increase to 50 percent by the mid-1950's and 86 percent by the end of the decade. Television began to cut into the newspapers' advertising revenue and audiences' reading time. Households that used to take two or three papers cut back to one.

Newspapers learned to coexist with the emerging media by focusing on their strengths: news coverage (particularly of local news), advertising coupons, and flexibility. Network news at that time was given in fifteen-minute slots and still relied heavily on newspapers. Announcers sometimes read stories directly from the papers. The "serious" journalists still were working for newspapers. Thus, despite crossover by both media, even the audience members quickly determined that television was primarily for entertainment, and newspapers were primarily for information.

The number of daily newspapers changed little between the end of World War II and 1959. With some fluctuations, the figure remained slightly more than 1,700. Many new newspapers, both dailies and weeklies, were started in small towns and suburbs as printing methods got easier and less expensive, and such locales could afford to begin a newspaper of their own.

The number of cities with two or more separately owned daily newspapers began to decline. In 1945, there were 117 such cities; by 1970 there were only 63. Major cities (New York, Los Angeles, Chicago, Detroit, Dallas) still supported two large dailies. Nevertheless, most dailies experienced an increase in advertising revenue. They dominated all other media in advertising support. Circulation numbers continued to rise throughout the decade.

Most papers, even larger ones, were still owned by one family, although chain ownership and concentration of ownership was increasing. In some cases, this meant a single company or family owned more than one media outlet. In some instances, a single owner claimed numerous small newspapers in different towns.

Headline Stories Newspapers of the 1950's almost always devoted their front pages to a dominant headline of the main story of the day. That trend was clear in the summer of 1950. Communist North Korea attacked the Republic of South Korea on June 25, 1950, and newspapers began intensive coverage of the ensuing war. The *Chicago Tribune* ran the first action story written by an onsite newspaper correspondent. Others, including the *New York Herald Tribune*, the *Chicago Daily News*, the *Christian Science Monitor,* and *The New York Times,* soon sent their own correspondents. As in previous wars, newspapers reporters and photographers risked their lives to do their jobs. One of the first female foreign correspondents, Marguerite Higgins, earned a Pulitzer Prize with her coverage of the war for the *New York Herald Tribune.*

Journalists wrangled with field commander General Douglas MacArthur over press freedoms, as he went from a complete lack of military censorship of war information to instituting a policy so stringent it subjected journalists to court martial for serious violations. The conflicts between President Harry S. Truman and General MacArthur led to headlines and moved many newspapers to take sides in their editorial pages.

Newspapers and television provided extensive coverage of Senator Joseph McCarthy's accusations of communism against public and private figures. Often, the persons defending themselves did not get the same amount of attention in the media. A debate

at the 1953 meeting of the Associated Press Managing Editors Association centered on McCarthy's manipulation of the media. Newspaper coverage of political figures and social events would never be the same again. Journalists became more critical and more concerned about objectivity versus truth. Objectivity had always meant printing both sides. Suddenly, "truth" meant finding the real story and not merely printing what a prominent person said.

Innovations and Improvements Newspapers improved in the quality and variety of news coverage in the 1950's. They spent more money on newsprint, increasing the number of pages devoted to both news and advertising. Inside pages featured straight news stories alongside lengthy features and comics. Editors discovered quickly that coverage of the new television industry would appeal to readers. They also expanded coverage of international news, sports, and hobbies. Many appealed to women with new or transformed women's (society) sections that included—along with the traditional coverage of club activities, food, fashion, and weddings—articles on careers, volunteerism, the arts, and politics.

The most significant technological change for newspapers was the widespread use of the Teletypesetter system. It replaced the Linotype system, which had dominated typesetting for decades. The Teletypesetter system made it easier and less expensive for newspapers to use wire service material. Because of Teletype, more newspapers began relying on the professionally produced stories of national wire service writers for the United Press and International News Service (later merged into the United Press International) and the Associated Press. Often, numerous small papers would run identical stories on news happening thousands of miles away, thus setting a precedent for future news coverage. Furthermore, during the mid-1950's, the Associated Press began work on the first version of its stylebook, later used by thousands of newspapers as a guideline for punctuation, spelling, abbreviations, and grammar.

Because of the way the Teletypesetter machines produced news copy, newspapers developed narrow columns. Many large papers looked much the same, with eight narrow columns of type dominated by one large headline and broken up by a few smaller ones. With only a black-and-white picture or two, the overall effect was a wash of gray. Color printing, first introduced during the 1890's, was widely used for the Sunday comics. However, color was still a costly luxury for many smaller newspapers.

Impact The decade of Senator McCarthy, the Korean War, the emergence of the Civil Rights movement, and Cold War politics, combined with an increasingly affluent, consumer-driven society, provided the right ingredients for the success of newspapers and their advertisers during the 1950's. The media form found that it could hold its own under competition from television and worked to distinguish itself with more balanced news coverage and more hard-hitting questions from its journalists. Furthermore, the endless discussion of loyalty, responsibility, and truth was intensified during the decade as the Cold War introduced new political realities for the government that at times aroused conflict-of-interest suspicions.

Subsequent Events During the 1970's, journalism schools and newspapers enjoyed a resurgence in popularity. Some newspaper reporters, such as Bob Woodward and Carl Bernstein, who broke the Watergate scandal for the *Washington Post*, became celebrities. During the 1980's, *USA Today* reinvented the look of newspapers with its introduction of shorter stories; wide, modular layouts; and lots of color.

Further Reading

Aronson, James. *The Press and the Cold War.* Indianapolis: Bobbs-Merrill, 1970. The author offers insight into the media's emerging role as a watchdog of human rights between the 1940's and the 1960's, with particular focus on McCarthyism.

Barnhurst, Kevin G., and John Nerone. *The Form of News: A History.* New York: Guilford Press, 2001. A collection of writings on the style, production, and social meaning of newspapers from the mid-eighteenth century to 2000.

Marsh, Harry D. "The Media in Transition, 1945-1974." In *The Media in America: A History,* edited by William David Sloan and James D. Startt. 4th ed. Northport, Ala: Vision Press, 1999. An overview of the effects the different types of media had on one another and on the political and social issues of the time period.

Nixon, Raymond B., and Jean Ward. "Trends in Newspaper Ownership and Inter-Media Competition." *Journalism Quarterly* 38 (1961): 15-24. An analysis of the growth of daily newspapers and competition with television and radio.

Tebbel, John. *The Media in America.* New York: Thomas Y. Crowell, 1974. This book is a comprehensive look at the media, particularly their role in political and social issues, from the eighteenth century through the early 1970's.

Sherri Ward Massey

See also Advertising; Censorship; Cold War; Communications in the United States; News magazines; *Peanuts; Pogo;* Presidential press conferences; Television in the United States.

■ Niagara Treaty

Identification Treaty between the United States and Canada delineating water usage of the Niagara River

Date Signed into law on February 27, 1950

The Niagara Treaty provided for an increase in the output of the Niagara River to provide consumers with cheaper electricity and also helped to maintain the scenic beauty of Niagara Falls.

In 1909, the United States and Canada signed the International Boundary Waters Treaty Act. It created the International Joint Commission (IJC) to determine all matters involving the use, obstruction, and diversion of the Niagara River. After forty years, however, the terms of the 1909 treaty no longer dealt effectively with the matter of how much water each country could use for the purposes of generating electricity.

The purpose of the Niagara Treaty of 1950 was to increase water output while at the same time preserving the natural beauty of Niagara Falls. At the time, the U.S. State Department acknowledged a dire situation in the northeastern section of the United States, which was facing a serious power shortfall. Previous agreements centered mainly on preserving water for Niagara Falls, but the 1950 treaty allowed the United States and Canada to provide a minimum water output level for Niagara Falls while diverting the rest of the water to meet the demand for affordable electricity. Article 5 of the treaty stated that any water not expressly reserved for scenic reasons would be used to generate electric power. According to the terms of the pact, Canada and the United States agreed that the water made available for purposes of hydroelectric power gener-

In October, 1951—the year after Canada and the United States signed the Niagara Treaty—the future queen Elizabeth and her husband, the duke of Edinburgh, drew a crowd at Niagara Falls during their tour of Canada. (Hulton Archive | by Getty Images)

ation were to be divided equally between Canada and the United States.

Impact Critics claimed that the treaty decreased 75 percent of the Niagara River's natural volume, and therefore stripped Niagara Falls of its natural splendor. However, the Niagara Treaty increased electric output and kept electric power costs low for consumers.

Further Reading

Jackson, John N. *The Mighty Niagara.* Amherst: Prometheus Books, 2003. An excellent history of the Niagara River and Niagara Falls.

Preservation and Enhancement of the American Falls at Niagara. Ottawa: International Joint Commission, 1975. A summary of the key aspects of the treaty can be found in this report.

Justin P. Coffey

See also Canada and U.S. investments; Foreign policy of Canada; Foreign policy of the United States; Natural resources; Water pollution.

■ Nielsen ratings

Definition Recording and evaluation of television viewing habits of households and individuals for the purpose of informing advertising marketing

The Nielsen rating system allowed 1950's advertisers to target their marketing efforts in order to influence the most likely viewers of particular television programming, thereby increasing sales.

Nielsen Media Research provides an independent, third-party measurement of the viewing patterns of a random sample of individual and household viewers of broadcast and other television programming, in the United States and Canada, to inform marketing and programming decisions.

The original A. C. Nielsen Company was created in 1923 by a twenty-six-year-old engineer, Arthur C. Nielsen, Sr. He essentially founded the field of modern market research. Initially he created a market analysis system by which he physically visited stores

Top-rated U.S Television Programs, 1950-1959

Season	No. 1	No. 2	No. 3
1950-1951	Texaco Star Theater	Fireside Theatre	Philco TV Playhouse
1951-1952	Arthur Godfrey's Talent Scouts	Texaco Star Theater	I Love Lucy
1952-1953	I Love Lucy	Arthur Godfrey's Talent Scouts	Arthur Godfrey and His Friends
1953-1954	I Love Lucy	Dragnet	Arthur Godfrey's Talent Scouts
1954-1955	I Love Lucy	The Jackie Gleason Show	Dragnet
1955-1956	The $64,000 Question	I Love Lucy	The Ed Sullivan Show
1956-1957	I Love Lucy	The Ed Sullivan Show	General Electric Theater
1957-1958	Gunsmoke	The Danny Thomas Show	Tales of Wells Fargo
1958-1959	Gunsmoke	Wagon Train	Have Gun Will Travel
1959-1960	Gunsmoke	Wagon Train	Have Gun Will Travel

Source: Tim Brooks and Earle Marsh. *The Complete Directory to Prime Time Network and Cable TV Shows,* 2003.

in various geographic areas in order to track the sales of different brands—what would later become known as "market share" information. Later, he transferred this type of market analysis into the broadcasting arena and began to measure the tuning habits of radio listeners. Nielsen first used the acquired technology of "audimeters," which could record exactly when individual radio sets were on and to what stations their dials were set. This technology made it possible to monitor the listening patterns of large numbers of households objectively and accurately.

In March of 1950, Nielsen purchased C. E. Hooper's national radio and television ratings company and began the largest media-monitoring company in the United States. During the early 1950's, Nielsen began monitoring television audiences to discover their watching patterns. Television viewing increased dramatically over the next few years and soon eclipsed radio listening. For television, a version of the audimeter, now referred to as the "Nielsen black box," was used to measure the viewing of television households. Nielsen could measure when a television was on and what channel it was set to at that time. Presumably, someone in the household was watching the set while it was on, but measurements about the specific audience were unrecorded. The original ratings provided only estimates of television audience size and composition. These household ratings did not measure the viewing habits of individuals along demographic lines.

To determine individual viewing demographics, Nielsen added the reporting element of weekly television diaries filled out by company-chosen "Nielsen families," who were picked to participate through a scientifically random sampling process. Based on a scientific principle of analyzing what people actually did, Nielsen developed random sample, national and local television audience measurements, called the National Television Index (NTI) and Nielsen Station Index (NSI), respectively.

Impact During the 1950's, television programs reached audiences enjoying unprecedented prosperity. Advertisers hoping to take advantage of this prosperity often sponsored entire programs. To maximize their marketing dollars, television advertisers needed reliable and projectable information about which television programs were being viewed and by whom. Without market research to guide them, companies had no way of knowing how best to spend their advertising dollars. In both Canada and the United States, consumer industries relied on the collected data of television viewing demographics provided by the Nielsen Media Company. During the 1950's, the activities and innovations of the Nielsen Media Company set the stage for the research of subsequent decades, when Nielsen became the key provider of viewing information for marketing and programming decision making and greatly influenced a world commerce economy. "Nielsen" became synonymous with "television ratings."

Further Reading

Beeville, Hugh Malcolm. *Audience Ratings: Radio, Television, and Cable.* Rev. ed. Hillsdale, N.J.: Erlbaum, 1988. Chronicles the development of television ratings.

Webster, James G., and Lawrence W. Lichty. *Ratings Analysis: Theory and Practice.* 2d ed. Hillsdale, N.J.: Erlbaum, 2000. Explores the methodology of ratings analysis and how ratings impact television and radio.

Megali Stuart

See also Advertising; Affluence and the new consumerism; Baby boomers; DuMont network; Gallup polls; *I Love Lucy; Leave It to Beaver; Mickey Mouse Club;* Television in Canada; Television in the United States; *Tonight Show.*

■ Nixon, Richard M.

Identification U.S. congressman and vice president
Born January 9, 1913; Yorba Linda, California
Died April 22, 1994; New York, New York

Richard M. Nixon's rise to national prominence during the 1950's, culminating in his eight years as President Dwight D. Eisenhower's vice president, set the stage for his candidacy for the presidency in 1960.

Richard Milhous Nixon entered political life in 1946, when he challenged incumbent democratic U.S. representative Jerry Voorhis. Nixon employed a hard-hitting campaign strategy that would become a trademark throughout his political career. He beat Voorhis decisively and joined a national tide that saw the Republican Party take control of Congress after the 1946 elections.

Nixon entered the 1950's primed for political success. In 1948, he catapulted to national prominence after his questioning of Alger Hiss before the House Committee on Un-American Activities (HUAC). He capitalized on this event by running for the U.S. Senate from California in 1950 against Democrat Helen Gahagan Douglas. Nixon won an overwhelming victory by alleging that Douglas was a communist sympathizer. During his two years in the Senate, Nixon became one of the most vocal Republican opponents of Democratic president Harry S. Truman's domestic and international policies.

Nixon's youth, conservative pedigree, and popularity with party regulars led Dwight D. Eisenhower to add him to the 1952 Republican ticket. However, his status as the vice presidential nominee was jeopardized when the press reported that he maintained a secret political fund financed by private interests. He vindicated himself in a nationally televised speech that argued the fund was not for personal use, but rather supplemented the meager administrative allowance members of Congress were given at the time. His "Checkers" speech succeeded, leading Eisenhower to keep him on the ticket that easily captured the presidency in November.

Nixon's aggressive partisanship as vice president polarized the public and almost led to his removal from the 1956 Republican ticket. However, he remained and served under Eisenhower for two terms. He was considered an effective vice president and successfully filled in for Eisenhower during the several debilitating illnesses that Eisenhower suffered between 1955 and 1957.

Nixon's activities during the 1950's can be summarized by three major themes: his untiring efforts in supporting the Republican Party, his leadership in the anticommunist movement, and his use of the vice presidency to prepare for his presidential campaigns during the 1960's.

Vice Presidential Years Nixon's rise to prominence within the Republican Party during the 1950's was enigmatic. His aggressive attacks on Democrats polarized the public, while his ability to bridge ideological fissures among Republicans united disparate wings of the party. Nixon's tireless speaking schedule on behalf of Republican candidates and causes established him as the party's most popular speaker. In the Senate, Nixon focused on attacking the Truman administration for its policies relating to the Korean War, for internal corruption, and for allegations of communist infiltration. As vice president, he served as the administration's partisan voice, allow-

Congressman Richard M. Nixon delivering an impromptu speech in a coastal California town while campaigning for the U.S. Senate in 1950. Nixon won the election, and two years later he was elected vice president of the United States. (AP/Wide World Photos)

ing President Eisenhower to have the appearance of being above politics.

Nixon was one of the most ardent anticommunists of the 1950's. He believed that the Democrats' New Deal policies begun under President Franklin D. Roosevelt during the 1930's were leading America toward socialism. He also argued that communism was expanding overseas. Like many Republicans of the era, he charged that numerous Democrats were communist sympathizers and that the Truman administration was soft on communism at home and abroad. However, Nixon opposed Truman's policy of containing communism and took the conservative stance that communist nations must be liberated. He softened his tone as vice president, especially regarding claims that subversives were embedded in the U.S. government. Instead, Nixon

turned his attention to promoting anticommunism abroad, as witnessed in his July, 1959, "kitchen debate" with Soviet premier Nikita Khrushchev, during which he espoused the virtues of capitalism and deplored the lack of freedom under communism.

Eisenhower vowed to make Nixon the most informed vice president in history to ensure a seamless transition in the event of his death or incapacitation. Nixon was actively involved in domestic and foreign policy debates and served as a primary administration liaison to Congress. Major trips to Asia, the Middle East, South America, and the Soviet Union bettered his diplomacy with world leaders. These experiences, combined with the nationwide party contacts he developed while campaigning, helped him develop the political portfolio that secured his presidency in 1968.

Impact Nixon's eight years as vice president changed the role of the office. Eisenhower allowed Nixon to be engaged in administration deliberations and provided him with opportunities to represent the country abroad. In turn, Nixon used his time in Congress and his vice president role to create the national connections that established him as a Republican presidential candidate during the 1960's.

Subsequent Events Nixon received the Republican nomination for president in 1960 and lost one of the closest elections in history to John F. Kennedy. After Nixon lost the 1962 California gubernatorial race, his political career appeared to be finished. However, he campaigned tirelessly for Republicans in 1964 and 1966 and emerged as the only presidential candidate acceptable to all factions of the party in 1968. He defeated Hubert H. Humphrey in November, 1968, and was reelected in 1972. Nixon's greatest accomplishments were in foreign policy: He stabilized relations with the Soviet Union, opened relations with China, and ended the war in Vietnam. This legacy was marred by the Watergate scandal that forced him to become the only president in American history to resign. Nixon spent the rest of his life trying to rehabilitate his image.

Further Reading

Ambrose, Stephen E. *Nixon: The Education of a Politician, 1913-1962.* New York: Simon & Schuster,

1987. Comprehensive study of Nixon's prepresidential career, with an emphasis on his career in Congress and his vice presidency.

Gelman, Irwin F. *The Contender: Richard M. Nixon, the Congress Years, 1946-1952*. New York: Free Press, 1999. Examines Nixon's congressional career and his role in the 1952 presidential campaign.

Nixon, Richard. *Six Crises*. Garden City, N.Y.: Doubleday, 1962. Nixon's personal account of the most important events of his political career during the 1950's.

Parmet, Herbert S. *Richard M. Nixon and His America*. New York: Smithmark, 1990. Study of the "Age of Nixon" and his influence on American politics during the 1950's and the rest of the twentieth century.

J. Wesley Leckrone

See also Army-McCarthy hearings; Barkley, Alben W.; Eisenhower, Dwight D.; Eisenhower's heart attack; Elections in the United States, midterm; Elections in the United States, 1952; Elections in the United States, 1956; Gallup polls; Hoover, J. Edgar; House Committee on Un-American Activities; Nixon's "Checkers" speech; Nixon's "kitchen debate"; Nixon's Latin America tour.

hower's running mate. He responded by defending himself on national television and in a brilliantly delivered speech gave a full accounting of his personal finances and made a stinging attack on the Democrats. He also vowed never to return a dog, named Checkers by his daughter Tricia, that had been sent to his family as a gift. Following the speech, Republicans rallied behind Nixon, and he was greeted as "my boy" by Eisenhower.

Impact The speech attracted fifty-five million viewers—the largest audience in television history until Nixon's 1960 debate with John F. Kennedy—and established television as a force in American politics. Moreover, it saved the political career of Nixon and possibly that of Eisenhower as well.

Further Reading

Ryan, Halford. "Senator Richard M. Nixon's Apology for 'The Fund.'" In *Oratorical Encounters: Selected Studies and Sources of Twentieth-Century Political Accusations and Apologies*, edited by Halford Ryan. New York: Greenwood Press, 1988. An analysis of the rhetorical strategies used by Nixon in confronting his accusers.

■ Nixon's "Checkers" speech

The Event Nationally televised speech delivered by vice presidential candidate Richard M. Nixon

Date September 23, 1952

Richard M. Nixon's emotional response to charges that he had misused political funds was so well received that it preserved his place on the ballot and ensured the continuation of a political career that would eventually lead him to the presidency.

During the middle of the 1952 presidential campaign, a newspaper story charged that thousands of dollars had been funneled to Nixon through a secret political fund. Although the fund was neither illegal nor particularly unusual, Nixon faced the threat of being dropped as Dwight D. Eisen-

Charged with improperly taking campaign funds for his own personal use, Nixon went on television and delivered an emotional appeal that saved his place on the Republican ticket and ensured that his political career would continue. (AP/Wide World Photos)

Wicker, Tom. *One of Us: Richard M. Nixon and the American Dream.* New York: Random House, 1991. Contains a chapter on the speech as a pivotal event in Nixon's life.

Lawrence W. Haapanen

See also Cold War; Elections in the United States, 1952; Khrushchev's visit to the United States; Nixon, Richard M.; Television in the United States.

■ Nixon's "kitchen debate"

The Event Impromptu discussion between U.S. vice president Richard M. Nixon and Soviet premier Nikita Khrushchev about the merits of capitalism and communism
Date July 24, 1959
Place Model kitchen at an American cultural exhibit in Moscow

This widely publicized event helped to improve United States-Soviet relations temporarily and enhanced Nixon's reputation as a skilled foreign diplomat because of his composure and use of humor.

As part of an attempt to improve United States-Soviet relations during the Cold War, both countries planned cultural exchange exhibits in New York City and Moscow. On July 24, 1959, Nixon and Khrushchev met at the Kremlin and began a discussion about capitalism and communism which continued at the U.S. exhibit and was recorded on an Ampex color videorecorder, the world's first.

Debating in the kitchen of the exhibit's model house, Khrushchev complained that the plywood construction of the dwelling would last only twenty years and would be unable to house the children and grandchildren of its owners. Nixon responded that the tastes of the children and grandchildren might be different, and Khrushchev retorted in that case they should change the furniture, not the house. The videotape of the encounter shows Nixon smiling and maintaining his composure as Khrushchev suggested that if the United States wanted to test Soviet resolution, the Soviets would teach the United States a lesson.

At the official opening of the U.S. exhibit, Nixon extolled the American freedoms of press, speech,

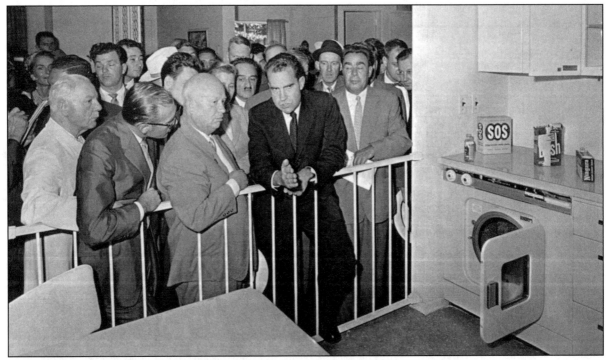

The verbal confrontation between U.S. vice president Richard M. Nixon (right) and Soviet premier Nikita Khrushchev (left) at an American trade exhibition in Moscow in 1959 helped win Nixon a reputation as a tough anticommunist. (To the right of Nixon is future Soviet premier Leonid Brezhnev.) (AP/Wide World Photos)

and travel as well as the wealth and security afforded to the typical American family. In a rare move, Khrushchev had the full text of Nixon's impromptu speech published in the Soviet press. The two men toured the banks of the Moscow River conversing with Russians, and Khrushchev asked Nixon if the people he met seemed to be the victims of communist oppression.

Impact As the Cold War tensions increased, the kitchen debate proved important for its role in highlighting, in lay terms, the differences in ideology and the quality of life between the United States and the Soviet Union for the average citizen. The debate also helped cement Nixon's prestige domestically. Nixon's visit set the stage for Khrushchev's visit to the United States and a visit by President Dwight D. Eisenhower to the Soviet Union.

Further Reading
Ambrose, Stephen E. *Nixon: The Education of a Politician, 1913-1962.* New York: Simon & Schuster, 1987. An overview of Nixon's career that includes discussion of the kitchen debate.
Nixon, Richard M. *Six Crises.* New York: Simon & Schuster, 1962. An early immediate account by Nixon himself, with a chapter on the kitchen debate.

Mark C. Herman
See also Cold War; Foreign policy of the United States; Khrushchev's visit to the United States; Nixon, Richard M. Nixon's Latin America tour.

■ Nixon's Latin America tour

The Event Accompanied by his wife, Vice President Richard M. Nixon undertook a goodwill tour of several Latin American countries to show American support for the region's anticommunist governments
Date May, 1958

Anti-American public demonstrations in several Latin American countries that Nixon visited revealed that there was growing resentment among Latin Americans toward the United States. The Eisenhower administration reevaluated its policy toward Latin America after the trip.

Richard M. Nixon embarked on a tour of Latin America in May, 1958, and his itinerary included visits to the capitals of eight countries: Uruguay, Argentina, Paraguay, Bolivia, Peru, Ecuador, Columbia,

and Venezuela. In each country he met with heads of state or foreign ministers. However, crowds with hecklers met Nixon and his wife at most stops, and the crowd that met them in Caracas, Venezuela, was the most violent. Onlookers spat on the Nixons after they arrived at the Caracas airport. As their motorcade drove into the city, a mob converged on the convoy and brought it to a halt. Nixon's car was pummeled by rocks; its windows smashed, the crowd pressed against the car, rocked it back and forth, and tried to roll it over. The driver saw an opening in the crowd and sped away.

Impact Nixon's visit dispelled American diplomats' illusion that supporting corrupt or dictatorial regimes solely because they were anticommunist would build political support for democracy in the Latin American region. In particular, the vice president's narrow escape in Caracas awakened U.S. leaders to the level of antipathy felt by Latin Americans toward the United States. In response, the Eisenhower administration continued to give economic and military aid to anticommunist governments, but it also provided more money to social, health, and educational programs in the region.

Further Reading
Eisenhower, Milton S. *The Wine Is Bitter: The United States and Latin America.* Garden City, N.Y.: Doubleday, 1963. The author was President Eisenhower's brother and a close adviser on Latin American affairs. He describes the Nixon trip and the policy shift that followed it.
Nixon, Richard M. *The Memoirs of Richard M. Nixon.* New York: Grosset & Dunlap, 1978. Nixon provides a firsthand account of the visit.
_____. *Six Crises.* New York: Simon & Schuster, 1990. One chapter details the visit to Latin America.

Richard A. Crooker
See also Cuban Revolution; Eisenhower Doctrine; Foreign policy of the United States; Guatemala invasion; Latin America; Mexico; Nixon, Richard M.; Nixon's "kitchen debate"; Organization of American States.

■ Nobel Prizes

Identification Prizes awarded annually by the Nobel Foundation of Sweden

The Nobel Prize foundation underwent several changes during the 1950's, including increasing its international scope and making investment changes that bolstered its funds.

Alfred Bernhard Nobel was born in Stockholm, Sweden, in 1833, and he eventually engaged in the making of gunpowder and munitions of war in Sweden and then in Russia. The use of his munitions in the Prussian-Austrian war of 1866 gave him a handsome return; during the Franco-Prussian war of 1870, he sold to both warring sides. Nobel also benefited financially from participation in the development and exploitation of the Baku oil fields of Russia. As a result, by the time of his death in 1896, he had amassed a large fortune. The Nobel Prizes trace their origin to Nobel's will: The Nobel Foundation was established as the repository of the funds left by

him. The income derived from the investment of more than thirty-one million Swedish kronor—then about 9 million U.S. dollars—was to be divided equally each year among recipients who had made the most important discoveries or efforts benefiting humankind in five fields or areas: physics, chemistry, physiology or medicine, literature, and peace. A sixth prize in economics was created in 1968.

Impact Until the 1950's, the method whereby the Nobel Prize winners were decided on was a very complex and secretive one. In that decade, however, a more open approach began. The Nobel Prizes awarded from 1901 to 1950 went primarily to Europeans. During these decades, for example, the Peace Prize centered on European problems and figures. After 1950, however, notable figures from all over the world were selected as laureates; candidates

Nobel Prize winners of 1956 included, from left to right, Walter Brattain (physics) and Dickinson W. Richards (physiology or medicine) of the United States; Cyril Norman Hinshelwood (chemistry) of Great Britain; Nikolay Semyonov (chemistry) of the Soviet Union; John Bardeen (physics), André Cournand (physiology or medicine), and William Shockley (physics) of the United States, and Werner Forssmann (physiology or medicine) of West Germany. (Hulton Archive | by Getty Images)

Nobel Prize Winners

1950
Literature: Bertrand Russell, Great Britain
Peace: Ralph Bunche, United States
Physics: Cecil Powell, Great Britain
Chemistry: Otto Diels and Kurt Alder, West Germany
Physiology or Medicine: Philip S. Hench, United States;
 Edward C. Kendall, United States; Tadeusz
 Reichstein, Switzerland

1951
Literature: Pär Lagerkvist, Sweden
Peace: Léon Jouhaux, France
Physics: Sir John Cockcroft, Great Britain; Ernest
 Walton, Ireland
Chemistry: Edwin McMillan and Glenn Seaborg,
 United States
Physiology or Medicine: Max Theiler, South Africa

1952
Literature: François Mauriac, France
Peace: Albert Schweitzer, France
Physics: Felix Bloch and Edward Purcell, United
 States
Chemistry: Archer Martin and Richard Synge,
 Great Britain
Physiology or Medicine: Selman A. Waksman,
 United States

1953
Literature: Winston Churchill, Great Britain
Peace: George C. Marshall, United States
Physics: Frits Zernike, Netherlands
Chemistry: Hermann Staudinger, West Germany
Physiology or Medicine: Fritz A. Lipmann, United
 States; Sir H. A. Krebs, Great Britain

1954
Literature: Ernest Hemingway, United States
Peace: Office of the U.N. High Commissioner for
 Refugees
Physics: Max Born, Great Britain; Walther Bothe,
 West Germany
Chemistry: Linus Pauling, United States
Physiology or Medicine: John F. Enders, Thomas H.
 Weller, and Frederick Robbins, United States

1955
Literature: Halldór Laxness, Iceland
Peace: No award
Physics: Willis Lamb, Jr., and Polykarp Kusch, United
 States
Chemistry: Vincent du Vigneaud, United States
Physiology or Medicine: Axel Hugo Theorell, Sweden

1956
Literature: Juan Ramón Jiménez, Spain
Peace: No award
Physics: William Shockley, John Bardeen, and Walter
 Brattain, United States
Chemistry: Nikolay Semyonov, Soviet Union; Sir Cyril
 Hinshelwood, Great Britain
Physiology or Medicine: Werner Forssmann, West
 Germany; Dickinson Richards, United States;
 André F. Cournand, United States

1957
Literature: Albert Camus, France
Peace: Lester B. Pearson, Canada
Physics: Tsung-Dao Lee and Chen Ning Yang, China
Chemistry: Sir Alexander Todd, Great Britain
Physiology or Medicine: Daniel Bovet, Italy

1958
Literature: Boris Pasternak, Soviet Union (declined)
Peace: Dominique Georges Pire, Belgium
Physics: Pavel A. Cherenkov, Ilya M. Frank, and Igor Y.
 Tamm, Soviet Union
Chemistry: Frederick Sanger, Great Britain
Physiology or Medicine: George W. Beadle, Edward L.
 Tatum, and Joshua Lederberg, United States

1959
Literature: Salvatore Quasimodo, Italy
Peace: Philip Noel-Baker, Great Britain
Physics: Emilio Segrè and Owen Chamberlain, United
 States
Chemistry: Jaroslav Heyrovsky, Czechoslovakia
Physiology or Medicine: Severo Ochoa and Arthur
 Kornberg, United States

696 North American Aerospace Defense Command
The Fifties in America

from the United States increased in particular. The number of women and Canadians receiving the award also increased beginning during the 1950's.

The decade's best-known recipients of Nobel Prizes included Ralph Bunche (1950), Albert Schweitzer (1952), and George C. Marshall (1953) for their efforts at global peace; Winston Churchill (1953) and Ernest Hemingway (1954) for their literary works; and Linus Pauling (1954) for his work in chemistry.

Under the terms of Nobel's will, up until the 1950's the Foundation's funds were invested in conservative but low-yielding investments. In that decade, a change was made to those providing a higher yield. This resulted in a sizable augmentation in Nobel Foundation funds which made it possible for the monetary amounts of the prizes to keep pace with inflation. Thus, the value of each prize in 1901 was about forty thousand dollars but by 1950, this figure had declined to a little over thirty-one thousand dollars. Since 1950, it has steadily grown and stood at about one million dollars by the beginning of the twenty-first century. As a result, the Nobel Prizes have continued to certify and handsomely reward that which is outstanding in science, literature, and work for peace.

Further Reading

Feldman, Burton. *The Nobel Prize: A History of Genius, Controversy, and Prestige.* New York: Arcade, 2000. An indispensable historical account of the origin, administration, and development of the Nobel Prizes together with comment on the controversies involving the nomination and awarding of all of the prizes over the first hundred years.

Hargittai, Istvan. *The Road to Stockholm: Nobel Prizes, Science, and Scientists.* New York: Oxford University Press, 2001. A study of the interplay among scientists and scientific bodies in the selection of Nobel Prize winners in science.

McGrayne, Sharon Bertsch. *Nobel Prize Women in Science: Their Lives, Struggles, and Momentous Discoveries.* Secaucus, N.J.: Carol, 1998. Biographical studies of women recipients of Nobel Prizes

Joseph C. Kiger

See also Bellow, Saul; Bunche, Ralph; Einstein, Albert; Eliot, T. S.; Hemingway, Ernest; Marshall, George C.; Medicine; Pauling, Linus; Pearson, Lester B.; Seaborg, Glen; Steinbeck, John; Transistors; Watson, James D.

■ North American Aerospace Defense Command

Identification Defense alliance between Canada and the United States

Date Founded in August, 1957, as the North American Air Defense Command (NORAD)

The NORAD alliance represented the growing integration of the Canadian and American militaries in the defense of North America in the face of perceived Soviet aggression during the Cold War.

On August 1, 1957, the Canadian government of Prime Minister John Diefenbaker announced that for the first time, Canada and the United States had formed a new "integrated operational control" for the air defense of both nations.

The first step toward NORAD began in 1940, when the Canadian government, fearful that its prime ally, Great Britian, would be conquered by Nazi Germany, sought the assistance of the administration of U.S. president Franklin D. Roosevelt in its defense. The result was the Permanent Joint Board on Defense, which coordinated the defense of the northern half of North America. Although it was never publicly debated, the arrangement marked the beginning of a much closer Canadian relationship with Canada's southern neighbor, and, as such, the arrangement was popularly received by Canadians.

The military relationship between Canada and the United States became even more important after the end of World War II. With the onset of the Cold War, the United States had a new military rival in the form of the Soviet Union. War with that enemy would likely involve a Soviet air attack, possibly with nuclear weapons, against the continental United States. The route of Soviet aircraft to their intended targets would carry them over Canada. Accordingly, the extent of Canadian military preparation had a direct bearing on American security.

The U.S. government repeatedly pressed several Canadian governments for stronger military ties. In 1951, the first Royal Canadian Air Force officers began liaison assignments at the U.S. Air Force's headquarters in Colorado Springs, Colorado. This closer cooperation involved the use of American money to erect on Canadian soil a series of radar defense lines designed to provide warning of an impending Soviet air assault. Should that assault materialize, Prime

Minister Louis St. Laurent's government gave permission to the U.S. military to attack incoming Soviet aircraft in Canadian airspace. Diefenbaker's government went one step further and gave approval to the United States to use missiles to shoot down Soviet planes over Canada.

Integrated Command From the perspective of U.S. military planners, even more integration was desired, although they remained conscious of offending the strong nationalist sensibilities of Canadians. Instead, subtle pressure was applied through the Canadian armed forces. In December of 1956, a committee formed from the two nations' militaries recommended an integrated command with a single overall commander for the air defense of North America. In March, 1957, the Eisenhower administration added its support to the plan.

In Canada, a federal election interrupted before Ottawa's final approval could be given. With little consultation, newly elected Prime Minister John Diefenbaker signed his approval to the agreement, falsely portraying it to the Canadian public as being merely an extension of the North Atlantic Treaty Organization (NATO). A Canadian officer was appointed as second in command to his American superior, and NORAD command posts (in the side of a mountain in Colorado Springs and down a mineshaft in North Bay, Ontario) were established in both nations.

Impact NORAD represented a significant and long-lasting 1950's development in the military and political relationship between Canada and the United States and showcased the importance of allied defense in the Cold War era. Although it never faced an attack during the Cold War, the defense system remained in place into the twenty-first century, by which time it was officially known as the North American *Aerospace* Defense Command—a name that refleted NORAD's role in space detection and tracking.

Further Reading

Crosby, Ann Denholm. *Dilemmas in Defence Decision-Making: Constructing Canada's Role in NORAD, 1958-96.* New York: St. Martin's Press, 1998. Systematic look at Canadian participation in NORAD.

Granatstein, J. L., and Norman Hillmer. *For Better or for Worse: Canada and the United States to the 1990's.* Toronto: Copp Clark Pitman, 1991. Detailed examination of Canada's relationship with the United States.

Steve Hewitt

See also Atomic bomb; Avro Arrow; Cold War; Continentalism; DEW Line; Diefenbaker, John G.; Eisenhower, Dwight D.; Foreign policy of Canada; St. Laurent, Louis.

■ North Atlantic Treaty Organization

Identification Military alliance among Western European democracies, the United States, and Canada

Date Formed on April 4, 1949

The North Atlantic Treaty Organization (NATO) was formed as a measure to protect its members against aggression from the Soviet Union or its satellite nations. An attack on a European NATO member would act as a tripwire, automatically bringing the United States into conflict and intending to act as a deterrent force against Soviet aggression in the Cold War era.

The original members of NATO when the treaty was signed in 1949 included the United States, Canada, Belgium, Britain, Denmark, France, Iceland, Luxembourg, the Netherlands, Norway, Portugal, and West Germany. During the late twentieth century, the alliance accepted several newly formed Central and Eastern European and Baltic democracies. NATO incorporates the idea of "collective security," according to which all members agree to come to the aid militarily of any members who are attacked.

Cold War Context The NATO treaty and its significance for the United States and the American public must be seen in the context of the Cold War. Most significantly, it was the first peacetime treaty of its kind entered into by the United States. Creating NATO meant that for the first time in its history, the United States was committing itself to an alliance that would oblige it to enter a war automatically upon any attack on a fellow member nation.

The pact's existence marked a more definitive break with the United States' isolationist past than did its membership in the United Nations (U.N.). At the United Nations, the United States could veto any Security Council resolution it wished, thereby avoiding any military action it opposed. However, with

NATO, there was no such veto power, and an assault on a European member would automatically bring the United States into the fray.

NATO must also be seen as part of the "containment" doctrine, crafted in 1947 at the outset of the Cold War by the American diplomat George Kennan, then stationed in Moscow. According to this strategy, the West was to find means to oppose attempts at Soviet expansion. NATO fit the bill perfectly as a means of deterring or thwarting Soviet overt or covert adventures in redrawing the map of Europe.

It is notable that no American politician of any stature attacked NATO or urged American withdrawal from the organization during the key decade of the 1950's, when Western policies attempted and succeeded in politically stabilizing Western Europe. Europe found itself able to continue its recovery efforts from death and destruction of World War II with less anxiety over the Soviet menace than would otherwise have been possible.

American Reaction American NATO membership had a marked effect on the American public. Over a period of time NATO accustomed the public as never before to an acceptance of its international responsibilities. It paved the way for further treaty obligations, including the Southeast Asian Treaty Organization (SEATO). Moreover, NATO fostered among the American public an acceptance of a continuing, open-ended obligation to enter wars ignited by Cold War forces and ideology. Although NATO was geographically far from Vietnam, some historians suggest that U.S. membership in NATO, far more than U.N. membership, psychologically helped smooth the way toward the American public's initial acceptance of entry into what became a divisive political and military quagmire in that country.

NATO gave the American public a sense of integration with Europe and its European allies, making it next to impossible for isolationist forces—never wholly absent from the American scene—to gain significant political ground. For example, once NATO established its credibility, any isolationist proposal of leaving Germany alone and untended in Europe, rather than occupied by tens of thousands of American soldiers, would never gain credence with the postwar American public. The gradual political transformation of West Germany, under the watchful eye

of its fellow NATO members, into a modern, well-behaved, market-economy, and democratic nation was watched closely by Americans. The fact that the new Germany committed itself via NATO as a full partner in the defense of Europe against the danger of communist subversion or onslaught heightened the American public's sense of security.

Canadian Reaction In Canada, the impact of NATO was somewhat different. Canadians were used to their country being part of a regime of mutual international obligations because of their historically close relationship to Great Britain and their consequent membership in the British Commonwealth. Canadians entered World War I early in the struggle, unlike the Americans, who held back initially. The main consequence of NATO membership for Canadians was that Canada was bound ever tighter to its southern neighbor, a fact some Canadian politicians disliked.

When radar stations were placed in Canada as part of the early warning defense against Soviet attack, Canada was placed at risk from Soviet attack. For Canada, which was drawn into the Cold War during the 1940's with the discovery of Soviet spies on its soil, being part of the Western defense system was nothing out of the ordinary; the nation's international political relations had long placed its armies in harm's way. However, the possibility of missile attack was a new feature of international life for Canadians.

Subsequent Events NATO has been called the most successful alliance in world history. It is credited for keeping the peace in Europe and for playing a significant role, along with policies such as the Marshall Plan, in keeping Western Europe out of the hands of communists. The alliance that took root during the 1950's lasted through the entire course of the Cold War and continued in subsequent decades.

Further Reading

Kaplan, Lawrence S. *The Long Entanglement: NATO's First Fifty Years.* Westport, Conn.: Praeger, 1999. Details the skepticism that America traditionally accorded foreign alliances and examines the alliance from its birth through the 1950's and beyond, the crises that beset it, and its current state.

_____. *NATO and the United States: The Enduring Alliance.* Rev. ed. New York: Twayne, 1994. Details

A session of the conference of NATO leaders in Paris in December, 1957. Canadian prime minister John Diefenbaker is second from the left, and U.S. president Dwight D. Eisenhower is at the far right, next to British prime minister Harold Macmillan. (Hulton Archive | by Getty Images)

the history of the organization, looking at key figures in its development, like John Foster Dulles, how it was received during the 1950's, and how its mission evolved as the Cold War ended.

Mayers, David Allan. *George Kennan and the Dilemmas of U.S. Foreign Policy.* New York: Oxford University Press, 1990. A focus on the containment policies of the United States gives good background for understanding the success of NATO.

Schmidt, Gustav, ed. *A History of NATO: The First Fifty Years.* New York: Palgrave Macmillan, 2001. A comprehensive history and assessment of the alliance by more than sixty contributors, many of them Europeans.

Charles F. Bahmueller

See also Acheson, Dean; Canada as a middle power; Cold War; Eisenhower, Dwight D.; Foreign policy of Canada; Foreign policy of the United States; Geneva Summit Conference; Isolationism; Lodge, Henry Cabot; North America Aerospace Defense Command; Pearson, Lester B.; Southeast Asia Treaty Organization; Suez Crisis; Warsaw Pact.

O

■ Oerter, Al

Identification Olympic discus thrower
Born September 19, 1936; Astoria, New York

The greatest discus thrower in history, Al Oerter eventually became the first Olympic athlete to win four consecutive gold medals in a single event.

Known as one of the greatest Olympic competitors, Al Oerter grew up in Hyde Park, New York, with no intention of becoming a world-class athlete. In high school, however, he emerged as a talented discus thrower, setting a national high school record and earning a track and field scholarship to the University of Kansas.

Always considered the underdog because of his untimely injuries and notable competitors, Oerter had a propensity for launching winning throws in important competitions. He earned international recognition at the 1956 Olympic Games in Melbourne, Australia. As a twenty-year-old sophomore, ranked sixth in the world, he was not expected to win against such well-known throwers as world record holder Fortune Gordien. However, his winning throw of 184 feet, 10.5 inches easily won the gold medal and set an Olympic record. Oerter won the

During the 1956 Olympics, U.S. athletes swept the men's discus throw medals. From left to right: Desmond Koch, third place; Al Oerter, first place; and Fortune Gordien, second place. (AP/Wide World Photos)

National Collegiate Athletic Association (NCAA) discuss championships in 1957 and 1958 and won six national championships between 1957 and 1966. In 1959, he won the gold medal at the Pan-American Games. He went on to win gold medals at the Olympic Games in Rome in 1960, Tokyo in 1964, and Mexico City in 1968.

Impact Oerter dominated discuss throwing in four consecutive Olympic Games. Through 2004, he and long-jumper Carl Lewis were the only two athletes to win gold medals in the same events in four consecutive Olympics. Oerter made a brief comeback during the late 1970's, earning a spot as an alternate for the 1980 U.S. Olympic team that boycotted the Moscow games. Injury prevented him from competing for a place on the 1984 Olympic team. Oerter was inducted into the National Track and Field Hall of Fame in 1974 and the Olympic Hall of Fame in 1983.

Further Reading

Baldwin, David. *Track and Field Record Holders: Profiles of the Men and Women Who Set World, Olympic, and American Marks, 1946-1995.* Jefferson, N.C.: McFarland, 1996. Profiles Oerter and details his contributions to the sport.

McMane, Fred. *Superstars of Men's Track and Field.* New York: Chelsea House, 1998. A book aimed at young adults that profiles athletes important to the sport of track and field, including Oerter.

Mark R. Ellis

See also Bowden, Don; Connolly, Olga; Mathias, Bob; Olympic Games of 1956; Sports.

■ Oklahoma football team

Identification Most successful college football program during the 1950's

The Oklahoma Sooners set records that have never been surpassed and inspired emulation and local pride.

During the 1950's, Coach Bud Wilkinson's University of Oklahoma Sooner football teams were national champions three times, won three out of four postseason bowl games, and won their conference championship every year of the decade. Their thirty-one-game winning streak ended in 1950, but a new streak beginning in 1953 ran to forty-seven games, setting a national collegiate record that remained unchallenged among major conference teams through 2004.

Oklahoma's loss to the University of Nebraska in 1959 was its first conference defeat in twelve years. Sportswriters referred to the Big Eight as "Oklahoma and the Seven Dwarfs," but many of the team's conference victories were actually close-run affairs, and the team regularly scheduled the most powerful national opponents. The team's overall record for the decade was ninety-one wins against ten losses and a pair of ties. Through that period, the team also produced a total of twenty-five all-American players, as well as many major award winners.

Wilkinson's tenure was not without some controversy. For example, he allowed players to receive subsidies from fans, sometimes turned a blind eye to player high jinks, and indulged in recruiting practices that would not be permitted in later decades. Nonetheless, Wilkinson also served as a positive role model. Many of his players were from poor local families and had weak academic backgrounds. Wilkinson ensured that his players were effectively tutored and taught his entire squad so well that, by the mid-1950's, many area high school coaches were his trainees and sent him their best players.

Impact Wilkinson pioneered observation, analysis, and play techniques later adopted by the emerging professional leagues. The team built pride in an area suffering from a poor "backwater" self-image. University president George Cross successfully lobbied for appropriations and gifts that would build a school of which the football team could be proud. The successful racial integration of the team during the late 1950's was also an important local milestone.

Wilkinson's team-building techniques were widely emulated in the Big Eight and elsewhere, eventually even by powerhouse schools on both coasts and by professional football leagues. The 1950's Sooners remain an unrivaled source of pride for Oklahomans.

Further Reading

Dent, Jim. *The Undefeated: The Oklahoma Sooners and the Greatest Winning Streak in College Football.* New York: St. Martin's Press, 2001. A detailed look at the achievement and the milieu.

Upchurch, Jay, and Mike McKenzie. *Tales from the Sooner Sidelines.* New York: Sports Publishing, 2003. Provides behind-the-scenes glimpses of the building of a football tradition.

J. Quinn Brisben

See also Football; Sports.

■ Olympic Games of 1952

The Event First Olympic Games of the post-World War II era in which both the United States and the Soviet Union competed

Date Held July 19-August 3, 1952

Organizers of the 1952 Helsinki Olympic Games came to refer to the event as the "last real Olympic Games" because the event was relatively unmarred by politics or commercialism and showed exceptional sportsmanship among the athletes.

The 1952 Summer Games marked the first time that the Soviet Union participated in the Olympics. The Soviets sent 381 athletes to Helsinki and won twenty-two gold and seventy-one total medals. It was not until the final day of competition that United States athletes overtook their Soviet counterparts to win the most medals of the Games. The Soviet medal tally was especially impressive because for many Soviet athletes, the 1952 Olympics marked the first time they had competed against world-class athletes from many countries.

The Soviet Union contributed to the Allied victory in World War II, but diplomatic relations between the Soviet Union and the United States eroded quickly after the war. The Marshall Plan, the Truman Doctrine, the Berlin Airlift, the Soviets' successful test of an atomic bomb, and the commencement of the Korean War each served to increase tensions between the two countries and among allies of each and led to the Cold War. The 1952 Olympics were impacted by the international climate as many wondered whether the political stresses affecting the American-Soviet relationship would extend to the sports world. Moreover, because the Helsinki Olympics marked the first time that Soviet and American athletes would meet in such large numbers and in such an internationally recognized event, the interaction between the two sides took on a more compelling interest.

Scoring System Controversy In Helsinki, additional factors caused friction between the East and West. One factor stemmed from the unofficial scoring system used to determine which nations earned the most number of points in the medal race. Throughout its history, the International Olympic Committee (IOC) has never regarded the country that earns the most medals as the "winner" of the Games; rather, the IOC promotes participation and friendship as more important than winning and losing. In 1952, Western media organizations reported that a gold medal was worth ten points; a silver medal, five; and a bronze medal, four; with three, two, and one points being awarded for fourth, fifth, and sixth places. However, the Soviets chose to adopt a new system that gave seven points for a gold medal and maintained the five-through-one Western system.

The scoring issue grew in importance as the Games progressed. Soviet athletes did especially well during the first week, with Soviet women dominating the gymnastics and track-and-field competitions. However, during the second week, American athletes began to give strong performances and steadily narrowed the medal and point gaps between them and their Soviet competitors.

With only two days of competition left, the Soviets began to assert that they would be the overall winners of the Games. This statement was based on their calculations from their own unique scoring system. Nevertheless, the Americans' strong showing in swimming, diving, and boxing led Western-based news agencies to conclude that the U.S. team had overtaken that of the Soviet Union, given that the traditional scoring method was employed. These news organizations also noted that a scoreboard that stood

---

Highlights of the Winter Games of 1952

Dates: February 14-25, 1952

Host city: Oslo, Norway

Events: 22

Participating nations: 30

Participating athletes: 585 men, 109 women

First gold medal: Andrea Mead Lawrence (U.S.A.) in women's giant slalom—the first giant slalom win for the United States; Lawrence also won the slalom

Ice hockey champion: Canada, which tied the United States, 3 to 3, in the final game

Men's figure skating champion: Dick Button (U.S.A.)

Other highlights: Germany and Japan were both readmitted to the Olympics for the first time since World War II. After the Winter Games, Oslo's Olympic Village was used to alleviate Norway's severe postwar housing shortage.

World Records Set in the 1952 Summer Games

Event	Athletes	Country	Record
Men's track and field			
4×400 meter relay	Wint, Laing, McKenley, and Rhoden	Jamaica	3:03.09
50 kilometer walk	Giuseppi Dordoni	Italy	45:28:07.8
triple jump	Adhemar Ferreira da Silva	Brazil	53 feet, 2.5 inches
hammer throw	Jozsef Cermak	Hungary	197 feet, 11.75 inches
decathlon	Bob Mathias	United States	7,887 points
Women's track and field			
80 meter hurdles	Shirley Strickland	Australia	10.9
shot put	Galina Zybina	Soviet Union	50 feet, 1.5 inches
Women's swimming			
4 × 100 meter relay	I. Novak, Temes, E. Novak, Szoke	Hungary	Time: 4:24.4
Weightlifting			
featherweight	Rafael Chimishyan	Soviet Union	743.5 pounds
middle-heavyweight	Norbert Schemansky	Soviet Union	981 pounds

outside the Soviets' Olympic village since the commencement of the Games came down once the American team passed the Soviet squad in points. The debate continued after the Games with the Soviet Union claiming that its athletes and those from the United States had scored the same number of points.

Athlete Interaction The Olympic Village has been a staple of the Games since 1936. However, in 1952, the Soviet Union chose not to allow its athletes to stay in the village with athletes from around the world. Instead, Soviet athletes, along with those from their Eastern Bloc allies, stayed at a separate location. This decision to segregate the athletes added more tension in the days leading up to the Games.

In the days immediately prior to the Olympics, Soviet and American athletes were informally and regularly meeting one another. The encounters were not friendly at first, but goodwill soon developed. For example, one news report described yachtsmen from both countries staring at one another during a practice session. Soon, rowers from both teams were

working out together, and one American official later described the Soviet team in friendly terms. During the Games, the personal exchanges continued. Soviet weight lifters hosted their American counterparts at their village, a Soviet and American were photographed shaking hands after the conclusion of their track-and-field competition, and the Soviet rowing team hosted a dinner for members of the American team one day after the United States had defeated the Soviets for the gold medal in the sport.

Athletic Highlights Although political posturing captured a great deal of attention at the Games, the sports matches and athletic accomplishments were also hailed by the media. Notably, several track-and-field events captured the hearts of the global audience. Emil Zatopek of Czechoslovakia won the 5,000- and 10,000-meters races as well as the marathon. Competing despite a gland infection and doctors' warnings against doing so, Zatopek ran with a pained gait and was the antithesis of the elegant distance runner gliding over the track. A number of women in the track-and-field category earned the respect of spectators and judges alike: Marjorie Jackson of Australia won two medals, while Soviet discus thrower Nina Romashkova became the first Soviet athlete to win Olympic gold.

The American team, including shot-putter Parry O'Brien, pole-vaulter Bob Richards, runner Malvin Whitefield, and decathlete Bob Mathias garnered much media coverage. O'Brien won the shot, making his seemingly effortless gliding technique famous. Richards was singled out because he was a church minister. Whitfield narrowly beat Arthur Wint of Jamaica by two-tenths of a second in the 800-meters run, an exact rematch of their 1948 Olympics race in London. Finally, Mathias defended his 1948 decathlon title when he won the event at the 1952 Games.

In other sports, new rules in equestrianism allowed nonmilitary officers and women to compete. Lis Hartel of Denmark, paralyzed below the knees after being infected with polio, became the first woman to win a medal (silver) in that event. The Soviet women's gymnastics team dominated their sport and won the team competition easily, beginning a streak that would continue for forty years until the Soviet Union broke up into separate republics.

Impact Although the Soviet government used its athletes as part of its Cold War propaganda and at times tried to demonstrate that success on the athletic field was linked to the virtues of socialism, in the end, the Games displayed uncharacteristically good sportsmanship among all teams, which belied the international tensions of the era. The Summer Games in 1956 would be clouded by more overt political ideologies, and several subsequent international boycotts of the Games would ensue in the 1970's and 1980's.

Further Reading

Buchanan, Ian, and Bill Mallon. *Historical Dictionary of the Olympic Movement.* 2d ed. Lanham, Md.: Rowman & Littlefield, 2001. Provides short, crisp descriptions of various individuals and events that played an important role in the development of the Olympics.

Guttmann, Allen. *The Olympics: A History of the Modern Games.* 2d ed. Urbana: University of Illinois Press, 2002. Easy-to-read and comprehensive account that traces the development of the modern Olympics from their birth during the late nineteenth century to their maturity in the twentieth century.

Anthony Moretti

See also British Empire Games; Hockey; Kono, Tommy; Mathias, Bob; Newspapers in the United States; Olympic Games of 1956.

■ Olympic Games of 1956

The Event First Olympic Games of the modern era scarred by a wide-scale boycott
Date November 22-December 8, 1956
Place Melbourne, Australia

The Olympic Games of 1956 became an arena for Cold War rivalries and served as affirmation that nations could use athletic boycotts as symbolic, yet powerful political weapons against other nations pursuing controversial political programs.

The 1956 Summer Olympics in Melbourne, Australia, marked the first time that the Games were held in the Southern Hemisphere. Enthusiasm over the event was dampened by controversy stemming from a multination boycott. Spain, Switzerland, and the Netherlands refused to compete because of the Soviet Union's suppression of the Hungarian revolt. Egypt, Lebanon, and Iraq chose to boycott in response to the developing crisis in the Suez. Moreover, the Games also proved controversial because of the triumph of the Soviet Union over all nations in the so-called medal and points races. The country's dominance rekindled the debate about how to define an amateur athlete.

The International Scene Hungary experienced a public revolt in 1956, as citizens critical of Soviet domination of the country demanded political reforms. In October, a new Hungarian prime minister said Soviet troops should leave and added that Hungary was preparing to exit the Warsaw Pact. Soviet troops soon invaded the capital, Budapest, and quickly squashed the rebellion. A change in political leadership followed, and the uprising ended. Three countries—Spain, Switzerland, and the Netherlands—chose to skip the Olympics after the International Olympic Committee (IOC) ruled that Soviet athletes, despite the actions of their government, should not be barred from competing in Melbourne.

The Suez Crisis also occurred in 1956, when Egypt's president, Gamal Abdel Nasser, nationalized the globally important Suez Canal, which had been operated by the British and French. The European countries entered into an alliance with Israel, which launched a surprise attack on Egypt one month before the start of the Olympics. The British and the French soon ordered the Israelis and the Egyptians out of the canal, and when neither acquiesced, the Europeans began a series of air strikes. The United States and the Soviet Union called on the British, French, and Israelis to cease their military actions. Nasser demanded that British and French athletes be barred from competition in the Olympics, but the IOC refused, prompting Egypt to pull out of the Games. In support, Lebanon and Iraq did the same.

Amateur Status During the 1950's, the IOC adopted a strict code for amateurism. The IOC argued that the Olympics were supposed to celebrate amateurism and be reserved for those athletes who participated because of their love of sport and not for monetary gain.

In the post-World War II years, the amateur question took on a new twist because of concerns about whether the Soviet Union was following Olympics rules. One of the principal concerns the IOC had was whether the Soviet Union was paying (or at least subsidizing) its athletes. Although the Soviet Union maintained it was complying with Olympics rules, the achievements of Soviet athletes in 1952

World Records Set in the 1956 Summer Games

Event	Athletes	Country	Record
Men's track and field			
javelin throw	Egil Danielsen	Norway	281 feet, 2.25 inches
4×100 meter relay	Bobby Morrow, Ira Murchison, Leamon King, Thane Baker	United States	39.5
Women's track and field			
80 meter hurdles	Shirley Strickland	Australia	10.7
long jump	Elzbieta Krzesinska	Poland	20 feet, 11 inches
high jump	Mildred McDaniel	United States	5 feet, 9.25 inches
4×100 meter relay	Strickland, Crocker, Mellon, Cuthbert	Australia	44.5
Men's swimming			
4×200 meter relay	Rose, Hendricks, Devitt, O'Halloran	Australia	8:26.6
Women's swimming			
100 meter butterfly	Shelley Mann	United States	1:11.0
4×100 meter relay	Crapp, Fraser, Leach, Morgan	Australia	4:17.1
Weightlifting			
bantamweight	Charles Vinci	United States	754 pounds
featherweight	Isaac Berger	United States	776.5 pounds
middleweight	Fyodor Bogdanovsky	Soviet Union	925.75 pounds
light heavyweight	Tamio Kono	United States	986.5 pounds
middle heavyweight	Arkady Vorobiev	Soviet Union	1,019.25 pounds

Highlights of the Winter Games of 1956

Dates: November 22-December 8, 1956
Host city: Cortina D'Ampezzo, Italy
Events: 24
Participating nations: 32
Participating athletes: 687 men, 134 women
Ice hockey champion: Soviet Union, which defeated the U.S. team after the U.S. team upset the Canadian team
Women's figure skating champion: Tenley Albright (U.S.A.), who skated on an injured ankle
Other highlights: First skier to win three gold medals in one Winter Olympics—Anton Sailer (Austria)

Women's figure skating champion Tenley Albright. (AP/Wide World Photos)

and 1956 raised concerns that the country was violating the spirit, if not the letter, of the rules of amateurism.

In early 1956, Avery Brundage, the American IOC president, demonstrated that he would play no favorites in the amateurism debate by directing the banishment of a top American track-and-field ath-

lete from the Olympics. Brundage called for an investigation of Wes Santee after reading newspaper reports suggesting Santee had accepted more expense money than he should have for competing in several U.S. events. That investigation confirmed Santee had taken too much money, and in February, 1956, he was banned for life from the Olympics. Two American newspapers were divided about whom to blame for this episode. The *Los Angeles Times* chose to criticize America's sports-governing bodies and the IOC, which it suggested was caving in to pressure from the Soviet Union. However, *The New York Times* argued that Santee knew the rules and simply did not follow them.

Key Events During the Games, the most memorable water polo match in Olympic history was played. The Soviet and Hungarian teams met in the pool, with the latter still in contention for the gold medal. The Hungarians won the game (and later the gold medal), but many spectators were astounded by the brutality of the match. At one point, a Hungarian player was fouled by his Soviet counterpart and exited the water with blood pouring down his face. Pictures of that athlete were disseminated throughout the world. The antagonism soon spread into the stands, and Australian police had to put down a potential riot.

The Soviet Union also won more medals than any other country in Melbourne (thirty-seven gold and ninety-eight total), prompting Soviet officials to boast that their team had shattered the larger-than-life image of the American team, which took home thirty-two gold and seventy-four total medals.

Impact Throughout the second half of the twentieth century, the Olympics were tarnished by boycotts and the vexing question of amateurism. The most recognizable boycotts occurred in 1980 and 1984, when the United States and the Soviet Union encouraged many nations to skip the Games. The idea that Olympic athletes could be used as political pawns had its origins in 1956. Although none of the six nations that skipped the Games that year was an athletic powerhouse, their absence nevertheless suggested that the IOC's goal of separating sports and politics was unattainable.

Further Reading

Espy, Richard. *The Politics of the Olympic Games.* Berkeley: University of California Press, 1979. Espy's account draws heavily on primary sources and provides a detailed narrative of various political issues that have affected the post-World War II Olympics.

Peppard, Victor, and James Riordan. *Playing Politics: Soviet Sports Diplomacy to 1992.* Greenwich, Conn.: JAI Press, 1993. Penetrating analysis of Soviet participation in the Olympics and the Soviet Union's use of sports as a political tool.

Senn, Alfred E. *Power, Politics, and the Olympic Games.* Champaign, Ill.: Human Kinetics Books, 1999. Senn's narrative covers many of the same issues as Espy's book, but it was written twenty years later and has fresher material.

Anthony Moretti

See also Bowden, Don; British Empire Games; Cold War; Connolly, Olga; Hockey; Hungarian revolt; Kono, Tommy; Newspapers in the United States; Oerter, Al; Olympic Games of 1952; Sports; Suez Crisis.

■ *On the Beach*

Identification Film about an imaginary nuclear holocaust
Director Stanley Kramer (1913-2001)
Date Released in 1959

Based on a novel of the same title by Nevil Shute, On the Beach *depicts the relationships between an American commander of a nuclear submarine and a group of Australians who await death from drifting radioactive clouds after a nuclear war. It is considered to be the first important film to deal with a nuclear holocaust, and it heightened the Cold War fears of the American public.*

On the Beach is one of Stanley Kramer's "message movies," adapted from the 1957 novel by Nevil Shute. Its title comes from a 1925 poem by T. S. Eliot titled *The Hollow Men.* A nuclear war between the world's major powers has killed most of the earth's human population. Only the population of Australia has temporarily escaped annihilation, but radioactive clouds are slowly drifting from the Northern Hemisphere to Australia. An American nuclear submarine, the USS *Sawfish,* commanded by Commander Dwight Towers (played by Gregory Peck) sails into Melbourne and is placed under the command of the

Royal Australian Navy. The mission of the *Sawfish* is to check levels of radiation as far north as Alaska and investigate sporadic radio signals coming from San Diego, California. In its journey, the crew finds desolate wastelands, devoid of human presence, and the mysterious radio signals prove not to be of human origin. Presented with the reality of their own impending deaths within a matter of a few months, the residents of Melbourne must each deal with their mortality. Parents not only face the choice of dying from radioactive infection or committing suicide by swallowing cyanide pills but also must deal with the horrific task of killing their infant children to prevent them from the extensive suffering caused by radioactive infection. The film cast also included actors such as Anthony Perkins, Fred Astaire, and Ava Gardner.

Director Kramer paints a chilling scenario of a dying planet and the actions of the people who remain. The movie makes clear that there can be no international reprieve from annihilation, no taking back of past transgressions, and no frantic appeals for mercy; it is simply the end of the human race. The film predicts not the end of all life on Earth but merely the end of the human race. In its extinction, humanity represents a failed experiment in which its inability to coexist brings about its own self-destruction. The film presents a horrific black-and-white apocalyptic vision without showing any physical destruction of cities or fields of rotting corpses; these images are left to the viewer's imagination.

Impact *On the Beach* was released while the Cold War was escalating between the United States and the Soviet Union. It placed before the American public one possible scenario of the harsh consequences of a nuclear war and emphasized that there can be no winners in such a conflict. The American public, already imbued with a fear of nuclear war, viewed this film as a possible harbinger of things to come. In the political spectrum, views of the film differed widely. Senator Wallace Bennett of the Senate Atomic Energy Committee viewed the movie as an unrealistic portrayal of reality, as well as being unscientific and misleading. Conversely, Nobel Peace Prize winner Linus Pauling considered the film as a movie that might save the world.

Further Reading

Engelhardt, Tom. *End of Victory Culture: Cold War America and the Disillusioning of a Generation.* 2d ed.

Amherst: University of Massachusetts Press, 1998. Explores the way in which Cold War fears were embedded in television and films of the era.

Shute, Nevil. *On the Beach*. New York: Ballantine Books, 1957. The original novel from which the screenplay for *On the Beach* was adapted.

Jose C. de Leon

See also Atomic bomb; Bomb shelters; Cold War; DEW Line; Film in the United States.

■ On the Road

Identification Novel about the lifestyle of the Beat generation
Author Jack Kerouac (1922-1969)
Date Published in 1957

On the Road is an American classic that established Jack Kerouac's reputation as the voice of the Beat writers.

Jack Kerouac's *On the Road* is a fictionalized portrait of the travels and adventures of Kerouac and his friends in the Beat generation during the late 1940's, as they traveled back and forth across the United States, relinquishing responsibility in favor of living for the moment. The main character of the novel is Dean Moriarty, based on Neal Cassady, a man whom Kerouac considered an uninhibited model of a romantic hero. Kerouac himself is Sal Paradise, the narrator of the story, who admires and emulates Dean's manic spontaneity.

The structure of the novel is picaresque, moving with the unfocused energy of its characters through a series of adventures without strong character or plot development. The method of spontaneous prose was characteristic of the Beat writers.

Impact Reviews of the novel were mixed when it was published in 1957. Some readers were shocked by the book's revelations of drug and alcohol abuse and sexual promiscuity. Others saw the novel as an important record of the lifestyle of the rebellious youth of the Beat generation. The book was a popular success, and critics began to see the lifestyle of the Beats as a journey or a spiritual quest. *On the Road* has entered the literary tradition of road literature and helped inspire the road literature and wandering of the hippie generation of the 1960's.

Further Reading
Cassady, Carolyn. *Off the Road: My Years with Cassady, Kerouac, and Ginsberg.* New York: Penguin Books,

1990. Neal Cassady's wife writes about her adventures with the Beats.

Swartz, Omar. *The View from "On the Road": The Rhetorical Vision of Jack Kerouac.* Carbondale: Southern Illinois University Press, 1999. Analysis of *On the Road* explains Kerouac's methods and his vision of an alternative culture.

Susan Butterworth

See also Automobiles and auto manufacturing; Beat generation; Burroughs, William; Ginsberg, Allen; Kerouac, Jack; Literature in the United States; *Naked Lunch*; Youth culture and the generation gap.

■ On the Waterfront

Identification Academy Award-winning film about union corruption on the New York waterfront
Director Elia Kazan (1909-2003)
Date Released in 1954

On the Waterfront was a showcase film for its ensemble cast of Actors Studio personnel, its depiction of criminal involvement in a labor union, and the controversial reputation of its director.

On the Waterfront focuses on the fate of two brothers—Terry Malloy (played by Marlon Brando), a former prizefighter turned dockworker and his brother, Charlie (Rod Steiger), a lawyer who works for the corrupt head of a Longshoreman's Union—who are caught in the middle of an investigation into the corrupt activities of the union's leadership. As the film opens, Terry is enjoying good jobs on the waterfront, which his brother's privileged position affords him. However, as the narrative unfolds, he is forced to acknowledge the corruption of the union and the consequences of the violence its leadership employs to maintain power over union members. Initially encouraged to cooperate with the crime commission by a local priest (Karl Malden) and later by the sister of one of the murdered workers (Eva Marie Saint), with whom he falls in love, Terry must make a decision whether or not to "come clean" or to play "deaf and dumb," as his brother and the leadership want him to do. The film concludes with Terry's testimony before the commission in which he reveals the details of the union's corrupt activities and accuses its president, Johnny Friendly (Lee J. Cobb), of responsibility for the murder of his girlfriend's brother.

Marlon Brando as the brooding Terry Malloy in On the Waterfront. *(AP/Wide World Photos)*

Senator Estes Kefauver's congressional investigations into crime in the United States publicized the widespread influence of criminal activities in all aspects of American life. *On the Waterfront* became perhaps the best-known film to dramatize the impact that organized crime had on the lives of ordinary people. The actions of Terry Malloy, who goes against the mob, also reflected indirectly on director Elia Kazan's own testimony earlier in the decade before the House Committee on Un-American Activities, when he named Hollywood figures who allegedly supported communist causes.

Impact *On the Waterfront*'s evocative black-and-white photography, location shooting in New York City, and outstanding cast marked it aesthetically as one of the most memorable films of Kazan's career and of the period.

Further Reading
Biskind, Peter. *Seeing Is Believing: How Hollywood Taught Us to Stop Worrying and Love the Fifties.* Rev. ed. New York: Pantheon Books, 2000. A lively dis-

cussion of the Hollywood films of the 1950's and how they reflect various social and political issues of the period.

Hey, Kenneth R. "Ambivalence as a Theme in *On the Waterfront*: An Interdisciplinary Approach to Film Study." In *Hollywood as Historian: American Film in a Cultural Context.* Lexington: University Press of Kentucky, 1983. Discusses the artistic collaboration on the film in the context of the film's origin.

Charles L. P. Silet

See also Academy Awards; Actors Studio; Bernstein, Leonard; Brando, Marlon; House Committee on Un-American Activities; Kazan, Elia; Kefauver Committee; Miller, Arthur; Organized crime; Unionism in the United States.

■ Operation Wetback

The Event Campaign of the U.S. Immigration and Naturalization Service (INS) to expel undocumented aliens from the United States
Date Program began on June 17, 1954
Place Southwestern United States

This campaign removed illegal aliens, or "wetbacks" (so-called because a primary method for immigrants entering the United States illegally was to swim across the Rio Grande), from the United States, ended migration into the country from Mexico, and secured the Mexican-U.S. border against further illegal immigration for more than a decade.

Labor shortages in the United States increased both legal and illegal migration into the country during the 1950's. The bracero program of the 1940's brought foreign nationals into the United States to work legally, while also increasing illegal migration from Mexico. Although many Americans welcomed the labor of illegal aliens, especially in agriculture, the majority of Americans grew alarmed at the growing numbers of immigrants within the country's borders.

Sensationalized media accounts about "wetbacks" increased public pressure to solve the influx of immigrants. Even after the passage of the Immigration and Nationality Act of 1952, legislation designed to make it more difficult to enter the United States, illegal immigration continued to increase into 1954. Between 1944 and 1954, the number of immigrants illegally entering from Mexico increased by 6,000 percent, and experts estimated that in 1954 alone, before the start of Operation Wetback, more than one million workers crossed the Rio Grande illegally. However, veterans from World War II and the Korean War needed jobs, and immigrants were blamed for depressing wages and for taking jobs away from U.S. citizens. They were also accused of making it more difficult to unionize workers. Health officials attributed increasing rates of communicable diseases to them. In this xenophobic atmosphere, immigrants increasingly were charged with increasing crime, welfare costs, and illegal drug traffic.

Fear of communist infiltration also fueled the drive to solve the wetback problem. Some claimed that communists were infiltrating the United States disguised as farmworkers. Critics of the INS claimed it was either complacent or incompetent to stem the rising tide of illegal immigration. American economic, social, and political security required complete control of the U.S. border.

The Campaign In response to growing public demand, the Eisenhower administration launched Operation Wetback on June 17, 1954, under the leadership of General Joseph May Swing. Federal, state, and local authorities worked in concert to rid the country of illegal aliens in a series of ever-expanding dragnets. Although it concentrated its efforts in the Southwest, no area of the country was spared. Illegal workers in industries in midwestern cities were also targeted. Nearly five thousand illegal aliens were apprehended on the first day, and officials claimed that more than one million people were deported to Mexico in 1954 alone, 90 percent of whom were Mexican nationals. Thousands of U.S. citizens were also deported. Many thousands more illegal aliens returned to Mexico voluntarily. The numbers of illegal aliens deported after 1954 dropped off sharply. In 1957, the INS declared the wetback problem to be solved. Very few illegal aliens remained in the wake of Operation Wetback's brutal efficiency.

Impact In the wake of Operation Wetback, the bracero program expanded to provide more temporary workers. It gave employers greater control over workers and brought them higher profits. The presence of illegal aliens in the workforce did not reach 1950's numbers again until the late 1970's.

Operation Wetback devastated Mexican American families by deporting the Mexican nationals among them. The campaign also disrupted Mexican American businesses. Interethnic tensions grew in border areas. Critics claim that the INS abused Mexi-

can Americans as well as the illegal aliens among them in their zeal to find and remove illegal immigrants. Moreover, Mexican Americans became less interested in assimilation and prouder of their ethnic heritage as a result.

Further Reading

Calavita, Kitty. *Inside the State: The Bracero Program, Immigration, and the INS.* New York: Routledge, 1992. Explains how Operation Wetback improved the reputation of the INS and the profitability of American agriculture.

García, Juan Ramon. *Operation Wetback: The Mass Deportation of Mexican Undocumented Workers in 1954.* Westport, Conn.: Greenwood Press, 1980. The classic and most complete study of Operation Wetback.

Samora, Julian. *Los Mojados: The Wetback Story.* Notre Dame: University of Notre Dame Press, 1971. Describes how Operation Wetback was one of several campaigns in U.S. history designed to regain control of immigration.

Evelyn Toft

See also Agriculture in the United States; Bracero program; Immigration and Nationality Act of 1952; Immigration to the United States; Latin America; Latinos; Mexico; Unemployment in the United States.

■ Oppenheimer, J. Robert

Identification American theoretical physicist
Born April 22, 1904; New York, New York
Died February 18, 1967; Princeton, New Jersey

After leading the project that built the first atomic bomb, J. Robert Oppenheimer became a leading advocate for the control of atomic energy and a strong opponent of the hydrogen bomb in his position as a scientific adviser to the federal government. The 1950's era of fears over subversive behavior among Americans ultimately led to his trial over treason and the revoke of his federal security clearance, effectively ending his role in the public sector.

Julius Robert Oppenheimer was born in New York City to affluent parents who could afford to indulge his interests in science, culture, and philosophy. After graduation from the elite private Ethical Culture School, Oppenheimer enrolled at Harvard as a chemistry student. Quickly, his interest shifted to physics, and he was given the opportunity to work in

Percy Bridgman's laboratory. He completed his undergraduate studies in only three years.

Interested in theoretical physics, Oppenheimer applied for a position at Cambridge University under Ernest Rutherford, who had discovered the atom's nucleus. Rutherford rejected Oppenheimer's application. Oppenheimer then sought a position with J. J. Thomson, who was recognized as the discoverer of the electron. Thomson accepted that application, and Oppenheimer was able to begin graduate work at Cambridge. There he met theorists Neils Bohr and Paul Ehrenfest and worked with other young students who would go on to have landmark careers in physics.

Oppenheimer was urged to study Paul Dirac's version of quantum theory, which ultimately led to an invitation to do doctoral research at the University of Göttingen under theorist Max Born. In less than one year, Oppenheimer completed his doctoral work. In 1929, Oppenheimer returned to the United States and received a dual appointment at the University of California at Berkeley and the California Institute of Technology. He was asked in 1942 to direct Manhattan Project research at Los Alamos, New Mexico. Following World War II, Oppenheimer returned to academia.

A Voice of Conscience During the 1940's and 1950's, Oppenheimer became well known to the general public, perhaps second only to fellow scientist Albert Einstein. After leading the team that developed the atomic bomb in Los Alamos, New Mexico, Oppenheimer was named to the directorship of Princeton University's Institute for Advanced Study in 1947, a group that included Einstein. However, Oppenheimer also seemed to shoulder the moral conscience of the scientists involved in atomic research and the subsequent deployment of the atomic bomb in Japan at the end of World War II. After witnessing the first atomic explosion, the Trinity test, on July 16, 1945, Oppenheimer claimed to have recalled a line from Hindu scripture: "I am become death, the shatterer of worlds." Although Oppenheimer recommended dropping the atomic bomb on Japan rather than merely arranging a demonstration of power to bring the Japanese to the negotiating table, he later came to regret his action.

Later, as chair of the Atomic Energy Commission general advisory committee, Oppenheimer worked to promote tight controls on further development of nuclear weapons and nuclear technology. His opposition to the development of the hydrogen bomb eventually led to questioning of his loyalty and suitability to receive classified information. In a vigorous campaign to build the H-bomb, Edward Teller actively used his own political connections to brush Oppenheimer's objections aside.

Oppenheimer's security clearance was revoked in December, 1953. He was granted a congressional hearing to clear himself, and, with an impeccable record of management of atomic bomb development and the support of the vast majority of his fellow atomic and nuclear scientists, Oppenheimer was declared a loyal American. However, in the era of McCarthyism, and as a result of his past involvement during the Depression years in socialist and communist groups, Oppenheimer's security clearance remained revoked. Many in the physics community never forgave Teller for his roughshod treatment of Oppenheimer in pursuit of H-bomb development, yet Oppenheimer remained revered for his unique intellect and contributions to the rise of American theoretical physics.

Impact Although Oppenheimer is most generally remembered for his Manhattan Project contributions, he also played a central role in the development of advanced theoretical physics in the United States. During the first two decades of the twentieth century, American physics was already acclaimed for its experimental research, but Europe remained the center for great advances in theoretical physics. American theoretical physics took quantum leaps as a result of the massive effort to understand the structure of the nucleus and release its energy. Oppenheimer attracted talented young students who went on to have brilliant careers in physics, but he also provided fundamental advances in different areas of physics. He collaborated with Born to develop the Born-Oppenheimer approximation, which permits certain types of quantum mechanical calculations involving atomic and molecular systems; he provided a basic understanding of electron extraction from metal surfaces under electric fields, which led to the development of the scanning electron microscope several decades later; and he applied general relativity to understanding stellar collapse, some of the first work that would eventually propose the existence of neutron stars and black holes.

President Lyndon B. Johnson presented Oppenheimer with the Atomic Energy Commission's Enrico Fermi Award in 1963. Oppenheimer concluded his scientific career at Princeton in 1966; however, that retirement was brief. Only eight months later, he died from throat cancer.

Further Reading

Davis, Nuel Pharr. *Lawrence and Oppenheimer.* New York: Simon & Schuster, 1968. Showcases the academic and research career of Oppenheimer at Berkeley.

Polenberg, Richard. *In the Matter of J. Robert Oppenheimer: The Security Clearance Hearing.* Ithaca, N.Y.: Cornell University Press, 2002. Objective review of the Oppenheimer security clearance hearings.

Rhodes, Richard. *The Making of the Atomic Bomb.* New York: Simon & Schuster, 1986. Perhaps the most comprehensive history of the Manhattan Project.

David G. Fisher

See also Atomic bomb; Atomic Energy Act of 1954; Disarmament movement; Einstein, Albert; Hydrogen bomb; Pauling, Linus; *Savannah*; Science and technology; Seaborg, Glenn; Teller, Edward.

■ O'Ree, Willie

Identification Canadian hockey player
Born October 15, 1935; Fredericton, New Brunswick, Canada

When Willie O'Ree donned a Boston Bruins uniform for a two-game trial in 1958, he became the first black player in the National Hockey League and helped integrate a sport that lagged behind others in racial integration.

Willie O'Ree grew up playing both ice hockey and baseball. In 1956, he was invited to a Milwaukee Braves baseball training camp in Georgia, where he found the racially discriminatory climate of the American South to be in sharp contrast to Canada's more tolerant society. Consequently, O'Ree decided to drop baseball and concentrate on hockey. He was a forward throughout his career, playing both left and right wing.

After a few years in Canada's junior leagues, O'Ree embarked upon a professional career that relegated him primarily to hockey's minor leagues. When he was twenty-one, he was hit in the face with a puck and lost almost all sight in his right eye, which limited his playing abilities.

Nevertheless, in January, 1958, O'Ree played in two games for the Boston Bruins, becoming the first person of African descent to play in the National Hockey League (NHL). He played forty-three more games for the Bruins during the 1960-1961 season, tallying four goals and ten assists. However, that was the extent of his NHL experience, although he played professionally for twenty-one years, retiring in 1979.

Impact By becoming the NHL's first black player, Willie O'Ree broke the color barrier of the last of North America's major team sports to integrate. In 1988, NHL leaders created a Diversity Task Force and appointed O'Ree to be its director. The panel's purpose was to educate members of minorities about hockey and to help develop the talents of minority players. This initiative was part of an effort to dispel hockey's reputation as a sport played only by white athletes and to make hockey more accessible and attractive to athletes of all races.

Further Reading

Harris, Cecil. *Breaking the Ice: The Black Experience in Professional Hockey.* Toronto: Insomniac Press, 2004. Profiles of notable black athletes in ice hockey.

O'Ree, Willie, with Michael McKinley. *The Autobiography of Willie O'Ree: Hockey's Black Pioneer.* New York: Somerville House, 2000. O'Ree's life and career in his own words.

Roger D. Hardaway

See also Hockey; Minorities in Canada; Racial discrimination; Sports.

■ *The Organization Man*

Identification Sociological treatise on the relationships between organizations and American society during the 1950's
Author William H. Whyte (1917-1999)
Date Published in 1956

In The Organization Man, *William H. Whyte argued that America's highly touted individualism was being eroded by a new organizational social ethic of conformity.*

The Organization Man appeared at a time when Americans lived in the shadow of the Cold War but enjoyed unprecedented access to consumer goods. William H. Whyte, then the managing editor of *Fortune* magazine, drew attention to a widespread shift in the relationships between individuals and large organizations—universities, the government, and most important, corporations. Whyte noted that although most Americans professed adherence to the "Protestant ethic" of individualism, self-reliance, and personal independence, a new ethic of social conformity was emerging.

Whyte called this conformity the "social ethic," which was based on three ideas: the group or organization was the ultimate source of creativity; membership in a social group, or "belongingness," was essential for individual happiness; and the idea that social problems could be solved or "engineered" with the help of social science. The new conformist ideology helped legitimate social pressures against the individual. Moreover, rather than resist the social ethic, the new "organization man" embraced it as a source of material and spiritual well-being although he would still use the language of individualism.

Impact Whyte admitted that social values were important but complained that in the age of the giant organization, they did not need to be emphasized because they stifled individual initiative and imagination and encouraged a tyranny of normalcy. *The Organization Man* had wide readership among academics and the general public.

Further Reading
Jackall, Robert. *Moral Mazes: The World of the Corporate Manager.* New York: Oxford University Press, 1989. Explores the process of moral decision making in the world of managers.
Putnam, Robert D. *Bowling Alone: The Collapse and Revival of American Community.* New York: Simon & Schuster, 2001. Details the deterioration of America's sense of community.

Edward W. Maine

See also Affluence and the new consumerism; *Affluent Society, The*; Cold War; Conformity, culture of; *Lonely Crowd, The*; *Man in the Gray Flannel Suit, The*; Mills, C. Wright.

■ Organization of American States

Identification Political organization of Western Hemisphere nations
Date Formed in 1948

Although often used as a means to combat the spread of communism, the Organization of American States (OAS) was established to defend countries in the Western Hemisphere from aggression, peacefully resolve conflicts, and build regional cooperation for social welfare.

In the post-World War II period, the political and economic needs of the United States, Canada, and the twenty independent Latin American countries converged, allowing the formation of the Organization of American States. For the Latin American countries, economic assistance and nonaggression provisions were the primary reasons for signing the pact. Several times during the 1950's, peacekeeping operations were necessary to stop conflicts in the region that were international in scope.

Programs for social welfare ranged from universal suffrage to the construction of the Pan-American Highway. However, differences in priorities between the United States and the other member countries were evident in events such as in the 1957 Latin American proposal to form an inter-American bank: While the United States initially refused to support the proposal, the bank eventually was established in 1959. The slowness of the United States to respond to Latin American needs resulted in many Latin American economic proposals being addressed through the United Nations rather than the OAS, a fact that weakened the latter organization.

American Priorities As the Cold War intensified, the United States considered the OAS primarily a mechanism for resisting communist infiltration in the Western Hemisphere. Under intense American pressure, the March, 1954, Caracas Conference, passed a resolution that any communist-related government in the Americas was a threat to everyone. With this justification, the United States assisted a coup in Guatemala against a government that had leftist policies, an action that undercut support for the United States throughout the region. After the Guatemalan intervention, there was an obvious split between the way in which the United States viewed the organization and its purpose and the views of Latin America.

In early 1959, Fidel Castro overthrew the government of Cuba, then an OAS member, and quickly took steps to nationalize American financial interests in that country. This event initiated a new crisis for the United States and within the OAS. Castro's goal of expanding his revolution beyond Cuba caused many Latin American governments to seek

Charter Members of the Organization of American States

Argentina	Haiti
Bolivia	Honduras
Brazil	Mexico
Chile	Nicaragua
Colombia	Panama
Costa Rica	Paraguay
Cuba	Peru
Dominican Republic	United States
Ecuador	Uruguay
El Salvador	Venezuela
Guatemala	

assistance from the United States in order to combat socialist expansion, a movement that had the effect of creating closer ties among many of the region's nations.

Impact The ideals of the Organization of American States generally were not achieved, and its existence had mixed results. By giving a forum for the exchange of ideas and for diplomatic negotiations, the OAS played a positive role in ongoing relations between the United States and Latin America. However, differing views regarding the organization's primary purpose and goals also caused increased tensions between the two regions.

Subsequent Events In January of 1962, Cuba was expelled from the OAS on the grounds that it was no longer a democratic country. Throughout the 1960's, the anticommunist stance of the organization remained strong. Although by the early twenty-first century Cuba had not been allowed to rejoin the OAS, all other independent countries of the Western Hemisphere remained members. While the OAS supported peacekeeping operations in crisis situations throughout the latter decades of the twentieth century, it spent more resources on increasing living standards throughout Latin America.

Further Reading

Stoetzer, O. Carlos. *The Organization of American States.* 2d ed. New York: Praeger, 1993. An overview of the structure of the OAS and its history.

Thomas, Christopher R., and Juliana T. Magloire. *Regionalism Versus Multilateralism: The Organization*

of American States in a Global Changing Environment. Boston: Kluwer Academic, 2000. Examines the activities of the organization and how it has changed during its history.

Donald A. Watt

See also Castro, Fidel; Cold War; Cuban Revolution; Foreign policy of the United States; Guatemala invasion; Latin America; Nixon's Latin America tour.

■ Organized crime

During the 1950's, the broad problem of organized crime was narrowly identified as being exclusively synonymous with an alien, conspiratorial society known as the Mafia.

The 1950's was a decade when both political forces and popular culture perpetuated fears of foreign-based threats to the nation's security and social well-being. The threats appeared all the more real as they were played out during an era known as the Cold War and before an audience mesmerized by the latest miracle of television.

In February of 1950, Senator Joseph McCarthy announced that he had a list of more than two hundred State Department employees who were members of the Communist Party. His virulent witch-hunt into alleged subversive activities within government, the entertainment industry, publishing circles, and even the military marked one of the darkest periods of American politics. It lasted for four turbulent years until the senator was censured by his colleagues. Three months after McCarthy had initially warned the public about security threats linked to the Soviet Union, a different peril, one having ties to Sicily, was about to be exposed by another U.S. senator.

In May of 1950, Estes Kefauver of Tennessee conducted the first of several widely televised hearings of the Special Committee to Investigate Organized Crime in Interstate Commerce. Hearings were held in more than one dozen cities and introduced television viewers to such colorful figures as Frank Costello, a reputed New York City crime boss.

Kefauver's conclusions regarding the lack of effective cooperation among law enforcement agencies and the extent of illegal gambling, assisted by local and statewide corruption, were credible revelations. These findings were, however, overshadowed by the more sensational conclusion that organized crime owed its existence to an alien society known as the Mafia. Furthermore, this society was described by the committee as a highly secretive, conspiratorial organization that had infiltrated the ranks of state and local governments, a threat similar in nature to McCarthy's allegations regarding communists.

Ethnic Ties and Stereotypical Portrayals Organized crime, in fact, included past and present activities of native-born Anglo-Saxons as well as individuals having immigrant Irish, Jewish, Polish, Russian, Asian, Hispanic, and African American backgrounds. Nonetheless, equating organized crime with Italian heritage and the Mafia dominated the public consciousness throughout the 1950's. In 1956, Senator McClellan of Arkansas investigated the relationship between organized crime and the Teamsters Union and eventually produced a star witness, Jo-

seph Valachi, who would solidify the Mafia image for future decades. Newspapers, films, and books of the 1950's mirrored the government's version of organized crime. Stories focused on high-profile ethnic crime bosses in New York and Chicago. Men with names such as Luciano, Genovese, Profaci, Bonnano, and Giancana dominated headlines, were the subject of paperbacks, and often became models for gangster films.

Television seized on this theme with its widely popular show *The Untouchables*, which recounted 1920's crime fighter Elliot Ness's battles with Al Capone's bootlegging empire. The series included references to many gangster-bootleggers of the period, practically all of whom had names that ended in a vowel, thus perpetuating the "ethnic" stereotype of gangsters. Not one episode made reference to Kennedy-family patriarch Joseph Kennedy's extensive ventures involving the bootlegging of Scotch

Reputed New York City crime boss Frank Costello (left) with his attorney, George Wolf, at a hearing of the Senate's Crime Investigating Committee in March, 1951. Costello's refusal to testify earned him an eighteen-month prison sentence for contempt of the Senate. (AP/ Wide World Photos)

whiskey through Canada during Prohibition. The senior Kennedy's son, John Fitzgerald, was a rising star in Democratic politics at the time the television series was running and would go on to become president in 1961.

Gambling Revenue and Law Enforcement By mid-century, the primary source of revenue for organized crime had become gambling. Syndicate interest in prostitution began to wane even before the beginning of Prohibition, due largely to reform movements followed by the passage of restrictive legislation. With the end of Prohibition during the early 1930's, crime syndicates were left with much wealth and with well-established organizational skills. These advantages favored successful ventures in labor racketeering, loan-sharking, and the eventual monopolization of otherwise legitimate concerns such as urban waste collection and construction projects. Though much of their gambling activities centered around illegal slot machines, floating card games, and the like, organized crime groups turned increasingly to the opportunities provided by legalized casino gambling in Nevada.

Organized crime inroads began in Las Vegas when Benjamin (Bugsy) Siegel opened the Flamingo Hotel in 1946, which was followed during the early 1950's by large-scale cooperative investments, principally by Jews and Italians. Despite the ethnic mix involved in organized crime, law enforcement circles continued to reinforce the Italian image of the problem.

In November of 1957, a state trooper patrolling around Apalachin, New York, a small rural town over the Pennsylvania border, spotted an unusually large number of cars convening on the estate of Joseph Barbara. Trooper Croswell, who previously had placed Barbara's home under surveillance for "suspicious" activities, called in other state and local officers to assist in a raid on the residence. Many of Barbara's guests tried to flee, but some were rounded up, arrested, and later tried on charges of conspiracy

and obstruction of justice. None of the convictions held on appeal when a court found that the raid and subsequent actions were conducted without probable cause to believe that criminal activity was underway. Several credible reasons for the Apalachin meeting existed, many of which did not support the belief that its purpose was that of charting the course of organized crime in the United States. Nevertheless, the official government interpretation claimed that activities there were solid proof of a nationwide Mafia conspiracy. This view of organized crime, sustained by the Apalachin affair, would carry over into the 1960's.

Impact Televised committee hearings of the 1950's, bolstered by the decade's press, popular culture, and law enforcement activities, firmly established the belief that the sole cause of organized crime was an alien, secret society known as the Mafia. Years later, the influential President's Task Force on Organized Crime endorsed this assessment when it also concluded that the core of organized crime in the United States was controlled "exclusively [by] men of Italian descent."

Further Reading

Abadinsky, Howard. *Organized Crime.* Belmont, Calif.: Wadsworth/Thomson, 2003. Excellent overview of the history of organized crime in the United States.

Bernstein, Lee. *The Greatest Menace: Organized Crime in Cold War America.* Amherst: University of Massachusetts Press, 2002. Interesting historical essay describing the politics behind portrayals of organized crime as an exclusively Mafia phenomenon.

Henry W. Mannle

See also Cold War; Hoffa, Jimmy; Hoover, J. Edgar; Kefauver, Estes; Kefauver Committee; Landrum-Griffin Act of 1959; McCarthy, Joseph; McClellan Committee; Motorcycle gangs; Turner-Stompanato scandal.

P

Packard, Vance

Identification American writer and social critic
Born May 22, 1914; Granville Summit, Pennsylvania
Died December 12, 1996; Martha's Vineyard, Massachusetts

A major critic of consumerism, Vance Packard argued that the manipulations of advertisers and the pursuit of status symbols inspired Americans to fritter away their 1950's-era wealth in mindless attempts to satisfy unconscious wants and alleviate unconscious fears.

The youngest of three children in a religious farming family, Packard honed his journalistic skills on student publications at Pennsylvania State University and spent his early career as a feature writer for magazines. He began his book-writing career writing nonfiction with sociological themes in 1956 and produced three best-sellers in a row.

In *The Hidden Persuaders* (1957), Packard argued that advertisers, guided by motivational research, create pseudo-needs, which link products to unconscious wants and fears. He argued that such manipulations were needed in economies that produce and sell unneeded products.

Packard's *The Status Seekers: An Exploration of Class Behavior in America and the Hidden Barriers That Affect You, Your Community, Your Future* (1959) placed the symbols of status among those pseudo-needs he explored in his prior book. The relentless pursuit of arbitrary status symbols, he charged, nourishes and even intensifies class divisions in the United States. In the *The Waste Makers* (1960), he cited the wastefulness that results from consumers' tendency to throw away products when trends turn and the products become obsolescent or unfashionable.

Although Packard continued to critique consumerism and mass marketing, none of his post-1960 works of social criticism approached the impact of his 1950's best-sellers.

Impact Packard was among several writers of the 1950's who pointed out the dark side of America's postwar affluent society. Critics charged that his thesis was overstated, yet it resonated with an increasing number of Americans who could afford all their material needs and still felt unfulfilled. Packard's writings anticipated those of later, more intense and focused critics such as Rachel Carson and Ralph Nader.

Further Reading

Cohen, Elizabeth. *A Consumer's Republic: The Politics of Mass Consumption in Postwar America.* New York: Knopf, 2003. Examines the way in which affluence and consumerism were linked to issues of citizenship (the encouragement to buy for "the good of the nation") in postwar America.
Horowitz, David. *American Social Classes in the 1950's: Selections from Vance Packard's "The Status Seekers."* New York: St. Martin's Press, 1995. Provides excerpts from *The Status Seekers* and an introduction by Horowitz that places Packard in the context of 1950's social criticism.
_____. *Vance Packard and American Social Criticism.* Chapel Hill: University of North Carolina Press, 1994. A comprehensive review of Packard's life and works in the context of the era.

Thomas E. DeWolfe

See also Advertising; Affluence and the new consumerism; *Affluent Society, The;* American Dream; Conformity, culture of; Mills, C. Wright.

Paint-by-numbers movement

Identification Production of oil paintings using kits that included numbered diagrams stamped on canvases, more than twenty premixed oil paints, and brushes
Developer Dan Robbins, an employee of Palmer Paint Company in Detroit, Michigan
Date Popularity peaked in 1954

Part of the do-it-yourself movement and the general interest in learning to paint, paint-by-numbers kits were the de-

cade's most popular hobby product and became emblematic of the growing leisure time of most Americans.

Max Klein, owner of Palmer Paint Company, was interested in expanding his products into something suitable for the entire family. Dan Robbins believed his paint-by-numbers idea would work; he recalled that the Italian Renaissance artist Leonardo da Vinci taught students and apprentices to paint by numbering parts of a canvas and assigning basic colors to them. The Palmer company's Craft Master sets received their first major exposure at Macy's department store in New York City in November, 1950. In slightly more than a year, the company sold more than fifteen million kits, and thirty-five other companies entered the market. Paintings mainly depicted animals, seascapes, landscapes, still-lifes, and religious themes. The most popular kit was one depicting the Last Supper of Jesus Christ. Advertising slogans for the kits claimed that "Every man is a Rembrandt!" and "A beautiful painting the first time you try!"

Impact Although professional artists, art historians, and art educators decried the paintings as "not real art," consumers found them an enjoyable use of increased leisure time and a way to satisfy creative yearnings. The boom ended in 1959, but the kits remained a standard hobby item into the early twenty-first century. During the 1990's, collectors began purchasing canvases painted during the 1950's and 1960's.

Further Reading

Bird, William L. *Paint by Numbers.* Washington, D.C.: Smithsonian Institution, 2001. This copiously illustrated, well-documented book details the product's development and rise in popularity as well as critical responses.

Robbins, Dan. *Whatever Happened to Paint-by-Numbers?* Delavan, Wis.: Possum Hill, 1998. Humorously written, in-depth account by the product's inventor.

Glenn Ellen Starr Stilling

See also Art movements; Fads; Famous Artists School; Painters Eleven.

■ Painters Eleven

Identification Group of Canadian abstract painters
Date Active from 1953 to 1960

The Painters Eleven played a major role in developing and stimulating awareness of abstract art in Canada during the 1950's.

Amid the growing prosperity and rapid change of postwar Canada, many artists felt a sense of isolation and constraint. Abstraction, so predominant in American and European artwork, had appeared in various isolated exhibitions in Toronto but was regarded only marginally by influential art institutions such as the Royal Canadian Academy of Arts and the Ontario Society of Artists.

Beginnings Toronto-area artists interested in the liberating style of abstraction formed Painters Eleven in 1953. William Ronald was instrumental in bringing seven of the members together in *Abstracts at Home*, an exhibition at Simpson's department store. Ronald's work appeared alongside paintings by Jack Bush, Oscar Cahen, Tom Hodgson, Alexandra Luke, Ray Mead, and Kazuo Nakamura. Pleased with the show, the artists met at Luke's lakeside studio to discuss future exhibits. They also invited Hortense Gordon, Jock Macdonald, Harold Town, and Walter Yarwood to join them.

Painters Eleven was a lively and informal group. Town suggested that they adopt the generic name of "Painters Eleven" in reference to the number of members. The new group had neither pretense of a common philosophy nor a group leader. The members' individual styles were as diverse as their backgrounds and experience. Nevertheless, they were united by their collective dissatisfaction with the conservatism of Toronto's art world and their desire to paint in the more spontaneous, less restrictive style of abstraction. They shared stylistic commonalities of boldness, energy, and a sense of experimentation. They also shared the practical purpose of developing opportunities to exhibit and promote abstract art.

Exhibitions Although relatively unstructured, the group was the Toronto area's first organization dedicated to abstract and nonobjective painting. Its members had a productive exhibition schedule. In 1954, Bush secured Toronto's Roberts Gallery for their first exhibition. They exhibited there periodically over the next two years. In 1956, through Ronald's contacts, they were invited to show with the *American Abstract Artists* at New York's Riverside Museum, where they were highly acclaimed. In addition to a variety of individual exhibits, the group also presented work at the University of Toronto's Hart House and the Park Gallery. In 1958 and 1959, the National Gallery of Canada circulated a Painters Eleven exhibition.

The group suffered several setbacks. In 1956, Cahen died in a car accident. The following year Ronald resigned, and Mead moved to Montreal. With the opening of new contemporary art galleries in Toronto, there was less need for collaboration. In 1960, the remaining members met at Hodgson's studio and, feeling that they had attained their original goals, decided to disband. An overview of the group's work remains at the Robert McLaughlin Gallery in Oshawa, Ontario.

Impact With their experiments in abstraction, Painters Eleven emerged during the 1950's as one of the first avant-garde art groups in Canada. Their impact on subsequent artists, museums, galleries, and collectors revolutionized the Toronto art world and influenced the development of modernist art in Canada. Due in part to the efforts of this group, Canadian art came to be viewed as a force in the larger North American and international art worlds.

Further Reading

Leclerc, Dennis. *The Crisis of Abstraction in Canada: The 1950's.* Ottawa: National Gallery of Canada, 1992. Published to accompany the 1992-1994 exhibition of the same title, this work underscores the 1950's as a transitional time in Canadian art.

Murray, Joan. *Canadian Art in the Twentieth Century.* Toronto: Dundurn Press, 1999. Concentrates on the variety and innovation of Canadian art, with emphasis on cultural context.

Ord, Douglas. *The National Gallery of Canada: Ideas, Art, Architecture.* Montreal: McGill-Queen's University Press, 2003. Explores the gallery's historical development and discusses public acceptance of avant-garde art.

Cassandra Lee Tellier

See also Abstract expressionism; Art movements; Famous Artists School; Paint-by-numbers movement.

■ Parker, Suzy

Identification American actor and fashion model
Born October 28, 1932; Long Island, New York
Died May 3, 2003; Montecito, California

Appearing numerous times on the covers of major fashion magazines, the willowy, redheaded Suzy Parker was the most prominent American fashion model of the 1950's.

Born Cecilia Ann Renee Parker, the tall, auburn-haired beauty later known as Suzy Parker began her modeling career at the age of fourteen and became one of the best-known faces during the 1950's as well as one of the highest-paid and most sought-after models of her generation.

Parker's striking photogenic looks captured the imagination of the public to such an extent that she eventually acquired the status of a celebrity. Chic and high-spirited, she was a favorite model of many of the top fashion designers of the day, especially Coco Chanel, who used her as her designated "face" of the 1950's. *Funny Face* (1957), a film directed by Stanley Donen and starring Audrey Hepburn, was based on Parker's modeling career. Parker herself also appeared in the film and enjoyed a short career of her own as a Hollywood actor.

Impact Parker's elegant manner and sophisticated style made her the quintessential female fashion icon of the 1950's. Her spectacular success was a forerunner of the fashion industry's "supermodel" trend of subsequent decades.

Further Reading

Baudot, Francois. *Chanel.* New York: Universe, 1996. Reviews Coco Chanel's work and features an indispensable full-page color photograph of Parker in a classic 1950's red Chanel evening gown; places Parker in the context of 1950's fashion.

Liaut, Jean-Noel. *Cover Girls and Supermodels, 1945-1965.* New York: Consortium Books, 1996. Profiling the major fashion models and cover girls of the postwar era, this book places Parker within the context of the era's image of femininity as adult and sophisticated in contrast to the childlike image that became popular during the late 1960's.

Margaret Boe Birns

See also Advertising; Affluence and the new consumerism; Bardot, Brigitte; Fashions and clothing; Kelly, Grace; Miss American pageants; Monroe, Marilyn; Taylor, Elizabeth.

■ Parks, Rosa

Identification Civil rights activist
Born February 14, 1913; Tuskegee, Alabama

Rosa Parks became an icon in African American history when her arrest for refusing to give up her bus seat to a white man triggered the bus boycott that galvanized the Civil Rights movement.

On December 1, 1955, Rosa Parks was headed home from work in Montgomery, Alabama. She boarded a crowded public bus and sat in the middle section in which African Americans were permitted to sit, so long as all white passengers were already seated. However, Parks's bus stopped, and a number of white people entered. The bus driver asked that the black passengers move to the back, and most of them complied. Parks, however, did not. The driver repeated his demand, but Parks refused again. He then threatened to have her arrested. Parks replied, "You may do that," a statement that helped her become an icon of the modern Civil Rights movement.

Impact Rosa Parks's arrest was not an accident. The National Association for the Advancement of Colored People (NAACP) sought a test case to confront the segregation laws. Parks, who had been a secretary for the NAACP and had worked with Martin Luther King, Jr., volunteered to be the person to test the seating laws on buses. Her act of civil disobedience was politically and legally significant: It galvanized the African American community and sparked the Montgomery bus boycott, and it provided the foundation for the *NAACP v. Alabama* 1958 Supreme Court case, which ultimately found the segregation laws unconstitutional.

Rosa Parks being fingerprinted by a Montgomery, Alabama, police officer after her arrest for refusing to surrender her bus seat to a white man. (AP/Wide World Photos)

Further Reading

Brinkley, Douglas. *Rosa Parks.* New York: Viking, 2000. Biography examining Parks's lifelong commitment to civil rights, not merely her act of resistance in 1955.

Parks, Rosa, and Gregory J. Reed. *Quiet Strength.* Grand Rapids, Mich.: Zondervan, 1994. A collection of Parks's speeches and thoughts that reflect her commitment to civil rights as an outgrowth of her religious faith.

Maurice Hamington

See also African Americans; Civil Rights movement; King, Martin Luther, Jr.; Montgomery bus boycott; National Association for the Advancement of Colored People; Southern Christian Leadership Conference; Women and the roots of the feminist movement.

■ Patterson, Floyd

Identification African American boxing champion
Born January 4, 1935; Waco, North Carolina

Floyd Patterson was a boxer who made history during the 1950's by becoming the first dethroned world heavyweight champion to regain his title.

When Patterson was a child, his family moved from North Carolina to New York City. As he grew up, he was prone to fighting other children in the neighborhood, so his mother sent him to Wiltwyck Reform School, where he learned the art of boxing. Patterson returned home and was discovered by boxing trainer legend Gus D'Amato.

Patterson gained early boxing fame by winning the Amateur Golden Gloves title and earning a gold medal in the 1952 Helsinki Olympics. He continued to box and in 1952 defeated Tommy Jackson. As a result of this win, he was given the opportunity to fight Archie Moore for the world heavyweight championship. Patterson made boxing history in 1956 by defeating Moore and became the youngest heavyweight champion in history—a distinction he held for thirty years.

In a highly publicized championship bout, Patterson lost his title to Sweden's Ingemar Johansson in June of 1959. One year later, Patterson defeated Johansson and remade boxing history by becoming the first heavyweight champion to regain his title. Many sport historians consider Patterson's punch that knocked Johansson out "the best punch in box-

ing." This fight secured Patterson's star status in Sweden and throughout Europe, and he embarked on a successful European exhibition tour after that rematch.

Impact Patterson was a humble and popular heavyweight boxing champion. His historic boxing achievements included being the youngest heavyweight boxing champion, the first heavyweight to regain his title, and the first Olympic gold medalist to win a world boxing title. After his retirement from boxing, Patterson trained other fighters and was appointed chairman of the New York Athletic Commission.

Further Reading

Brooke-Ball, Peter. *Great Fights: Fifty Epic Encounters from the History of Boxing.* London: Anness, 2001. Recounts important fights from the sport.

Patterson, Floyd. *Victory over Myself.* New York: Random House, 1962. Patterson's autobiography.

Dana D. Brooks

See also African Americans; Marciano, Rocky; Robinson, Sugar Ray; Sports; Walcott, Jersey Joe.

■ Pauling, Linus

Identification Physical chemist and peace activist
Born February 28, 1901; Portland, Oregon
Died August 19, 1994; Big Sur, California

As a Nobel laureate in chemistry, Linus Pauling began his successful campaign against the testing of nuclear weapons in the atmosphere during the 1950's.

Despite the loss of his father at a very early age, Linus Pauling was able to help support his mother and two sisters and graduate summa cum laude from Oregon Agricultural College. He went on to get his doctorate from the California Institute of Technology in 1925. Through the next twenty-five years, his research at Caltech led to pivotally important discoveries in the fields of structural chemistry and molecular biology.

Pauling worked on many military projects during World War II, but his concern about the dangers that the atomic bomb posed for humanity led him to to include pleas for peace in the speeches he gave throughout the United States and in several foreign countries. These speeches dealt with his discovery that sickle-cell anemia was a molecular disease and with his discoveries, published in 1951, of the three-dimensional arrangements of atoms in such biological materials as hair, wool, and muscle.

Throughout the 1950's, Pauling warned the public about the dangers of the proliferation and testing of nuclear weapons and their potential for causing a worldwide disaster. Officials in the State Department, worried that his criticisms of the U.S. program to develop the hydrogen bomb were not in the best interests of American security, took away his passport. In 1954, when Pauling learned that he had received the Nobel Prize in Chemistry, the State Department granted him a passport to travel to Sweden to receive the award.

As a Nobel laureate, Pauling was able to use his enhanced prestige to convince an ever-growing number of scientists that nuclear testing was immoral, since it caused cancers in adults and multiple birth defects in babies. He debated Edward Teller, a bomb-test advocate, on television, and he signed many peace appeals, including the Russell-Einstein Manifesto, which called for an international congress of scientists to discuss the dangers of nuclear war. The first of a long series of these conferences was held in Pugwash, Nova Scotia, in 1957.

Linus Pauling (right) and fellow Caltech scientist George Beadle, around 1952. (California Institute of Technology)

During the late 1950's, Pauling became increasingly involved in the debate over nuclear fallout, especially through the Scientists' Bomb-Test Appeal, which he helped write and circulate. Eventually signed by more than ten thousand scientists from forty-nine nations, this document was presented by Pauling and his wife to Dag Hammarskjöld, secretary-general of the United Nations, on January 15, 1958. In 1959, Pauling published *No More War!* and brought a lawsuit against the Defense Department and the Atomic Energy Commission to prevent them from conducting further nuclear tests.

Impact Pauling's crusade did not bear fruit until the early 1960's, when, after several years of negotiations, the United States and the Soviet Union reached an agreement on a test ban treaty. In October of 1963, when the treaty became effective, Pauling was awarded the Nobel Peace Prize for 1962. For the Nobel Committee and many others, Pauling exemplified the social conscience of concerned scientists of the 1950's.

Pauling's peace activism continued throughout the rest of his life, and his concern for the health of humanity also led to his advocacy of large amounts of vitamins, especially vitamin C, which, he believed, would help reduce human suffering.

Further Reading

Divine, Robert A. *Blowing on the Wind: The Nuclear Test Ban Debate, 1954-1960.* New York: Oxford University Press, 1978. An analysis of the controversies, both political and scientific, over nuclear tests.

Hager, Thomas. *Force of Nature: The Life of Linus Pauling.* New York: Simon & Schuster, 1995. One of the most comprehensive of the several biographies written about Pauling.

Pauling, Linus. *No More War!* New York: Dodd, Mead, 1983. The anniversary edition of this book was updated by Pauling a decade before his death.

Robert J. Paradowski

See also Atomic bomb; Bomb shelters; Cold War; Disarmament movement; Einstein, Albert; Nobel Prizes; Oppenheimer, J. Robert; Seaborg, Glenn; Teller, Edward.

■ Pay television

Definition Television programming sold directly to customers through special broadcast stations, which transmitted scrambled signals that were decoded by boxes connected to subscribers' television sets

During the 1950's, pay television was vigorously opposed by the American movie theater and commercial television industries, which saw it as a major economic threat to their own entertainment offerings. Regulatory delays stifled its growth in the decades ahead.

Pay television is nearly as old as the television industry itself, but it had difficult beginnings and never achieved the heights envisioned by its early promoters. Supporters of pay television campaigned for broadcast rights as early as 1950, but the Federal Communications Commission (FCC) refused to authorize pay service except in a few experimental cases. Supporters saw pay television as a practical option toward building a national television system. The FCC, however, argued that pay television should be supplemental to free television and passed stringent laws to prevent it from siphoning away viewers. The National Association of Theater Owners and the Joint Committee Against Toll Television asked the courts to uphold the FCC rules to protect their business interests. Magazine and newspaper advertisements sponsored by these groups portrayed pay television as an assault on free television, a burden to low-income viewers, and a threat to basic American ideals.

Impact Characterized by rapid growth and major economic restructuring, the 1950's was the formative period for American television. Subscription stations sprouted around the United States on the UHF (ultrahigh frequency) band but only in those areas permitted by the FCC. A subscription station, for example, was not permitted to be established until at least four commercial television stations were in an area. Section 303 of the Federal Communications Act required the FCC to experiment with new uses of broadcasting. For example, it permitted pay-television company Skiatron to test its system on WOR-TV New York in 1950 and Telemeter to broadcast over KTLA Los Angeles in 1951.

Subsequent Events The campaign to stop pay television intensified during the 1960's. Strong opposition from the film industry in California led to a state referendum prohibiting pay television in 1964. The referendum was later ruled unconstitutional. Furthermore, legal restrictions imposed by the FCC stifled the growth of this industry for two decades. No substantial growth occurred in pay television until the late 1960's, when the FCC lifted its restrictions in response to mounting pressure from the film and cable industries. The film industry, for example, saw potential in providing films specifically for pay television. Because film companies could save money on marketing and distribution, pay television was potentially more lucrative than the country's dying movie theaters. In 1977, the U.S. Court of Appeals for the District of Columbia ruled the FCC restrictions unconstitutional on the grounds that siphoning had not been demonstrated during the 1950's prior to the restrictions being imposed.

Pay or subscription television was the antecedent of cable, satellite, and various interactive forms of pay television such as pay-per-view and programming on demand. Unlike cable television, pay television did not need to string wires or follow complicated franchise procedures. Always a free enterprise endeavor, pay television was competitive against cable television during the 1970's and early 1980's but waned in importance and passed quietly into television history during the late 1980's.

Further Reading

Boddy, William. *Fifties Television: The Industry and Its Critics.* Urbana: University of Illinois Press, 1994. Includes discussion of early regulations, programming, and economic issues.

Smith, Anthony, ed. *Television: An International History.* New York: Oxford University Press, 1995. A collection of articles on the origins and forms of television around the world.

Ann M. Legreid

See also Communications in Canada; Communications in the United States; Drive-in theaters; Film in Canada; Film in the United States; Television in Canada; Television in the United States.

■ Peale, Norman Vincent

Identification Minister at the oldest protestant church in the United States, author, and motivational speaker
Born May 31, 1898; Bowersville, Ohio
Died December 24, 1993; New York, New York

In 1952, Norman Vincent Peale published The Power of Positive Thinking, *a book destined to sell more than twenty million copies over the next half century. His book became a model for the thousands of self-help books that followed.*

Peale was ordained in the Methodist Episcopal Church in 1922 and held several pastorates. In 1932, he changed his affiliation to the Dutch Reformed Church so that he could become the pastor of Marble Collegiate Church, a Dutch Reformed Church founded in Manhattan in 1628. He remained the pastor of Marble Collegiate for fifty-two years. He and his wife founded *Guideposts* magazine in 1945, and by the 1950's, it was the largest circulating religious magazine in the United States. Peale's life was the subject of a 1964 movie titled *One Man's Way.*

Peale acknowledged having had an inferiority complex during his younger days and felt that his feeling of inferiority had held him back. As a result, he preached a message that merged theology and psychology: maintaining that a positive attitude would lead to success. He was subsequently called the father of the self-esteem gospel, a mixture of modern psychology and the Bible.

Impact Peale was one of North America's most influential clergymen during the 1950's and throughout the remainder of his life. For fifty-four years, he broadcast a daily radio show, and in later years, his sermons were broadcast on television. He was constantly in demand as a motivational speaker. Throughout his lifetime, he authored forty-six books. His best-selling book, *The Power of Positive Thinking*, was published in forty-one languages.

Further Reading

George, Carol V. *God's Salesman: Norman Vincent Peale and the Power of Positive Thinking.* New York:

Oxford University Press, 1994. Author uses interviews and access to Peale's personal archives to tell his life story and to explore the impact of his writings.

Peale, Norman Vincent. *The True Joy of Positive Living: An Autobiography.* New York: Morrow, 1984. Combines autobiographical information with further words of personal motivation.

Dale L. Flesher

See also Carnegie, Dale; Graham, Billy; Religion in the United States; Sheen, Fulton J.

■ Peanuts

Identification Syndicated comic strip
Artist Charles Schulz (1922-2000)
Date First published on October 2, 1950

By using psychological and social commentary, Peanuts *helped introduce pop psychology and philosophy to the public and became a cultural phenomenon during the 1950's.*

Using child cartoon characters who seemed to speak as adults but without the inhibitions usually developed by adulthood was the signature approach to the *Peanuts* personae developed by artist Charles Schulz, who had experienced a sense of bland anonymity as a child. After serving in the military in World War II, Schulz was employed by *Timeless Topix*, a Roman Catholic comics magazine that was the first to print his cartoons. In 1947, the *St. Paul Pioneer Press* became the first to publish his newspaper strip, which then was known as *L'il Folks*. By age twenty-seven, Schulz found himself speaking through Charlie Brown, Shermy, and Patty in *Peanuts*, his renamed strip. Schulz considered his art a calling and, in his mind, his way of preaching. Believing that cartoons and humor should have a message, he invested his work with experience, reflection, and meaning.

The children who populated the world of *Peanuts* were identifiable personality types who laid out human gifts and foibles in a time when the American citizenry was becoming more familiar not only with psychological thought but also with understanding the sheer humanness of ordinary folk. The bland-faced, long-suffering Charlie Brown, the overbearing Lucy, the musical Schroeder, the thinking Linus, and others brought to life ordinary human quirks, grappled with concerns, and shared the values of honesty and friendship. By 1955, *Peanuts* and its growing cast of characters had taken such hold that Schulz was presented his first Reuben Award, the highest honor afforded cartoonists.

Impact Putting forth psychological and social commentary, the comic strip provided contemplative reflection on the human condition as people recognized themselves in the comic strip characters. This was a new idea for mid-twentieth century Americans, who were far more accustomed to comic strips that were action- or comedy-oriented. By the late 1950's the members of the *Peanuts* contingent were becoming household words. Phrases such as "security blanket" found their way into ordinary vocabulary. Cross-generational conversations were opened by and used the shorthand of *Peanuts* characters and their dialogue. *Peanuts* had become a cultural meeting point. The characters were printed on greeting cards, seen on television specials and in any number of books, quoted in sermons, and used by theologian Robert Short in his works *The Gospel According to Peanuts* (1965) and *The Parables of Peanuts* (1968). The impact of the comic strip and its artist was recognized by the United States when Schulz was awarded the Congressional Medal of Honor in 2000.

Further Reading

Inge, M. Thomas. *Charles M. Schulz: Conversations.* Jackson: University Press of Mississippi, 2001. Schulz discusses his life, theology, sports, the art of the comic strip, and the human condition in general.

Schulz, Charles. *Peanuts: The Art of Charles M. Schulz.* New York: Pantheon Books, 2003. Uses archived material from the Charles M. Schulz Museum and includes early strips, storyboards, and personal scrapbooks.

Frances R. Belmonte

See also Capp, Al; Comic books; *Kukla, Fran and Ollie*; Newspapers in the United States; *Pogo*; Snead, Sam; Youth culture and the generation gap.

■ Pearson, Drew

Identification American journalist and radio commentator
Born December 13, 1897; Evanston, Illinois
Died September 1, 1969; Washington, D.C.

Pearson was the most widely read and most influential of the newspaper and radio journalists of the 1950's and played a key role in undermining Senator Joseph McCarthy's anticommunist witch-hunts.

By 1950, Drew Pearson was very influential as a columnist for newspapers that had a combined circulation of forty million; he also reached another twenty million radio listeners. He was involved in two of the most controversial events of the 1950's: President Harry S. Truman's firing of General Douglas MacArthur during the Korean conflict and the rise and fall of Senator Joseph McCarthy of Wisconsin.

After his initial success in the Korean War, MacArthur wanted both to use air strikes and naval shelling on Communist China and to bring Formosa (now Taiwan) into the war. Fearful of a third world war, Truman resisted, and after the disaster at the Yalu River, MacArthur was fired, despite his enormous popularity in the United States. Pearson, who had long been critical of the general, supported Truman and unearthed information that suggested that MacArthur had in fact made three tactical errors in the Yalu rout.

Pearson's involvement in the McCarthy affair was more direct. In 1950, he disproved McCarthy's charge that there were 205 communists in the State Department. Pearson found only three people whose loyalty might be questioned. Although his associate Jack Anderson was initially a friend of McCarthy, Pearson continued his attacks on the junior senator from Wisconsin in his syndicated *Washington Merry-Go-Round* column. McCarthy counterattacked by encouraging a successful "patriotic" boycott of products advertised on Pearson's radio show, which was taken off the air. Called a "left-wing mockingbird" and assaulted by fellow columnists Walter Winchell and Westbrook Pegler, Pearson responded by writing a 1951 exposé of McCarthy, alleging that his war record was phony, that he cheated on his income taxes, and that he was in the pay of the real estate lobby. The assaults on Pearson became physical when McCarthy attacked him at the Sulgrave Club in Washington, D.C., in December, 1950.

Though he was not a professed liberal, Pearson espoused liberal causes such as integration, civil rights, the welfare system, foreign aid, and peace. He was an outspoken opponent of right-wing radicals and campaigned against censorship and corruption in the military-industrial complex. He may have been more critical of Republican presidents than

Democratic ones, but he incurred the wrath of President Truman when he criticized the singing of the president's wife and daughter. Speaking to the "outsiders," the people from the rural Midwest, he battled the powerful elite by pushing for change and exposing the "insiders." Because of his controversial views, he was often sued, and he responded in kind, winning all but one case that went to trial. Even though he was a muckraking investigative journalist reporting on domestic and political intrigue in Washington, he was also a crusader.

Impact Pearson made muckraking respectable and gave American citizens inside information about events within Washington. After his death, his colleague Jack Anderson continued his column. Pearson's willingness to confront Washington power brokers established a tradition of exposing political wrongdoing that later helped lead to the resignation of President Richard M. Nixon.

Further Reading

Abell, Tyler, ed. *Drew Pearson Diaries, 1949-1959.* New York: Holt, Rinehart and Winston, 1974. Highlights previously unpublished material.

Anderson, Jack, and James Boyd. *Confessions of a Muckraker.* New York: Random House, 1979. Details the collaboration between Pearson and Anderson.

Pilat, Oliver. *Drew Pearson: An Unauthorized Biography.* New York: Harper & Row, 1973. Balanced account of Pearson's life and accomplishments.

Shapiro, Bruce, ed. *Shaking the Foundations: Two Hundred Years of Investigative Journalism in America.* New York: Thunder's Mouth Press, 2002. Includes a discussion of Pearson's contribution to the field of investigative reporting.

Thomas L. Erskine

See also MacArthur, Douglas; McCarthy, Joseph; Newspapers in the United States; Radio; Truman, Harry S.

■ Pearson, Lester B.

Identification Canadian politician and Nobel Peace Prize winner

Born April 23, 1897; Newtonbrook, Ontario, Canada

Died December 27, 1972; Ottawa, Ontario, Canada

Lester Bowles Pearson was minister of external affairs in the Canadian government of Prime Minister Louis St. Laurent between 1948 and 1957. For his peacemaking efforts in response to the Suez Crisis in 1956, he was awarded the 1957 Nobel Peace Prize.

Born into an Irish-Canadian family, Lester Pearson attended the University of Toronto before enlisting in the Canadian military during World War I. After the war, he won a scholarship to Oxford University, a path that led him initially into an academic career at the University of Toronto. In 1928, however, he became a senior civil servant in the Department of External Affairs. Over the next twenty years, he played a prominent role at various Canadian diplomatic missions including those in London and in Washington.

Political Career In 1948, Pearson chose to play a more direct role in Canadian diplomatic policy making. In that year, he sought election for the first time, winning a seat in the federal House of Commons as a member of the Liberal Party; he was promptly appointed as minister of external affairs by the new prime minister, Louis St. Laurent.

As a prominent cabinet minister, Pearson played a leading role in determining Canada's place in world affairs. His first major role was on behalf of his government in the creation of the North Atlantic Treaty Organization (NATO). In 1956, the Suez Crisis erupted. As Canada's minister of external affairs, Pearson took a direct role in the debate for a solution to the conflict at the General Assembly of the United Nations. He was the driving force behind a resolution that created a United Nations peacekeeping force that was deployed between the opposing forces in the Suez. Afterward, he received the 1957 Nobel Peace Prize, which created a sense of pride in Canadians over their nation's role in the establishment of international peacekeeping.

In 1957, Pearson also had to deal with the suicide of Herbert Norman, Canada's ambassador to Egypt, after a U.S. Senate subcommittee publicized allegations about Herbert's being a Soviet agent. Canadians—and in particular Pearson, who was a friend of Herbert—blamed the suicide on McCarthyism. However, despite the anger, Pearson ensured that the incident would not do permanent damage to American-Canadian relations.

With the defeat of the Liberals in the 1957 election, St. Laurent retired, and Pearson won the lead-

Lester B. Pearson. (Library of Congress)

ership of the party, in the process becoming the leader of the opposition. In that position he would be a staunch critic of the Progressive Conservative government of Prime Minister John Diefenbaker until 1963, when St. Laurent defeated Diefenbaker and began a five-year stint as Canada's prime minister. Pearson retired from public life in 1968.

Impact Lester Pearson had a significant impact during the 1950's not only on Canadian policy but, in the case of the Suez Crisis and the creation of a United Nations peacekeeping force, on international affairs as well.

Further Reading

English, John. *The Worldly Years: The Life of Lester Pearson, 1949-1957.* Toronto: Knopf Canada, 1992. Definitive biography of Pearson.

Whitaker, Reg, and Gary Marcuse. *Cold War Canada: The Making of a National Insecurity State, 1945-1957.* Toronto: University of Toronto Press, 1996. Detailed examination of Canada's role during the early years of the Cold War.

Steve Hewitt

See also Canada and Great Britain; Canada as a middle power; Diefenbaker, John G.; Elections in Canada; Foreign policy of Canada; Israel; North Atlantic Treaty Organization; St. Laurent, Louis; Suez Crisis; United Nations.

■ *Perry Mason*

Identification Dramatic television series about a defense attorney who virtually never loses a case
Producer Paisano Productions
Date Aired from 1957 to 1966

Perry Mason popularized the genre of legal drama as well as adding to the popularity of television in general when the medium was still in its infancy.

After five films and a long-running radio drama had been made from Erle Stanley Gardner's Perry Mason novels, in 1956, the author formed his own production company, Paisano Productions, with family friends Correl Jackson and Gail Patrick Jackson to create a television series that shaped the history of the televised medium. The show, titled *Perry Mason,* starred Raymond Burr as Mason and had an ensemble cast that included Barbara Hale as secretary Della Street, William Hopper as detective Paul Drake, William Talman as District Attorney Hamilton Burger, and Ray Collins as Lieutenant Arthur Tragg.

The formula for *Perry Mason* seldom varied: Each week Mason took on a client to whom all evidence pointed as the culprit in a murder and, through both thorough investigation and clever courtroom maneuvers, managed to exonerate the defendant and expose the real murderer. Audiences of the 1950's made the show a hit almost immediately. Both Burr and Hale won Emmy Awards for their performances in 1959, and Burr took home two additional Emmy Awards for his *Perry Mason* performances in 1960 and 1961.

Impact By combining investigative work with courtroom drama, *Perry Mason* provided a format that captured viewers' attention and built a loyal audience. Shows with similar formulas would continue to garner large television audiences for the remainder of the twentieth century. The show also established Raymond Burr as a major television star and provided a role that he would reprise in made-for-television films during the 1980's and 1990's.

Further Reading

Kelleher, Brian, and Diana Merrill. *The Perry Mason TV Show Book.* New York: St. Martin's Press, 1987. Detailed history of the show's creation, including actors' biographies. Includes synopses of each episode filmed during the show's nine-year run.

Martindale, David. *The Perry Mason Casebook.* Las Vegas: Pioneer Books, 1991. Details the creation of the series, summarizes each episode, and comments on subsequent revivals.

Myers, Richard. *TV Detectives.* San Diego, Calif.: A. S. Barnes, 1981. Places the series in the context of other shows featuring attorneys as detectives.

Laurence W. Mazzeno

See also *Dragnet*; Emmy Awards; Spillane, Mickey; Pulp magazines; Television in the United States.

■ Peter Pan

Identification Animated Disney film based on Scottish playwright James M. Barrie's 1904 play and 1911 novel of the same title

Directors Clyde Geronimi (1901-1989) and Wilfred Jackson (1906-1988)

Date Released in 1953

Peter Pan, an account of the boy who never grew up, was one of the popular animated films released by Disney Studios during the 1950's.

Beginning in 1905, the story of *Peter Pan* appeared in several musical adaptations and productions, including a Jerome Kern adaptation in 1924 and a 1950 production by composer-conductor Leonard Bernstein, featuring Boris Karloff and Jean Arthur. Jerome Robbins produced the Broadway version in 1954, starring Mary Martin. However, Walt Disney's animated version arguably became the story's most widely known version.

Disney acquired the rights to *Peter Pan* from London's Great Ormond Street Hospital in 1939, but World War II delayed production. The animators based their work on a complete costumed version and leading songwriters created an entirely new musical score. The Disney version continued the tradition of having the same actor play Mr. Darling and Captain Hook but did not have a woman play Peter, a decision that broke with previous stage productions. The film was released to theaters in 1953. Its initial four-million-dollar budget was rapidly recovered.

Impact The Disney version of *Peter Pan*, along with the other animated films made by Disney during the era and the increasingly sophisticated world of animated filmmaking, helped shape the tastes of the post-World War II generation of children. It was an upbeat story well suited to the energetic mood of the United States during the 1950's. Six rereleases, video and DVD versions, overseas releases, and merchandizing have made Disney's *Peter Pan* one of the all-time highest money-makers for film. Its songs and characters are readily recognized by millions.

Further Reading

Barrie, James M. *Peter Pan: The Complete and Unabridged Text.* New York: Viking Press, 1991. A newer edition of Barrie's original story reminds readers that the tale is not only a delightful children's story but also a wry and pleasurable read for adults.

Geis, Darlene. *Walt Disney's Treasury of Children's Classics: Favorite Disney Films, 1937-1977.* New York: Disney Press, 1995. A book geared for children, it gives a behind-the-scenes look at the production of seventeen classic Disney films based on well-known fairy tales, folktales, and short stories.

Rebecca Lovell Scott

See also Bernstein, Leonard; Broadway musicals; Disneyland; Film in the United States; *Kukla, Fran and Ollie.*

■ Peterson, Oscar

Identification Canadian jazz pianist

Born August 15, 1925; Montreal, Canada

Considered one of the greatest jazz musicians, Oscar Peterson refined his style and consolidated his career during the 1950's.

Born in Canada of West Indian parents, Peterson was a musical prodigy who achieved fame in Canada while still a teenager. He was brought to New York to play at Carnegie Hall in 1949, and he formed a trio with bassist Ray Brown and guitarist Herb Ellis in 1951. The Peterson-led combo enjoyed a worldwide reputation, touring North America, Europe, and Japan from 1953 to 1958 and recording extensively.

Peterson not only was an accompanist to outstanding vocalists of the 1950's such as Ella Fitzgerald and Frank Sinatra but also enjoyed a reputation as a virtuoso soloist. His style did not fall into any specific jazz category: blending the swing music of the 1940's and the be-bop style of the 1950's, he became known for his extraordinary technical mastery and inventive improvisations. Throughout the 1950's, Peterson was voted best pianist in the *Down Beat* magazine reader polls.

Impact Peterson's music was indicative of the transition from the previous big band decades to postwar "modern jazz" of the 1950's, but he stands as a great jazz artist who transcends any one era.

Further Reading

Lees, Gene, and Graham Lees. *Oscar Peterson.* Roseville, Calif.: Prima Lifestyles, 1991. Knowledgeable study of the life and work of Peterson. Based on extensive interviews, enhanced by authors' knowledge of the jazz world.

Marin, Reva. *Oscar: The Life and Music of Oscar Peterson.* Toronto: Groundwood Books, 2003. Inspirational biography of Peterson, tracking his rise from poverty, his overcoming of racism, his life as a jazz musician, and his musical ideas. Includes profiles of fellow jazz artists, photos, and a reading-and-listening guide.

Margaret Boe Birns

See also African Americans; Brubeck, Dave; Fitzgerald, Ella; Jazz; Music; Newport Jazz Festival; Sinatra, Frank.

■ *Peyton Place*

Identification Sensational novel about dark secrets in a small New England town
Author Grace Metalious (1924-1964)
Date Published in 1956

One of the best-selling fiction books of all time, Peyton Place *was among the most controversial novels of the 1950's.*

During the mid-1950's, Grace Metalious, a small-town mother of three who had never published a word, sat down at her typewriter and proceeded to write a book that shocked the nation. Like Henry Bellaman's *Kings Row* (1940) sixteen years earlier, Metalious's novel, *Peyton Place*, described the secrets and scandals of life in a small town. Stories of the townsfolk are intertwined, but the main narrative revolves around three women: sophisticated Constance MacKenzie; her daughter, aspiring writer Allison, whose illegitimacy is Constance's most closely guarded secret; and Selena Cross, a working-class girl who murders her lecherous stepfather in self-defense.

In an age of caution and conformity, Metalious's unconventional views on hypocrisy, sexuality, violence, power, and powerlessness were shocking and disturbing to many. Metalious saw poverty as a social failure rather than an individual one—an uncommon viewpoint for the era. She wrote frankly about sexual abuse at a time when newspapers generally used words no stronger than "molested." Her daring viewpoints quickly earned her the nickname "Pandora in blue jeans."

Sensational content aside, *Peyton Place* struck a powerful chord with women. A decade before Betty Freidan's *The Feminine Mystique* (1963) and Helen Gurley Brown's *Sex and the Single Girl* (1962), Metalious wrote about issues that would become central to the feminist cause: rape, abortion, battered women, and sexual freedom. "Rather than showing rape as a male rite of passage," writes biographer Emily Toth, Metalious showed it "as it appeared to a woman: ugly, violent, a destruction of innocence—and having nothing to do with sexual pleasure." In Metalious's vision, abortion could be a life-saving act, and incest was a crime justifiably punished by murder. Her women were sexually desirous beings, in stark contrast to the attitudes commonly established by male writers of the day; like their author, her fictional women refused to be confined by the 1950's notion of a woman's place.

Impact *Peyton Place* was both a literary blockbuster and a sociological phenomenon. It spawned a sequel, *Return to Peyton Place* (1959); a feature film (1957); and a long-running television soap opera (1964-1969).

The phrase "Peyton Place" quickly became shorthand for any small town that appeared calm and pretty to outsiders but whose dark secrets spilled out when one scratched the surface. Metalious noted that while these towns appear "peaceful as a postcard," further examination would unearth oddities and secrets that townspeople clearly were aware of but hoped to keep hidden.

Because of its language and subject matter, the novel was denounced as "literary sewage" and banned from many library shelves; Canada refused to import it. Nonetheless, *Peyton Place* quickly surpassed Margaret Mitchell's _Gone with the Wind_ (1936) as the top-selling fiction book of all time, holding that distinction for several years and selling millions of copies worldwide. Metalious had the last laugh, famously retorting to her critics, "If I'm a lousy writer, then an awful lot of people have lousy taste."

Further Reading

Hendler, Jane. _Best Sellers and Their Film Adaptations in Postwar America: "From Here to Eternity," "Sayonara," "Giant," "Auntie Mame," "Peyton Place."_ New York: Peter Lang, 2001. Examines the way in which several novels of the 1950's, including _Peyton Place_, disrupted commonly held notions of gender identity in both print and filmed forms.

Toth, Emily. _Inside Peyton Place: The Life of Grace Metalious._ Garden City, N.Y.: Doubleday, 1981. In this poignant biography, Toth writes sympathetically of Metalious: the eccentric, fun-loving friend; haphazard wife and mother; and compulsive writer.

Jennifer Davis-Kay

See also Book publishing; Censorship; _Lady Chatterley's Lover_; Literature in the United States; _Lolita_; Sex and sex education; Women and the roots of the feminist movement.

■ Photography

Definition Process of using light-sensitive media to make permanent images of objects

During the 1950's, advancements in film and camera technology enabled greatly increased use of photography in science, criminology, and photojournalism and improved the efforts of amateur photographers.

Experiments with photography date back to Leonardo da Vinci's fifteenth century camera obscura—a box with a small hole or lens in one wall that admits light, forming at its back an image of a scene. Two centuries later, Johann Schulze discovered that silver salts were light sensitive and used sunlight to make crude images. The nineteenth century witnessed rapid advancements in photography through the work of Joseph Niepce, a French physicist; Louis Daguerre, a French painter-inventor, who made daguerreotypes on silver iodide-coated plates; and William Talbot, a British scientist who invented light-sensitive, silver-salt-coated paper to make negatives and prints.

George Eastman's simple Kodak cameras and development kits of the late nineteenth century stimulated millions of amateurs to take and print cheaper photos. Inventions in the first half of the twentieth century simplified photo-making through improved lenses, which yielded very fast photos, and brought forth flashbulbs and electronic flashes, expanding the possibilities of photo subjects. Photos were taken by millions of amateurs, and professional photographers developed abstract photography and took part in photojournalism and nature photography.

Science, Criminalistics, and Everyday Uses The improvements in photography during the 1930's and 1940's spilled over into the 1950's, and photography advanced even more. During the 1950's, improved manufacturing processes increased light sensitivity of black-and-white and color film. For example, color film speeds rose tenfold, better enabling the capture of moving subjects and increasing the clarity of photos. Also, electronic light amplifiers developed to intensify dim illumination, making it possible for astronomers to record very faint light emitted by distant stars. In addition, shorter film exposure times combined with super-fast shutters enabled finer analysis of processes involving motion. The advances enhanced the quality of amateur and professional photos.

Consequences of advances included much greater use of photography in science. In the field of biology, much better illustrations of bioprocesses became possible. Moreover, increased shutter speeds allowed scientists to document in separate photos things such as the individual beats of a hummingbird wing. The new techniques also gave biologists, biochemists, chemists, and physicists more useful photos—by using film sensitive to visible, infrared, and ultraviolet light—for careful exploration of fundamental phenomena in their fields, including undersea, weather, and microscopy studies.

Polaroid cameras became invaluable to criminalistics (forensic science), allowing police to document crime scenes thoroughly with the use of near-instant photographs. They could quickly identify crime-scene areas that needed better filming, without waiting for film processing at the police station, which in turn made it unnecessary to return to a crime scene later, when evidence might be tampered with, removed, or obscured. Better film quality and fine enlargement techniques also enabled the clear dissection of crime scenes to find clues. Black-and-white photography was used predominantly since it picks up much more detail than color film. Infrared and ultraviolet photos also had criminalistic uses, particularly in identifying document forgeries, inks, and special aspects of fabrics or papers that could aid their individualization and criminal prosecution.

For the general public, Polaroid cameras enabled better documentation of important family celebrations and excursions that would never recur. Furthermore, higher-quality photos and higher speeds of conventional color films engendered precise color photos of things people wanted to remember exactly. In addition, improved home development kits let amateurs easily crop and enlarge parts of photos precisely as they wanted them.

Impact The 1950's photographic advances led to an increased popularity of picture taking and increased photography use in science, portraiture, and photojournalism. These impacts increased revenues of the industry and, in turn, spurred further advances. In addition, 1950's photos advanced the understanding of natural sciences and made it clearer to legislators and voters the importance of carrying out social reforms. Photojournalism "shrunk" the world, better familiarizing people with their own countries and those of others. Furthermore, Polaroid police photos increased the arrest and conviction rates of criminals. Finally, inexpensive photo equipment led increasing numbers of Americans to fall in love with amateur photography.

Subsequent Events The 1960's development of color Polaroid film enabled amateur photographers to make color prints in approximately one minute. In subsequent years, more advances in photography occurred, including even better cameras, lenses,

This picture by amateur photographer Virginia Schau—who used a Kodak Brownie camera—won the 1954 Pulitzer Prize for photography. The accident shown in the picture occurred on a bridge over Shasta Lake in Northern California in May, 1953. After the driver and codriver were pulled to safety, their truck's cab caught fire and fell to the rocks below. (AP/Wide World Photos)

and film; the development of prints at pharmacies and supermarkets; and the development of "throwaway" cameras for vacations. By the 1990's, development of computer science and digital technology produced digital cameras, which used computer technology to let amateurs cut, zoom, shrink, and otherwise improve photos.

Further Reading

Dantzic, Jerry. *Jerry Dantzic's New York: The Fifties in Focus.* New York: Edition Stemmle, 2002. Documents the work of famed photojournalist Jerry Dantzic, including the sights and people of New York City during the 1950's. Discusses his early gelatin-silver work.

Hirsch, Robert. *Seizing the Light: A History of Photography.* Boston: McGraw-Hill, 2000. Thorough, well-illustrated, educational description of photography history.

London, Barbara, and John Upton. *Photography.* 6th ed. New York: Longman, 1998. Includes history and technology of photography. Bibliography and index.

Rosenblum, Naomi. *A World History of Photography.* 3d ed. New York: Abbeville Press, 1997. Well-illustrated history of photography.

Sanford S. Singer

See also Advertising; Astronomy; Instant photography; *Life*; News magazines; *Playboy*.

■ Photovoltaic cell

The Event Invention of a device that converts light energy into electricity
Date Developed during the early 1950's
Place Murray Hill, New Jersey

Photovoltaic cells are long-lasting, reliable devices that produce electricity from light; their numerous practical applications range from the space program to simple consumer products.

Generating electrical current from sunlight was first reported in 1839 by French physicist Edmund Becquerel. Albert Einstein later discovered the scientific basis for this process. When photons, the particles associated with electromagnetic radiation, are absorbed by a material, they impart energy to some of the electrons in the material, freeing those electrons to participate in electric current flow. This is known as the photovoltaic or photoelectric effect.

During the early 1950's, Bell Laboratories conducted extensive research on the photovoltaic effect and built the first photovoltaic cell using layers of pure silicon. In 1954, Bell researchers found that silicon doped with certain impurities could serve as the semiconductor in their photovoltaic cell, and the Bell Solar Battery was invented. In 1958, the first space photovoltaic cell was flown in *Vanguard I*. As cell costs decreased during the 1970's and 1980's, myriad applications were found. The earliest cells were about 1 percent efficient in converting light to electricity, but with technological advancements, efficiencies grew to more than 17 percent by the early twenty-first century.

Impact Photovoltaic cells, also known as solar cells, became an important component of the space program during the 1960's, particularly in satellites. Starting during the 1970's, they were used to provide power for commercial and residential uses. During the 1980's, they became a popular power source for consumer electronic devices, including calculators, radios, and watches.

Further Reading

Archer, Mary D., and Robert Hill. *Clean Electricity from Photovoltaics.* London: Imperial College Press, 2001. Details photovoltaic cell technology, applications, and future prospects.

Bube, Richard H. *Photovoltaic Materials.* River Edge, N.J.: World Scientific, 1998. Examines the materials used in photovoltaic power generation.

Alvin K. Benson

See also Computers; Einstein, Albert; Inventions; Science and technology.

■ *Playboy*

Identification American men's magazine
Publisher Hugh Hefner (1926-   )

Playboy helped start the sexual revolution by supporting a positive and more liberal attitude toward sexual behavior, while also defining the American urban male as one who could enjoy "the good life."

Playboy was the brainchild of its publisher, Hugh Hefner, who was born in Chicago into a strict middle-class Methodist family. After serving in World War II, Hefner entered the University of Illinois, where he focused on the student newspaper and humor magazine. After college, Hefner married and worked briefly for *Esquire* magazine in the circulation department.

When *Esquire* moved to New York, Hefner stayed in Chicago and found himself jobless. The experience made him determined to succeed in a business venture of his own. Unable to sell his comic strip and magazine ideas, he decided to produce his own magazine with his limited funds. His major asset was a nude photograph of film star Marilyn Monroe. The photo had been taken for a calendar company years earlier, and despite its existence being widely known, no mainstream magazine would publish it for fear of prosecution under the restrictive obscenity laws of the time.

In November of 1953, the first issue of *Playboy* was published with Monroe's image on the cover. The first issue had no date (there was not enough money to publish a second issue, so there was no way of knowing how long the shelf life of the magazine would be) and contained only forty-four pages. Hefner wrote in his introduction, "If we are able to give the American male a few extra laughs and a little diversion from the anxieties of the Atomic Age, we'll feel we've justified our existence."

The first issue was a huge success, beginning what became the magazine's decades-long tenure. Throughout the 1950's, the magazine increased in circulation and status, until the October, 1959, issue, which sold more than one million copies.

Because the success of *Playboy* was hard to duplicate, the magazine created a niche for itself that lasted for decades. The magazine's most brilliant move came in 1956 with the campaign "What is a Playboy?" The promotion defined the Playboy reader as a man who "must see life not as a vale of tears, but a happy time; he must take joy in his work, without regarding it as the end and all of living . . ." In this campaign, *Playboy* defined its readership not as it was but as it aspired to be. The magazine then provided a forum for discussion of the things of the sophisticated good life: literature, clothes, apartments, and beautiful women.

Formula for Success Throughout the 1950's, *Playboy* followed a simple formula for its success: provocative, but not entirely explicit, photographs of beautiful women and a mixture of articles on the swinging urban bachelor's "good life." The principal woman featured in each issue was labeled "Playmate of the Month." The very earliest photographs published in the magazine were similar to the Marilyn Monroe picture, purchased from calendar companies or other freelance photographers. *Playboy* started publishing its own photographs—often in what came to be its signature, artistic manner—in mid-1955. Soon after, Janet Pilgrim (born Charlaine Karalus), who was the magazine's subscription manager, became the playmate of the month. She reappeared in December of that year and was the first of the "girl-next-door" types, rather than professional models, that the magazine heralded. Hefner believed that it was better to make the playmates seem natural and friendly rather than merely exotic or unattainable. Another of the 1950's most famous play-

Hugh Hefner, the founder and publisher of Playboy, *sitting in front of a collage made up of "Playmate" centerfolds from his magazine.* (Hulton Archive | by Getty Images)

mates was Betty Page, featured in January, 1955, who would go on to become a pinup cult figure. Each month's playmate was featured in a double-page spread, called "a centerfold," until March of 1956, when the feature became a triple-page fold.

Hefner regarded the era as one that needed civilizing and felt his male readers needed "polish" if they were to be successful. He steered his magazine toward an intellectual emphasis on everything from fiction to fashion and ensured that his pages could boast serious criticism about art, literature, culture, and design. Therefore, readers could find *Playboy* articles about "Mixing the Perfect Martini" (1955), or a series called "Penthouse Apartment," which featured bachelor pad accoutrements. Profiles of celebrities such as Louis Armstrong and Lenny Bruce were also a part of the magazine's format.

Fiction proved an important aspect of the magazine and helped win critical approval. Ray Bradbury published sections of his novel *Fahrenheit 451* (1953) in 1954 and published several short stories in the magazine's pages throughout the decade. The magazine soon became a showcase for works by esteemed authors such as Erskine Caldwell, John Steinbeck, and Evelyn Waugh.

Cartoons also played a surprisingly important role in *Playboy* during this period. Two of the most important cartoonists were Shel Silverstein and Alberto Vargas. Silverstein specialized in comic drawings and poems and would continue his affiliation with *Playboy* until he became a successful songwriter and children's book author. Vargas drew unique pictures of beautiful girls in a signature style until his death in 1982.

Outside the Covers The success of *Playboy* soon spilled into other ventures beyond the magazine. In August of 1959, *Playboy* sponsored a jazz festival in Chicago that featured the most outstanding talent of the era and began the magazine's regular sponsorship of events, signaling that Hugh Hefner's *Playboy* empire was underway. In October of that year, a nationally syndicated television program was launched titled *Playboy's Penthouse*. The show featured Hefner as the host of a party in his bachelor pad surrounded by celebrity guests and beautiful women. Guests on the show included many of the magazine's playmates as well as entertainers and intellectuals, such as singer Ella Fitzgerald and poet Carl Sandburg. The most successful and influential venture was planned throughout the late 1950's but did not open until February, 1960: the first Playboy Club, a nightclub that featured waitresses dressed as "bunnies."

Impact The publication of the provocative *Playboy* proved to be one of the decade's cultural milestones. The magazine's impact went far beyond critics' impression of it as an upscale "girlie" magazine with pretentious pornography and instead became a symbol of sophisticated urbanity and freethinking. *Playboy* represented a startling contrast to the conservative values of the 1950's. The magazine celebrated hedonism and free sexual attitudes before such views were widely accepted. It also represented a powerful marketing force by linking upward mobility to sexual freedom and by defining its audience in an epicurean manner. The magazine continued its success into the twenty-first century.

Further Reading
Peterson, James R. *Playboy: Fifty Years—the Photographs.* San Francisco: Chronicle Books, 2003. A collec-

tion of photographs from the first fifty years of the magazine.
Scott, Kathryn Leigh. *The Bunny Years: The Surprising Inside Story of the Playboy Clubs, the Women Who Worked as Bunnies, and Where They Are Now.* New York: Pomegranate Press, 1999. Gives an account of the early days of the Playboy Clubs.

Charles C. Howard

See also Affluence and the new consumerism; Bardot, Brigitte; Kinsey Report; *MAD*; Monroe, Marilyn; *Roth v. United States*; Sahl, Mort; Sex and sex education.

■ Pledge of Allegiance

The Event Insertion by the U.S. Congress of the phrase "under God" into the Pledge of Allegiance
Date Flag Day, June 14, 1954

The addition of "God" to the Pledge of Allegiance blurred the First Amendment line drawn between church and state, sparking a decades'-long controversy.

The Pledge of Allegiance, written to commemorate the four hundredth anniversary of Columbus Day, was first published in 1892 in a children's magazine, *The Youth's Companion.* Its original words were: "I pledge allegiance to my flag and to the Republic for which it stands: one nation, indivisible, with liberty and justice for all." In 1923, the phrase "the flag of the United States" replaced "my flag." In 1924, "of America" was added.

By 1935, forty state legislatures had passed laws requiring mandatory recitation of the pledge by schoolchildren, which led to a court challenge on behalf of young Jehovah's Witnesses who refused on religious grounds to salute the flag. In 1940, the U.S. Supreme Court upheld the constitutionality of the mandatory pledge, citing the overriding priorities of national unity and patriotism. However, the Court

---

The Revised Pledge of Allegiance

"I pledge allegiance to the flag of the United States of America and to the republic for which it stands, <u>one nation under God</u>, indivisible, with liberty and justice for all."

reversed its decision in 1943, in reaction to a series of more than three hundred vicious attacks on Jehovah's Witnesses, making recitation of the pledge voluntary.

The phrase "under God" was included on Flag Day, June 14, 1954, after intense lobbying by the Knights of Columbus, a Roman Catholic men's service organization, and various clergy, including President Dwight D. Eisenhower's Presbyterian pastor, George Docherty. The pastor echoed the views of many Americans at the height of the Cold War when he asserted that the secular American pledge could equally serve as the pledge of the atheistic Soviet Union. The pastor argued that the pledge should be changed to reflect Americans' overwhelming belief in a supreme being, in contrast to the lack of faith of the godless communists.

Ironically, the pledge's author, Francis Bellamy, had been a socialist clergyman who shared the egalitarian and freethinking ideals of his cousin, Edward Bellamy, author of the socialist utopian novel *Looking Backward* (1887). Francis Bellamy would probably not have been happy with the inclusion of "under God," according to his granddaughter, who reported that Bellamy had been forced to leave his church in 1891 because of the negative reception to his socialist sermons. In fact, he eventually stopped going to church altogether because of the racial bigotry he encountered in the congregation he joined upon his retirement to Florida.

Impact The 1954 change turned the pledge into a combination of patriotic oath and public prayer and became emblematic of the nation's "religious revival" of the 1950's. It was a time when Norman Vincent Peale, Billy Graham, and Bishop Fulton J. Sheen rose to prominence, and prayer became entrenched in Washington, D.C.: President Eisenhower inaugurated the "prayer breakfast" and Congress created a prayer room in the Capitol. Organized protest and appeals to change the wording of the pledge began in earnest during the 1960's in conjunction with the furor ignited over prayer in schools.

Subsequent Events Two years after inclusion of "under God" in the pledge, "In God We Trust" was declared the official motto of the United States, surviving a court challenge of the Ninth Circuit Court of Appeals in 1970. The court ruled that references to God in the motto and elsewhere were ceremonial and patriotic, not religious. Nonetheless, the same Ninth Circuit Court declared "under God" in the pledge unconstitutional on June 26, 2002. To quell the resulting storm of protest, the judge who wrote the ruling issued a stay to postpone its being put into effect. In April, 2003, the Ninth Circuit declined to review its decision, but the federal government subsequently petitioned the U.S. Supreme Court to overturn the ruling. On Flag Day, June 14, 2004, the Supreme Court overruled the lower court's ruling that the Pledge of Allegiance is unconstitutional, while sidestepping the issue of separation of church and state.

Further Reading

Clausen, Christopher. "Opening Exercises." *American Scholar* 72, no. 1 (Winter, 2003): 35-44. History of the pledge within the context of the Ninth Circuit Court of Appeals' 2002 decision that the words "under God" are unconstitutional.

Jones, Jeffrey Owen. "The Pledge's Creator." *Smithsonian* 34, no. 8 (November, 2003): 113-117. Reflections on what the author of the Pledge of Allegiance might have thought of the controversy caused by the 2002 Ninth Circuit Court of Appeals decision.

Sue Tarjan

See also Cold War; Graham, Billy; "In God We Trust" on U.S. currency; Loyalty oaths; Peale, Norman Vincent; Religion in the United States; Sheen, Fulton J.

■ *Pocho*

Identification Coming-of-age novel about a young Mexican in an immigrant family in Depression-era California
Author José Antonio Villarreal (1924-   )
Date Published in 1959

Pocho was the first novel by a Hispanic American writer released by a major U.S. publisher.

A slang term, "pocho" is used in a derogatory manner to describe a Mexican immigrant who has abandoned his heritage and traditions in favor of assimilation. In José Antonio Villarreal's semiautobiographical novel, his protagonist, Richard Rubio, must deal both with growing tensions between his immigrant parents and with the divergent pull of traditional Mexican and contemporary American cultures as he seeks his own identity in life. Living in Santa Clara (later part of the Silicon Valley), Richard deals with the strains of bilingualism and the experience of discrimination, not only against Latinos by the dominant culture but also among different groups within the Latino community. In high school, he encounters the rise of the pachuco culture (characterized by those wearing "zoot suits") and the responsibility to be the man of the house when his father deserts the family. Ultimately, he resolves to create his own future and joins the Navy.

Impact Although a product of the 1950's, *Pocho* had little cultural influence or attention until it was reissued as a paperback in 1970. At that time, the rise of the Chicano movement led many Mexican Americans to search for an earlier artistic voice that expressed the perspectives of their people. Some argued the novel's resolution and tone did not convey adequately enough resolve in confronting and critiquing the dominant culture. However, most readers came to recognize the work as a forerunner and a model for the significant expansion in Chicano literary works that occurred in the last three decades of the twentieth century.

Further Reading

Pitti, Stephen J. *The Devil in Silicon Valley: Northern California, Race, and Mexican Americans.* Princeton, N.J.: Princeton University Press, 2003. This readable narrative provides a historical context for the Santa Clara County Villarreal actually lived in and described in *Pocho.*

Sedore, Timothy S. "Solace in Solitude: An American Adamic Alienation and José Antonio Villarreal's *Pocho.*" *Literary Interpretation Theory* 11, no. 2 (2000): 239-259. Argues that *Pocho*'s "outsider" focus merits greater recognition in mainstream American literature.

Scot M. Guenter

See also Bracero program; Demographics of the United States; Latinos; Literature in the United States; Mexico; Racial discrimination.

■ Poetry

During the 1950's, poetry underwent a transformation from modernism to the contemporary, or postmodern, period. Experimentation with form and content reflected the counterculture movement that began at this time.

Modern poets such as T. S. Eliot and Ezra Pound, who wrote in a style that drew heavily on the classical education they had received, greatly influenced the poets who came after them. However, postmodern poets also began to experiment outside the boundaries of form and content. They sought a more organic style of poetry that took shape according to the subject matter rather than starting with an existing form and making the subject matter conform to that structure. This style was known as free verse and drew from a tradition that began with Walt Whitman, who is considered the founder of American poetry and who wrote long, sprawling lines in the American vernacular of the mid-nineteenth century. William Carlos Williams brought this style into the twentieth century and influenced the generation of poets who followed him. Although another poet of Williams's time, Robert Frost, described free verse as similar to playing tennis without a net, postmodern poets found that it allowed them greater freedom and better accommodated the more personal and political subject matter that they addressed in their poems.

Some poets, such as Richard Wilbur and Anthony Hecht, continued to write using the formal style of fairly strict meter and rhyme. However, other poets made a transition from what they had learned from modern poets to a new style that permitted more experimentation. Adrienne Rich, under the tutelage and mentorship of W. H. Auden and considered one of the finest formalist poets of that period, was an important proponent of this style. At the beginning of the 1950's, she wrote in a style derivative of the modern poets who had influenced her. As the decade progressed, so too did her writing, as she attempted to find her own poetic voice outside the boundaries of classical poetry. She continued her experimentation into the 1960's in a quest to break free from what she saw as a patriarchal language. Eventually, Rich developed a political style of poetry that was more focused on exposing the limitations of language and its use as a means of destruction than it was an expression of inward thought and emotion.

Prominent Poets and Movements Rather than considering language as a restriction, confessionalists used the formal style, with strict rhyme and meter, to provide a controlled framework for subject matter that was considered highly personal. Robert Lowell is considered the founder of this movement and in-

Twenty-three-year-old Sylvia Plath in 1955. (Sophia Smith Collection, Smith College)

that poetry should follow breathing patterns rather than prefabricated meter and emulate the rhythms of human speech. This theory, developed by Charles Olson, came to be known as projective verse. Advocating an organic form, poets of this school believed that the form of a poem should emerge from the content and that artificial order should not be imposed on the spontaneity and irregularity of human speech. Poets within this movement included Robert Creeley, Robert Duncan, and Denise Levertov. Although criticized as writing from a more theoretical than visceral perspective, Black Mountain poets gained a reputation as risk-taking writers who sought to open up new opportunities for poets to reach a wider audience.

Reacting against what they saw as the complacency of the 1950's, Beat poets took this movement toward reaching a wider audience further, incorporating elements of both confessionalism and the Black Mountain style into poems that explored taboo subjects with colloquial language, even profanity, in lines that were Whitmanesque in their length and breadth. Allen Ginsberg's 1956 poem "Howl," in which he openly portrayed drug-using and homosexual subcultures, was the most famous example of this movement. Moreover, at this time, the idea of poetry as spoken word rather than merely words to be read on a page became popular. The term "Beat" not only referred to the jazz rhythm that poets were striving for but also symbolized the feeling of being beaten down by a society that forced one to conform to what the Beats considered a culture in denial rather than having the freedom to express one's true self. Poets in this movement also included Gregory Corso, Lawrence Ferlinghetti, and Gary Snyder.

fluenced other confessional poets such as Anne Sexton, Sylvia Plath, and W. D. Snodgrass. Confessionalism also was marked by its use of "I" and other first-person pronouns in poems that showed no clear delineation between the poet and the speaker, hence the term "confessional." The poems from this movement suggested the baring of the poet's soul regardless of what was considered proper during the 1950's and early 1960's and included taboo subject matter such as sexual abuse and mental illness. Despite its controversial and even offensive nature to some, confessional poetry was recognized for its control of highly volatile material by using highly skilled attention to form and style. The poets explored emotions and experiences that were seen as a threat to happiness and stability, characteristics considered so important in what Robert Lowell called the "tranquilized" 1950's.

The Black Mountain poets also became known as groundbreakers during the early 1950's. Originating at Black Mountain College, an experimental school in North Carolina, this movement proposed

Impact Using what their modern mentors taught them about the power of language and poetry as a way of manipulating it to create certain effects, poets of the 1950's sought new ways to transform their experiences and observations into works of art that would reach not only an educated, academic audience, but also the common man or woman. They sought to explore the intellectual and emotional terrain that had been off limits to more classically trained poets and opened up new possibilities for poetry to reach its readers and listeners.

Further Reading

Davison, Peter. *The Fading Smile: Poets in Boston from Robert Lowell to Sylvia Plath.* New York: W. W.

The Fifties in America

Norton, 1996. A description, written by a contemporary poet himself, of the creative atmosphere in Boston during the 1950's and those who inhabited it, including some of the best-known confessionalists.

Hoover, Paul, ed. *Postmodern American Poetry.* New York: W. W. Norton, 1994. An effective introduction to the major poetic movements of the 1950's and early 1960's, with discussions of the Beat, Black Mountain, and New York poets, as well as examples of their work.

McClatchy, J. D., ed. *The Vintage Book of Contemporary Poetry.* New York: Vintage Books, 2003. An anthology providing a wide selection of poetry from the mid-twentieth century to the twenty-first century.

Weinberger, Eliot, ed. *American Poetry Since 1950: Innovators and Outsiders.* New York: Marsilio, 1993. An examination of four generations of poets considered representative of the movement from modernism toward postmodernism.

Holly L. Norton

See also Armour, Richard; Beat generation; Book publishing; Corso, Gregory; Eliot, T. S.; Ferlinghetti, Lawrence; Ginsberg, Allen; Jazz; Kerouac, Jack; Literature in the United States; Pound, Ezra; Rexroth, Kenneth; San Francisco Renaissance.

■ Pogo

Identification Syndicated comic strip about a possum living in a southern swamp
Artist Walt Kelly (1913-1973)
Dates Ran from 1948 to 1973

One of the most widely read comic strips of the 1950's, Pogo *blended entertainment with political and social satire*

In 1941, cartoonist Walt Kelly created Pogo, a southern possum, as a character in the strip called *Albert the Alligator,* which was part of Dell Comics' *Animal Comics.* In 1948, Kelly became the art director and political cartoonist for the *New York Star.* Albert the Alligator and his other animal neighbors moved from comic books to the comic pages of the *Star* in a daily comic strip called *Pogo.* When the *Star* folded in 1949, *Pogo* moved to the *New York Post.* By the early 1950's, *Pogo* was syndicated, and in 1958, it appeared in more than five hundred newspapers.

By the time Pogo and his neighbors had moved to newspaper comic strips, the strip's human characters had been left behind. Political figures appeared but in the form of animal characters. The most famous to appear during the 1950's was Senator Joseph McCarthy, who appeared as a lynx, Simple J. Malarkey. Political figures were not the only targets of Kelly's pen. In 1952, he parodied rival Harold Gray's comic strip *Little Orphan Annie* in a sequence titled "Li'l Arf An' Nonny."

Impact *Pogo* became one of the most popular comic strips of the 1950's, but when it skewered political figures, it was sometimes moved to the editorial page or removed altogether from newspapers. *Pogo* stretched the bounds of the medium and would influence cartoonists for decades to come.

Further Reading

Harvey, Robert C. *The Art of the Funnies.* Jackson: University Press of Mississippi, 1994. Good history of comics, including *Pogo.*

Wertham, Fredric. *Seduction of the Innocent.* Mattituck, N.Y.: Amereon, 1996. A reprint of Wertham's influential 1954 book that encouraged censorship of comics.

Robert E. Haag

See also Capp, Al; Censorship; Comic books; House Committee on Un-American Activities; *Kukla, Fran and Ollie;* McCarthy, Joseph; Newspapers in the United States; *Peanuts.*

■ Poitier, Sidney

Identification African American film actor
Born February 20, 1927; Miami, Florida

Sidney Poitier made headlines during the 1950's for his well-received roles in films and theater; he was the first male African American actor to be nominated for an Academy Award for his role in 1958's The Defiant Ones.

Born in Miami, Florida, but raised in the Bahamas, Sidney Poitier was the youngest child of Evelyn and Reginald Poitier. At age fifteen, he returned to Miami to live with an older brother, and at age sixteen, he relocated to New York City after serving briefly in the U.S. Army. Illiterate and without any acting experience, Poitier unsuccessfully auditioned at the American Negro Theatre. His failure at this first audition inspired him to teach himself how to read and speak without a Caribbean accent. Six months later, he returned to the American Negro Theatre and, in exchange for janitorial work, received free acting lessons.

In 1946, Poitier earned the role of Harry Belafonte's understudy in the play *Days of Our Youth* and shortly thereafter, was hired for a small part in the production of the Greek comedy *Lysistrata.* In 1950, Poitier made his film debut in the movie *No Way Out.* With that film's success, Poitier starred in several other films, including *Cry, the Beloved Country* (1952), *Blackboard Jungle* (1955), *Edge of the City* (1957), and *Something of Value* (1957). In 1959, he starred as Walter Lee Younger in the first Broadway production of Lorraine Hansberry's play *A Raisin in the Sun.*

Impact A popular film actor during the 1950's, Poitier enjoyed successes in film and theater that redefined the cultural barriers confronting African American actors. In 1964, Poitier became the first African American to win a best-acting Academy Award for his role in *Lilies of the Field* (1963). Throughout the next four decades, he continued to act and direct.

Further Reading

Goudsouzian, Aram. *Sidney Poitier: Man, Actor, Icon.* Chapel Hill: University of North Carolina Press, 2004. Details the highs and lows of Poitier's career and provides apt commentary on his films.

Poitier, Sidney. *The Measure of a Man: A Spiritual Autobiography.* San Francisco: Harper, 2000. Poitier's life and career in his own words.

Bernadette Zbicki Heiney

See also Academy Awards; African Americans; Belafonte, Harry; *Blackboard Jungle*; Film in the United States; Theater in the United States.

■ Polaris missiles

Identification First practical submarine-based intercontinental ballistic weapon
Date First launched in April, 1959

Polaris missiles constituted an important part of U.S. strategic nuclear deterrence during the Cold War.

Throughout the early years of the Cold War, the United States began experimenting with the concept of submarine-launched ballistic missiles (SLBM) to be aimed at the Soviet Union. Preliminary efforts—such as the air-breathing *Regulus II,* an early cruise missile—were feasible technically but required submarines to surface in order to fire. Another stumbling block was reliance upon liquid fuel propellants, which were highly unstable and could be disastrous to a submarine if ignited prematurely.

However, by the mid-1950's, great strides had been made in the field of safer, solid fuel rocketry that would allow a submarine to carry its ordnance safely while still submerged. A vessel thus armed would be almost impossible to detect and therefore would be immune to destruction through a surprise, preemptive strike. In 1956, the U.S. Navy commissioned the Lockheed Corporation to develop such a weapon, possession of which would grant the United States tremendous strategic advantages over the Soviet Union in the event of war.

The resulting Polaris weapon, also known as the A-1, was a relatively small device, 28 feet long with a diameter of only 54 inches. The design was deliberately kept compact to facilitate the missile's storage in firing tubes aboard a submarine. The missile was ejected from the tube by compressed air to minimize any chance of damage to the submarine, and once on the surface, the rocket motors ignited, propelling the missile and its nuclear warhead into low orbit. The Polaris was then guided to its target through an intricate inertial guidance system.

Accuracy in the A-1 was minimal by later standards; it was limited to within one mile of its target. This fact, coupled with the missile's low-yield warhead and a one-thousand-mile range, made it less than ideal as a strategic weapon initially, but greater advances were anticipated over time. The Polaris was successfully test launched in April, 1959, and the following year, it deployed at sea onboard the USS *George Washington*, the world's first atomic-powered missile submarine. This union of nuclear power with missile technology resulted in a powerful form of strategic deterrence, and thereafter submarines constituted the third rung of America's triad nuclear strategy, following land-based missiles and piloted bombers.

Impact Lockheed ultimately constructed 1,150 Polaris missiles, placed on twenty-one American ballistic submarines. The missiles were the first and only nuclear weapons exported abroad; in 1963 British prime minister Harold Macmillan agreed to accept the missiles for Royal Navy submarines. The last Polaris was finally retired from the fleet in 1981, replaced by the more powerful Poseidon missile. The British retained their missiles in front-line service until the 1990's, making the Polaris missile system one of the longest-serving and most successful nuclear deterrents of the Cold War era.

Further Reading

Moore, John E. *The Impact of Polaris: The Origins of Britain's Seaborne Nuclear Deterrent.* Huddersfield, England: Richard Netherwood, 1999. A detailed policy study behind Macmillan's decision to accept the *Polaris* for British use.

Solomon, James B. *The Multilateral Force: America's Nuclear Solution for NATO, 1960-1965.* Annapolis, Md.: U.S. Naval Academy, 1999. High-level strategic study regarding the American emphasis on nuclear deterrence.

Spinardi, Graham, et al., eds. *From Polaris to Trident: The Development of U.S. Fleet Ballistic Missile Technology.* Cambridge, England: University of Cambridge Press, 1994. Uses the *Polaris* missiles as a starting point for its discussion on the development of the ballistic missile program.

John C. Fredriksen

See also Cold War; DEW Line; Foreign policy of the United States; Hydrogen bomb; Military-industrial complex; *Nautilus*, USS; Teller, Edward.

■ Polio

Definition Viral disease that produced hysteria and fear among North Americans fearing its transmission during the 1950's

Before the 1950's, hundreds of thousands of North Americans were paralyzed or killed by polio, whose onset appeared to be an ordinary summer flu. The occurrence of the disease terrified millions of people and kept social activities that could lead to exposure at a minimum. Development of the polio vaccines during the decade nearly eradicated the disease and increased public confidence in biomedical science.

Polio attacks brain and spinal cord gray matter. Called "infantile paralysis" until the early 1950's, it was thought to be a disease of children that always resulted in paralysis. It was soon understood, however, that people of any age could catch polio and that victims were not always paralyzed. Historians suggest polio has afflicted humans since ancient times, because of biblical depictions of people with withered

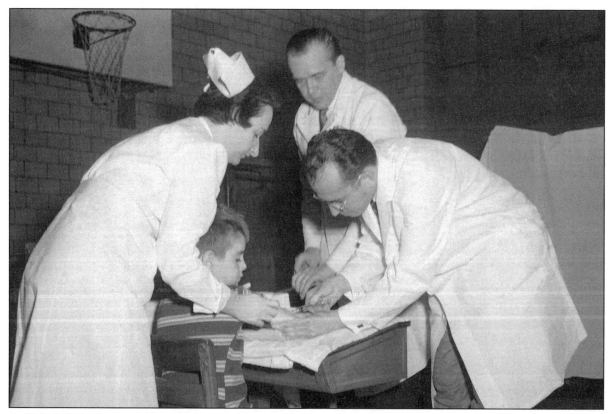

Dr. Jonas Salk, the discoverer of the first polio vaccine, inoculating an elementary school child in Pittsburgh, Pennsylvania, in February, 1954. (AP/Wide World Photos)

limbs. In modern times, polio was first described in 1840 by the German physician Jacob von Heine. In 1902, Karl Landsteiner discovered three polio virus strains: Brunhilde, Lansing, and Leon.

Vaccines At the beginning of the 1950's, continuation of worldwide polio epidemics that began during the 1940's became a medical crisis in the United States. In 1950, for example, 3,400 severe cases occurred. In 1951, even more cases developed, and by 1952, there were 58,000 cases. That year, polio epidemics occurred in Europe, China, India, Japan, Korea, and the Philippines.

For Americans, the aftermath of polio was painfully clear in photos of President Franklin D. Roosevelt, who contracted the disease in 1921 and had to wear heavy steel braces on his legs. Walking was so difficult for him that he spent most of his time in a wheelchair. During the late 1940's and early 1950's, as the polio epidemic was at its worst, posters advertising the March of Dimes contained heartbreaking pictures of children on crutches and in iron lungs—the cumbersome mechanical aids that enabled polio victims with paralyzed rib cages to breathe. Before a polio vaccine became available, many parents throughout the United States and Canada panicked, keeping their children away from schools and other public facilities, such as movie theaters and swimming pools.

To counter this epidemiological crisis, the National Foundation for Infantile Paralysis funded research that led to development of vaccines by Jonas E. Salk and Albert B. Sabin during the decade. A major problem that had slowed vaccine development—the inability of polio viruses to grow outside live cells—was obviated by 1949, when Harvard researchers John Enders, Frederick C. Robbins, and Thomas H. Weller developed means to grow the polio virus outside the body. Using their technique, Salk, a University of Pittsburgh physician, developed an injected vaccine made from killed polio viruses of all three strains.

After 1954, field trials on approximately two million American children—a scope unprecedented in U.S. medical history—began. The results were immediate, and the vaccine was pronounced safe and effective for widespread use. In 1955, mass inoculation began around the United States and the world. At the end of the 1950's, a live and oral form of the vaccine was developed by Sabin to counter problems

The March of Dimes and the Salk Vaccine

During the early twentieth century, polio became an epidemic health problem in the United States. The reason was ironic: Because of improved sanitation, Americans had less contact with the organisms in sewers and open drains that had formerly allowed them to build up immunities to the polio virus.

In 1927 polio sufferer Franklin D. Roosevelt founded the nonprofit Warm Springs Foundation, and in 1938 he established the National Foundation for Infantile Paralysis, whose campaign became known as the March of Dimes. Funds were raised with the aid of posters—typically showing children on crutches—and radio campaigns. Listeners throughout the United States mailed dimes to the foundation, which provided thousands of dollars to help people care for their stricken family members. The campaign also financed Jonas Salk's attempts to grow the three known types of the polio virus in his laboratory and materially contributed to the creation of an effective vaccine during the early 1950's. The March of Dimes also financed the development of Albert Sabin's oral vaccine, which became available to the public in 1962.

with the Salk vaccine. The Salk and Sabin vaccines (the latter was not used until the 1960's) protected against all polio virus types. The number of polio cases declined dramatically after vaccines began being used.

Impact The 1950's saw near eradication of this catastrophic disease that had killed or disabled millions of people worldwide. Salk's killed vaccine and Sabin's live vaccine are deemed by many historians to be among the most important medical discoveries of the twentieth century. Polio still occurred by the end of the 1950's, although rarely, but people no longer feared the summer months, when polio infections had been most numerous. Also, development of the tissue culture methods of Enders, Robbins, and Weller opened the door for later use of mammalian tissue cultures for advances in molecular biology that identified viral causes of cancer and acquired immunodeficiency syndrome (AIDS).

Subsequent Events Sabin's oral vaccine, licensed in 1961, quickly replaced Salk's injected vaccine as the standard U.S. polio immunizing agent because of easy administration and the belief that its live viruses would work longer than Salk's killed viruses. Despite the effectiveness of the vaccine, polio vulnerability of unimmunized people was shown to be quite high throughout the world after the 1950's. In 1979, this was made painfully obvious by epidemics among unvaccinated Amish Americans. Retrospective studies by the World Health Organization, published in 1994, showed that once the vaccines were widely used, the Western Hemisphere quickly became free of naturally occurring polio.

Continued and minor paralytic polio outbreaks after the late 1950's occurred in situations where virus attenuation was incomplete; these outbreaks caused rethinking of the vaccine use. Reliance on the Sabin vaccine decreased in stages as time went by. In 1997, to reduce vaccine-related polio, the U.S. Centers for Disease Control (CDC) recommended that all children get two doses of injected (killed) vaccine, followed by two oral doses of attenuated vaccine. In 2000, to eliminate risks of vaccine-related polio, the CDC revised its recommendation to four injections of killed virus by age four.

Further Reading

Daniel, Thomas M., and Frederick C. Robbins, eds. *Polio*. Rochester, N.Y.: University of Rochester Press, 1997. Fine reference for the history and epidemiology of the disease. Includes illustrations, bibliography, and index

Gould, Tony. *A Summer Plague: Polio and Its Survivors.* New Haven, Conn.: Yale University Press, 1995. An excellent reference with illustrations, bibliography, and index.

Sherrow, Victoria. *Jonas Salk.* New York: Facts On File, 1993. Describes Salk and his contributions to science.

Sanford S. Singer

See also Cancer; Health care systems in Canada; Health care systems in the United States; Medicine; Science and technology.

■ Pollock, Jackson

Identification American artist
Born January 28, 1912; Cody, Wyoming
Died August 11, 1956; East Hampton, Long Island, New York

Jackson Pollock became the most influential American abstract expressionist artist during the 1950's through his bold and innovative painting techniques.

Paul Jackson Pollock was born on a sheep farm in Cody, Wyoming, to LeRoy Pollock and Stella May McClure Pollock. He was the youngest of five sons. By 1928, the family was living in Los Angeles, California. Pollock attended Manual Arts High School, where he received some instruction in painting and drawing. In 1930, he joined his brother Charles in New York City and enrolled at the Art Students League (ASL). For more than two years, Pollock studied painting, composition, and life drawing with the noted "regionalist" artist Thomas Hart Benton. He went to work for the Federal Art Project of the Works Project Administration (WPA) in 1935. However, by the late 1930's, Pollock was developing a serious problem with alcohol that would trouble him through the rest of his life. By embracing a bold abstract approach to his painting, Pollock came to the attention of the legendary art patron Peggy Guggenheim, who gave him his first one-person show in November of 1943.

The Artist and Mythic Figure In 1945, Pollock married fellow artist Lee Krasner. As his wife, confidante, and caretaker, Krasner did her best to channel Pollock's energy into his art. During the late 1940's, Pollock experimented with what would become known as his "drip" technique of painting after the couple had relocated to a house on Long Island in the community of East Hampton. He would put down a large canvas on his studio floor and begin to splatter and drip paint onto the canvas. Through this approach, Pollock attempted to give expression to what was in his unconscious. He maintained that his paintings were not mere accidents but were in actuality the finished products of what came together out of his inner self.

In 1949, *Life* magazine did an in-depth article on Pollock titled "Jackson Pollock: Is He the Greatest Living Painter in the United States?" In 1950, Pollock completed some of his most spectacular mural-sized paintings, including *Lavender Mist* and *Autumn Rhythm*; did a radio interview with William Wright; and was documented while painting in a study by noted photographer Hans Namuth. Namuth also filmed the artist, and one of the filmed sequences involved Pollock painting on a pane of glass. Pollock completed thirty-two paintings during 1950, making it his most productive year as an artist. He was rapidly becoming the face of contemporary American art. While for the most part the general public was dubious about Pollock's drip creations, many art critics began to champion his genius.

In 1951, the completed Namuth film was premiered at the Museum of Modern Art. Although Pollock had difficulty making a living selling his paintings during the early 1950's, he continued to experiment and to push himself creatively. He also began to drink heavily again and had episodes of deep depression. Pollock had his last one-person show in 1954 at the Sidney Janis Gallery in New York City. Frustrated with Pollock's rapid deterioration, Krasner escaped to Europe in July, 1956, for a visit to Peggy Guggenheim. On August 11, 1956, a drunk and self-destructive Pollock died in a car accident.

Impact It might be argued not only that Pollock was the most important American artist of the 1950's, but also that he must be recognized as one of the most important artists that the United States has ever produced. Pollock was not one who looked for truth in what may be called rational experience. During the late 1940's and early 1950's, he found the strength to channel his own personal demons into his art. While *Time* magazine sarcastically dubbed him "Jack the Dripper" in 1956, thereby dismissing what it did not understand, the shadow that Pollock cast on the art world since his untimely death has been large. Many artists who came after him paid homage to him as a great liberator, as someone who made art a deeply personal statement.

Further Reading

Karmel, Pepe, ed. *Jackson Pollock: Interviews, Articles, and Reviews.* New York: Museum of Modern Art, 1999. Includes essential documents by and about Pollock.

Naifeh, Steven, and Gregory White Smith. *Jackson Pollock: An American Saga.* New York: Clarkson N. Potter, 1989. A massive and truthful biography that is never less than compelling.

Jeffry Jensen

See also Abstract expressionism; Art movements; de Kooning, Willem; Guggenheim Museum; Johns, Jasper; Kline, Franz; Motherwell, Robert; Painters Eleven; Rauschenberg, Robert.

■ Postage stamps

U.S. and Canadian postage stamps became more colorful, more numerous, and higher in face value during the 1950's.

During the early 1950's, the most frequently used postal stamps in the United States were those of the Presidential Series, first issued in 1938-1939. The stamps in that series featured all the then-deceased American presidents in order, from George Washington on the one-cent stamp through Calvin Coolidge on the five-dollar stamp. The series also included Benjamin Franklin on a one-half-cent stamp, Martha Washington on a one-and-one-half-cent stamp, and the White House on a four-and-one-half-cent stamp.

As with all definitives, the stamps in the Presidential Series were the same small size and were reprinted when supplies ran out. The stamps featured a common design: a bust of the president on the left, the words "UNITED STATES POSTAGE" on the upper right, and the denomination on the bottom. The stamps with denominations of one dollar or more were a slightly fancier, two-color version of the same theme. At the beginning of the decade, since the basic postage rate was three cents, the most commonly used stamp was the three-cent one portraying the third U.S. president, Thomas Jefferson.

In 1954, the Presidential Series began to be supplanted by a new set known as the Liberty Series. Most of the stamps in the new series were portraits of presidents or other famous men (no women were included), but there were a few pictures of monuments and famous buildings. The stamp priced at the first-class postage rate when the set began (three cents) portrayed the Statue of Liberty, but when first-class postage was raised to four cents in 1958, most letters began bearing the stamp portraying Abraham Lincoln.

Commemorative Stamps The United States began issuing stamps in honor of specific events in 1893, with a sixteen-stamp set honoring the four-hundred-year anniversary of Christopher Columbus's first voyage to America. The number of stamps in the Columbus set and their high denominations made them unpopular at first, but commemoratives—stamps issued for a particular event, in smaller runs than the definitives, and typically taken off sale after a few years—continued to be produced.

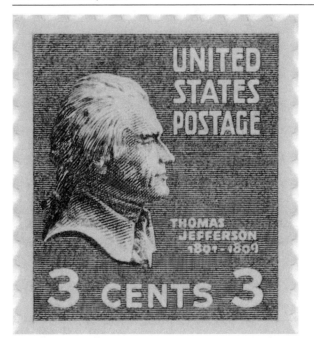

From 1938 until 1958, when the U.S. Post Office raised the price of mailing a first-class letter to four cents, this three-cent Thomas Jefferson stamp in the Presidential Series was the most commonly used postage stamp in the United States. (Arkent Archive)

Before World War II, there were typically about four commemoratives issued per year for generally agreed-upon subjects. However, with representatives and senators urging commemoration of their own constituents' interests, the numbers of separate commemorative issues increased in 1948 to an unprecedented twenty-eight, including such unusual subjects as the American poultry industry, the American Turners Association (a gymnastics group), and Moina Michael, creator of the memorial poppy. Complaints brought the number down to six the next year. By the end of the 1940's, the average number of stamps per year crept back up to the high teens and continued to increase, eventually reaching three figures.

Stamps had traditionally been engraved using a single color, but by 1950, foreign countries, particularly small European principalities such as Monaco and San Marino, began issuing multicolored stamps. Like commemoratives, two-colored stamps had been tried in the nineteenth century, but they too fell from sight for a while. In 1952, a stamp was issued in honor of the International Red Cross and was mostly blue but included the organization symbol in red. In 1957, there was a stamp showing the

American flag in full color; a new one was issued in 1959, when the flag expanded to forty-nine stars. A 1959 Forest Conservation stamp—showing a brown tree trunk, a gold-leaved tree, and green leaves—gave an indication of the colorful beauty that could be placed on the small canvas of a stamp. A themed series of stamps, called Champions of Liberty and honoring foreign heroes, began late in the decade and included depictions of Philippine president Ramon Magsaysay, Hungarian politician and journalist Lajos Kossuth, and South American revolutionary leaders José San Martin and Simón Bolívar.

Canadian Stamps Canadian stamps were similar to U.S. stamps of the time. Because Canada was part of the British Commonwealth, its definitives pictured the contemporary ruling monarch of Great Britain. A set portraying King George VI appeared in 1950, and after his death a set portraying Queen Elizabeth II was issued in 1953.

Impact The 1950's continued the postal service's commitment to using stamps to depict the American experience to a world audience. Most subjects that appear on U.S. stamps are suggested by the public, which can submit proposals on any number of topics. In 1957, the postal service began the Citizen's Stamp Advisory Committee to help assess these topics for their merit and to help decide the appearance of the stamps. Subject matter that was deemed educational and interesting by the advisory committee was passed to the postmaster general, who decided which stamps to issue, thus setting the precedent for the process as it continued in later decades.

Further Reading
Boggs, Winthrop. *The Postage Stamps and Postal History of Canada.* Boston: Quarterman, 1974. Chronicles key developments in Canada's postal history.
Youngblood, Wayne L. *All About Stamps: An Illustrated Encyclopedia of Philatelic Terms.* Iola, Wis.: Krause, 2000. Gives information on stamps issued during the 1950's.

Arthur D. Hlavaty
See also Art movements; Monroe, Marilyn.

■ Pound, Ezra

Identification American poet and writer
Born October 30, 1885; Hailey, Idaho
Died November 1, 1972; Venice, Italy

Ezra Pound's iconoclastic and innovative poetry and writing style shaped the international modernist literary movement. While his activities during World War II earned him infamy, his treason case and subsequent incarceration in a mental hospital galvanized the literary world during the 1950's.

Ezra Pound was born in a small Western mining town in 1885, but the Pound family left it for New York City when he was two years old and he was reared in the East. At the age of twelve, he began his regular travel to Europe. Following a disastrous attempt at an academic career in the United States, Pound left for London in 1908. He became closely involved with such literary figures as Ford Maddox Ford, James Joyce, and T. S. Eliot and began his writing career there. In 1914, Pound married Dorothy Shakespear, and they moved to Paris, where he continued his writing and became close with such writers as Ernest Hemingway and Gertrude Stein. Olga Rudge, a well-known American violinist, became his mistress at this time. In 1924, the Pounds moved to Rapallo, Italy. By this time, Pound's poetry, much of it appearing in his decades-long *Cantos* project, began to earn him international renown.

World War II and After As World War II loomed, Pound delivered increasing oral and written attacks on Jews. He alleged that they had a nefarious cultural and economic influence worldwide, particularly in the United States and Great Britain. He flooded literary, political, and economic leaders in the United States and Europe with letters and articles expounding these views. As the United States increased its participation in the war against the Axis powers, Pound offered his services as a radio broadcaster and writer for the Italian government. His subsequent broadcasts were aimed at American troops and were vitriolic in their attacks on U.S. politicians and war policies. In his aired statements, Pound made it clear that he believed such politicians and policies were controlled by Jews.

Pound was seized by American occupation forces in Italy in 1945, and on the basis of his wartime activities, he was indicted for treason by U.S. authorities. Transported and tried in the United States (he was still an American citizen), he was judged to be insane, and in 1946, he was admitted to Washington, D.C.'s St. Elizabeth's Hospital. While there, his receipt of the prestigious Bollingen Prize in Poetry occasioned much controversy, primarily because of his profascist, anti-Semitic beliefs during the war.

Following repeated appeals and pleadings for Pound's release by such distinguished literary friends as Ernest Hemingway, Robert Frost, Archibald Macleish, and T. S. Eliot, the U.S. government dismissed his indictment and ordered his release in 1958. Pound returned to Italy in that year and took up residence with Olga Rudge in a Venetian house. He entered a period that he called "the silence" and rarely spoke to anyone. Pound was in ill health during the last decade of his life and died in Venice in 1972.

Impact Despite Pound's infamous anti-Semitism and role in Fascist politics during World War II, most critics agree that he was the literary figure most responsible for defining and promoting the Modernist literary aesthetic. He snubbed convention and challenged a world and literary establishment, yet his influence was substantial. During his incarceration throughout the late 1940's and the 1950's, Pound produced some of his most notable poetry, including *The Pisan Cantos* (1948), and numerous translations from the Chinese and Greek. The support from his literary friends made headlines during the late 1950's.

Further Reading

Tytell, John. *Ezra Pound: The Solitary Volcano.* Chicago: Ivan R. Dee, 2004. An excellent biography of Pound based on interviews as well as published and unpublished Pound documents.

Wilhelm, James J. *Ezra Pound: The Tragic Years, 1925-1972.* University Park: Pennsylvania State University Press, 1994. A detailed study of Pound's life between 1925 and 1972.

Joseph C. Kiger

See also Eliot, T. S.; Hemingway, Ernest; Literature in the United States; Poetry.

■ Powell, Adam Clayton, Jr.

Identification African American politician
Born November 29, 1908; New Haven, Connecticut
Died April 4, 1972; Miami, Florida

As one of the few African Americans in Congress during the 1950's, Adam Clayton Powell, Jr., helped lead the fight for civil rights.

The son of a noted minister, Adam Clayton Powell grew up in Harlem, where his father headed the Abyssinian Baptist Church. After attending public schools in New York City, he earned a bachelor's degree from Colgate University in 1930 and a master's degree from Columbia University in 1932. He joined his father's staff at the expanding Abyssinian church and got involved in social work and the early Civil Rights movement. When he took over as pastor in 1937, the church's membership had reached thirteen thousand members. This huge flock provided the core of his support as he moved into politics and became the first black person on the New York City Council in 1941.

Serving in Congress In 1944, Powell won a seat representing Harlem in the U.S. Congress, where he quickly established himself as an advocate for racial equality. As one of only two African Americans in the House of Representatives, he challenged segregation and discrimination wherever he found it, including in Congress itself. In 1946, he attached an amendment to an appropriations bill for school lunches that would deny federal funds to any facility that discriminated on the basis of race. He would continue to add these "Powell Amendments" to innumerable pieces of legislation throughout the 1950's. In advocating racial justice, he often ran headlong into resistance from southern legislators and on one occasion was even punched by Representative Cleveland Bailey of West Virginia.

During the 1950's, Powell served on the House's Education and Labor Committee, and he eventually became its chair during the early 1960's. During his early tenure with the committee, crucial legislation such as the National Defense Education Act, the Vocational Education Act, and Head Start were all passed. Powell ultimately was responsible for helping to pass sixty major bills, the most by any member of the House of Representatives in history. Powell also paid some attention to American relations with the less-developed world, attending an important conference of nonaligned nations in Bandung, Indonesia, in 1955.

Impact Controversial and colorful, Powell was a hero to his constituents and to all who fought for civil rights. During the 1950's, Powell was one of the best-known leaders of the black community. His hard work for civil rights and fiery sermons made him extremely popular in his Harlem district and gained respect from like-minded people around the world. At the same time, his outspokenness and flamboyant lifestyle made him a target for criticism from opponents of racial integration. Eventually his critics helped to end his career, when he was stripped of his seat in Congress during the late 1960's because of alleged financial impropriety. He retired to the Bahamas in 1971 and died in Miami in 1972.

Further Reading

Hamilton, Charles. *Adam Clayton Powell, Jr.: The Political Biography of an American Dilemna.* New York: Atheneum, 1991. A balanced and well-researched biography with a political focus.

Haygood, Wil. *King of the Cats: The Life and Times of Adam Clayton Powell, Jr.* Boston: Houghton Mifflin, 1993. A good biography of Powell.

Andy DeRoche

Congressman Adam Clayton Powell, Jr. (Library of Congress)

See also African Americans; Civil Rights movement; Congress, U.S.; Liberalism in U.S. politics; School desegregation.

■ Presidential press conferences

Definition Occasions on which U.S. presidents appear before gatherings of journalists and respond to questions

Although presidential press conferences had an earlier history spanning several decades, during the 1950's, they evolved into a fixture of the television age and made the president a regular guest on American television screens.

A major change in the way in which presidential press conferences took place occurred in 1950, when President Harry S. Truman moved the scene of his press conferences from the White House to the Indian Treaty Room in the State Department building across the street. In addition to this change in venue, press conferences took on a more formal air as correspondents arose upon the president's entrance and introduced themselves by name when asking questions. Beginning in his second term, Truman allowed radio broadcasts of excerpts from his press conferences, and, after President Dwight D. Eisenhower took office in 1953, the press conferences continued to be recorded, and newspapers were allowed to quote the president directly as long as they used the officially approved transcript.

The single most important innovation occurred in January of 1955, when press conferences began to be filmed for broadcast by the television networks, subject to editing by the White House. This step was taken by Eisenhower and his press secretary, Jim Hagerty, in an effort to bypass the press corps and reach the American public directly without relying on what they perceived as slanted news coverage. Eisenhower also frequently prefaced his press conferences with brief statements on current actions or policies of his administration, taking further advantage of his opportunity to address the viewing public.

President Truman averaged 3.4 press conferences per month during his almost eight years in office, about half the frequency of his predecessor, President Franklin D. Roosevelt. During President Eisenhower's two terms, the monthly average fell to 2.0. The longest stretch without a regular press conference (24 weeks) occurred after his September,

1955, heart attack. Both Truman and Eisenhower maintained cordial relations with the press, but Eisenhower, with his considerable experience in public relations while in the army, was more forthcoming in his answers during the events. Truman, on the other hand, approached the press conference as if it were a battle of wits with reporters.

On occasion, press conferences reflected the adversarial relationship between press and president as reporters asked persistent or irritating questions; on one occasion during the Korean War, Truman was trapped into saying that the use of the atomic bomb was always under consideration, a statement from which he later retreated. Later, Eisenhower was so angered by a question about Senator Joseph McCarthy that he abruptly walked out of a press conference.

Impact As it adapted to the age of television, the presidential press conference demonstrated during the 1950's that it would be a permanent institution in American politics, providing citizens with their best opportunity to witness public give-and-take on the part of the president and giving the president a prime-time public relations opportunity. Only one additional step was needed to create the modern presidential press conference as Americans would come to know it, and that was taken in 1961, when President John F. Kennedy's press conferences began to be broadcast on live television.

Further Reading

Allen, Craig. *Eisenhower and the Mass Media: Peace, Prosperity, and Prime-Time TV.* Chapel Hill: University of North Carolina Press, 1993. A scholarly book that argues that Eisenhower rightfully deserves the title of the first television president.

Parry-Giles, Shawn J. *The Rhetorical Presidency, Propaganda, and the Cold War, 1945-1955.* Westport, Conn.: Praeger, 2002. This book takes an analytical view of presidents Truman and Eisenhower, the use of propaganda, and the news.

Smith, Carolyn. *Presidential Press Conferences: A Critical Approach.* New York: Praeger, 1990. This book describes the history, structure, and function of presidential press conferences.

Lawrence W. Haapanen

See also Eisenhower, Dwight D.; Newspapers in the United States; Television in the United States; Truman, Harry S.

■ Presley, Elvis

Identification American rock-and-roll singer
Born January 8, 1935; Tupelo, Mississippi
Died August 16, 1977; Memphis, Tennessee

A clean-cut, good-looking, and charismatic white south-erner who combined country, gospel, and rhythm-and-blues music, Elvis Presley blurred and challenged the social and racial barriers of the time, becoming the most celebrated popular music phenomenon of his era. During the late 1950's, he used his sexuality and distinctive vocal style to revolutionize and popularize rock-and-roll music.

The son of Gladys and Vernon Presley, Elvis Presley was raised as an only child after his twin brother, Jesse Garon, was stillborn. He remained extraordinarily close to his parents throughout his life and expressed a particular devotion to his mother, whose death in 1958 Presley called the greatest tragedy of his life. The Presleys lived slightly above the poverty line and attended the First Assembly of God Church, whose Pentecostal services first exposed Presley to music. His fundamentalist Christian background and his spirituality remained in the fabric of his music throughout his life. On his eleventh birthday, Presley received his first guitar and thereafter began private lessons with his Uncle Vester. His guitar would be a constant companion in his life.

In 1948, Vernon Presley took a job at the Precision Tool Company and moved his family to Memphis, Tennessee, where the younger Presley soaked up the rich musical tradition of the Mississippi River city. Elvis graduated from Memphis's L. C. Humes High School in 1953. That same year, he recorded two ballads as a birthday present to his mother. The songs garnered the attention of Sam Phillips, the owner of the legendary Sun Records in Memphis, who signed Presley to a recording contract. Presley's debut disc on Sun featured the single "That's All Right, Mama," which showcased his rich voice and his unique rockabilly blend of country music with the blues. It produced immediate fan-

fare. Word of Presley's talent and tantalizing performances spread quickly, and appearances throughout the South, including at the legendary Grand Ole Opry, fueled his instant popularity.

Early RCA Years and Films Presley came under the management of Colonel Tom Parker, a dominant manager of several country artists, who struck a deal with Sam Phillips to release the young talent to the major label of RCA Records for $35,000 in late 1955. Presley reportedly received a $5,000 advance that he used to purchase a pink Cadillac for his mother. Similar expressions of generosity—including expensive and lavish gifts, often to total strangers, and extraordinary donations to local, national, and international causes—would soon be-

This photo of Elvis Presley performing in 1956 was used on the cover of his first record album. (AP/Wide World Photos)

come part of the mystique of Presley that would define him for life.

On January 10, 1956, Presley's debut session at RCA produced "Heartbreak Hotel." The record's startling originality and intensity riveted the American public, who subsequently helped push the single to number one in an astounding eight weeks. During that same month, Presley made his national television debut, displaying his sexually enticing gyrations before an audience whose alleged outrage temporarily persuaded producers to film the star exclusively from the waist up. With his exposure extending to both radio and television, Presley's fan base swelled to global proportions almost overnight, and he hit number one for a second time with the ballad "I Want You, I Need You, I Love You." A resolute perfectionist, Presley next released what was to become the most commercially successful double-sided single in pop history, "Hound Dog"/"Don't Be Cruel." Though it sounded like it was recorded in one breathless plunge, Presley demanded thirty-one takes before agreeing to the final cut. The single remained at number one in the United States for eleven weeks. In 1956 alone, Presley turned out ten singles that became certified gold. He used his profits from these releases to purchase Graceland, a former Memphis church that he lavishly converted into a twenty-three-room mansion. He would live there until his death in 1977.

As the first rock star to cross over into films with consistent commercial success, Presley appeared in the first of his thirty-three films, *Love Me Tender*, in 1957. Although his acting received mixed reviews, the picture was a box-office smash, recouping its $1 million filming cost in only three days. A string of record singles continued in earnest through 1957, including another big hit in "All Shook Up." Presley's film release schedule was stepped up as rumors of his U.S. Army draft loomed. RCA and Twentieth Century-Fox paired to release three major films in the next two and a half years, including *Loving You* (1957) and *Jailhouse Rock* (1957). Presley's fourth motion picture, *King Creole*, widely regarded as his finest film and a classic of this era, was released in 1958 after he was inducted into the U.S. Army.

After entering the Army on March 24, 1958, Presley served his country as a model soldier mainly in Germany from 1958 until 1960. He was awarded a leave a few months later to be with his sick mother, and on August 14, 1958, Gladys Presley died at age

Presley checking into a U.S. Army base in Friedberg, Germany, where he performed most of his Army service. (AP/Wide World Photos)

forty-six, only one day after Presley's return to Memphis. Throughout Presley's stint in the Army, his manager kept him on the airwaves with timely releases of hits such as "Wear My Ring Around Your Neck," "Hard Headed Woman" and "A Big Hunk O' Love." In 1958 alone, Presley earned more than $2 million.

Impact Presley had unprecedented success in the music industry, establishing benchmarks for the most charted singles (114), the most top-ten singles (38), and the most weeks in the number-one position on the record charts (80). Many of his achievements remained unparalleled in subsequent decades. The importance of Presley in popular music remains incalculable. The most celebrated phenomenon of his era, and for many, the purest embodiment of rock and roll, Presley's personal fusion of black and white musical influences in the 1950's produced some of the finest and most enduring recordings of the century. Presley ushered in a whole new era of American music and popular culture with his unique sound and showmanship, and he possessed a generous spirit and a sense of humor and humility that enhanced his natural charisma and made him a natural performer. His music and style inspired new generations of performers and thousands of imitators who continued to pay tribute to his legacy both as an innovator and as an icon in the decades following the 1950's.

The myriad awards and accolades bestowed on Presley throughout his life and posthumously included fourteen Grammy nominations (three wins) from the National Academy of Recording Arts and Sciences; the Grammy Lifetime Achievement Award, which he received at age thirty-six; and being named one of the Ten Outstanding Men of the Nation for 1970 by the United States Jaycees organization. In 1986, nine years following his death, he was among the first group of inductees into the Rock and Roll Hall of Fame.

Subsequent Events Upon his release from the Army in 1960, Presley resumed his place of prominence in radio, television, and music, releasing a string of five number-one hits during the early 1960's. Though overshadowed by the English invasion and the Beatles, who took hold of American pop culture during the 1960's, Presley managed to reemerge with a December, 1968, television special that has since become one of the most celebrated moments in pop music broadcasting history. Resembling the consummate pop idol of the 1950's, Elvis helped rekindle America's love affair with him by presenting his 1950's classics. He concluded with a passionate delivery of "If I Can Dream." Because of the overwhelming response to his broadcast, Presley undertook his most significant recording in years. With producer Chips Moman overseeing the sessions in January, 1969, Presley recorded in Memphis for the first time since 1955, producing enough material to fill two critically acclaimed albums that featured some of the finest music of his career, including "In the Ghetto," "Don't Cry, Daddy" and "Kentucky Rain." "Suspicious Minds" became his first number-one single since "Good Luck Charm" in 1962 and his last number-one pop hit.

During the late 1960's and through the 1970's, Presley embarked on a series of live performances, particularly in Las Vegas, where he managed to break all existing attendance records. By the mid-1970's, Presley made appearances as an overweight and ostentatiously outfitted performer. His long-term addiction to prescription pain medication caused him to collapse several times on stage. He suffered a fatal heart attack in his Graceland home on August 16, 1977, an event that sparked an outpouring of love and remembrance worldwide. He was forty-two years old.

Further Reading

Flowers, Clare. *The World According to Elvis*. New York: Michael O'Mara Books, 2003. A standard biography of Presley.

Guralnick, Peter. *Last Train to Memphis: The Rise of Elvis Presley*. New York: Little, Brown, 1994. A two-volume work that focuses its attention on Presley's early years as an entertainer, ending its discussion in 1958.

Mason, Bobbie Ann. *Elvis Presley*. New York: Viking Adult, 2002. A personal interpretation of Presley's life by an important novelist that pays considerable attention to his early career.

Nash, Alanna. *The Colonel: The Extraordinary Story of Colonel Tom Parker and Elvis Presley*. New York: Simon & Schuster, 2003. Uses primary documents to uncover surprising details about Parker's life and, in the process, sheds light on Presley's career.

Jan Giel

See also *American Bandstand*; Berry, Chuck; Boone, Pat; Dance, popular; Diddley, Bo; Hairstyles; Lewis, Jerry Lee; Little Richard; Music; Rock and roll; Sullivan, Ed; Top 40 radio; Valens, Ritchie; Youth culture and the generation gap.

■ *Profiles in Courage*

Identification Collection of political essays
Author John F. Kennedy (1917-1963)
Date Published in 1956

This study of American politicians who risked their careers to defend their principles received a Pulitzer Prize in 1957 and helped lift Kennedy to national prominence.

In 1954, John F. Kennedy, then a first-term U.S. senator from Massachusetts, conceived an idea for a magazine article profiling several prominent politicians who took political risks to defend principles that were fundamental to the preservation of the American republic. When a series of back operations during the mid-1950's left Kennedy bedridden, he decided to use his period of convalescence to expand the article idea into a full-length book.

Profiles in Courage was a collection of essays focusing on critical junctures in the careers of eight U.S. politicians in which each had demonstrated exceptional political courage, a quality that Kennedy believed was lacking in many of his contemporaries. Among his subjects were Daniel Webster, who sacrificed a chance to become president by defending the Compromise of 1850, and Robert Taft, a Republican senator who opposed the Nuremberg Trials of Nazi war criminals on legal grounds. The book was published in January of 1956 to much critical acclaim and quickly became a best-seller, winning the Pulitzer Prize for biography in 1957.

Impact The success of *Profiles in Courage* helped establish Kennedy as a nationally known political figure with the potential to become president by dispelling popular perceptions of him as an affable playboy who lacked the initiative and intellectual rigor to hold higher office. This boost to Kennedy's reputation helped re-elect him to the Senate in 1958 and helped provide the basis for his election to the U.S. presidency in 1960.

Further Reading

Dallek, Robert. *An Unfinished Life: John F. Kennedy, 1917-1963.* New York: Little, Brown, 2003. Biography of Kennedy reveals previously unpublished details of his life and career.

Reeves, Richard. *Profile of Power.* New York: Touchstone Books, 1994. Discusses the relevance of *Profiles in Courage* to the Kennedy presidency.

Michael H. Burchett

See also Elections in the United States, midterm; Kennedy, John F.; Literature in the United States.

■ Puerto Rican nationalist attack on Congress

The Event Four Puerto Rican nationalists fired bullets at members of Congress on the floor of the House of Representatives

Date March 1, 1954

As a violent reaction against the creation of the commonwealth of Puerto Rico, the attack on Congress was met with extensive repression of Puerto Rican nationalists and a progressive decline in the popularity of independence as a political option.

On March 1, 1954, four Puerto Rican nationalists—Rafael Cancel Miranda, Andres Figueroa Cordero, Irvin Flores Rodríguez, and Lolita Lebrón—seated themselves as tourists in the visitors' gallery of the U.S. House of Representatives. When Lebrón unfurled the Puerto Rican flag and shouted "Free Puerto Rico now," her comrades fired down upon the floor, wounding five congressmen. Cancel, Figueroa, and Lebrón were immediately apprehended, and Flores was later captured in a bus station.

"I did not come here to kill; I came here to die," Lebrón cried out during the assault. A note in her purse explained that she was willing to give her life to free her homeland from the subjugation of the United States. She denounced the "barbarous torture" of the leader of the Partido Nacionalista, Don Pedro Albizu Campos, who preached that only revolutionary action would lead to Puerto Rican independence.

A cycle of violence and repression had begun in 1935, when three nationalists were killed in a gun battle at the University of Puerto Rico, leading the following year to the assassination of the chief of police and the imprisonment of Albizu. Violence continued on Palm Sunday in 1937, when nineteen nationalists were killed in an unauthorized parade held in Ponce, where Albizu Campos had been born, producing yet another round of assassination and retaliation. In 1950, with the proposal to transform Puerto Rico into a commonwealth, nationalists attacked seven Puerto Rican towns and the governor's official residence and attempted to assassinate U.S. president Harry S. Truman. Albizu was jailed again until he was pardoned by Governor Luis Muñoz Marín in September, 1953, five months before the attack on Congress. Albizu was re-imprisoned until Muñoz Marín pardoned him again in 1964.

Lebrón and her fellow revolutionaries were condemned to life imprisonment by a U.S. court. In 1976, after outgoing U.S. president Gerald Ford suggested that Puerto Rico should be made a state, the revolutionary Armed Forces of National Liberation (FALN) sent letter bombs to federal officials and set off three bombs in Manhattan, New York. When

Police officers removing Lolita Lebrón (center), Andres Figueroa Cordero (in disheveled jacket), and Rafael Cancel Miranda (behind Lebrón) from the Capitol Building, in which they used rifles to fire into a session of the House of Representatives from the visitors' gallery, while shouting "Free Puerto Rico!" A fourth member of the Puerto Rican nationalist group, Irvin Flores Rodríguez, was captured at a bus station. (AP/Wide World Photos)

Figueroa was diagnosed with terminal cancer the following year, it was feared that his death would make a martyr for the Puerto Rican underground, and he was pardoned by President Jimmy Carter. In 1979, with increasing commentary that the imprisoned Puerto Rican nationalists were political prisoners, they were all pardoned and were received warmly upon returning to Puerto Rico.

Impact The assault on Congress did little to advance Puerto Rico toward independence, as it discredited

the use of violence and led to continued repression of nationalists. The Partido Independista Puerto-rriqueño (PIP) swore loyalty to the constitution creating the commonwealth but denounced it as a colonial farce. Ideologically divided between Marxists and militant Roman Catholics, the PIP obtained only 86,386 votes in 1956, and only 24,103 in 1960. In official plebiscites, independence repeatedly decreased in popularity to less than 3 percent of the total vote. Members of the FALN committed some 130 terrorist acts between 1974 and 1983, but most were pardoned eventually by President Bill Clinton.

Further Reading

Fernandez, Ronald. *Prisoners of Colonialism: The Struggle for Justice in Puerto Rico.* Monroe, Maine: Common Courage Press, 1994. A defense of various champions of Puerto Rican independence.

Ribes Tovar, Federico. *A Chronological History of Puerto Rico.* New York: Educational Publishers, 1973. A chronology of Puerto Rican history, including accounts of nationalist revolutionary actions during the decade.

Bland Addison

See also Latin America; Latinos; Puerto Rico as a commonwealth; Truman assassination attempt.

■ Puerto Rico as a commonwealth

The Event Political process that transformed Puerto Rico's colonial status into a "Commonwealth"

Date July 25, 1952

Because Puerto Rico's commonwealth status neither established the island's complete independence nor admitted it as a state of the Union, this ambiguous relationship between the former colony and American power became a festering source of debate.

Public Law 600, signed by President Harry S. Truman on July 3, 1950, launched a political process that led to the declaration of the commonwealth of Puerto Rico on July 25, 1952. The process required two Puerto Rican referenda and a constitutional convention, as well as final congressional approval. The governing statutes, known as the Federal Relations Act of 1952, repealed those aspects of the Jones Act (1917) that dealt with local government and created a new but unclear relationship between the United States and Puerto Rico. Not entirely free of vestiges of colonialism, commonwealth status did not make Puerto Rico independent or a state of the Union.

The idea of a commonwealth was developed by Puerto Rico's first elected governor, Luis Muñoz Marín, who by force of personality and in a compromise solution to the question of political status kept the Partido Popular Democrático (PPD) continually in power from 1949 to 1968. The commonwealth was to be created "in the nature of a compact" between Puerto Rico and the United States, an ambiguous wording that Muñoz Marín interpreted to mean that Puerto Rico had autonomy but not independence. However, both the Senate and House reports stated that Public Law 600 "would not change Puerto Rico's fundamental political, social, and economic relationship to the United States." *Independistas* and *Nacionalistas* charged that the commonwealth solution would not repeal the colonial status deriving from the Treaty of Paris (1898), which had ended the Spanish-American War and recognized the plenary power of Congress over the territory of Puerto Rico. To compound the ambiguity, the Constitutional Assembly formally translated the term "Commonwealth of Puerto Rico" into Spanish as *Estado Libre Asociado de Puerto Rico*, which means "free associated state of Puerto Rico."

Autonomy under the concept of the commonwealth could, however, be viewed favorably by advocates of statehood as at least a step toward ultimate union with the United States, and this interpretation was championed by the Partido Estadista Republicano (PER), which emerged during the mid-1950's. However, members of the Nationalist Party, inspired by the fiery ideology of Pedro Albizu Campos, rejected "autonomy" as only a confirmation of colonial status and reacted violently to the proposal to associate with the United States by attacking seven Puerto Rican towns on October 30, 1950, and attempting to assassinate Muñoz Marín in the governor's official residence. On November 1, two nationalists tried to assassinate Truman in his temporary residence at Blair House in Washington, D.C. In March, 1954, after the commonwealth had been proclaimed and Albizu Campos released from prison, nationalists wounded five American congressmen in an attack upon the U.S. House of Representatives. Repression of nationalist violence and increasing prosperity during the 1950's channeled desires for independence into the political activities of the Partido Independentista Puertorriqueño (PIP).

Internationally, the creation of the commonwealth occurred in the context of increasing Cold War accusations from the Soviet Union that Puerto Rico was an exploited American colony in violation of the Atlantic Charter (1941) and the United Nations Charter (1945). By stressing the nature of the bilateral compact that had established the commonwealth, the United States was released by the General Assembly in November, 1953, from having to report on Puerto Rico as a "non-self-governing territory." Furthermore, to counter charges of economic exploitation, the United States took steps to promote industrialization in Puerto Rico through Operation Bootstrap and made it into a "showcase" for Latin American development. The hardships of the economic transformation from an agricultural to an industrial society during the decade brought a half million Puerto Ricans to seek a better life in the United States, thus tightening the bonds between the two cultures.

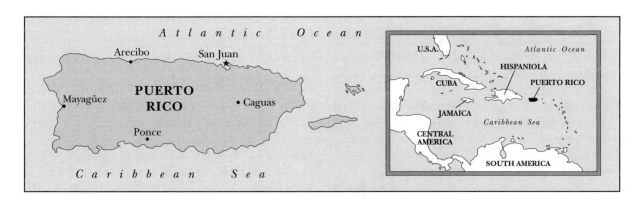

Impact The creation of the commonwealth was an important stage in a century-long effort to associate Puerto Rico with the United States without providing actual statehood. Puerto Ricans—considered American citizens since 1917 and serving as U.S. soldiers in both world wars—sought higher political dignity than being colonial subjects under congressional rule. During the initial years of the commonwealth, Puerto Rico experienced rapid economic growth and increased prosperity but was not able to overcome nagging problems of poverty, unemployment, and crime, which opponents of the Partido Popular Democrático blamed on the failure to achieve either independence or statehood.

Subsequent Events A plebiscite in 1967 asserted a desire for an enhanced commonwealth by 60 percent, while statehood garnered 39 percent of the vote and independence less than 1 percent. However, efforts to extend Puerto Rican sovereignty under the concept of the commonwealth repeatedly failed, and among many limitations, without voting representation in Congress, U.S. laws continued to be applied to the Puerto Rican people without their consent. In a 1993 plebiscite, the commonwealth position won 49 percent of the vote, while the statehood position had advanced to 46 percent, and independence to 4 percent. In a 1998 plebiscite, less than half of one percent voted for commonwealth, only 2.5 percent voted for independence, and 46.5 percent voted for statehood, but by a slim majority, 50.3 percent voted to reject all of the possibilities offered.

Further Reading

Morrales Carrión, Arturo. *Puerto Rico: A Political and Cultural History.* New York: W. W. Norton, 1983. Chapter 14 details the factors leading to the creation of the commonwealth.

Perusse, Roland. *The United States and Puerto Rico: The Struggle for Equality.* Malabar, Fla.: R. E. Krieger, 1990. An analysis of the political concepts involved in the creation of the commonwealth, and subsequent attempts to modify its structure.

Trías Monge, José. *Puerto Rico: The Trials of the Oldest Colony in the World.* New Haven, Conn.: Yale University Press, 1997. A balanced critique of the limitations of commonwealth status, the historical factors leading to its creation, and the ongoing debate about its future by the distinguished former chief justice of Puerto Rico.

Bland Addison

See also Alaska statehood; Congress, U.S.; Hawaii statehood; Latin America; Latinos; Puerto Rican nationalist attack on Congress; Truman assassination attempt; *West Side Story.*

■ Pulp magazines

Definition Inexpensive periodicals printed on untrimmed seven-by-ten-inch pulpwood paper, featuring lurid stories in such genres as adventure, Western, romance, crime, fantasy, horror, and science fiction

After a fifty-year period when pulp magazines provided millions of Americans with entertaining, escapist reading, most of these publications failed during the 1950's, mainly as a result of competition from paperback books, comic books, and television.

From their origin at the end of the nineteenth century to their demise during the 1950's, the mass-market magazines called "pulps" became the chief form of recreational reading for many North Americans. Most scholars of popular culture trace the beginning of pulp magazines to 1896, when publisher Frank Munsey changed *The Argosy* from a boy's magazine specializing in inspirational stories by writers such as Horatio Alger to a low-priced periodical for young adults concentrating on adventure stories. The new approach worked, and by the early twentieth century, *Argosy* was selling a half-million copies per month. Other publishers, particularly Street and Smith, profited from Munsey's example, and they starting pioneering new markets by specializing with such pulps as *Western Story, Detective Story, Love Story,* and *Sport Story.* Writers such as Edgar Allan Poe, Arthur Conan Doyle, Robert Louis Stevenson, and H. Rider Haggard had already developed these genres, but pulp writers, most of whom earned two cents a word or even less, needed to churn out much material quickly in order to make a living, which resulted in stories with conventional characters and formulaic plots. Some famous pulp writers were Edgar Rice Burroughs, who created the character of Tarzan in 1912, and Frederick Schiller Faust, who wrote hundreds of Western stories under the name of Max Brand.

By the 1920's, pulp magazines had become standardized: 128 pages containing several short stories and one or two novelettes. Their covers, printed in color on coated stock, were often tantalizing to catch a potential reader's attention at the newsstand. Not all pulps catered to the mass market. Some, such as *Weird Tales* and *Black Mask*, generated small but passionate followings, and these magazines also offered apprenticeships for many new American writers. For example, *Weird Tales* published stories by writers such as Robert Bloch, August Derleth, Fritz Leiber, and Ray Bradbury. Tennessee Williams published his first story, "The Vengeance of Nitocris," in *Weird Tales* in 1928. Such "hard-boiled" detective writers as Dashiell Hammett, Carroll John Daly, and Raymond Chandler perfected their styles, characters, and plots while writing for *Black Mask* and other pulps. These magazines peaked in popularity during the mid-1930's, when more than ten million readers, one of whom was President Franklin D. Roosevelt, regularly purchased copies from the selection of two hundred kinds of pulps either by subscription or at newsstands. The magazines' stories about heroes overcoming harrowing difficulties provided a theme with which many people in the Depression could identify. Some genres gave readers other worlds into which they could escape. For example, Hugo Gernsback, a former electrical engineer and inventor, founded *Amazing Stories* in 1926, and by 1930, when he named this new genre "science fiction," his magazine had reached a circulation of 100,000.

The Pulps' Demise World War II marked the beginning of the end of pulp magazines. Readers and writers became involved in the war effort, and publishers were confronted with paper shortages and a breakdown in their distribution systems. Increased production costs continued into the postwar years, when certain enterprising publishers mass merchandized twenty-five-cent paperback books, causing a deep decline in pulp magazine sales. The war also created a new audience, more sophisticated than Depression readers. These new readers were eager to explore entertainment in the new medium of television.

By 1950, pulp magazines were no longer a significant form of popular diversion. Young people were reading comic books, and young adults were reading paperbacks. Both young and old were watching television, whose shows were often based on Western, crime, adventure, mystery, and detective stories that had been developed earlier by pulp writers. In fact, characters who had become familiar through serializations in the pulps now appeared on television: Detective characters Sam Spade, Philip Marlow, Perry Mason, and Nick Carter are examples.

Another serious competitor of the pulps was the "slick" magazine, so-called because it was printed on high-quality glossy paper. These magazines, such as the *Saturday Evening Post*, published both nonfiction and fiction and were attractively illustrated. Some pulp writers moved to the more lucrative pulps during the 1950's. Others began writing for publishers of paperbacks, whose sales were so large during the 1950's and 1960's that their numbers were greater than all the books that had been published in the period since the invention of movable type.

Although most pulp magazines ceased publication by the early 1950's, a small number struggled on. For example, adventure stories, a staple of the early pulps, continued to be written and read. William Coleman Tuttle had, for three decades, published a series of stories combining the adventure, mystery, and Western genres in *Adventure Magazine*. This series, which featured Hashknife Hartley, a picaresque cowboy who solved mysteries for the fun of it, lasted into the early 1950's. Pure pulp Westerns also continued to be published, though with declining readers, before meeting their end during the 1960's. As the Western pulps declined and died, writers and publishers sought reasons for their lost readership. Some cited competition from the commercial slicks and television, while others blamed publishers who compromised the genre by combining it with alien forms such as, for example, the "soap horse opera" in the pulps *Ranch Romances* and *Romantic Range*.

Television helped to keep the plots and characters of the traditional pulp Westerns in the public eye. In the second half of the 1950's, for example, more than thirty Western series appeared on television, many of them based on pulp approaches, but others, such as *Gunsmoke* and *The Rifleman*, formed a new genre, the "adult Western." So powerful was television that the only Western pulps to survive the 1950's were a few magazines that anthologized old stories.

Some detective pulps managed to survive into the 1950's, including *Black Mask*, although it became a bimonthly and subsequently was incorporated into *Ellery Queen's Mystery Magazine*, which for several years reprinted old stories by pulp mystery writers. *Detective Story*, *Detective Tales*, and *Mystery Magazine* were also commercially marketable for a while, but, like other specialized pulps, they encountered increasing competition from paperbacks, television, motion pictures, slick magazines, and even the weekly mystery in some newspapers. Some mystery writers for the pulps made the transition into this new environment by writing scripts for television and contributing to the outpouring of novels that ushered in what critics would later call the golden age of mystery writing. However, others failed to make this transition. For example, after writing stories that proved very popular during the 1920's and 1930's, Carroll John Daly encountered increasing difficulties during the 1940's and 1950's as pulp markets waned. He tried changing his style, and he even left New York for California, where he hoped to become a television writer, but he met with rejection. He died in 1958, destitute and forgotten.

Popularity of Science Fiction The one specialized pulp genre that did not die with the others was science fiction. Fans of this genre were passionate about their pulp magazines, and they formed fan clubs and fanzines, or amateur magazines that kept their enthusiasms alive and growing. During the early 1950's, more than twenty-five science-fiction pulp magazines existed, including such new ventures as *Galaxy Science Fiction*, edited by Herbert Gold, and the *Magazine of Fantasy and Science Fiction*, edited by Anthony Boucher. Fans also pressured publishers into reissuing classic pulp stories from earlier periods. Their enduing popularity was proved when, by the end of the twentieth century, new and old science-fiction novels formed a significant percentage—some say 25 percent—of all novels published. The new science-fiction readers tended to be different from earlier readers of the 1930's. Though they were still predominantly young and male, they were now better educated and wealthier. These readers were better able to appreciate scientific ideas, sophisticated plots, complex characterizations, and stylistic brilliance. Some science-fiction writers who exhibited these traits became prominent during the 1950's, including Ray Bradbury, whose *Martian Chronicles* (1950), *Fahrenheit 451* (1953), and many other works made him one of the world's best-selling science-fiction writers.

Impact By the 1950's, the golden age of pulp fiction was over, with a residue of scattered, specialized pulps that were diminishing in numbers and readers. Though attempts, mainly nostalgic, to revive such pulps as *Weird Tales* and *Black Mask* occurred, these efforts came to naught. The pulps' time had come and gone. For a few decades, pulps had been the chief entertainment for millions of Americans. During their heyday, literary critics paid little attention to these very popular magazines whose writings were, for them, close to worthless. Theodore Sturgeon, a pulp writer, once responded to this criticism by admitting, "Sure, 90 percent of science fiction is crud. That's because 90 percent of everything is crud." (Sturgeon is usually quoted as having used the word "crap," instead of "crud.") It is true that, like most magazines, the pulps contained material that varied greatly in quality, much of it reprehensibly inept. However, some pulp stories have withstood the test of time, and critics now consider them as classic American literature.

The pulps also provided the necessary experience for many young writers who went on to make significant literary contributions: Williams became a distinguished playwright, and Hammett proved that detective stories could be serious works of art. Although pulp publishers and writers wanted to make money rather than create literature, many scholars consider pulp magazines as an important part of American cultural history. Pulp stories reflected the society in which they were written. When the pulps were most popular, during the 1930's, Americans were suffering through the Depression, seeking release from a disheartening world. The improved economy of the 1950's created new needs that were satisfied by new forms of entertainment.

Though pulp magazines died out, the genre lived on in other forms in subsequent decades. Hollywood director Quentin Tarantino deliberately titled one of his most successful films *Pulp Fiction* (1994), since he made use of pulp plot devices, characters, and style. Furthermore, plays, films, comics, and other media continued to take advantage of such pulp characters as Tarzan, Sam Spade, and Zorro. American culture certainly changed during the 1950's and afterward, but the emotions on which pulp writers capitalized continued to be very much a part of human nature.

Further Reading

Dinan, John A. *The Pulp Western: A Popular History of the Western Fiction Magazine.* San Bernardino, Calif.: Borgo Press, 1983. This monograph, part of the series Studies in the Philosophy and Criticism of Literature, analyzes the significance of "this most maligned of literatures." Illustrations and index.

Goldstone, Tony. *The Pulps: Fifty Years of American Pop Culture.* New York: Bonanza Books, 1970. This anthology contains representative examples of stories from many genres. A helpful survey history of a century of pulp fiction begins the book, which also has introductions to each of the genres.

Goulart, Ron. *An Informal History of the Pulp Magazines.* New York: Ace Books, 1972. Paperback reprint of a work originally titled *Cheap Thrills* that analyzes popular fiction from the dime novels of the nineteenth century to the paperbacks of the late twentieth century, with an emphasis on the period between the two world wars.

Tebbel, John, and Mary Ellen Zuckerman. *The Magazine in America: 1741-1990.* New York: Oxford University Press, 1991. The authors explore pulp fiction in chapters on "Developing the Mass Market" and "Pulps and Science Fiction."

Robert J. Paradowski

See also Book publishing; Comic books; Fads; *Fahrenheit 451*; Literature in Canada; Literature in the United States; *MAD*; *Saturday Evening Post*; Spillane, Mickey; Television in Canada; Television in the United States; Television Westerns.

■ Racial discrimination

The 1950's was a watershed period in racial discrimination in the United States. During that decade, efforts to combat racial discrimination that had begun to gain momentum during the 1920's reached their height, following a liberal wind of change that swept across the country.

Although racial discrimination violates the principles of equality enshrined in the U.S. Constitution, the history of the United States is replete with examples of overt racial discrimination practiced by the white majority. Racial and ethnic discrimination has generally been related to patterns of immigration and migration, particularly in the flow of newcomers to northern cities. Immigrants and migrants to the cities have, as groups, tended to occupy the lowest social and economic levels—a fact that has contributed to the discrimination practiced against them.

During the late nineteenth century, southern states circumvented the Fifteenth Amendment, which guaranteed African American men the right to vote, by inventing devices such as poll taxes, grandfather clauses, and literacy tests to bar former slaves and their descendants from the ballot box. Racial discrimination was not, however, directed only against African Americans. Asians and Latinos were also discriminated against. For example, Chinese laborers who arrived in Hawaii and California to work on farms and in mines, were often resented by white workers, who felt threatened by their willingness to work for lower wages. Discriminatory federal immigration laws later limited the numbers of Asians who could immigrate to the United States.

Other forms of discrimination prevailed in the delivery of public services, education, housing, transportation, and virtually all aspects of life. Even the nation's capital city, Washington, D.C., was not immune. There, the federal government itself operated racially segregated schools and provided separate eating and working places for its African American civil servants. Public facilities, including rest rooms, were marked "White Only" and "Colored," and the U.S. military services remained racially segregated. However, a wind of change began to blow through the United States in the 1950's during the postwar industrialization that fostered migration from the South to the North and from villages to towns and cities.

Roots and Forms of Racial Discrimination Although the post-Civil War Fourteenth and Fifteenth Amendments to the Constitution were clear on the rights of African Americans to full citizenship, it soon became evident that some segments of American society were unwilling to extend the full rights of citizenship to former slaves and their descendants. Jim Crow laws in southern states institutionalized segregation in almost every aspect of life. Racial discrimination was also practiced outside the South, but in northern states it was generally enforced by custom, rather than by law.

The McCarran-Walter Act of 1952 was designed to eliminate racial discrimination from immigration laws. However, although the law ended the so-called Asiatic Barred Zone, it also limited immigration from what was referred to as the Asia-Pacific Triangle to only two thousand persons per year. Moreover, the law included all immigrants of Asian descent in that quota, even if they were native residents or citizens of Western nations. The restriction applied exclusively to Asians and remained in force until more sweeping immigration reforms were enacted during the 1960's.

The Liberal Revolution The changes in postwar American society during the mid-twentieth century were tumultuous. A scarcity of labor triggered by restrictions on European immigration during the 1920's resulted in a labor shortage that contributed to drawing African Americans to large urban centers. At the same time, new technologies in agriculture were enabling farmers to mechanize their operations, thereby helping to drive black farmworkers to seek employment in the cities. The growing migration of rural African Americans to cities increased urban congestion, poverty, and racial tensions. Meanwhile, whites tended to move away from city centers to suburban areas. In 1950, 43 percent of African Americans lived in central metropolitan areas, and that figure steadily rose during the 1950's.

During the 1930's, as the Great Depression eroded the prosperity of the previous decade, Americans welcomed the relief provided by President Franklin D. Roosevelt's New Deal programs. The New Deal not only addressed economic issues but also provided a legislative framework for dismantling segregated institutions and extending political rights to members of minority groups that carried over into the 1950's. After Democratic president Harry S. Truman won the 1948 election, his administration seized the opportunity to intensify domestic reforms. In his inaugural address, he called for a "Fair Deal" that was essentially an extension of Roosevelt's New Deal. After Republican Dwight D. Eisenhower was elected president in 1952, his administration continued many of the previous administration's economic and social reforms as a matter of political exigency while Democrats retained majorities in the House of Representatives and Senate.

During the mid-1950's, Lyndon B. Johnson, the Democratic majority leader in the Senate, persuaded both Republicans and northern and western Democrats to accept a limited civil rights bill designed primarily to protect the voting rights of African Americans. Southern senators permitted the measure to pass without a filibuster. The resulting Civil Rights Act of 1957 created a bipartisan Commission on Civil Rights with power to subpoena witnesses and authority to investigate violations of voting rights. It also provided for a new assistant attorney general to initiate civil rights suits in federal district courts. To most observers, the 1957 law—the first civil rights act since 1875—was a landmark.

Meanwhile, the appointment of Earl Warren as chief justice, brought an additional boost to the reform movement. President Eisenhower appointed the Republican former governor of California to the post, thinking him a conservative on social issues, but was stunned by Warren's ideological shift. During his tenure as chief justice, Warren expressed deep concern for civil rights and liberties and worked to extend the role of the Court in social reform. During the early 1950's, the Supreme Court ruled that no citizen could be excluded from voting in state primaries or from serving on juries on ac-

count of race; that restrictive covenants—agreements by sellers of houses not to sell to persons of certain races or religions—were not permissible; and that segregation in interstate transportation and public recreational facilities was illegal.

Civil Rights Struggles The Civil Rights movement of the 1950's and 1960's helped promote the passage of important legislation. Supreme Court decisions and regulations of federal agencies also contributed greatly to fighting discrimination. Spearheading the struggle against Jim Crow in the courts was the legal team of the Legal Defense Fund of the National Association for the Advancement of Colored People (NAACP), which included such Howard University-trained attorneys as future Supreme Court justice Thurgood Marshall. The NAACP's initial strategy was to test the separate-but-equal principle established in the Supreme Court's 1896 *Plessy v. Ferguson* ruling by demanding that separate facilities truly be equal. By the late 1940's, the NAACP was shifting its focus to challenge segregation in education. After winning a case that forced the University of Texas Law School to admit a black student, in *Sweatt v. Painter* (1950), the NAACP legal team took on segregation in public schools. Challenges to segregated school systems in Kansas, South Carolina, and Virginia led to the Supreme Court's landmark ruling in *Brown v. Board of Education* in 1954. The Court's unanimous ruling finally reversed the separate-but-equal principle by unequivocally stating that "in the field of public education the doctrine of 'separate but equal' has no place" because segregated schools are "inherently unequal." The decision held that the plaintiffs were in fact "deprived of the equal protection of the laws guaranteed by the Fourteenth Amendment."

Despite the Supreme Court's clear ruling against school segregation, it would take some years for the decision to be fully implemented. However, by 1957, school desegregation was well advanced in the federally administered District of Columbia and in neighboring states. Efforts at desegregation were also underway in North Carolina, Tennessee, Arkansas, and Texas, and the majority of the formerly all-white public colleges and universities in the South were starting to admit African Americans.

By contrast, the *Brown* decision was meeting a well-orchestrated program of white resistance in Virginia and states in the Deep South. Southern state legislatures denounced the ruling as unconstitutional and mandated that their public schools would be closed if they had to be desegregated. In September 1957, the first overt defiance of court-ordered desegregation took place in Little Rock, Arkansas, where President Eisenhower had to send in federal troops to supervise a high school's integration. However, segregationist strongholds eventually began to crumble. In 1959, Virginia finally allowed its local schools boards to obey federal court orders if they wished to keep their public schools open. Georgia's legislature followed by permitting limited desegregation in Atlanta. By 1961, only South Carolina, Alabama, and Mississippi still resisted school desegregation.

Impact The social reforms of the 1950's were brought about by a combination of factors: postwar industrialization that drove African Americans to northern cities, legal pressure from the NAACP, and a willingness of the Supreme Court to help force social change. The fact that the changes that occurred were rapidly absorbed into existing institutions bears testimony to the capacity of the American social-political system to accommodate change within its established norms and founding instruments.

Further Reading

Berman, William C. *The Politics of Civil Rights in the Truman Administration.* Columbus: Ohio State University Press, 1970. Review of the issues and politics of civil rights under the Truman administration as they relate to the growing political influence of African Americans in the Democratic Party.

Fix, Michael, and Raymond Struyk, eds. *Clear and Convincing Evidence.* Washington, D.C.: Urban Institute, 1993. Important contribution to the debate over the continuing existence and nature of discrimination in American society, especially in the areas of housing and employment.

Hamilton, Dona Cooper, and Charles V. Hamilton. *The Dual Agenda.* New York: Columbia University Press, 1997. This book replaces existing ideology with historical analysis demonstrating the consequences of race-based opposition to civil rights and social welfare and its impact on the quality of life for the entire nation.

Irons, Peter. *Jim Crow's Children: The Broken Promises of the "Brown" Decision.* New York: Penguin, 2004. Study of desegregation during the 1950's that characterizes the period as one of slow, misdirected, and ultimately flawed progress for African Americans in education.

Raffel, Jeffrey. *Historical Dictionary of School Segregation and Desegregation: The American Experience.* Westport, Conn.: Greenwood Press, 1998. Encyclopedic reference work on school segregation and desegregation.

Weisbrot, Robert. *Freedom Bound: A History of America's Civil Rights Movement.* New York: Penguin, 1991. Fine comprehensive history of the Civil Rights movement.

Austin Ogunsuyi

See also Asian Americans; California's Alien Land Laws; Civil Rights Act of 1957; Civil Rights movement; Commission on Civil Rights; Interracial marriage laws; Jewish Americans; Ku Klux Klan; Latinos; Minorities in Canada; Native Americans; Till lynching; Vinson, Fred M.; White Citizens' Councils.

■ Radio

Definition Wireless mode of audio communication developed during the 1920's that provides listeners with a variety of entertainment and information programming

Despite the rising success of television during the 1950's, radio still proved popular, especially with new programming formats designed to emphasize radio's informative and service-oriented nature.

During the early 1950's, radio remained an amazing invention. With a simple twist of the dial, a listener could tune in the greatest personalities in world affairs and show business. Radio brought current events and entertainment directly into homes and cars. Listeners could hear their favorite comedy programs and entertainers, such as *Amos and Andy,* Jack Benny, and George Burns and Gracie Allen, or their favorite music programs, such as *Arthur Godfrey's Talent Scouts,* and musicians, such as Bing Crosby and Gene Autry. Other programs, such as the courtroom drama *Perry Mason,* the detective series *Dragnet,* the soap opera *The Guiding Light,* and the Western *The Lone Ranger* still made up the bulk of radio's programming in 1950, but this type of format would quickly change.

Television Competition The golden age of radio began to fade during the 1950's with more Americans turning to television for their main source of entertainment. Television advanced rapidly during its first nine years of commercial existence. In a short time, television preempted radio as the preferred source for dramas, sports, soap operas, variety programming, comedies, Westerns, and children's shows. By the end of the 1950's, network radio had become a supplementary, secondary entertainment source as most of its programming, talent, advertising revenue, and ratings shifted to television. To survive the impact of television, radio had to find a new niche where it could best serve the public.

At first many considered television a complement to radio broadcasting, calling it "sight radio," "radio vision," or "radio moving pictures." However, with the massive shift of radio programs to television, what had begun as "sight radio" began to destroy its "hearing-only" competition. Many well-known radio personalities such as Milton Berle, Ed Sullivan, Fred Allen, Jack Benny, George Burns, and Gracie Allen began appearing on television. Several radio series–*The Lone Ranger, The Original Amateur Hour,* and *Break the Bank*—became television series. By 1950, some of the best television programs—*The Goldbergs, Suspense, Arthur Godfrey's Talent Scouts, The Life of Riley,* and *Stop the Music!*—came directly from network radio, several continuing to feature the same sponsors and stars. For example, after fifteen years on radio, *Your Hit Parade* brought the week's top popular songs to television; the radio quiz show *Truth or Consequences* and its ten-year host, Ralph Edwards, also switched to television as did the radio comedy *Your Show of Shows,* starring Sid Caesar.

The impact of television on radio became even more apparent when television began its daytime programming. Soap operas, radio's last principal form of nonmusic entertainment, followed the comedies, Westerns, and dramas to the rival medium— *The Guiding Light* in 1952, *Valiant Lady* in 1953, and *Portia Faces Life* in 1954. Even new television soap operas, such as *Search for Tomorrow, Love of Life,* and *Hankins Falls,* resembled in format the radio soap opera.

By the 1950's, radio, which had become accustomed to being the primary entertainment medium in American households, had to be satisfied with television's "leftovers"—listeners who did not own television sets, those who did not like the television programs being offered, and automobile listeners. With the loss of its advertisers, ratings, talent,

Walter Winchell in 1955. (Hulton Archive I by Getty Images)

and nonmusic programming to the televised medium, radio had to reinvent itself if it hoped to survive.

Innovations in Radio Programming In November, 1950, NBC radio tried to offset television's impact on radio audiences by introducing *The Big Show,* a lavish ninety-minute Sunday evening variety program that featured the biggest stars in show business, including Groucho Marx, Ethel Barrymore, Jimmy Durante, and Fred Allen. *The Big Show* originated in New York and offered each week a lineup of talent drawn from stage, screen, nightclubs, and recordings. Broadway stars performed scenes from their hit plays and musicals. Despite good talent and good ratings, *The Big Show* proved to be too expensive to produce and was canceled after two seasons, succumbing to the growing popularity of *The Ed Sullivan Show* on television, which was well on its way to becoming a national institution.

In 1951, radio networks resorted to big-name stars to attract audiences away from television. NBC had Hollywood actor Cary Grant and his real-life wife, Betsy Drake, in the comedy *Mr. and Mrs. Blandings*. Humphrey Bogart and Lauren Bacall starred in *Bold Venture*, which was syndicated to more than four hundred markets. In 1952, the top evening network radio shows continued to include favorite personalities, including Jack Benny, Walter Winchell, Bing Crosby, and Gene Autry.

Radio also tried to regain the audience it had lost to television with adult series in science fiction and Westerns—genres that had traditionally been children's fare in radio. NBC radio's *Dimension X* and *X Minus One* presented serious science fiction based on stories by leading writers in the field. CBS radio focused on the adult Western with *Gunsmoke* in 1952. CBS later introduced *Fort Laramie, Luke Slaughter of Tombstone, Frontier Gentleman*, and as late as 1958, an adaptation of the television series *Have Gun, Will Travel*. NBC radio also experimented with adult Westerns with *Dr. Six-Gun* and Jimmy Stewart's *The Six-Shooter*. Radio detective dramas became more sophisticated and informative. Police dramas such as *Dragnet, Broadway Is My Beat*, and *Twenty-First Precinct* painted a grim, unglamorous picture of law enforcement in an urban context. Private investigator programs such as *Yours Truly, Johnny Dollar*, and *Night Beat* also highlighted heroes operating within an adult environment.

In the waning days of the radio drama during the 1950's, the networks still produced several dramatic series such as *NBC Star Playhouse, Philco Playhouse*, and *Your Nutrilite Radio Theater*. Radio networks' last attempts at substantive radio drama consisted of NBC's *Your Radio Theater*, a fifty-five minute showcase that featured well-known plays, and CBS's revival of *The CBS Radio Workshop*. Touted as "dedicated to man's imagination—the theater of the mind," *The CBS Radio Workshop* featured the network's finest talents performing a series of unsponsored, experimental, one-of-a-kind broadcasts for a twenty-month run before signing off for the last time at the end of 1957.

Despite these programming efforts, radio could not compete with the sights and sounds of television. The December, 1955, Nielsen ratings did not list a single evening radio program among its top ten programs. The most popular evening radio show was *Dragnet*, which was tied for fourteenth place, well behind the soap operas and variety shows of daytime radio. In 1960, network radio finally abandoned its attempt to compete with television in family enter-

tainment programming and the two last survivors of the great days of radio went off the air: *Amos and Andy* (airing since 1928) and *National Barn Dance* (airing since 1932).

Radio's Transformation The key to radio's transformation and economic survival was its ability to do better those things that television could not do. Radio concentrated on its portability—something television could not match. Using the slogan "Radio—your constant companion," radio promoted mobility and intimacy. With its mobility, radio could provide more frequent on-the-spot news coverage, and the vast car-radio audience began to receive special attention with innovative, immediate programming, such as frequent traffic condition reports. Radio listening did not require audiences' complete attention. Therefore, radio was able to keep the interest of housewives as they cleaned and of families as they ate or were out for a drive.

Radio networks and independent radio stations created more service programming of the kind television could not do well: programs for the beach, automobile, restaurants, shops, factories, and elevators. These programs focused on music, foreign-language audiences, sports, and local news and entertainment. Radio sought out new audiences in the hours when most television stations had signed off the air. Midnight-to-dawn programs flourished, especially in big cities with listeners who stayed up late.

For the most part, recorded music was the mainstay for the radio industry. The 1950's saw an increase in the number of independent radio stations that specialized in classical music and other sophisticated material. Usually broadcasting on FM, classical stations often attracted the attention of high-fidelity sound enthusiasts. Classical music was not the only music genre radio used to reinvent itself in the face of the growing popularity of television. Rock-and-roll music was becoming popular in American culture. Musicians such as Bo Diddley, Chuck Berry, and Elvis Presley helped radio find another niche to serve the public by providing listeners with an innovative rock-and-roll music format.

The Top 40 Format and Disc Jockeys In 1955, a recording by a pop music group called Bill Haley and His Comets became the number-one radio play. The group's hit song "Rock Around the Clock" ushered in the era of rock-and-roll music on radio and, with it, a new audience that would prove to be radio's economic salvation. The Top 40 music format marked the beginning of a long relationship between radio and the recording industry: Radio and the music industry depended upon each other for their economic survival. The recording industry produced the popular, youth-oriented music radio needed, and radio, in turn, provided the necessary exposure to create a market for the music. From the recording industry's perspective, radio was the perfect promotional vehicle for showcasing its established and up-and-coming artists.

The simple radio announcer who played phonograph records soon became a disc jockey, who had a huge following of fans attracted to him because of his personality and the music he played. The format of the disc jockey show—music and patter—made it ideal for spot advertising in the midst of playing records. With the demise of "live" music on radio, the disc jockeys had a huge influence on the music industry. As the role of rock and roll and local programming continued to grow, so did the role of the disc jockey. In 1959, there were between fifteen hundred and two thousand record companies, turning out 50 to 250 new records each week. Because of their influence in record promotion, by the end of the 1950's, disc jockeys had become the recipients of impressive—but at times unethical—perks.

Payola and Plugola Scandals Job-related dividends—called "payola"—included cash for playing certain records to make them hits as well as expensive gifts and stock in record companies. At the same time, there were accusations of "plugola"—when disc jockeys or show hosts accepted gifts or cash from companies in exchange for the mention ("plug") on radio programs of particular products, while the stations received no remuneration.

Disc jockeys' involvement in payola and plugola came under public scrutiny shortly after the 1958 television quiz show scandals. Federal Communication Commission (FCC) hearings and congressional investigations in 1959 and much of 1960 revealed that a large number of disc jockeys, including some of the most respected ones, took bribes in exchange for promoting certain records. In November, 1959, the House Subcommittee on Legislative Oversight began an investigation into the allegations of plugola and payola on radio and discovered unethical radio station activities all over the country. Testi-

mony before a Senate Commerce subcommittee in 1958 revealed that in order for songs to get radio airtime, record producers had to pay disc jockeys in cash; some disc jockeys made $300 to $500 a week above their annual salaries of $25,000 to $50,000.

In December, 1958, the Federal Trade Commission (FTC) formally charged RCA, London Records, and Bernard Lowe, Inc., as well as six distributors in Philadelphia and Cleveland, with bribing disc jockeys. Although it admitted no guilt, RCA reached a consent agreement with the FTC and agreed to stop paying disc jockeys to play RCA records unless the listening public was told that the station or the disc jockey had been paid to play the record. In the wake of the scandals, the FCC started its own sweeping investigation by ordering all 5,326 radio and television licensees (including educational broadcast stations) to report on all programs and commercials broadcast after November 1, 1958, for which their employees received payments of money or gifts not identified over the air. In addition, the National Association of Broadcasters toughened its ethics code, banning payola and plugola.

The Radio News Documentary Radio broadcasting had originated in news, and by the 1950's, as radio searched for new ways to retain audiences, it returned to news. The war in Korea increased news audiences and restored radio's role in journalism. Because the June, 1950, Korea invasion occurred on a Sunday, a day without afternoon newspapers, radio gained a war news exclusive. Radio coverage of the Korean War eradicated the usual summer slump in radio ratings and encouraged increased sponsorship of news shows. A special Hoover study (the precursor to the Nielsen ratings) for July 5-11, 1950, showed a 63 percent increase in listeners for network radio news programs.

In June, 1955, NBC introduced *Monitor,* a weekend news magazine with the flexibility of network programming along with both local and national spot advertising. From Saturday mornings until Sunday evenings, listeners heard forty hours of news, features, music, comedy, and interviews. *Monitor* represented a new concept in radio with its combination of interviews, remote pick-ups, comedy briefs, music, and news.

The perfection of the tape recorder in the late 1940's made it practical for radio to include the voices of newsmakers in its programs, and the radio documentary became a successful program form during the 1950's. Radio documentaries ranged in focus from studies of gambling and illegal immigration from Mexico to narcotics and the threat of organized crime. On December 15, 1950, CBS radio launched *Hear It Now*, considered to be an ambitious innovation of the radio documentary. Produced and written by the CBS team of Edward R. Murrow and Fred W. Friendly, *Hear It Now* was patterned after a series of successful record albums also produced by Murrow and Friendly. Narrated by Murrow, the *I Can Hear It Now* albums brought voices of newsmakers of the prior thirty years into the homes of millions. The radio venture wanted to follow the same path for current newsmakers by creating, in Friendly's words, "pictures for the ear." On the premier program, listeners heard actual interviews from Korea, Montana, and New York. Broadcast during prime time on Friday nights, *Hear It Now* enjoyed immediate popularity and received a Peabody Award after its first few months on the air. NBC and ABC quickly imitated the *Hear It Now* format with their own news magazine programs. *Hear It Now* eventually gave way to television. After leaving the air in June, 1951, it reappeared five months later as a CBS televised series, *See It Now*.

Impact Radio did not die out at the end of the 1950's as many had predicted it would. Rather, it experienced a metamorphosis, becoming once again an influential communication medium. By 1959, radio had lost to television the programming that had made it so popular during the 1930's and 1940's. However, by the end of the 1950's, radio had discovered new and innovative programming that played to its strengths of portability and immediacy. In 1959, the United States had about 156 million radio receivers—more than three times the number of television sets. Automobiles accounted for 26 percent of these radios while the rest were in homes. Radio began to draw audiences as large as ever at times when television could not be viewed comfortably. The medium always had reflected the values and realities of its environment, and by 1960, it reflected a mobile, affluent, and commercialized American society that was committed to television for its creative amusement but still turned to radio for music and instantaneous information.

Further Reading

Blue, Howard. *Words at War: World War II Era Radio Drama and the Postwar Broadcasting Industry Blacklist.* Landham, Md.: Scarecrow Press, 2002. History of American radio broadcasting during World War II and the subsequent Cold War era.

Cox, Jim. *Say Goodnight, Gracie: The Last Years of Network Radio.* Jefferson, N.C.: McFarland, 2002. Gives a good account of radio's history, from the fading of radio's golden age during the 1950's through its post-golden years of the 1960's.

Douglas, Susan. *Listening In: Radio and the American Imagination.* New York: Times Books, 1999. In-depth cultural history of radio.

The First Fifty Years of Broadcasting: The Running Story of the Fifth Estate. Washington, D.C.: Broadcasting, 1982. Detailed history of the first fifty years of broadcasting as told through the more than two thousand issues of *Broadcasting* magazine.

Hilliard, Robert, and Michael C. Keith. *The Broadcast Century: A Biography of American Broadcasting.* 3d ed. Boston: Focal Press, 2001. History of broadcast media, including coverage of the anticommunist blacklists of the 1950's.

Hilmes, Michele. *Radio Voices: American Broadcasting, 1922-1952.* Minneapolis: University of Minnesota Press, 1997. Sociological study of radio as part of the U.S. culture.

Keith, Michael C., ed. *Talking Radio: An Oral History of American Radio in the Television Age.* Armonk, N.Y.: M. E. Sharpe, 2000. Nearly one hundred former radio personalities and reporters review American radio after World War II and the development of television.

Maltin, Leonard. *The Great American Broadcast: A Celebration of Radio's Golden Age.* New York: Penguin Putnam, 1997. History of radio's achievements using interviews with many of radio's leading personalities from the 1940's and 1950's.

Sterling, Christopher H., ed. *The Museum of Broadcast Communications Encyclopedia of Radio.* New York: Fitzroy Dearborn, 2004. Contains more than six hundred entries related to radio history, including *Amos and Andy*, Jack Benny, Bing Crosby, and *The Lone Ranger.*

Eddith A. Dashiell

See also *Amos and Andy*; Canadian Broadcasting Corporation; Communications in Canada; Freed, Alan; Linkletter, Art; Murrow, Edward R.; Music; Mutual Broadcasting System scandal; Radio Free Europe; Rock and roll; Television in the United States; Television soap operas; Top 40 radio.

■ Radio Free Europe

Identification U.S. radio station that broadcast
    propaganda to Eastern Europe
Date Started broadcasting in 1950

*Radio Free Europe (RFE) served as a U.S. government
short-wave broadcasting service to Eastern Europe and was
established as a front for the Central Intelligence Agency
(CIA) to promote democratic values and institutions to
countries behind the Iron Curtain during the Cold War era.*

Radio Free Europe was a short-wave service that was
incorporated in 1949 as the broadcast division of the
National Committee for a Free Europe (NCFE) and
was designed to deliver local news and features to
East European countries from transmitters in Germany. NCFE was established by former Office of
Strategic Services officers as a CIA-front organiza-
tion, and its existence was originally kept not only
from the American people but also from the press
and the U.S. Congress. It began its broadcasts on
July 4, 1950, with a program beamed to Czechoslovakia from the Lamperthein transmitter site in Germany.

Crusade for Freedom, a fund-raising project of
the American Heritage Foundation, was also a cover
for NCFE activities, which enabled it to appear as a
popular movement. Both NCFE (under the motto
"To Halt Communism and Save Freedom") and Crusade for Freedom ("The Struggle for the Souls of
Men") were organized "to liberate" central Europe.
Radio Free Europe was considered the most important part of the NCFE operation. Its objective was to
broadcast to communist-dominated Eastern Europe
and to expose the problems of communist regimes
in Albania, Bulgaria, Czechoslovakia, Hungary, Poland, and Romania. RFE featured music and news,
skits, satires, and speeches by exiled leaders; moni-
tored the broadcasts of all central and eastern Europe; and managed the use of information compiled
from the intelligence community. The governments
of the target countries worked constantly to jam RFE
signals.

Impact The Committee for a Free Europe developed a full-scale plan for the liberation of Eastern
Europe. Between April, 1954, and November, 1956,
Radio Free Europe's predecessor, Free Europe Committee, Inc., regularly delivered printed leaflets and
informational booklets by balloon to Czechoslova-

kia, Hungary, and Poland in order to help amend
the lack of free exchange of information in those
countries.

During the severe labor unrest in Poland in 1956,
RFE was praised for its balanced broadcasts and for
its initiative to foster a climate that led to a temporary restoration of peace. However, in that same
year, the Soviet occupation of Hungary closed many
independent stations, leaving only RFE, outside the
Iron Curtain, to broadcast to Hungary. The political
troubles of 1956 led to new RFE management, which
resulted in more factual news broadcasts with more
reliance on major news bureaus, less dependence on
the stories of refugees who had recently escaped the
Iron Curtain, and more audience surveys to determine programming.

Subsequent Events RFE's front organization status
was revealed after a series of 1967 articles in *The New
York Times*. In August, 1972, President Richard M.
Nixon appointed a presidential study commission
on international broadcasting that found that RFE
and Radio Liberty, with their flow of "free and un-
censored information to peoples deprived of it," actually contributed to a climate of détente. In 1973,
the two radio stations were placed under the juris-
diction of the Board for International Broadcasting;
three years later RFE and RL merged, but after the
end of the Cold War during the early 1990's, RFE/
RL struggled to define its mission.

Further Reading

Mickelson, Sig. *America's Other Voices: Radio Free Eu-
    rope and Radio Liberty.* New York: Praeger, 1983.
    Reveals little-known facts about the international
    politics and intelligence community background
    of RFE.
Puddington, Arch. *Broadcasting Freedom: The Cold
    War Triumph of Radio Free Europe and Radio Liberty.*
    Lexington: University Press of Kentucky, 2000. A
    former staff member of the RFE chronicles the
    history of the station.
Urban, George R. *Radio Free Europe and the Pursuit of
    Democracy: My War Within the Cold War.* New Haven,
    Conn.: Yale University Press, 1997. Former direc-
    tor of RFE provides behind-the-scenes details of
    the station.

Martin J. Manning

See also Central Intelligence Agency; Cold War;
Hungarian revolt; Radio; Truman Doctrine; United
States Information Agency.

■ Railroad seizure

The Event President Harry S. Truman confronted a strike by railroad workers at the onset of the Korean War
Date June-September, 1950

The seizure of the railroads during a labor dispute by President Truman in the interest of national defense called into question his use of executive authority in this instance and weakened his already tenuous relationship with organized labor.

President Truman's relationship with organized labor was tenuous during the postwar years, and strikes by union workers became commonplace during his administration. In 1946, the United States was already in the midst of three major strikes from the coal, steel, and railroad industries. Labor representatives depicted the president as a traitor and a dictator. Negotiations between railroad management and their unions over higher wages dragged on for months.

By the early 1950's, the economy was suffering from inflation rates in the double digits and high taxes. Moreover, with the Korean War underway, regulations were imposed to minimize budget deficits. Truman received congressional approval for the use of executive powers to control wages and prices, allocate materials, and construct defense plants for the wartime economy. Stable labor relations and an increase in wartime production were vital once the Korean conflict began. The country relied on carriers for passenger and freight transportation in times of military necessity, but another railroad strike loomed during the president's second term in office.

Truman's labor problems continued to worsen during the 1950's. Strikes occurred again in the automobile, lumber, textile, coal, and steel industries. To complicate matters, railroad switchmen decided to go on strike, and on June 25, 1950, four thousand members of the Switchmen's Union of North America walked off their jobs on five midwestern and western carriers. Truman stated in a news conference during the first week of July that the strike was having drastic effects on wheat and cattle shipments. Subsequently, the union called off the strikes against four of the carriers but continued to strike against the Chicago, Rock Island, and Pacific Railroad companies.

Truman proceeded to convene a mediation board under the Railway Labor Act in order to settle the dispute. The board consisted of a Supreme Court justice, a former member of the Indiana high court, and an economics professor from California. The board recommended that the switchmen return to work, but union members did not accept the compromise. Truman believed he had no choice but to issue Executive Order 10141 on July 8, taking control of the nation's railroads. The president, as commander in chief, considered the strike a threat to national security in the light of the Korean War. He also invoked the Army Appropriation Act of August, 1916—legislation created on the verge of the U.S. entry into World War I. The act allowed the government to seize control of railroads, steamship lines, inland waterways, and telephone-telegraph companies in the interest of national defense.

The secretary of the army assumed control of the railroads, although daily operations remained in the hands of railroad personnel. The president also demanded that strikers return to work or they would face dismissal and loss of seniority benefits. A settlement was finally reached in early September with the help of the presidential assistant and acting chairman of the National Security Resources Board, John R. Steelman. A new contract was negotiated with cost of living adjustments, an increase in wages, and a five-day workweek that would take effect the following year.

Impact Truman decided against running for reelection in 1952. The president believed he had been betrayed by postwar promises from union leaders for cooperation with the federal government. Truman's use of executive power to seize operations of both the railroad and steel industries raised constitutional concerns and questions about whether he had exceeded his authority in these instances. However, the issues during the 1952 election focused more on the economy, the Korean War, the communist threat, and government corruption. These factors contributed to Democratic candidate Adlai Stevenson's defeat in his presidential race against the popular Dwight D. Eisenhower.

Further Reading
Gosnell, Harold F. *Truman's Crises: A Political Biography of Harry S. Truman.* Westport, Conn.: Greenwood Press, 1980. Analyzes Truman's leadership abilities and political career. Author balances

scholarship on the two schools of thought regarding Truman's career. Includes extensive use of maps.

Hamby, Alonzo L. *Man of the People: A Life of Harry S. Truman.* New York: Oxford University Press, 1995. Scholarly work that focuses on Truman's perspective toward international politics and the definition of the U.S. role in the world. Truman's ideological views toward liberal democratic politics are also addressed.

Lee, R. Alton. *Truman and Taft-Hartley: A Question of Mandate.* Lexington: University Press of Kentucky, 1966. Lee uses the Taft-Hartley Act as a case study and illustrates how national labor policy is influenced by public opinion, and ideological and policy differences between the legislative and executive branches.

McCullough, David. *Truman.* New York: Simon & Schuster, 1992. Extensively researched and award-winning biography of Truman. The author chronicles Truman's childhood, career in politics, and postwar life. Includes archival materials and interviews with family, friends, and fellow politicians.

Truman, Harry S. *Memoirs: Years of Trial and Hope, Vol. II.* Garden City, N.Y.: Doubleday, 1956. Truman's memoirs in three volumes. Volume II focuses on his years as president.

Gayla Koerting

See also Business and the economy in the United States; Elections in the United States, 1952; Income and wages in the United States; Inflation in the United States; Korean War; Steel mill closure; Truman, Harry S.; Unionism in the United States.

■ Rapid eye movement (REM)

The Event Discovery of the existence of a period during sleep characterized by specific eye movement and electrical activity in the brain
Date Discovered in December, 1951

Prior to the 1950's, psychoanalysts dominated the study of dreams, and scientists believed that the brain was inactive during sleep. The discovery that sleep included periods of brain activity spurred scientific research specifically on sleep.

Eugene Aserinsky, a medical student at the University of Chicago, discovered REM in the sleep laboratory of his physiology professor, Nathaniel Kleitman.

Kleitman had assigned Aserinsky to study the eye movements of sleeping infants. Aserinsky detected distinct cycles of eye movements, and in subsequent studies with adults, he detected the same cycles. Studying brainwave activity with electroencephalogram (EEG) recordings, he found that brainwave activity increased during the periods of rapid eye movement. The increased brainwave activity was not consistent with EEG recordings during other periods of sleep. When he woke subjects during periods of REM, he found that most recalled their dreams and could describe them in detail.

Impact Aserinsky and Kleitman's publication of their discovery in *Science* in September, 1953, was the catalyst for further scientific research on sleep. During the 1950's, William Dement, another medical student, conducted studies with Kleitman to verify the relationship between REM sleep and dreams and to develop a classification system to identify stages of sleep.

Further Reading

Brown, Chip. "The Stubborn Scientist Who Unraveled a Mystery of the Night." *Smithsonian* 34, no. 7 (October, 2003): 92. In this magazine article, the author recounts the story of the discovery of REM in the context of the lives of the principal researchers.

Dement, William, and Christopher Vaughan. *The Promise of Sleep: A Pioneer in Sleep Medicine Explores the Vital Connection Between Health, Happiness, and a Good Night's Sleep.* New York: Dell, 1999. This book contains Dement's personal account of sleep research during the 1950's and beyond.

John F. Marszalek III

See also Genetics; Medicine; Science and technology.

■ Rauschenberg, Robert

Identification American artist
Born October 22, 1925; Port Arthur, Texas

By combining painting and objects, Rauschenberg created artworks that blurred the line between traditional painting and sculpture.

During the mid-1950's, Robert Rauschenberg surprised the New York art world by creating a new art form that combined elements of painting and sculpture. Mixing the painterly gestures of the prevalent

"Combine" artist Robert Rauschenberg at a New York beach in 1959. (Hulton Archive | by Getty Images)

abstract expressionist movement with found objects from everyday life, Rauschenberg called his hybrid creations "combines." These works included materials scavenged from the street or found in junk shops, such as rusted metal, wood scraps, and discarded packaging, along with found images and expressionistic painting.

Rauschenberg's most famous combine, *Monogram* (1955-1959), features a stuffed goat encircled by an automobile tire, mounted on a platform covered with scraps of found wood and metal, printed images, and oil paint. In *Bed*, a combine from 1955, Rauschenberg literally turned a quilt, sheet, and pillow into a canvas for his expressive brushwork. The artist's goal was to create works that bridged the gap between art and life.

Rauschenberg further stretched the boundaries of conventional art by collaborating with musician John Cage and dancer/choreographer Merce Cunningham to create innovative performances incorporating art, music, and dance.

Impact Rauschenberg expanded the definition of modern art, influencing an entire generation of artists and providing a transition between the abstract expressionist movement of the 1940's and 1950's, and the pop art of the 1960's.

Further Reading

Hopps, Walter, and Susan Davidson. *Robert Rauschenberg: A Retrospective.* New York: Guggenheim Museum, 1997. Well-illustrated history of Rauschenberg's career, including a detailed chronology.

Steinberg, Leo. *Encounters with Rauschenberg (A Lavishly Illustrated Lecture).* Chicago: University of Chicago Press, 2000. An art critic's intriguing look at Rauschenberg and the New York art scene of the 1950's and 1960's.

Paula C. Doe

See also Abstract expressionism; Art movements; de Kooning, Willem; Guggenheim Museum; Johns, Jasper; Pollock, Jackson.

■ Rayburn, Sam

Identification Speaker of the United States House of Representatives through most of the 1950's
Born January 6, 1882
Died November 16, 1961

Perhaps the most powerful legislative leader in the history of the United States, Sam Rayburn served as Speaker of the House more than twice as long as any of his predecessors and had more than forty-eight years of continuous service as an elected House official.

Sam Rayburn was born in Tennessee, the son of William Marion and Martha (Waller) Rayburn. In 1887, the family moved near Bonham, Texas, in Fannin County, which became Rayburn's lifelong home. After graduation from East Texas Normal College, Rayburn taught school for two years before being elected as a Democrat to the Texas House of Representatives in 1906. Between legislative sessions, he completed law school at the University of Texas. He rose to Texas House Speaker before his election to the U.S. Congress in 1912. That election began a tenure ending with his death forty-eight years later. He served on the Interstate and Foreign Commerce Committee, specializing in railroad legislation. He became House majority leader in 1937 and speaker in 1940. He remained speaker, with the short exceptions of Republican control (between 1947-1949 and 1953-1955), until his death in 1961.

Legislative Leader During the 1950's, Rayburn ranked as the second-most powerful man in the United States in a *Look* magazine poll. Working with Democratic president Harry S. Truman early in the decade and Republican president Dwight D. Eisenhower later, Rayburn was integrally involved in all legislative policies enacted during that decade. He opposed Senator Joseph McCarthy's radical anticommunism and later worked with fellow Texan, Senate Majority Leader Lyndon B. Johnson, his protégé. Rayburn earned fame putting together coalitions within the House to accomplish legislative goals. A clear example of this influence came in the passage of the 1957 Civil Rights Act, the first such act passed since the Reconstruction era after the Civil War. While Rayburn had not been a notable advocate for civil rights during his tenure in Congress, he saw that the time had come for passage of an act guaranteeing universal voting rights. His support for the bill made passage in Congress possible and set the stage for a Democratic Party during the mid-1960's that was far different from that of Rayburn's own era.

Political Leader Rayburn chaired the Democratic national conventions in 1948, 1952, and 1956, at the dawn of the age of television and briefly considered running for president himself in 1952. Throughout Rayburn's career he was a strong supporter of Democratic nominees for president, a position that often placed him in conflict with the conservative wing of the Texas Democratic Party. That conflict was most intense during the 1950's, when Rayburn supported Adlai E. Stevenson for president, even though most state elected officials supported Eisenhower. Rayburn became a leader among the "regular" Democrats in Texas politics, opposing the "Shivercrats" headed by conservative governor Allan Shivers. He was a strong supporter of Lyndon B. Johnson for president in 1960 and had a large role in Johnson's decision to accept the vice presidential nomination under John F. Kennedy in 1960. After contracting cancer, Rayburn died at the age of seventy-nine, and his funeral was attended by presidents Truman, Ei-

senhower, and Kennedy, as well as future president Lyndon Johnson, in his hometown of Bonham.

Impact Rayburn's nearly half-century in office was marked by an independence of action that at times diverted sharply from party aims. He was a formidable congressional adversary, yet his personal integrity and fairness earned him numerous admirers from both parties. The 1950's witnessed Rayburn's mastery of the political process as he worked in tandem with Lyndon Johnson and other party members on countless important legislative goals.

Further Reading

Champagne, Anthony. *Congressman Sam Rayburn.* New Brunswick, N.J.: Rutgers University Press, 1984. Excellent study of Rayburn as a political leader.

Cheney, Richard, and Lynne B. Cheney. *Kings of the Hill: Power and Personality in the House of Representatives.* New York: Simon & Schuster, 1996. Profiles great leaders of the House of Representatives, including Sam Rayburn.

Hardeman, D. B., and Donald C. Bacon. *Rayburn: A Biography.* Austin: Texas Monthly Press, 1987. One of the most complete biographies of Rayburn, written by close associates.

James Riddlesperger

See also Alaska statehood; Civil Rights Act of 1957; Congress, U.S.; Conservatism in U.S. politics; Eisenhower, Dwight D.; Elections in the United States, midterm; Elections in the United States, 1952; Elections in the United States, 1956; House Committee on Un-American Activities; McCarthy, Joseph; Stevenson, Adlai.

■ *Reader's Digest*

Identification American general interest magazine
Publisher Reader's Digest Association, founded by DeWitt and Lila Wallace
Date First published in 1922

Reader's Digest *started out as DeWitt Wallace's dream to provide a valuable service for busy readers and quickly became the world's best-selling magazine and the flagship product of an international corporation. During the 1950's, the magazine maintained its stance as a conservative publication with a subject-matter focus on the average person rather than the celebrity.*

In 1920, DeWitt Wallace borrowed six hundred dollars from his family to create a sample magazine. His ambition was to create a publication full of condensed articles for readers too busy to read full-length magazines or books. He established the Reader's Digest Association in 1921. He and his new wife, Lila, opened their first office later that year. In February, 1922, they published their first copy of the magazine and sold it through the mail for twenty-five cents a copy. One-year subscriptions in 1923 sold for $2.75. The publishers first offered *Reader's Digest* on newsstands in 1929.

Format The magazine was formatted as a pocket-sized, general-interest monthly magazine and was recognizable by a front cover that looked like a table of contents and a back cover that featured a painting or drawing. It targeted middle-American families, with articles on health and nutrition, humor, finances and money management, personal relationships, biographies, do-it-yourself projects, and inspirational real-life stories. The magazine featured a number of popular columns, including "Word Power," "You Be the Judge," "The Best Medicine," "Life in These United States," and "Personal Glimpses." It averaged around 170 pages in length during the 1950's.

The magazine specialized in reprinting articles from numerous other publications—among them *Saturday Evening Post, Life, McCall's, Popular Science, Newsweek,* and *Redbook.* The editors solicited original work and column briefs from freelance writers and *Digest* readers, and the magazine printed excerpts from novels in its book section.

Social Commentary *Reader's Digest* has never been known for taking obvious strong stances on political or social issues, but its founders' conservative, religious, and anticommunist views were clear in the articles chosen for publication during the 1950's. The magazine did not shy from the important news issues of the decade, publishing articles on worldwide communism conflicts, U.S. and international government and social leaders, human rights issues, U.S. politics, atomic power, big business, and the Korean War. The magazine also prohibited tobacco advertisements in its U.S. edition, a policy that has remained in place throughout its existence. During the mid-1950's, *Reader's Digest* featured a series of articles, including "Negroes Among Us" and "Jews Among Us," which offered historical background and discussion of equal rights issues for members of minority groups in the United States.

Impact The 1950's were significant years for the magazine's parent company as it evolved into a major corporation and expanded both its products and its international distribution. The corporation established the Reader's Digest Condensed (Select Editions) Books, first sold in the United States and Canada. The U.S. edition of the magazine began accepting paid advertising for the first time in 1955. In 1959, the company started offering music products, its first nonprint line. Moreover, *Reader's Digest* began to be distributed in New Zealand, Argentina, Spain, and Denmark during the decade. By the mid-1950's, the magazine was printed in sixteen languages and boasted more than thirty million readers. By the twenty-first century, *Reader's Digest,* was published in forty-eight editions and nineteen languages. With millions of readers, it is, by most accounts, the most widely read magazine in the world.

Further Reading

Canning, Peter. *American Dreamers: The Wallaces and "Reader's Digest": An Insider's Story.* New York: Simon & Schuster, 1996. Offers a comprehensive biography of the publishers and an inside look at the company.

Heidenry, John. *Theirs Was the Kingdom: Lila and DeWitt Wallace and the Story of the "Reader's Digest."* New York: W. W. Norton, 1993. An engaging chronicle of the Wallaces' rise to prominence.

January, Brendan. *DeWitt and Lila Wallace: Charity for All.* New York: Children's Press, 1998. A young-adult book that focuses on the publishers as philanthropists who generously shared their fortune with educational and arts projects.

Sharp, Joanne P. *Condensing the Cold War: "Reader's Digest" and American Identity.* Minneapolis: University of Minnesota Press, 2000. Examines the magazine's coverage of the standoff between the United States and the Soviet Union during the Cold War.

Sherri Ward Massey

See also Advertising; Book publishing; *Life; Look;* News magazines; *TV Guide.*

■ Reagan, Ronald

Identification American actor and president of the Screen Actors' Guild (SAG)

Born February 6, 1911; Tampico, Illinois

Died June 5, 2004; Los Angeles, California

During the 1950's, Ronald Reagan emerged from a waning film-acting career to become spokesman for the General Electric Company, a position that catapulted him into politics.

Born into a family of modest means, Ronald Wilson Reagan, the son of John Edward and Nellie Wilson Reagan, was raised in Dixon, Illinois. He played high school football and worked summers as a life guard: He was credited with seventy-eight rescues. The Reagans moved around a great deal during the first decade of Ronald's life. He learned early that it was unwise to develop strong attachments to people from whom he might soon be separated. Upon completing high school, he entered Eureka College, from which he was graduated as an economics major. While he was there, he served as student body president, played football, and was captain of the swim team. He worked as a radio sports announcer from 1932 until 1938, when he launched his career as an actor, a career that saw him complete fifty-three

films between 1938 and 1957. In 1947, he became president of the Screen Actors Guild (SAG).

Transitional Years The 1950's were times of considerable transition for Reagan. In 1948, his eight-year marriage to actress Jane Wyman ended. Shattered by his divorce, Reagan mused that he should have devoted less time to his duties as president of SAG and more to saving his faltering marriage. Nevertheless, having learned emotional detachment early, he moved ahead, putting the divorce behind him.

A plea from Nancy Davis in 1949 asking him, as president of SAG, to investigate the rumor that her name had appeared on a list of suspected communists in the film industry led to a date between the two. They married in 1952 and later had two children; Reagan also had two children from his first marriage.

Reagan's service as president of SAG helped him mature dramatically as an effective negotiator and honed his exceptional communication skills. In

In 1951, Ronald Reagan starred in Bedtime for Bonzo, *in which he played a college professor conducting an experiment that brought a chimpanzee into his home, which included a pretend wife, played by Diana Lynn (holding chimpanzee).* (Museum of Modern Art, Film Stills Archive)

1954, the General Electric Company appointed Reagan its official spokesman, a position in which he hosted the General Electric Theater for television and acted in some of its productions. He regularly traveled to General Electric plants throughout the United States to speak about his experiences in Hollywood and about America's promise. As he perfected these speeches for presentation, his political philosophy gradually changed. He blamed an ever-expanding government for encroaching on the liberties Americans had traditionally taken for granted.

Emerging Political Career Although Reagan had consistently been a liberal and a staunch Democrat—which he officially remained until 1960 when he changed his voter registration to Republican—he grew increasingly conservative as he thought through the problems facing the United States at mid-century. He voted for Dwight D. Eisenhower during the 1952 and 1956 elections, and during the late 1950's, he organized and promoted the Democrats-for-Nixon campaign.

If Reagan had once expected government to resolve society's problems, he now reached the conclusion that government *was* the problem and had to be changed by minimizing its role in the lives of Americans. His work with General Electric became the catapult for an unanticipated political career that would lead to his becoming governor of California for two terms and ultimately president of the United States for two terms.

Reagan's negotiating skills were evident to all who worked with him during his presidency of SAG. Although he officially left that office in 1952, he was persuaded to return as president in 1959 to lead SAG's strike against movie producers, an effort that he helped SAG win. Charlton Heston called him a tough and shrewd bargainer who converted to his side even those who fundamentally disagreed with him. Reagan later credited his successful negotiations with Mikhail Gorbachev during the 1980's to the experience he had gained in working with actors and producers during his service to SAG during the 1950's.

Impact Although the political career of Ronald Reagan was in its earliest stages of development during the 1950's, it burgeoned into a full-fledged and highly successful career in the following two decades. His election as governor of California in 1966

marked a turn toward conservatism in American politics that was to be repeated in 1980, when Reagan was elected the fortieth president of the United States. In this capacity, he used his exceptional negotiating skills to bring about an end to the Cold War. His demand that Chairman Gorbachev take down the wall that separated East and West Berlin was a symbolic gesture that resonated throughout the world and led to a lessening of the international tensions that had plagued the 1950's and 1960's. It became a major step in promoting future diplomatic negotiations that resulted in such important agreements as nuclear disarmament and a ban on nuclear testing.

Further Reading
Benson, Gigi, ed. *The President and Mrs. Reagan.* New York: Harry N. Abrams, 2003. A touching account of the Reagans. Introduction by their daughter, Patti Davis.

Judson, Karen. *Ronald Reagan.* Springfield, N.J.: Enslow, 1997. A reliable and readable biography of Ronald Reagan.

Morris, Edmund. *Dutch: A Memoir of Ronald Reagan.* New York: Random House, 1999. A comprehensive and somewhat controversial portrait of Reagan by the man appointed his official biographer in 1985.

R. Baird Shuman

See also *Confidential*; Disneyland; Eisenhower, Dwight D.; Elections in the United States, midterm; Elections in the United States, 1952; Elections in the United States, 1956; Film in the United States; Nixon, Richard M.

■ Rebel Without a Cause

Identification Film about restless American teenagers and their families
Director Nicholas Ray (1911-1979)
Date Released in 1955

This legendary film represented the angst of middle-class white adolescents during the 1950's, and established James Dean as an icon of cool, hip, estranged youth.

Original posters advertising *Rebel Without a Cause* screamed, "Jim Stark—a kid in the year 1955—what makes him tick . . . like a bomb?" In a post-World War II era punctuated by widespread fear of nuclear disaster, what makes Jim (played by James Dean) ex-

Natalie Wood and James Dean during a quiet moment in Rebel Without a Cause. (Museum of Modern Art, Film Stills Archive)

plosive is a sterile middle-class world inhabited by ineffectual, distant parents. Signaling the problems America faced during the 1950's, this film, based on a true story, centers on three lonely adolescents who are desperate for the attention of their families. Their wildness and self-destructive impulses develop from their unsatisfactory relationships with their fathers.

Wrestling with 1950's attitudes toward gender roles, Jim is anguished by the question he asks his henpecked, apron-clad father, "What do you have to do to be a man?" Angered by being called "chicken," Jim needs support and yearns for a role model, neither of which his submissive, inadequate father can provide. Literally howling that the bickering between his parents is "tearing me apart," Jim begs his father to stand up to his domineering mother, who "makes mush" out of his father, who "eats him alive and he takes it." As social outsiders, Jim and his friends attempt to establish their identities apart both from the peer pressure of the gang that controls their high school and from the conformist, materialistic ("Don't I buy everything you want?") values of their parents.

Impact This film struck such responsive chords in audiences of the 1950's that it inspired a succession of films dealing with rebellious adolescents.

Further Reading

Hofstede, David. *James Dean: A Bio-Bibliography.* Westport, Conn.: Greenwood Press, 1996. Includes a short biography of Dean and an extensive annotated bibliography.

Rock and Roll Generation: Teen Life in the 1950's. Alexandria, Va.: Time-Life Books, 1998. Illustrated exploration of 1950's youth culture, which was both promoted and reflected in *Rebel Without a Cause.*

Spoto, Donald. *Rebel: The Life and Legend of James Dean.* New York: HarperCollins, 1996. This biography demythologizes its subject.

Deborah D. Rogers

See also Automobiles and auto manufacturing; Baby boomers; *Blackboard Jungle*; *Catcher in the Rye, The*; Conformity, culture of; Dean, James; *Giant*; Wide-screen movies; *Wild One, The*; Youth culture and the generation gap.

■ Recession of 1957-1958

The Event Sustained general decline in American business activity and consumer spending that lasted eight months

Date August, 1957-April, 1958

This most severe recession of the 1950's caused the highest unemployment levels of the decade and alerted officials to the limitations of using fiscal and monetary policies to prevent economic downturns.

The 1957-1958 recession was the third recession that occurred in the United States after World War II. Although the decline in business activity was rapid, the length of the economic decline was relatively short, lasting only eight months.

The recession began in August, 1957 and ended in April, 1958. During this period industrial production dropped by 13.5 percent compared to 9 percent during the 1953-1954 recession. The unemployment rate doubled during the recession, but even after the recovery began in the spring of 1958, unemployment continued to rise, reaching a maximum level of 7.7 percent in August, 1958. This was the highest monthly unemployment rate experienced during the decade of the 1950's.

Typically, a downturn in unemployment lags several months behind an upswing in production because employers are reluctant to recall laid-off workers until they are fairly certain that business conditions have improved. Moreover, normal growth in the labor force must be absorbed, and employees who were released during the recession period must be rehired.

During the 1957-1958 recession, gross national product declined 3.2 percent. However, disposable personal income changed little because of the impact of the automatic stabilizers such as unemployment insurance, which provided financial support to laid-off workers.

William Martin, chairman of the Federal Reserve Board, testifying before the Senate Banking Committee in February, 1958. Martin told the committee that the nation should recover from the recession without having to institute a major tax cut to increase spending or having to create a massive public works program to increase incomes. (AP/Wide World Photos)

Affected Sectors The recession did not affect all sectors of the economy uniformly. One of the hardest-hit sectors was the capital goods industry. Business expenditures on plant and equipment dropped by 16 percent. Consumer durables expenditures also declined, especially for automobiles. The manufacturing and goods-producing sectors were quantitatively more important during the 1950's than in subsequent decades, and thus the decline in those sectors during this recession had a major impact on the overall economy. By contrast, the service sector was little affected by the recession.

Causes The causes of the recession can be traced to the prosperity period of the mid-1950's. Inflationary pressures began to develop during this time, and the level of inventories became very high. To prevent serious inflation, the Federal Reserve Board followed

a highly restrictive monetary policy. Bank reserve requirements were raised, and the rediscount rate was increased on several occasions. These steps had the effect of moderating the rate of increase of economic activity in the 1956-1957 period.

One of the major factors leading to the decline both in production and, more broadly, in the gross national product was the liquidation of inventories. In the third quarter of 1957, inventories were being accumulated at a rate of more than $2 billion a year. However, during the first quarter of 1958, inventory liquidation reached an annual rate of $9.5 billion and continued at the relatively high level of $8 billion during the second quarter of that year. Inventory accumulation and liquidation played a major role in the movements of the business cycle during the 1950's as techniques of inventory control were relatively imprecise compared to those of later decades.

A number of other casual factors also contributed to the 1957-1958 recession, including the decline in capital goods expenditures, particularly on plant and equipment. The latter had grown more rapidly than the overall increase in demand for goods and services, which led to excess capacity and the subsequent fall in business investment. Another cause of the recession was the changing composition of consumer expenditures. Proportionally less money was spent on durable goods and more on nondurables and services, thus causing some economic dislocation.

Shifts in foreign trade also affected the economy during the 1957 downturn. Exports of goods and services increased during the early part of 1957 because of the Suez Crisis in Egypt and the Middle East, which resulted in the short term closure of the Suez Canal and the attendant disruption of oil exports from that region. However, once the Suez Canal was reopened in 1958, U.S. oil exports declined as importers returned to their traditional sources of supply.

Finally, during 1956, the real money supply (adjusted for inflation) fell. As a result, interest rates rose as output increased. In 1957, the growth rate of total output began to decline, partly because of the tight monetary policy followed during the previous year. This had a negative impact, for example, on the growth of the housing industry as a result of reduced credit availability and higher monthly mortgage payments. Instead of adopting an easier monetary policy to stimulate the growth of output, the Federal Reserve policy remained restrictive, thus aggravating the 1957-1958 recession. In this case the monetary authorities seemed more concerned about preventing inflation than ameliorating the effects of the business cycle.

Recovery Economic activity reached a low point in April, 1958, and then began to increase. The gains in production came in part from the ending of inventory liquidation in the last quarter of 1958 and because of some increase in inventories during the first quarter of 1959. In addition, a major force for recovery came from the consumer sector as expenditures increased on nondurable goods and services. As interest rates declined, increases in residential construction also occurred, and mortgage funds were made more readily available under Federal Housing Administration (FHA) and Veterans Administration (VA) programs.

The first half of 1959 was a period of strong economic recovery. However, the economy suffered a severe setback when the longest steel strike on record began during the summer. When the steel strike ended in October, 1959, the economy rebounded.

Higher government expenditures were important in stimulating economic activity. Federal government expenditures increased by almost $3 billion from the third quarter of 1957 to the third quarter of 1958, and state and local government expenditures increased by almost $4 billion. Moreover, tax receipts fell off sharply, and this factor, combined with increased spending, caused a federal deficit in 1959 of $12.4 billion. While this was the largest deficit in peacetime history, it also helped stimulate the recovery from the 1957-1958 recession.

Impact The recession of 1957-1958 made economists and policy makers aware that the tools of monetary and fiscal policy alone were not capable of preventing severe economic downturns. Moreover, it alerted officials and consumers to the uneven pace of economic growth. In addition, the recession ushered in a protracted period of high unemployment that continued until 1965.

Further Reading

Hansen, Alvin. *Business Cycles and Depressions.* New York: Garland, 1997. A theoretical and empirical treatment of the causes and consequences of business cycles.

Ross, Arthur, ed. *Unemployment and the American Economy.* New York: John Wiley & Sons, 1964. A policy-oriented study of the unemployment problems created by the 1957-1958 recession.

Valentine, L. *Business Cycles and Forecasting.* 7th ed. Mason, Ohio: Southwestern, 1987. Presents methodologies for forecasting fluctuations in economic activity.

Vatter, Harold G. *The U.S. Economy in the 1950's: An Economic History.* Westport, Conn.: Greenwood, 1984. Traces the important developments of the economic cycles during the 1950's.

Alan L. Sorkin

See also Automobiles and auto manufacturing; Business and the economy in the United States; Economic Stabilization Agency; Income and wages in Canada; Income and wages in the United States; Inflation in the United States; Small Business Administration; Steelworkers strike; Unemployment in the United States.

■ Red Monday

The Event Day on which the U.S. Supreme Court passed down four rulings defending civil liberties

Date June 17, 1957

The Supreme Court aroused fierce opposition from anticommunists by limiting previously accepted invasions of civil liberties that were believed necessary for national security during the Cold War era.

The Supreme Court routinely upheld actions of Congress and the executive branch of the government taken in the name of national security during the early years of the Cold War. In *Dennis v. United States* (1951), for example, the Court upheld the conviction of eleven national leaders of the U.S. Communist Party for violating the 1940 Smith Act that made it a crime to advocate forceful overthrow of the government.

By the late 1950's, however, the national mood had shifted, and people seemed less fearful of communist subversion. The composition of the Court changed with the arrival of Chief Justice Earl Warren and associate justices John Marshall Harlan, William Brennan, and Charles Whittaker. In 1957, the Court examined several appeals involving political dissent, weighing constitutional rights of defendants against national security concerns.

Four Decisions The Court's *Yates v. United States* (1957) decision overturned the conviction of fourteen leaders of the California Communist Party. The justices rejected the government's argument that, under the Smith Act, membership in the Communist Party was sufficient evidence of conspiracy. They ruled six to one that advocating concrete action to overthrow the government, not simply expounding abstract principles, was necessary for a criminal conviction.

In another case, John T. Watkins, a labor organizer, testified before the House Committee on Un-American Activities (HUAC) concerning his own activities but refused to name communists with whom he had been associated. In *Watkins v. United States*, the Court overturned his conviction, six to one, asserting that the HUAC failed to prove a legislative need for such information and ruling that Congress did not have the power to expose merely for the sake of exposing.

Sweezy v. New Hampshire reversed, in a 6-2 decision, the conviction of Paul Sweezy, who had refused to answer questions from a state attorney general concerning a lecture Sweezy had given at the University of New Hampshire, as well as queries concerning his activities in the Progressive Party in the 1948 election.

In *Service v. Dulles*, the Court examined John Stewart Service's dismissal from the diplomatic corps. Service had criticized the Nationalist Chinese government while serving in China during World War II. Upon his return to the United States, he was subjected to a series of loyalty hearings; when none produced evidence justifying his dismissal, the secretary of state fired him. The Court declared this act had violated the State Department's established procedures and unanimously ordered Service reinstated.

Impact The Court's four decisions won praise from civil libertarians. They especially hailed Justice Felix Frankfurter's powerful defense of academic freedom in his concurring opinion in *Sweezy.* The standard of proof demanded in the *Yates* decision effectively ended use of the Smith Act; the Department of Justice never reindicted the California communists and no further prosecutions under that act occurred.

Conservatives complained furiously that the Court had aided communist subversion. They protested that *Watkins* unfairly limited the investigative powers of congressional committees, that *Sweezy* prevented states from protecting students from subversive teachers, and that *Yates* made it practically impossible to prosecute conspirators against America. The Georgia legislature called for the impeachment of Earl Warren, a demand the ultraconservative John Birch Society turned into a national movement. Legislators proposed more than one hundred bills to limit the power of the Court to review lower court decisions or rule laws unconstitutional. Despite the furor, none of the measures was passed.

Further Reading

Cray, Ed. *Chief Justice: A Biography of Earl Warren.* New York: Simon & Schuster, 1997. Examines Red Monday decisions in the light of Warren's career.

Lewis, Thomas T., and Richard Wilson, eds. *Encyclopedia of the U.S. Supreme Court.* Pasadena, Calif.: Salem Press, 2000. Covers major cases of the Supreme Court and discusses their significance.

Sabin, Arthur J. *In Calmer Times: The Supreme Court and Red Monday.* Philadelphia: University of Pennsylvania Press, 1999. Places the decisions in the context of decreasing fear of the menace of communism.

Milton Berman

See also Cold War; *Dennis v. United States*; House Committee on Un-American Activities; John Birch Society; Warren, Earl; *Yates v. United States.*

■ Release time

Definition Practice of allowing religious instruction for public school students during school time

The U.S. Supreme Court decision on release time handed down in Zorach v. Clauson *(1952) created the possibility that some government assistance for religious instruction as part of public education might be constitutionally permissible.*

Public endorsement or support of religious practices in public institutions, referred to by some as "public religion," became increasingly controversial after World War II. As religious pluralism became more prominent, conservative groups called for more accommodation of religion within public institutions and discourse, while liberals sought to strengthen the separation between church and state. Cold War concerns with "atheistic communism" heightened the tensions over where to draw the line between the church and state.

During the nineteenth century there were numerous occasions of accommodation between church and state when public funds were not involved. These included "blue laws," which required businesses to close on Sunday, and the offering of prayer to commence legislative sessions and other public events. An unofficial, largely Protestant "public religion" was routine in many of the public schools, as evidenced by some schools' inclusion of Bible reading and prayer at the beginning of the school day.

Prior to World War II and the advent of the Cold War, another accommodationist exercise was present in many of the nation's public schools. Religious education classes, often taught by members of the clergy, were offered in the schools during regular school hours. The instructors were under the supervision of school officials, and the permission of parents was required for their children to participate. Implemented largely for the benefit of Roman Catholic students not able to attend parochial schools, these "release-time" programs appealed also to Protestant and Jewish students.

During the 1940's, the public schools of Champaign, Illinois, implemented a release-time program in cooperation with neighborhood churches and synagogues. Students who chose not to participate in weekly instruction held in school classrooms went to study halls. Attendance was taken of both release-time participants and nonparticipants.

Supreme Court Involvement Responding to a lawsuit initiated by Vashti McCollum, parent of a Champaign high school student, the Court's 6-3 decision in *McCollum v. Board of Education* (1948) ruled that the practice of religious instruction was in violation of the First Amendment. The Court maintained that the separation of church and state was breached because the program allowed for the superintendent's approval of the instructors, the use of public schools classrooms, and the inclusion of compulsory attendance laws.

Four years later, the Court partly retreated in *Zorach v. Clauson.* That 6-3 decision supported a practice of New York City schools, which allowed students to be released from school for one hour a week to participate in religious instruction at a religious center of their choice. Unlike the Champaign program, the New York City release-time practice (sometimes called "dismissed-time") did not include the superintendent's approval of the instructors, the use of public school classrooms, or the use of public funds. Justice William O. Douglas, who ruled with the majority in *McCollum,* ruled also with the majority in *Orach* and declared that religious instruction followed the established traditions of the country.

Impact The teaching of religion in public schools goes to the heart of the issue of separation of church and state. The *Zorach* decision, allowing for religious classes away from school property, expanded the accommodationist principle, but any encouragement to supporters of religion in the schools resulting from *Zorach* was short-lived as a result of several Court decisions during the following decade concerning prayer and Bible reading in schools.

Further Reading

Hall, Kermit L., ed. *The Oxford Companion to the Supreme Court of the United States.* New York: Oxford University Press, 1992. Includes excellent entries pertaining to key Court cases relevant to release-time.

Pritchett, C. Herman. *Constitutional Civil Liberties.* Englewood Cliffs, N.J.: Prentice-Hall, 1984. Includes thorough coverage of release-time in a chapter on "Religious Freedom and Establishment."

Robert R. Mathisen

See also Cold War; Religion in the United States; Supreme Court decisions, U.S.

■ Religion in Canada

Canada's religious patterns have reflected a unique combination of historical and geographical factors and have deviated markedly from the norm of sectarianism in the United States. The post-World War II era saw challenges to the old ecclesiastical orders, growing secularization, and the beginnings of change in the religious marketplace.

Religion played a central role in the opening and development of Canada, and from the beginning, Canada was a strongly religious country, dominated by the high church formality of the Anglican and Roman Catholic Churches. In contrast to the religious dissent and schism on the American frontier, the religious landscape in Canada was dominated by large, powerful churches linked to powerful business and political elites, all of which bore close resemblances to the ecclesiastical elites of Europe. Canada's religious oligopoly was reinforced by the special status of Roman Catholicism in Quebec, where ethnicity, language, and religion were tightly intertwined in the French Triune.

In 1925, a third religious body, the United Church of Canada, was established through the merger of several Protestant groups, the Methodists, Congregationalists, Brethren, and 70 percent of the Presbyterians. Canada's Christian churches have been defined by tradition, formality, service, and sophisticated organization at the national level. Understandably, they have helped to shape the country's development and identity in myriad ways. The Constitution Act of 1791, for example, legally established the Church of England as a bulwark against

revolution in the king's realm. It was known officially as the Church of England in Canada until 1955.

A Move Toward Liberalism Victorian Christianity was orthodox, tradition-bound, and controlling; at the same time it was vibrant and left a legacy of sacred and secular imprints on Canada's political party system, social programs, foreign policy, and citizens' attitudes toward law and order. Canada's patterns in the post-World War II era were typical of modern, industrialized societies undergoing secularization, yet the Canadian patterns showed significant deviations from the norms in the United States. Before World War II, Canadian churches were closely allied with right-wing politics. With the defeat of fascism, the churches shifted to a more liberal, left-wing position favoring the development of social welfare programs. From the 1950's forward, the United Church was a major force in promoting social programs as well as the rights of workers, prisoners, and indigenous peoples. The Catholic and Anglican denominations also drifted to the Left. Thus, the traditional established churches of Canada became the foremost exponents of liberation theology, socialism, and communitarian values in the decades following World War II.

Contrasts with the United States In contrast to the United States, Canada experienced a slow, nonviolent separation from Great Britain, and dealing with disparate groups was central to its emergence as an independent state. Similarly, religious groups were expected to cooperate for service, enjoying government support as a matter of tradition. Full religious freedom was guaranteed to Canadians through the Charter of Rights and Freedoms, rights that were set in place not by public debate but by a group of political elites.

Canada's religious landscape also was not shaped by religious dissent. Pollsters taking the country's religious pulse have shown religion to be much less sectarian, voluntary, and evangelical than in the United States. Gallup polls taken during the 1960's showed that Canadian churches were less moralistic and fundamentalistic and more permissive in social attitudes than American churches. Anglophones, or English-speaking Canadians, were more inclined toward fundamentalism than Canadian francophones. French-speaking Catholics in Canada, for example, have consistently been the most

A drive-in church in Scarborough, Ontario, reflects the impact of automobile culture on religion in North America during the 1950's. (Hulton Archive | by Getty Images)

The "Big Three" Churches The "Big Three" religious institutions—the Roman Catholic, Anglican, and United Churches—became the dominant components of Canada's religious landscape, with the Catholic Church the largest single religious entity. During the 1950's, more than 90 percent of Canadians were affiliated with one of these three. The next largest Protestant denominations were the Presbyterians, Lutherans, and Baptists.

The Big Three institutions are all hierarchical with spatially well-defined territories. The Catholic Church is organized into dioceses overseen by bishops and archdioceses or provinces overseen by archbishops. The highest-ranking Catholic clergy in Canada are cardinals. The Anglican Church, headquartered in Toronto, is organized into regional groupings also known as dioceses, each one with its own bishop or bishops. The head of the national church is called the primate and the general synod is its chief governing body. The United Church, the largest Protestant group, is headquartered in Toronto and organized into regional conferences. The Lutherans are also hierarchical in nature, while other groups have a looser organization—such as the Baptists—or are locally autonomous, such as nondenominational groups. The Canadian Council of Churches, established in 1944, is a Christian ecumenical network or umbrella group designed to offer support, leadership, and education to its members.

While the Big Three held considerable sway over Canadian religious life, indigenous religions were not given the same recognition as those of the Euro-Canadians. Native religions had no official status during the 1950's. Moreover, many nonnatives lacked basic knowledge of their communities' spiritual heritage and related events and concepts such as potlatch, dual divinity, and tribal creation stories. Christian missionaries, in fact, contributed to the decline of native spiritualism through genera-

liberal on moral issues such as living together before marriage and birth control. Christian fundamentalism has not had the same media presence and fervor in Canada that it has witnessed in the United States.

Content analyses of print media reveal that religious themes are more than twice as common in the United States. Fundamentalism has grown in Canada over the decades but not to the extraordinary heights seen in the United States. Canadians are not inclined to switch from mainline churches to fundamentalist ones, suggesting a strong allegiance to tradition and the desire to stay with churches with which they have had a long identification. In 1950, there were only 1.1 million evangelical Protestants in Canada, less than 5 percent of the population; by 2000, the number had increased to 2.5 million, 8 percent of the total population.

tions of contact conversion. Many native groups in Canada followed a combination of traditional and Christian beliefs and thus recognized more than one god.

Influence on the Built Environment During the 1950's, Canada's religious bodies supported an abundance of theological schools and colleges, boarding schools, and related institutions and programs. The Catholic Church of Canada sponsored the greatest number of educational institutions such as St. Paul's University in Ottawa and St. Thomas University in Fredrickton, New Brunswick. The Anglican Church sponsored Trinity College in Toronto and Queen's College in St. John's, Newfoundland. Canterbury College, also Anglican, was incorporated in 1957 as a part of the University of Windsor. The United Church sponsored Emmanuel College of Victoria University in Toronto. The Presbyterians supported Knox College, also in Toronto. The interdenominational McGill University Faculty of Religious Studies in Montreal was given its initial accreditation in 1952. The Baptist's McMaster Divinity College in Hamilton, Ontario, received initial accreditation in 1954. Most theological seminaries and programs in Canada, however, were established in the decades following the 1950's. Religious treasures and landmarks abound, from basilicas to bell towers and special works of art. The Basilica of Sainte Anne de Beaupre near Quebec City and the Basilica of Notre Dame in Montreal are two of the most famous religious landmarks.

Growing Secularization The peace and prosperity of the 1950's set the stage for dramatic changes in the country's religious climate. The gradual decline in churchgoing during the 1950's gave way to a dramatic decline in the following decades. Polls following World War II showed that 60 percent of Canadians were attending church weekly, against only 40 percent in the United States. In later decades, 25 percent of Canadians attended church weekly while the American figure has held steady at approximately 40 percent.

The most precipitous drop in church attendance has been in Quebec among the French Catholics. During the 1950's, 85 percent of the population of Quebec attended church weekly; that proportion later dropped to 14 percent. Catholicism, however, remains an important component in the cultural identity of Canada's francophones. A majority of French Canadians—86 percent—continued to identify themselves as Catholic in the decades following the 1950's; many of them continued to enroll their children in Catholic schools. The "Quiet Revolution" in Quebec—a period during the 1960's in which values and attitudes of the past were rejected and the province began its modernization efforts—brought wide-ranging disillusionment with the church and a decline of the old ecclesiastical order. Many people viewed the church as rigid, aloof, and intolerant. As a consequence, the speed and scale of secularization in Quebec has been unmatched by any other Canadian province.

The Anglican Church, once holding a privileged position, began to diminish in status after World War II as political, economic, and cultural ties with Great Britain weakened. During the 1950's, the Anglicans were about 16 percent of the country's population; by the early twenty-first century, they represented only 8 percent, half of whom reside in Ontario. Unlike the Catholic Church, the Anglican Church did not have a vast network of educational institutions to aid its growth. The United Church of Canada, founded in 1925, was faced with the difficult task of holding together diverse strands of Protestantism. The church experienced an upsurge following World War II, but its numbers began to diminish during the late 1950's. Affiliation with the United Church fell from a high of 20 percent to a low of 11 percent by 2001. Except for Catholicism in Quebec, the greatest erosion in Christianity has been in the Anglican and United Churches.

Impact Canada has become one of the most religiously diverse countries in the world, especially in southeast Ontario; this change has been attributed to the change in immigration policy and the integration of non-Western, non-Christian immigrants. In 1901, Canada was about 98 percent Christian and 2 percent non-Christian. During the 1950's, it was about 95 percent Christian and 5 percent non-Christian; by 2001 it was 72 percent Christian and 28 percent non-Christian. The percentage of Christians dropped about 0.9 percent per year, with Protestantism falling off the fastest; small non-Christian religious groups have increased in number and popularity. The French have always constituted the core of the Canadian Catholic community. Quebec was unrivaled as the religion's geographical core during the 1950's, but by the twenty-first century, 52 percent of Canada's Catholics lived outside the province.

In the early twenty-first century, 72 percent of the Canadian population professed Christianity, down 20 percent from the 1950's. Another 20 percent had no religious beliefs, and about 8 percent adhered to Islam—the largest non-Christian group; Buddhism; Hinduism; Sikhism; neopaganism; New Age Spirituality; and other varieties. Although ecclesiastical power has been greatly diluted since the war, secularization has not killed religion across Canada. Recent polling suggests a resurgence in the mainline churches as well as a new and elevated degree of interest in the fundamentalist groups. Canada has never forged a fundamentalist, emotionally charged civil religion as in the United States, and given its past, sectarianism is likely to remain a minor part of the Canadian religious landscape.

Further Reading

Bibby, Reginald Wayne. *Unknown Gods: The Ongoing Story of Religion in Canada.* Toronto: Stoddart, 1993. Focuses on change in religious patterns and practice in recent decades.

Christie, Nancy, and Enrico Cumbo. *Households of Faith: Family, Gender, and Community in Canada, 1760-1969.* Montreal: McGill-Queen's University Press, 2003. Examines the impact of religion on family, community, and national identity.

Hewitt, W. E., ed. *The Sociology of Religion: A Canadian Focus.* Toronto: Butterworths, 1993. A collection of readings on diverse topics such as civil religion, evangelism, and nonbelief.

MacKey, Eva. *The House of Difference: Cultural Politics and National Identity in Canada.* Studies in Culture and Communication. New York: Routledge, 2000. Examines the contradictions and ambiguities of national identity in past and current public culture.

Menendez, Albert J. *Church and State in Canada.* Amherst, N.Y.: Prometheus Books, 1996. Shows religious impact on education, law, and politics with some comparisons to the United States.

Ann M. Legreid

See also Canadian regionalism; Education in Canada; Health care systems in Canada; Immigration to Canada; Jewish Americans; Religion in the United States; Revised Standard Version of the Bible; World Council of Churches convention.

■ Religion in the United States

Religions in the United States were well defined, structured, and clearly established during the 1950's. Spirituality was denominationally based and rooted in community and class values. Churches and synagogues were well respected and their authority was largely unquestioned. However, there were also faint rumblings that later would be instrumental in bringing about sweeping changes in religious values and practice.

In his 1967 book, *The Sacred Canopy: Elements of a Sociological Theory of Religion,* Peter Berger describes religion during the 1950's as a "sacred canopy." He noted that just as a tent covers a certain area, keeping out bad weather and making the inside a place of comfort and shelter from the elements, religion in the United States during this era provided a way of looking at the world that, in retrospect, was an enclosed worldview. Berger defines religion as the establishment of a sacred order, that is, a view of the world and the cosmos that imposes a certain meaning and creates order out of the chaos or meaninglessness of life.

During the 1950's, social institutions such as school systems, work, the church, family life, and gender roles were considered part of a sacred cosmic frame of reference established by God, while authority was considered God's instrument on Earth. The father of a family was God's agent; the priests, bishops, and ministers were the voice of God for lay people. By participating in this institutional order, people participated in a kind of divine order. Even though these social institutions were designed and created by humankind, religion legitimated them by viewing them as ultimate reality. Religion gave them a semblance of inevitability, firmness and durability, qualities that are ascribed to God. Many religious followers in this era felt that if one failed to participate in this schema, one might lose all connection with the sacred and be swallowed up by disorder and chaos.

Among religious practitioners, social institutions often were linked to the underlying structure of the universe and were grounded in sacred time. In a sense, then, they became immortal. To step into a church was to escape into a world beyond, a sacred space, quiet and with subdued lighting. For Roman Catholics, the language was from a different time and had a mystical sense about it. The altar was often located on a distant, massive platform. Sunday mass obligation was very strict, and the faithful feared the punishment of Hell if they did not attend. Divorce was very rare, and the family structure was sacrosanct. Children learned their religion from catechism classes, where the answers were sure and unquestioned.

Preachers and Evangelists Many preachers and evangelists worked to maintain an insular world view. In 1952, when television began to be popular, Rex Humbard of Akron, Ohio, decided to use this new technology for preaching. However, most religious programming was sponsored by the National Council of Churches, which was careful not to allow free airtime to the evangelicals. During the early

1950's, evangelist Billy Graham purchased airtime for an interview program, but his audience was very small.

In 1954, Oral Roberts and his wife, Evelyn, filmed a series of thirty-minute studio programs patterned on Roberts's radio program, but they were not successful. However, Roberts was convinced that more "souls" could be reached through television than through other means. His idea was to capture on camera the charged atmosphere of the revival tent. He filmed what was called at the time a "crusade"—his preaching from Akron. These programs not only included his sermons but also the altar calls, when people lined up to be healed; the performance of "miracles"; and the reactions of the congregation to the words they were hearing. Roberts believed he

In July, 1958, more than ninety thousand Jehovah's Witnesses gathered in New York's Yankee Stadium for the opening of an eight-day convention. (AP/Wide World Photos)

had found a way to introduce the nation to the remarkable healing revival.

In 1957, Billy Graham took a similar step. He decided to air his Saturday-evening services from Madison Square Garden in New York City. Graham contracted with ABC to air four programs, thereby establishing a precedent for broadcasting crusade services. Other evangelical broadcasters found it more difficult to get aired or to generate popular response. Many stations feared that selling time to revivalists would sully their images. The general feeling was that evangelist preachers only were exploiting hysteria and ignorance by showing adherents in trances or shouting their prayers. Throughout this period, the National Council of Churches lobbied Congress to ban the sale of television time for religious purposes. However, these programs gradually became more acceptable to the public. Roberts's mail doubled after one month on television; his mailing list grew to more than one million names by the end of the 1950's. Graham began receiving between 50,000 and 75,000 letters each week.

Bishop Fulton J. Sheen's television program, *Life Is Worth Living*, aired from 1952 to 1957. Sheen earned an Emmy Award in 1952 as television's most outstanding personality. His message not only was constructed around the tenets of medieval Roman Catholicism but also included messages that met the challenge of Cold War communism. Sheen was so charismatic a preacher that he was able to draw a number of famous people into the Roman Catholic Church, including Henry Ford II, journalist-congresswoman Clare Boothe Luce, journalist Heywood Broun, and actor Virginia Mayo. Sheen was a man of his times, a 1950's Catholic who thought that tradition was best and that complex political problems could be addressed reasonably by medieval philosophers. He accepted invitations to preach across the country as well as throughout the world. Thousands of average Americans joined the Catholic Church because of Sheen's efforts.

Synagogue Architecture and the Creation of Israel
During the 1950's and 1960's approximately one thousand new synagogues were consecrated in the United States. This number represented a large increase for the Jewish religion, but it also presented a problem because the second commandment pro-

hibited any rendering of human or animal form that could be worshiped as a deity. When synagogues began to be commissioned in the modern style, and employing such leading architects as Erich Mendelsohn and Percival Goodman, Jews began to adopt a new attitude toward synagogue art, viewing art not as a separate entity but as an integral part of a synagogue's architecture that must be taken into account at the preliminary stages of the building's design. They decided that abstract art could be allowed, and this provided many abstract artists with an opportunity to use their talents in religious as well as in secular venues. Abstract art resolved the age-old dilemma of creating a Jewish art that was not in violation of the second commandment's prohibition against the depiction of human or animal forms, and for this reason, it was welcomed in the synagogue. B'nai Israel in Millburn, New Jersey, is a good example of this religious-secular blend of architectural elements. It was designed in 1952 by Sidney Goodman and incorporated the sculpture of Herbert Ferber, the painting of Robert Motherwell, and the ark curtain design of Adolph Gottlieb.

During this time, shortly after World War II and the Holocaust, abstract art was especially meaningful. Jews became aware of themselves as a physical community and as a congregation. Jewish leaders and designers specifically wanted modern buildings. They felt that a new synagogue should reflect the modern Jewish experience, which involved freedom from persecution. They were happy to approve of the idea to employ contemporary abstract artists for the new buildings.

Another meaningful development for the Jews of the 1950's was the creation of the state of Israel in 1948. This event also contributed to the Jewish sense of being a physical congregation. They could now feel that they had a homeland in which they could take pride, and this fact nurtured both their Jewish inner selves and their need for "normal" status within the United States. The time after World War II was a time of sustained prosperity. Younger Jews were more affluent and tended to be less strict in their adherence to Judaism. Modern abstract art was one important way in which the Jewish community could express the forging of a new Jewish identity. A new spirit of Judaism and an increased self confidence and pride arose from their new status as Americans with a homeland.

Anticommunism and Religious Protest When the Soviet Union became identified with "godless communism" during the Cold War, many Americans saw the United States as a protector of religion. The phrase "under God" was added to the Pledge of Allegiance during the 1950's so that the public would commit themselves at public events to living in "one nation, under God, indivisible, with liberty and justice for all." Roman Catholics, Protestants, and Jews commonly were united in their opposition to communism. Billy Graham was a fervent anticommunist and supporter of the atomic bomb—a stance that he later repudiated. The Roman Catholic Holy Year of 1950 aimed to strengthen the church against communism. During that year, more than three million pilgrims from almost every country in the world made their way to Saint Peter's Basilica in Rome. Later, in April, 1959, Pope John XXIII forbade Catholics to vote for parties supporting communism.

World War II had a lasting effect on the culture of the 1950's. Dorothy Day was representative of many groups of people both who were antiwar and anti-atom bomb and who called on religious beliefs in their protests. Day founded the Catholic Worker movement in several cities to help the poor and homeless. During the mid-1950's, she and her community refused to participate in New York state's civil defense drill. When the sirens sounded on June 15, 1955, Day was among a small group of people sitting in front of her town's city hall. A Catholic Worker leaflet explained that "In the name of Jesus, who is God, who is Love, we will not obey this order to pretend, to evacuate, to hide. We will not be drilled into fear. We do not have faith in God if we depend upon the Atom Bomb." Day described her civil disobedience as an act of penance for the U.S. use of nuclear weapons on Japanese cities. When the crowd in front of city hall swelled to more than two thousand protesters, Day was eventually arrested and jailed.

Eastern Religions A new interest among Americans in Eastern religions was sparked in part by the rise of the Beat generation. This was a group of men and women writers and visual artists who protested against the conformity of the postwar era. They wrote and sang about a false and conformist United States. Although the word "beat" held connotations of "spent" or "beaten down," it also referred to a sense of the "beatific," "sacred," or "holy." Jack Kerouac, a devout Roman Catholic and one of the leading Beat writers, explained that he was trying to capture in his writing the secret holiness of the downtrodden. Furthermore, Allen Ginsberg's poems "Kaddish," and "Howl" expressed despair over the beaten state of the individual and society.

Kerouac became a close friend of the young Zen poet Gary Snyder. His book *The Dharma Bums* (1958) describes a mountain climbing trip that he and Snyder shared and captures the tentative steps he and his friends were taking toward spiritual realization. Kerouac found enlightenment through the Buddhist religion and tried to follow Snyder's lead in communing with nature. Ultimately, the Beat generation helped awaken a popular interest in Eastern religions, including Hinduism, Daoism, and Zen Buddhism, and related practices including meditation, yoga, and acupuncture.

Religious Schools and Bible Study During the 1950's, Catholic schools as well as the religious congregations that staffed them were at their most numerous and most influential. As far back as 1908, the system encompassed more than twenty thousand teachers and more than one million pupils, and cost more than fifteen million dollars to operate annually. Religious schools began very early after the founding of the American colonies, when missionaries emigrated to the United States to open schools for their religions. As circumstances changed from that of a missionary country to that of a country regularly provided with a fixed ecclesiastical organization, the schools came to be recognized as a function of organized parish work. Many schools, including those in the Catholic, Episcopalian, and Presbyterian faiths, asked for and received public monies.

By the 1950's, Catholic schools were staffed almost exclusively by nuns, women from hundreds of different religious congregations, under the leadership of the diocesan bishops and priests. The schools were known for their strict disciplinary practices, their education in religion and morals, and their ability to function at a very low cost. Most American Catholic children attended Catholic schools during this era. In 1956, there were 9,385 Catholic elementary schools with 3,349,293 students; 2,399 Catholic high schools with 693,607 students; and 247 Catholic colleges and universities with 219,706 students.

Some religious schools of other denominations also continued.

Doubts about the historicity of the Bible narratives had been raised throughout the history of Bible study. However, during the 1950's, Bible study took a new turn. Traditional belief held that the first five books of the Bible, known as the Pentateuch, had been written by Moses and that Moses had lived in about 1,200 B.C.E. During the nineteenth century, however, scholars questioned this premise. They argued that Moses could not have known or experienced some of the things that he was writing about. During the nineteenth century, especially, Protestant scholars worked to apply literary and form criticism to biblical text. Literary criticism showed that the texts had developed over a long period of time and that they had been written and rewritten. They showed various strands of writing within the same text. Form criticism attempted to discern the genre of the writing; that is, that which constituted creeds, law codes, hymns, morality stories, or accounts of historical events. Moreover, scholars realized that during the early history there was a disregard of anything written and that traditions were passed down orally. They concluded that the first books of the Bible were not written until about 500 B.C.E. or perhaps somewhat earlier.

Much of this scholarly work, however, was resisted by church authorities, who feared that it was sacrilegious to apply modern literary criticism to a book that was divinely inspired. A breakthrough came in 1943, when Pope Pius XII published "Divino Afflante Spiritu." In this letter, the pope opened the door to Catholic scholarship in all areas of biblical study. During the 1950's, therefore, biblical scholars were invited to study the criticism and the findings of other related sciences such as archaeology and social history. As a result, Catholic and non-Catholic scholars were free to work together in their study and interpretations, which sparked a degree of ecumenical cooperation. Roland DeVaux, Albert Clamer, and Bruce Vawter were among the first scholars during this decade to take advantage with the new scholarly freedom. In 1958, Pope Pius XII recognized the new science-based study of the Bible and sent a message to the first Catholic International Biblical Conference of Brussels. He referred with gratification to the beneficial results of his encyclical letter fifteen years before. Another result of the new freedom during this era was the development of

a progressive program for preparing ministers, and a new generation of highly competent scholars emerged.

However, the new scholarship of the 1950's stayed mostly hidden in seminaries and universities because it was either too difficult or too disturbing for lay people to understand. It was only much later that these ideas became better known. For example, the Catholic Almanac of 1956 makes no mention of "Divino Afflante Spiritu" but only refers to a previous papal letter in 1927.

Impact Religion during the 1950's was largely a matter of following the Ten Commandments and rules and staying within the framework set up by churches or synagogues. During the 1960's, people began to want more than a rule-abiding spirituality. They risked stepping out from under the sacred canopy where order and discipline took top priority in order to seek the sacred on their own terms. People began to look for a deeper meaning to their lives, sometimes by experimenting with various religions and philosophies or sometimes by simply turning their back on religious teachings. During the 1960's, the second Vatican Council recognized this need and worked to provide a theology that was community based, a ritual that was more meaningful, and a spirituality that was more concerned with social justice.

Further Reading

Berger, Peter. *The Sacred Canopy: Elements of a Sociological Theory of Religion*. Garden City, N.Y.: Anchor Books, 1967. This book uses the image of the sacred canopy to describe religion.

Dawson, Lorne L. "Anti-Modernism, Modernism, and Postmodernism: Struggling with the Cultural Significance of New Religious Movements." *Sociology of Religion* 59, no. 2 (1998): 131-136. An article that delves into the characteristics of new religious movements and how they vary from the more staid aspects of the 1950's.

Epstein, Joseph. "My 1950's." *Commentary* 96, no. 3 (September, 1993): 37-42. Discusses the author's view of the social and political conditions during the 1950's and includes some discussion of the religious climate.

Harrell, David Edwin, Jr. "Pentecost at Prime Time." *Christian History* 15, no. 1 (1996): 52-54. This is an interesting review of Pentecostal preachers and their discovery of television during the 1950's.

Pells, Richard H. *The Liberal Mind in a Conservative Age: American Intellectuals in the 1940's and 1950's.* New York: Harper & Row, 1985. Pells shows that the 1950's was a lively time for liberal thinking, even though the majority culture was overly conservative.

Wall, James. "Changes in Attitude: The Lost World of the 1950's." *The Christian Century,* October 18, 1995, 947-948.

Wong, Janay Jadine. "Synagogue Art in the 1950's." *Art Journal,* Winter 53, no. 4 (1994), 37-43. This article recounts the important changes in architecture in the building of synagogues and how modern art liberated and spurred enormous new growth in religious-oriented architecture.

Winifred Whelan

See also Baby boomers; Beat generation; Graham, Billy; "In God We Trust" on U.S. currency; *Inherit the Wind*; Jewish Americans; Peale, Norman Vincent; Pledge of Allegiance; Release time; Religion in Canada; Revised Standard Version of the Bible; Sheen, Fulton J.; World Council of Churches convention.

■ Revised Standard Version of the Bible

Identification First major translation of the Protestant Bible in half a century
Date Changes spanned from 1946 to 1957

The Revised Standard Version (RSV) of the Bible was an interdenominational Protestant attempt to modernize the language of the Bible for both private and public worship and study. While widely received, the RSV stirred up considerable controversy among Christians.

For three hundred years, the Authorized (King James) Version of the Protestant Bible had been formative and normative for the English-speaking world. By the 1880's, it was evident that a new translation was needed. Better ancient biblical texts (such as the Codex Sinaiticus) had been recovered, and the English language had changed. While at least 150 translations of all or parts of the Bible had been published between 1611 and 1881, none was considered official, and none caught the public imagination. By 1885, a revised version was produced in Great Britain, and it was adopted, with some changes, for use in the United States as the American Revised Version (ARV) in 1901. Perhaps because of its stodgy presentation, the ARV was not widely read. Meanwhile, the potential audience for a readable English Bible was evidenced by the explosion of the number of English speakers, from six million in 1611, to more than 600 million by 1989.

In 1929, Thomas Nelson Publishers surrendered the copyright on the ARV to the International Council of Religious Education. Within a year, an American Standard Bible Revision Committee of eight Old Testament and eight New Testament scholars met. Three scholars familiar with the literary needs of Bible translation joined them. However, because of the Great Depression, the committee met only once.

In 1938 the revision committee was reformed, with a group of thirty-two American and Canadian scholars, divided into Old and New Testament sections. The committee desired a readable modern text, utilizing the latest manuscript discoveries, critical scholarship, and historical insight. In spite of World War II, translators worked diligently, publishing revised versions of the New Testament in 1946, the Old Testament in 1952, and the Apocrhypha in 1957.

A New Audience The RSV became one of the most noted translations of the 1950's in striving to meet the varied requirements of Bible readers at that time. It was a book suitable not only for both liturgical and devotional use but also useful for study and for appreciation as a literary classic. The Bible was produced from an ecumenical perspective—pan-Protestant with consideration of Roman Catholic, Jewish, and humanist viewpoints. It attempted to do justice to legitimate scholarly disagreement yet also meet the need for a genuinely popular book. This was to be a book for a new audience, that of the United States amid a 1950's religious awakening.

Impact The RSV received an amazing variety of responses. While it quickly became the mainstream Protestant Bible of the decade, it also triggered a revival of interest in the King James version, both by religious conservatives and by those with a passion for literature, who regarded the Authorized Version as an English-language classic. The revision sparked a proliferation of translations that sought to find relevance among the faithful in the next decades, including the *Living Bible* (1971), The Good News Bible (1976), the Cotton Patch versions (1970's, cast in the African American dialects of the Deep South), and even a New Revised Standard Version (1989). Furthermore, the text of the RSV, while reflecting the conservative religious mood of the United States during the 1950's, was soon eclipsed by the social changes of the 1960's, and pressure was felt to address issues such as inclusive language (which was ignored by the RSV). Though intended to be timeless, the RSV remains a reflection of American letters and Protestant religion in 1950's.

Further Reading

Bruce, F. F. *The English Bible.* London: Oxford University Press, 1961. A definitive study by an accomplished scholar.

Daniell, David. *The Bible in English.* New Haven, Conn.: Yale University Press, 2003. A thorough examination of the translations of the Bible and the impact successive versions of it have had on the people and communities that read them.

Greenslade, Stanley L., ed. *The Cambridge History of the Bible.* Cambridge, England: Cambridge University Press, 1963. An authoritative text on the Bible in English.

MacGregor, Geddes. *A Literary History of the Bible.* Nashville: Abingdon, 1968. A readable and reliable study of the Scriptures as both a religious and cultural phenomenon.

C. George Fry

See also Graham, Billy; Peale, Norman Vincent; Religion in Canada; Religion in the United States.

■ Rexroth, Kenneth

Identification American poet and literary critic
Born December 22, 1905; South Bend, Indiana
Died June 6, 1982; Montecito, California

Kenneth Rexroth's leadership in the San Francisco literary community during the 1950's helped establish regional and national poetry movements.

An avid reader and self-taught writer, Kenneth Rexroth lived in San Francisco from 1927 through the late 1960's. In 1948 and 1949, he received Guggenheim grants enabling him to promote his writing and literary philosophy. By the early 1950's, he had become a respected author of poetry, plays, and critical essays. Long associated with leftist and anarchist groups, Rexroth advocated resistance to abusive government and decried academic elitism.

Rexroth played a central role in the success of the 1950's San Francisco Renaissance. He arranged gatherings, helped found a poetry center where he gave readings and taught workshops, hosted a book-review radio program, and published several books of poetry. He also wielded critical influence through articles written for periodicals such as *The Nation*, the *San Francisco Chronicle*, and *The New York Times Book Review.*

Impact Throughout the 1950's, Rexroth used his influence to encourage younger poets, including such Beat generation members as Lawrence Ferlinghetti and Allen Ginsberg. Poetry readings with jazz accompaniment had become common, and Rexroth frequently read "Thou Shalt Not Kill," a long, incendiary poem honoring Welsh poet Dylan Thomas and condemning the violent and depersonalizing nature of contemporary society.

Rexroth's sizable contribution to American poetry as a writer and translator has been largely overshadowed by his 1950's activities as a mentor to the Beat poets.

Further Reading

Gutierrez, Donald. *The Holiness of the Real: The Short Verse of Kenneth Rexroth.* Madison, N.J.: Fairleigh Dickinson University Press, 1995. Examines Rexroth's shorter poems and addresses his accomplishments as a social critic and journalist.

Hamalian, Linda. *A Life of Kenneth Rexroth.* New York: Norton, 1991. A biography documenting Rexroth's diverse activities and talents.

Margaret A. Dodson

See also Beat generation; Burroughs, William; Ferlinghetti, Lawrence; Ginsberg, Allen; Kerouac, Jack; Literature in the United States; Poetry; San Francisco Renaissance.

■ Ribonucleic acid (RNA)

The Event Using an enzyme extracted from bacteria, RNA—the material that transmits genetic information from deoxyribonucleic acid (DNA) for protein production—was synthesized in a cell-free system
Date Discovery published on November 11, 1955

The structure of DNA had been defined only two years before, published simultaneously by James Watson, Francis Crick, Maurice Wilkins, and Rosalind Franklin. The synthesis of RNA in test tubes, outside of a cell, provided a mechanism for understanding the process by which genetic information is translated into protein.

In the mid-1950's, Marianne Grunberg-Manago, a French biochemist working with Severo Ochoa at New York University, was studying the process by which energy-rich phosphate bonds are utilized in biochemical reactions. Ochoa had isolated an enzyme that would soon be called polynucleotide phosphorylase (PNP) from the bacterium Azotobacter. Grunberg-Manago observed that if one mixed the enzyme with ribonucleotide diphosphates and appropriate accessory atoms and molecules, that the ribonucleotides could be assembled into a polymer of RNA. At the time, the researchers believed this was the actual RNA-synthesizing enzyme in the cell.

Within a year, it became clear that the function of the enzyme was not RNA synthesis; somewhat ironically, it represented a mechanism for the cell to degrade RNA. Nevertheless, the significance of the work included the demonstration that it is possible to synthesize RNA in a test tube, and that the enzyme provides one mechanism to do so in the laboratory.

Impact The ability to synthesize RNA strands that could direct the formation of protein in cell-free systems was instrumental in defining the genetic code by the early 1960's, and important to the understanding of protein synthesis itself.

Further Reading

Chamberlin, M., and P. Berg. "Deoxyribonucleic Acid-directed Synthesis of Ribonucleic Acid by an Enzyme from *Escherichia coli.*" *Proceedings of the National Academy of Sciences USA* 48 (1962): 81-94. Description of the process by which the authors synthesized RNA in a test tube.

Echols, Harrison. *Operators and Promotors.* Berkeley: University of California Press, 2001. History of molecular biology and the role played by leading scientists in its development. The presence of numerous diagrams and glossary help simplify the presentation.

Judson, Horace. *The Eighth Day of Creation.* New York: Cold Spring Harbor Laboratory Press, 1996. Probably the most complete work dealing with the history of molecular biology in a format for the nonspecialist.

Richard Adler

See also DNA (deoxyribonucleic acid); Genetics; Nobel Prizes; Science and technology; Watson, James D.

■ Ridgway, Matthew B.

Identification American commander during the Korean War
Born March 3, 1895; Fort Monroe, Virginia
Died July 26, 1993; Fox Chapel, Pennsylvania

As commander of U.S. Eighth Army in Korea, Matthew Ridgway launched a counteroffensive by United Nations (U.N.) forces that drove the Chinese out of South Korea.

The son of a field artillery colonel, Ridgway graduated from the military academy at West Point in 1917. He received a number of stateside and overseas posts that included China, Nicaragua, Bolivia, Panama, and the Philippines in the peacetime years. During World War II, Ridgway assumed commands of the Eighty-Second Airborne Division and later the Eighteenth Airborne Corps, which assisted with the invasions and assaults on Sicily, Normandy, the Netherlands, Belgium, and Germany. He was appointed the commander of the Caribbean Defense Command in July, 1948, and the next year became the Army's deputy chief of staff.

Korea Ridgway entered the Korean War during a dismal period for American forces. The Eighth Army experienced a demoralizing defeat from Chinese offensives that forced them to retreat below the thirty-eighth parallel. Their leader, General Walton Walker, died in a jeep accident, and Ridgway was named as his successor on December 22, 1950. General Douglas MacArthur gave control of ground forces over to Ridgway. Ridgway rallied and began to regroup his troops. In late January, 1951, he launched a successful counteroffensive and eventually recaptured Seoul. On April 11, President Harry S. Truman relieved MacArthur of command, turning over supreme command to Ridgway. Truce negotiations began a few months later but dragged on for two more years.

In 1952, Truman made Ridgway the head of the North Atlantic Treaty Organization (NATO), and the following year, Ridgway was appointed chief of staff. By the mid-1950's, Ridgway was an outspoken critic of the Eisenhower administration and its ad-

General Matthew B. Ridgway shortly after taking command of U.N. forces in Korea in mid-1951. (National Archives)

herence to the doctrine of massive retaliation and atomic power at the expense of ground forces. He retired from the army in 1955 and, over the next five years, became the chairman for the board of trustees at the Mellon Institute for Industrial Research in Pittsburgh. In 1956, Ridgway wrote *Soldier: The Memoirs of Matthew B. Ridgway.*

Impact Although considered an innovator in airborne warfare during World War II, Ridgway proved his tactical and strategic prowess in Korea. His skillful deployment of troops under adverse conditions illustrated his leadership abilities. The general also was prophetic. In a detailed report, Ridgway's warning to avoid involvement in Indochina persuaded President Dwight D. Eisenhower not to intervene in Vietnam.

Further Reading

Appleman, Roy E. *Ridgway Duels for Korea.* College Station: Texas A&M University Press, 1990. Comprehensive volume that chronicles the Korean War from November of 1950 to July of 1951. Author utilizes official records, military reports, and correspondence and interviews with soldiers to uncover battlefield events.

Mitchell, George C. *Matthew B. Ridgway: Soldier, Statesman, Scholar, Citizen.* Mechanicsburg, Pa.: Stackpole Books, 2002. An authorized biography of Ridgway; the author describes Ridgway's combat performance and military skills.

Soffer, Jonathan M. *General Matthew B. Ridgway: From Progressivism to Reaganism, 1895-1993.* Westport, Conn.: Praeger, 1998. Account focuses on Ridgway's ideology and politics. Author considers Ridgway a soldier-diplomat, who maintained his ideals despite growing political pressures.

Gayla Koerting

See also Atomic bomb; China; Eisenhower, Dwight D.; Korean War; MacArthur, Douglas; Truman, Harry S.

■ Ringling Brothers and Barnum and Bailey Circus

Identification Largest circus in the United States through most of the twentieth century

The 1950's was a time of challenge and modernization for circuses, which survived in the face of major social and technological changes. Moreover, during this period, tented circuses gave way to indoor circuses with sponsored shows in auditoriums.

The history of the circus in the United States is dominated by the rags-to-riches story of the seven Ringling brothers from Wisconsin. On May 19, 1884, the Ringlings staged the first performance of the Yankee Robinson and Ringling Brothers Circus in Baraboo, Wisconsin. Baraboo would serve as the Ringling wintering grounds for the next thirty-four years before the family's move to Bridgeport, Connecticut, and subsequently to Sarasota, Florida.

The Ringlings promptly converted their show into a railroad circus, bought out the competition, and built their reputation to equal that of the Barnum and Bailey Circus of Connecticut. With the purchase of Barnum and Bailey in 1907, the Ringlings were crowned "Kings of the Circus World," and the two circuses were permanently merged in 1918 into the largest circus of all time. The circus offered a kaleidoscope of entertainment, from high-wire stunts, animal acts, and acrobatics to clowns and equestrian shows. Elephant acts were the hallmark of the Ringling circus; in the most famous show of all, thirty-six elephants wore tutus in the "elephant ballet" in 1942.

The Ringling circus held its final tented performance in Pittsburgh, Pennsylvania, on July 16, 1956. In the previous season, the circus traveled twenty thousand miles to 170 cities and entertained audiences totaling two million. No element did more direct harm to the circus than American television. Audiences could view circus acts on the *The Ed Sullivan Show* or watch a circus clown, Red Skelton, in the comfort of their homes.

The decline of the circus actually had roots during the 1930's and the Great Depression; the show was further hurt by war restrictions, rising transportation costs, labor shortages, the Ringling family quarrels, and the normal hazards of fires, train wrecks, and blowdowns. Faced with falling revenue, brothers John and Henry Ringling North began the modernization of the circus during the 1950's, streamlining its operations. Only a few motorized, tented circuses traveled the circuit in subsequent decades; most circuses, including Ringling, now perform indoors in temperature-controlled auditoriums.

Impact The Ringlings helped define the golden age of the circus and made it an American institution. Director Cecil B. DeMille's *The Greatest Show on Earth* (1952), filmed at Sarasota, Florida, using live-action film footage, won an Academy Award for best picture in 1952. The movie featured a string of Ringling stars, such as clowns Emmett Kelly, Otto Giebling, Paul Jung, and Lou Jacobs; the bareback riding Zoppes; and aerialists Antoinette Concello and Fay Alexander. The tramp clown, Emmett Kelly, remains one of the most recognized names in circus history. The Flying Wallendas gained fame for the art of flying trapeze and their high-wire pyramids; Alfredo Codona as an aerial gymnast; and Gunther Gebel-Williams as a superb animal trainer. The circus has played to packed audiences in North America and Europe for more than a century.

Further Reading

Culhane, John. *The American Circus: An Illustrated History.* New York: Henry Holt, 1990. A thorough and chronological history of the circus through its many phases.

Eckley, Wilton. *The American Circus.* Boston, Mass.: G. K. Hall, 1984. A detailed history of the various circus arts, from high-wire acts to clowning.

Fox, Charles Philip, and Tom Parkinson. *The Circus in America.* Waukesha, Wis.: Country Beautiful, 1969. A history of the circus with photographs and copies of original posters.

Ann M. Legreid

See also Sullivan, Ed; Television for children; Television in the United States.